Trigonometry

Work It Out Like your instructors, authors Ratti and McWaters encourage you to practice this material frequently. Each chapter includes ample opportunities to master the material by solving problems and applying your understanding.

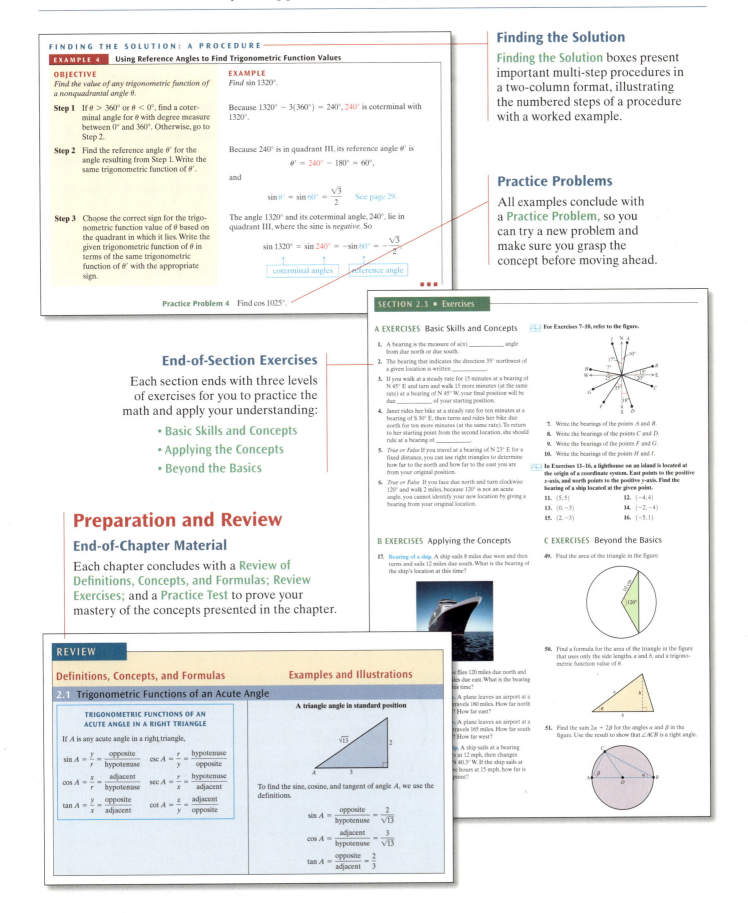

FINDING THE SOLUTION: A PROCEDURE

EXAMPLE 4 Using Reference Angles to Find Trigonometric Function Values

OBJECTIVE
Find the value of any trigonometric function of a nonquadrantal angle θ.

Step 1 If $\theta > 360°$ or $\theta < 0°$, find a coterminal angle for θ with degree measure between 0° and 360°. Otherwise, go to Step 2.

Step 2 Find the reference angle θ′ for the angle resulting from Step 1. Write the same trigonometric function of θ′.

Step 3 Choose the correct sign for the trigonometric function value of θ based on the quadrant in which it lies. Write the given trigonometric function of θ in terms of the same trigonometric function of θ′ with the appropriate sign.

EXAMPLE
Find $\sin 1320°$.

Because $1320° - 3(360°) = 240°$, 240° is coterminal with 1320°.

Because 240° is in quadrant III, its reference angle θ′ is
$$\theta' = 240° - 180° = 60°,$$
and
$$\sin \theta' = \sin 60° = \frac{\sqrt{3}}{2} \quad \text{See page 29.}$$

The angle 1320° and its coterminal angle, 240°, lie in quadrant III, where the sine is *negative*. So
$$\sin 1320° = \sin 240° = -\sin 60° = -\frac{\sqrt{3}}{2}.$$

coterminal angles   reference angle

Practice Problem 4 Find $\cos 1025°$.

Finding the Solution

Finding the Solution boxes present important multi-step procedures in a two-column format, illustrating the numbered steps of a procedure with a worked example.

Practice Problems

All examples conclude with a **Practice Problem,** so you can try a new problem and make sure you grasp the concept before moving ahead.

End-of-Section Exercises

Each section ends with three levels of exercises for you to practice the math and apply your understanding:
- **Basic Skills and Concepts**
- **Applying the Concepts**
- **Beyond the Basics**

SECTION 2.3 ▪ Exercises

A EXERCISES Basic Skills and Concepts

1. A bearing is the measure of a(n) _____ angle from due north or due south.

2. The bearing that indicates the direction 35° northwest of a given location is written _____.

3. If you walk at a steady rate for 15 minutes at a bearing of N 45° E and turn and walk 15 more minutes (at the same rate) at a bearing of N 45° W, your final position will be due _____ of your starting position.

4. Janet rides her bike at a steady rate for ten minutes at a bearing of S 30° E, then turns and rides her bike due north for ten more minutes (at the same rate). To return to her starting point from the second location, she should ride at a bearing of _____.

5. *True or False* If you travel at a bearing of N 23° E for a fixed distance, you can use right triangles to determine how far to the north and how far to the east you are from your original position.

6. *True or False* If you face due north and turn clockwise 120° and walk 2 miles, because 120° is not an acute angle, you cannot identify your new location by giving a bearing from your original location.

For Exercises 7–10, refer to the figure.

7. Write the bearings of the points *A* and *B*.
8. Write the bearings of the points *C* and *D*.
9. Write the bearings of the points *F* and *G*.
10. Write the bearings of the points *H* and *I*.

In Exercises 11–16, a lighthouse on an island is located at the origin of a coordinate system. East points to the positive *x*-axis, and north points to the positive *y*-axis. Find the bearing of a ship located at the given point.

11. $(5, 5)$ 12. $(-4, 4)$
13. $(0, -3)$ 14. $(-2, -4)$
15. $(2, -3)$ 16. $(-5, 1)$

B EXERCISES Applying the Concepts

17. *Bearing of a ship.* A ship sails 8 miles due west and then turns and sails 12 miles due south. What is the bearing of the ship's location at this time?

C EXERCISES Beyond the Basics

49. Find the area of the triangle in the figure.

50. Find a formula for the area of the triangle in the figure that uses only the side lengths, *a* and *b*, and a trigonometric function value of θ.

51. Find the sum $2\alpha + 2\beta$ for the angles α and β in the figure. Use the result to show that $\angle ACB$ is a right angle.

Preparation and Review

End-of-Chapter Material

Each chapter concludes with a Review of Definitions, Concepts, and Formulas; Review Exercises; and a Practice Test to prove your mastery of the concepts presented in the chapter.

... flies 120 miles due north and ... les due east. What is the bearing ... his time?

... A plane leaves an airport at a ... travels 180 miles. How far north ... ? How far east?

... A plane leaves an airport at a ... travels 165 miles. How far south ... ? How far west?

... p. A ship sails at a bearing ... s at 12 mph, then changes ... N 40.3° W. If the ship sails at ... e hours at 15 mph, how far is ... point?

REVIEW

Definitions, Concepts, and Formulas   **Examples and Illustrations**

2.1 Trigonometric Functions of an Acute Angle

TRIGONOMETRIC FUNCTIONS OF AN ACUTE ANGLE IN A RIGHT TRIANGLE

If *A* is any acute angle in a right triangle,

$$\sin A = \frac{y}{r} = \frac{\text{opposite}}{\text{hypotenuse}} \quad \csc A = \frac{r}{y} = \frac{\text{hypotenuse}}{\text{opposite}}$$

$$\cos A = \frac{x}{r} = \frac{\text{adjacent}}{\text{hypotenuse}} \quad \sec A = \frac{r}{x} = \frac{\text{hypotenuse}}{\text{adjacent}}$$

$$\tan A = \frac{y}{x} = \frac{\text{opposite}}{\text{adjacent}} \quad \cot A = \frac{x}{y} = \frac{\text{adjacent}}{\text{opposite}}$$

A triangle angle in standard position

To find the sine, cosine, and tangent of angle *A*, we use the definitions.

$$\sin A = \frac{\text{opposite}}{\text{hypotenuse}} = \frac{2}{\sqrt{13}}$$

$$\cos A = \frac{\text{adjacent}}{\text{hypotenuse}} = \frac{3}{\sqrt{13}}$$

$$\tan A = \frac{\text{opposite}}{\text{adjacent}} = \frac{2}{3}$$

Trigonometry

J. S. Ratti

University of South Florida

Marcus McWaters

University of South Florida

Addison-Wesley

Boston San Francisco New York
London Toronto Sydney Tokyo Singapore Madrid
Mexico City Munich Paris Cape Town Hong Kong Montreal

Executive Editor:	Anne Kelly
Sr. Project Editor:	Joanne Dill
Editorial Assistant:	Sarah Gibbons
Senior Managing Editor:	Karen Wernholm
Senior Production Supervisor:	Peggy McMahon
Text Designer:	Carolyn Deacy Design
Cover Designer:	Barbara T. Atkinson
Cover Image:	Fountain. Las Palmas-Alberto Paredes/Age fotostock
Photo Researcher:	Beth Anderson
Senior Media Producer:	Ceci Fleming
Math XL Project Supervisor:	Edward Chappell
QA Manager, Assessment Content:	Marty Wright
Senior Marketing Manager:	Katherine Greig
Market Development Manager:	Dona Kenly
Marketing Assistant:	Katherine Minton
Senior Media Buyer:	Ginny Michaud
Digital Assets Manager:	Marianne Groth
Senior Author Support/ Technology Specialist:	Joe Vetere
Rights and Permissions Advisor:	Michael Joyce
Sr. Manufacturing Manager:	Carol Melville
Production Coordination, Technical Illustrations, and Composition:	Pre-Press PMG
Situational Art:	Scientific Illustrators, Pre-Press PMG

The Library of Congress has already cataloged the Student Edition as follows:

Library of Congress Cataloging-in-Publication Data

Ratti, J. S.
 Trigonometry / J.S. Ratti, Marcus McWaters.
  p. cm.
 ISBN 0-321-56798-6 (student ed.) — ISBN 0-321-56506-1
(annotated instructor's ed.)
 1. Trigonometry—Textbooks. I. McWaters, Marcus M. II. Title.
 QA531.R34 2009
 516.24—dc22

2009005444

1 2 3 4 5 6 7 8 9 10—QWT—11 10 09

Addison-Wesley
is an imprint of

PEARSON

ISBN-13 978-0-321-56798-7
ISBN-10 0-321-56798-6

To

Javis G. Ratti
Jayden G. Ratti
Dr. Marcia Abide
Mrs. Sharon A. Larzelere
Dr. Kathy McWaters

Foreword

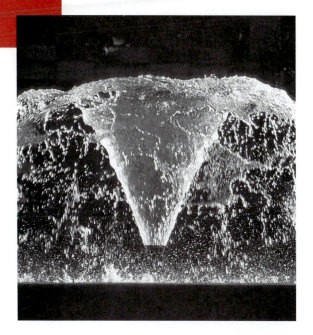

Many challenges face today's trigonometry students and instructors. Students arrive in this course with varying levels of comprehension from their previous courses. Students often resort to memorization to pass the course instead of learning the concepts presented. As a result, a textbook needs to get students to a common starting point and engage them in becoming active learners, without sacrificing the solid mathematics that is necessary for conceptual understanding. Instructors are faced with the task of producing students who understand trigonometry, are prepared for the next step, and find mathematics useful and interesting. Our goal is to help students and instructors achieve all of this and more.

In this text, there is a strong emphasis on both concept development and real-life applications. The clearly explained, well-developed, and in-depth coverage of topics such as trigonometric functions, graphing, solving equations, and identities provides thorough preparation for the study of calculus and will substantially improve all students' comprehension of mathematics in general. Just-in-time review throughout the text ensures that all students are beginning with the same foundation of algebra skills. Numerous applications are used to motivate students to apply the concepts and skills they learn in trigonometry to other courses, including the physical and biological sciences, engineering, and economics, and to on-the-job and everyday problem solving. Students are given ample opportunities throughout this book to think about important mathematical ideas and to practice and apply algebraic skills.

Another goal was to create a book that clearly shows the relevance of the material that students are learning. Throughout the text, we emphasize why the material being covered is important and how it can be applied. Because the text thoroughly develops mathematical concepts with clearly defined terminology, students see the *why* behind those concepts, paving the way for deeper understanding, better retention, less reliance on rote memorization, and (ultimately) more success.

This focus on students does not mean that we neglected instructors. As instructors ourselves, we know how essential it is to use a book in which you believe and that helps you teach mathematics. To that end, the level of the book was carefully selected so that the material would be accessible to students and provide them with an opportunity to grow. Our hope is that once you have looked through this textbook, you will see that we fulfilled our initial goals of writing for today's students as well as for you, the instructor.

Contents

CHAPTER 1

Trigonometric Functions 1

CHAPTER 2

Right Triangle Trigonometry 57

CHAPTER 3

Radian Measure and Circular Functions   91

CHAPTER 4

Graphs of the Circular Functions   131

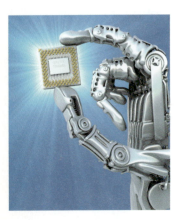

APPENDIX A

Review 379

Preface

This text is written with specific attention to overcoming the traditional hurdles that students meet when studying trigonometry. The pace has been slowed, using short sections that allow students to learn a topic thoroughly before going forward. Graphic and geometric elements are used to provide visual cues that help students understand and retain the material. Exercise sets provide extensive practice to reinforce basic skills, while some exercises are still included for students who need to be challenged. At the end of each chapter is a complete review of the chapter material so that students can easily prepare for exams.

Features

CHAPTER OPENER Each chapter opener includes a description of applications relevant to the content of the chapter, a series of images related to these and other applications, and the list of topics that will be covered in the chapter. In one page, students see what they are going to learn and why they are learning it.

REVIEW On the first page of each section is a list of topics that students should review prior to starting the chapter. Section references accompany the suggested review material so that students can readily find the material. The **Objectives** of the section are clearly stated and numbered. Each numbered objective is paired with a similarly numbered subsection so that students can quickly find the section material for an objective.

APPLICATION The discussion in each section begins with a motivating anecdote or piece of information that is tied to an application problem. This problem is solved in an example later in the section or revisited in an exercise, using the mathematics covered in the section.

SECTION OPENERS These section openers lend continuity to the section and its content, utilizing material from a variety of fields: the physical and biological sciences (including health sciences), economics, art and architecture, the history of mathematics, and more. Of special interest are contemporary topics such as the greenhouse effect and global warming, CAT scans, and computer graphics.

DEFINITIONS AND THEOREMS All are boxed for emphasis and titled for ease of reference, as are lists of rules and properties.

FIGURES All figures are titled to make it easy to identify what is being illustrated.

EXAMPLES The examples include a wide range of computational, conceptual, and modern applied problems carefully selected to build confidence, competency, and understanding. Every example has a title that indicates its purpose. For every example, clarifying side comments are provided for each step in the detailed solution.

PRACTICE PROBLEM All examples are followed by a Practice Problem for students to try so that they can check their understanding of the concept covered.

PROCEDURE BOXES These boxes, interspersed throughout the text, present important procedures in numbered steps. Special **Finding the Solution** boxes present important multistep procedures, such as the steps for graphing a trigonometric function, in a two-column format. The steps of the procedure are given in the left column, and following these steps, an example is worked in the right column. This approach provides students with a clear model with which they can compare when encountering difficulty in their work. These boxes are a part of the numbered examples.

MAIN FACTS These boxes summarize information related to equations and their graphs, such as those of the conic sections.

HISTORICAL NOTES When appropriate, historical notes appear in the margin, giving students information about key people or ideas in the history and development of mathematics. This information is included to add flavor to the subject matter.

TECHNOLOGY CONNECTIONS Although the use of graphing calculators is optional in this book, Technology Connections give students tips on using calculators to solve problems, check answers, and reinforce concepts.

WARNINGS Warnings boxes appear as appropriate throughout the text to let students know of common errors and pitfalls that can trip them up in their thinking or calculations.

RECALL Periodically, students are reminded in a margin Recall note of a key idea they learned earlier in the text that will help them work through a current problem.

STUDY TIPS Students are given hints for handling newly introduced concepts.

BY THE WAY These margin notes provide students with additional interesting information on nonessential topics to keep them engaged in the mathematics presented.

EXERCISES The heart of any textbook is its exercises. Knowing this, we made sure that the quantity, quality, and variety of exercises meet the needs of all students. The problems in each exercise set are carefully graded to strengthen the skills developed in the associated section. Exercises are divided into three categories: **A: Basic Skills and Concepts** (developing fundamental skills), **B: Applying the Concepts** (using the section's material to solve real-world problems), and **C: Beyond the Basics** (providing more challenging exercises that give students an opportunity to reach beyond the material covered in the section). Exercises are paired so that the even-numbered A Exercises closely follow the preceding odd-numbered exercises. All application exercises are titled and relevant to the topics of the section. The A and B Exercises are intended for a typical student, while the C Exercises, generally more theoretical in nature, are suitable for honors students, special assignments, or extra credit. **Critical Thinking** exercises, appearing as appropriate, are designed to develop students' higher-level thinking skills, and calculator problems are included where needed. Finally, **Group Projects** are provided at the end of many exercise sets so that students can work together to reinforce and extend one another's comprehension of the material.

END-OF-CHAPTER The chapter-ending material includes a complete **Review of Definitions**, **Concepts, and Formulas**; **Review Exercises**; and **a Chapter Test**. The chapter review, a thorough description of key topics indicating where the material occurs in the text, encourages students to reread sections rather than memorize definitions out of context. The Review Exercises provide students with an opportunity to practice what they have learned in the chapter. Then students can take the Chapter Test. All tests are designed to increase student comprehension and verify that students have mastered the skills and concepts in the chapter. Mastery of these materials should indicate a true comprehension of the chapter and the likelihood of success on the associated in-class examination.

APPENDIX The appendix gives a review of the fundamental concepts of algebra and geometry required for the study of trigonometry. Each section of the appendix is complete with exercises the student can use to verify their readiness to use the material in that section in the study of trigonometry.

Supplements

FOR THE STUDENT

Student's Solutions Manual

- By Beverly Fusfield
- Provides detailed worked-out solutions to the odd-numbered end-of-section and Chapter Review exercises and solutions to all of the Practice Problems and the Chapter Test
- ISBN-13: 978-0-321-64464-0; ISBN-10: 0-321-64464-6

Graphing Calculator Manual

- By Darryl Nester, *Bluffton University*
- Provides instructions and keystroke operations for the TI-83/83+, TI-84+, TI-86, and TI-89
- Keyed directly to text Examples and Technology Connections
- ISBN-13: 978-0-321-64467-1; ISBN-10: 0-321-64467-0

Video Resources on DVD with Optional Subtitles

- Videos feature Section Summaries and Example Solutions. Section Summaries cover key definitions and procedures for most sections. Example Solutions walk students through the detailed solution process for selected examples in the textbook.
- Videos are ideal for distance learning or supplemental instruction on a home computer or in a campus computer lab.
- Videos include optional subtitles in English and Spanish.
- ISBN-13: 978-0-321-64459-6; ISBN-10: 0-321-64459-X

A Review of Algebra

- By Heidi Howard, *Florida Community College at Jacksonville*
- Provides additional support for those students needing further algebra review
- ISBN-13: 978-0-201-77347-7; ISBN-10: 0-201-77347-3

FOR THE INSTRUCTOR

Annotated Instructor's Edition

- Answers included on the same page beside the text exercises where possible for quick reference
- ISBN-13: 978-0-321-56506-8; ISBN-10: 0-321-56506-1

Instructor's Solutions Manual

- By Beverly Fusfield
- Complete solutions provided for all end-of-section exercises, including the Critical Thinking and Group Projects, Practice Problems, Chapter Review exercises, and Chapter Test
- ISBN-13: 978-0-321-64460-2; ISBN-10: 0-321-64460-3

Instructor's Testing Manual

- By James Lapp
- Includes diagnostic pretests, chapter tests, and additional test items, grouped by section, with answers
- Available online within MyMathLab or from the Instructor Resource Center at www.pearsonhighered.com/irc

TestGen®

- Enables instructors to build, edit, print, and administer tests
- Features a computerized bank of questions developed to cover all text objectives
- Available for download from Pearson Education's online catalog: www.pearsonhighered.com/testgen

PowerPoint® Lecture Slides

- Features presentations written and designed specifically for this text, including figures and examples from the text
- Available online within MyMathLab or from the Instructor Resource Center at www.pearsonhighered.com/irc

Pearson Math Adjunct Support Center

The **Pearson Math Adjunct Support Center** (www.pearsontutorservices.com/math-adjunct.html) is staffed by qualified instructors with more than 50 years of combined experience at both the community college and university level. Assistance is provided for faculty in the following areas:

- Suggested syllabus consultation
- Tips on using materials packed with the book
- Book-specific content assistance
- Teaching suggestions, including advice on classroom strategies

Media Resources

MyMathLab® Online Course (access code required)

MyMathLab® is a text-specific, easily customizable online course that integrates interactive multimedia instruction with textbook content. MyMathLab gives you the tools you need to deliver all or a portion of your course online, whether your students are working in a lab setting or are working from home.

- **Interactive homework exercises**, correlated to your textbook at the objective level, are algorithmically generated for unlimited practice and mastery. Most exercises are free-response and provide guided solutions, sample problems, and learning aids for extra help.
- **Personalized Study Plan**, generated when students complete a test or quiz, indicates which topics have been mastered and links to tutorial exercises for topics students have not mastered.
- **Multimedia learning aids** such as video lectures, animations, and a complete multimedia textbook help students independently improve their understanding and performance.
- **Assessment Manager** lets you create online homework, quizzes, and tests that are automatically graded. Select just the right mix of questions from the MyMathLab exercise bank, instructor-created custom exercises, and/or TestGen® test items.
- **Gradebook**, designed specifically for mathematics and statistics, automatically tracks students' results and gives you control over how to calculate final grades. You can also add off-line (paper-and-pencil) grades to the gradebook.
- **MathXL Exercise Builder** allows you to create static and algorithmic exercises for your online assignments. You can use the library of sample exercises as an easy starting point.
- **Pearson Tutor Center** (www.pearsontutorservices.com) access is automatically included with MyMathLab. The Tutor Center is staffed by qualified math instructors who provide textbook-specific tutoring for students via toll-free phone, fax, e-mail, and interactive Web sessions.

MyMathLab is powered by CourseCompass™, Pearson Education's online teaching and learning environment, and by MathXL®, Pearson Education's online homework, tutorial, and assessment system. MyMathLab is available to qualified adopters. For more information, visit www.mymathlab.com or contact your Pearson sales representative.

MathXL® Online Course (access code required)

MathXL® is an online homework, tutorial, and assessment system that accompanies Pearson's textbooks in mathematics and statistics.

- **Interactive homework exercises**, correlated to your textbook at the objective level, are algorithmically generated for unlimited practice and mastery. Most exercises are free-response and provide guided solutions, sample problems, and learning aids for extra help.
- **Personalized Study Plan**, generated when students complete a test or quiz, indicates which topics students have mastered and links to tutorial exercises for topics students have not mastered.
- **Multimedia learning aids** such as video lectures and animations help students independently improve their understanding and performance.

- **Assessment Manager** lets you create online homework, quizzes, and tests that are automatically graded. Select just the right mix of questions from the MathXL exercise bank, instructor-created custom exercises, and/or TestGen® test items.
- **Gradebook**, designed specifically for mathematics and statistics, automatically tracks students' results and gives you control over how to calculate final grades.
- **MathXL Exercise Builder** allows you to create static and algorithmic exercises for your online assignments. You can use the library of sample exercises as an easy starting point.

MathXL® is available to qualified adopters. For more information, visit www.mathxl.com or contact your Pearson sales representative.

MathXL® Tutorials on CD (ISBN-13: 978-0-321-64466-4; ISBN-10: 0-321-64466-2)

This interactive tutorial CD-ROM provides algorithmically generated practice exercises that are correlated at the objective level to the exercises in the textbook. Every practice exercise is accompanied by an example and a guided solution designed to involve students in the solution process. Selected exercises may also include a video clip to help students visualize concepts. The software provides helpful feedback for incorrect answers and can generate printed summaries of students' progress.

Video Resources on DVD

Video Resources on DVD with Optional Subtitles (ISBN-13: 978-0-321-64459-6; ISBN-10: 0-321-64459-X)

The video lectures for this text are available on DVD-Rom, making it easy and convenient for students to watch the videos from a computer at home or on campus. The videos feature an engaging team of mathematics instructors who present Section Summaries and Example Solutions. Section Summaries cover key definitions and procedures from most sections. Example Solutions walk students through the detailed solution process for selected examples in the textbook. The format provides distance-learning students with comprehensive video instruction for most sections in the book, but also allows students needing only small amounts of review to watch instruction on a specific skill or procedure. The videos have optional text subtitles, which can be easily turned off or on for individual student needs. Subtitles are available in English and Spanish.

InterAct Math Tutorial Web site: www.interactmath.com

Get practice and tutorial help online! This interactive tutorial Web site provides algorithmically generated practice exercises that correlate directly to the exercises in the textbook. Students can retry an exercise as many times as they like with new values each time for unlimited practice and mastery. Every exercise is accompanied by an interactive guided solution that provides helpful feedback for incorrect answers. Students also can view a worked-out sample problem that takes them through an exercise similar to the one they're working on.

Acknowledgments

We would like to express our gratitude to the reviewers of this edition, who provided such invaluable insights and comments. Their contributions helped shape the development of the text and carry out the vision stated in the preface.

Contributors

J. Michael Albanese, *Central Piedmont Community College*
Linda E. Barton, *Ball State University*
Gus Brar, *Delaware County Community College*
Irene Brown, *Mercyhurst College*
Alicia Collins, *Mesa Community College*
Said Fariabi, *San Antonio College*
Antanas Gilvydis, *Richard J. Daley College*
Nina R. Girard, *University of Pittsburgh at Johnstown*
Gloria P. Hernandez, *Louisiana State University—Eunice*
Alicia K. Jefferson, *Jackson State University*
Robert A. Johnson, *Salisbury University*
Jennifer R. McNeilly, *University of Illinois—Urbana-Champaign*
Christine S. Mirbaha, *The Community College of Baltimore County*
Denise M. Nunley, *Glendale Community College*
Paul O'Heron, *Broome Community College*
Robin Ruffato, *Ball State University*
Deoki N. Sharma, *DeVry University*
Cindy Soderstrom, *Salt Lake Community College*
Leslie A. Soltis, *Mercyhurst College*
Katrina N. Staley, *North Carolina A&T State University*
Linda Tansil, *Southeast Missouri State University*
Marilyn Toscano, *University of Wisconsin—Superior*

Reviewers

David Garth, *Truman State University*
James Henson, *Edinboro University of Pennsylvania*
Carol Lerch, *Daniel Webster College*
Rabindra N. Mukherjee, *Reading Area Community College*

Our sincerest thanks go to the legion of dedicated individuals who worked tirelessly to make this book possible. We express special thanks to Carrie Green for the excellent work she did as the development editor on the text. We would also like to express our gratitude to our typist, Beverly DeVine-Hoffmeyer, for her amazing patience and skill. We must also thank Dr. Praveen Rohatgi, Dr. Nalini Rohatgi, and Dr. Bhupinder Bedi for the consulting they provided on all material relating to medicine. We particularly want to thank Professor Mile Krajcevski for many helpful discussions and suggestions, particularly for improving the exercise sets. Further gratitude is due to Irena Andreevska, Gokarna Aryal, Ferene Tookos, and Christine Fitch for their assistance on the answers to the exercises in the text. In addition, we would like to thank Alicia Gordon, Cindy Trimble & Associates, and Lauri Semarne for their meticulous accuracy in checking the text. Thanks are due as well to Laura Hakala and Pre-Press PMG for their excellent production work. Finally, our thanks are extended to the professional and remarkable staff at Addison-Wesley. In particular, we would like to thank Greg Tobin, Publisher; Anne Kelly, Executive Editor; Joanne Dill, Senior Project Editor; Peggy McMahon, Senior Production Supervisor; Katherine Greig, Senior Marketing Manager; Dona Kenly, Market Development Manager; Katherine Minton, Marketing Assistant; Barbara Atkinson, Cover Designer; Ceci Fleming, Senior Media Producer; Karen Wernholm, Senior Managing Editor; and Joe Vetere, Senior Author Support/ Technology Specialist.

We invite all who use this book to send suggestions for improvements to Marcus McWaters at mmm@cas.usf.edu.

About the Authors

J. S. Ratti

EDUCATION

PhD Mathematics Wayne State University

TEACHING

Wayne State University (teaching assistant and instructor)

University of Nevada at Las Vegas (instructor)

Oakland University (assistant professor)

University of South Florida (professor and past chairman)

Undergraduate courses taught: college algebra, trigonometry, finite mathematics, calculus (all levels), set theory, differential equations, linear algebra

Graduate courses taught: number theory, abstract algebra, real analysis, complex analysis, graph theory

AWARDS

USF Research Council Grant

USF Teaching Incentive Program (TIP) Award

USF Outstanding Undergraduate Teaching Award

Academy of Applied Sciences grants

RESEARCH

Complex analysis, real analysis, graph theory, probability

PERSONAL INTERESTS

Fan of Tampa Bay Buccaneers

Marcus McWaters

EDUCATION

BS Major: mathematics   Minor: physics
Louisiana State University New Orleans

PhD Major: mathematics   Minor: philosophy
University of Florida

TEACHING

Louisiana State University (teaching assistant)

University of Florida (teaching assistant and graduate fellow)

University of South Florida (associate professor and department chair)

Undergraduate courses taught: college algebra, trigonometry, finite mathematics, calculus, business calculus, life science calculus, advanced calculus, vector calculus, set theory, differential equations, linear algebra

Graduate courses taught: graph theory, number theory, discrete mathematics, geometry, advanced linear algebra, topology, mathematical logic, modern algebra, real analysis

AWARDS

Graduate Fellow, University of Florida (Center of Excellence Grant)

USF Research Council grant

USF Teaching Incentive Program (TIP) Award

Provost's Award

RESEARCH

Topology, algebraic topology, topological algebra

Founding member, USF Center for Digital and Computational Video

PERSONAL INTERESTS

Traveling with his wife and two daughters, theater, water-skiing, racquetball

Trigonometric Functions

Angles are vital for activities ranging from taking photographs to designing layouts for city streets. Scientists use angles and basic trigonometry to measure remote distances such as the distance between mountain peaks and the distances between planets. Angles are universally used to specify locations on Earth via longitude and latitude. In this chapter, we begin the study of trigonometry and its many uses.

Angles

George Ferris (1859–1896)

FERRIS WHEEL

A Ferris wheel is an amusement park ride. It is a structure consisting of an upright wheel with passenger gondolas (cars) suspended from the rim. It is named after the Pennsylvania bridge builder George Ferris, who designed and built the 80-meter-tall wheel for the World's Columbian Exposition in Chicago in 1893. Now China has built the world's largest Ferris wheel, called the Great Beijing Wheel. It was completed in 2009, with a height of 208 meters (682 feet) and the ability to accommodate 1920 passengers.

In Exercise 67, we consider the revolutions of a Ferris wheel. ■

1 Learn the vocabulary associated with angles.

Angles

A **ray** is a half-line made up of a point on a line, called the **endpoint**, and all of the points on one side of the endpoint. An **angle** is formed by rotating a ray about its endpoint. The angle's **initial side** is the ray's original position; the angle's **terminal side** is its position after rotation. The endpoint is called the **vertex** of the angle. A curved arrow drawn in the interior of the angle's vertex indicates both the direction and amount of rotation from the initial side to the terminal side. Capital letters at the vertex, or the Greek letters α (alpha), β (beta), γ (gamma), and θ (theta) are often used to name angles. The symbol $\angle$ is used to denote an angle.

In Figure 1.1, the vertex of an angle θ is labeled A and the points B and C are each on one side of θ. We may refer to the angle θ in Figure 1.1 in any of the following ways:

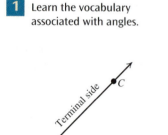

FIGURE 1.1 Angle θ

Angle θ	Angle A	Angle BAC	Angle CAB
$\angle\theta$	$\angle A$	$\angle BAC$	$\angle CAB$

If the rotation of the initial side to the terminal side is in a counterclockwise direction, the angle formed is a **positive angle**. If the rotation is in a clockwise direction, the angle formed is a **negative angle**. See Figure 1.2.

Terminal side

θ

Initial side

Angle θ is positive.

(a)

Initial side

θ

Terminal side

Angle θ is negative.

(b)

FIGURE 1.2 Positive and negative angles

Degree Measure

We measure angles by determining the amount and direction of rotation from the initial side to the terminal side. Two common units for measuring angles are *degrees* and *radians*. (Radian measure will be discussed in Section 3.1.)

DEGREE MEASURE OF ANGLES

An angle formed by rotating the initial side counterclockwise one complete revolution (so the terminal side coincides with the initial side) is assigned the measure **360 degrees**, written **360°**. An angle of **one degree**, written 1°, represents an angle formed by $\dfrac{1}{360}$ of one complete revolution in the counterclockwise direction.

Angles are classified according to their measures. As illustrated in Figure 1.3, an **acute angle** has measure between 0° and 90°; a **right angle** has measure 90°, or one-fourth of a counterclockwise revolution; an **obtuse angle** has measure between 90° and 180°; and a **straight angle** has measure 180°, or half of a counterclockwise revolution.

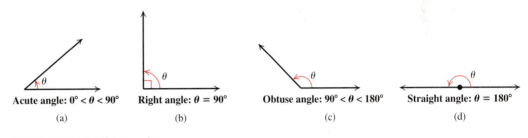

Acute angle: 0° < θ < 90°   Right angle: θ = 90°   Obtuse angle: 90° < θ < 180°   Straight angle: θ = 180°

(a)   (b)   (c)   (d)

FIGURE 1.3 Classifying angles

In Figure 1.4, we have used angle θ in two different ways: to name the angle (vertex) and to represent the measure of the angle. Some authors write the measure of angle θ as $m(\angle\theta) = 60°$. We adopt the informal notation $\theta = 60°$.

A plane angle is often measured by a *protractor*. See Figure 1.5(a). One device used by engineers and surveyors for measuring angles is called a *transit*. See Figure 1.5(b).

θ = 60°

FIGURE 1.4

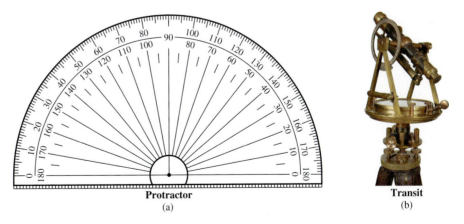

Protractor
(a)

Transit
(b)

FIGURE 1.5 Angle measuring devices

Complements and Supplements

Two positive angles are **complements** (or **complementary angles**) if the sum of their measures is 90°. So two angles with measures 50° and 40° are complements because 50° + 40° = 90°. Each angle is the complement of the other.

Two positive angles are **supplements** (or **supplementary angles**) if the sum of their measures is 180°. So two angles with measures 120° and 60° are supplements because 120° + 60° = 180°.

EXAMPLE 1   **Finding Complements and Supplements**

Find the complement and the supplement of the given angle or explain why the angle has no complement or no supplement.

a. 73°   **b.** 110°

SOLUTION

a. If θ represents the complement of 73°, then $\theta + 73° = 90°$; so $\theta = 90° - 73° = 17°$. The complement of 73° is 17°. If α represents the supplement of 73°, then $\alpha + 73° = 180°$; so $\alpha = 180° - 73° = 107°$. The supplement of 73° is 107°.

b. There is no complement of a 110° angle because 110° > 90°. If β represents the supplement of 110°, then $\beta + 110° = 180°$; so $\beta = 180° - 110° = 70°$. The supplement of 110° is 70°.   ■ ■ ■

Practice Problem 1   Find the complement and the supplement of 67°.   ■

2 Convert between decimal degree and degree-minute-second notations.

Decimal Degree (DD) and Degree-Minute-Second (DMS)

Today it is common to divide degrees into fractional parts using **decimal degree (DD)** notation such as 30.5°. Traditionally, however, the fractional parts of a degree were expressed in terms of *minutes* and *seconds*. A degree is subdivided into 60 equal parts called **minutes**, denoted by the symbol ($'$). A minute is further subdivided into 60 equal parts called **seconds**, denoted by the symbol ($''$). An angle measuring 27 degrees, 14 minutes, and 39 seconds is written as $27°14'39''$ in **degree-minute-second (DMS)** notation.

RELATIONSHIP BETWEEN DEGREES, MINUTES, AND SECONDS

$$1° = 60' \qquad\qquad 1' = 60'' \qquad\qquad 1° = 60(1') = 60(60'') = 3600''$$

$$1' = \frac{1}{60}(1°) = \left(\frac{1}{60}\right)° \quad 1'' = \frac{1}{60}(1') = \left(\frac{1}{60}\right)' \quad 1'' = \frac{1}{3600}(1°) = \left(\frac{1}{3600}\right)°$$

Arithmetic calculations are sometimes more cumbersome in DMS notation than in DD notation.

EXAMPLE 2   **Adding and Subtracting in DMS Notation**

Let $\alpha = 46°42'12''$ and $\beta = 31°54'17''$.

a. Find the sum: $\alpha + \beta$.

b. Find the difference: $\alpha - \beta$.

SOLUTION

a.

$$\alpha = 46°42'12'' = 46° + 42' + 12'' \qquad \text{Rewrite.}$$
$$+\beta = +31°54'17'' = \underline{+31° + 54' + 17''} \qquad \text{Rewrite.}$$
$$\alpha + \beta = 77° + (96') + 29'' \qquad \text{Add.}$$
$$= 77° + (1° + 36') + 29'' \qquad \begin{array}{l}\text{Carry, as in addition.} \\ 96' = 60' + 36' = 1° + 36'.\end{array}$$
$$= (77° + 1°) + 36' + 29'' \qquad \text{Regroup.}$$
$$= 78° + 36' + 29'' \qquad \text{Simplify.}$$
$$= 78°36'29'' \qquad \text{DMS notation}$$

b. Because $54' > 42'$ and $17'' > 12''$, we first write α in the following form:

$$\alpha = 46°42'12'' = 46° + 42' + 12'' \qquad \text{Rewrite.}$$
$$= 45° + (1° + 42') + 12'' \qquad 46° = 45° + 1°; \text{regroup.}$$
$$= 45° + 102' + 12'' \qquad 1° + 42' = 60' + 42' = 102'$$
$$= 45° + 101' + (1' + 12'') \qquad 102' = 101' + 1'; \text{regroup.}$$
$$= 45° + 101' + 72'' \qquad 1' + 12'' = 60'' + 12'' = 72''$$

$$\alpha = 46°42'12'' = 45° + 101' + 72''$$
$$-\beta = -31°54'17'' = \underline{-(31° + 54' + 17'')}$$
$$\alpha - \beta = (45 - 31)° + (101 - 54)' + (72 - 17)'' \qquad \text{Subtract.}$$
$$= 14° + 47' + 55'' \qquad \text{Simplify.}$$
$$= 14°47'55'' \qquad \text{Rewrite.} \qquad ■ ■ ■$$

Practice Problem 2 Let $\alpha = 37°12'37''$ and $\beta = 24°15'45''$.

a. Find the sum: $\alpha + \beta$.   **b.** Find the difference: $\alpha - \beta$.   ■

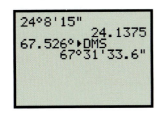

EXAMPLE 3   **Converting from DMS to DD Notation**

Convert $24°8'15''$ to DD notation, rounded to two decimal places.

SOLUTION

$$24°8'15'' = 24° + 8 \cdot 1' + 15 \cdot 1'' \qquad \text{Rewrite.}$$
$$= 24° + 8\left(\frac{1}{60}\right)° + 15\left(\frac{1}{3600}\right)° \qquad 1' = \left(\frac{1}{60}\right)°; 1'' = \left(\frac{1}{3600}\right)°$$
$$\approx 24.14° \qquad \text{Use a calculator.} \qquad ■ ■ ■$$

Practice Problem 3 Convert $13°9'22''$ to DD notation, rounded to two decimal places.   ■

EXAMPLE 4   **Converting from DD to DMS Notation**

Convert $67.526°$ to DMS notation, rounded to the nearest second.

SOLUTION

$$67.526° = 67° + 0.526 \cdot 1° \qquad \text{Rewrite.}$$
$$= 67° + 0.526(60') \qquad 1° = 60'$$
$$= 67° + 31.56' \qquad \text{Use a calculator.}$$
$$= 67° + 31' + 0.56 \cdot 1' \qquad \text{Rewrite.}$$
$$= 67° + 31' + 0.56(60'') \qquad 1' = 60''$$
$$= 67° + 31' + 33.6'' \qquad \text{Use a calculator.}$$
$$\approx 67°31'34'' \qquad \text{Rounded to nearest second} \qquad ■ ■ ■$$

Practice Problem 4 Convert $41.275°$ to DMS notation, rounded to the nearest second.   ■

3 Draw angles in standard position.

FIGURE 1.7(a) **45° angle**

FIGURE 1.7(b) **135° angle**

FIGURE 1.7(c) **−240° angle**

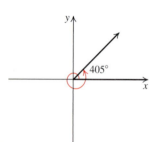

FIGURE 1.7(d) **405° angle**

4 Find coterminal angles.

Standard Position

An angle in a rectangular coordinate system is in **standard position** if its vertex is at the origin and its initial side is the positive *x*-axis. All of the angles in Figure 1.6 are in standard position. An angle in standard position is **quadrantal** if its terminal side lies on a coordinate axis; it is said to **lie in a quadrant** if its terminal side lies in that quadrant.

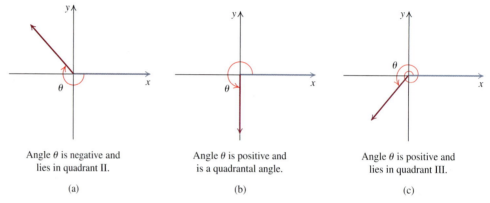

Angle θ is negative and lies in quadrant II.

(a)

Angle θ is positive and is a quadrantal angle.

(b)

Angle θ is positive and lies in quadrant III.

(c)

FIGURE 1.6 **Three angles in standard position**

The size (magnitude) of an angle in standard position is measured from the positive *x*-axis to the terminal side. The measure of an angle has no numerical limit because the terminal side can be rotated indefinitely.

EXAMPLE 5   **Drawing an Angle in Standard Position**

Draw each angle in standard position and state the quadrant in which it lies.

a. 45°   **b.** 135°   **c.** −240°   **d.** 405°

SOLUTION

a. Because $45 = \frac{1}{2}(90)$, a 45° angle is $\frac{1}{2}$ of a 90° angle and lies in quadrant I. See Figure 1.7(a).

b. Because $135 = 90 + 45$, a 135° angle is a counterclockwise rotation of 90°, followed by half of a 90° counterclockwise rotation. It lies in quadrant II. See Figure 1.7(b).

c. Because $-240 = -180 - 60$, a −240° angle is a clockwise rotation of 180° followed by a clockwise rotation of 60°. It lies in quadrant II. See Figure 1.7(c).

d. Because $405 = 360 + 45$, a 405° angle is one complete counterclockwise rotation of 360°, followed by $\frac{1}{2}$ of a 90° counterclockwise rotation. It lies in quadrant I. See Figure 1.7(d).   ■ ■ ■

Practice Problem 5   Draw a 225° angle in standard position.   ■

Coterminal Angles

Two angles with different measures that have the same initial and terminal sides are called **coterminal angles**. The angles 45° and 405° (405° = 45° + 360°) of

Figures 1.7(a) and 1.7(d), respectively, are coterminal angles. Note that for an angle θ in standard position, one more complete rotation of 360° clockwise or counterclockwise results in an angle with the same initial and terminal side as θ.

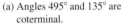

COTERMINAL ANGLES

An angle θ, measured in degrees, is coterminal with the angle

$$\theta + n \cdot 360°,$$

where n is any integer.

Any angle in standard position is coterminal with an angle whose measure is between 0° and 360°.

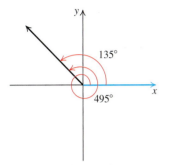

(a) Angles 495° and 135° are coterminal.

EXAMPLE 6   Finding Coterminal Angles

Find the angle between 0° and 360° that is coterminal with each of the angles. Then write all coterminal angles.

a. 495°   **b.** −150°

SOLUTION

Coterminal angles are obtained by adding or subtracting multiples of 360° to (or from) the given angle. If the given angle has measure more than 360°, we should subtract. For negative angles, we should add.

a. Because 495° is a positive angle greater than 360°, we subtract 360° to get an angle between 0° and 360°: 495° − 360° = 135°. The 495° and 135° angles are coterminal. See Figure 1.8(a). All angles that are coterminal with 135° can be written in the form 135° + $n \cdot$ 360°, where n is an integer.

b. By adding 360° to −150°, we obtain an angle between 0° and 360°: −150° + 360° = 210°.

The 210° and −150° angles are coterminal. See Figure 1.8(b). All angles that are coterminal with 210° can be written in the form 210° + $n \cdot$ 360°, where n is an integer. ■ ■ ■

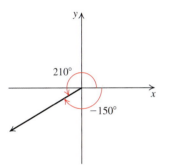

(b) Angles 210° and −150° are coterminal.

FIGURE 1.8 Coterminal angles

Practice Problem 6 Repeat Example 6 for the following angles.

a. 765°   **b.** −570° ■

EXAMPLE 7   Finding Coterminal Angles

The terminal side of an angle θ in standard position passes through the point $(-2, 2)$. Write all possible degree measures of this angle.

SOLUTION

In Figure 1.9, segment OP is the diagonal of the 2 × 2 square $PQOR$. So OP bisects the right angle QOR. Therefore, $\theta = 90° + \frac{1}{2}(90°) = 90° + 45° = 135°$. There are infinitely many angles with OP as the terminal side. Each of these angles differs by 360°. So $\theta = 135° + n \cdot 360°$, n any integer. ■ ■ ■

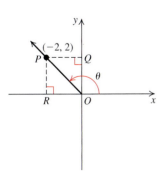

FIGURE 1.9

Practice Problem 7 Repeat Example 7 assuming that the terminal side of θ passes through the point $(-3, -3)$. ■

5 Recall vocabulary associated with angles and lines.

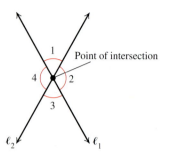

FIGURE 1.10 Intersecting lines and vertical angles

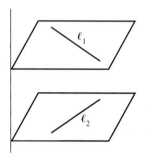

FIGURE 1.11 Skew lines

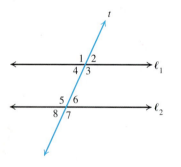

FIGURE 1.12 A transversal

Angles and Lines

From geometry, we recall some definitions and facts about angles and lines. Two lines in the same plane are called **coplanar lines**. Two lines having a point in common are called **intersecting lines**. Figure 1.10 shows two intersecting lines, ℓ_1 and ℓ_2. Four angles are formed at the point of intersection, indicated by the numbers 1, 2, 3, and 4.

The pairs of **vertical angles** are **(i)** $\angle 1$ and $\angle 3$ and **(ii)** $\angle 2$ and $\angle 4$.

VERTICAL ANGLES PROPERTY

If two lines intersect at a point, the pairs of vertical angles are equal in measure.

In Figure 1.10, $\qquad\qquad \angle 1 = \angle 3$ and $\angle 2 = \angle 4$.

Two coplanar lines that do not intersect are called **parallel lines**. Two lines on different planes that do not intersect are called **skew lines**. See Figure 1.11. A **transversal** is a line that intersects two or more coplanar lines, each at a different point. Figure 1.12 shows parallel lines ℓ_1 and ℓ_2 with the transversal t intersecting these lines. Eight angles are formed at the points of intersection, indicated by the numbers 1 through 8.

1. The pairs of **corresponding angles** are
   (i) $\angle 1$ and $\angle 5$, **(ii)** $\angle 2$ and $\angle 6$, **(iii)** $\angle 3$ and $\angle 7$, and **(iv)** $\angle 4$ and $\angle 8$.
2. The pairs of **alternate interior angles** are
   (i) $\angle 3$ and $\angle 5$ and **(ii)** $\angle 4$ and $\angle 6$.
3. The pairs of **interior angles on the same side of the transversal** are
   (i) $\angle 3$ and $\angle 6$ and **(ii)** $\angle 4$ and $\angle 5$.

The following important properties hold.

PROPERTIES OF ANGLES FORMED BY PARALLEL LINES CUT BY A TRANSVERSAL

Let a transversal intersect two parallel lines. See Figure 1.12.

1. Each pair of corresponding angles is equal in measure:
$$\angle 1 = \angle 5; \ \angle 2 = \angle 6; \ \angle 3 = \angle 7; \ \angle 4 = \angle 8$$
2. Each pair of alternate interior angles is equal in measure:
$$\angle 3 = \angle 5; \ \angle 4 = \angle 6$$
3. Interior angles on the same side of the transversal are supplementary:
$$\angle 3 + \angle 6 = 180°; \ \angle 4 + \angle 5 = 180°$$

EXAMPLE 8   Finding Angle Measures

In Figure 1.12, find the measures of $\angle 2$ and $\angle 5$ assuming that $\angle 2 = (2x + 61)°$ and $\angle 5 = (7x + 11)°$.

SOLUTION

$$\angle 4 = \angle 2 \qquad \text{Vertical angles}$$
$$\angle 4 = (2x + 61)° \qquad \angle 2 = (2x + 61)°$$
$$\angle 4 + \angle 5 = 180° \qquad \text{Property 3}$$
$$(2x + 61)° + (7x + 11)° = 180° \qquad \text{Substitute values.}$$

Solve for x in the equation:

$$(2x + 61) + (7x + 11) = 180$$
$$9x + 72 = 180 \qquad \text{Combine terms.}$$
$$9x = 180 - 72 = 108 \qquad \text{Isolate the } x \text{ term and simplify.}$$
$$x = 12 \qquad \text{Solve for } x.$$

So

$$\angle 2 = (2x + 61)° = (2(12) + 61)° = 85° \qquad \text{Replace } x \text{ with 12 and simplify.}$$
$$\angle 5 = (7x + 11)° = (7(12) + 11)° = 95° \qquad \text{Replace } x \text{ with 12 and simplify.}$$

■ ■ ■

Practice Problem 8   In Figure 1.12, find the measures of $\angle 2 = (6x - 3)°$ and $\angle 7 = (8x + 43)°$.

■

SECTION 1.1 ■ Exercises

A EXERCISES Basic Skills and Concepts

1. The degree measure of one complete revolution is

   _____ .

2. The sum of two complementary angles is _____ .

3. An angle is in standard position if the _____ side is the positive x-axis and the vertex is at the origin.

4. For any integer n, an angle of $\theta° + n \cdot 360°$ has the same terminal side as the angle of _____ degrees.

5. *True or False* Counterclockwise rotation of a ray about its endpoint results in positive angles, and clockwise rotation results in negative angles.

6. *True or False* An angle in standard position is quadrantal if its terminal side lies in a quadrant.

In Exercises 7–12, find (a) the complement and (b) the supplement of each angle or explain why the angle has no complement or no supplement.

7. $47°$

8. $75°$

9. $120°$

10. $160°$

11. $210°$

12. $-50°$

13. Write the complement of an acute angle of $\theta°$.

14. Write the complement of an obtuse angle of $\theta°$.

15. Write the supplement of an acute angle of $\theta°$.

16. Write the supplement of an obtuse angle of $\theta°$.

17. Is there an angle that is its own complement? If so, what is it?

18. Is there an angle that is it own supplement? If so, what is it?

In Exercises 19–30, find (a) the sum $\alpha + \beta$ and (b) the difference $\alpha - \beta$ of the two angles.

19. $\alpha = 34°12'$, $\beta = 27°5'$

20. $\alpha = 64°37'$, $\beta = 23°12'$

21. $\alpha = 47°54'$, $\beta = 12°14'$

22. $\alpha = 35°43'$, $\beta = 15°35'$

23. $\alpha = 15°38'$, $\beta = 13°45'$

24. $\alpha = 28°42'$, $\beta = 16°56'$

25. $\alpha = 70°12'15''$, $\beta = 54°18'$

26. $\alpha = 16°15'12''$, $\beta = 12°23'$

27. $\alpha = 12°15'22''$, $\beta = 8°27'36''$

28. $\alpha = 89°45'40''$, $\beta = 56°35'46''$

29. $\alpha = 187°56'33''$, $\beta = 220°34'67''$

30. $\alpha = 240°35'48''$, $\beta = 335°6'54''$

In Exercises 31–36, convert each angle to decimal degree notation. Round your answer to two decimal places. Verify your answer from the ANGLE menu of your calculator.

31. $70°45'$

32. $38°38'$

33. $23°42'30''$

34. $45°50'50''$

35. $-15°42'57''$

36. $-70°18'13''$

In Exercises 37–42, convert each angle to DMS notation. Round your answer to the nearest second. Verify your answer from the ANGLE menu of your calculator.

37. $27.32°$

38. $120.64°$

39. $13.347°$

40. $110.433°$

41. $19.0511°$

42. $82.7272°$

In Exercises 43–50, draw each angle in standard position and state the quadrant in which it lies.

43. 495°   **44.** 315°

45. 765°   **46.** 855°

47. −45°   **48.** −135°

49. −225°   **50.** −315°

In Exercises 51–58, find an angle between 0° and 360° that is coterminal with each angle. Then write all coterminal angles.

51. 400°   **52.** 700°

53. 1785°   **54.** 2064°

55. −50°   **56.** −225°

57. −400°   **58.** −700°

In Exercises 59–66, the terminal side of an angle in standard position passes through the given point. Write all possible degree measures of this angle.

59. $(3, 3)$ **60.** $(4, -4)$

61. $(-5, 5)$ **62.** $(-2, -2)$

63. $(1, 0)$ **64.** $(0, 2)$

65. $(-3, 0)$ **66.** $(0, -4)$

B EXERCISES Applying the Concepts

67. **Ferris wheel.** A Ferris wheel makes six revolutions in 20 minutes. Through how many degrees does a rider in a car move in ten seconds?

68. **Revolutions of a saw blade.** A circular saw blade makes 500 revolutions per minute. Find the number of degrees a point on the edge of the saw blade moves in one second.

69. **Clock hands.** Through how many degrees does the minute hand of a clock move from 4:20 P.M. to 5:10 P.M.?

70. **Clock hands.** Through how many degrees does the hour hand of a clock move from 3:15 P.M. to 7:45 P.M.?

71. **Geometry.** In the adjoining figure, AOB is a line. Find the value of x.

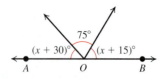

72. **Geometry.** In the adjoining figure, AOB is a line. Find the measure of each marked angle.

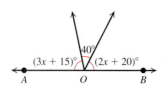

73. **Geometry.** In the adjoining figure, the lines ℓ_1 and ℓ_2 intersect. The measure of angle α is 3 times the measure of angle β. Find the measures of α, β, γ, and θ.

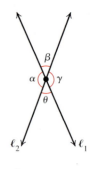

74. **Geometry.** Use the figure of Exercise 73 to find α, β, γ, and θ for $\alpha = (4x + 2)°$ and $\beta = (3x + 3)°$.

75. **Geometry.** In the adjoining figure, ℓ_1 and ℓ_2 are parallel lines and t is a transversal. Assuming that $\alpha = (5x + 70)°$ and $\beta = (4x + 29)°$, find the measures of α and β.

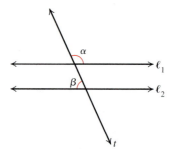

76. **Geometry.** Repeat Exercise 75 assuming that $\alpha = (7x + 94)°$ and $\beta = (5x - 10)°$.

77. **Geometry.** In the adjoining figure, rays AB and CD are parallel. Assuming that $\alpha = 40°$ and $\beta = 30°$, find the measure of $\angle BOC$.

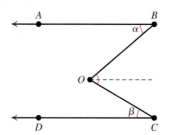

78. **Geometry.** In the adjoining figure, ray AB is parallel to ray CD and to ray EF. $\angle \alpha = 60°$, and line segment CE bisects $\angle BCD$. Find the measure of $\angle CEF$.

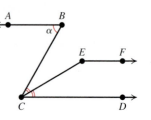

C EXERCISES Beyond the Basics

79. In the adjoining figure, the lines AB and CD intersect at the point O and $\angle COE = 90°$. Find the values of x, y, and z.

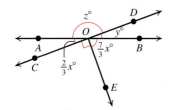

80. AB and CD are parallel lines and P and Q are points as shown in the figure.
  a. Find $\angle BPD$.
  b. Find $\angle ABQ + \angle BQD + \angle CDQ$.

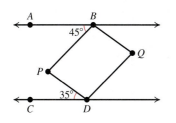

81. AB and CD are parallel lines, and a transversal intersects these lines at M and N, respectively. (See the figure.) Show that the bisectors of the interior angles form a rectangle.

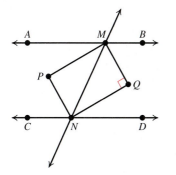

82. In Exercise 81, assuming that the transversal is perpendicular to the parallel lines, show that the bisectors of the interior angles form a square.

83. In the figure, AB, CD, and EF are parallel rays. Find the difference of the angles α and β.

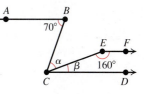

Critical Thinking

84. Four lines are in a plane, no two of which are parallel. Find the maximum number of points of intersections of these lines.

Triangles

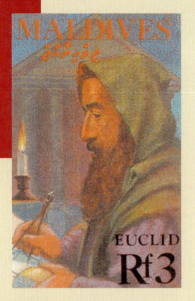

Euclid (315–270 BC)

Before Starting this Section, Review
1. Solving quadratic equations (Appendix)

Objectives
1   Classify triangles.
2   State and use the Pythagorean theorem.
3   Define 45°–45°–90° and 30°–60°–90° triangles.
4   Compare congruent and similar triangles.

EUCLID

Euclid, also known as Euclid of Alexandria, is popularly called the "Father of Geometry." Euclid's *Elements* includes 13 books on plane geometry, number theory, algebra, and other branches of mathematics. Although many of the results in *Elements* originated with earlier mathematicians, one of Euclid's accomplishments was to present them in a logically coherent way. His method of mathematical proofs has been a basic tool of mathematics during the last 24 centuries. Properties of similar triangles stated in Euclid's theorem (see page 19) are most important in the development of trigonometry. ■

---

1   Classify triangles.

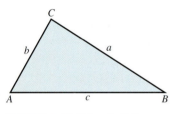

FIGURE 1.13   **Triangle *ABC***

Triangles

A triangle is a plane polygon with three vertices and three sides. For a triangle ABC, we follow the usual practice of labeling the length of the side opposite each vertex by the corresponding lowercase letter. So a, b, c are the lengths of the sides opposite the vertices A, B, C, respectively. See Figure 1.13.

BASIC TRIANGLE FACTS

In any triangle ABC (Figure 1.13), the following hold:

(i) Angle sum property. The sum of the measures of all three angles is 180°.

$$A + B + C = 180°$$

(ii) Triangle inequality. The sum of the lengths of any two sides is greater than the length of the third side.

$$a + b > c, \quad b + c > a, \quad c + a > b$$

(iii) Angle-side property. Larger angles have larger opposite sides.

$$\text{If } A > B, \text{ then } a > b.$$

(iv) Area. The area K of a triangle is given by

$$K = \frac{1}{2}(\text{base})(\text{height}).$$

The term *base* denotes the length of any side, and *height* denotes the length of a perpendicular to the side (or side extended) from the vertex opposite the side.

EXAMPLE 1   **Using the Angle Sum Property**

Find the angles of the triangle in Figure 1.14.

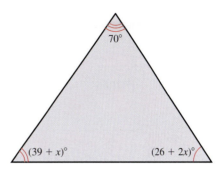

FIGURE 1.14

SOLUTION

We have $70 + (39 + x) + (26 + 2x) = 180$ Angle sum property

$$135 + 3x = 180 \qquad \text{Simplify.}$$
$$3x = 180 - 135 = 45$$
$$x = 15 \qquad \text{Solve for } x.$$

So $39 + x = 39 + 15 = 54$ and $26 + 2x = 26 + 2(15) = 56$. The angles of the triangle are $70°$, $54°$, and $56°$.   ▪ ▪ ▪

Practice Problem 1   Find the angles of the triangle in Figure 1.15.   ▪

We classify triangles according to the relative measures of their angles and sides.

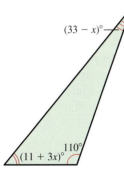

FIGURE 1.15

Type	Description	Figure
Acute Triangle	All three angles are acute.	
Right Triangle	One angle is a right angle.	
Obtuse Triangle	One angle is an obtuse angle.	Obtuse angle
Equilateral Triangle	All three sides are equal. All three angles have equal measure $60°$.	$60°$ $60°$ $60°$

continued on the next page

Type	Description	Figure
Isosceles Triangle	Two sides are equal. The two angles opposite equal sides are also equal.	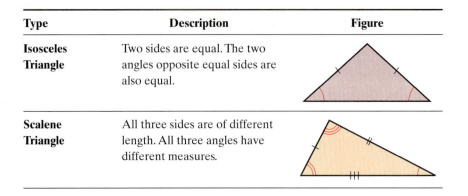
Scalene Triangle	All three sides are of different length. All three angles have different measures.	

The concepts of right triangles and *similar triangles* are important in trigonometry.

2 State and use Pythagorean theorem.

Right Triangle

In a right triangle, the side opposite the right angle is called the **hypotenuse**; it is the longest side in the right triangle. The other two sides are the **legs** of the triangle. Because the sum of the angles in any triangle is 180°, the other two angles in a right triangle are acute and complementary. A central theorem for right triangles is the Pythagorean theorem.

PYTHAGOREAN THEOREM

In any right triangle, the square of the length of the hypotenuse equals the sum of the squares of the lengths of the other two sides:

$$c^2 = a^2 + b^2$$

The converse of the Pythagorean theorem also is true: If the lengths of the sides of a triangle are a, b, and c and satisfy the relation $c^2 = a^2 + b^2$, then the triangle is a right triangle.

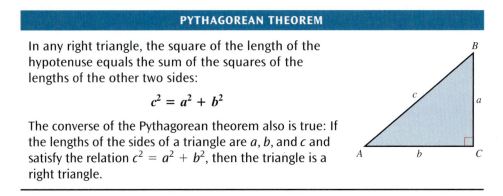

A Proof of the Pythagorean Theorem

There are hundreds of proofs of the Pythagorean theorem. We offer one that is based on the formulas for the areas of a rectangle and a triangle. We write the area of the square of length $a + b$ in two ways. See Figures 1.16 and 1.17.

Area of the square in Figure 1.16 = Area of the square in Figure 1.17.

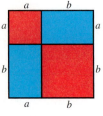

FIGURE 1.16

Areas of the two red squares	+	Areas of the two blue rectangles	=	Area of the red square	+	Areas of the four blue triangles
$a^2 + b^2$	+	$2(ab)$	=	c^2	+	$4\left(\dfrac{1}{2}ab\right)$
$a^2 + b^2$	+	$2ab$	=	c^2	+	$2ab$
		$a^2 + b^2$	=	c^2		Subtract $2ab$ from both sides.

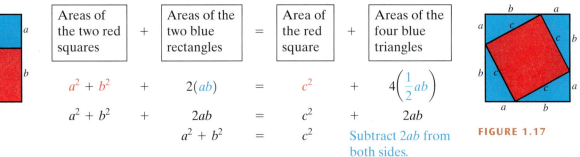

FIGURE 1.17

So the right triangle of the lower right corner of Figure 1.17 with legs of lengths a and b and hypotenuse of length c satisfies the relation $a^2 + b^2 = c^2$. Since a and b can be the lengths of the legs of any right triangle, the relation $a^2 + b^2 = c^2$ holds for all right triangles.

We can use the Pythagorean theorem to find the third side of a right triangle if any two sides are known.

EXAMPLE 2 Using the Pythagorean Theorem

A 26-foot ladder placed 10 feet from a house reaches the top of the chimney of the house. How high is the top of the chimney above the ground?

SOLUTION

Figure 1.18 shows a diagram of the situation.

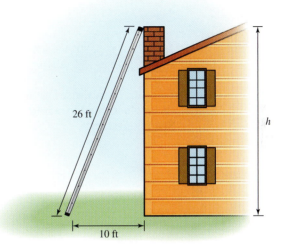

FIGURE 1.18

You can see that the height h of the top of the chimney is the third side of a right triangle in which two sides are known.

$$h^2 + 10^2 = 26^2 \qquad \text{Pythagorean theorem}$$
$$h^2 = 26^2 - 10^2 \qquad \text{Subtract } 10^2 \text{ from both sides.}$$
$$h^2 = 676 - 100 = 576 \qquad \text{Simplify.}$$
$$h = \sqrt{576} = 24 \qquad \text{Take the square root.}$$

The top of the chimney is 24 feet above the ground. ■ ■ ■

Practice Problem 2 Find the sides of the triangle in Figure 1.19. ■

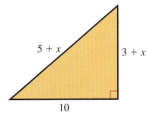

FIGURE 1.19

3 Define **45°–45°–90°** and **30°–60°–90°** triangles.

Some Special Right Triangles

A right triangle in which both acute angles are 45° is called a **45°–45°–90° triangle**. Such a triangle is an isosceles right triangle. So the two legs of the right triangle are of equal length. Let x be the length of each of the two legs. As is customary, we let c = length of the hypotenuse.

$$x^2 + x^2 = c^2 \qquad \text{Pythagorean theorem}$$
$$2x^2 = c^2$$
$$c = x\sqrt{2} \qquad c \text{ is a positive number.}$$

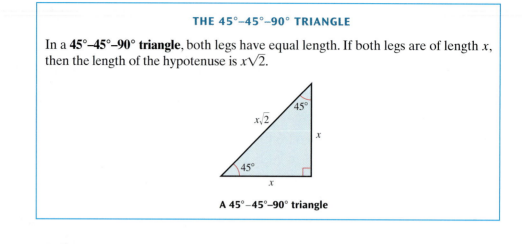

THE 45°–45°–90° TRIANGLE

In a **45°–45°–90° triangle**, both legs have equal length. If both legs are of length x, then the length of the hypotenuse is $x\sqrt{2}$.

A 45°–45°–90° triangle

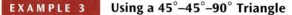

EXAMPLE 3   **Using a 45°–45°–90° Triangle**

Find the vertical rise (to the nearest foot) for a ski lift with cable length 2400 feet if the angle formed by a horizontal line at the bottom terminal and the lift cable is 45°. See Figure 1.20.

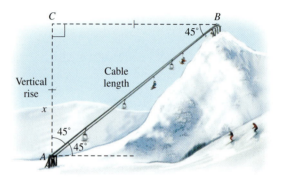

FIGURE 1.20

SOLUTION

We note that $\angle BAC$ in Figure 1.20 is 45°.

Consider the 45°–45°–90° triangle ABC. Let $AC = x$ be the vertical rise. Then the cable length $AB = x\sqrt{2}$. So

$$x\sqrt{2} = 2400 \qquad \text{Cable length is 2400 feet.}$$

$$x = \frac{2400}{\sqrt{2}} \qquad \text{Divide both sides by } \sqrt{2}.$$

$$x = \frac{2400}{\sqrt{2}} \cdot \frac{\sqrt{2}}{\sqrt{2}} \qquad \text{Rationalize the denominator.}$$

$$x = 1200\sqrt{2} \text{ ft} \qquad \text{Simplifying gives the exact answer.}$$

$$x \approx 1697 \text{ ft} \qquad \text{Use a calculator.} \qquad ■■■$$

Practice Problem 3   Repeat Example 3 assuming that the cable length is 3420 ft.   ■

Figure 1.21(a) shows an equilateral triangle with each side having length $2x$ and each angle equaling 60°. A segment from the vertex of one of the angles drawn perpendicular to the opposite leg produces two congruent triangles. The third angle of each congruent triangle is $180° - (90° + 60°) = 30°$. See Figure 1.21(b).

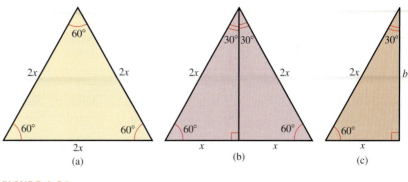

FIGURE 1.21

The right triangle in Figure 1.21(c) is called a **30°–60°–90° triangle**. We can find the length, b, of the third side of this triangle.

$$x^2 + b^2 = (2x)^2 \qquad \text{Pythagorean theorem}$$
$$x^2 + b^2 = 4x^2 \qquad (2x)^2 = (2x)(2x) = 4x^2$$
$$b^2 = 4x^2 - x^2 = 3x^2 \qquad \text{Solve for } b^2.$$
$$b = x\sqrt{3} \qquad b > 0 \text{ because } b \text{ represents length.}$$

THE 30°–60°–90° TRIANGLE

In a **30°–60°–90° triangle**, if the shortest leg (the side opposite the 30° angle) is of length x, then the hypotenuse (longest side) is of length $2x$ (2 times the length of the shortest leg) and the other leg (the side opposite the 60° angle) is of length $x\sqrt{3}$ ($\sqrt{3}$ times the length of the shortest leg).

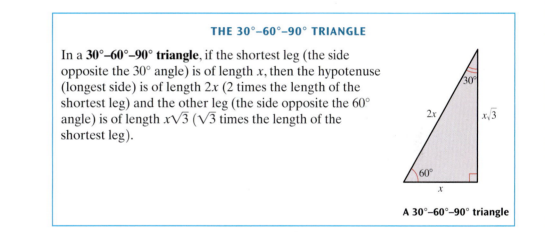

A 30°–60°–90° triangle

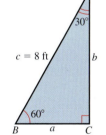

FIGURE 1.22

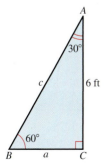

FIGURE 1.23

EXAMPLE 4　Finding Side Lengths in a 30°–60°–90° Triangle

Find the lengths of the sides of the triangle in Figure 1.22 rounded to the nearest tenth of a foot.

SOLUTION

The triangle ABC in Figure 1.22 is a 30°–60°–90° triangle. So the side a (opposite the 30° angle) is the shortest side.

$$8 = 2a \qquad \text{Hypotenuse} = 2 \cdot (\text{shortest side})$$
$$4 = a \qquad \text{Solve for } a.$$
$$b = a\sqrt{3} \qquad \text{Side opposite 60° angle} = \sqrt{3} \cdot (\text{shortest side})$$
$$= 4\sqrt{3} \approx 6.9 \qquad \text{Replace } a \text{ with 4 and use a calculator.}$$

The sides of the triangle are $a = 4$ ft, $b = 6.9$ ft, and $c = 8$ ft.　■ ■ ■

Practice Problem 4　Find the lengths of the sides of the triangle in Figure 1.23 rounded to the nearest tenth of a foot.　■

4 Compare congruent and
similar triangles.

Congruent and Similar Triangles

Recall from geometry that two figures are *congruent* if it is possible to place one of them on top of the other so that they coincide. The symbol $\cong$ is usually used for congruence. For angles, this means that their measures (in degrees or radians) are equal, and for segments, their lengths are equal. You'll also need to remember that a side of a triangle that lies between two angles is called the **included side** of the angles, and that the angle formed by two sides is the **included angle** of the sides.

CONGRUENT TRIANGLES

Two triangles are **congruent** if their corresponding sides and corresponding angles are congruent.

RECALL

The **corresponding sides** are the sides opposite the equal angles in each triangle.

In Figure 1.24, triangles *ABC* and *DEF* are congruent. The corresponding congruent sides are marked with small straight line segments called *hash marks*. The corresponding congruent angles are marked with small *arcs*.

$\angle A \cong \angle D, a \cong d$
$\angle B \cong \angle E, b \cong e$
$\angle C \cong \angle F, c \cong f$

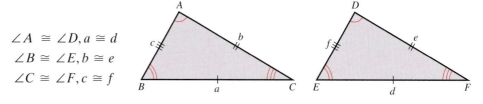

FIGURE 1.24 **Two congruent triangles**

Fortunately, not every part of the definition for congruent (or similar) triangles must be verified to decide whether two triangles are congruent (or similar).

CONGRUENT-TRIANGLE THEOREMS

SAS (Side–Angle–Side). If two sides and the included angle of one triangle are equal to the corresponding sides and the included angle of a second triangle, the two triangles are congruent.
ASA (Angle–Side–Angle). If two angles and the included side of one triangle are equal to the corresponding two angles and the included side of a second triangle, the two triangles are congruent.
SSS (Side–Side–Side). If the three sides of one triangle are equal to the corresponding sides of a second triangle, the two triangle are congruent.

Two congruent triangles have the same shape and same size. Two triangles are *similar* if they have the same shape but not necessarily the same size. If two triangles are similar (same shape), then one is an enlargement of the other. This means that two similar triangles have equal (congruent) angles and their corresponding sides are in the same proportion.

SIMILAR TRIANGLES

Two triangles are **similar** if their corresponding angles are equal and their corresponding sides are proportional.

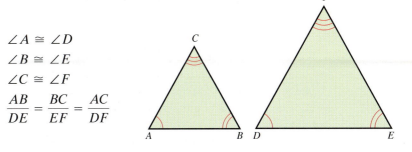

$$\angle A \cong \angle D$$
$$\angle B \cong \angle E$$
$$\angle C \cong \angle F$$
$$\frac{AB}{DE} = \frac{BC}{EF} = \frac{AC}{DF}$$

FIGURE 1.25 Two similar triangles

In fact, Euclid proved that if the angles of one triangle are equal to the angles of another triangle, then their corresponding sides are proportional.

EUCLID'S THEOREM

Two triangles are **similar** if the angles of one are equal (congruent) to the angles of the other. In this case, the lengths of their corresponding sides are proportional.

EXAMPLE 5   Finding Side Lengths in Similar Triangles

Triangles ABC and DEF in Figure 1.26 are similar. Find the lengths x and y of the unknown sides of the two triangles.

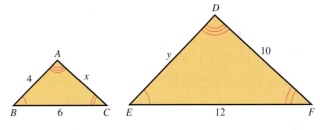

FIGURE 1.26

SOLUTION

Because the given triangles are similar, their corresponding sides are proportional. To find x, we use the proportion that contains x and three known sides.

$$\frac{AC}{DF} = \frac{BC}{EF} \qquad \text{Corresponding sides are proportional.}$$

$$\frac{x}{10} = \frac{6}{12} \qquad \text{Substitute values.}$$

$$x = \frac{6(10)}{12} = 5 \qquad \text{Multiply both sides by 10 and simplify.}$$

To find y, we use the following proportion:

$$\frac{BC}{EF} = \frac{AB}{DE}$$

$$\frac{6}{12} = \frac{4}{y} \qquad \text{Substitute values.}$$

$$6y = 12(4) \qquad \text{Cross multiply.}$$

$$y = \frac{12(4)}{6} = 8 \qquad \text{Solve for } y \text{ and simplify.} \qquad ■ ■ ■$$

STUDY TIP

The proportions for similar triangles were given as $\frac{AB}{DE} = \frac{BC}{EF} = \frac{AC}{DE}$. They could also have been given as $\frac{DE}{AB} = \frac{EF}{BC} = \frac{DE}{AC}$.

When solving problems choose the most convenient proportions. In Example 5, choosing $\frac{EF}{BC} = \frac{DE}{AB}$ leads to $\frac{12}{6} = \frac{y}{4}$. Make this choice if you prefer to work with variables in the numerator.

Practice Problem 5 Find the unknown side lengths for the similar triangles in Figure 1.27.

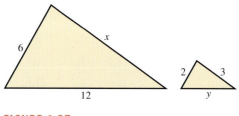

FIGURE 1.27

Many problems involving similar triangles have one triangle on top or inside of another triangle.

EXAMPLE 6 **Finding Side Lengths in Similar Triangles**

In Figure 1.28, the segment DE is parallel to the side BC.

a. Show that the triangles ADE and ABC are similar.

b. Find the unknown segment lengths x and y.

SOLUTION

a. Because DE is parallel to BC, the line through D and B is a transversal crossing the parallel lines containing the sides DE and BC. We have

$$\angle ADE = \angle ABC \qquad \text{Corresponding angles}$$
$$\angle AED = \angle ACB \qquad \text{Corresponding angles}$$

Both triangles share angle A. So the triangles ADE and ABC are similar because they have equal corresponding angles.

b. To find x, we use the proportion:

$$\frac{AE}{AC} = \frac{AD}{AB} \qquad \text{Corresponding sides are proportional.}$$

$$\frac{x}{x+7} = \frac{3}{9} \qquad \text{Substitute values.}$$

$$9x = 3(x+7) \qquad \text{Cross multiply.}$$

$$9x = 3x + 21 \qquad \text{Distribute.}$$

$$9x - 3x = 21 \qquad \text{Subtract } 3x \text{ from both sides.}$$

$$6x = 21 \qquad \text{Simplify.}$$

$$x = \frac{21}{6} = 3.5 \qquad \text{Solve for } x \text{ and simplify.}$$

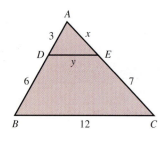

FIGURE 1.28

To find y, we use the proportion:

$$\frac{DE}{BC} = \frac{AD}{AB} \qquad \text{Corresponding sides are proportional.}$$

$$\frac{y}{12} = \frac{3}{9} \qquad \text{Substitute values.}$$

$$y = 12\left(\frac{3}{9}\right) = 4 \qquad \text{Multiply both sides by 12 and simplify.} \qquad ■■■$$

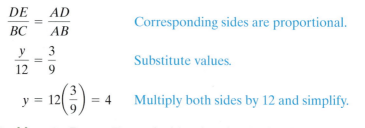

FIGURE 1.29

Practice Problem 6 Repeat Example 6 for the triangles in Figure 1.29.

SECTION 1.2 ■ Exercises

A EXERCISES Basic Skills and Concepts

1. The sum of the measures of the three angles of a triangle is _____.

2. In an isosceles triangle, the two angles opposite equal sides are _____.

3. In a 30°–60°–90° triangle, the hypotenuse is _____ times the length of the shortest side and the side opposite the 60° angle is _____ times the length of the shortest side.

4. In similar triangles, the lengths of the corresponding sides are _____.

5. *True or False* If two triangles are congruent, then they are similar.

6. *True or False* If two triangles are similar, then they are congruent.

In Exercises 7–14, refer to a triangle ABC.

7. If $A = 50°$ and $B = 72°$, find C.

8. If $B = 64°$ and $C = 48°$, find A.

9. If $A = 48°15'$ and $C = 98°$, find B.

10. If $A = 34°$ and $B = 67°45'$, find C.

11. If $A = 46.72°$ and $C = 65°$, find B.

12. If $A = 69°$ and $B = 54.67°$, find C.

13. If $A = 60°$, $B = (57 - x)°$, and $C = (25 + 3x)°$, find B and C.

14. $A = (50 + 4x)°$, $B = 50°$, and $C = (80 - 2x)°$, find A and C.

15. Find the angles of the triangle ABC assuming that $A = x°$, $B = 2x°$, and $C = 3x°$.

16. Find the angles of the triangle ABC assuming that $A = 2x°$, $B = 3x°$, and $C = 4x°$.

In Exercises 17–24, refer to the right triangle ABC with $C = 90°$.

17. Assuming that $a = 5$ and $b = 12$, find c.

18. Assuming that $a = 7$ and $b = 24$, find c.

19. Assuming that $a = 5$ and $c = 13$, find b.

20. Assuming that $a = 20$ and $c = 29$, find b.

21. Assuming that $a = 8 - x$, $b = 9 + x$, and $c = 13$, find a and b.

22. Assuming that $a = 17 - 2x$, $b = 24$, and $c = 15 + 2x$, find a and c.

23. Assuming that $a = 5 + x$, $b = 6 + 3x$, and $c = 5 + 4x$, find a, b, and c.

24. Assuming that $a = 2x - 1$, $b = 10 + 6x$, and $c = 6 + 7x$, find a, b, and c.

In Exercises 25–32, find the remaining sides of a 45°–45°–90° triangle from the given information.

25. The shorter sides each have length 4.

26. The shorter sides each have length 5.

27. The shorter sides each have length $\frac{1}{2}$.

28. The shorter sides each have length $\frac{3}{5}$.

29. The hypotenuse has length $3\sqrt{2}$.

30. The hypotenuse has length $6\sqrt{2}$.

31. The hypotenuse has length 4.

32. The hypotenuse has length 6.

In Exercises 33–38, find the remaining sides of a 30°–60°–90° triangle from the given information.

33. The length of the shortest side is 4.

34. The length of the shortest side is 6.

35. The length of the side opposite the 60° angle is 4.

36. The length of the side opposite the 60° angle is 6.

37. The length of the hypotenuse is 4.

38. The length of the hypotenuse is 6.

In Exercises 39–44, a pair of similar triangles is given. Write the corresponding angles and the ratios of the corresponding sides.

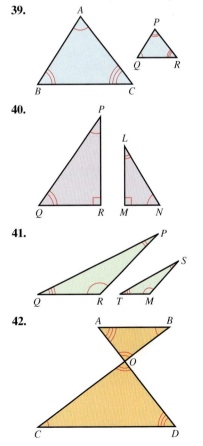

39.

40.

41.

42.

43.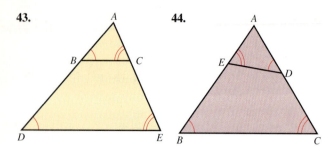

44.

In Exercises 45–47, explain why each pair of triangles is similar. Write the ratios of the corresponding sides.

45.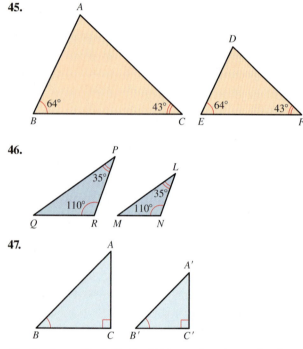

46.

47.

48. Angle–angle similarity. If two angles of one triangle are equal to two angles of another triangle, then the two triangles are similar. Explain why this statement is always true.

In Exercises 49–52, explain why the two triangles *AOB* and *COD* are similar. Find the lengths of the unknown segments labeled with the variables *x*, *y*, and *z*.

49. *AB* and *CD* are parallel.   **50.** *AB* and *CD* are parallel.

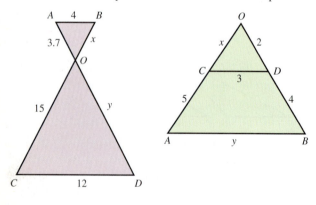

51.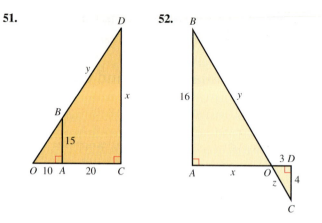

52.

B EXERCISES Applying the Concepts

53. Distance. The distance between the tops of two trees 47 feet and 39 feet high is 17 feet. Find the horizontal distance between the trees.

54. Distance between cars. Two cars leave a city at the same time. One heads north at 30 miles per hour, and the other heads west at 40 miles per hour. What is the distance between the two cars after two hours?

55. Flagpole. The shadow of a flagpole is 20 feet long when the angle between the shadow end and the top of the flagpole is 60°. How tall is the flagpole?

56. Ladder length. A ladder leaning against a vertical wall makes an angle of 45° with the ground. The foot of the ladder is 9 feet from the wall. Find the length of the ladder.

57. Meteorology. A balloon is connected to a meteorological station by a cable of length 200 meters inclined at 60° to the horizontal. Find the height of the balloon from the ground.

58. Shadow length. The sun is 30° above the horizontal. Find the length of the shadow of a building that is 150 feet tall.

59. Area of a rectangle. In a rectangle, the angle between a diagonal and a side is 30° and the length of the diagonal is 6 centimeters. Find the area of the rectangle.

60. Repeat Exercise 59 assuming that the angle between a diagonal and a side is 45°.

61. Height of a building. A surveyor measures the shadow of a building to be 32 feet. At the same time, the shadow of his 6-foot-tall assistant is 4 feet. How tall is the building?

62. Height of a tower. A tower casts a shadow 60 feet long. At the same time, the shadow of a 5.7-foot-tall groundskeeper is 11.4 feet. Find the height of the tower.

63. Tennis. Find the height h at which the tennis ball must be hit so that it will just pass over the middle of the net and land 13 feet from the base of the net. See the diagram.

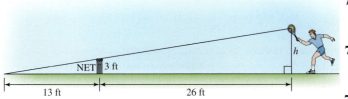

NET 3 ft

13 ft   26 ft

64. Tennis. Suppose the tennis ball from Exercise 63 is hit 7.5 feet above the ground and it just crosses the middle of the net and lands 15 feet from the base of the net. Find the distance the ball traveled.

C EXERCISES Beyond the Basics

65. In triangle ABC, let AD be perpendicular to BC. If angle C is acute, show that

$$AB^2 = BC^2 + AC^2 - 2BC \cdot CD.$$

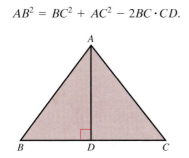

66. In Exercise 65, assuming that $C = 60°$, show that $c^2 = a^2 + b^2 - ab$.

67. In triangle ABC, let $\angle C$ be an obtuse angle and AD be perpendicular to BC (extended). Show that

$$AB^2 = BC^2 + AC^2 + 2BC \cdot CD.$$

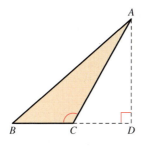

68. In Exercise 67, if $C = 120°$, show that $c^2 = a^2 + b^2 + ab$.

69. In a triangle ABC, show that angle C is a right angle, an obtuse angle, or an acute angle accordingly as $c^2 = a^2 + b^2$, $c^2 > a^2 + b^2$, or $c^2 < a^2 + b^2$, respectively.

70. The sides of a triangle are 13 cm, 16 cm, and 10 cm. Is the triangle right-angled, acute, or obtuse?

71. In an equilateral triangle ABC, let AD be perpendicular to BC. Show that $3AB^2 = 4AD^2$.

72. In a right triangle ABC with $A = 90°$, let AD be perpendicular to BC. Let the length of AD be p. Show that

$$\frac{1}{p^2} = \frac{1}{b^2} + \frac{1}{c^2}.$$

73. Show that the line segment joining the midpoints of any two sides of a triangle is parallel to the third side and equal to one-half of it.

74. Show that the line segments joining the midpoints of the sides of a triangle form four triangles, each of which is similar to the original triangle.

75. Show that in two similar triangles, the ratio of the two corresponding sides is equal to the ratio of their corresponding heights.

76. Show that the ratio of the areas of two similar triangles is equal to the ratio of the squares of any two corresponding sides.

77. The areas of two similar triangles are 49 cm² and 81 cm². If a side of the smaller triangle is of length 35 cm, find the length of the corresponding side of the bigger triangle.

78. The areas of two similar triangles are 12 ft² and 48 ft². If the height of the smaller triangle is 3.2 ft, find the corresponding height of the larger triangle.

Exercises 79–82 refer to a regular n-gon (an n-sided polygon in which all sides are of equal length and all angles are of equal measure).

79. Show that each angle of a regular n-gon is $\frac{180}{n}(n-2)$ degrees.

80. The sides of a regular pentagon (five-sided polygon) are extended to form a star. Find the measure of the angle at each point of the star.

81. Repeat Exercise 80 for a regular n-gon ($n \geq 5$).

82. The sides of a regular n-gon ($n \geq 5$) are extended to form a star. Assuming that the sum of the measures of the angles of the star is 540°, find the number of sides of the polygon.

Critical Thinking

83. In a triangle ABC, which of the following is always true?

(i) $c^2 = a^2 + b^2$ (ii) $c - a = b$

(iii) $c - a > b$ (iv) $c - a < b$

Trigonometric Functions

Before Starting this Section, Review

1. Distance formula (Appendix)
2. Angle in standard position (Section 1.1)
3. Similar triangles (Section 1.2)
4. 30°–60°–90° triangle (Section 1.2)
5. 45°–45°–90° triangle (Section 1.2)

Objectives

1. Define the trigonometric functions of an angle.
2. Find the trigonometric function values of quadrantal angles.
3. Find trigonometric function values of 30°, 45°, and 60°.
4. Determine signs of the trigonometric functions.

GOLF AND THE SINE FUNCTION

The sine and cosine functions show up in surprising places.

The angle that a golf ball makes with the ground on take off and its initial speed determine the rest of its flight. Moreover, the time it takes for the ball to hit the ground after reaching its maximum height is exactly the same as if the ball had been dropped straight down from that height. The horizontal motion has no effect on the vertical motion. Suppose we ignore air resistance and measure time in seconds and distance in feet. Then the equation $h = v_0 t \sin \theta - 16t^2$ gives the height, h, of the golf ball after t seconds, where θ is the initial angle the ball makes with the ground and v_0 is its initial speed. The horizontal distance, d, the ball travels in t seconds is $d = t v_0 \cos \theta$. In Example 10, we use these equations to investigate the flight of a golf ball. ■

---

1 Define the trigonometric functions of an angle.

Trigonometric Functions of Angles

Consider an angle θ in standard position. Let $P = (x, y)$ be any point (other than the origin) on the terminal ray of θ. The distance, r, between the origin $O = (0, 0)$ and the point $P = (x, y)$ is $r = \sqrt{(x - 0)^2 + (y - 0)^2} = \sqrt{x^2 + y^2}$. Then $r > 0$.

We define the six trigonometric functions, **sine**, **cosine**, **tangent**, **cosecant**, **secant**, and **cotangent**, of the angle θ using the abbreviations **sin**, **cos**, **tan**, **csc**, **sec**, and **cot**, respectively.

DEFINITION OF THE TRIGONOMETRIC FUNCTIONS OF AN ANGLE θ

Let $P(x, y)$ be any point (other than the origin) on the terminal ray of an angle θ in standard position and let $r = \sqrt{x^2 + y^2}$. We define

$$\sin \theta = \frac{y}{r} \qquad\qquad \csc \theta = \frac{r}{y} \quad (y \neq 0)$$

$$\cos \theta = \frac{x}{r} \qquad\qquad \sec \theta = \frac{r}{x} \quad (x \neq 0)$$

$$\tan \theta = \frac{y}{x} \quad (x \neq 0) \qquad\qquad \cot \theta = \frac{x}{y} \quad (y \neq 0)$$

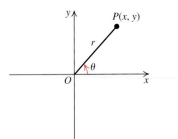

FIGURE 1.30 Standard position

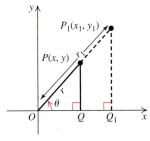

FIGURE 1.31

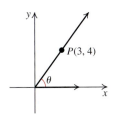

FIGURE 1.32

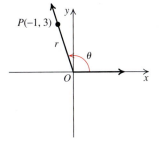

FIGURE 1.33

We make the following observations:

1. You can see (Figure 1.30) that the trigonometric functions of an angle are just the names of the six possible ratios of two out of the three numbers x, y, and r.

2. Because the value of each trigonometric function of an angle in standard position is determined by the position of the terminal side, all *coterminal angles* are assigned identical values by the six trigonometric functions.

3. In Figure 1.31, triangles POQ and P_1OQ_1 are similar by angle–angle similarity, so the ratios of corresponding sides are equal. Letting $r = \sqrt{x^2 + y^2}$ and $r_1 = \sqrt{x_1^2 + y_1^2}$, we have $\sin \theta = \dfrac{y}{r} = \dfrac{y_1}{r_1}$, $\cos \theta = \dfrac{x}{r} = \dfrac{x_1}{r_1}$, and so on. This shows that the values of the trigonometric functions do not depend on the choice of the point $P(x, y)$ on the terminal side of θ.

EXAMPLE 1   **Finding Trigonometric Function Values**

The terminal side of an angle θ in standard position contains the point $(3, 4)$. Find the values of the six trigonometric functions of θ.

SOLUTION

Because $x = 3$ and $y = 4$ (see Figure 1.32), we have

$$r = \sqrt{x^2 + y^2} \qquad \text{Definition of } r$$
$$= \sqrt{3^2 + 4^2} \qquad \text{Replace } x \text{ with 3 and } y \text{ with 4.}$$
$$= \sqrt{25} = 5 \qquad \text{Simplify.}$$

Replacing x with 3, y with 4, and r with 5 in the definition of the trigonometric functions, we have

$$\sin \theta = \frac{y}{r} = \frac{4}{5} \qquad \csc \theta = \frac{r}{y} = \frac{5}{4}$$

$$\cos \theta = \frac{x}{r} = \frac{3}{5} \qquad \sec \theta = \frac{r}{x} = \frac{5}{3}$$

$$\tan \theta = \frac{y}{x} = \frac{4}{3} \qquad \cot \theta = \frac{x}{y} = \frac{3}{4} \qquad ■ ■ ■$$

Practice Problem 1   The terminal side of an angle α in standard position contains the point $(-5, -12)$. Find the values of the six trigonometric functions of α.   ■

We will assume all angles to be in standard position unless stated otherwise.

EXAMPLE 2   **Finding Trigonometric Function Values**

The terminal side of an angle θ contains the point $P(-1, 3)$. Find the exact values of the six trigonometric functions of θ.

SOLUTION

Because $x = -1$ and $y = 3$ (see Figure 1.33), we have

$$r = \sqrt{x^2 + y^2} \qquad \text{Definition of } r$$
$$= \sqrt{(-1)^2 + 3^2} \qquad \text{Replace } x \text{ with } -1 \text{ and } y \text{ with 3.}$$
$$= \sqrt{10} \qquad \text{Simplify.}$$

STUDY TIP

We rationalize the denominator to remove radicals from it. For example,

$$\frac{3}{\sqrt{10}} = \frac{3}{\sqrt{10}} \cdot \frac{\sqrt{10}}{\sqrt{10}}$$

$$= \frac{3\sqrt{10}}{(\sqrt{10})^2} = \frac{3\sqrt{10}}{10}$$

Replacing x with -1, y with 3, and r with $\sqrt{10}$ in the definition of the trigonometric functions, we have

$$\sin\theta = \frac{y}{r} = \frac{3}{\sqrt{10}} = \frac{3\sqrt{10}}{10} \qquad \csc\theta = \frac{r}{y} = \frac{\sqrt{10}}{3}$$

$$\cos\theta = \frac{x}{r} = \frac{-1}{\sqrt{10}} = -\frac{\sqrt{10}}{10} \qquad \sec\theta = \frac{r}{x} = \frac{\sqrt{10}}{-1} = -\sqrt{10}$$

$$\tan\theta = \frac{y}{x} = \frac{3}{-1} = -3 \qquad \cot\theta = \frac{x}{y} = \frac{-1}{3} = -\frac{1}{3} \qquad ■■■$$

Practice Problem 2 The terminal side of an angle θ contains the point $P(2, -5)$. Find the exact values of the six trigonometric functions of θ. ■

2 Find trigonometric function values of quadrantal angles.

Trigonometric Functions of Quadrantal Angles

Recall that an angle in standard position is a quadrantal angle if its terminal side coincides with a coordinate axis. The angles with measure $0°$, $\pm90°$, $\pm180°$, $\pm270°$, $\pm360°$, $\pm450°$, and so on, are quadrantal angles. In general, an angle θ of the form $\theta = n \cdot 90°$, where n is any integer, is a quadrantal angle.

In the definitions of the trigonometric functions, notice that if one of the coordinates of a point on the terminal side of an angle is 0, then this coordinate cannot appear in a denominator.

If the terminal side is on the x-axis, then the y-coordinate is 0 and the cotangent $\left(\cot\theta = \dfrac{x}{y}\right)$ and the cosecant $\left(\csc\theta = \dfrac{r}{y}\right)$ functions are undefined. If the terminal side is on the y-axis, then the x-coordinate is 0 and the tangent $\left(\tan\theta = \dfrac{y}{x}\right)$ and the secant $\left(\sec\theta = \dfrac{r}{x}\right)$ functions are undefined.

EXAMPLE 3 **Finding the Values of the Trigonometric Functions of Quadrantal Angles**

Find the values (if any) of the six trigonometric functions of each angle.

a. $\theta = 0°$ **b.** $\theta = 90°$

SOLUTION

First choose a point on the terminal side of each angle, as shown in Figure 1.34. Then use the definitions of the trigonometric functions.

a. $\theta = 0°$; choose $P(1, 0)$, then $x = 1$, $y = 0$, and $r = \sqrt{1^2 + 0^2} = 1$,

$$\sin 0° = \frac{y}{r} = \frac{0}{1} = 0 \qquad \cos 0° = \frac{x}{r} = \frac{1}{1} = 1$$

$$\tan 0° = \frac{y}{x} = \frac{0}{1} = 0 \qquad \sec 0° = \frac{r}{x} = \frac{1}{1} = 1$$

Because the y-coordinate of P is 0, $\csc 0°$ and $\cot 0°$ are undefined.

b. $\theta = 90°$; choose $Q(0, 1)$, then $x = 0$, $y = 1$, and $r = \sqrt{0^2 + 1^2} = 1$,

$$\sin 90° = \frac{y}{r} = \frac{1}{1} = 1 \qquad \cos 90° = \frac{x}{r} = \frac{0}{1} = 0$$

$$\csc 90° = \frac{r}{y} = \frac{1}{1} = 1 \qquad \cot 90° = \frac{x}{y} = \frac{0}{1} = 0$$

Because the x-coordinate of Q is 0, $\sec 90°$ and $\tan 90°$ are undefined. ■■■

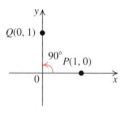

FIGURE 1.34 Quadrantal angles 0° and 90°

Practice Problem 3   Find the values (if any) of the six trigonometric functions of each angle.

a. $\theta = 180°$ **b.** $\theta = 270°$ ■

Table 1.1 summarizes the facts about nonnegative quadrantal angles less than 360°.

TABLE 1.1 Trigonometric Function Values of Quadrantal Angles

θ (degrees)	$\sin \theta$	$\cos \theta$	$\tan \theta$	$\cot \theta$	$\sec \theta$	$\csc \theta$
0°	0	1	0	undefined	1	undefined
90°	1	0	undefined	0	undefined	1
180°	0	−1	0	undefined	−1	undefined
270°	−1	0	undefined	0	undefined	−1

FINDING THE SOLUTION: A PROCEDURE

EXAMPLE 4   **Finding the Trigonometric Function Values of Coterminal Quadrantal Angles**

OBJECTIVE
Find the trigonometric function values of quadrantal angles greater than or equal to 360° or less than 0°.

Step 1   For a given angle α, find the nonnegative angle θ less than 360° that is coterminal with the given angle.

   (i) If $\alpha \geq 360°$, subtract multiples of 360° to find θ.

   (ii) If $\alpha < 0°$, add multiples of 360° to find θ.

Step 2   Now α and θ are coterminal angles. They have the same trigonometric function values. Use Table 1.1 to write the trigonometric function values of α.

EXAMPLE
Find the trigonometric function values of 990°.

Because 990° > 360° we subtract multiples of 360° until the resulting angle is less than 360°.

$$990° - 360° = 630°$$

$990° - 2(360°) = 270°$, and $270° < 360°$. Because $270° = 990° - 2(360°)$, the angle 270° is coterminal with 990°.

Using Table 1.1, we have

$$\sin 990° = \sin 270° = -1$$
$$\csc 990° = \csc 270° = -1$$
$$\cos 990° = \cos 270° = 0$$
$$\sec 990° = \sec 270° = \text{undefined}$$
$$\tan 990° = \tan 270° = \text{undefined}$$
$$\cot 990° = \cot 270° = 0$$ ■ ■ ■

Practice Problem 4   Find the trigonometric function values of 1170°.   ■

EXAMPLE 5   **Finding Trigonometric Function Values**

Find the trigonometric function values of −1260°.

SOLUTION
Since $-1260° < 0°$, we add multiples of 360° to find its coterminal quadrantal angle in Table 1.1. Because $-1260° + 4(360°) = -1260° + 1440° = 180°$, the angles 180° and −1260° are coterminal angles.

Using Table 1.1, we have

$$\sin(-1260°) = \sin 180° = 0 \qquad \csc(-1260°) = \csc 180° = \text{undefined}$$
$$\cos(-1260°) = \cos 180° = -1 \qquad \sec(-1260°) = \sec 180° = -1$$
$$\tan(-1260°) = \tan 180° = 0 \qquad \cot(-1260°) = \cot 180° = \text{undefined}$$

▪ ▪ ▪

Practice Problem 5   Find the trigonometric function values of $-630°$.   ▪

3 Find trigonometric function values of 30°, 45°, and 60°.

Trigonometric Function Values of Special Angles

In the previous section, we introduced two special triangles: the 30°–60°–90° triangles and the 45°–45°–90° triangles. Figure 1.35 shows both types of triangles when the length of the shortest side is 1.

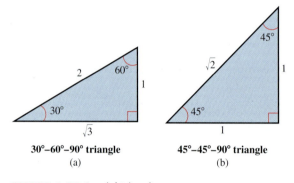

30°–60°–90° triangle
(a)

45°–45°–90° triangle
(b)

FIGURE 1.35 Special triangles

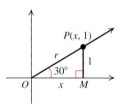

FIGURE 1.36

EXAMPLE 6   **Finding Trigonometric Function Values of 30°**

Find the trigonometric function values of 30°.

SOLUTION
Place an angle of measure 30° in standard position. Choose the point P on its terminal side with y-coordinate equal to 1. The triangle POM in Figure 1.36 is a 30°–60°–90° triangle.
So, $x = \sqrt{3}, y = 1$, and $r = 2$. See Figure 1.35.

$$\sin 30° = \frac{y}{r} = \frac{1}{2} \qquad\qquad \csc 30° = \frac{r}{y} = \frac{2}{1} = 2$$

$$\cos 30° = \frac{x}{r} = \frac{\sqrt{3}}{2} \qquad\qquad \sec 30° = \frac{r}{x} = \frac{2}{\sqrt{3}} = \frac{2\sqrt{3}}{3}$$

$$\tan 30° = \frac{y}{x} = \frac{1}{\sqrt{3}} = \frac{\sqrt{3}}{3} \qquad \cot 30° = \frac{x}{y} = \frac{\sqrt{3}}{1} = \sqrt{3}$$ ▪ ▪ ▪

Practice Problem 6   Find the trigonometric function values of 60°.   ▪

EXAMPLE 7   **Finding Trigonometric Function Values of 45°**

Find the trigonometric function values of 45°.

SOLUTION
Place an angle of measure 45° in standard position. Choose the point P with y-coordinate equal to 1. The triangle POM in Figure 1.37 is a 45°–45°–90° triangle.

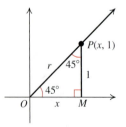

FIGURE 1.37

So, $x = 1, y = 1$, and $r = \sqrt{2}$. See Figure 1.35.

$$\sin 45° = \frac{y}{r} = \frac{1}{\sqrt{2}} = \frac{\sqrt{2}}{2} \qquad \csc 45° = \frac{r}{y} = \frac{\sqrt{2}}{1} = \sqrt{2}$$

$$\cos 45° = \frac{x}{r} = \frac{1}{\sqrt{2}} = \frac{\sqrt{2}}{2} \qquad \sec 45° = \frac{r}{x} = \frac{\sqrt{2}}{1} = \sqrt{2}$$

$$\tan 45° = \frac{y}{x} = \frac{1}{1} = 1 \qquad \cot 45° = \frac{x}{y} = \frac{1}{1} = 1 \qquad \blacksquare\,\blacksquare\,\blacksquare$$

Practice Problem 7   Find the trigonometric function values of $405° = 45° + 360°$.   ■

The trigonometric function values of the *common angles* $0°, 30°, 45°, 60°,$ and $90°$ are used frequently and are summarized in Table 1.2.

TABLE 1.2 Trigonometric Function Values of Common Angles

θ	$\sin\theta$	$\cos\theta$	$\tan\theta$	$\cot\theta$	$\sec\theta$	$\csc\theta$
0°	0	1	0	undefined	1	undefined
30°	$\frac{1}{2}$	$\frac{\sqrt{3}}{2}$	$\frac{\sqrt{3}}{3}$	$\sqrt{3}$	$\frac{2\sqrt{3}}{3}$	2
45°	$\frac{\sqrt{2}}{2}$	$\frac{\sqrt{2}}{2}$	1	1	$\sqrt{2}$	$\sqrt{2}$
60°	$\frac{\sqrt{3}}{2}$	$\frac{1}{2}$	$\sqrt{3}$	$\frac{\sqrt{3}}{3}$	2	$\frac{2\sqrt{3}}{3}$
90°	1	0	undefined	0	undefined	1

4 Determine signs of the trigonometric functions.

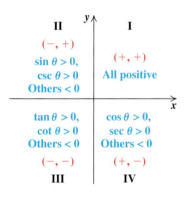

FIGURE 1.38 Signs of the trigonometric functions

Signs of the Trigonometric Functions

Suppose angle θ is not a quadrantal angle and its terminal side contains a point (x, y) other than the origin. We know that $r = \sqrt{x^2 + y^2}$ is positive. Therefore, the signs of x and y determine the signs of the trigonometric functions.

If θ lies in quadrant I, then both x and y are positive; so all six trigonometric function values are positive. However, if θ lies in quadrant II, then x is negative and y is positive, which means that only $\sin\theta = \frac{y}{r}$ and $\csc\theta = \frac{r}{y}$ are positive. If θ lies in quadrant III, then x and y are both negative; so only $\tan\theta = \frac{y}{x}$ and $\cot\theta = \frac{x}{y}$ are positive. If θ lies in quadrant IV, then x is positive and y is negative, which means that only $\cos\theta = \frac{x}{r}$ and $\sec\theta = \frac{r}{x}$ are positive. Figure 1.38 and Table 1.3 summarize the signs of the trigonometric functions.

TABLE 1.3 Signs of Trigonometric Functions

Functions	Positive in Quadrants	Negative in Quadrants
Sine and cosecant	I and II	III and IV
Cosine and secant	I and IV	II and III
Tangent and cotangent	I and III	II and IV

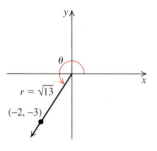

FIGURE 1.39

EXAMPLE 8   **Determining the Quadrant in Which an Angle Lies**

Assuming that $\tan \theta > 0$ and $\cos \theta < 0$, in which quadrant does θ lie?

SOLUTION

Because $\tan \theta > 0$, θ must lie in quadrant I or in quadrant III. However, $\cos \theta > 0$ for θ in quadrant I, so θ must lie in quadrant III. ■ ■ ■

Practice Problem 8   Assuming that $\sin \theta > 0$ and $\cos \theta < 0$, in which quadrant does θ lie? ■

EXAMPLE 9   **Evaluating Trigonometric Functions**

Given that $\tan \theta = \dfrac{3}{2}$ and $\cos \theta < 0$, find the exact values of $\sin \theta$ and $\sec \theta$.

SOLUTION

Because $\tan \theta > 0$ and $\cos \theta < 0$, angle θ lies in quadrant III. We identify a point (x, y) in quadrant III that is on the terminal side of θ. We have

$$\tan \theta = \frac{y}{x} = \frac{3}{2},$$

and because the point (x, y) is in quadrant III, both x and y must be negative. See Figure 1.39. If we choose $x = -2$ and $y = -3$, then

$$\tan \theta = \frac{y}{x} = \frac{-3}{-2} = \frac{3}{2}.$$

Further, $r = \sqrt{x^2 + y^2} = \sqrt{(-2)^2 + (-3)^2} = \sqrt{4 + 9} = \sqrt{13}$.

From $x = -2$, $y = -3$, and $r = \sqrt{13}$, we can find $\sin \theta$ and $\sec \theta$.

$$\sin \theta = \frac{y}{r} = \frac{-3}{\sqrt{13}} = -\frac{3\sqrt{13}}{13} \qquad \sec \theta = \frac{r}{x} = \frac{\sqrt{13}}{-2} = -\frac{\sqrt{13}}{2} \quad ■■■$$

Practice Problem 9   Given that $\tan \theta = -\dfrac{4}{5}$ and $\cos \theta > 0$, find the exact values of $\sin \theta$ and $\sec \theta$. ■

EXAMPLE 10   **Flight of a Golf Ball**

A golf ball is hit on a level fairway with an initial velocity of 128 ft/sec and an initial angle of flight of 30°. Find its range (the horizontal distance it traveled before hitting the ground) and its maximum height to the nearest foot.

SOLUTION

We use the height equation from the section introduction on page 24.

$$h = v_0 t \sin \theta - 16t^2$$
$$h = 128 \, t \sin 30° - 16t^2 \qquad \text{Replace } v_0 \text{ with 128 and } \theta \text{ with 30°.}$$
$$= 64t - 16t^2 = -16t(t - 4) \qquad \text{Replace } \sin 30° \text{ with } \frac{1}{2} \text{ and simplify.}$$

The graph of $h = 64t - 16t^2$ is a parabola; the portion of the graph with $h(t) \geq 0$ represents the height of the ball and the time the ball was in flight. See Figure 1.40. The vertex is $(2, 64)$, because $t = \dfrac{-64}{2(-16)} = 2$ and $h(2) = 64(2) - 16(2)^2 = 64$.

So the maximum height of the ball is 64 feet, and because $h(4) = 0$, the ball remains in flight for 4 seconds.

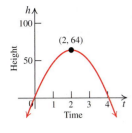

FIGURE 1.40

The distance traveled after 4 seconds is the range.

$$d = t\,v_0 \cos\theta$$ Horizontal distance equation

$$d = 4(128)\cos\theta = 4(128)\cos 30°$$ Replace v_0 with 128 and θ with 30°.

$$= 4(128)\frac{\sqrt{3}}{2} \approx 443 \text{ ft}$$ Use a calculator.

The ball reaches a maximum height of 64 feet and has a range of 443 feet.   ■ ■ ■

Practice Problem 10   Repeat Example 10 for a ball with an initial velocity of 140 ft/sec and an initial angle of flight of 45°.   ■

SECTION 1.3 ■ Exercises

A EXERCISES Basic Skills and Concepts

1. For a point $P(x, y)$ on the terminal side of an angle θ in standard position, we let $r =$ _____ .

In Exercises 2 and 3, use the notations from Exercise 1.

2. $\sin\theta =$ _____ , $\cos\theta =$ _____ ,
   $\tan\theta =$ _____

3. $\csc\theta =$ _____ , $\sec\theta =$ _____ ,
   $\cot\theta =$ _____

4. If θ_1 and θ_2 are coterminal angles, then $\sin\theta_1$
   _____ $\sin\theta_2$.

5. *True or False* The value of a trigonometric function of θ depends on the choice of the point $P(x, y)$ on the terminal side of θ.

6. *True or False* In each quadrant, cosine and cosecant are both positive or both negative.

In Exercises 7–22, the terminal side of an angle θ in standard position contains the given point. Find the values of the six trigonometric functions of θ.

7. $(-3, 4)$ **8.** $(4, -3)$

9. $(5, 12)$ **10.** $(-12, 5)$

11. $(7, 24)$ **12.** $(-24, 7)$

13. $(-24, -7)$ **14.** $(-7, 24)$

15. $(1, 1)$ **16.** $(-3, -3)$

17. $(\sqrt{2}, \sqrt{2})$ **18.** $(-3, \sqrt{3})$

19. $(\sqrt{3}, -1)$ **20.** $(\sqrt{13}, \sqrt{3})$

21. $(5, -2)$ **22.** $(-3, 5)$

In Exercises 23–34, find the exact value. If any are not defined, write *undefined*.

23. $\sin 450°$ **24.** $\cos 450°$

25. $\cos(-90°)$ **26.** $\sin(-90°)$

27. $\tan 450°$ **28.** $\cot 540°$

29. $\tan(-540°)$ **30.** $\sec 1080°$

31. $\csc 900°$ **32.** $\csc 1080°$

33. $\sin(-1530°)$ **34.** $\cos(-2610°)$

In Exercises 35–44, find the exact value of each expression.

35. $\sin 60° + \sin 30°$ **36.** $\cos 60° + \cos 30°$

37. $\sin 60° - \cos 60°$ **38.** $\sin 30° - \cos 30°$

39. $\sin 45° \cos 45°$ **40.** $\sin 30° \cos 60°$

41. $\cos 30° \tan 30°$ **42.** $\sin 60° \cot 60°$

43. $(\sin 30° + \cos 30°)^2$ **44.** $(\sin 30° - \cos 30°)^2$

In Exercises 45–52, use the given information to find the quadrant in which θ lies.

45. $\sin\theta < 0$ and $\cos\theta < 0$ **46.** $\sin\theta < 0$ and $\tan\theta > 0$

47. $\sin\theta > 0$ and $\cos\theta < 0$ **48.** $\tan\theta > 0$ and $\csc\theta < 0$

49. $\cos\theta > 0$ and $\csc\theta < 0$ **50.** $\cos\theta < 0$ and $\cot\theta > 0$

51. $\sec\theta < 0$ and $\csc\theta > 0$ **52.** $\sec\theta < 0$ and $\tan\theta > 0$

53. Find the value of x assuming that the point $(x, -5)$ is on the terminal side of θ in quadrant III and $\sin\theta = -\dfrac{5}{13}$.

54. Repeat Exercise 53 assuming that θ lies in quadrant IV.

55. Find the value of y assuming that the point $(7, y)$ is on the terminal side of θ in quadrant I and $\cos\theta = \dfrac{7}{25}$.

56. Repeat Exercise 55 assuming that θ lies in quadrant IV.

In Exercises 57–64, find the exact values of the remaining trigonometric functions of θ from the given information.

57. $\cos\theta = -\dfrac{5}{13}$, θ in quadrant III

58. $\tan\theta = -\dfrac{3}{4}$, θ in quadrant IV

59. $\cot \theta = -\dfrac{3}{4}, \theta$ in quadrant II

60. $\sec \theta = \dfrac{4}{\sqrt{7}}, \theta$ in quadrant IV

61. $\sin \theta = \dfrac{3}{5}, \tan \theta < 0$

62. $\cot \theta = \dfrac{3}{2}, \sec \theta > 0$

63. $\sec \theta = 3, \sin \theta < 0$

64. $\tan \theta = -2, \sin \theta > 0$

B EXERCISES Applying the Concepts

In Exercises 65–72, use the following discussion.

Projectile Motion

Suppose a projectile is launched from the origin into the first quadrant with an initial velocity v_0 feet per second at an angle θ with the horizontal. If the only force acting on the projectile is the force of gravity (with acceleration, $g = 32$ ft/sec^2), then the equation of motion (see the figure) is given by the following:

$$y = x \tan \theta - \frac{16 \sec^2 \theta}{v_0^2} x^2$$

Maximum height $H = \dfrac{1}{64}(v_0 \sin \theta)^2$

Time of flight $t = \dfrac{v_0 \sin \theta}{16}$

Horizontal range $R = \dfrac{v_0^2 \sin \theta \cos \theta}{16}$

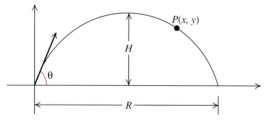

65. Golf. A golf ball is hit with an initial velocity of 44 ft/sec with an angle $\theta = 30°$. Find $H, t,$ and R.

66. Repeat Exercise 65 assuming that $\theta = 45°$.

67. Repeat Exercise 65 assuming that $\theta = 60°$.

68. Repeat Exercise 65 assuming that $\theta = 90°$.

69. Football. A football is kicked with an initial velocity of 80 ft/sec with an angle $\theta = 45°$.
  a. Write the equation of motion of the ball.
  b. What is the height of the ball at a point $x = 100$ feet from the origin?

70. Find the maximum height attained by the football in Exercise 69.

71. Find the time of flight for the ball in Exercise 69.

72. Find the range of the ball in Exercise 69.

73. Light refraction. A fish swimming d feet below the surface is viewed from a line of sight that makes an angle of θ degrees from the vertical. Because the light is refracted by the water, the fish appears to be A feet below the surface, where

$$A = \frac{3d \cos \theta}{\sqrt{7 + 9 \cos^2 \theta}}.$$

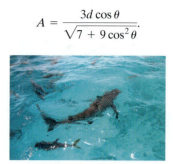

What is the apparent depth of a fish swimming 2 feet below the surface when viewed at an angle of 60° from the vertical?

74. Sound levels. The decibel level, D, of a sound directed eastward is measured 3 yards from the source. If the ray from the sound source through a point 3 yards away makes an angle θ with an eastward ray from the source point, then

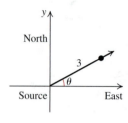

$$D = 25 + 15 \cos \theta.$$

Find the decibel level at a point 3 yards from the sound source assuming that
  a. The point is due east of the sound source.
  b. The point is due west of the sound source.
  c. The point is due south of the sound source.

75. Height of a kite. A kite is flying at the end of 100 feet of string that is in a taut straight line. The height, h, of the kite is given by $h = 100 \sin \theta$, where θ is the angle the string makes with the ground. Find the kite's height assuming the following:
  a. $\theta = 30°$
  b. $\theta = 60°$

C EXERCISES Beyond the Basics

In Exercises 76–79, let $P(x, y)$ denote the point of intersection of the terminal side of an angle θ in standard position and the circle with center $(0, 0)$ and radius r so that $x^2 + y^2 = r^2$.

76. If $r = 5$ and $x = 3$ and $0° < \theta < 90°$, find $\sin \theta$.

77. If $r = 5$ and $x = -3$ and $90° < \theta < 180°$, find $\sin \theta$.

78. If $r = 13$ and $y = 5$ and $90° < \theta < 180°$, find $\cos \theta$.

79. If $r = 1$ and $x = \dfrac{1}{2}$ and $270° < \theta < 360°$, find $\sin \theta$.

In Exercises 80–83, use the figure to find a triangle congruent to triangle *POM* that justifies the statements in each exercise.

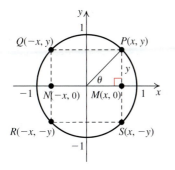

80. $\sin(-\theta) = -\sin\theta, \cos(-\theta) = \cos\theta$, and $\tan(-\theta) = -\tan\theta$

81. $\sin(180° - \theta) = \sin\theta, \cos(180° - \theta) = -\cos\theta$, and $\tan(180° - \theta) = -\tan\theta$

82. $\sin(180° + \theta) = -\sin\theta, \cos(180° + \theta) = -\cos\theta$, and $\tan(180° + \theta) = \tan\theta$

83. $\sin(360° - \theta) = -\sin\theta, \cos(360° - \theta) = \cos\theta$, and $\tan(360° - \theta) = -\tan\theta$

In Exercises 84–87, use the results of Exercises 80–83.

84. Find $\sin(-45°)$ and $\tan(-60°)$.

85. Find $\sin 135°, \cos 135°$, and $\tan 120°$.

86. Find $\sin 225°, \cos 240°$, and $\tan 210°$.

87. Find $\sin 315°, \cos 300°$, and $\tan 330°$.

88. Show that for any angle $\theta, -1 \le \sin\theta \le 1$ and $-1 \le \cos\theta \le 1$.

89. In the figure, show that triangles *POM* and *QON* are congruent.
   a. Find coordinates of the point Q.
   b. Show that $\sin(\theta + 90°) = \cos\theta$, $\cos(\theta + 90°) = -\sin\theta$, and $\tan(\theta + 90°) = -\cot\theta$.

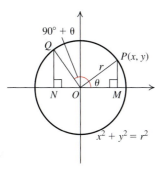

90. Suppose $\tan\theta = \cot\theta$. Find
   a. θ assuming that $0° < \theta < 90°$.
   b. θ assuming that $180° < \theta < 270°$.

91. Assuming that $\sin(A - B) = \dfrac{1}{2}$ and $\cos(A + B) = \dfrac{1}{2}$, find the values of acute angles A and B.

92. In an acute triangle ABC, find the value of $\tan(A + B) + \tan C$.

93. What is the smallest positive value for $\sec\theta$?

94. What is the largest negative value for $\csc\theta$?

In Exercises 95–98, without evaluating the functions, explain why each statement is false.

95. $\cos 105° = \cos 60° + \cos 45°$

96. $\sin 260° = 2\sin 130°$

97. $\tan 123° = \tan 61° + \tan 62°$

98. $\sec 380° = \sec 185° + \sec 195°$

Critical Thinking

99. *True or False* $\cos(\sin\theta°)° = \sin(\cos\theta°)°$. Explain.

100. *True or False* $\sec\theta° > \tan\theta°$ for every angle θ. Explain.

Reference Angles

Before Starting this Section, Review

1. Angle in standard position
   (Section 1.1)
2. Trigonometric functions of angles
   (Section 1.3)

Objectives

1 Find a reference angle.

2 Use reference angles to find trigonometric function values.

3 Find angles from a given trigonometric function value.

THE LONDON EYE

The **London Eye**, also known as the **Millennium Wheel**, was constructed in 1999 and is located on the bank of the River Thames in London, England. It is 135 meters high and is the tallest wheel in Europe. The wheel carries 32 sealed and air-conditioned passenger capsules attached to its external circumference. It rotates at a slow rate to complete one revolution in 30 minutes. This slow rotation speed allows passengers to walk on or off the moving capsules at ground level without any need to stop the wheel. Over 3 million people visit the wheel a year, making it the most popular paid tourist attraction in the United Kingdom. In Example 8, we discuss the height of a passenger capsule. ■

1 Find a reference angle.

Reference Angle

For any nonquadrantal angle θ, there is a corresponding acute angle called its *reference angle* θ' whose trigonometric function values are identical to those of θ, except possibly for the sign.

DEFINITION OF A REFERENCE ANGLE

Let θ be an angle in standard position that is not a quadrantal angle. The **reference angle** for θ is the positive acute angle θ' (theta prime) formed by the terminal side of θ and the *x*-axis.

If θ lies in quadrant I, then $\theta' = \theta$. The rules for finding the reference angle θ' for a positive angle θ ($0° < \theta < 360°$) in each of the four quadrants are given in Figure 1.41.

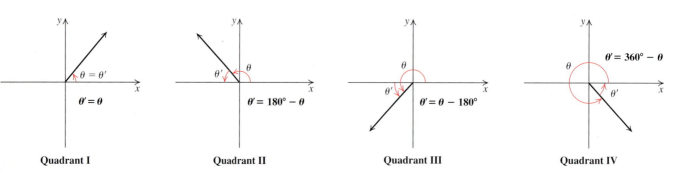

Quadrant I   **Quadrant II**   **Quadrant III**   **Quadrant IV**

FIGURE 1.41 **Reference angles**

EXAMPLE 1   Finding Reference Angles

Find the reference angle θ' for each angle θ.

a. $\theta = 250°$ **b.** $\theta = 297°15'$

SOLUTION

a. Because $250° = 180° + 70°$, the angle $\theta = 250°$ lies in quadrant III. So

$$\theta' = \theta - 180° \qquad \text{Rule from Figure 1.41}$$
$$\theta' = 250° - 180° = 70° \qquad \text{Substitute } \theta = 250° \text{ and simplify.}$$

b. Because $\theta = 297°15' = 270° + 27°15'$, the angle θ lies in quadrant IV. So

$$\theta' = 360° - \theta \qquad \text{Rule from Figure 1.41}$$
$$\theta' = 360° - 297°15' = 62°45' \qquad \text{Substitute for } \theta \text{ and simplify.} \qquad ■■■$$

Practice Problem 1   Find the reference angle θ' for each angle θ.

a. $\theta = 175°$ **b.** $\theta = 210°30'$ ■

Because the reference angle for an angle θ is the acute angle θ' formed by the terminal side of θ and the *x*-axis, all coterminal angles have the same reference angle. So to find the reference angle for an angle α, we use the following procedure.

FINDING THE SOLUTION: A PROCEDURE

EXAMPLE 2   Finding the Reference Angle for Any Angle

OBJECTIVE

Find the reference angle α' for a nonquadrantal angle α that is greater than 360° or is a negative angle.

Step 1 For the given angle α, find a coterminal angle θ between 0° and 360°.

Step 2 Use the rules given in Figure 1.41 to find the reference angle θ' for the angle θ resulting from Step 1.

Step 3 The reference angle θ' in Step 2 is also the reference angle α' for the given angle α. That is, $\alpha' = \theta'$.

EXAMPLE

Find the reference angle α' for $\alpha = 828°$.

1. Subtracting multiples of 360° from 828°, we have $828° - 2(360°) = 108°$. The angles $\alpha = 828°$ and $\theta = 108°$ are coterminal angles.

2. Because $108° = 90° + 18°$, the angle $\theta = 108°$ lies in quadrant II. So

$$\theta' = 180° - \theta \qquad \text{Rule from Figure 1.41}$$
$$\theta' = 180° - 108° = 72°$$

3. $\alpha' = 72°$ Because $\alpha' = \theta'$

■■■

Practice Problem 2   Find the reference angle α' for $\alpha = 2025°$.   ■

EXAMPLE 3   Finding the Reference Angle for a Negative Angle

Find the reference angle α' for $\alpha = -523°$.

SOLUTION

Step 1 Adding multiples of 360° to $-523°$, we have $2(360°) - 523° = 720° - 523° = 197°$. The angle $\alpha = -523°$ is coterminal with the angle $\theta = 197°$.

Step 2   Because $197° = 180° + 17°$, the angle $\theta = 197°$ lies in quadrant III. So

$$\theta' = \theta - 180° \qquad \text{Rule from Figure 1.41}$$
$$\theta' = 197° - 180° = 17° \qquad \text{Substitute and simplify.}$$

Step 3 $\alpha' = 17°$ $\alpha' = \theta'$ ■ ■ ■

Practice Problem 3   Find the reference angle α' for $\alpha = -70°$.   ■

---

2 Use reference angles to find trigonometric function values.

Using Reference Angles

A reference angle is used to find the values of trigonometric functions of any nonquadrantal angle θ. (The procedure on page 27 is used for quadrantal angles.) For example, consider the reference angle θ' of the angle θ in Figure 1.42. Let $P(x, y)$ be a point on the terminal side of θ in quadrant III. Then $Q\big(|x|, |y|\big)$ is in quadrant I. From the definition of trigonometric functions, we have

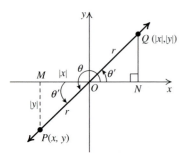

$$\cos \theta = \frac{x}{r} = \frac{-|x|}{r} = -\frac{|x|}{r} \qquad \text{Because } x \text{ is negative, } |x| = -x, \text{ or } -|x| = x.$$

The right triangles POM and QON in Figure 1.42 are congruent by SAS. We have

$$\cos \theta' = \frac{|x|}{r}.$$

So, $\cos \theta = -\dfrac{|x|}{r} = -\cos \theta'$.

FIGURE 1.42

In general, $\cos \theta$ and $\cos \theta'$ have the same value except possibly for the sign; that is, $\cos \theta = \pm \cos \theta'$. The same is true for the other five trigonometric functions.

FINDING THE SOLUTION: A PROCEDURE

EXAMPLE 4   Using Reference Angles to Find Trigonometric Function Values

OBJECTIVE
Find the value of any trigonometric function of a nonquadrantal angle θ.

EXAMPLE
Find $\sin 1320°$.

Step 1   If $\theta > 360°$ or $\theta < 0°$, find a coterminal angle for θ with degree measure between $0°$ and $360°$. Otherwise, go to Step 2.

Because $1320° - 3(360°) = 240°$, $240°$ is coterminal with $1320°$.

Step 2   Find the reference angle θ' for the angle resulting from Step 1. Write the same trigonometric function of θ'.

Because $240°$ is in quadrant III, its reference angle θ' is

$$\theta' = 240° - 180° = 60°,$$

and

$$\sin \theta' = \sin 60° = \frac{\sqrt{3}}{2} \qquad \text{See page 29.}$$

Step 3   Choose the correct sign for the trigonometric function value of θ based on the quadrant in which it lies. Write the given trigonometric function of θ in terms of the same trigonometric function of θ' with the appropriate sign.

The angle $1320°$ and its coterminal angle, $240°$, lie in quadrant III, where the sine is *negative*. So

$$\sin 1320° = \sin 240° = -\sin 60° = -\frac{\sqrt{3}}{2}.$$

coterminal angles   reference angle

■ ■ ■

Practice Problem 4   Find $\cos 1025°$.   ■

EXAMPLE 5   **Find the Exact Value of tan 330°**

Find the exact value of tan 330°.

SOLUTION

Step 1   Because 330° is between 0° and 360°, we proceed to find its reference angle.

Step 2   Because 330° is in quadrant IV, its reference angle θ' is

$$\theta' = 360° - 330° = 30°.$$

$$\tan \theta' = \tan 30° = \frac{\sqrt{3}}{3} \qquad \text{See Table 1.2 on page 29.}$$

Step 3   In quadrant IV, $\tan \theta$ is *negative*. So

$$\tan 330° = -\tan 30° = -\frac{\sqrt{3}}{3}. \qquad ■ ■ ■$$

Practice Problem 5   Find the exact value of cot 120°.   ■

EXAMPLE 6   **Finding the Trigonometric Function Value of a Negative Angle**

Find the exact value of $\cos(-480°)$.

SOLUTION

Step 1   Since $2(360°) - 480° = 240°$, the angles $-480°$ and $240°$ are coterminal.

Step 2   Because $240° = 180° + 60°$, the angle $240°$ is in quadrant III. Its reference angle is 60°. Therefore, the reference angle, θ', for the angle $-480°$ is also 60°.

$$\cos \theta' = \cos 60° = \frac{1}{2} \qquad \text{See Table 1.2 on page 29.}$$

Step 3   In quadrant III, $\cos \theta$ is *negative*. So

$$\cos(-480°) = -\cos 60° = -\frac{1}{2}. \qquad ■ ■ ■$$

Practice Problem 6   Find the exact value of $\sin(-510°)$.   ■

EXAMPLE 7   **Finding the Trigonometric Function Values of an Angle**

Find the trigonometric function values of $\alpha = -210°$.

SOLUTION

Step 1   We find an angle θ between 0° and 360° that is coterminal with α.

Since $360° - 210° = 150°$, the trigonometric function values of $\alpha = -210°$ and $\theta = 150°$ are identical.

Step 2   Because $150° = 180° - 30°$, the angle $\theta = 150°$ lies in quadrant II. Its reference angle is $\theta' = 30°$.

Step 3   Recall that the sine and cosecant functions are positive in quadrant II and that the other four functions are negative. Using Table 1.2, we have

$$\sin(-210°) = \sin 150° = \sin 30° = \frac{1}{2} \qquad \csc(-210°) = \csc 150° = \csc 30° = 2$$

$$\cos(-210°) = \cos 150° = -\cos 30° = -\frac{\sqrt{3}}{2} \qquad \sec(-210°) = \sec 150° = -\sec 30° = -\frac{2\sqrt{3}}{3}$$

$$\tan(-210°) = \tan 150° = -\tan 30° = -\frac{\sqrt{3}}{3} \qquad \cot(-210°) = \cot 150° = -\cot 30° = -\sqrt{3}$$

■ ■ ■

Practice Problem 7   Find the trigonometric function values of $\alpha = 570°$.   ■

EXAMPLE 8   **The Millennium Wheel**

The height h (in meters) of a passenger capsule on the Millennium Wheel above the Wheel's base is given by $h = 67.8 - 67.2\cos\theta$, where θ is the angle the capsule arm makes with a vertical ray downward from the wheel's center. See Figure 1.43. How high is the capsule when

a. $\theta = 135°$?   **b.** $\theta = 300°$?   **c.** $\theta = 870°$?

SOLUTION

a. $\theta = 135°$ is in QII; so $\theta' = 180° - 135° = 45°$ and $\cos\theta = -\cos\theta'$

$$\begin{aligned} h &= 67.8 - 67.2\cos 135° & \theta = 135° \\ &= 67.8 - 67.2(-\cos 45°) & \theta' = 45°; \cos 135° = -\cos 45° \\ &= 67.8 - 67.2\left(-\frac{\sqrt{2}}{2}\right) & \text{Replace } \cos 45° \text{ with } \frac{\sqrt{2}}{2}. \\ &= 67.8 + (33.6)\sqrt{2} \approx 115.3 \text{ meters} & \text{Use a calculator} \end{aligned}$$

b. $\theta = 300°$ is in Q IV; so $\theta' = 360 - 300 = 60°$ and $\cos\theta = \cos\theta'$.

$$\begin{aligned} h &= 67.8 - 67.2\cos 300° & \theta = 300° \\ &= 67.8 - 67.2\cos 60° & \theta' = 60°; \cos 300° = \cos 60°. \\ &= 67.8 - 67.2\left(\frac{1}{2}\right) & \text{Replace } \cos 60° \text{ with } \frac{1}{2}. \\ &= 34.2 \text{ meters} \end{aligned}$$

c. $\theta = 870° = 2(360) + 150$; so $870°$ and $150°$ are coterminal angles in QII.

$$\theta' = 180° - 150° = 30° \text{ and } \cos 870° = \cos 150° = -\cos 30° = -\frac{\sqrt{3}}{2}$$

$$\begin{aligned} h &= 67.8 - 67.2\cos 870° & \theta = 870° \\ &= 67.8 - 67.2\left(-\frac{\sqrt{3}}{2}\right) & \text{Replace } \cos 870° \text{ with } -\frac{\sqrt{3}}{2}. \\ &= 67.8 + 33.6\sqrt{3} \text{ meters} \approx 125.1 \text{ meters} & \text{Use a calculator.} \end{aligned}$$

■ ■ ■

Practice Problem 8   In Example 8, find the height of the capsule when $\theta = 600°$.   ■

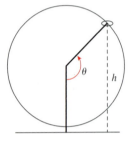

FIGURE 1.43

3 Find angles from a given trigonometric function value.

Angles with Given Trigonometric Function Value

So far, we have discussed a procedure to find the trigonometric function values of an angle θ. Now we reverse the process. Suppose we are given a trigonometric function value, say $\sin\theta = -\frac{1}{2}$. How do we find all angles θ whose sine is $-\frac{1}{2}$?

The signs of the trigonometric functions together with a knowledge of reference angles are used to find all angles with a given trigonometric function value.

FINDING THE SOLUTION: A PROCEDURE

EXAMPLE 9   **Finding All Angles with a Given Trigonometric Function Value**

OBJECTIVE	EXAMPLE
Find all values of θ with a given trigonometric function value.	*Find all values of θ with* $\sin\theta = -\dfrac{1}{2}$.

Step 1 Find the absolute value of the given function value. Find the acute angle θ' associated with this absolute value.

1. $\left|-\dfrac{1}{2}\right| = \dfrac{1}{2}$. So $\sin\theta' = \dfrac{1}{2}$ gives (see Table 1.2 on page 29)

$$\theta' = 30°.$$

Step 2 Use Table 1.3 (Section 1.3) and the sign of the given value to find the two quadrants in which θ may lie.

2. Because $\sin\theta = -\dfrac{1}{2}$ is negative, θ lies in quadrant III or in quadrant IV.

Step 3 Use the result of Step 2 to find two possible values, θ_1 and θ_2, in the interval $[0°, 360°)$ with reference angle θ'. From page 34, we have

quadrant I, $\theta = \theta'$.
quadrant II, $\theta = 180° - \theta'$.
quadrant III, $\theta = 180° + \theta'$.
quadrant IV, $\theta = 360° - \theta'$.

3. We have

$$\theta_1 = 180° + 30° = 210° \quad \textcolor{blue}{\theta_1 \text{ in quadrant III}}$$
$$\theta_2 = 360° - 30° = 330° \quad \textcolor{blue}{\theta_2 \text{ in quadrant IV}}$$

Step 4 All values of θ are given by

$$\theta = \theta_1 + n \cdot 360° \text{ or } \theta = \theta_2 + n \cdot 360°.$$

4. $\theta = 210° + n \cdot 360°$, or
$\theta = 330° + n \cdot 360°$ *n* is any integer.

Practice Problem 9 Find all values of θ with $\tan\theta = \sqrt{3}$.

SECTION 1.4 ■ Exercises

A EXERCISES Basic Skills and Concepts

1. The reference angle θ' for a nonquadrantal angle θ in standard position is the acute angle formed by the terminal side of θ and the _____ .

In Exercises 2–4, assume θ is in the interval $(0°, 360°)$.

2. If θ is in quadrant II, then $\theta' =$ _____ .

3. If θ is in quadrant III, then $\theta' =$ _____ .

4. If θ is in quadrant IV, then $\theta' =$ _____ .

5. *True or False* Trigonometric function values of an angle and its reference angle are the same.

6. *True or False* At most, there are two possible angles in the interval $[0°, 360°)$ having the same value for a given trigonometric function.

In Exercises 7–22, write the reference angle for each angle.

7.	46°	8.	87°
9.	96°	10.	126°
11.	192°	12.	220°
13.	290°	14.	305°
15.	−145°	16.	−190°
17.	−260°	18.	−320°
19.	1570°	20.	1900°
21.	−1360°	22.	−2040°

In Exercises 23–34, complete the table with exact trigonometric function values. If a function is not defined for a value, write *undefined*.

	θ	$\sin\theta$	$\cos\theta$	$\tan\theta$	$\cot\theta$	$\sec\theta$	$\csc\theta$
23.	120°		$-\dfrac{1}{2}$		$-\dfrac{\sqrt{3}}{3}$	-2	
24.	135°	$\dfrac{\sqrt{2}}{2}$		-1			$\sqrt{2}$
25.	150°				$-\sqrt{3}$	$-\dfrac{2\sqrt{3}}{3}$	2
26.	180°	0	-1				undefined
27.	210°	$-\dfrac{1}{2}$			$\sqrt{3}$		-2
28.	225°		$-\dfrac{\sqrt{2}}{2}$	1			$-\sqrt{2}$
29.	240°		$-\dfrac{1}{2}$	$\sqrt{3}$		-2	
30.	270°	-1	0		0		
31.	300°	$-\dfrac{\sqrt{3}}{2}$	$\dfrac{1}{2}$			2	
32.	315°		$\dfrac{\sqrt{2}}{2}$		-1	$\sqrt{2}$	
33.	330°	$-\dfrac{1}{2}$			$-\sqrt{3}$		-2
34.	360°	0	1	0			

In Exercises 35–46, find the exact value of each expression.

35. $\sin(-300°)$
36. $\cos(-330°)$
37. $\tan(-315°)$
38. $\csc(-330°)$
39. $\sec(-240°)$
40. $\cot(-240°)$
41. $\sin(-225°)$
42. $\cos(-210°)$
43. $\tan(-150°)$
44. $\sec(-135°)$
45. $\sin(-60°)$
46. $\cos(-45°)$

In Exercises 47–54, find the exact value of each expression.

47. $\sin 1470°$
48. $\cos 1860°$
49. $\tan 1125°$
50. $\sec 2190°$
51. $\csc(-2130°)$
52. $\sec(-1410°)$
53. $\tan(-690°)$
54. $\cot(-2100°)$

In Exercises 55–70, find possible value(s) of θ in the interval $[0°, 360°)$ with the given trigonometric function value.

55. $\cos\theta = \dfrac{1}{2}$
56. $\sin\theta = -\dfrac{\sqrt{3}}{2}$
57. $\tan\theta = -\sqrt{3}$
58. $\sec\theta = -2$
59. $\csc\theta = \dfrac{\sqrt{3}}{2}$
60. $\sec\theta = -\dfrac{\sqrt{3}}{2}$
61. $\cot\theta = \sqrt{3}$
62. $\cos\theta = -\dfrac{1}{2}$

63. $\sin\theta = 1$
64. $\cos\theta = 1$
65. $\cos\theta = -1$
66. $\sin\theta = -1$
67. $\cos\theta = 0$
68. $\sin\theta = 0$
69. $\sin\theta = 2$
70. $\sin\theta = -2$

In Exercises 71–74, find all values of θ with the given trigonometric function value.

71. $\sin\theta = -\dfrac{\sqrt{2}}{2}$
72. $\cos\theta = -\dfrac{\sqrt{3}}{2}$
73. $\tan\theta = \dfrac{\sqrt{3}}{3}$
74. $\sec\theta = 2$

In Exercises 75–84, find the value of θ in the interval $[0°, 360°)$ that satisfies the given conditions.

75. $\sin\theta = -\dfrac{\sqrt{2}}{2}$ and θ in quadrant III
76. $\sin\theta = -\dfrac{\sqrt{2}}{2}$ and θ in quadrant IV
77. $\cos\theta = -\dfrac{1}{2}$ and θ in quadrant II
78. $\cos\theta = -\dfrac{1}{2}$ and θ in quadrant III
79. $\tan\theta = -\sqrt{3}$ and θ in quadrant II
80. $\tan\theta = -\sqrt{3}$ and θ in quadrant IV
81. $\sin\theta = \dfrac{\sqrt{2}}{2}$ and θ in quadrant II
82. $\cos\theta = \dfrac{\sqrt{3}}{2}$ and θ in quadrant IV
83. $\tan\theta = \sqrt{3}$ and θ in quadrant III
84. $\sec\theta = 2$ and θ in quadrant IV

B EXERCISES Applying the Concepts

85. **A safety chain.** A piece of heavy equipment has two 8-foot metal arms that make a V with the horizontal plane and form an angle of 120° at their base. A contractor wants to put a chain from the top of one arm to the top of the other arm for safety. (See the figure.) How long must the chain be?

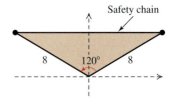

86. **Removing a buoy.** A crane is situated on the edge of a sheer cliff. It has a 12-foot arm that makes an angle of 120° with the horizontal and drops a hook straight down to a metal buoy that must be pulled from the water. (See the figure.) How far is the center of the buoy from the cliff?

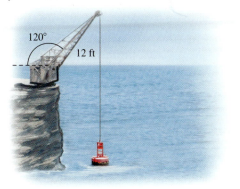

C EXERCISES Beyond the Basics

87. Find all values of θ with $-360° < \theta < 0°$, for which $\tan \theta = 1$.

88. Find a formula for the reference angle θ' of a negative angle θ with $-180° < \theta < -90°$.

89. Find a formula for the reference angle θ' of a negative angle θ with $-270° < \theta < -180°$.

90. Find a formula for the reference angle θ' of a negative angle θ with $-360° < \theta < -270°$.

In Exercises 91–93, use the following figure to explain why each relation is true.

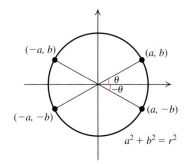

91. **a.** $\sin (-\theta) = -\sin \theta$
   b. $\cos (-\theta) = \cos \theta$
   c. $\tan (-\theta) = -\tan \theta$

92. **a.** $\sin (180° - \theta) = \sin \theta$
   b. $\cos (180° - \theta) = -\cos \theta$
   c. $\tan (180° - \theta) = -\tan \theta$

93. **a.** $\sin (180° + \theta) = -\sin \theta$
   b. $\cos (180° + \theta) = -\cos \theta$
   c. $\tan (180° + \theta) = \tan \theta$

In Exercises 94–98, evaluate each expression.

94. $\sin 300° \cos 150° + \cos 300° \sin 150°$

95. $\cos 270° \cos 120° + \sin 270° \sin 120°$

96. $\cos 690° \cos 780° - \sin 690° \sin 780°$

97. $\dfrac{\tan 780° + \tan 330°}{1 - \tan 780° \tan 330°}$

98. $\dfrac{\tan 1470° - \tan 1230°}{1 + \tan 1470° \tan 1230°}$

In Exercises 99 and 100, find all angles α and β between 0° and 360° that satisfy the given pair of equations.

99. $\tan (\alpha + \beta) = 1, \sin (\alpha - \beta) = \dfrac{1}{2}$

100. $\sec (\alpha + \beta) = 2, \csc (\alpha - \beta) = 2$

Critical Thinking

101. Find all angles $\theta, 0° \le \theta \le 360°$ for which $\csc \theta = -\sec \theta$.

102. Find all angles $\theta, 0° \le \theta \le 360°$ for which $\sec \theta = \tan \theta$.

Fundamental Trigonometric Identities

Before Starting this Section, Review

1. Definitions of trigonometric functions (Section 1.3)
2. Pythagorean theorem (Section 1.2)

Objectives

1. State the reciprocal identities.
2. State the quotient identities.
3. State the Pythagorean identities.
4. Simplify a complicated trigonometric expression.

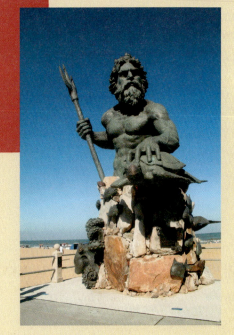

MYTHOLOGICAL GODS AND SUPERHEROES

Many mythological gods had two identities, one Roman and one Greek. For example, the Ruler of the Seas was known as Poseidon (Greek) and Neptune (Roman), and the Goddess of Love and Beauty was known as Aphrodite (Greek) and Venus (Roman). Perhaps the two best-known fictitious American dual identities are Batman (Bruce Wayne) and Superman (Clark Kent). In this section, you investigate the many disguises that expressions in trigonometry wear and learn why it's important to be able to recognize them.

An **identity** is an equation that is satisfied by all values of the variable for which both sides are defined. The equations

$$2(x + 3) = 2x + 6,$$
$$x^2 - 9 = (x + 3)(x - 3), \text{ and}$$
$$\frac{2}{x - 2} + \frac{3}{x + 2} = \frac{5x - 2}{x^2 - 4}$$

are examples of identities. However, the equation $x^2 - 4 = 0$ is not an identity. Such an equation is called a **conditional equation** because it is true for some values of x (2 and -2) but not for all values of x (say $x = 3$) for which both sides are defined.

Let $P(x, y)$ be a point on the terminal side of an angle θ in standard position and $r = \sqrt{x^2 + y^2} > 0$. We defined the six trigonometric functions in terms of x, y, and r. (See page 24.) We use these definitions to explore relationships involving the trigonometric functions. ■

---

1 State the reciprocal identities.

Reciprocal Identities

Recall from the definitions on page 24 that $\sin \theta = \dfrac{y}{r}$ and $\csc \theta = \dfrac{r}{y}$ $(y \neq 0)$. Then $\sin \theta \csc \theta = \dfrac{y}{r} \cdot \dfrac{r}{y} = 1$. The equation $\sin \theta \csc \theta = 1$ means that this equation is satisfied by all angles θ for which both $\sin \theta$ and $\csc \theta$ are defined. So the equation $\sin \theta \csc \theta = 1$ is an identity. This identity can also be written in equivalent forms

$$\sin \theta = \frac{1}{\csc \theta} \quad \text{and} \quad \csc \theta = \frac{1}{\sin \theta}.$$

The last two forms show that $\sin \theta$ and $\csc \theta$ are reciprocals.

Similarly, we note that

$$\cos \theta \sec \theta = \frac{x}{r} \cdot \frac{r}{x} = 1, \quad \cos \theta = \frac{1}{\sec \theta}, \quad \text{and} \quad \sec \theta = \frac{1}{\cos \theta}$$

and that

$$\tan \theta \cot \theta = \frac{y}{x} \cdot \frac{x}{y} = 1, \qquad \tan \theta = \frac{1}{\cot \theta}, \qquad \text{and} \qquad \cot \theta = \frac{1}{\tan \theta}.$$

In summary, the following reciprocal relations hold for any angle θ that does not lead to a 0 denominator.

RECIPROCAL IDENTITIES

$$\sin \theta = \frac{1}{\csc \theta} \qquad\qquad \csc \theta = \frac{1}{\sin \theta}$$

$$\cos \theta = \frac{1}{\sec \theta} \qquad\qquad \sec \theta = \frac{1}{\cos \theta}$$

$$\tan \theta = \frac{1}{\cot \theta} \qquad\qquad \cot \theta = \frac{1}{\tan \theta}$$

EXAMPLE 1   **Using Reciprocal Identities**

a. Assuming that $\sin \theta = \dfrac{3}{4}$, find $\csc \theta$.

b. Assuming that $\sec \theta = \dfrac{5}{3}$, find $\cos \theta$.

c. Assuming that $\cot \theta = -\dfrac{7}{12}$, find $\tan \theta$.

SOLUTION

a. $\csc \theta = \dfrac{1}{\sin \theta} = \dfrac{1}{\dfrac{3}{4}} = \dfrac{4}{3}$ Replace $\sin \theta$ with $\dfrac{3}{4}$.

b. $\cos \theta = \dfrac{1}{\sec \theta} = \dfrac{1}{\dfrac{5}{3}} = \dfrac{3}{5}$ Replace $\sec \theta$ with $\dfrac{5}{3}$.

c. $\tan \theta = \dfrac{1}{\cot \theta} = \dfrac{1}{-\dfrac{7}{12}} = -\dfrac{12}{7}$ Replace $\cot \theta$ with $-\dfrac{7}{12}$.   ■ ■ ■

Practice Problem 1

a. Assuming that $\csc \theta = 5$, find $\sin \theta$.

b. Assuming that $\cos \theta = -\dfrac{1}{2}$, find $\sec \theta$.

c. Assuming that $\tan \theta = \dfrac{5}{11}$, find $\cot \theta$.   ■

2 State the quotient identities.

Quotient Identities

Let's consider the quotient of $\sin \theta$ and $\cos \theta$. If $\cos \theta \neq 0$, then

$$\frac{\sin \theta}{\cos \theta} = \frac{y}{r} \div \frac{x}{r} = \frac{y}{r} \cdot \frac{r}{x} = \frac{y}{x} = \tan \theta.$$

Similarly, if $\sin\theta \neq 0$, then

$$\frac{\cos\theta}{\sin\theta} = \frac{x}{r} \div \frac{y}{r} = \frac{x}{\cancel{r}} \cdot \frac{\cancel{r}}{y} = \frac{x}{y} = \cot\theta.$$

We have the quotient identities.

QUOTIENT IDENTITIES

$$\tan\theta = \frac{\sin\theta}{\cos\theta} \qquad\qquad \cot\theta = \frac{\cos\theta}{\sin\theta}$$

EXAMPLE 2   **Using Quotient Identities**

Given $\sin\theta = \dfrac{3}{5}$ and $\cos\theta = -\dfrac{4}{5}$, find $\tan\theta$ and $\cot\theta$.

SOLUTION

$$\tan\theta = \frac{\sin\theta}{\cos\theta} \qquad\qquad \text{Quotient identity}$$

$$= \frac{\dfrac{3}{5}}{-\dfrac{4}{5}} = -\frac{3}{4} \qquad\qquad \text{Substitute the values and simplify.}$$

$$\cot\theta = \frac{1}{\tan\theta} \qquad\qquad \text{Reciprocal identity}$$

$$= \frac{1}{-\dfrac{3}{4}} = -\frac{4}{3} \qquad\qquad \text{Substitute the value and simplify.}$$

So $\tan\theta = -\dfrac{3}{4}$ and $\cot\theta = -\dfrac{4}{3}$. ■ ■ ■

Practice Problem 2   Assuming that $\sin\theta = -\dfrac{5}{17}$ and $\cos\theta = \dfrac{12}{17}$, find $\cot\theta$. ■

EXAMPLE 3   **Using Reciprocal and Quotient Identities**

Assuming that $\tan\theta = 4$ and $\sec\theta = -\sqrt{17}$, find the values of the remaining trigonometric functions of θ.

SOLUTION
We have

$$\cot\theta = \frac{1}{\tan\theta} \qquad\qquad \text{Reciprocal identity}$$

$$= \frac{1}{4} \qquad\qquad \text{Replace } \tan\theta \text{ with } 4$$

$$\cos\theta = \frac{1}{\sec\theta} \qquad\qquad \text{Reciprocal identity}$$

$$= \frac{1}{-\sqrt{17}} \qquad\qquad \text{Replace } \sec\theta \text{ with } -\sqrt{17}$$

$$= -\frac{1}{\sqrt{17}} \cdot \frac{\sqrt{17}}{\sqrt{17}} = -\frac{\sqrt{17}}{17} \qquad\qquad \text{Rationalize the denominator.}$$

$$\sin \theta = \cos \theta \tan \theta \qquad \text{Multiply both sides of } \frac{\sin \theta}{\cos \theta} = \tan \theta \text{ by } \cos \theta.$$

$$= -\frac{\sqrt{17}}{17} \cdot 4 \qquad \text{Substitute values for } \cos \theta \text{ and } \tan \theta.$$

$$= -\frac{4\sqrt{17}}{17} \qquad \text{Rewrite.}$$

$$\csc \theta = \frac{1}{\sin \theta} \qquad \text{Reciprocal identity}$$

$$= -\frac{17}{4\sqrt{17}} \qquad \text{Substitute value of } \sin \theta \text{ and simplify.}$$

$$= -\frac{\sqrt{17}}{4} \qquad \text{Rationalize the denominator.}$$

So the values of the remaining trigonometric functions are:

$$\sin \theta = -\frac{4\sqrt{17}}{17}, \quad \cos \theta = -\frac{\sqrt{17}}{17}, \quad \csc \theta = -\frac{\sqrt{17}}{4}, \quad \text{and} \quad \cot \theta = \frac{1}{4}. \quad ■ ■ ■$$

Practice Problem 3 Assuming that $\cot \theta = 2$ and $\csc \theta = -\sqrt{5}$, find the values of the remaining trigonometric functions of θ. ■

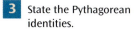

3 State the Pythagorean identities.

Pythagorean Identities

For any angle θ in standard position whose terminal side passes through the point $P(x, y)$, other than the origin (see Figure 1.44), the Pythagorean theorem requires that

$$x^2 + y^2 = r^2 \qquad \text{Where } r \text{ is the distance between } P \text{ and the origin}$$

$$\frac{x^2}{r^2} + \frac{y^2}{r^2} = \frac{r^2}{r^2} \qquad \text{Divide both sides by } r^2.$$

$$\left(\frac{x}{r}\right)^2 + \left(\frac{y}{r}\right)^2 = 1 \qquad \frac{a^2}{b^2} = \left(\frac{a}{b}\right)^2$$

$$(\cos \theta)^2 + (\sin \theta)^2 = 1 \qquad \cos \theta = \frac{x}{r}, \quad \sin \theta = \frac{y}{r}$$

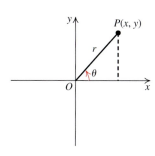

FIGURE 1.44 Standard position

It is customary to write $\cos^2 \theta$ instead of $(\cos \theta)^2$ and $\sin^2 \theta$ instead of $(\sin \theta)^2$. A similar convention holds for powers of all trigonometric functions. So,

$$\cos^2 \theta + \sin^2 \theta = 1.$$

The equation $x^2 + y^2 = r^2$ gives two other useful identities.

$$x^2 + y^2 = r^2$$

$$\frac{x^2}{x^2} + \frac{y^2}{x^2} = \frac{r^2}{x^2} \qquad \text{Divide both sides by } x^2 \neq 0.$$

$$1 + \left(\frac{y}{x}\right)^2 = \left(\frac{r}{x}\right)^2 \qquad \text{Simplify, } \frac{a^2}{b^2} = \left(\frac{a}{b}\right)^2.$$

$$1 + (\tan \theta)^2 = (\sec \theta)^2 \qquad \tan \theta = \frac{y}{x}, \quad \sec \theta = \frac{r}{x}$$

$$1 + \tan^2 \theta = \sec^2 \theta$$

Dividing both sides of the equation $x^2 + y^2 = r^2$ by $y^2 \neq 0$ leads to the identity

$$1 + \cot^2 \theta = \csc^2 \theta.$$

The three identities resulting from the equation $x^2 + y^2 = r^2$ are called the **Pythagorean identities** because the Pythagorean theorem is the basis for these identities.

> **PYTHAGOREAN IDENTITIES**
>
> $$\cos^2\theta + \sin^2\theta = 1 \qquad 1 + \tan^2\theta = \sec^2\theta \qquad 1 + \cot^2\theta = \csc^2\theta$$

The identity $\sin^2\theta + \cos^2\theta = 1$ can be expressed in several forms.

$\sin^2\theta + \cos^2\theta = 1$	Pythagorean identity
$\sin^2\theta = 1 - \cos^2\theta$	Subtract $\cos^2\theta$ from both sides.
$\sin\theta = \pm\sqrt{1 - \cos^2\theta}$	Solve for $\sin\theta$.

Similarly, we have

$\cos^2\theta = 1 - \sin^2\theta$	Subtract $\sin^2\theta$ from both sides of $\sin^2\theta + \cos^2\theta = 1$.
$\cos\theta = \pm\sqrt{1 - \sin^2\theta}$	Solve for $\cos\theta$.

So the identity $\sin^2\theta + \cos^2\theta = 1$ yields four equivalent forms:

$$\sin^2\theta = 1 - \cos^2\theta, \quad \text{and} \quad \cos^2\theta = 1 - \sin^2\theta;$$
$$\sin\theta = \pm\sqrt{1 - \cos^2\theta}, \quad \text{and} \quad \cos\theta = \pm\sqrt{1 - \sin^2\theta}.$$

In the same way, we can express each of the identities $1 + \tan^2\theta = \sec^2\theta$ and $1 + \cot^2\theta = \csc^2\theta$ in four equivalent forms.

STUDY TIP

You can also work Example 4 as we did in Section 1.3 (Example 9), by drawing the angle θ in the appropriate quadrant. Find x, y, and r and then use definitions of the trigonometric functions.

EXAMPLE 4 **Using Pythagorean Identities**

a. Given $\sin\theta = \dfrac{1}{3}$ and $\cos\theta < 0$, find $\cos\theta$ and $\tan\theta$.

b. Given $\sec\theta = -2$ and $\tan\theta > 0$, find $\tan\theta$ and $\sin\theta$.

SOLUTION

a. Use the Pythagorean identity involving $\sin\theta$.

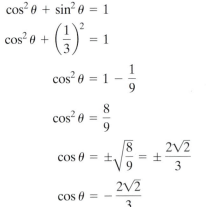

$\cos^2\theta + \sin^2\theta = 1$	Pythagorean identity
$\cos^2\theta + \left(\dfrac{1}{3}\right)^2 = 1$	Replace $\sin\theta$ with $\dfrac{1}{3}$.
$\cos^2\theta = 1 - \dfrac{1}{9}$	Subtract $\dfrac{1}{9} = \left(\dfrac{1}{3}\right)^2$ from both sides.
$\cos^2\theta = \dfrac{8}{9}$	Simplify.
$\cos\theta = \pm\sqrt{\dfrac{8}{9}} = \pm\dfrac{2\sqrt{2}}{3}$	Square root property
$\cos\theta = -\dfrac{2\sqrt{2}}{3}$	$\cos\theta < 0$ is given.

Then, $\quad \tan\theta = \dfrac{\sin\theta}{\cos\theta} = \dfrac{\dfrac{1}{3}}{-\dfrac{2\sqrt{2}}{3}}$	Replace $\sin\theta$ with $\dfrac{1}{3}$ and $\cos\theta$ with $-\dfrac{2\sqrt{2}}{3}$.
$= -\dfrac{1}{2\sqrt{2}}$	Simplify.
$= -\dfrac{\sqrt{2}}{4}$	Rationalize the denominator.

b. Use the Pythagorean identity involving $\sec \theta$.

$$1 + \tan^2 \theta = \sec^2 \theta \qquad \text{Pythagorean identity}$$
$$1 + \tan^2 \theta = (-2)^2 \qquad \text{Replace } \sec \theta \text{ with } -2.$$
$$\tan^2 \theta = 3 \qquad \text{Subtract 1 from both sides and simplify.}$$
$$\tan \theta = \pm\sqrt{3} \qquad \text{Square root property}$$
$$\tan \theta = \sqrt{3} \qquad \tan \theta > 0 \text{ is given.} \qquad \blacksquare \ \blacksquare \ \blacksquare$$

Then, $\qquad \cos \theta = \dfrac{1}{\sec \theta} = \dfrac{1}{-2} = -\dfrac{1}{2}$

$$\sin \theta = \cos \theta \tan \theta = \left(-\frac{1}{2}\right)\sqrt{3} = -\frac{\sqrt{3}}{2}$$

Practice Problem 4   Given $\cos \theta = -\dfrac{2}{3}$ and $\sin \theta > 0$, find $\sin \theta$ and $\tan \theta$. $\blacksquare$

EXAMPLE 5   Using the Fundamental Trigonometric Identities

If $\cot \theta = \dfrac{3}{4}$ and $180° < \theta < 270°$, find the values of the remaining trigonometric functions of θ.

SOLUTION

From the given value of $\cot \theta$, we can find the value of the related function $\csc \theta$ by using the identity $\csc^2 \theta = 1 + \cot^2 \theta$.

$$\csc^2 \theta = 1 + \cot^2 \theta \qquad \text{Pythagorean identity}$$
$$= 1 + \left(\frac{3}{4}\right)^2 \qquad \text{Replace } \cot \theta \text{ with } \frac{3}{4}.$$
$$= 1 + \frac{9}{16} \qquad \left(\frac{3}{4}\right)^2 = \frac{9}{16}$$
$$\csc^2 \theta = \frac{25}{16} \qquad \text{Simplify.}$$
$$\csc \theta = \pm\sqrt{\frac{25}{16}} = \pm\frac{5}{4} \qquad \text{Square root property}$$
$$\csc \theta = -\frac{5}{4} \qquad \theta \text{ is in quadrant III, so } \csc \theta \text{ is negative.}$$
$$\sin \theta = -\frac{4}{5} \qquad \sin \theta = \frac{1}{\csc \theta}$$

Multiply both sides of the quotient identity $\dfrac{\cos \theta}{\sin \theta} = \cot \theta$ by $\sin \theta$ to get

$$\cos \theta = \cot \theta \sin \theta$$
$$= \left(\frac{3}{4}\right)\left(-\frac{4}{5}\right) \qquad \text{Substitute values of } \cot \theta \text{ and } \sin \theta.$$
$$= -\frac{3}{5} \qquad \text{Simplify.}$$

We have the following values of the trigonometric functions of θ.

$$\sin \theta = -\frac{4}{5} \qquad\qquad \csc \theta = -\frac{5}{4}$$

$$\cos \theta = -\frac{3}{5} \qquad\qquad \sec \theta = \frac{1}{\cos \theta} = -\frac{5}{3}$$

$$\cot \theta = \frac{3}{4} \qquad\qquad \tan \theta = \frac{1}{\cot \theta} = \frac{4}{3} \qquad \blacksquare \ \blacksquare \ \blacksquare$$

Practice Problem 5   Assuming that $\tan \theta = -1$ and $90° < \theta < 180°$, find the values of the remaining trigonometric functions of θ.   ■

4 Simplify a complicated trigonometric expression.

Simplifying a Trigonomeric Expression

The basic trigonometric identities are often used for simplifying complicated trigonometric expressions. Recall that when simplifying algebraic expressions, we may use properties of real numbers, factoring techniques, and special product formulas. We may also rationalize the denominator. To simplify trigonometric expressions, we use these same techniques together with the fundamental trigonometric identities.

EXAMPLE 6   **Simplifying by Expressing All Trigonometric Functions in Terms of Sines and Cosines**

Rewrite $\cot \theta + \tan \theta + \csc \theta \sec \theta$ in terms of sines and cosines and then simplify the resulting expression.

SOLUTION

$\cot \theta + \tan \theta + \csc \theta \sec \theta$

$$= \frac{\cos \theta}{\sin \theta} + \frac{\sin \theta}{\cos \theta} + \frac{1}{\sin \theta} \cdot \frac{1}{\cos \theta} \qquad \text{Quotient and Reciprocal identities}$$

$$= \frac{\cos^2 \theta}{\sin \theta \cos \theta} + \frac{\sin^2 \theta}{\sin \theta \cos \theta} + \frac{1}{\sin \theta \cos \theta} \qquad \text{Write each fraction with the common denominator } \sin \theta \cos \theta$$

$$= \frac{\cos^2 \theta + \sin^2 \theta + 1}{\sin \theta \cos \theta} \qquad \text{Add numerators.}$$

$$= \frac{1 + 1}{\sin \theta \cos \theta} \qquad \sin^2 \theta + \cos^2 \theta = 1$$

$$= \frac{2}{\sin \theta \cos \theta} \qquad \blacksquare\blacksquare\blacksquare$$

Practice Problem 6   Rewrite the expression in terms of sines and cosines and then simplify the resulting expression.

$$\frac{\tan \theta}{\sec \theta + 1} + \frac{\tan \theta}{\sec \theta - 1} \qquad \blacksquare$$

EXAMPLE 7   **Proving That an Equation Is Not an Identity**

Prove that the equation $(\sin \theta - \cos \theta)^2 = \sin^2 \theta - \cos^2 \theta$ is not an identity.

SOLUTION

We prove that the given equation is not an identity by finding at least one value of θ for which both sides are defined but for which the two sides of the equation have different values.

Let $\theta = 0°$. We know that $\sin 0° = 0$ and $\cos 0° = 1$.

The left side $= (\sin \theta - \cos \theta)^2 = (0 - 1)^2 = 1$.   Replace θ with $0°$.

The right side $= \sin^2 \theta - \cos^2 \theta = (0)^2 - (1)^2 = -1$.   Replace θ with $0°$.

Because for $\theta = 0°$ the two sides of the equation are not equal, the given equation is not an identity.   ■■■

Practice Problem 7   Prove that the equation $\cos \theta = 1 - \sin \theta$ is not an identity.   ■

SECTION 1.5 ■ Exercises

A EXERCISES Basic Skills and Concepts

1. Trigonometric functions $\sec\theta$, $\csc\theta$, and $\cot\theta$ are, respectively, the reciprocals of _____, _____, and _____.

2. The quotient identities are $\dfrac{\sin\theta}{\cos\theta} =$ _____ and $\dfrac{\cos\theta}{\sin\theta} =$ _____.

3. The identity $\sin^2\theta + \cos^2\theta = 1$ can also be written in equivalent forms $1 - \cos^2\theta =$ _____, $1 - \sin^2\theta =$ _____, $\sin\theta = \pm\sqrt{1 - \cos^2\theta}$, and $\cos\theta = \pm\sqrt{1 - \sin^2\theta}$.

4. Equivalent forms of the identity $1 + \tan^2\theta = \sec^2\theta$ are $\sec^2\theta - \tan^2\theta =$ _____, $\sec^2\theta - 1 =$ _____, $\sec\theta = \pm\sqrt{1 + \tan^2\theta}$, and $\tan\theta = \pm\sqrt{\sec^2\theta - 1}$.

5. Equivalent forms of the identity $1 + \cot^2\theta = \csc^2\theta$ are $\csc^2\theta - \cot^2\theta =$ _____, $\csc^2\theta - 1 =$ _____, $\csc\theta = \pm\sqrt{1 + \cot^2\theta}$, and $\cot\theta = \pm\sqrt{\csc^2\theta - 1}$.

6. *True or False* The equation $\sin\theta\cot\theta = \cos\theta$ is true for every value of θ for which both sides are defined, is an identity.

In Exercises 7–12, use the reciprocal identities to find the indicated function value.

7. $\sin\theta = \dfrac{2}{3}$, find $\csc\theta$

8. $\cos\alpha = -\dfrac{3}{4}$, find $\sec\alpha$

9. $\sec\beta = 5$, find $\cos\beta$

10. $\csc\beta = 5$, find $\sin\beta$

11. $\tan\theta = -\dfrac{2}{7}$, find $\cot\theta$

12. $\cot\theta = \dfrac{3}{5}$, find $\tan\theta$

In Exercises 13–16, use quotient identities to find the indicated function value.

13. $\sin\theta = \dfrac{5}{13}$, $\cos\theta = \dfrac{12}{13}$; find $\tan\theta$

14. $\sin\theta = \dfrac{5}{\sqrt{61}}$, $\cos\theta = -\dfrac{6}{\sqrt{61}}$; find $\cot\theta$

15. $\sin\theta = \dfrac{2}{\sqrt{13}}$, $\cot\theta = \dfrac{3}{2}$; find $\cos\theta$

16. $\cos\alpha = \dfrac{1}{\sqrt{10}}$, $\tan\alpha = -3$; find $\sin\alpha$

In Exercises 17–20, use the reciprocal and quotient identities to find the indicated function value.

17. $\tan\theta = \dfrac{2}{3}$, $\sin\theta = -\dfrac{2}{\sqrt{13}}$; find $\cos\theta$

18. $\cot\theta = -\dfrac{5}{2}$, $\cos\theta = \dfrac{5}{\sqrt{29}}$; find $\sin\theta$

19. $\sec\alpha = \dfrac{\sqrt{17}}{4}$, $\tan\alpha = 4$; find $\sin\alpha$

20. $\csc\alpha = \dfrac{\sqrt{34}}{3}$, $\cot\alpha = \dfrac{5}{3}$; find $\cos\alpha$

In Exercises 21–26, use Pythagorean identities to find the indicated function value.

21. $\sin\theta = -\dfrac{12}{13}$, $180° < \theta < 270°$; find $\cos\theta$

22. $\cos\theta = -\dfrac{2}{\sqrt{13}}$, $90° < \theta < 180°$; find $\sin\theta$

23. $\tan\theta = 3$, $180° < \theta < 270°$; find $\sec\theta$

24. $\sec\theta = \dfrac{5}{4}$, $270° < \theta < 360°$; find $\tan\theta$

25. $\cot\theta = \dfrac{1}{2}$, $180° < \theta < 270°$; find $\csc\theta$

26. $\csc\theta = 3$, $90° < \theta < 180°$; find $\cot\theta$

In Exercises 27–48, use the basic trigonometric identities and the given information to find the exact values of the remaining trigonometric functions.

27. $\sin\theta = -\dfrac{3}{5}$ and $180° < \theta < 270°$

28. $\cos\theta = -\dfrac{12}{13}$ and $90° < \theta < 180°$

29. $\tan\theta = 2$ and $0 < \theta < 90°$

30. $\sec\theta = -3$ and $90° < \theta < 180°$

31. $\csc\theta = -\dfrac{3}{2}$ and $180° < \theta < 270°$

32. $\cot\theta = -2$ and $90° < \theta < 180°$

33. $\cos\theta = -\dfrac{3}{5}$ and $\sin\theta = \dfrac{4}{5}$

34. $\cos\theta = \dfrac{3}{5}$ and $\sin\theta = -\dfrac{4}{5}$

35. $\sin\theta = \dfrac{\sqrt{3}}{3}$ and $\cos\theta = \dfrac{\sqrt{6}}{3}$

36. $\sin\theta = \dfrac{\sqrt{3}}{3}$ and $\cos\theta = -\dfrac{\sqrt{6}}{3}$

37. $\tan\alpha = \dfrac{1}{2}$ and $\sec\alpha = -\dfrac{\sqrt{5}}{2}$

38. $\tan\alpha = \dfrac{1}{2}$ and $\sec\alpha = \dfrac{\sqrt{5}}{2}$

39. $\sec\beta = 3$ and $\cot\beta = \dfrac{\sqrt{2}}{4}$

40. $\sec\beta = 3$ and $\cot\beta = -\dfrac{\sqrt{2}}{4}$

41. $\cot\theta = \dfrac{12}{5}$ and $\sin\theta = -\dfrac{5}{13}$

42. $\cot\theta = -\dfrac{12}{5}$ and $\sin\theta = -\dfrac{5}{13}$

43. $\sin\theta = \dfrac{3}{4}$ and $\cos\theta < 0$

44. $\cos\theta = \dfrac{4}{5}$ and $\tan\theta < 0$

45. $\tan\theta = 2$ and $\sin\theta < 0$

46. $\cot\theta = -2$ and $\sec\theta > 0$

47. $\sec\theta = \dfrac{5}{2}$ and $\sin\theta < 0$

48. $\csc\theta = 2$ and $\tan\theta < 0$

In Exercises 49–62, use the basic identities to find the numerical value of each expression.

49. $(1 - \sin\theta)(1 + \sin\theta) + \sin^2\theta$

50. $(\cos\theta + 1)(\cos\theta - 1) + \sin^2\theta$

51. $(1 + \tan\theta)(1 - \tan\theta) + \sec^2\theta$

52. $(\sec\theta - 1)(\sec\theta + 1) - \tan^2\theta$

53. $(\sec\theta + \tan\theta)(\sec\theta - \tan\theta)$

54. $(\csc\theta + \cot\theta)(\csc\theta - \cot\theta)$

55. $\dfrac{\sec^2\theta - 4}{\sec\theta - 2} - \sec\theta$

56. $\dfrac{9 - \csc^2\theta}{3 + \csc\theta} + \csc\theta$

57. $\sin\theta\cos\theta\,(\tan\theta + \cot\theta)$

58. $\dfrac{\sec\theta\csc\theta\,(\sin\theta + \cos\theta)}{\sec\theta + \csc\theta}$

59. $\dfrac{1}{\sec\theta - \tan\theta} + \dfrac{1}{\sec\theta + \tan\theta} - 2\sec\theta$

60. $\dfrac{1}{\csc\theta - \cot\theta} - \dfrac{1}{\csc\theta + \cot\theta} - 2\cot\theta$

61. $\dfrac{\tan^2\theta - 2\tan\theta - 3}{\tan\theta + 1} - \tan\theta$

62. $\dfrac{\tan^2\theta + \sec\theta - 1}{\sec\theta - 1} - \sec\theta$

In Exercises 63–72, prove that the given equation is not an identity.

63. $(\sin\theta + \cos\theta)^2 = \sin^2\theta + \cos^2\theta$

64. $(1 - \cos\theta)^2 = 1 - \cos^2\theta$

65. $\sin(\theta + 45°) = \sin\theta + \sin 45°$

66. $\cos(\theta + 45°) = \cos\theta + \cos 45°$

67. $\sin 2\theta = 2\sin\theta$

68. $\cos 2\theta = 2\cos\theta$

69. $\tan^2\theta - 1 = \sec^2\theta$

70. $\cot^2\theta + 1 = \sec^2\theta$

71. $\sqrt{\sec^2\theta - 1} = \sec\theta - 1$

72. $\sqrt{\csc^2\theta + 1} = \csc\theta + 1$

B EXERCISES Applying the Concepts

73. **Length of a ladder.** A ladder x feet long makes an angle θ with the horizontal and reaches a height of 20 feet. Then $x = \dfrac{20}{\sin\theta}$. Use a reciprocal identity to rewrite this formula.

74. **Distance from a building.** From a distance of x feet to a 60-foot-high building, the angle of elevation is θ degrees. Then $x = \dfrac{60}{\tan\theta}$. Use a reciprocal identity to rewrite this formula.

75. **Area of a polygon.** The area of a regular n-sided polygon circumscribed about a circle of radius r is given by $A = nr^2 \dfrac{\sin\left(\dfrac{180°}{n}\right)}{\cos\left(\dfrac{180°}{n}\right)}$. Use a quotient identity to rewrite this formula in terms of a single trigonometric function.

76. Use the formula you develop in Exercise 75 to find the area of a square circumscribed about a circle of radius 3 feet.

77. **Angle between two lines.** Two lines with slopes m_1 and m_2 (with $m_1 > m_2$) intersect at a point. The angle θ between these lines at the point of intersection satisfies the equation $(1 + m_1 m_2)\sin\theta = m_1\cos\theta - m_2\cos\theta$. Rewrite this equation in terms of a single trigonometric function.

78. Use the formula you developed in Exercise 77 to find the angle between the lines $y = 4x + 8$ and $y = \dfrac{3}{5}x - 6$.

C EXERCISES Beyond the Basics

In Exercises 79–88, simplify to find the numerical value of each expression.

79. $(\sin\alpha\cos\beta + \cos\alpha\sin\beta)^2 + (\cos\alpha\cos\beta - \sin\alpha\sin\beta)^2$

80. $(\sin\alpha\cos\beta - \cos\alpha\sin\beta)^2 + (\cos\alpha\cos\beta + \sin\alpha\sin\beta)^2$

81. $3(\sin^4\alpha + \cos^4\alpha) - 2(\sin^6\alpha + \cos^6\alpha)$

82. $\sin^6\alpha + \cos^6\alpha + 3\cos^2\alpha - 3\cos^4\alpha$

83. $\dfrac{1 - \cos\theta}{1 + \cos\theta} + \dfrac{1 + \cos\theta}{1 - \cos\theta} - 4\cot^2\theta$

84. $\dfrac{\cos^3\theta + \sin^3\theta}{\cos\theta + \sin\theta} + \dfrac{\cos^3\theta - \sin^3\theta}{\cos\theta - \sin\theta}$

85. $\dfrac{\sec^2\theta + 2\tan^2\theta}{1 + 3\tan^2\theta}$

86. $\dfrac{\csc^2\alpha + \sec^2\alpha}{\csc^2\alpha - \sec^2\alpha} - \dfrac{1 + \tan^2\alpha}{1 - \tan^2\alpha}$

87. $\cos^2\alpha(3 - 4\cos^2\alpha)^2 + \sin^2\alpha(3 - 4\sin^2\alpha)^2$

88. $(\sin\theta + \csc\theta)^2 + (\cos\theta + \sec\theta)^2 - \tan^2\theta - \cot^2\theta$

89. Assming that $\tan\theta + \cot\theta = 2$, show that $\tan^2\theta + \cot^2\theta = 2$.

90. Assuming that $\sec\theta + \cos\theta = 2$, show that $\sec^2\theta + \cos^2\theta = 2$.

91. Assuming that $5\tan\theta = 4$, find the value of $\dfrac{5\sin\theta - 3\cos\theta}{5\sin\theta + 2\cos\theta}$.

92. Assuming that $4\cot\theta = 3$, find the value of $\dfrac{\sin\theta - \cos\theta}{\sin\theta + \cos\theta}$.

93. Assuming that $\tan\theta = \dfrac{1}{\sqrt{7}}$, find the value of

$\dfrac{\csc^2\theta - \sec^2\theta}{\csc^2\theta + \sec^2\theta}$.

94. Assuming that $\cot\theta = \dfrac{1}{\sqrt{3}}$, find the value of $\dfrac{1 - \cos^2\theta}{2 + \sin^2\theta}$.

Critical Thinking

95. Consider the equation $\cos\theta = \sqrt{1 - \sin^2\theta}$.
 a. Why is this equation an identity for $0 \le \theta \le 90°$?
 b. Show that the equation is not an identity for $0 \le \theta \le 180°$.

96. *True or False* In algebra, we note that for any real numbers $a, b,$ and c, the equation $c(a - b) = ca - cb$ is an identity. Therefore, by analogy, the equation $\cos(\alpha - \beta) = \cos\alpha - \cos\beta$ is an identity. Explain.

97. Can $\sin\theta$, $\cos\theta$, and $\tan\theta$ all be negative for any angle θ? Explain.

REVIEW

Definitions, Concepts, and Formulas	Examples and Illustrations

1.1 Angles

▪ **Angle** An angle is formed by rotating a ray about its endpoint, called the vertex. The angle's initial side is the ray's original position, and its terminal side is the ray's position after rotation.	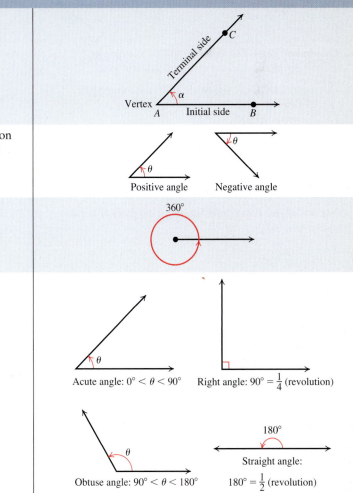
▪ **Positive and negative angles** A counterclockwise rotation of the ray gives a positive angle, and a clockwise rotation gives a negative angle.	
▪ **Degree measure** An angle can be measured in degrees, where $1° = \dfrac{1}{360}$ revolution, or 1 revolution $= 360°$.	
▪ **Types of angles**	

■ **Complements and supplements**

a. Angles $\alpha > 0$ and $\beta > 0$ are complementary if $\alpha + \beta = 90°$.

b. Angles $\alpha > 0$ and $\beta > 0$ are supplementary if $\alpha + \beta = 180°$.

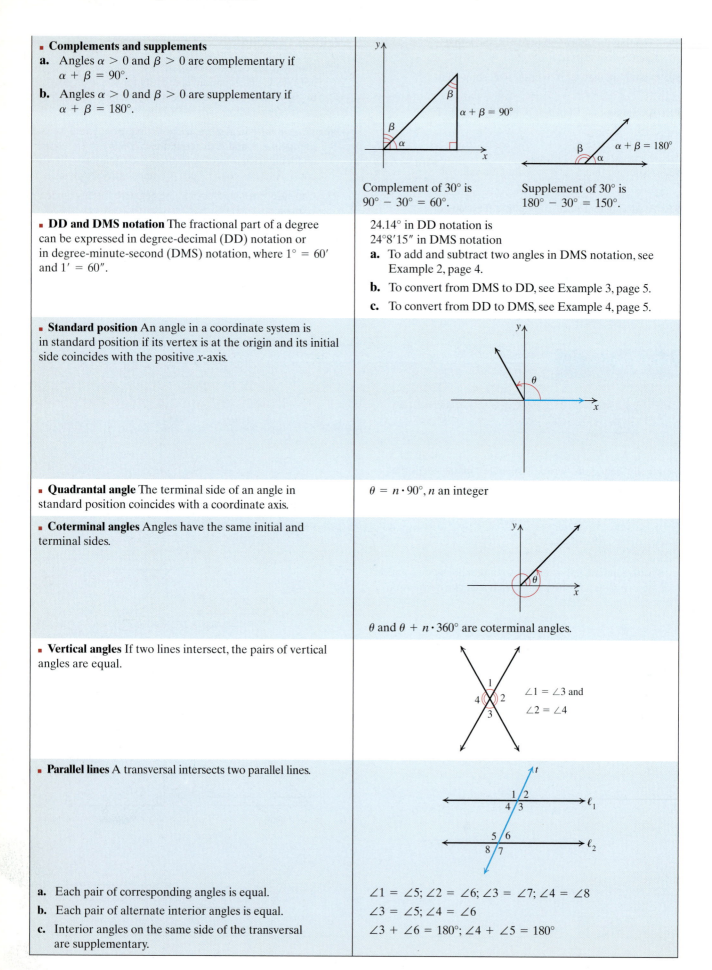

Complement of 30° is $90° - 30° = 60°$.

Supplement of 30° is $180° - 30° = 150°$.

■ **DD and DMS notation** The fractional part of a degree can be expressed in degree-decimal (DD) notation or in degree-minute-second (DMS) notation, where $1° = 60'$ and $1' = 60''$.

24.14° in DD notation is 24°8′15″ in DMS notation

a. To add and subtract two angles in DMS notation, see Example 2, page 4.

b. To convert from DMS to DD, see Example 3, page 5.

c. To convert from DD to DMS, see Example 4, page 5.

■ **Standard position** An angle in a coordinate system is in standard position if its vertex is at the origin and its initial side coincides with the positive x-axis.

■ **Quadrantal angle** The terminal side of an angle in standard position coincides with a coordinate axis.

$\theta = n \cdot 90°$, n an integer

■ **Coterminal angles** Angles have the same initial and terminal sides.

θ and $\theta + n \cdot 360°$ are coterminal angles.

■ **Vertical angles** If two lines intersect, the pairs of vertical angles are equal.

$\angle 1 = \angle 3$ and $\angle 2 = \angle 4$

■ **Parallel lines** A transversal intersects two parallel lines.

a. Each pair of corresponding angles is equal.

b. Each pair of alternate interior angles is equal.

c. Interior angles on the same side of the transversal are supplementary.

$\angle 1 = \angle 5$; $\angle 2 = \angle 6$; $\angle 3 = \angle 7$; $\angle 4 = \angle 8$

$\angle 3 = \angle 5$; $\angle 4 = \angle 6$

$\angle 3 + \angle 6 = 180°$; $\angle 4 + \angle 5 = 180°$

1.2 Triangles

■ Angle sum property The sum of the measures of all three angles of a triangle is 180°.

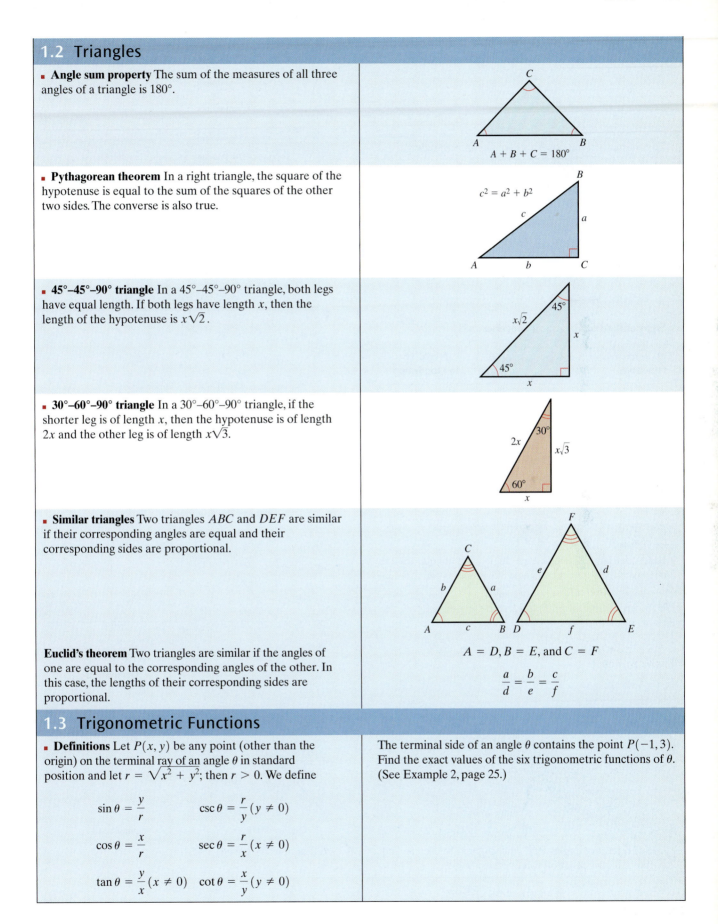

$$A + B + C = 180°$$

■ Pythagorean theorem In a right triangle, the square of the hypotenuse is equal to the sum of the squares of the other two sides. The converse is also true.

$$c^2 = a^2 + b^2$$

■ 45°–45°–90° triangle In a 45°–45°–90° triangle, both legs have equal length. If both legs have length x, then the length of the hypotenuse is $x\sqrt{2}$.

■ 30°–60°–90° triangle In a 30°–60°–90° triangle, if the shorter leg is of length x, then the hypotenuse is of length $2x$ and the other leg is of length $x\sqrt{3}$.

■ Similar triangles Two triangles ABC and DEF are similar if their corresponding angles are equal and their corresponding sides are proportional.

Euclid's theorem Two triangles are similar if the angles of one are equal to the corresponding angles of the other. In this case, the lengths of their corresponding sides are proportional.

$$A = D, B = E, \text{ and } C = F$$

$$\frac{a}{d} = \frac{b}{e} = \frac{c}{f}$$

1.3 Trigonometric Functions

■ Definitions Let $P(x, y)$ be any point (other than the origin) on the terminal ray of an angle θ in standard position and let $r = \sqrt{x^2 + y^2}$; then $r > 0$. We define

$$\sin\theta = \frac{y}{r} \qquad \csc\theta = \frac{r}{y}\,(y \neq 0)$$

$$\cos\theta = \frac{x}{r} \qquad \sec\theta = \frac{r}{x}\,(x \neq 0)$$

$$\tan\theta = \frac{y}{x}\,(x \neq 0) \quad \cot\theta = \frac{x}{y}\,(y \neq 0)$$

The terminal side of an angle θ contains the point $P(-1, 3)$. Find the exact values of the six trigonometric functions of θ. (See Example 2, page 25.)

■ Trigonometric Function Values of Quadrantal Angles

θ (degrees)	$\sin \theta$	$\cos \theta$	$\tan \theta$	$\cot \theta$	$\sec \theta$	$\csc \theta$
0°	0	1	0	undefined	1	undefined
90°	1	0	undefined	0	undefined	1
180°	0	−1	0′	undefined	−1	undefined
270°	−1	0	undefined	0	undefined	−1
360°	0	1	0	undefined	1	undefined

■ Trigonometric Function Values of Common Angles

Trigonometric Function Values of Common Angles

θ	$\sin \theta$	$\cos \theta$	$\tan \theta$	$\cot \theta$	$\sec \theta$	$\csc \theta$
0°	0	1	0	undefined	1	undefined
30°	$\dfrac{1}{2}$	$\dfrac{\sqrt{3}}{2}$	$\dfrac{\sqrt{3}}{3}$	$\sqrt{3}$	$\dfrac{2\sqrt{3}}{3}$	2
45°	$\dfrac{\sqrt{2}}{2}$	$\dfrac{\sqrt{2}}{2}$	1	1	$\sqrt{2}$	$\sqrt{2}$
60°	$\dfrac{\sqrt{3}}{2}$	$\dfrac{1}{2}$	$\sqrt{3}$	$\dfrac{\sqrt{3}}{3}$	2	$\dfrac{2\sqrt{3}}{3}$
90°	1	0	undefined	0	undefined	1

■ **Signs of the Trigonometric Functions**

Functions	Positive in Quadrants	Negative in Quadrants
Sine and cosecant	I and II	III and IV
Cosine and secant	I and IV	II and III
Tangent and cotangent	I and III	II and IV

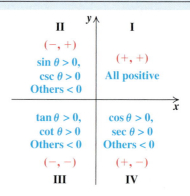

Signs of the Trigonometric Functions

1.4 Reference Angles

■ **Reference angle** The reference angle for a nonquadrantal angle θ is the positive acute angle θ' formed by the terminal side of θ and the x-axis.

For the procedure for finding reference angles, see Example 2, page 35.

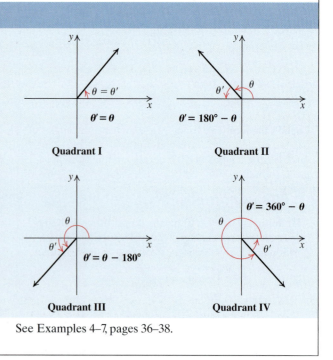

See Examples 4–7, pages 36–38.

■ **Use of reference angles** Reference angles are used to find the trigonometric function values of any angle.

1.5 Fundamental Trigonometric Identities

■ **Reciprocal identities**

$$\csc\theta = \frac{1}{\sin\theta} \qquad \sec\theta = \frac{1}{\cos\theta} \qquad \cot\theta = \frac{1}{\tan\theta}$$

$$\sin\theta = \frac{1}{\csc\theta} \qquad \cos\theta = \frac{1}{\sec\theta} \qquad \tan\theta = \frac{1}{\cot\theta}$$

Quotient identities

$$\tan\theta = \frac{\sin\theta}{\cos\theta} \qquad \cot\theta = \frac{\cos\theta}{\sin\theta}$$

■ **Pythagorean identities**

$$\cos^2\theta + \sin^2\theta = 1; \sin\theta = \pm\sqrt{1 - \cos^2\theta};$$
$$\cos\theta = \pm\sqrt{1 - \sin^2\theta},$$
$$\sec^2\theta = 1 + \tan^2\theta;$$
$$\sec\theta = \pm\sqrt{1 + \tan^2\theta};$$
$$\tan\theta = \pm\sqrt{\sec^2\theta - 1},$$
$$\csc^2\theta = 1 + \cot^2\theta;$$
$$\csc\theta = \pm\sqrt{1 + \cot^2\theta};$$
$$\cot\theta = \pm\sqrt{\csc^2\theta - 1}$$

If $\sin\theta = \dfrac{3}{5}$ and $90° < \theta < 180°$, then $\csc\theta = \dfrac{1}{\sin\theta} = \dfrac{5}{3}$.

$$\cos\theta = -\sqrt{1 - \sin^2\theta} = -\sqrt{1 - \left(\frac{3}{5}\right)^2} = -\frac{4}{5}$$

$$\sec\theta = \frac{1}{\cos\theta} = -\frac{5}{4}$$

$$\tan\theta = \frac{\sin\theta}{\cos\theta} = \frac{\frac{3}{5}}{-\frac{4}{5}} = -\frac{3}{4}$$

$$\cot\theta = \frac{1}{\tan\theta} = -\frac{4}{3}$$

The choice of $+$ or $-$ depends on the quadrant in which θ lies. For example, if θ is in QII, then

$$\sin\theta = \sqrt{1 - \cos^2\theta},$$
$$\cos\theta = -\sqrt{1 - \sin^2\theta},$$
$$\tan\theta = -\sqrt{\sec^2\theta - 1},$$
$$\sec\theta = -\sqrt{1 + \tan^2\theta},$$
$$\csc\theta = \sqrt{1 + \cot^2\theta}, \text{ and}$$
$$\cot\theta = -\sqrt{\csc^2\theta - 1}.$$

REVIEW EXERCISES

1. Find the complement of $67.8°$.

2. Find the supplement of $123.4°$.

3. Convert $64°15'30''$ to decimal-degrees notation rounded to two decimal places.

4. Convert $34.742°$ to degrees-minutes-seconds notation rounded to the nearest second.

5. Draw each angle in standard position and state the quadrant in which it lies.
   a. $-135°$ **b.** $240°$ **c.** $600°$ **d.** $-750°$

6. Find the angle between $0°$ and $360°$ that is coterminal with each angle.
   a. $580°$ **b.** $1460°$ **c.** $-675°$ **d.** $-1345°$

7. The terminal side of an angle in standard position passes through the given point. Write all possible degree measures of this angle.
   a. $(-2, 0)$ **b.** $(3, -3)$

8. In a right triangle, one of the acute angles is $45°$ and the length of its shortest side is 6 cm. Find the lengths of the other two sides.

9. Repeat Exercise 8 assuming that one of the acute angles is $30°$.

10. Find the angles of the triangle ABC assuming that $A = (2x + 10)°$, $B = (3x - 20)°$, and $C = (3x + 30)°$.

11. *True or False* If all three sides of a triangle are of different length, then all three angles have different measure.

12. *True or False* All scalene triangles are acute triangles.

In Exercises 13–20, the terminal side of an angle θ in standard position contains the given point. Find the values of the six trigonometric functions of θ.

13. $(-3, 4)$ 14. $(-5, -12)$

15. $(2, -3)$ 16. $(3, 5)$

17. $(2, 0)$ 18. $(0, 3)$

19. $(-4, 0)$ 20. $(0, -5)$

In Exercises 21–26, find the quadrant in which θ lies.

21. $\tan\theta < 0$ and $\sin\theta > 0$

22. $\cot\theta > 0$ and $\csc\theta < 0$

23. $\cot\theta > 0$ and $\sec\theta < 0$

24. $\sec\theta < 0$ and $\csc\theta > 0$

25. $\sec\theta > 0$ and $\tan\theta < 0$

26. $\sin\theta < 0$ and $\cot\theta < 0$

In Exercises 27–30, find the exact values of the remaining trigonometric functions of θ from the given information.

27. $\cot \theta = -\dfrac{5}{12}$ and θ in quadrant II

28. $\cot \theta = -\dfrac{5}{12}$ and θ in quadrant IV

29. $\sin \theta = \dfrac{3}{5}$ and $\cos \theta > 0$

30. $\sec \theta = \dfrac{13}{12}$ and $\sin \theta < 0$

In Exercises 31–34, find the reference angle θ' for each angle θ.

31. $\theta = 260°$ **32.** $\theta = 530°$

33. $\theta = -275°$ **34.** $\theta = -1315°$

In Exercises 35–38, find the exact values of the six trigonometric functions of θ.

35. $\theta = 390°$ **36.** $\theta = -390°$

37. $\theta = -495°$ **38.** $\theta = 1020°$

In Exercises 39–46, use the basic trigonometric identities and the given information to find the exact values of the remaining trigonometric functions.

39. $\sin \theta = \dfrac{5}{13}$ and $\cos \theta = \dfrac{12}{13}$

40. $\csc \theta = \dfrac{5}{3}$ and $\sec \theta = \dfrac{5}{4}$

41. $\sin \theta = \dfrac{1}{2}$ and $90° < \theta < 180°$

42. $\cos \theta = \dfrac{1}{2}$ and $270° < \theta < 360°$

43. $\tan \theta = 4$ and $180° < \theta < 270°$

44. $\csc \theta = 3$ and $90° < \theta < 180°$

45. $\cot \theta = -2$ and $270° < \theta < 360°$

46. $\tan \theta = -\dfrac{7}{4}$ and $90° < \theta < 180°$

In Exercises 47–50, use the basic identities to find the numerical value of each expression.

47. $(1 - \cos \theta)(1 + \cos \theta) - \sin^2 \theta$

48. $(\csc \theta - 1)(\csc \theta + 1) - \cot^2 \theta$

49. $\dfrac{\cot^2 \theta + \cot \theta - 2}{\cot \theta - 1} - \cot \theta$

50. $\dfrac{\sin \theta}{1 - \sin \theta} - \dfrac{\sin \theta}{1 + \sin \theta} - 2 \tan^2 \theta$

CHAPTER TEST

1. Find the supplement of $61°31'$.

2. Write all possible quadrantal angles.

3. Two lines AB and CD intersect at point O. If the sum of three adjacent angles at O is $260°$, find each of the four angles at O.

4. Find the angles of a triangle with measures $(x + 15)°$, $(x + 30)°$, and $(x + 45)°$.

5. The measure of three angles of a triangle are in the ratio $2 : 3 : 5$. Find the angles of the triangle.

6. In a right isosceles triangle, the length of the hypotenuse is 20 cm. Find the length of the remaining two sides.

7. *True or False* Two congruent triangles are similar. Explain.

8. A 3-foot shrub is 4.5 feet away from a 12-foot streetlight. What is the length of the shadow cast by the shrub?

9. Assuming that $(2, -1)$ is a point on the terminal side of θ, find $\sin \theta$.

10. Assuming that $(-2, -3)$ is a point on the terminal side of θ, find $\csc \theta$.

11. Assuming that $\sin \theta > 0$ and $\sec \theta < 0$, find the quadrant in which θ lies.

12. Assuming that $\cot \theta < 0$ and $\csc \theta < 0$, find the quadrant in which θ lies.

13. Find the reference angle for $845°$.

14. Find the reference angle for $-640°$.

15. Assuming that $\sin \theta = \dfrac{4}{7}$ and $90° < \theta < 180°$, find $\cos \theta$.

16. Assuming that $\tan \theta = -\dfrac{5}{12}$ and θ in quadrant IV, find $\sec \theta$.

17. Show that $1 + \tan \theta = \sec \theta$ is not an identity.

18. Show that $\csc \theta = \sqrt{1 + \cot^2 \theta}$ is not an identity.

19. Simplify: $\sin \theta \cot \theta - \sec \theta \cos^2 \theta$

20. Simplify: $\dfrac{2 \sin^2 \theta + \sin \theta - 1}{2 \sin \theta - 1} - \sin \theta$

Right Triangle Trigonometry

An understanding of the use of the trigonometric expressions associated with right triangles is essential for the successful application of trigonometry to real-world problems. In this chapter, we investigate the relationships between the sides and the angles of triangles and the many applications of these relationships to problems we encounter in our everyday experiences.

Trigonometric Functions of an Acute Angle

Before Starting this Section, Review

1. Similar triangles (Section 1.2)
2. Pythagorean theorem (Section 1.2)
3. Identities (Section 1.5)

Objectives

1 Define the trigonometric functions using right triangles.

2 Use cofunction identities.

3 Find the trigonometric function values for an acute angle in a right triangle.

4 Find trigonometric function values with a calculator.

CHRISTMAS TREE AT ROCKEFELLER CENTER

Millions of New Yorkers and tourists come to see the Rockefeller Center Christmas Tree in Rockefeller Plaza. Typically, the tree is a Norway spruce. It is native to Northern Europe but has been successfully planted in the United States, where it grows to excellent size. The minimum requirement is that the tree be 65 feet tall and 35 feet wide; however, the preferred tree is between 75 and 90 feet tall and proportionally wide. It is carefully prepared for travel before being cut. A 180-ton hydraulic crane is used to handle the cut tree, which is loaded on a custom-made telescoping trailer and transported in the middle of the night to Rockefeller Center. In Exercise 58, you find the height of the tree used one year in Rockefeller Center. ■

---

1 Define the trigonometric functions using right triangles.

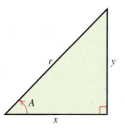

FIGURE 2.1 A right triangle

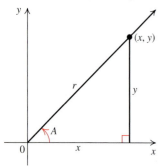

FIGURE 2.2 A triangle angle in standard position

Right Triangle Trigonometry

Suppose A is an acute angle in a right triangle having sides of length x and y and hypotenuse of length r. See Figure 2.1. To find the trigonometric function values of angle A, we place it in standard position as shown in Figure 2.2. Then the point (x, y) is on the terminal side of A and r is the distance between (x, y) and the origin. We can now write the definitions of the six trigonometric functions of the angle A in terms of the sides of the triangle. We use the words *opposite* for the length of the side opposite the angle A, *adjacent* for the length of the side adjacent to the angle A, and *hypotenuse* for the length of the hypotenuse.

TRIGONOMETRIC FUNCTIONS OF AN ACUTE ANGLE IN A RIGHT TRIANGLE

If A is any acute angle in a right triangle, labeled as in Figure 2.1,

$$\sin A = \frac{y}{r} = \frac{\text{opposite}}{\text{hypotenuse}} \qquad \csc A = \frac{r}{y} = \frac{\text{hypotenuse}}{\text{opposite}}$$

$$\cos A = \frac{x}{r} = \frac{\text{adjacent}}{\text{hypotenuse}} \qquad \sec A = \frac{r}{x} = \frac{\text{hypotenuse}}{\text{adjacent}}$$

$$\tan A = \frac{y}{x} = \frac{\text{opposite}}{\text{adjacent}} \qquad \cot A = \frac{x}{y} = \frac{\text{adjacent}}{\text{opposite}}$$

Note that the ratios in the second column in the box on page 58 are the reciprocals of those in the first column.

EXAMPLE 1 **Finding Trigonometric Function Values of Right Triangle Angles**

Find the sine, cosine, and tangent of angles A and B in the right triangle in Figure 2.3.

SOLUTION

We use the lengths of the hypotenuse and the sides opposite and adjacent to each angle.

$$\sin A = \frac{\text{opposite}}{\text{hypotenuse}} = \frac{3}{5} \qquad \cos A = \frac{\text{adjacent}}{\text{hypotenuse}} = \frac{4}{5} \qquad \tan A = \frac{\text{opposite}}{\text{adjacent}} = \frac{3}{4}$$

$$\sin B = \frac{\text{opposite}}{\text{hypotenuse}} = \frac{4}{5} \qquad \cos B = \frac{\text{adjacent}}{\text{hypotenuse}} = \frac{3}{5} \qquad \tan B = \frac{\text{opposite}}{\text{adjacent}} = \frac{4}{3}$$

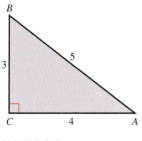

FIGURE 2.3

Note that the side opposite A is the side adjacent to B and the side adjacent to A is the side opposite B. ▪ ▪ ▪

Practice Problem 1 Find the cosecant, secant, and cotangent of angles A and B for the right triangle in Figure 2.3. ▪

2 Use cofunction identities.

Cofunctions

In Example 1, we see that $\sin A = \cos B$ and $\cos A = \sin B$. This is true for acute angles A and B in any right triangle. As Figure 2.4 suggests,

$$\sin A = \frac{\text{opposite } A}{\text{hypotenuse}} = \frac{a}{c} = \frac{\text{adjacent to } B}{\text{hypotenuse}} = \cos B$$

$$\cos A = \frac{\text{adjacent to } A}{\text{hypotenuse}} = \frac{b}{c} = \frac{\text{opposite } B}{\text{hypotenuse}} = \sin A$$

$$\tan A = \frac{\text{opposite } A}{\text{adjacent to } A} = \frac{a}{b} = \frac{\text{adjacent to } B}{\text{opposite } B} = \cot B$$

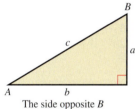
The side opposite A is the side adjacent to B.
The side opposite B is the side adjacent to A.

FIGURE 2.4 Cofunction values

Similarly, $\csc A = \sec B$, $\sec A = \csc B$, and $\cot A = \tan B$. Because $A + B = 90°$, angles A and B are complementary angles with $\sin A = \cos B$. The sine and cosine are called **cofunctions**. The tangent and cotangent are also cofunctions, as are secant and cosecant. Because $A + B = 90°$, $B = 90° - A$, so $\sin A = \cos B = \cos (90° - A)$. Similar results, known as the *cofunction identities*, relate the values of the cofunctions of complementary angles.

COFUNCTION IDENTITIES

For an acute angle A,

$$\sin A = \cos (90° - A) \qquad \cos A = \sin (90° - A) \qquad \tan A = \cot (90° - A)$$
$$\csc A = \sec (90° - A) \qquad \sec A = \csc (90° - A) \qquad \cot A = \tan (90° - A)$$

EXAMPLE 2 Using the Cofunction Identities

Express each function value in terms of its cofunction.

a. sin 13°   **b.** tan 67°   **c.** csc 81°

SOLUTION

a. Because the cosine is the cofunction of the sine,

$$\sin 13° = \cos (90° - 13°) = \cos 77°.$$

b. Because the tangent and cotangent are cofunctions,

$$\tan 67° = \cot (90° - 67°) = \cot 23°.$$

c. Because the secant and cosecant are cofunctions,

$$\csc 81° = \sec (90° - 81°) = \sec 9°.$$ ■ ■ ■

Practice Problem 2 Express each function value in terms of its cofunction.

a. cos 43°   **b.** cot 70°   **c.** sec 54°   ■

EXAMPLE 3 Finding One Solution for an Equation

Find one value of θ that is a solution of the given equation.

a. $\cos 15° = \sin (\theta - 15°)$ **b.** $\cot \theta = \tan (\theta + 20°)$

SOLUTION

a. The cofunction identity $\cos 15° = \sin (90° - 15°)$ shows that $\theta = 90°$ is one solution of $\cos 15° = \sin (\theta - 15°)$.

b. Because the tangent and cotangent are cofunctions, $\cot A = \tan B$ if A and B are acute angles and $A + B = 90°$. So $\cot \theta = \tan (\theta + 20°)$ if θ and $\theta + 20°$ are acute angles and

$$\theta + (\theta + 20°) = 90°$$
$$2\theta = 70° \quad \theta + \theta = 2\theta; \text{ subtract } 20° \text{ from both sides.}$$
$$\theta = 35° \quad \text{Solve for } \theta.$$ ■ ■ ■

Practice Problem 3 Find one value of θ that is a solution of the equation $\cos (\theta + 40°) = \sin \theta$.   ■

3 Find the trigonometric function values for an acute angle in a right triangle.

Trigonometric Function Values

If the lengths of two sides of a right triangle are known, the Pythagorean theorem can be used to find the remaining length.

EXAMPLE 4 Finding Trigonometric Function Values for Angles in a Right Triangle

Triangle ABC is a right triangle with sides of lengths a, b, and c and a right angle at C. Assuming that $a = 5$ and $c = 13$, find the six trigonometric function values of A.

SOLUTION

First, sketch the triangle ABC. See Figure 2.5.

$$a^2 + b^2 = c^2 \qquad \text{Pythagorean theorem}$$
$$5^2 + b^2 = 13^2 \qquad \text{Replace } a \text{ with 5 and } c \text{ with 13.}$$
$$b^2 = 13^2 - 5^2 = 169 - 25 = 144 \qquad \text{Subtract } 5^2 \text{ from both sides; simplify.}$$
$$b = \sqrt{144} = 12 \qquad \text{Solve for } b.$$

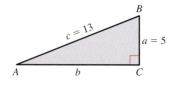

FIGURE 2.5 Right triangle

Now use $a = 5 =$ opposite, $b = 12 =$ adjacent, and $c = 13 =$ hypotenuse.

$$\sin A = \frac{a}{c} = \frac{5}{13} \qquad\qquad \csc A = \frac{c}{a} = \frac{13}{5}$$

$$\cos A = \frac{b}{c} = \frac{12}{13} \qquad\qquad \sec A = \frac{c}{b} = \frac{13}{12}$$

$$\tan A = \frac{a}{b} = \frac{5}{12} \qquad\qquad \cot A = \frac{b}{a} = \frac{12}{5}$$

■ ■ ■

Practice Problem 4   Rework Example 4 with $a = 1$ and $c = 5$.   ■

EXAMPLE 5   **Finding the Length of A Rope**

A boat, attached by a rope at water level, is tethered to a dock that is 5 feet above the water, as shown in Figure 2.6. Find the length of the rope assuming that the angle between the rope and the dock is $60°$.

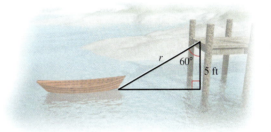

FIGURE 2.6

SOLUTION

The rope is the hypotenuse of a right triangle having a $60°$ angle with an adjacent side of length 5 feet. If r is the length of the rope in feet, we have

$$\cos 60° = \frac{5}{r} \qquad \cos\theta = \frac{\text{adjacent}}{\text{hypotenuse}}$$

$$\frac{1}{2} = \frac{5}{r} \qquad \text{Replace } \cos 60° \text{ with } \frac{1}{2}; \text{ see page 29.}$$

$$r = 10 \qquad \text{Solve for } r.$$

The rope is 10 feet long.   ■ ■ ■

Practice Problem 5   Represent the distance that the boat in Example 5 is from the dock using a trigonometric function of $60°$, then compute that distance.   ■

4 Find trigonometric function values with a calculator.

Trigonometric Function Values with a Calculator

Calculators with keys for the sine, $\boxed{\text{SIN}}$; cosine, $\boxed{\text{COS}}$; and tangent, $\boxed{\text{TAN}}$ functions can be used to find the trigonometric function values for all six trigonometric functions.

To find the values for the cosecant, secant, and cotangent functions, you use the $\boxed{\text{SIN}}$, $\boxed{\text{COS}}$, and $\boxed{\text{TAN}}$ keys with an appropriate reciprocal identity. Although we have discussed only degree measure of angles, we will soon learn an equally important unit of angle measure called *radian* measure. To find a trigonometric function value of an angle measured in degrees, you must set the calculator to *Degree mode*.

The screens below show the results found in Example 6.

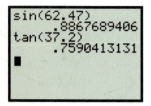

The Ans⁻¹ on the third line of the next screen indicates that the next number displayed is the reciprocal of the previous one.

The screens below show the results found in Example 7.

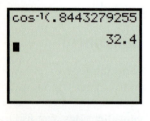

EXAMPLE 6 **Finding Trigonometric Function Values Using a Calculator**

Find the approximate value of each expression, rounded to four decimal places.

a. sin 62.47°   **b.** tan 37°12′   **c.** sec 86.342°

SOLUTION

Set your calculator to Degree mode.

a. $\sin 62.47° \approx 0.8867689406 \approx 0.8868$

b. Convert 37°12′ to decimal degrees:

$$\tan 37°12′ = \tan 37.2° \approx 0.7590413131 \approx 0.7590$$

c. To find sec 86.342°, use the reciprocal identity $\sec\theta = \dfrac{1}{\cos\theta}$. First, find cos 86.342°; then use the reciprocal key, $\boxed{x^{-1}}$, to get

$$\sec 86.342 \approx 15.67378941 \approx 15.6738. \quad ■■■$$

Practice Problem 6 Find approximate values for each expression, rounded to four decimal places.

a. cos 25.39°   **b.** cot 56°18′   ■

Finding Angles Using a Calculator

We used the $\boxed{\text{SIN}}$, $\boxed{\text{COS}}$, and $\boxed{\text{TAN}}$ keys to find the value of a trigonometric function of an angle. However, sometimes we want to find the measure of an angle that has a certain trigonometric function value. Many calculators have keys marked $\boxed{\text{SIN}^{-1}}$, $\boxed{\text{COS}^{-1}}$, and $\boxed{\text{TAN}^{-1}}$ that can be used for this purpose. These keys are for *inverse functions*, which we will study in a later chapter. For now, we want to use them to find the measure of an angle in quadrant I having a specific trigonometric function value. This can be done when the trigonometric function value is positive.

EXAMPLE 7 **Finding an Angle with a Specific Trigonometric Function Value**

Find an angle θ between 0° and 90° having the specified function value. Round your answer to the nearest tenth of a degree.

a. $\cos\theta \approx 0.8443279255$ **b.** $\csc\theta \approx 1.053878471$

SOLUTION

Set your calculator to Degree mode.

a. Enter the value 0.8443279255 and use the $\boxed{\text{COS}^{-1}}$ key to get:

$$\cos^{-1}(0.8443279255) \approx 32.4°$$

b. Because $\csc\theta = \dfrac{1}{\sin\theta}$, enter 1.053878471 and use the $\boxed{x^{-1}}$ key to find $\sin\theta \approx 0.9488760113$. Then use the $\boxed{\text{SIN}^{-1}}$ key to find θ.

We have,

$$\sin^{-1}(0.9488760113) \approx 71.59999994 \approx 71.6°. \quad ■■■$$

Practice Problem 7 Find an angle θ between 0° and 90° having the specified function value. Round your answer to the nearest tenth of a degree.

a. $\sin\theta \approx 0.8358073614$ **b.** $\cot\theta \approx 5.050369047$ ■

FIGURE 2.7

| EXAMPLE 8 | **Finding the Angle a Ladder Makes with a Building** |

A 25-foot ladder leans against a building, and the foot of the ladder is 4 feet from the building. What angle, to the nearest tenth of a degree, does the ladder make with the building?

SOLUTION

First, sketch a diagram as shown in Figure 2.7. If θ is the angle between the ladder and the building, we have

$$\sin \theta = \frac{4}{25} = 0.16.$$

Then θ is the acute angle with $\sin \theta = 0.16$. Put your calculator in Degree mode and use the $\boxed{\text{SIN}^{-1}}$ key to find

$$\theta = \sin^{-1}(0.16) \approx 9.2°.$$

■ ■ ■

Practice Problem 8 Rework Example 8 for a 20-foot ladder whose foot is 5 feet from the building.

■

SECTION 2.1 ■ Exercises

A EXERCISES Basic Skills and Concepts

1. In a right triangle ABC with right angle at C, $\sin A = $ _____ , $\cos A = $ _____ , and $\tan A = $ _____ .

2. If θ and α are two acute angles (measured in degrees) in a right triangle and $\cos \theta = \sin \alpha$, then $\theta + \alpha = $ _____ .

3. To find the value of $\csc 63°$ on a scientific calculator, we find _____ and then use the $\boxed{x^{-1}}$ key.

4. *True or False* If θ is an acute angle in a right triangle and $\tan \theta = \frac{2}{5}$, then $\sin \theta = 2$ and $\cos \theta = 5$.

5. *True or False* The leg adjacent to angle θ in a right triangle is the leg opposite the angle $90° - \theta$.

6. *True or False* If the length of the side opposite angle A in a right triangle is shorter than the length of the side adjacent to A, then $\sin A < \cos A$.

In Exercises 7–12, find the exact values for the six trigonometric functions of the angle in each figure. Rationalize the denominator where necessary.

7. 8.

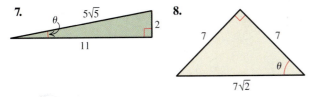

9.   10.   11.   12.

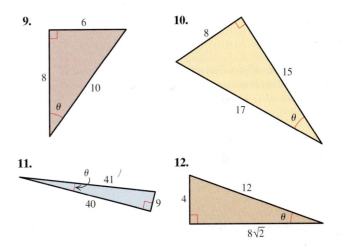

In Exercises 13–18, express each function in terms of its cofunction.

13. $\sin 58°$ 14. $\cos 37°$
15. $\tan 27°$ 16. $\cot 49°$
17. $\sec 65°$ 18. $\csc 78°$

In Exercises 19–26, find one value of θ that is a solution to the given equation.

19. $\sin \theta = \cos(\theta + 30°)$ 20. $\cot \theta = \tan(\theta + 10°)$
21. $\sec \theta = \csc(\theta - 30°)$ 22. $\cos \theta = \sin(\theta - 10°)$
23. $\tan(\theta + 5°) = \cot(\theta + 15°)$
24. $\csc(\theta + 8°) = \sec(\theta + 32°)$

25. $\sin 3\theta = \cos(\theta + 30°)$

26. $\cot(4\theta + 2°) = \tan(\theta + 43°)$

In Exercises 27–32, triangle ABC is a right triangle with sides of lengths a, b, and c and a right angle at C. Find the six trigonometric function values of A. Rationalize denominators containing radicals.

27. $a = 9, b = 12$

28. $a = 3, b = \sqrt{7}$

29. $a = 21, c = 29$

30. $a = 2, c = 5$

31. $b = \sqrt{13}, c = 7$

32. $b = 1, c = \sqrt{5}$

In Exercises 33–42, find the approximate value of each expression, rounded to four decimal places.

33. $\cos 59.27°$

34. $\sec 82.11°$

35. $\sec 28.43°$

36. $\cot 2.75°$

37. $\tan 33°14'$

38. $\sin 72°45'$

39. $\sec 27°42'$

40. $\cos 41°24'$

41. $\cot 19°30'$

42. $\sec 5°48'$

In Exercises 43–46, rewrite the expression as a value of the sine, cosine, or tangent function before using a calculator to find the approximate value, rounded to four decimal places.

43. $\dfrac{1}{\sec 11.8°}$

44. $\dfrac{1}{\cot 55.8°}$

45. $\cot(90° - 31.16°)$

46. $\cot 80°$

In Exercises 47–54, find an angle θ between 0° and 90° having the specified function value. Round your answer to the nearest tenth of a degree.

47. $\cos\theta \approx 0.9163627296$

48. $\sin\theta \approx 0.6665324702$

49. $\tan\theta \approx 1.609070042$

50. $\tan\theta \approx 4.915157031$

51. $\csc\theta \approx 1.673289695$

52. $\sec\theta \approx 1.765517282$

53. $\cot\theta \approx 1.56365642$

54. $\cot\theta \approx 0.4705642812$

B EXERCISES Applying the Concepts

55. Bracing a tree. A tree is supported by a rope anchored in the ground and attached to the tree 4 feet above the ground. If the ground is flat and the rope makes a 45° angle with the tree, how far is the rope anchored from the base of the tree?

56. Ramp height. A 15-foot ramp forms an angle of 8° with the ground. How high is the end of the ramp above the ground? Round your answer to one decimal place.

57. Height of a flagpole. A flagpole is supported by a 30-foot tension wire attached to the flagpole and to a stake in the ground. If the ground is flat and the angle the wire makes with the ground is 40°, how high up the flagpole is the wire attached? Round your answer to the nearest foot.

58. Height of a Christmas tree. In 2008, the angle from the top of the Rockefeller Center Christmas tree to a point

100 feet from its base (on flat ground) was found to be 40°. Find the height of the tree, to the nearest foot.

59. Adjusting a spotlight. A spotlight illuminates a spot on the stage that is 20 feet below and 35 feet in front of the light. What angle is formed by the light beam and a vertical line through the spotlight? Round your answer to the nearest degree.

60. Red light violations. A camera is attached to a traffic signal 18 feet above the road. What angle does the camera's line of sight make with the vertical when a car at a horizontal distance of 40 feet from the base of the signal is viewed? Round your answer to the nearest degree.

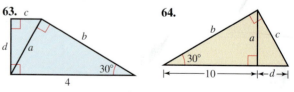

C EXERCISES Beyond the Basics

61. Find $\tan\theta$, where θ is the angle that the diagonal of a cube makes with the lower corner of the cube. (See the figure.)

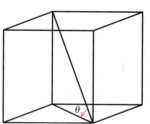

62. A rectangle is formed by doubling the width of a square while leaving the length unchanged. What angle does the diagonal of the rectangle make with its longer side? Round your answer to the nearest tenth of a degree.

In Exercises 63 and 64, find the exact value of each side labeled in the figure.

63.

64.

65. Find the distance between A and C in the figure.

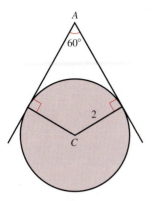

66. In a right triangle with acute angle θ, what value must the hypotenuse have for the length of the opposite side to represent $\sin \theta$ and the length of the adjacent side to represent $\cos \theta$?

67. Use the result of Exercise 66 to compare $\sin \alpha$ and $\sin \beta$ and to compare $\cos \alpha$ and $\cos \beta$ assuming that α and β are acute angles and the measure of α is less than the measure of β.

68. In a right triangle with acute angle θ, what value must the adjacent side have for the length of the opposite side to represent $\tan \theta$?

69. Use the result of Exercise 68 to compare $\tan \alpha$ and $\tan \beta$ assuming that α and β are acute angles and the measure of α is less than the measure of β.

70. In the adjoining figure, ABC is a triangle with a right angle at C. The segment CL is perpendicular to AB. Show that $CL^2 = AL \cdot LB$.

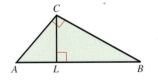

Critical Thinking

71. Draw a right triangle with acute angle θ. Then use the definitions of $\sin \theta$ and $\cos \theta$ together with the Pythagorean theorem to show that $\sin^2 \theta + \cos^2 \theta = 1$.

72. Sketch the line with equation $y = mx, m > 0$. What is the relationship between the slope of this line and the acute angle with vertex $(0, 0)$ in a triangle with vertices $(0, 0)$, $(x, 0)$, and (x, mx)?

GROUP PROJECT

All references are to the figure.

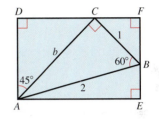

    (i) Find b and $\angle CAB$.
   (ii) Find $AD, DC,$ and $\angle ACD$.
  (iii) Find $\angle BCF$ and $\angle CBF$.
  (iv) Find CF and BF.
   (v) Find AE and BE.
  (vi) Find $\angle BAE$ and $\angle ABE$.
 (vii) Find $\sin 15°$ and $\cos 15°$.
(viii) Find $\sin 75°$ and $\cos 75°$.

Solving Right Triangles

Before Starting this Section, Review

1. Pythagorean theorem (Section 1.2)
2. Trigonometric functions of angles (Section 1.3)

Objectives

1. Identify significant digits.
2. Solve right triangles.
3. Solve problems involving angles of elevation or depression.

MEASURING MOUNT KILIMANJARO

Trigonometry developed as a result of attempts to solve practical problems in astronomy, navigation, and land measurement. The word *trigonometry*, coined by Pitiscus in 1594, is derived from two Greek words, *trigonon* (triangle) and *metron* (measure), and means "triangle measurement."

Measuring objects that are generally inaccessible is one of the many successes of trigonometry. In Example 6, we use trigonometry to approximate the height of Mount Kilimanjaro, Tanzania. Mount Kilimanjaro is the highest mountain in Africa. ■

1 Identify significant digits.

Significant Digits

In applied problems, we frequently work with numbers that result from measurement. The *significant digits* in these numbers (or in a number that results from calculations involving these numbers) are all of the digits known with certainty, together with a final digit about which there is some uncertainty. When a scientist says that a dog's weight is 72.6 lbs, to three significant digits, this means that the final digit, 6, is uncertain and that the actual weight is between 72.55 and 72.65 lbs. Uncertainty also occurs in approximations obtained from calculators and from rounded estimates.

RULES FOR IDENTIFYING SIGNIFICANT DIGITS

1. The digits 1, 2, 3, 4, 5, 6, 7, 8, and 9 are always significant.
2. Leading zeros are not significant; the first nonzero digit on the left is the first significant digit in a number.
3. Zeros between two nonzero digits are always significant.
4. Trailing zeros are considered significant only when the number contains a decimal point.

According to these rules,

743 has three significant digits.	Rule 1
30907 has five significant digits.	Rules 1 and 3
0.0014 has two significant digits.	Rules 1 and 2
500 has one significant digit.	Rule 4
500. has three significant digits.	Rule 4

Calculations with numbers that are approximations should be rounded to contain the same number of significant digits as the number in the calculation that has the *fewest significant digits*. Your result can be no more accurate than the least accurate number used in your calculation. Numbers that are not approximations, such as numbers that are theoretically derived, or that result from counting are not considered when this rounding rule is applied. For example, the digit 2 in the expression $2\pi r$ for the circumference of a circle is not an approximation. So although 2 has only one significant digit, this fact is ignored when the expression $2\pi r$ is used. If you are told to use 3.14 as an approximation for π and that the radius of a circle is 2.4 feet, then $2(3.14)(2.4) = 15.072$ is rounded to two significant digits (not one) and is reported as 15 feet.

2 Solve right triangles.

Solving Right Triangles

To solve a triangle means to find the lengths of all of the sides and the measures of all of the angles in the triangle. We use the familiar notation where a, b, and c denote the lengths of the sides opposite angles A, B, and C, respectively. In a right triangle, C always denotes the $90°$ angle. (So c denotes the length of the hypotenuse.) See Figure 2.8.

Table 2.1 gives the relationship between the accuracy of measurement of sides and angles in triangles. For example, if an angle is accurate to the nearest degree and a side is given to *three* significant digits, the remaining sides will be given to only *two* significant digits and the remaining angles to the nearest degree.

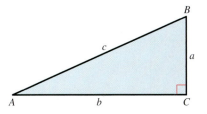

FIGURE 2.8 A right triangle

TABLE 2.1 Significant Digits in Right Triangle Measures

Accuracy of Sides	Accuracy of Angles
Two significant digits	Nearest degree
Three significant digits	Nearest 10 minutes or tenth of a degree
Four significant digits	Nearest minute or hundredth of a degree

When solving triangles, it is helpful to sketch and label a diagram. If rounding is required, round only the answers, not the numbers found in the intermediate steps. Finally, use the values given in the problem whenever possible, rather than values calculated in intermediate steps.

EXAMPLE 1   **Solving a Right Triangle Given an Angle and a Side**

Solve the right triangle ABC, where $A = 32.7°$ and $c = 14.3$ in.

SOLUTION

First, sketch a triangle and label it using the given information. See Figure 2.9.
    Because $A + B = 90°$,

$$B = 90° - A = 90° - 32.7° = 57.3°.$$

Next, find a.

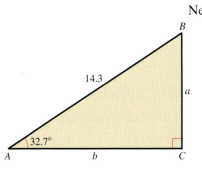

$$\sin 32.7° = \frac{a}{14.3} \qquad \sin A = \frac{\text{opposite}}{\text{hypotenuse}}$$

$$a = 14.3 \sin 32.7° \qquad \text{Multiply both sides by 14.3.}$$

$$a \approx 14.3(0.54024032) \qquad \text{Use a calculator.}$$

$$a \approx 7.73 \text{ in.} \qquad \text{Three significant digits}$$

FIGURE 2.9

To find b, we could use $a^2 + b^2 = c^2$, but this would require us to use the value for a found in the previous step. Instead, we use the given information when possible.

$$\cos 32.7° = \frac{b}{14.3} \qquad\qquad \cos A = \frac{\text{adjacent}}{\text{hypotenuse}}$$

$$b = 14.3 \cos 32.7° \qquad \text{Multiply both sides by 14.3.}$$

$$b \approx 14.3(0.84151078) \qquad \text{Use a calculator.}$$

$$b \approx 12.0 \text{ in.} \qquad \text{Three significant digits}$$

Notice that we rounded a and b to three significant digits because both $A = 32.7°$ and $c = 14.3$ have three significant digits. ■ ■ ■

Practice Problem 1 Solve the right triangle ABC, where $B = 49.2°$ and $c = 16.9$ in.
■

STUDY TIP

When solving a triangle, to find length, use the [SIN], [COS], and [TAN] keys and to find angles, use the [SIN⁻¹], [COS⁻¹], and [TAN⁻¹] keys.

EXAMPLE 2 **Solving a Triangle Given Two Sides**

Solve the right triangle ABC, where $a = 18.91$ cm and $b = 21.48$ cm.

SOLUTION

First, sketch a triangle and label it using the given information. See Figure 2.10.

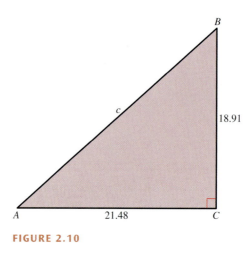

FIGURE 2.10

Then

$$\tan A = \frac{18.91}{21.48} \qquad\qquad \tan A = \frac{\text{opposite}}{\text{adjacent}}$$

$$A = \tan^{-1}\left(\frac{18.91}{21.48}\right) \qquad \text{Section 2.1}$$

$$A \approx 41.36° \qquad \text{Use a calculator.}$$

A is rounded to one hundredth of a degree because the sides are given with four significant digits.

Because $A + B = 90°$,

$$B = 90° - A \approx 90° - 41.36° = 48.64°.$$

To find c, we use

$$a^2 + b^2 = c^2 \qquad\qquad \text{Pythagorean theorem}$$

$$c = \sqrt{a^2 + b^2} \qquad\qquad \text{Take the square root of both sides } (c > 0).$$

$$c = \sqrt{(18.91)^2 + (21.48)^2} \approx 28.62 \text{ cm} \qquad \text{Use a calculator.}$$

Four significant digits are given for c because a and b were given with four significant digits. ■ ■ ■

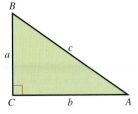

Practice Problem 2 Solve the right triangle *ABC*, where $a = 7.72$ in. and $b = 9.54$ in. ■

The following identities provide some of the fundamental relationships between the angles and sides of a right triangle. Most are consequences of the basic definitions; for example, multiplying both sides of the equation $\sin A = \dfrac{\text{opposite}}{\text{hypotenuse}} = \dfrac{a}{c}$ by c yields $a = c \sin A$. The cofunction identities, such as $\sin A = \cos B$, yield several others.

$$A + B = 90° \quad a = c \sin A \quad c = b \sec A$$
$$a^2 + b^2 = c^2 \quad b = c \cos A \quad a = b \tan A$$
$$c = a \csc A \quad b = a \cot A$$

EXAMPLE 3 **Solving a Right Triangle within Another Right Triangle**

Use the information in Figure 2.11 to solve for *x*, the distance in feet between *D* and *C*.

SOLUTION

From right triangle *BCD*, we have

$$\tan 50° = \frac{h}{x} \qquad \tan 50° = \frac{\text{opposite}}{\text{adjacent}}$$
$$h = x \tan 50° \qquad \text{Multiply both sides by } x.$$

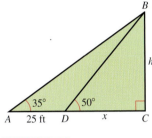

FIGURE 2.11

From right triangle *ABC*, we have

$$\tan 35° = \frac{h}{x + 25} \qquad \tan 35° = \frac{\text{opposite}}{\text{adjacent}}$$
$$h = (x + 25) \tan 35° \qquad \text{Multiply both sides by } x + 25.$$

Because $h = x \tan 50°$ and $h = (x + 25) \tan 35°$,

$x \tan 50° = (x + 25) \tan 35°$	Both expressions equal h.
$x \tan 50° = x \tan 35° + 25 \tan 35°$	Distributive property
$x \tan 50° - x \tan 35° = 25 \tan 35°$	Subtract $x \tan 35°$ from both sides.
$x(\tan 50° - \tan 35°) = 25 \tan 35°$	Factor out the common factor, x.
$x = \dfrac{25 \tan 35°}{\tan 50° - \tan 35°}$	Divide both sides by $\tan 50° - \tan 35°$.
$\approx \dfrac{25(0.70020754)}{0.49154605}$	Use a calculator.
≈ 36 ft	Round to two significant digits.

■ ■ ■

Practice Problem 3 Use the result of Example 3 to find the value (in feet) of *h* in Figure 2.11. ■

EXAMPLE 4 **EXAMPLE 4   Finding the Radius of a Circle**

A line segment from a point where a tangent line meets a circle to the center of the circle always makes a 90° angle with the line. See Figure 2.12. Assuming that the distance between A and P is 15 meters, find the radius r of the circle (in meters).

SOLUTION

Because r is also the distance between P and B, the distance between A and B is $15 + r$. Because ABC is a right triangle,

$$\sin 27° = \frac{r}{15 + r} \qquad \qquad \sin 27° = \frac{\text{opposite}}{\text{hypotenuse}}$$

$$(15 + r)\sin 27° = r \qquad \qquad \text{Multiply both sides by } 15 + r.$$

$$15 \sin 27° + r \sin 27° = r \qquad \qquad \text{Distributive property}$$

$$15 \sin 27° = r - r \sin 27° \qquad \qquad \text{Subtract } r \sin 27° \text{ from both sides.}$$

$$15 \sin 27° = r(1 - \sin 27°) \qquad \qquad \text{Factor out } r, \text{ the common factor.}$$

$$r = \frac{15 \sin 27°}{1 - \sin 27°} \qquad \qquad \text{Divide both sides by } 1 - \sin 27°.$$

$$\approx \frac{15(0.4539904997)}{1 - 0.4539904997} \qquad \text{Use a calculator.}$$

$$\approx 12 \text{ meters} \qquad \qquad \text{Round to two significant digits.} \quad ■ ■ ■$$

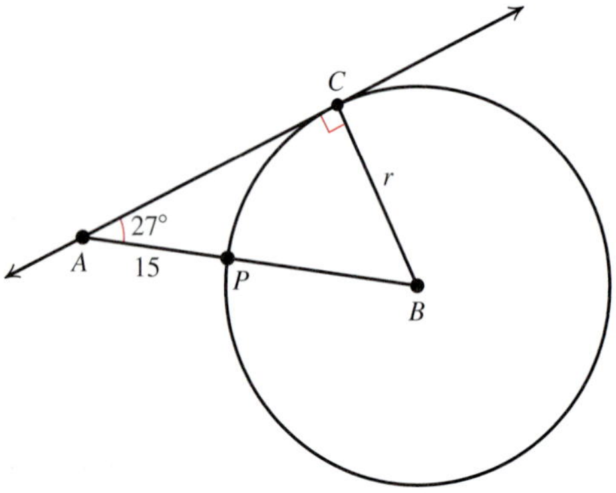

FIGURE 2.12

Practice Problem 4   Rework Example 4 assuming that the distance between A and P in Figure 2.12 is 25 inches. ■

3 Solve problems involving angles of elevation or depression.

Angles of Elevation and Depression

Angles that are measured between a line of sight and a horizontal line occur in many applications and are called *angles of elevation* or *angles of depression*. If the line of sight is *above* the horizontal line, the angle between the two lines is called the **angle of elevation**. If the line of sight is *below* the horizontal line, the angle between the two lines is called the **angle of depression**.

For example, suppose you are taking a picture of a friend who is standing on a balcony in the New Orleans French Quarter. See Figure 2.13. The angle your eyes rotate through as your gaze changes from looking straight ahead to looking at your friend is the angle of elevation.

STUDY TIP

Remember that an angle of elevation or an angle of depression is the angle between the line of sight and a *horizontal* line.

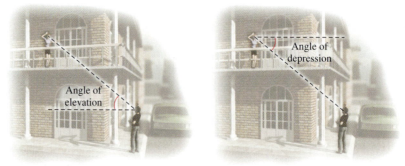

Angle of elevation

Angle of depression

FIGURE 2.13

The angle through which your friend's eyes rotate as she changes from looking straight ahead to looking down at you is the angle of depression.

68.2°

←— 150 ft —→

FIGURE 2.14

EXAMPLE 5   **Finding the Height of a Cloud**

To find the height of a cloud at night, a farmer shines a spotlight straight up to a spot on the cloud. The angle of elevation to this same spot on the cloud from a point located 150 feet horizontally from the spotlight is 68.2°. Find the height of the cloud to the nearest foot.

SOLUTION

We let h represent the height of the cloud in feet; so h is the length of side opposite the acute angle of 68.2° in the right triangle sketched in Figure 2.14. We have

$$\tan 68.2° = \frac{opposite}{adjacent} = \frac{h}{150} \qquad \tan A = \frac{opposite}{adjacent}$$

$$h = 150 \cdot \tan 68.2° \approx 375 \qquad \text{Use a calculator.}$$

The height of the cloud is approximately 375 feet, rounded to the nearest foot. ■ ■ ■

Practice Problem 5   From an observation deck 425 feet high on top of a lighthouse, the angle of depression of a ship at sea is 4.2°. How many miles is the ship from a point at sea level directly below the observation deck? ■

EXAMPLE 6   **Measuring the Height of Mount Kilimanjaro**

A surveyor wants to measure the height of Mount Kilimanjaro by using the known height of a nearby mountain. The nearby location is at an altitude of 8720 feet, the distance between that location and Mount Kilimanjaro's peak is 4.9941 miles, and the angle of elevation from the lower location is 23.75°. See Figure 2.15. Use that information to find the approximate height of Mount Kilimanjaro, to the nearest foot.

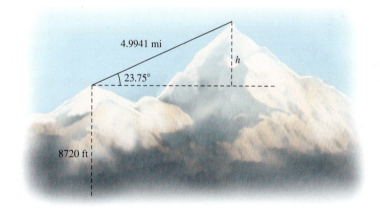

4.9941 mi

23.75°

h

8720 ft

FIGURE 2.15

SOLUTION

The sum of the side length h and the location height of 8720 feet gives the approximate height of Mount Kilimanjaro. Let h be measured in miles. Use the definition of $\sin \theta$, for $\theta = 23.75°$.

$$\sin \theta = \frac{opposite}{hypotenuse} = \frac{h}{4.9941}$$

$$h = (4.9941) \sin \theta \qquad \text{Multiply both sides by 4.9941.}$$

$$= (4.9941) \sin 23.75° \qquad \text{Replace } \theta \text{ with 23.75°.}$$

$$h \approx 2.0114 \qquad \text{Use a calculator.}$$

Because 1 mile = 5280 feet,

$$2.0114 \text{ miles} = (2.0114)(5280) \approx 10,620 \text{ feet.}$$

Thus, the height of Mount Kilimanjaro

$$\approx 10,620 + 8720 = 19,340 \text{ feet.}$$ ■ ■ ■

Practice Problem 6 The height of the nearby location to Mount McKinley, Alaska, is 12,870 feet; its distance to Mount McKinley's peak is 3.3387 miles; and the angle of elevation θ is 25°. What is the approximate height of Mount McKinley, to the nearest foot?   ■

SECTION 2.2 ■ Exercises

A EXERCISES Basic Skills and Concepts

1. The longest golf drive in competition was made by Mike Austin in 1974, and it was 515 yards. The range of values that would be reported as 515 yards is between _____ yards and _____ yards. (*Source:* www.wikipedia.org)

2. When solving a right triangle with side lengths given to three significant digits, the angles found should be given to the _____ of a degree.

3. If one acute angle in a right triangle is 26.4°, the other acute angle measures _____ degrees.

4. If the hypotenuse of a right triangle measures 10 feet and one side measures 8 feet, then the remaining side measures _____ feet.

5. *True or False* The NFL reports that Minnesota scored a record 556 points during the 1998 season. This means that the actual number of points scored could be any number between 555 and 557.

6. *True or False* There are three significant digits in 0.0101.

In Exercises 7–12, solve each right triangle.

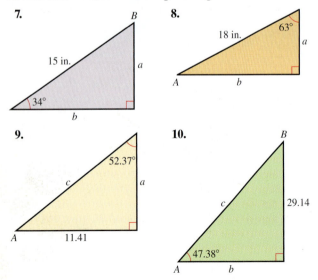

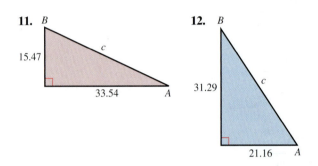

In Exercises 13–28, solve each right triangle ABC with $C = 90°$. Your answers should give angles in decimal degrees in Exercises 13–22 and in degrees and minutes in Exercises 27 and 28.

13. $A = 23.7°, c = 2.33$ cm

14. $A = 73.3°, c = 7.24$ cm

15. $B = 32.6°, c = 64.21$ ft

16. $B = 37.6°, c = 14.42$ ft

17. $A = 62.92°, b = 14.7$ ft

18. $A = 41.12°, b = 27.4$ ft

19. $B = 28.47°, a = 5.243$ m

20. $B = 71.43°, a = 22.14$ m

21. $A = 71.37°, a = 42.66$ cm

22. $B = 61.42°, b = 27.41$ cm

23. $a = 15.6$ cm, $b = 12.4$ cm

24. $a = 210$ cm, $b = 514$ cm

25. $a = 5.71$ m, $b = 18.39$ m

26. $b = 60.4$ m, $c = 192.8$ m

27. $A = 34°7', c = 5.278$ ft

28. $A = 75°26', c = 12.38$ ft

In Exercises 29–36, all references are to the figure, the distance between A and D is a, and the distance between D and C is x.

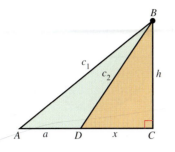

29. Assuming that $A = 37°$, $\angle BDC = 49°$, and $a = 17$, find h and x.

30. Assuming that $A = 21°$, $\angle BDC = 53°$, and $a = 8$, find h and x.

31. Assuming that $A = 27°$, $\angle BDC = 54°$, and $c_1 = 33$, find h, x, and a.

32. Assuming that $A = 14°$, $\angle BDC = 31°$, and $c_1 = 50$. find h, x, and a.

33. Assuming that $A = 39°$, $\angle BDC = 55°$, and $c_2 = 22$, find h, x, and a.

34. Assuming that $A = 28°$, $\angle BDC = 36°$, and $c_2 = 19$, find h, x, and a.

35. Assuming that $A = 13°$, $\angle DBC = 25°$, and $a = 11$, find h and x.

36. Assuming that $A = 24°$, $\angle DBC = 31°$, and $a = 40$. find h and x.

In Exercises 37–42, all references are to the figure, the distance between A and P is x, and the distance between A and C is y.

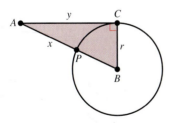

37. Assuming that $A = 35°$ and $r = 12$, find x and B.

38. Assuming that $B = 29°$ and $r = 18$, find x and A.

39. Assuming that $A = 41°$ and $x = 24$, find r and B.

40. Assuming that $B = 52°$ and $x = 19$, find r and A.

41. Assuming that $y = 62$ and $r = 11$, find A and x.

42. Assuming that $y = 39$ and $r = 20$. find A and x.

B EXERCISES Applying the Concepts

43. **Height of a cliff.** The angle of elevation from a rowboat moored 75 feet from a cliff is 73.8°. Find the height of the cliff to the nearest foot.

44. **Bracing a flagpole.** A flagpole is supported by a 30-foot tension wire attached to the flagpole and to a stake in the ground. If the angle of elevation from the stake to the point on the flagpole where the wire is attached is 40°, how high up the flagpole is the wire attached? Round your answer to the nearest foot.

45. **Measuring a tree.** Find the height of a pine tree that casts a 93-foot shadow on the ground assuming that the angle of elevation from the point on the ground at the tip of the shadow to the sun is 24°35′. Round your answer to the nearest foot.

46. **Flying a kite.** A girl is flying a kite. How long of a string must she have to raise the kite 200 feet above the ground if the angle of elevation from her eyes to the kite is 28°4′ and her eyes are 5 feet above the ground? Round your answer to the nearest foot.

47. **Measuring a tree.** Suppose a 45-foot tree casts a shadow 58 feet long. What is the angle of elevation with respect to the ground from the tip of the shadow to the top of the tree? Give your answer in decimal degrees, rounded to the nearest tenth of a degree.

48. **Sighting a forest fire.** A forest ranger in a fire tower 30 feet above the ground sees a small fire. The angle of depression from the ranger to the fire is 21°. How far is the fire from the base of the tower? Round your answer to the nearest foot.

49. **Mooring a boat.** A boat is attached by a taut line to a dock that is 3.5 feet above the water level. The angle of depression from the dock to the boat is 8°. How far is the boat from the base of the dock? Round your answer to the nearest foot.

50. **A bird spots a bug.** A bird is sitting on top of a utility pole. The angle of depression from the bird to a bug on the ground is 52°. The distance from the bird to the bug is 27 feet. How tall is the pole? Round your answer to the nearest foot.

51. **Spotting an alligator.** From an observation tower 35 feet above a swamp, a tourist sees an alligator at an angle of depression of 20.5°. How far is the alligator from the base of the tower? Round your answer to the nearest foot.

52. Airport location. A plane is 2.5 miles above the ground. The distance from the spot on the ground directly below the plane to the airport is 6.2 miles. What is the angle of depression from the airplane to the airport? Give your answer in decimal degrees, rounded to the nearest tenth of a degree.

C EXERCISES   Beyond the Basics

53. In the figure, show that $h = \dfrac{d}{\cot\alpha - \cot\beta}$.

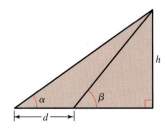

54. In the figure, show that $h = \dfrac{d}{\cot\alpha + \cot\beta}$.

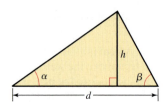

55. Find the area of this triangle.

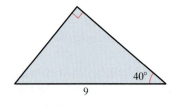

[*Hint:* Use Exercise 54.]

56. Find the area of triangle *ABC*.

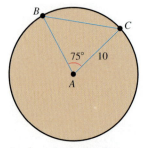

57. Find the exact value of *x* in the figure.

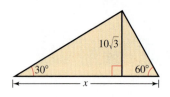

58. Write an expression for the value of *d*, the distance from *P* to the tangent line, in terms of θ and *r*. See the figure.

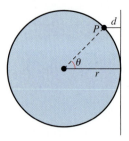

59. Show that the length of a side of a regular heptagon inscribed in a circle of radius *r* is $2r\sin\left(\dfrac{360°}{14}\right)$. See the figure.

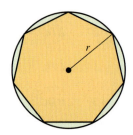

60. Write the area of the triangle inscribed in a semicircle of radius *r* as a function of θ. See the figure.

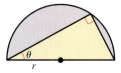

61. In the adjoining figure find
   a. $\cos\alpha$ **b.** $\tan\beta$

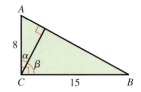

Critical Thinking

62. Explain how you can solve a right triangle when any two sides are given.

63. Explain why it is not possible to solve a right triangle when just the measures of the two acute angles are given.

Additional Applications of Right Triangles

Before Starting this Section, Review

1. Angles (Section 1.1)
2. Trigonometric functions of an acute angle (Section 2.1)

Objectives

1. Solve problems involving bearings.
2. Solve problems involving two related triangles.
3. Solve problems involving circular objects.

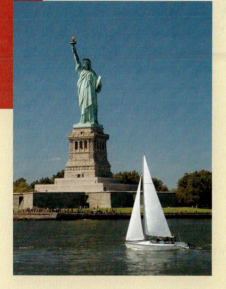

STATUE OF LIBERTY

The idea for France to give a monument to America as a memorial to Liberty came from French intellectuals who were opposed to the oppressive regime of Napoleon III. The sculptor who designed the Statue of Liberty, Frédéric Auguste Bartholdi, was fascinated by New York Harbor from the time he sailed in to it in 1871, saying it was "where people get their first view of the New World." Bartholdi patterned the Statue of Liberty after the Roman goddess Libertas, who personified freedom. The idea of this tribute to Liberty inspired contributions from many notables. For example, Alexandre Gustave Eiffel, the designer of the Eiffel Tower, designed the skeleton for the statue. Joseph Pulitzer, on hearing that the Statue of Liberty project was about to fail because of lack of funds, used his financial newspaper, *World*, to raise over $100,000 for the statue's completion. In Exercise 28, you find the height of the Statue of Liberty. ■

1. Solve problems involving bearings.

Bearings

In navigation and surveying, directions are usually given by using bearings. A **bearing** is the measure of an acute angle from due north or due south. The bearing N $\theta°$ E means $\theta°$ to the east of due north, whereas S $\theta°$ W means $\theta°$ to the west of due south. See Figure 2.16.

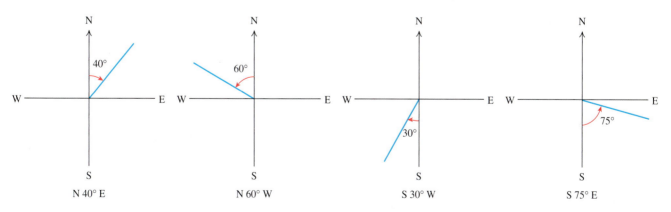

FIGURE 2.16

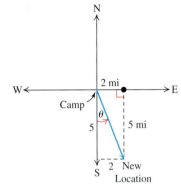

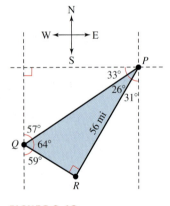

FIGURE 2.17

FIGURE 2.18

EXAMPLE 1   **Finding Bearings from a Campsite**

A camper leaves camp and hikes 2 miles due east and then turns and hikes 5 miles due south. From the camp, what is the bearing of her new location?

SOLUTION

Because we want the bearing of the new location *from* the camp, we draw a diagram with the origin of our N-S-E-W coordinate system at the camp. See Figure 2.17.

Because bearings are specified using *acute* angles from the north or south direction, we want to find the acute angle θ in Figure 2.17. We have $\tan \theta = \dfrac{\text{opposite}}{\text{adjacent}} = \dfrac{2}{5}$;

so $\theta = \tan^{-1}\left(\dfrac{2}{5}\right) \approx 22°$, to the nearest degree. The bearing of the new location from

camp is S 22° E.   ■ ■ ■

Practice Problem 1   The hospital where Latasha works is 7 miles due west and 4 miles due north from her home. What is the bearing of the hospital from Latasha's home?   ■

EXAMPLE 2   **Using Bearings to Compute a Distance**

The bearing from a disabled ship to a rescue vessel is S 59° E, and the bearing to the nearest port is N 57° E. The bearing from the port to the rescue vessel is S 31° W. Assuming that the rescue vessel is 56 miles from the port, find the distance between the rescue vessel and the disabled ship.

SOLUTION

First, draw a diagram. In Figure 2.18, the disabled ship (Q), the port (P), and the rescue vessel (R) form a triangle. The acute angle at P, in the right triangle with hypotenuse PQ formed by the east–west line through P, is $90° - 57° = 33°$. So $\angle QPR = 90° - 33° - 31° = 26°$. In Figure 2.18, $\angle PQR = 180° - 57° - 59° = 64°$. Because 26° and 64° are complementary angles, $\angle QRP = 90°$ and Q, P, and R determine a right triangle. Then

$$\tan 26° = \frac{\text{opposite}}{\text{adjacent}} = \frac{QR}{56}; \text{so}$$

$$QR = 56 \tan 26° \approx 27 \text{ miles, rounded to the nearest mile.}$$ ■ ■ ■

Practice Problem 2   In Example 2, how far is the disabled ship from the port?   ■

---

2   Solve problems involving two related triangles.

Related Triangles

EXAMPLE 3   **Using Right Triangles to Estimate a Location**

A ranger finds that the angle of elevation from his current location to the top of a tower is 28.3°. After walking another 50 feet toward the tower, he finds that the angle of elevation to the top of the tower is 31.2°. How far is the ranger from the tower, to the nearest foot?

SOLUTION

Draw a diagram to illustrate this situation. See Figure 2.19. From the right triangle BCD, we have

$$\tan 31.2° = \frac{h}{x} \qquad\qquad \tan 31.2° = \frac{\text{opposite}}{\text{adjacent}}$$

$$h = x \tan 31.2° \qquad \text{Multiply both sides by } x.$$

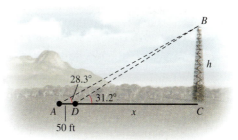

FIGURE 2.19

From right triangle ABC, we have

$$\tan 28.3° = \frac{h}{x + 50} \qquad \tan 28.3° = \frac{\text{opposite}}{\text{adjacent}}$$

$$h = (x + 50)\tan 28.3° \quad \text{Multiply both sides by } x + 50.$$

Because $h = x \tan 31.2°$ and $h = (x + 50)\tan 28.3°$,

$x \tan 31.2° = (x + 50)\tan 28.3°$	Both expressions equal h.
$x \tan 31.2° = x \tan 28.3° + 50 \tan 28.3°$	Distributive property
$x \tan 31.2° - x \tan 28.3° = 50 \tan 28.3°$	Subtract $x \tan 28.3°$ from both sides.
$x(\tan 31.2° - \tan 28.3°) = 50 \tan 28.3°$	Factor out x.
$x = \dfrac{50 \tan 28.3°}{\tan 31.2° - \tan 28.3°}$	Divide both sides by $\tan 31.2° - \tan 28.3°$.
≈ 401 feet	Round to the nearest foot. ■ ■ ■

Practice Problem 3 Find the height of the tower in Example 3, to the nearest foot. ■

EXAMPLE 4   **Using Triangles to Estimate the Height of a Monument**

Britany is not allowed to approach the stones when she visits Stonehenge. To measure the height to the top of a stone supported by two others, she stands at point A (see Figure 2.20) and finds that the angle of elevation to the top of the stone is 21.2°. She then turns 90° and walks 20.0 feet to the point B. If the angle between the line from point B to the base of the support stone and her path from A to B is 63.4°, how high is the top of the supported stone?

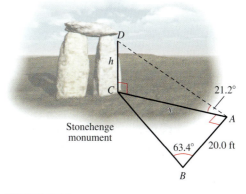

FIGURE 2.20

SOLUTION

First, we find the distance x in right triangle BAC.

$$\tan 63.4° = \frac{x}{20} \qquad \color{teal}{\tan 63.4° = \frac{\text{opposite}}{\text{adjacent}}}$$

$$x = 20 \tan 63.4° \qquad \color{teal}{\text{Multiply both sides by 20.}}$$

We want to find the height h in right triangle ACD.

$$\tan 21.2° = \frac{h}{x} \qquad \color{teal}{\tan 21.2° = \frac{\text{opposite}}{\text{adjacent}}}$$

$$h = x \tan 21.2° \qquad \color{teal}{\text{Multiply both sides by } x.}$$

$$= 20 \tan 63.4° \tan 21.2° \qquad \color{teal}{\text{Replace } x \text{ with } 20 \tan 63.4°.}$$

$$\approx 15.5 \text{ feet} \qquad \color{teal}{\text{Round to three significant digits; use a calculator.}}$$

The top of the supported stone is about 15.5 feet high. ■ ■ ■

Practice Problem 4 In Example 4, find the distance from point A to the point D without using the Pythagorean theorem. Round your answer to the nearest foot. ■

3 Solve problems involving circular objects.

Circular Objects

EXAMPLE 5   **Using Triangles to Estimate the Distance from the Moon to the Earth**

An observer at C in Figure 2.21 sees the moon on the horizon at the same time a second observer at P also sees the moon. By comparing their measurements of the moon relative to the stars, they determine that $\angle CMP$ is $0.95°$. If the radius of the earth is 3960 miles, how far is the moon from the surface of the earth, to the nearest mile?

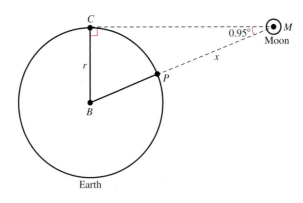

FIGURE 2.21

SOLUTION

In Figure 2.21, x is the distance we want to find. Because $r = 3960$ miles is also the distance between P and B, the distance between M and B is $3960 + x$. Because MCB is a right triangle,

$$\sin 0.95° = \frac{3960}{3960 + x} \qquad \color{teal}{\sin 0.95° = \frac{\text{opposite}}{\text{hypotenuse}}}$$

$$(3960 + x) \sin 0.95° = 3960 \qquad \color{teal}{\text{Multiply both sides by } 3960 + x.}$$

$$3960 \sin 0.95° + x \sin 0.95° = 3960 \qquad \color{teal}{\text{Distributive property}}$$

$$x \sin 0.95° = 3960 - 3960 \sin 0.95°$$ Subtract $3960 \sin 0.95°$ from both sides.

$$x = \frac{3960 - 3960 \sin 0.95°}{\sin 0.95°}$$ Divide both sides by $\sin 0.95°$.

$$\approx 234{,}884 \text{ miles}$$ Rounded to the nearest mile; use a calculator.

Practice Problem 5   In Figure 2.22 (not to scale), the plane at point A is 4.7 miles above the earth's surface. Assuming that $\angle CAB = 87.1°$, estimate the radius of the earth, to the nearest mile.

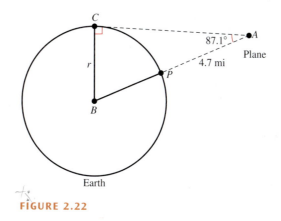

FIGURE 2.22

SECTION 2.3 ■ Exercises

A EXERCISES Basic Skills and Concepts

1. A bearing is the measure of a(n) _____ angle from due north or due south.

2. The bearing that indicates the direction 35° northwest of a given location is written _____.

3. If you walk at a steady rate for 15 minutes at a bearing of N 45° E and turn and walk 15 more minutes (at the same rate) at a bearing of N 45° W, your final position will be due _____ of your starting position.

4. Janet rides her bike at a steady rate for ten minutes at a bearing of S 30° E, then turns and rides her bike due north for ten more minutes (at the same rate). To return to her starting point from the second location, she should ride at a bearing of _____.

5. *True or False* If you travel at a bearing of N 23° E for a fixed distance, you can use right triangles to determine how far to the north and how far to the east you are from your original position.

6. *True or False* If you face due north and turn clockwise 120° and walk 2 miles, because 120° is not an acute angle, you cannot identify your new location by giving a bearing from your original location.

For Exercises 7–10, refer to the figure.

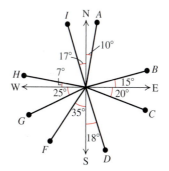

7. Write the bearings of the points A and B.

8. Write the bearings of the points C and D.

9. Write the bearings of the points F and G.

10. Write the bearings of the points H and I.

In Exercises 11–16, a lighthouse on an island is located at the origin of a coordinate system. East points to the positive x-axis, and north points to the positive y-axis. Find the bearing of a ship located at the given point.

11. $(5, 5)$ 12. $(-4, 4)$

13. $(0, -3)$ 14. $(-2, -4)$

15. $(2, -3)$ 16. $(-5, 1)$

B EXERCISES Applying the Concepts

17. Bearing of a ship. A ship sails 8 miles due west and then turns and sails 12 miles due south. What is the bearing of the ship's location at this time?

18. Bearing of a plane. A plane flies 120 miles due north and then turns and flies 200 miles due east. What is the bearing of the plane's location at this time?

19. Distance flown by a plane. A plane leaves an airport at a bearing of N 40.7° E and travels 180 miles. How far north of the airport is the plane? How far east?

20. Distance flown by a plane. A plane leaves an airport at a bearing of S 37.4° W and travels 165 miles. How far south of the airport is the plane? How far west?

21. Distance traveled by a ship. A ship sails at a bearing of N 49.7° E for two hours at 12 mph, then changes direction to a bearing of N 40.3° W. If the ship sails at this bearing for three more hours at 15 mph, how far is the ship from its starting point?

22. Distance traveled by a hiker. A hiker walks at a bearing of S 13.4° W for an hour and a half at 4 mph, then changes direction to a bearing of N 76.6° W. If the hiker walks at this bearing for two more hours at 5 mph, how far is he from his starting point?

23. Distance to a boat. A worker on an oil rig spots a boat due north of the rig at the same time a worker in another rig sees the same boat at a bearing of N 20.6° W. If the second rig is 3 miles due east of the first rig, how far is the boat from the first rig?

24. Distance to a radar station. Two radar stations are located on a north–south line 14 miles apart. They simultaneously pick up a plane due west of the southmost station at a bearing of S 61.7° W of the northmost station. How far is the plane from the northmost station?

25. Bearing of a ship. Two ships leave port at the same time, one sailing at a bearing of S 22.7° W at 14 mph and the other sailing at a bearing of N 67.3° W at 20 mph. What is the bearing from the second ship to the first ship after an hour?

26. Bearing of a plane. Two planes leave an airport at the same time, one flying at a bearing of N 53.2° E and the other flying at a bearing of S 36.8° E. If the first plane's average speed is 300 mph and the second plane's average speed is 450 mph, what is the bearing from the second plane to the first plane after two hours?

27. Tracking a bear. Angelina is watching a bear directly approach her observation deck. When she first notices the bear, the angle of depression to the bear is 6.5°. When she checks again, the angle of depression to the bear is 9.9°. If the observation deck is 35 feet high, how far did the bear walk between these measurements?

28. Height of the Statue of Liberty. While sailing toward the Statue of Liberty, a sailor in a boat observed that at a certain point, the angle of elevation of the tip of the torch was 25°. After sailing another 100 meters toward the statue, the angle of elevation became 41°50′. How tall is the Statue of Liberty?

29. Height of a statue. From a hot air balloon 30 feet above the ground, the angle of depression to the top of a statue of Paul Bunyan is 11.3° and the angle of depression to the bottom of the statue is 26.6°. How tall is the statue?

30. Height of a performer. A singer is standing against an 8.5-foot backdrop. From a point at stage level, the angle of elevation to the top of the backdrop is 13.6°, while the angle to the top of the singer's head is 8.7°. How tall is the singer?

31. Height of a building. A 12.5-meter statue sits on a corner on top of a building. The angle of elevation from a point on the ground to the bottom of the statue is 33.6° and to the top of the statue is 37.5°. Find the height of the building.

32. Height of a tree. A tourist wants to know the height of a tree growing on top of a cliff that is 40 meters high. From her boat, she finds that the angle of elevation to the bottom of the tree is 57.9° and to the top of the tree is 62.1°. Find the height of the tree.

33. Height of a painting. Raphael stands 12 feet from a large painting on a wall. He sets his camera 5 feet 6 inches above the floor. Assuming that the bottom edge of the painting is 4 feet above the floor and the angle of elevation from the camera to the top of the painting is 50°, find the height of the painting.

34. **Height of a building.** Assume that from the top of the Empire State Building (which is about 1250 feet high), the angle of depression to the top of a second building is 55.8° and the angle of depression to the bottom of the second building is 67.7°. Find the height of the second building.

35. **Distance between Earth and the moon.** If the radius of the earth is $r = 3960$ miles and the angle at the earth's center is $A = 89°3'$, find the distance between the moon and the surface of the earth.

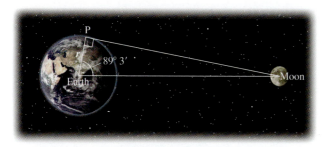

36. **Height of a satellite.** A communication satellite is orbiting far above Earth, as shown in the figure. If the radius of Earth is $r = 3960$ miles and the angle at S is 10.1°, how far is the satellite from the surface of the earth?

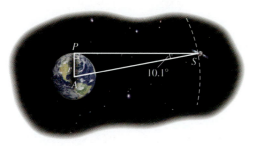

37. **Height of a silo.** Desi wants to estimate the height of a silo. She finds the angle of elevation from point A in the figure to the top of the silo to be 21.8°. She then turns 90° and walks 25 feet to point B. She next finds the angle between

a line through B and the base of the silo and the path from A to B is 72.6°. Find the height of the silo.

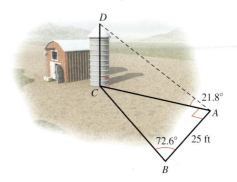

38. **Height of a tower.** Juan and Kathy want to estimate the height of an observation tower in a forest. The angle of elevation from the point on the ground where Juan is standing to the top of the tower is 50.1°. Kathy walks 50 feet from Juan at a right angle to the line from Juan to the base of the tower. She finds that the angle between the path from her new position to the base of the tower and the path she traveled from Juan is 60.2°. Find the height of the tower.

39. **Diameter of an emblem.** A circular emblem is suspended from the center of its sides by two wires, each 5 feet long. (See the figure.) If the angle between the wires is 23.5°, what is the emblem's diameter?

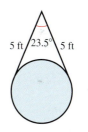

40. **Spotlight diameter.** A light 12 feet above a stage floor produces a cone of light. If the angle shown in the figure is 28°, what is the diameter of the circle of light on the floor?

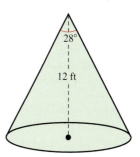

41. **Area of a field.** The diagonal of a rectangular field is 210.3 meters, while the shorter side is 87.72 meters. Find the area of the field.

42. **Traffic sign design.** A "yield" traffic sign is in the shape of an equilateral triangle. Assuming that the sign is 1.2 feet high, find the length of each side.

43. Traffic sign design. A "warning" traffic sign in the shape of a diamond (rhombus) is 1.6 meters wide. (See the figure.) If $\angle A = 48°$, find the length of each side.

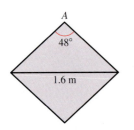

44. Area of land. Find the area of a section of land in the shape of a parallelogram assuming that two adjacent sides are 16 and 20 meters long and the included angle is 49.3°.

45. Height of a plane. From a tower 150 feet high with the sun directly overhead, an airplane and its shadow have an angle of elevation of 67.4° and an angle of depression of 8.1°, respectively. Find the height of the airplane.

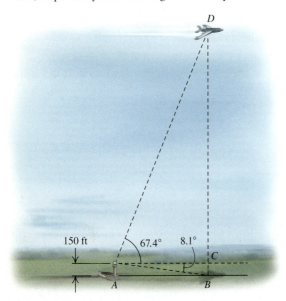

46. Height of a building. The WCNC-TV Tower in Dallas, North Carolina, is 600 meters high. Suppose a building is erected such that the base of the building is on the same plane as the base of the tower, the angle of elevation from the top of the building to the top of the tower is 75.24°, and the angle of depression from the top of the building to the foot of the tower is 60.05°. How high would the building have to be? (*Source:* http://en.wikipedia.org)

47. Height of a plane. A plane flies directly over two tracking stations that are 500 meters apart on a level plane. The plane flies in the direction from Station A to Station B. After the plane has passed Station B, an observer at Station B records the angle of elevation as 38.9°. At the same time, an observer at station A records the angle of elevation as 36.9°. What is the plane's altitude?

48. Speed of a plane. A plane flying at an altitude of 12,000 feet finds the angle of depression to the base of a building ahead of the plane to be 10.4°. With the building still straight ahead, two minutes later the angle of depression is 25.6°. Find the speed of the plane relative to the ground (in feet per minute).

C EXERCISES Beyond the Basics

49. Find the area of the triangle in the figure.

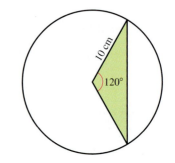

50. Find a formula for the area of the triangle in the figure that uses only the side lengths, a and b, and a trigonometric function value of θ.

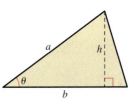

51. Find the sum $2\alpha + 2\beta$ for the angles α and β in the figure. Use the result to show that $\angle ACB$ is a right angle.

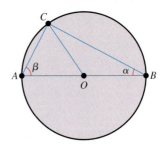

52. Find the value of x in the figure.

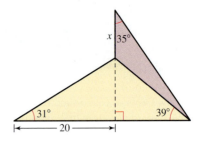

53. The figure is a regular pentagon, so all of the sides are equal and all of the angles are equal.

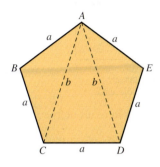

a. The dashed lines divide the pentagon into three triangles. Find the measure of ∠ABC (and each pentagon angle) by summing the angles in the three triangles and dividing by 5.

b. Find ∠BAC and ∠CAD.

c. Explain why $\cos 36° = \dfrac{1}{2}\dfrac{b}{a}$.

d. Explain why $\sin 18° = \dfrac{1}{2}\dfrac{a}{b}$.

54. Use the figure to find the exact value of $\cos 22.5°$, given that $AB = BD$.

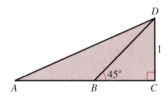

a. Show that $BC = 1$ and $BD = \sqrt{2}$.

b. Show that $AD = \sqrt{4 + 2\sqrt{2}}$.

c. Show that ∠BAD = 22.5°.

d. Show that $\cos 22.5° = \dfrac{1 + \sqrt{2}}{\sqrt{4 + 2\sqrt{2}}}$.

55. Modify the figure in Exercise 54 so that ∠CBD = 30°.

a. Show that $BD = 2$ and $BC = \sqrt{3}$.

b. Show that $AD = 2\sqrt{2 + \sqrt{3}}$ and $2\sqrt{2 + \sqrt{3}} = \sqrt{6} + \sqrt{2}$.

c. Show that ∠BAD = 15°.

d. Show that $\cos 15° = \dfrac{2 + \sqrt{3}}{\sqrt{6} + \sqrt{2}}$.

Critical Thinking

56. A second method for expressing bearings uses just one angle. For example, a bearing given as 120° means that this bearing is found by rotating a ray (initial side) pointing due north 120° clockwise. Convert each bearing from this notation to the notation introduced in this section.

a. 35°   **b.** 150°

c. 240°   **d.** 310°

REVIEW

Definitions, Concepts, and Formulas	**Examples and Illustrations**

2.1 Trigonometric Functions of an Acute Angle

TRIGONOMETRIC FUNCTIONS OF AN ACUTE ANGLE IN A RIGHT TRIANGLE If A is any acute angle in a right triangle, $\sin A = \dfrac{y}{r} = \dfrac{\text{opposite}}{\text{hypotenuse}} \qquad \csc A = \dfrac{r}{y} = \dfrac{\text{hypotenuse}}{\text{opposite}}$ $\cos A = \dfrac{x}{r} = \dfrac{\text{adjacent}}{\text{hypotenuse}} \qquad \sec A = \dfrac{r}{x} = \dfrac{\text{hypotenuse}}{\text{adjacent}}$ $\tan A = \dfrac{y}{x} = \dfrac{\text{opposite}}{\text{adjacent}} \qquad \cot A = \dfrac{x}{y} = \dfrac{\text{adjacent}}{\text{opposite}}$	**A triangle angle in standard position** 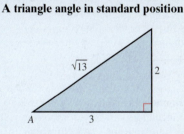 To find the sine, cosine, and tangent of angle A, we use the definitions. $\sin A = \dfrac{\text{opposite}}{\text{hypotenuse}} = \dfrac{2}{\sqrt{13}}$ $\cos A = \dfrac{\text{adjacent}}{\text{hypotenuse}} = \dfrac{3}{\sqrt{13}}$ $\tan A = \dfrac{\text{opposite}}{\text{adjacent}} = \dfrac{2}{3}$

■ **Cofunctions** For acute angles A and B in any right triangle, $\sin A = \cos B$ and $\cos A = \sin B$ because

$$\sin A = \frac{\text{opposite } A}{\text{hypotenuse}} = \frac{a}{c} = \frac{\text{adjacent to } B}{\text{hypotenuse}} = \cos B.$$

Similarly, $\tan A = \cot B$, $\csc A = \sec B$, and $\sec A = \csc B$. Because $A + B = 90°$, angles A and B are complementary. The sine and cosine functions are called **cofunctions**. The tangent and cotangent are also cofunctions, as are secant and cosecant. Because $A + B = 90°$, $B = 90° - A$, and $\sin A = \cos B = \cos(90° - A)$. Similar results, known as the *cofunction identities*, relate the values of the cofunctions of complementary angles.

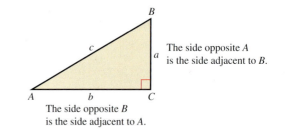

The side opposite A is the side adjacent to B.

The side opposite B is the side adjacent to A.

> **COFUNCTION IDENTITIES**
>
> For an acute angle A,
>
> $\sin A = \cos(90° - A)$ $\cos A = \sin(90° - A)$
>
> $\tan A = \cot(90° - A)$ $\csc A = \sec(90° - A)$
>
> $\sec A = \csc(90° - A)$ $\cot A = \tan(90° - A)$

We can express $\sin 18°$ in terms of its cofunction by

$$\sin 18° = \cos(90° - 18°) = \cos 72°.$$

We can express $\tan 62°$ in terms of its cofunction by

$$\tan 62° = \cot(90° - 62°) = \cot 28°.$$

We can express $\csc 80°$ in terms of its cofunction by

$$\csc 80° = \sec(90° - 80°) = \sec 10°.$$

■ **Finding trigonometric function values for angles in a right triangle** If the lengths of two sides of a right triangle are known, the Pythagorean theorem can be used to find the remaining length. Then the angles in the triangle can be found.

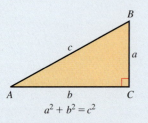

$a^2 + b^2 = c^2$

> **PYTHAGOREAN THEOREM**
>
> In any right triangle, the square of the length of the hypotenuse equals the sum of the squares of the lengths of the other two sides.

If triangle ABC is a right triangle with sides of lengths $a = 8$ and $c = 17$, we can find the six trigonometric function values of A.

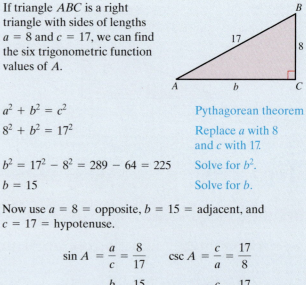

$a^2 + b^2 = c^2$	Pythagorean theorem
$8^2 + b^2 = 17^2$	Replace a with 8 and c with 17.
$b^2 = 17^2 - 8^2 = 289 - 64 = 225$	Solve for b^2.
$b = 15$	Solve for b.

Now use $a = 8 =$ opposite, $b = 15 =$ adjacent, and $c = 17 =$ hypotenuse.

$$\sin A = \frac{a}{c} = \frac{8}{17} \qquad \csc A = \frac{c}{a} = \frac{17}{8}$$

$$\cos A = \frac{b}{c} = \frac{15}{17} \qquad \sec A = \frac{c}{b} = \frac{17}{15}$$

$$\tan A = \frac{a}{b} = \frac{8}{15} \qquad \cot A = \frac{b}{a} = \frac{15}{8}$$

■ **Finding trigonometric function values using a calculator.** Calculators with keys for the sine, $\boxed{\text{SIN}}$; cosine, $\boxed{\text{COS}}$; and tangent, $\boxed{\text{TAN}}$ functions can be used to find the trigonometric values for all six trigonometric functions.

To evaluate values for the cosecant, secant, and cotangent functions, you use the $\boxed{\text{SIN}}$, $\boxed{\text{COS}}$, and $\boxed{\text{TAN}}$ keys with an appropriate reciprocal identity. To find a trigonometric function value of an angle measured in degrees, you must set the calculator to *Degree mode*.

To find an approximate value of $\sin 58.24°$, rounded to four decimal places, first set your calculator to Degree mode. Then

$$\sin 58.24° \approx 0.8502603704 \approx 0.8503.$$

To find an approximate value of $\csc 72.694°$, use the reciprocal identity $\csc \theta = \dfrac{1}{\sin \theta}$. First, find $\sin 72.694°$; then use the reciprocal key, $\boxed{x^{-1}}$, to get

$$\csc 72.694° \approx 1.047416928 \approx 1.0474.$$

■ **Finding angles using a calculator.** Sometimes we want to find the measure of an angle that has a certain trigonometric function value. Many calculators have keys marked $\boxed{\text{SIN}^{-1}}$, $\boxed{\text{COS}^{-1}}$, and $\boxed{\text{TAN}^{-1}}$ that can be used for this purpose. These keys are for *inverse functions*, which we will study in a later chapter. We can use them to find the measure of an angle in quadrant I having a specific trigonometric function value when that value is positive.

To find an angle θ between $0°$ and $90°$ having $\cos \theta \approx 0.8783169514$, enter the value 0.8783169514 and use the $\boxed{\text{COS}^{-1}}$ key. $\cos^{-1}(0.8783169514) \approx 28.6°$ to the nearest tenth of a degree.

To find an angle θ between $0°$ and $90°$ having $\sec \theta \approx 1.500302003$, use the fact that $\sec \theta = \dfrac{1}{\cos \theta}$. Enter the value 1.500302003 and use the $\boxed{x^{-1}}$ key to find $\cos \theta \approx 0.6665324701$. Then use the $\boxed{\text{COS}^{-1}}$ key to find θ; $\cos^{-1}(0.6665324701) \approx 48.2°$, to the nearest tenth of a degree.

2.2 Solving Right Triangles

■ **Significant digits** The *significant digits* in numbers that result from measurement (or in a number that results from calculations involving these numbers) are all of the digits known with certainty, together with a final digit about which there is some uncertainty.

Number	Rule(s)
824 has three significant digits.	1
60502 has five significant digits.	1 and 3
0.0037 has two significant digits.	1 and 2
800 has one significant digit.	4
800. has three significant digits.	4

> **RULES FOR IDENTIFYING SIGNIFICANT DIGITS**
>
> 1. The digits 1, 2, 3, 4, 5, 6, 7, 8, and 9 are always significant.
> 2. Leading zeros are not significant; the first nonzero digit on the left is the first significant digit in a number.
> 3. Zeros between two nonzero digits are always significant.
> 4. Trailing zeros are considered significant only when the number contains a decimal point.

■ **Calculations with significant digits** Calculations with numbers that are approximations should be rounded to contain the same number of significant digits as the number in the calculation that has the *fewest significant digits*. Your result can be no more accurate than the least accurate number used in your calculation. Numbers that are not approximations, such as numbers that are theoretically derived, or that result from counting are not considered when this rounding rule is applied.

For example, the digit 2 in the expression $2\pi r$ for the circumference of a circle is not an approximation. So although 2 has only one significant digit, this fact is ignored when the expression $2\pi r$ is used. If you are told to use 3.14 as an approximation for π and that the radius of a circle is 2.4 feet, then $2(3.14)(2.4) = 15.072$ is rounded to two significant digits (not one) and is reported as 15 feet.

■ **Solving right triangles** To solve a triangle means to find the lengths of all of the sides and the measures of all of the angles in the triangle. We use the familiar notation where a, b, and c denote the lengths of the sides opposite angles A, B, and C, respectively. In a right triangle, C always denotes the $90°$ angle. (So c denotes the length of the hypotenuse.) The table gives the relationship between the accuracy of measurement of sides and angles in triangles.

Significant Digits in Right Triangle Measures

Accuracy of Sides	Accuracy of Angles
Two significant digits	Nearest degree
Three significant digits	Nearest 10 minutes or tenth of a degree
Four significant digits	Nearest minute or hundredth of a degree

If an angle is accurate to the nearest degree and a side is given to *three* significant digits, then the remaining sides will be given to only *two* significant digits and the remaining angles to the nearest degree.

To solve the right triangle ABC, where $A = 28.1°$ and $c = 16.3$ cm, sketch a triangle and label it.

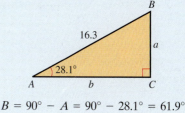

$$B = 90° - A = 90° - 28.1° = 61.9°$$

Next, find a.

$$\sin 28.1° = \frac{\text{opposite}}{\text{hypotenuse}} = \frac{a}{16.3}$$

$a = 16.3 \sin 28.1° \approx 7.68$ cm, to three significant digits.

When solving triangles, it is helpful to sketch and label a diagram. If rounding is required, round only the answers, not the numbers found in the intermediate steps. Finally, use the values given in the problem whenever possible, rather than values calculated in intermediate steps.

The following diagram shows some of the fundamental relationships between the angles and sides of a right triangle. The cofunction identities, such as $\sin A = \cos B$, yield several others.

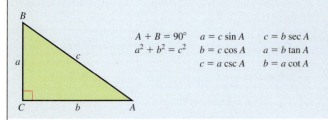

$$A + B = 90° \qquad a = c \sin A \qquad c = b \sec A$$
$$a^2 + b^2 = c^2 \qquad b = c \cos A \qquad a = b \tan A$$
$$\qquad\qquad c = a \csc A \qquad b = a \cot A$$

To find b, use the given information:

$$\cos 28.1° = \frac{b}{16.3}$$

$b = 16.3 \cos 28.1° \approx 14.4$ cm, to three significant digits.

We rounded a and b to three significant digits because both $A = 28.1°$ and $c = 16.3$ have three significant digits.

■ **Angles of elevation or depression** Angles that are measured between a line of sight and a horizontal line occur in many applications and are called *angles of elevation* or *angles of depression*. If the line of sight is *above* the horizontal line, the angle between these two lines is called the **angle of elevation**. If the line of sight is *below* the horizontal line, the angle between the two lines is called the **angle of depression**.

For example, suppose the headlights from a car parked on level pavement 4 feet from the wall of a garage hit a spot on the wall 6.5 feet above the floor. If the headlights are 3 feet above the floor, to find the angle of elevation of the head-lights to the nearest degree, we first sketch a diagram.

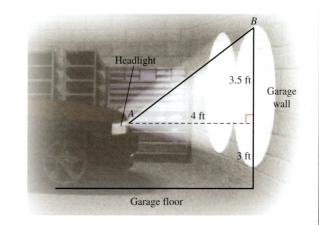

Because the headlights are 3 feet above the floor, the spot on the wall is $6.5 - 3 = 3.5$ feet above the center of the headlight. To find the angle of elevation, A, notice that

$$\tan A = \frac{3.5}{4}; \text{ so } A = \tan^{-1}\left(\frac{3.5}{4}\right) \approx 41°.$$

2.3 Additional Applications of Right Triangles

■ **Bearings** In navigation and surveying, directions are usually given by using *bearings*. A **bearing** is the measure of an acute angle from due north or due south. The bearing N $\theta°$ E means $\theta°$ to the east of due north, whereas S $\theta°$ W means $\theta°$ to the west of due south.

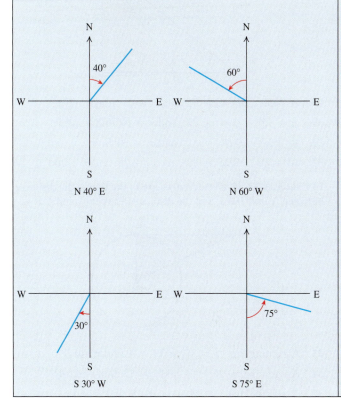

N 40° E

N 60° W

S 30° W

S 75° E

Suppose a boat leaves an island and travels 4 miles due east and then turns and sails 7 miles due south. To find the bearing of the boat's new location from the island, we draw a diagram with the origin of our N-S-E-W coordinate system at the camp.

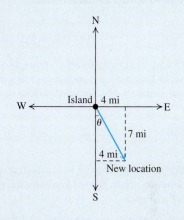

Because bearings are specified using *acute* angles from the north or south direction, we want to find the acute angle θ in the figure. We have $\tan \theta = \dfrac{\text{opposite}}{\text{adjacent}} = \dfrac{4}{7}$; so $\theta = \tan^{-1}\left(\dfrac{4}{7}\right) \approx 30°$, to the nearest degree. The bearing of the new location from camp is S 30° E.

REVIEW EXERCISES

In Exercises 1 and 2, find the exact values for the six trigonometric functions of the angle in each figure. Rationalize the denominator where necessary.

1.

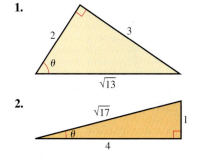

2.

In Exercises 3 and 4, express each function in terms of its cofunction.

3. $\cos 43°$

4. $\sec 32°$

In Exercises 5–8, find one value of θ that is a solution to the given equation.

5. $\sin 24° = \cos (\theta - 24°)$

6. $\tan \theta = \cot (\theta + 17°)$

7. $\sec (\theta + 4°) = \csc (\theta + 36°)$

8. $\cos 2\theta = \sin (\theta + 21°)$

In Exercises 9 and 10, triangle *ABC* is a right triangle with sides of lengths *a*, *b*, and *c* and a right angle at *C*. Find the six trigonometric function values of *A*. Rationalize denominators containing radicals.

9. $a = 4, b = 4\sqrt{3}$ **10.** $a = 5, c = 6$

In Exercises 11–14, find the approximate value of each expression, rounded to four decimal places.

11. $\sin 46.19°$ **12.** $\tan 68.42°$

13. $\sec 4.37°$ **14.** $\cos 78.22°$

In Exercises 15 and 16, rewrite the expression as a value of the sine, cosine, or tangent function before using a calculator to find the approximate value, rounded to four decimal places.

15. $\dfrac{1}{\csc 14.2°}$ **16.** $\cot(90° - 46.24°)$

In Exercises 17–20, find an angle θ between 0° and 90° having the specified function value. Round your answer to the nearest tenth of a degree.

17. $\sin \theta \approx 0.9659258263$ **18.** $\cos \theta \approx 0.0348994967$

19. $\tan \theta \approx 1.07236871$ **20.** $\sec \theta \approx 1.624269245$

In Exercises 21 and 22, solve each right triangle.

21.

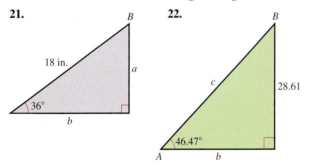

22.

18 in.   *a*   36°   *b*   *B*

28.61   *c*   46.47°   *A*   *b*   *B*

In Exercises 23–28, solve each right triangle *ABC* with $C = 90°$. Your answers should give angles in decimal degrees.

23. $A = 21.8°, c = 1.92$ cm

24. $A = 71.6°, c = 6.89$ cm

25. $A = 61.42°, b = 15.2$ ft

26. $A = 42.37°, b = 26.9$ ft

27. $a = 7.28$ m, $b = 20.42$ m

28. $a = 13.9$ m, $b = 14.2$ m

In Exercises 29–32, all references are to the figure, the distance between *A* and *D* is *y*, and the distance between *D* and *C* is *x*.

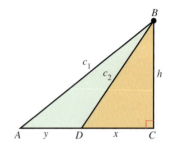

29. $A = 35°$, $\angle BDC = 51°$, and $y = 19$; find h and x.

30. $A = 15°$, $\angle DBC = 27°$, and $y = 14$; find h and x.

31. $A = 29°$, $\angle BDC = 51°$, and $c_1 = 30$; find h, x, and y.

32. $A = 32°$, $\angle BDC = 38°$, and $c_2 = 20$; find h, x, and y.

In Exercises 33–35, all references are to the figure, the distance between *A* and *P* is *x*, and the distance between *A* and *C* is *y*.

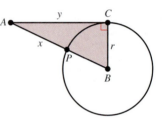

33. Assuming that $A = 31°$ and $r = 9$, find x and B.

34. Assuming that $B = 48°$ and $x = 18$, find r and A.

35. Assuming that $y = 51$ and $r = 15$, find A and x.

In Exercises 36–40, a ranger station on an island is located at the origin of a coordinate system. The positive *x*-axis points east, and the positive *y*-axis points north. Find the bearing of a campsite located at the given point.

36. $(5, 0)$ **37.** $(3, 3)$

38. $(0, -4)$ **39.** $(-1, -2)$

40. $(-5, 5)$

41. A support wire from one end of a circus tightrope makes a 30° angle with the ground. If the tightrope is 40 feet high, how long is the wire?

42. When a 2-foot pendulum makes a 45° angle with the vertical line through its pivot, how far is the tip of the pendulum from that line?

43. A spotlight will be set in the ground so that its beam makes a 40° angle with the ground. If the light is to hit a spot 7 feet above the ground on a vertical wall, how far from the wall should the light be placed?

44. A 24-foot ladder leaning against a building makes a 75° angle with the ground. How high up the building does the ladder reach?

45. A visiting engineer measures the angle of elevation to the top of the Marine Corps Memorial in Washington, D.C., as 34.1°. If the engineer took this measurement from a distance of 115 feet from the monument, how tall is the monument?

46. A "warning" traffic sign in the shape of a diamond (rhombus) is 1.8 meters wide. The top angle is 50°. Find the length of each side.

47. The diagonal of a rectangular field is 285.6 meters, while one side is 218.5 meters. Find the area of the field.

48. A plane leaves an airport at a bearing of N 37.4° W and travels 160 miles. How far north of the airport is the plane? How far west?

49. At a time when the sun's rays make a 35° angle with the horizontal, how long is the shadow cast by a man who is 6 foot 2 inches tall standing on the ground?

50. The angle of depression from the top of a tree to a point 85 feet from its base (on the ground) is found to be 12°. Find the height of the tree to the nearest foot.

51. The angle of depression to a rescue ship from a helicopter 850 feet directly above a crippled boat is 40°. How far is the rescue ship from the crippled boat?

52. Two ships leave port at the same time, one sailing at a bearing of N 21.3° E at 12 mph and the second sailing at a bearing of S 68.7° E at 18 mph. What is the bearing from the second ship to the first ship after an hour?

53. Renee sets her camera 5 feet 2 inches above the floor 6 feet away from a bust in a museum. Assuming that the bust sits on a 4-foot podium and the angle of elevation from the camera to the top of the bust is 30°, find the height of the bust.

54. A plane leaves an airport at a bearing of N 22° W. After flying 1 mile, the plane turns 90° toward the northeast. What bearing does the plane have from the airport after traveling 2.5 miles in the second direction?

55. Kaitlyn wants to estimate the height of an obelisk on the opposite side of a pond. The angle of elevation from the point on the ground where she is standing to the top of the obelisk is 4°. She then turns and walks 30 feet at a right angle to the line from her original position to the base of the obelisk. Assuming that the angle between the path she just walked and line between her new position and the base of the obelisk is 82.9°, find the height of the obelisk.

CHAPTER TEST

1. Find the sine, cosine, and tangent of angle A.

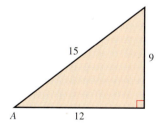

2. Assuming that $\sin 18° = \dfrac{1}{1 + \sqrt{5}}$, find $\cos 72°$.

3. Find one value of θ that is a solution of the equation $\cos 20° = \sin (2\theta - 20°)$.

4. Triangle ABC is a right triangle with sides of lengths a, b, and c and a right angle at C. Assuming that $a = 5$ and $b = 12$, find the sine, cosine, and tangent of angle A.

5. Find the approximate value of $\sec 76.531°$, rounded to four decimal places.

6. Find an angle θ between 0° and 90° with $\cos \theta \approx 0.9335804265$. Round your answer to the nearest tenth of a degree.

7. Solve the right triangle ABC with sides of lengths a, b, and c and a right angle at C assuming that $A = 28.7°$ and $c = 12.9$ in.

8. Solve the triangle ABC with sides of lengths a, b, and c and a right angle at C, where $a = 17.68$ cm and $b = 22.19$ cm.

9. Use the information in the figure to solve for x, the distance in feet between D and C.

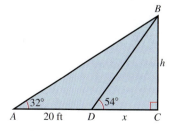

10. The distance between A and P in the figure is x, and the distance between A and C is y. Assuming that $A = 32°$ and $r = 10$, find x and B.

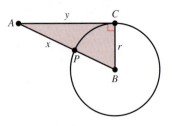

11. A boat is attached at water level by a taut line to a dock that is 4 feet above the water level. The angle of depression from the dock to the boat is 14°. How long is the rope? Round your answer to the nearest foot.

12. A horizontal wire between two houses is 100 feet long. The wire is replaced and lowered on one end so that it is now inclined at an angle of 10°. How long is the new wire?

13. A ship travels 140 miles at a bearing of N 30° W? How far north and how far east has the ship traveled?

14. Two ships leave port at the same time, one sailing N 15° E at 12 mph and the second sailing S 75° E at 16 mph. Find the bearing from the second ship to the first ship an hour later.

15. The angle of elevation to the top of a mural hanging on a wall from a camera placed 10 feet from the wall is 38°. The angle of depression from the camera to the bottom of the mural is 21°. Find the vertical height of the mural.

Radian Measure and Circular Functions

The trigonometric functions associated with angles turn up in a surprising number of applications. A wide range of problems involving objects moving in a circular path, ranging from seats on a Ferris wheel to heavenly bodies, are more conveniently handled when the trigonometric functions are functions of numbers rather than angles. Defining the trigonometric functions as functions of numbers is accomplished in this chapter through the introduction of a new way to measure angles.

Radian Measure

Before Starting this Section, Review

1. Angles (Section 1.1)
2. Definitions of the trigonometric functions (Section 1.3)
3. Signs of the trigonometric functions (Section 1.3)

Objectives

1. Define radian measure.
2. Convert between degree and radian measure.
3. Find trigonometric function values for angles.

THE IMPORTANCE OF UNITS

If you're told that your air conditioning will be out for "two," you instantly notice how important units are: two hours, two days, two weeks? It makes a difference. Two, without further qualification, is not very informative when referring to measurement.

In 1999, NASA lost a $125 million Mars orbiter because a Lockheed Martin engineering team used English units of measurement while NASA's team used the metric system for a key spacecraft operation. This difference in units resulted in miscommunication between the Mars Climate Orbiter spacecraft team in Denver, Colorado, and NASA's flight team at its Jet Propulsion Laboratory in Pasadena, California.

In this section, we discuss two units for the measurement of angles, degrees, and radians. Examples 1 and 2 show how to convert between these two units. ■

---

1 Define radian measure.

Radian Measure

An angle whose vertex is at the center of a circle is called a **central angle**. For convenience, in this book, a central angle means a positive central angle (unless otherwise specified).

RADIAN MEASURE OF A CENTRAL ANGLE

If a central angle, θ, intercepts an arc of length s in a circle of radius r, then

$$\theta = \frac{s}{r} \text{ radians.}$$

By agreement, the word *radian* may be omitted when giving the measure of an angle in radians. So $\theta = 5$ means $\theta = 5$ radians; to give the measure of θ in degrees, the degree symbol *must* be used, as in $\theta = 5°$. Radian measure can also be specified by using the notation $\theta = 5^r$, or $\theta = 5_r$, rather than simply $\theta = 5$.

To find the radian measure of any central angle, we divide the length of its intercepted arc by the radius of the circle. For example, if a central angle θ intercepts an arc of length 5 cm on a circle with radius 2 cm, then $\theta = \dfrac{5 \text{ cm}}{2 \text{ cm}} = 2.5$ radians. See Figure 3.1. (The central angle intercepts the arc along the circle from the initial side to the terminal side.)

$\theta = 2.5$ radians

FIGURE 3.1 Radian measurement

A central angle formed by rotating the initial ray through an arc of the circle of length equal to the radius of the circle has measure **1 radian** $\left(\theta = \dfrac{r}{r} = 1\right)$. See Figure 3.2.

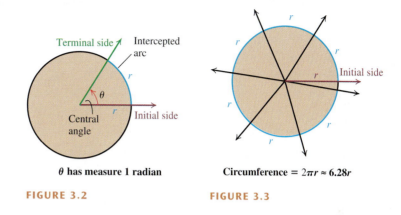

θ has measure 1 radian

FIGURE 3.2

Circumference $= 2\pi r \approx 6.28r$

FIGURE 3.3

Because the circumference of a circle of radius r is $2\pi r \approx 6.28r$, six arcs of length r can be consecutively marked off on a circle of radius r, leaving only a small portion of the circumference uncovered. See Figure 3.3.

Each of the (positive) central angles in Figure 3.3 that intercepts an arc of length r has measure 1 radian; so the measure of one complete revolution is a little more than 6 radians (approximately 6.28 radians and exactly 2π radians).

2 Convert between degree and radian measure.

Degree–Radian Conversion

We know that a $180°$ central angle in a circle of radius r intercepts an arc whose length, s, is one-half the circumference of the circle; that is, $s = \dfrac{1}{2}(2\pi r) = \pi r$. So to find the radian measure of $\theta = 180°$, we write:

$$\theta = 180° = \frac{s}{r} \text{ radians} \qquad \text{Radian measure formula}$$

$$= \frac{\pi r}{r} \text{ radians} \qquad \text{Replace } s \text{ with } \pi r.$$

$$= \pi \text{ radians} \qquad \text{Remove the common factor.}$$

We've found that **$180° = \pi$ radians**.

Dividing both sides of this equation first by 180 and then by π results in the two equations

$$1° = \frac{\pi}{180} \text{ radian} \qquad \text{and} \qquad 1 \text{ radian} = \frac{180}{\pi} \text{ degrees}.$$

To convert θ degrees to radians, multiply both sides of the first equation by θ. To convert θ radians to degrees, multiply both sides of the second equation by θ.

CONVERTING BETWEEN DEGREES AND RADIANS

$$\theta° = \theta\left(\frac{\pi}{180}\right) \text{ radians}$$

$$\theta \text{ radians} = \theta\left(\frac{180}{\pi}\right) \text{ degrees}$$

EXAMPLE 1   **Converting from Degrees to Radians**

Convert each angle from degrees to radians.

a. 30°   **b.** 90°   **c.** −225°   **d.** 55.8°

SOLUTION

To convert θ degrees to radians, multiply θ degrees by $\frac{\pi}{180°}$.

a. $30° = 30° \cdot \frac{\pi}{180°} = \frac{30\pi}{180} = \frac{\pi}{6}$ radian

b. $90° = 90° \cdot \frac{\pi}{180°} = \frac{90\pi}{180} = \frac{\pi}{2}$ radians

c. $-225° = -225° \cdot \frac{\pi}{180°} = \frac{-225\pi}{180} = -\frac{5\pi}{4}$ radians

d. $55.8° = 55.8° \cdot \frac{\pi}{180°} = \frac{55.8\pi}{180} \approx 0.97$ radian   Use a calculator.   ■ ■ ■

Practice Problem 1   Convert −45° to radians.   ■

Angles that are fractions of a complete rotation are usually expressed in radian measure as fractional multiples of π rather than as decimals. For example, we write 30° as $\frac{\pi}{6}$ radian, which is the exact value, instead of writing the approximation 30° ≈ 0.52 radian.

EXAMPLE 2   **Converting from Radians to Degrees**

Convert each angle in radians to degrees.

a. $\frac{\pi}{3}$ radians   **b.** $-\frac{3\pi}{4}$ radians   **c.** 1 radian   **d.** 3.75 radians

SOLUTION

To convert θ radians to degrees, multiply θ radians by $\frac{180°}{\pi}$.

a. $\frac{\pi}{3}$ radians $= \frac{\pi}{3} \cdot \frac{180°}{\pi} = \left(\frac{180}{3}\right)° = 60°$

b. $-\frac{3\pi}{4}$ radians $= -\frac{3\pi}{4} \cdot \frac{180°}{\pi} = \left(-\frac{3}{4}\right)180° = -135°$

c. 1 radian $= 1 \cdot \frac{180°}{\pi} \approx 57.3°$ Use a calculator.

d. 3.75 radians $= 3.75 \cdot \frac{180°}{\pi} \approx 214.9°$ Use a calculator.   ■ ■ ■

Practice Problem 2   Convert $\frac{3\pi}{2}$ radians to degrees.   ■

In Example 2, we saw that 1 radian is approximately 57.3°; so one radian corresponds to a much larger angle than does one degree. Figure 3.4 compares 30° and 30 radians.

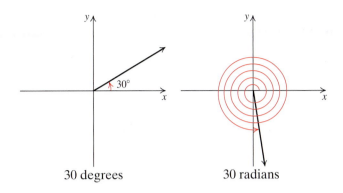

30 degrees   30 radians

FIGURE 3.4 Comparing degrees and radians

3 Find trigonometric function values for angles.

Trigonometric Function Values

Trigonometric function values can be found for angles regardless of whether the angle is given in degrees or radians. In Example 1, we found that $30° = \dfrac{\pi}{6}$ radian;

so $\sin\dfrac{\pi}{6} = \sin 30° = \dfrac{1}{2}$. Table 3.1 gives both the degree and radian measure for some commonly used angles, together with the exact value of the sine and cosine of each.

Figure 3.5 includes the degree and radian measures of some commonly used angles that are fractional multiples of π. With practice, you should be able to make these conversions without using the figure.

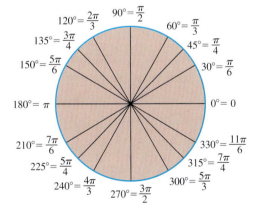

FIGURE 3.5 Common angle measures

TABLE 3.1 Degree and Radian Measures for Common Angles

θ Degrees	θ Radians (exact)	θ Radians (approximate)	$\sin\theta$	$\cos\theta$
0°	0	0	0	1
30°	$\dfrac{\pi}{6}$	0.52	$\dfrac{1}{2}$	$\dfrac{\sqrt{3}}{2}$
45°	$\dfrac{\pi}{4}$	0.79	$\dfrac{\sqrt{2}}{2}$	$\dfrac{\sqrt{2}}{2}$
60°	$\dfrac{\pi}{3}$	1.05	$\dfrac{\sqrt{3}}{2}$	$\dfrac{1}{2}$
90°	$\dfrac{\pi}{2}$	1.57	1	0
180°	π	3.14	0	−1
270°	$\dfrac{3\pi}{2}$	4.71	−1	0
360°	2π	6.28	0	1

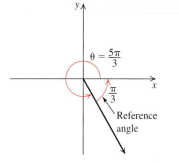

FIGURE 3.6

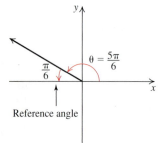

FIGURE 3.7

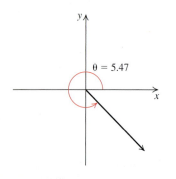

FIGURE 3.8

EXAMPLE 3 **Finding Trigonometric Function Values for Angles Measured in Radians**

a. Find $\sin \dfrac{5\pi}{3}$. **b.** Find $10 \cos \dfrac{5\pi}{6}$.

SOLUTION

a. By comparing $\dfrac{5\pi}{3} = \dfrac{10\pi}{6}$ with the quadrantal angle $\dfrac{3\pi}{2} = \dfrac{9\pi}{6}$, we find that $\dfrac{5\pi}{3}$ is in QIV; so its sine is negative. See Figure 3.6. Its reference angle is $2\pi - \dfrac{5\pi}{3} = \dfrac{6\pi}{3} - \dfrac{5\pi}{3} = \dfrac{\pi}{3}$.

Then,
$$\sin \frac{5\pi}{3} = -\sin\frac{\pi}{3} = -\frac{\sqrt{3}}{2}.$$

b. Comparing $\dfrac{5\pi}{6}$ with $\pi = \dfrac{6\pi}{6}$, we find that $\dfrac{5\pi}{6}$ is in QII; so its cosine is negative. See Figure 3.7. Its reference angle is

$$\pi - \frac{5\pi}{6} = \frac{6\pi}{6} - \frac{5\pi}{6} = \frac{\pi}{6}.$$

Then $10 \cos \dfrac{5\pi}{6} = 10\left(-\cos\dfrac{\pi}{6}\right) = 10\left(-\dfrac{\sqrt{3}}{2}\right) = -5\sqrt{3}.$ ■ ■ ■

Practice Problem 3 Find $-\sin\dfrac{7\pi}{6}$.   ■

EXAMPLE 4 **Locating the Terminal Side of θ When θ Is Given in Decimal Radians**

In what quadrant does $\theta = 5.47$ lie?

SOLUTION

Because no measure is specified, θ is assumed to be given in radians. Because $4.71 < 5.47 < 6.28$ and 4.71 and 6.28 are the approximate radian measures for $270°$ and $360°$, θ lies in QIV. See Figure 3.8 and Table 3.1.   ■ ■ ■

Practice Problem 4 In what quadrant does $\theta = 1.82$ lie?   ■

SECTION 3.1 ■ Exercises

A EXERCISES Basic Skills and Concepts

1. To convert θ degrees to radians, multiply θ by _____.

2. To convert θ radians to degrees, multiply θ by _____.

3. If a central angle θ intercepts an arc of length 3 on a circle of radius 2, then $\theta =$ _____.

4. If $\theta = 2$, then θ lies in Q _____.

5. *True or False* The arc intercepted by $\theta = 2$ is larger than the arc intercepted by $\alpha = 85°$.

6. *True or False* The value of $\cos 60 = \dfrac{1}{2}$.

In Exercises 7–12, find the radian measure of the central angle θ in a circle of radius r, assuming that θ intercepts an arc of length s.

7. $r = 2\,\text{cm}, s = 8\,\text{cm}$ **8.** $r = 3\,\text{ft}, s = 12\,\text{ft}$

9. $r = 5\,\text{m}, s = 13\,\text{m}$ **10.** $r = 2\,\text{in.}, s = 9\,\text{in.}$

11. $r = \dfrac{1}{2}\,\text{ft}, s = 3\,\text{ft}$ **12.** $r = \dfrac{1}{5}\,\text{m}, s = 2\,\text{m}$

In Exercises 13–24, convert each measure from degrees to radians. Express your answer as a multiple of π.

13. $45°$ **14.** $60°$

15. $150°$ **16.** $300°$

17. $315°$ **18.** $330°$

19. $-180°$ **20.** $-210°$

21. $480°$ **22.** $450°$

23. $-510°$ **24.** $-420°$

In Exercises 25–32, convert each measure from degrees to radians. Write your answers as decimals.

25. $19°$ **26.** $83°$

27. $22.4°$ **28.** $57.6°$

29. $125.23°$ **30.** $114.71°$

31. $94°26'$ **32.** $72°38'$

In Exercises 33–48, convert each measure from radians to degrees.

33. $\dfrac{\pi}{2}$ **34.** $\dfrac{3\pi}{4}$

35. $\dfrac{8\pi}{3}$ **36.** $\dfrac{15\pi}{4}$

37. $\dfrac{5\pi}{3}$ **38.** $\dfrac{11\pi}{6}$

39. $-\dfrac{5\pi}{4}$ **40.** $-\dfrac{3\pi}{2}$

41. $\dfrac{5\pi}{2}$ **42.** $\dfrac{17\pi}{6}$

43. $-\dfrac{11\pi}{4}$ **44.** $-\dfrac{7\pi}{3}$

45. $\dfrac{13\pi}{20}$ **46.** $\dfrac{3\pi}{5}$

47. $-\dfrac{7\pi}{60}$ **48.** $-\dfrac{17\pi}{30}$

In Exercises 49–56, convert each measure from radians to degrees. Round your answers to the nearest degree.

49. 7 **50.** 4

51. 2.89 **52.** 3.47

53. 6.84 **54.** 0.27

55. -9.0318 **56.** -16.2147

In Exercises 57–72, find the exact value of each expression.

57. $\sin\dfrac{\pi}{6}$ **58.** $\cos\dfrac{\pi}{4}$

59. $\tan\dfrac{\pi}{3}$ **60.** $\cot\dfrac{\pi}{6}$

61. $\sec\dfrac{\pi}{4}$ **62.** $\csc\dfrac{\pi}{3}$

63. $\cos\dfrac{\pi}{2}$ **64.** $\sin\pi$

65. $\tan\dfrac{5\pi}{6}$ **66.** $\cot\dfrac{5\pi}{3}$

67. $\sin\left(-\dfrac{7\pi}{6}\right)$ **68.** $\cos\left(-\dfrac{7\pi}{4}\right)$

69. $5\sin\pi$ **70.** $13\cos\dfrac{3\pi}{2}$

71. $4\cos\dfrac{11\pi}{6}$ **72.** $8\sin\dfrac{2\pi}{3}$

In Exercises 73–80, in what quadrant does each angle lie?

73. $\theta = 0.71$ **74.** $\theta = 0.44$

75. $\theta = 1.89$ **76.** $\theta = 1.85$

77. $\theta = 4.87$ **78.** $\theta = 5.02$

79. $\theta = 4.61$ **80.** $\theta = 6.21$

B EXERCISES Applying the Concepts

81. **Angles on a clock.** What is the radian measure of the smaller central angle made by the hands of a clock at 4:00? Express your answer as a rational multiple of π.

82. **Angles on a clock.** What is the radian measure of the larger central angle made by the hands of a clock at 7:00? Express your answer as a rational multiple of π.

83. **Pizza slices.** A slice of pizza left in a gym locker has a radius of 9 inches, and the outer crust edge is 4 inches long. What is the radian measure of the angle formed by its edges?

84. **Suspending a shark.** A shark is suspended by a wire wound around a pulley of radius 4 inches. The shark must be raised 6 inches more to be completely off the ground. Through how many degrees must the pulley be rotated counterclockwise to accomplish the 6-inch lift? Round your answer to the nearest degree.

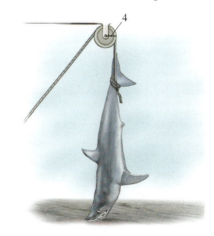

85. Pendulum angle. The tip of a 5-foot pendulum travels 2.62 feet as it swings through an angle. Find the radian measure of the angle.

86. Pushing a car A car with wheels having a 15-inch radius is pushed so that it rolls forward 90 inches.
   a. What is the radian measure of the angle through which the wheels turned?
   b. Did the wheels complete a full revolution?

C EXERCISES Beyond the Basics

In Exercises 87–90, find the exact value of each expression.

87. $\cos\dfrac{\pi}{4}\cos\dfrac{\pi}{6} + \sin\dfrac{\pi}{4}\sin\dfrac{\pi}{6}$

88. $\sin\dfrac{\pi}{6}\cos\dfrac{\pi}{3} + \cos\dfrac{\pi}{6}\sin\dfrac{\pi}{3}$

89. $\cos\dfrac{\pi}{3}\cos\dfrac{\pi}{6} - \sin\dfrac{\pi}{3}\sin\dfrac{\pi}{6}$

90. $\sin\dfrac{\pi}{4}\cos\dfrac{\pi}{6} - \cos\dfrac{\pi}{4}\sin\dfrac{\pi}{6}$

In Exercises 91–94, write each value as the sum or difference of two of the values $\dfrac{\pi}{6}, \dfrac{\pi}{4}, \dfrac{\pi}{3}, \dfrac{\pi}{2}$**, and** π**. For example,** $\dfrac{15\pi}{12} = \pi + \dfrac{\pi}{4}.$

91. $\dfrac{9\pi}{12}$ **92.** $\dfrac{7\pi}{12}$

93. $\dfrac{\pi}{12}$ **94.** $\dfrac{5\pi}{12}$

In Exercises 95–98, find the exact value of each expression assuming that $x = \dfrac{\pi}{3}$ **and** $y = \dfrac{\pi}{4}.$

95. $2\cos\left(x + \dfrac{\pi}{3}\right) - \sin 2y$

96. $5\sin\dfrac{x}{2} + 4\cos\left(3y - \dfrac{3\pi}{2}\right)$

97. $-3\cos\left(5x + 2y - \pi\right)$

98. $8\sin\left(4y - \dfrac{3x}{2}\right)$

99. The two equal legs of the isosceles triangle in the figures are joined by a hinge at A. If the third leg is made of copper and is bent to form an arc of a circle with center A, the measure of the angle at A will decrease. Find the new and old measures of the angle at A in degrees.

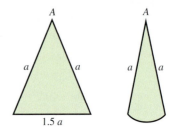

Critical Thinking

100. An angle with radian measure 1 has approximate degree measure 57.3°. Is it always true that angles with positive radian measure have a larger degree measure? Why or why not?

101. If you mark off the arc intercepted by an angle of 1° consecutively 360 times from any point on a circle, you return to your starting point. Is there an integer, n, so that if you mark off the arc intercepted by an angle of 1 radian consecutively n times from a point on a circle you will return to your starting point?

Applications of Radian Measure

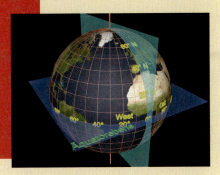

Before Starting this Section, Review

1. Radian measure of a central angle (Section 3.1)
2. Converting between radian and degree measure (Section 3.1)

Objectives

1. Find the length of an arc of a circle.
2. Find the area of a sector of a circle.

LATITUDE AND LONGITUDE

Any location on Earth can be described by two numbers, its *latitude* and its *longitude*. To understand how these two location numbers are assigned, we think of Earth as being a perfect sphere.

Lines of latitude are parallel circles of different sizes around the sphere representing Earth. The longest circle is the equator, with latitude 0, while at the poles, the circles shrink to a point. Lines of longitude (also called *meridians*) are circles of identical size that pass through the North Pole and the South Pole as they circle the globe. Each of these circles crosses the equator. The equator is divided into 360 degrees, and the longitude of a location is the number of degrees where the meridian through that location meets the equator. For historical reasons, the meridian near the old Royal Observatory in Greenwich, England, is the one chosen as 0 longitude.

Today this prime meridian is marked with a band of brass that stretches across the yard of the observatory. Longitude is measured from the prime meridian, with positive values going east (0 to 180) and negative values going west (0 to −180). Both ±180-degree longitudes share the same line in the middle of the Pacific Ocean. At the equator, the distance on Earth's surface for each one degree of latitude or longitude is just over 69 miles.

Every location on Earth is identified by the meridian and the latitude lines that pass through it. In Example 4, we explain how latitude values are assigned and how they can be used to compute distances between cities having the same longitude. ■

1 Find the length of an arc of a circle.

Arc Length

The formula for the radian measure θ of a central angle that intercepts an arc of length s is

$$\theta = \frac{s}{r}.$$

Multiplying both sides of this equation by r yields $s = r\theta$, a formula for the length s of the arc intercepted by a (positive) central angle with radian measure θ in a circle of radius r.

ARC LENGTH FORMULA

$s = r\theta, \quad \theta$ in radians

EXAMPLE 1   **Finding Arc Length of a Circle**

A circle has a radius of 18 inches. Find the length of an arc intercepted by a central angle with measure 210°.

SOLUTION

To use the arc length formula, we must first convert the central angle measure from degrees to radians.

$$s = r\theta \qquad \text{Arc length formula}$$

$$s = 18\left(\frac{7\pi}{6}\right) \qquad \theta = 210° = 210°\left(\frac{\pi}{180°}\right) = \frac{7\pi}{6} \text{ radians}$$

$$= 21\pi \qquad \text{Simplify.}$$

$$\approx 65.97 \text{ inches} \qquad \text{Use a calculator.} \qquad ■ ■ ■$$

Practice Problem 1   A circle has a radius of 2 meters. Find the length of an arc intercepted by a central angle with measure 225°.   ■

EXAMPLE 2   **Finding the Length of a Cable**

Supplies are being lowered into a mine shaft by using a spool of cable. If the diameter of the wrapped cable is 3 feet, how far will the supplies be lowered when the spool rotates 90° clockwise? See Figure 3.9.

SOLUTION

The length of cable that will be unwound during a 90° rotation is the arc length for a circle of diameter 3 feet and a central angle of 90°. We use the formula $s = r\theta$ with r = half the 3-foot diameter = 1.5 feet, and with θ converted to radian measure.

$$s = r\theta \qquad \text{Arc length formula}$$

$$= 1.5\left(\frac{\pi}{2}\right) \qquad r = \frac{3}{2} = 1.5; \theta = 90° = \frac{\pi}{2} \text{ radians}$$

$$\approx 2.4 \text{ feet} \qquad \text{Use a calculator.} \qquad ■ ■ ■$$

Practice Problem 2   Rework Example 2 assuming that the spool diameter is 3.5 feet and the spool rotates 120° clockwise.   ■

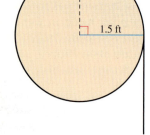

1.5 ft

FIGURE 3.9

EXAMPLE 3   **Finding a Relationship Between a Bike's Pedal and Wheel Sprockets**

The pedal sprocket, wheel sprocket, and chain of a bicycle are shown in Figure 3.10. Kyra says that for the wheel sprocket to rotate 60° every time the pedal sprocket rotates through 30°, the radius of the wheel sprocket should be half the radius of the pedal sprocket. Is Kyra correct?

r_2 Wheel sprocket

r_1 Pedal sprocket

FIGURE 3.10

SOLUTION

Let r_1 = the pedal sprocket radius and r_2 = the wheel sprocket radius. When the pedal sprocket rotates through 30°, a section of chain the length of the arc, s, intercepted by a central angle of 30° and radius r_1 moves around both the pedal sprocket and the wheel sprocket. See Figure 3.11. This same length of arc (or chain), s, will be intercepted by an angle of 60° on the wheel sprocket. We use the arc length formula $s = r\theta$ for both angles (with degrees converted to radians).

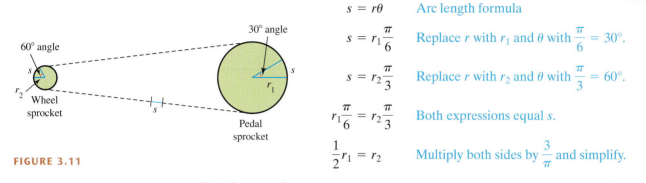

$$s = r\theta \qquad \text{Arc length formula}$$

$$s = r_1 \frac{\pi}{6} \qquad \text{Replace } r \text{ with } r_1 \text{ and } \theta \text{ with } \frac{\pi}{6} = 30°.$$

$$s = r_2 \frac{\pi}{3} \qquad \text{Replace } r \text{ with } r_2 \text{ and } \theta \text{ with } \frac{\pi}{3} = 60°.$$

$$r_1 \frac{\pi}{6} = r_2 \frac{\pi}{3} \qquad \text{Both expressions equal } s.$$

$$\frac{1}{2} r_1 = r_2 \qquad \text{Multiply both sides by } \frac{3}{\pi} \text{ and simplify.}$$

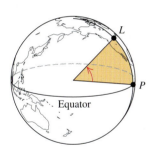

FIGURE 3.11

Kyra is correct! ■ ■ ■

Practice Problem 3   What is the relationship between the radii of the pedal and wheel sprockets if the wheel sprocket rotates 90° every time the pedal sprocket rotates through 30°? ■

EXAMPLE 4   **Finding the Distance Between Cities**

We obtain the latitude of a location L anywhere on Earth by first finding the point of intersection, P, between the great circle through the north and south poles through L and the equator. The latitude of L is the angle formed by rays drawn from the center of Earth to points L and P, with the ray through P being the initial ray. See Figure 3.12.

Billings, Montana, is due north of Grand Junction, Colorado. Find the distance between Billings (latitude 45°48′ N) and Grand Junction (latitude 39°7′ N) to the nearest mile. Use 3960 miles as the radius of Earth. The N in 45°48′ N means the location is north of the equator.

FIGURE 3.12

SOLUTION

Because Billings is due north of Grand Junction, the same great circle passes through both cities. The distance between the cities is then the length of the arc, s, on this meridian subtended by the central angle, θ, that is the difference in their latitudes. See Figure 3.13.

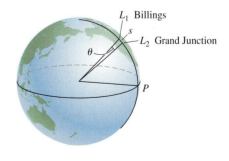

FIGURE 3.13

The measure of angle θ is $45°48' - 39°7' = 6°41'$. To use the arc length formula $s = r\theta$, we must first convert the angle $6°41'$ to radians.

$$\theta = 6°41' \approx 6.6833° = 6.6833\left(\frac{\pi}{180}\right) \text{ radian} \approx 0.1166 \text{ radian}.$$

We use this value of θ and $r = 3960$ miles in the arc length formula:

$$s = r\theta$$
$$s \approx (3960)(0.1166) \text{ miles} \approx 462 \text{ miles.} \quad \blacksquare \blacksquare \blacksquare$$

Practice Problem 4   Chicago, Illinois, is due north of Pensacola, Florida. Find the distance between Chicago (latitude 41°51′ N) and Pensacola (latitude 30°25′ N) to the nearest mile. Use the value $r = 3960$ miles.   ■

2 Find the area of a sector of a circle.

Area of a Sector

A **sector** of a circle is a region bounded by the two sides of a central angle and its intercepted arc.

Suppose that θ is the radian measure of a central angle of a circle of radius r. See Figure 3.14. To find a formula for the area of the sector of the circle formed by this central angle θ, we use the proportion:

$$\frac{\text{area of a sector}}{\text{area of a circle}} = \frac{\text{length of the intercepted arc}}{\text{circumference of the circle}}$$

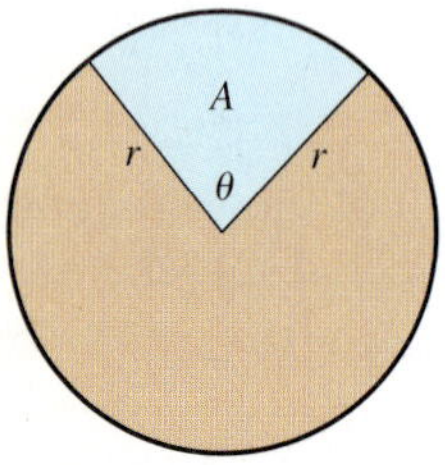

Letting A = area of the sector, this equation becomes

$$\frac{A}{\pi r^2} = \frac{r\theta}{2\pi r} \qquad \text{Area of a circle} = \pi r^2; \text{ circumference} = 2\pi r$$

Arc length formula: $s = r\theta$

$$A = \pi r^2\left(\frac{r\theta}{2\pi r}\right) \qquad \text{Multiply both sides by } \pi r^2.$$

$$= \frac{1}{2}r^2\theta \qquad \text{Simplify.}$$

FIGURE 3.14 Area of a sector of a circle

AREA OF A SECTOR

The area A of a sector of a circle of radius r formed by a central angle with radian measure θ is

$$A = \frac{1}{2}r^2\theta$$

EXAMPLE 5   **Finding the Area of a Sector of a Circle**

How many square inches of pizza have you eaten (rounded to the nearest square inch) if you eat a sector of a pizza 18 inches in diameter whose edges form an angle of 30°? See Figure 3.15.

SOLUTION

We must first convert 30° to radians in order to use the formula for the area of a sector. The radius of the pizza is $\frac{1}{2}$ the diameter, or 9 inches, and $30° = \frac{\pi}{6}$ radian.

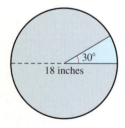

FIGURE 3.15

$$A = \frac{1}{2}r^2\theta$$ Area of a sector formula

$$= \frac{1}{2}9^2\left(\frac{\pi}{6}\right)$$ Replace r with 9 and θ with $\frac{\pi}{6}$.

$$\approx 21 \text{ square inches}$$ Use a calculator.

You have eaten about 21 square inches of pizza.   ■ ■ ■

Practice Problem 5 Find the area of a sector of the circle of radius 10 inches formed by an angle of 60°. Round your answer to two decimal places.   ■

SECTION 3.2 ■ Exercises

A EXERCISES Basic Skills and Concepts

1. The length, s, of the arc intercepted by a central angle with radian measure θ in a circle of radius r is _____.

2. If you double the measure of a central angle, the length of the arc intercepted will _____.

3. The area A of a sector of a circle of radius r formed by a central angle with radian measure θ is _____.

4. The formulas for both arc length and area of a sector require the angle involved to be measured in _____.

5. *True or False* The area of a sector of a circle of radius r and angle 30° is $\frac{1}{2}r^2(30) = 15r^2$.

6. *True or False* The area of a sector of a circle quadruples if the radius of the circle is doubled.

In Exercises 7 and 8, find the exact length of the arc intercepted by the central angle.

7.   8.

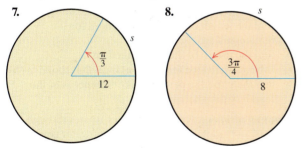

In Exercises 9–16, find the length of the arc intercepted by a central angle θ in a circle of radius r.

9. $\theta = 3, r = 5$ m

10. $\theta = 7, r = 2$ m

11. $\theta = \frac{\pi}{6}, r = 18$ ft

12. $\theta = \frac{\pi}{2}, r = 12$ ft

13. $\theta = \frac{3\pi}{5}, r = 10.2$ cm

14. $\theta = \frac{7\pi}{12}, r = 1.9$ cm

15. $\theta = 30°, r = 4.79$ in.

16. $\theta = 120°, r = 18.27$ in.

In Exercises 17–22, find the radius of a circle where a central angle θ intercepts an arc of length s.

17. $\theta = 1.2, s = 4.8$ cm

18. $\theta = 8.3, s = 24.9$ cm

19. $\theta = \frac{2\pi}{3}, s = 6\pi$ m

20. $\theta = \frac{3\pi}{4}, s = 12\pi$ m

21. $\theta = 300°, s = 10\pi$ ft

22. $\theta = 210°, s = 7\pi$ ft

In Exercises 23 and 24, find the area of each sector.

23.   24.

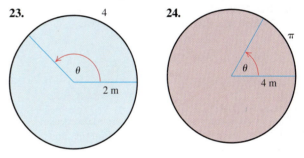

In Exercises 25–32, find the area of a sector of a circle with radius r and central angle θ.

25. $\theta = 3.4, r = 3$ m

26. $\theta = 4.7, r = 2$ m

27. $\theta = \frac{2\pi}{3}, r = 16.1$ ft

28. $\theta = \frac{5\pi}{6}, r = 31.4$ ft

29. $\theta = 47°, r = 9.1$ cm

30. $\theta = 135°, r = 22.4$ cm

31. $\theta = 115°, r = 20.0$ mi

32. $\theta = 82°, r = 60.0$ mi

33. Find the radius (to the nearest foot) of a circle in which a sector of area 60 ft^2 has a central angle of $\frac{\pi}{2}$.

34. Find the radius of a circle in which a sector of area $\frac{\pi}{3}$ in.^{2} has a central angle of 30°.

35. Find the radian measure of a central angle in a circle of radius 4 ft of a sector of area 33 ft^2.

36. Find the radian measure of a sector of area 100 in.^{2} in a circle of radius 20 in.

B EXERCISES Applying the Concepts

37. **Motorcycle movement.** As a motorcycle with tires having a 19-inch diameter rolls forward, its wheels rotate 120°. How many inches does the motorcycle move?

38. **Pendulum motion.** How far does the tip of a 5-foot pendulum travel as it swings through an angle of 30°?

39. **Lowering cargo.** Cargo is being lowered into the storage bay of a ship, using a spool of cable. If the diameter of the wrapped cable is 3.5 feet, how far will a cargo box be lowered when the spool rotates 100° clockwise?

40. **Loading a boat.** A boat is being pulled onto a trailer, using a spool of cable. If the diameter of the wrapped cable is 4 inches, how far forward will the boat travel when the spool rotates through 180°?

In Exercises 41 and 42, use the figure showing the pedal sprocket, wheel sprocket, and chain of a bicycle.

41. **Bicycle sprocket.** Assuming that the pedal sprocket rotates through 180° and $r_2 = 0.7r_1$, find the angle through which the wheel sprocket rotates.

42. **Bicycle sprocket.** Assuming that the wheel sprocket rotates 270° when the pedal sprocket rotates 90° and $r_1 = 4$ inches, find the value of r_2.

43. **Clock angles.** What is the radian measure of the angle made by the minute hand of a clock as it moves from 12 to 5? Express your answer as a rational multiple of π.

44. **Clock angles.** What is the radian measure of the angle made by the minute hand of a clock as it moves from 5 to 12? Express your answer as a rational multiple of π.

45. **Security cameras.** A security camera rotates through an angle of 120°. To the nearest foot, what is the arc width of the field of view 40 feet from the camera?

In Exercises 46–51, the latitude of any location on Earth is the angle formed by the two rays drawn from the center of Earth to the location and to the equator. The ray through the location is the initial ray. Use 3960 miles as the radius of Earth.

46. **Distance on Earth.** Indianapolis, Indiana, is due north of Montgomery, Alabama. Find the distance between Indianapolis (north latitude 39°44′ N) and Montgomery (latitude 32°23′ N).

47. **Distance on Earth.** Pittsburgh, Pennsylvania, is due north of Charleston, South Carolina. Find the distance between Pittsburgh (north latitude 40°30′ N) and Charleston (latitude 32°54′ N).

48. **Distance on Earth.** Amsterdam, the Netherlands, is due north of Lyon, France. Find the distance between Amsterdam (north latitude 52°23′ N) and Lyon (latitude 45°42′ N).

49. **Distance on Earth.** Adana, Turkey (north latitude 36°59′ N) is due north of Jerusalem, Israel (latitude 31°47′ N). Find the distance between Adana and Jerusalem.

50. **Distance on Earth.** Miles City, Montana, is 440 miles due north of Boulder, Colorado. Find the difference in the latitudes of these two cities.

51. **Distance on Earth.** Lincoln, Nebraska, is 554 miles due north of Dallas, Texas. Find the difference in the latitudes of these two cities.

52. **Nautical mile.** A nautical mile is the length of an arc of the equator subtended by a central angle of 1′. Using 3960 miles for the value of the radius of the earth, express 1 nautical mile in terms of standard (**statute**) miles.

53. **Approximation.** For small central angles with large radii, the length of the intercepted arc on a circle and the chord inscribed in the arc are good approximations of each other. For a 3° central angle in a circle of radius 4 miles,

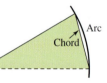

　　a. find the length of the inscribed chord for the intercepted arc.

　　b. find the length of the intercepted arc.

　　c. subtract the value found in (**a**) from that found in (**b**) and then find the percent this difference is of the length of the intercepted arc.

54. **Rotating sprinkler.** A water sprinkler rotates through an angle of 140° while spraying a stream of water covering a distance of 22 feet. (See the figure.) What is the area of lawn that receives water?

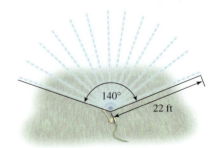

55. Rotating windshield wiper. A windshield wiper rotates through an angle of 100°. The length of the wiper arm is 20.5 inches, while the cleaning blade is 18 inches long. The shaded area in the figure shows the area cleaned by the blade. Find this area.

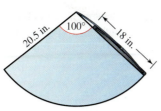

56. Area of land. A parcel of land that is bounded by a curved highway has one boundary that is the arc of a circle and includes a sector of land, as shown in the figure. Find the area of the parcel of land.

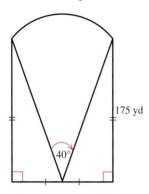

57. Grazing area. A goat is tethered to the corner of a fence by a 10-foot rope, as shown in the figure. Assuming that the goat can move freely to the full extent of the rope, find the area of the land on which the goat can graze.

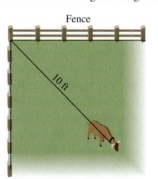

58. Grazing area. The goat in Exercise 57 is later tethered to the outside corner of the fence, as shown in the figure. Find the area of the land on which the goat can now graze.

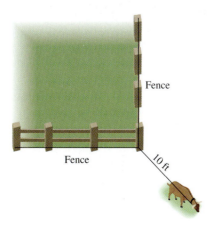

C EXERCISES Beyond the Basics

59. Find the shaded area of the circle that has a radius of 7 centimeters and a central angle of 120°.

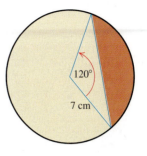

60. The perimeter of a circular sector with central angle θ and radius r is $2r + r\theta$. If the perimeter is 20 inches and the radius is 4 inches, find θ (in radians).

61. In this figure, the perimeter of the upper portion $ABCD$ is 22 cm.
   a. Find the degree measure of θ.
   b. Find the area of the upper portion, $ABCD$, of the figure.

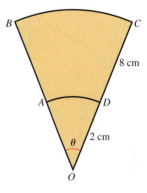

62. Assuming that BC is an arc of a circle, determine whether ABC or OBC is a sector of this circle, given that $\angle BAC = 30°$ and $\angle BOC = 26°$. Explain your answer.

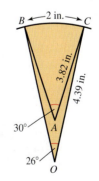

63. A traffic circle has four unevenly spaced roads, as shown in the figure. The diameter of the circle is 300 feet. Assuming that the central angles have measures ∠*AOH* = 85°, ∠*BOC* = 70°, ∠*DOE* = 50°, and ∠*FOG* = 75°, find the total feet of curbing needed for the outer arcs of the traffic circle.

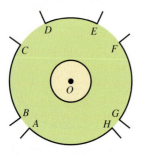

64. The area of a sector of a circle of radius *r* formed by a central angle with radian measure *θ* is *r*. What is the relationship between *r* and *θ*?

65. The chord in the sector of the circle of radius 1 shown in the figure has length 1. Show that the shaded area in the figure is given by $\dfrac{2\pi - 3\sqrt{3}}{12}$.

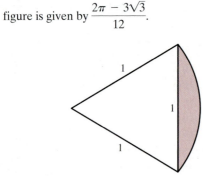

Critical Thinking

66. Arrange the following radian measures from smallest to largest: $\pi, \dfrac{3\pi}{2}, 3, 4$

67. Which line of latitude has a smaller radius, the line of latitude through a city of latitude 30°40′13″ or the line of latitude through a city of 40°30′13″ latitude?

GROUP PROJECT

In about 250 B.C., the philosopher Eratosthenes estimated the radius of Earth based on what might appear to be scant information. He knew that the city of Syene (modern Aswan) is directly south of the city of Alexandria and that Syene and Alexandria are (in modern units) about 500 miles apart. He also knew that in Syene at noon on a midsummer day, an upright rod casts no shadow but makes an angle with a vertical rod at Alexandria, and that then the sun's rays at Syene are effectively parallel to the sun's rays at Alexandria. Explain how, by measuring the length of the shadow in Alexandria at noon on the summer solstice (when 7°12′ there was no shadow in Syene), Eratosthenes could measure the circumference of the Earth.

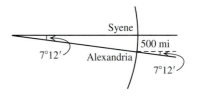

The Unit Circle and Circular Functions

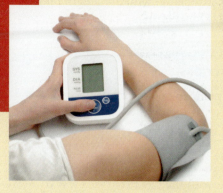

Before Starting this Section, Review

1. The equation of a circle (Appendix)
2. Definition of the trigonometric functions of an angle (Section 1.3)
3. Exact values of the trigonometric functions (Section 3.1)
4. Arc length formula (Section 3.2)

Objectives

1. Define circular functions.
2. Find exact values of circular functions.
3. Find approximate values of circular functions.
4. Identify the domains of the circular functions.
5. Apply circular functions.

BLOOD PRESSURE

In 1628, William Harvey wrote in his book *De Motu Cordis* (*On the Motion of the Heart*), "Just as the king is the first and highest authority in the state, so the heart governs the whole body!" He thereby announced to the world that the heart pumped blood through the entire body. There was a time, however, when even the fact that blood circulated at all was not accepted; the arteries were thought to carry air, not blood.

The first measurements of blood pressure were made in the early eighteenth century by Stephen Hales, an English botanist, physiologist, and clergyman. He found that pressure from a horse's heart filled a vertical glass tube with the horse's blood to a height of 8 feet 3 inches. He accomplished this by inserting a narrow brass pipe directly into an artery and fitting a 9-foot-long vertical glass tube to the pipe.

Fortunately, today a much safer, more convenient, and simplified method for measuring blood pressure is available everywhere. In Exercise 69, we use the circular functions to find blood pressure. ■

---

1 Define circular functions.

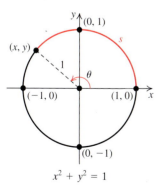

$x^2 + y^2 = 1$

FIGURE 3.16 The unit circle

Circular Functions

The relationship between the radian measure of a central angle and the length of the arc it intercepts allows us to define the trigonometric functions so that their domains are sets of numbers rather than angles. In many applications and in advanced mathematics, this is a more useful approach. We begin with a **unit circle**, a circle of radius 1 unit centered at the origin. See Figure 3.16. Recall (Appendix) that the equation for this circle is $x^2 + y^2 = 1$.

If s is any positive real number, we measure off an arc of length s (counterclockwise) beginning on the unit circle at $(1, 0)$ and ending at the point (x, y) on the unit circle. Then the point (x, y) is on the terminal ray of the central angle with radian measure θ that intercepts this arc. See Figure 3.17. Because the distance from the origin to (x, y) is $r = 1$, we have

$$\cos \theta = \frac{x}{r} = \frac{x}{1} = x \quad \text{and} \quad \sin \theta = \frac{y}{r} = \frac{y}{1} = y.$$

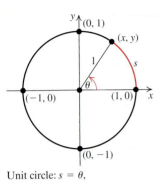

Unit circle: $s = \theta$,
$x = \cos \theta, y = \sin \theta$

FIGURE 3.17 Circular functions

Because $\theta = s$, we can write $\cos s = x$ and $\sin s = y$ and think of these functions as functions of the arc length, s, a real number. If s is a negative real number, we measure off an arc of length $|s|$ in a clockwise direction. Again, $\theta = s$, and we proceed as before. If $s = 0$, we let $(x, y) = (1, 0)$. All six trigonometric functions can now be defined as functions of numbers associated with arc length on a unit circle. When this is done, they are called **circular functions**.

CIRCULAR FUNCTIONS

If s is a real number and (x, y) is the related point on the unit circle described previously, then

$$\cos s = x \qquad\qquad \sin s = y \qquad\qquad \tan s = \frac{y}{x} \quad (x \neq 0)$$

$$\sec s = \frac{1}{x} \quad (x \neq 0) \qquad \csc s = \frac{1}{y} \quad (y \neq 0) \qquad \cot s = \frac{x}{y} \quad (y \neq 0)$$

If s is any real number, we can evaluate the trigonometric function values for s in three ways:

1. Find the endpoint (x, y) of the arc intercepted by the central angle (in standard position) of radian measure s on the unit circle and use the circular function definitions.

2. Use our earlier methods for finding the trigonometric function values for a central angle with radian measure s.

3. Convert s from radian measure to degree measure and use our earlier methods for finding trigonometric function values.

EXAMPLE 1   Using the Definition of the Circular Functions

Find $\sin s$, $\cos s$, and $\tan s$ for $s = \pi$.

SOLUTION

We want to find the endpoint of the arc intercepted by the central angle with radian measure π on the unit circle.

This arc has endpoint $(-1, 0)$. See Figure 3.18. So $x = -1$ and $y = 0$. Then

$$\sin \pi = y = 0 \quad \cos \pi = x = -1, \text{ and } \tan \pi = \frac{y}{x} = \frac{0}{-1} = 0. \qquad ■ ■ ■$$

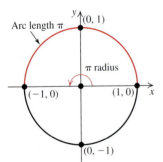

FIGURE 3.18

Practice Problem 1   Find $\sin s$, $\cos s$, and $\tan s$ for $s = \dfrac{3\pi}{2}$.   ■

2 Find exact values of circular functions.

Exact Circular Function Values

Figure 3.19 summarizes our earlier discussions of right triangles and reference angles, showing the connection between degree measure and radian measure of familiar angles, and the ordered pairs on the unit circle.

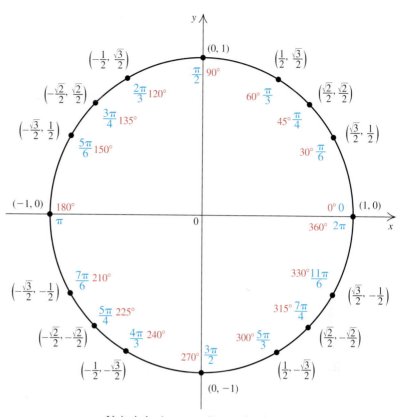

Unit circle: degrees, radians, ordered pairs

FIGURE 3.19 Degrees, radians, ordered pairs

EXAMPLE 2 Finding Exact Circular Function Values in Three Ways

Find $\sin \dfrac{5\pi}{6}$, $\cos \dfrac{5\pi}{6}$, and $\tan \dfrac{5\pi}{6}$ by

a. using Figure 3.19 to find the endpoint of the arc intercepted by $\theta = \dfrac{5\pi}{6}$ radians.

b. using reference angles and Table 3.1 from Section 3.1.

c. converting $\dfrac{5\pi}{6}$ to degrees.

SOLUTION

a. From Figure 3.19, we see that the endpoint of the arc intercepted by

$\theta = \dfrac{5\pi}{6}$ radians is $\left(-\dfrac{\sqrt{3}}{2}, \dfrac{1}{2}\right)$. So $\cos \dfrac{5\pi}{6} = -\dfrac{\sqrt{3}}{2}$, $\sin \dfrac{5\pi}{6} = \dfrac{1}{2}$, and

$$\tan \dfrac{5\pi}{6} = \dfrac{\sin \dfrac{5\pi}{6}}{\cos \dfrac{5\pi}{6}} = \dfrac{\dfrac{1}{2}}{-\dfrac{\sqrt{3}}{2}} = -\dfrac{1}{\sqrt{3}} = -\dfrac{\sqrt{3}}{3}.$$

b. We see that $\theta = \dfrac{5\pi}{6}$ radians is in QII, by either comparing $\dfrac{5\pi}{6}$ to $\dfrac{6\pi}{6}$ or referring to

Figure 3.19. So its cosine is negative and its sine is positive. The reference angle is

$$\pi - \dfrac{5\pi}{6} = \dfrac{6\pi}{6} - \dfrac{5\pi}{6} = \dfrac{\pi}{6}.$$

Then $\cos\dfrac{5\pi}{6} = -\cos\dfrac{\pi}{6} = -\dfrac{\sqrt{3}}{2}$, $\sin\dfrac{5\pi}{6} = \sin\dfrac{\pi}{6} = \dfrac{1}{2}$, and

$$\tan\frac{5\pi}{6} = \frac{\sin\dfrac{5\pi}{6}}{\cos\dfrac{5\pi}{6}} = \frac{\dfrac{1}{2}}{-\dfrac{\sqrt{3}}{2}} = -\frac{1}{\sqrt{3}} = -\frac{\sqrt{3}}{3}.$$

c. Converting $\dfrac{5\pi}{6}$ to degrees, we have $\dfrac{5\pi}{6} \cdot \dfrac{180}{\pi} = 150°$. Notice that Figure 3.19 also gives this information. Because $150°$ is in QII, $\cos 150°$ is negative, and its reference angle is $180° - 150° = 30°$.

Then $\cos\dfrac{5\pi}{6} = \cos 150° = -\cos 30° = -\dfrac{\sqrt{3}}{2}$,

$$\sin\frac{5\pi}{6} = \sin 150° = \sin 30° = \frac{1}{2}, \text{ and}$$

$$\tan\frac{5\pi}{6} = \frac{\sin\dfrac{5\pi}{6}}{\cos\dfrac{5\pi}{6}} = \frac{\dfrac{1}{2}}{-\dfrac{\sqrt{3}}{2}} = -\frac{1}{\sqrt{3}} = -\frac{\sqrt{3}}{3}.$$ ■ ■ ■

Practice Problem 2 Repeat Example 2 for $\sin\dfrac{7\pi}{6}$, $\cos\dfrac{7\pi}{6}$, and $\tan\dfrac{7\pi}{6}$. ■

EXAMPLE 3 **Finding Exact Circular Function Values for Negative Numbers**

Find $\sin\left(-\dfrac{\pi}{6}\right)$.

SOLUTION

The angles with radian measures $-\dfrac{\pi}{6}$ and $\dfrac{11\pi}{6}$ are coterminal and are in QIV. See Figure 3.20.

From Figure 3.19, we see that the endpoint of the intercepted arc is $\left(\dfrac{\sqrt{3}}{2}, -\dfrac{1}{2}\right)$.

Then $\sin\left(-\dfrac{\pi}{6}\right) = -\dfrac{1}{2}$. ■ ■ ■

Practice Problem 3 Find $\cos\left(-\dfrac{5\pi}{4}\right)$. ■

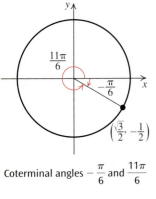

Coterminal angles $-\dfrac{\pi}{6}$ and $\dfrac{11\pi}{6}$

FIGURE 3.20

 3 Find approximate values of circular functions.

Approximate Circular Function Values

To find approximate circular function values of real numbers, your calculator must be in Radian mode.

EXAMPLE 4 **Using a Calculator to Find Approximate Circular Function Values**

Use a calculator to approximate each circular function value (rounded to four decimal places).

a. $\sin 1.76$ **b.** $\tan(-3.17)$ **c.** $\sec 4.27$

In Radian mode, finding sec 4.27 requires two steps.

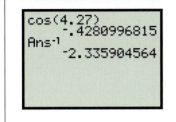

SOLUTION

a. Put your calculator in Radian mode and use the $\boxed{\text{SIN}}$ key to find sin 1.76 ≈ 0.9822.

b. Use the $\boxed{\text{TAN}}$ key to find tan (−3.17) ≈ −0.0284.

c. To find the secant, cosecant, and cotangent values, use the reciprocal identities and the reciprocal key $\boxed{x^{-1}}$. Still in Radian mode, first use the $\boxed{\text{COS}}$ key, then the $\boxed{x^{-1}}$ key.

$$\sec 4.27 = \frac{1}{\cos 4.27} \approx -2.3359$$ ■ ■ ■

Practice Problem 4   Use a calculator to approximate each circular function value.

a. cos 1.43   **b.** csc 2.11   **c.** cot (−4.03)   ■

4 Identify the domains of the circular functions.

Domains of the Circular Functions

If s is any real number, the arc intercepted by the central angle on the unit circle with radian measure s determines a point (x, y) on the unit circle. Because $\cos s = x$ and $\sin s = y$, both functions are defined at s; so the domain of these functions is the set of all real numbers.

However, $\tan s = \dfrac{y}{x}$ and $\sec s = \dfrac{1}{x}$; so these functions are not defined for $x = 0$. This occurs only at the points $(0, 1)$ and $(0, -1)$ when $s = \dfrac{\pi}{2}, -\dfrac{\pi}{2}, \dfrac{3\pi}{2}, -\dfrac{3\pi}{2}, \dfrac{5\pi}{2},$

$-\dfrac{5\pi}{2},$ and so on. See Figure 3.19. These values can be described as "odd integer multiples of $\dfrac{\pi}{2}$," which can be written $(2n + 1)\dfrac{\pi}{2}$ or $\dfrac{\pi}{2} + n\pi$. So the domain of the tangent and secant functions is all real numbers s satisfying

$$s \neq (2n + 1)\frac{\pi}{2}, n \text{ any integer.}$$

Similarly, because $\cot s = \dfrac{x}{y}$ and $\csc s = \dfrac{1}{y}$, these functions are not defined when $y = 0$, corresponding to the points $(1, 0)$ and $(-1, 0)$. This occurs when $s = \pi, -\pi, 2\pi, -2\pi, 3\pi, -3\pi,$ and so on. To eliminate values of s that result in $y = 0$, the domain for these functions is the set of all real numbers s satisfying

$$s \neq n\pi, n \text{ any integer.}$$

We summarize these results next.

DOMAINS OF THE CIRCULAR FUNCTIONS

sin s, cos s	All real numbers; $(-\infty, \infty)$
tan s, sec s	All real numbers s; $s \neq (2n + 1)\dfrac{\pi}{2}, n$ any integer
cot s, csc s	All real numbers s; $s \neq n\pi, n$ any integer

---

To find the number in the interval $\left[0, \dfrac{\pi}{2}\right]$ that has a specific circular function value, your calculator must be in Radian mode.

When a nonnegative number is input, the calculator keys $\boxed{\text{COS}^{-1}}$, $\boxed{\text{SIN}^{-1}}$, and $\boxed{\text{TAN}^{-1}}$ display approximate values for numbers in $\left[0, \dfrac{\pi}{2}\right]$ having the input value of cosine, sine, and tangent, respectively.

EXAMPLE 5 Finding Numbers Having Specific Circular Function Values

Use a calculator to find an approximate value for s in $\left[0, \dfrac{\pi}{2}\right]$.

a. $\cos s = 0.6291$ **b.** $\sec s = 3.4295$

SOLUTION

a. With your calculator in Radian mode, use the $\boxed{\text{COS}^{-1}}$ key to find
$$s = \cos^{-1}(0.6291) \approx 0.8904.$$

b. Because $\sec s = \dfrac{1}{\cos s}$, we have $\cos s = \dfrac{1}{\sec s}$. So we want to find s, where
$$\cos s = \frac{1}{\sec s} = \frac{1}{3.4295}.$$ As in part **a**, in Radian mode, use the $\boxed{\text{COS}^{-1}}$ key.

$$s = \cos^{-1}\left(\frac{1}{3.4295}\right) \approx 1.2749$$ ■ ■ ■

Practice Problem 5 Repeat Example 5 for these circular functions.

a. $\sin s = 0.2011$ **b.** $\csc s = 4.7162$ ■

---

5 Apply circular functions.

An Application

EXAMPLE 6 Finding an Angle of Refraction

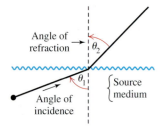

Angle of refraction → θ_2

θ_1 { Source medium

Angle of incidence

FIGURE 3.21

Suppose we have two media, such as water and air, one containing a light source. If the velocity of light in the medium with the light source is v_1 and the velocity of light in the second medium is v_2, then Snell's law says that

$$\frac{v_1}{v_2} = \frac{\sin \theta_1}{\sin \theta_2},$$

where θ_1 and θ_2 are the angles identified in Figure 3.21.

Assuming that the angle of incidence is $45°$ and light travels 20% faster in the second medium than in the light source medium, find the angle of refraction to the nearest degree.

SOLUTION

We know that v_2 is 20% faster than v_1; so

$$v_2 = v_1 + 0.2v_1 = 1.2v_1.$$

Then $\dfrac{v_2}{v_1} = 1.2.$ Divide both sides by v_1.

From $\dfrac{v_1}{v_2} = \dfrac{\sin \theta_1}{\sin \theta_2}$, we have

$$\sin \theta_2 = \frac{v_2}{v_1}\sin \theta_1 \qquad \text{Multiply both sides by } \frac{v_2}{v_1}\sin \theta_2.$$

$$\sin \theta_2 = 1.2 \sin 45° \qquad \text{Replace } \frac{v_2}{v_1} \text{ with 1.2 and } \theta_1 \text{ with } 45°.$$

$$\sin \theta_2 = 1.2 \left(\frac{\sqrt{2}}{2}\right) \qquad \text{Remember that } \sin 45° = \frac{\sqrt{2}}{2}, \text{ or see}$$

Table 3.1 in Section 3.1.

$$\theta_2 = \sin^{-1}\left[1.2\left(\frac{\sqrt{2}}{2}\right)\right] \qquad \text{Use the } \boxed{\text{SIN}^{-1}} \text{ key on a calculator.}$$

$$\approx 1.0132$$

$$\theta_2 \approx (1.0132)\frac{180}{\pi} \approx 58° \qquad \text{Convert radians to degrees.} \qquad \blacksquare\;\blacksquare\;\blacksquare$$

Practice Problem 6   Rework Example 6 assuming that v_2 is 50% faster than v_1 and $\theta_1 = 30°$.   ■

SECTION 3.3 ■ Exercises

A EXERCISES Basic Skills and Concepts

1. A unit circle is a circle with center at the _____ and radius = _____.

2. When the trigonometric functions are defined as functions of numbers associated with an arc length on a unit circle, they are called _____.

3. If (x, y) is the endpoint of an arc that begins at $(1, 0)$ and is intercepted by the central angle of radian measure s on the unit circle, then $x = $ _____.

4. The domain of the circular function sine is _____.

5. *True or False* If (x, y) is the endpoint on the unit circle for finding the circular function values of the number s and $\tan s$ is undefined, then we must have $x = 0$.

6. *True or False* If $\sin s$ is negative, then s must be a negative number.

In Exercises 7–12, use Figure 3.19 and the definition of the circular functions to find the exact values for sin s, cos s, and tan s.

7. $s = \dfrac{\pi}{2}$

8. $s = \dfrac{3\pi}{2}$

9. $s = \dfrac{4\pi}{3}$

10. $s = \dfrac{5\pi}{4}$

11. $s = -\dfrac{7\pi}{4}$

12. $s = -\dfrac{11\pi}{6}$

In Exercises 13–28, find the exact circular function value.

13. $\cos\dfrac{5\pi}{3}$

14. $\sin\dfrac{2\pi}{3}$

15. $\tan\dfrac{3\pi}{2}$

16. $\cot\pi$

17. $\sin\dfrac{5\pi}{3}$

18. $\cos\dfrac{3\pi}{4}$

19. $\sec 2\pi$

20. $\csc\dfrac{3\pi}{2}$

21. $\tan 3\pi$

22. $\cot\dfrac{5\pi}{2}$

23. $\cos\left(-\dfrac{\pi}{2}\right)$

24. $\sin(-\pi)$

25. $\sec\left(-\dfrac{11\pi}{6}\right)$

26. $\csc\left(-\dfrac{5\pi}{3}\right)$

27. $\sin\dfrac{14\pi}{6}$

28. $\cos\dfrac{25\pi}{3}$

In Exercises 29–40, use a calculator to approximate each circular function value (rounded to four decimal places).

29. $\sin 1.42$

30. $\cos 0.57$

31. $\tan 2.04$

32. $\cot 3.71$

33. $\sec 5.241$

34. $\csc 7.943$

35. $\cos(-3.208)$

36. $\sin(-0.0743)$

37. $\cot(-4.632)$

38. $\tan(-6.449)$

39. $\csc(-0.0024)$

40. $\sec(-0.4114)$

In Exercises 41–50, state which circular functions are undefined for the given value of s.

41. $\dfrac{\pi}{2}$

42. 2π

43. π

44. $\dfrac{3\pi}{2}$

45. $-\pi$

46. $-\dfrac{\pi}{2}$

47. $-\dfrac{17\pi}{2}$

48. $-\dfrac{211\pi}{2}$

49. $\dfrac{57\pi}{2}$

50. 412π

In Exercises 51–56, use a calculator to find an approximate value for s in $\left[0, \dfrac{\pi}{2}\right]$ having each circular function value.

51. $\cos s = 0.4361$

52. $\sin s = 0.7295$

53. $\cot s = 0.3174$

54. $\tan s = 1.1433$

55. $\csc s = 2.4736$

56. $\sec s = 5.1498$

In Exercises 57–62, do not use a calculator. Use Figure 3.19 to find an exact value of s in the specified interval with the given circular function value.

57. $\sin s = \dfrac{1}{2}, \left[\dfrac{\pi}{2}, \pi\right]$

58. $\cos s = -\dfrac{\sqrt{2}}{2}, \left[\dfrac{\pi}{2}, \pi\right]$

59. $\tan s = -1, \left[\dfrac{3\pi}{2}, 2\pi\right]$

60. $\cot s = 1, \left[\pi, \dfrac{3\pi}{2}\right]$

61. $\sec s = -\sqrt{2}, \left[\dfrac{\pi}{2}, \pi\right]$

62. $\csc s = -2, \left[\pi, \dfrac{3\pi}{2}\right]$

In Exercises 63–68, use the figure to approximate the given circular function values to within successive tenths. For example, you might have $0.1 <$ value < 0.2. Then use a calculator to find approximate values to the nearest hundredth.

63. $\cos 1, \sin 1$

64. $\cos 3, \sin 3$

65. $\cos 5, \sin 5$

66. $\cos(-1), \sin(-1)$

67. $\cos(-3), \sin(-3)$

68. $\cos(-5), \sin(-5)$

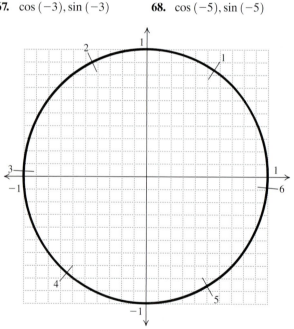

Grid lines are 0.1 unit apart. The arc lengths are marked along the circle

B EXERCISES Applying the Concepts

69. Blood pressure. Maurice's blood pressure (in millimeters of mercury) while resting is given by the function $R(t) = 25 \sin(2\pi t) + 100$, where t is time in seconds. Find his blood pressure after
  a. 1 second   **b.** 1.75 seconds

70. Ferris wheel motion. The height (in feet) of a seat on a Ferris wheel at a state fair is given by the function

$$H(t) = 27.5 + 25 \sin\left(\dfrac{\pi}{40}t - \dfrac{\pi}{2}\right),$$ where t is in seconds.

How high is the seat when
  a. $t = 0$?   **b.** $t = 10$?
  c. $t = 40$?   **d.** $t = 60$?

71. Resistance in blood vessels. When two blood vessels branch apart, the branching angle, θ, that minimizes resistance to the flow of blood is given by $\cos\theta = \left(\dfrac{r_2}{r_1}\right)^4$, where r_2 is the smaller radius and r_1 is the larger radius for the two vessels. Find θ assuming that r_1 is twice as large as r_2.

72. Water over a dam. The amount of water flowing across a V-shaped dam (in m³/sec) at a fixed height is $Q(\theta) = 22 \tan\dfrac{\theta}{2}$, where θ is the angle of the V. When the angle is changed from 20° to a larger angle θ and the height is kept fixed, the amount of water flowing across the dam doubles. Find θ to the nearest degree.

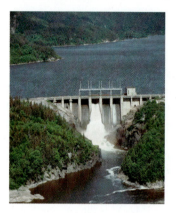

C EXERCISES Beyond the Basics

In Exercises 73–76, find the exact value of each expression.

73. $\sin\dfrac{\pi}{2} + \sin\dfrac{7\pi}{6}$

74. $\cos\dfrac{4\pi}{3} + \cos\dfrac{5\pi}{4}$

75. $2\sin\dfrac{3\pi}{4} - 5\tan\dfrac{7\pi}{4}$

76. $-5\cot\dfrac{\pi}{6} + 7\tan\dfrac{5\pi}{4}$

In Exercises 77–82, the point (x, y) is the endpoint of an arc on the unit circle beginning at $(1, 0)$ and intercepted by an angle of radian measure s.

77. Assuming that $y = \dfrac{1}{2}$ and $x < 0$, find the exact value of $\cos s$.

78. Assuming that $y = \dfrac{\sqrt{2}}{2}$ and $x > 0$, find the exact value of $\sin s$.

79. Assuming that $x = \sqrt{3}\, y$ and $y < 0$, find the exact value of $\cos s$ and $\sin s$.

80. Assuming that $x \cdot y = 0$ and $x < 0$, find the exact value of $\cos s$ and $\sin s$.

81. Find approximate values of $\cos s$ and $\sin s$ assuming that $s = 4.3$.

82. Find approximate values of $\cos s$ and $\sin s$ assuming that $s = -3.7$.

83. Find all values in the interval $[3000\pi, 3010\pi]$ that are not in the domain of tan s.

84. Find all values in the interval $[3000\pi, 3010\pi]$ that are not in the domain of csc s.

85. How many numbers in the interval $[0, 2000\pi]$ are not in the domain of cot s?

86. How many numbers in the interval $[0, 2000\pi]$ are not in the domain of sec s?

87. Find the domain of $y = \tan\left(s + \dfrac{\pi}{2}\right)$.

88. Find the domain of $y = \cot\left(s + \dfrac{\pi}{2}\right)$.

Critical Thinking

In Exercises 89–91, the points (x, y), $(-x, y)$, $(x, -y)$, and $(-x, -y)$ are the endpoints of the arcs on the unit circle beginning at $(1, 0)$ and intercepted by angles of s, t, u, and v radians, respectively.

89. How are sin s and cos s related to cos t and sin t?

90. How are sin s and cos s related to cos u and sin u?

91. How are sin s and cos s related to cos v and sin v?

Angular and Linear Speed

EARTH'S ROTATION

The earth is usually described as a sphere, although it has a bulge that makes it more elliptical than spherical. The earth rotates around its own axis toward the east. This means that every point on Earth is traveling at a certain speed around Earth's axis. Because the earth also orbits around the sun, the earth is traveling at some speed around the sun. In this section, we discuss two distinct ways of measuring speed for objects on a circular path, and in Exercises 50 and 51, we investigate the speed of a point on the equator as it travels around the earth and the speed of the earth as it travels around the sun. ■

1 Define angular and linear speed.

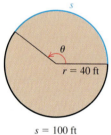

$s = 100$ ft
$\theta = 2.5$ radians

FIGURE 3.22

Angular and Linear Speed

If you are driving at 50 mph in a straight line, your linear speed is 50 mph. If the road bends or curves and your speedometer says 50 mph, your linear speed is still 50 mph. (Think of straightening the road.) Even if you were driving around a circular track, you would still have a linear speed (again, think of straightening the track), but with a circular path, the idea of *angular speed* can also be introduced.

We begin with slower speeds and smaller dimensions in an indoor setting. Suppose a skater skates 100 feet in 5 seconds, then her *average speed*, v, is given by

$$v = \frac{\text{distance}}{\text{time}} = \frac{100 \text{ feet}}{5 \text{ seconds}} = 20 \text{ feet per second.}$$

Suppose now that the skater is skating around the circumference of a circular skating rink with radius 40 feet. See Figure 3.22. In 5 seconds, the skater travels an arc of length 100 feet and moves through an angle θ, where

$$\theta = \frac{s}{r} = \frac{100}{40} = 2.5 \text{ radians.} \qquad \text{\color{blue}{Replace } } s \text{ \color{blue}{by 100 and }} r \text{ \color{blue}{by 40.}}$$

We say that the skater is traveling at an (average) *angular speed* of ω (omega), where $\omega = \dfrac{\theta}{t} = \dfrac{2.5}{5} = 0.5$ radian per second.

We call the average speed, 20 feet per second, the *linear speed* to distinguish it from the (average) *angular speed*, which is 0.5 radian per second.

If a beam of light from the center of the rink is focused on the skater, then (since her angular speed is 0.5 radian per second) the beam will sweep out an angle of 0.5 radian (about 28.6°) in 1 second. See Figure 3.23.

Notice that the linear speed is the product of the radius and the angular speed; that is, $v = 20 = 40(0.5) = r\omega$.

We will come back to this later.

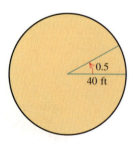

FIGURE 3.23

LINEAR AND ANGULAR SPEED

Suppose an object travels around a circle of radius r. If the object travels through an angle of θ radians and an arc of length s, in time t, then

1. $v = \dfrac{s}{t}$ is the (average) **linear speed** of the object; and

2. $\omega = \dfrac{\theta}{t}$ is the (average) **angular speed** of the object.

EXAMPLE 1   **Finding Angular and Linear Speed**

A point on a circle rotates through $\dfrac{5\pi}{4}$ radians in 5 seconds.

a. Find the angular speed of the point.

b. How long does it take the point to rotate through $90°$?

SOLUTION

a. The point rotates through the angle $\theta = \dfrac{5\pi}{4}$ radians in $t = 5$ seconds. Then

$$\omega = \frac{\theta}{t} \qquad \text{Angular speed formula}$$

$$\omega = \frac{\dfrac{5\pi}{4}}{5} \qquad \text{Replace } \theta \text{ with } \frac{5\pi}{4} \text{ and } t \text{ with } 5.$$

$$\omega = \frac{\pi}{4} \text{ radian/sec} \qquad \text{Simplify.}$$

b. We now know that the angular speed, ω, is $\dfrac{\pi}{4}$ radian/sec. The point rotates through $90°$ when $\theta = 90° = \dfrac{\pi}{2}$ radians. We have

$$\omega = \frac{\theta}{t} \qquad \text{Angular speed formula}$$

$$\frac{\pi}{4} = \frac{\dfrac{\pi}{2}}{t} \qquad \text{Replace } \omega \text{ with } \frac{\pi}{4} \text{ and } \theta \text{ with } \frac{\pi}{2}.$$

$$t = \frac{\pi}{2} \cdot \frac{4}{\pi} \qquad \text{Multiply both sides by } t\frac{4}{\pi}.$$

$$t = 2 \text{ seconds} \qquad \text{Simplify.}$$

It takes two seconds for the point to rotate through $90°$.   ■ ■ ■

Practice Problem 1   A point on a circle rotates through $\dfrac{3\pi}{4}$ radians in 6 seconds.

a. Find the angular speed of the point.

b. How long does it take for the point to rotate through $90°$?   ■

2 Relate angular and linear speeds.

Relationship Between Angular and Linear Speeds

The linear speed, v, of an object moving through an arc of length s during time t on a circle of length r is

$$v = \frac{s}{t} \qquad \text{Linear speed formula}$$

If the object travels through θ radians during this time, then $s = r\theta$; so

$$v = \frac{s}{t} = \frac{r\theta}{t} \qquad \text{Replace } s \text{ with } r\theta.$$

Because $\omega = \dfrac{\theta}{t}$,

$$v = \frac{r\theta}{t} = r\left(\frac{\theta}{t}\right) = r\omega \qquad \text{Replace } \frac{\theta}{t} \text{ with } \omega.$$

This relationship between angular and linear speed is often useful.

RELATING ANGULAR AND LINEAR SPEED

$$v = r\omega$$

Linear Speed   Angular Speed

EXAMPLE 2 **Finding Angular and Linear Speeds from Revolutions per Minute**

A model plane is attached to a swivel so that it flies in a circular path at the end of a 12-foot wire at the rate of 15 revolutions per minute. Find the angular speed and the linear speed of the plane.

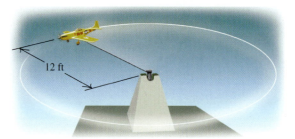

12 ft

SOLUTION

Since angular speed is measured in radians per unit of time, we must convert revolutions per minute to radians per minute. Because 1 revolution is 2π radians, 15 revolutions is $15 \cdot 2\pi = 30\pi$ radians. So $\omega = 30\pi$ radians per minute and

$$
\begin{aligned}
v &= r\omega && \text{Angular and linear speed relationship} \\
&= 12 \cdot 30\pi \text{ feet per minute} && \text{Replace } r \text{ with 12 and } \omega \text{ with } 30\pi \\
& && \text{radians per minute.} \\
&\approx 1131 \text{ feet per minute} && \text{Use a calculator.} \qquad \blacksquare\ \blacksquare\ \blacksquare
\end{aligned}
$$

Practice Problem 2   Repeat Example 2 assuming that the wire is 10 feet long and the plane flies at a rate of 18 revolutions per minute.   ■

EXAMPLE 3   **Finding the Speed of a River**

A waterwheel has a radius of 8 feet. Assuming that the wheel makes 12 revolutions per minute, find

a. the speed of the river in feet per minute.

b. the angular and linear speed of a point 6 feet from the wheel's center. See Figure 3.24.

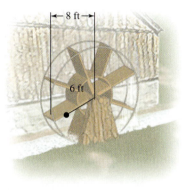

FIGURE 3.24

SOLUTION

a. Since a point on the outer edge of the wheel moves at the same rate as the river, the speed of the river can be approximated by finding the linear speed of a point on the outer edge of the wheel.

Because 1 revolution is 2π radians, 12 revolutions is $12 \cdot 2\pi = 24\pi$ radians, and $\omega = 24\pi$ radians per minute.

Then	$v = r\omega$	Angular and linear speed relationship
	$v = 8(24\pi)$	Replace r with 8 and ω with 24π.
	$v \approx 603 \text{ ft/min}$	Use a calculator.

b. Every point on the wheel rotates at the same angular speed, $\omega = 24\pi$ radians per minute. However, the radius of the circle around which this point travels is 6 feet, which affects the point's linear speed.

$v = r\omega$	Angular and linear speed relationship
$v = 6(24\pi)$	Replace r with 6 and ω with 24π.
$v \approx 452 \text{ ft/min}$	Use a calculator.

■ ■ ■

Practice Problem 3   Repeat Example 3 assuming that the radius of the wheel is 10 feet and the wheel makes 9 revolutions per minute.   ■

SECTION 3.4 ■ Exercises

A EXERCISES Basic Skills and Concepts

1. When distance traveled is divided by the time it takes to travel that distance, the result is _____ speed.

2. When an object travels on a circular path through an angle of θ radians, the _____ speed results from dividing θ by the time it takes to travel through θ radians.

3. The product of the radius and the angular speed of an object results in its _____.

4. The points on the second hand of a clock all have the same _____ speed but different _____ speeds.

5. *True or False* If two objects traveling on circular paths with different radii both travel through θ radians in 20 seconds, the angular speed of the object on the circle with the larger radius will be greater.

6. *True or False* The numerical values (but not the units) for the angular speed and the linear speed of an object traveling on a circle of radius 1 are identical.

In Exercises 7–12, find the linear speed of a point traveling a circular path, where *s* is distance traveled in time *t*.

7. $s = 6\ \text{ft}, t = 2\ \text{min}$ 8. $s = 12\ \text{ft}, t = 3\ \text{min}$

9. $s = 20\ \text{m}, t = 4\ \text{sec}$ 10. $s = 15\ \text{m}, t = 5\ \text{sec}$

11. $s = 100\ \text{yd}, t = 10\ \text{sec}$ 12. $s = 300\ \text{yd}, t = 60\ \text{sec}$

In Exercises 13–18, find the angular speed of a point traveling through θ radians in time *t*.

13. $\theta = \dfrac{\pi}{2}, t = 5\ \text{sec}$ 14. $\theta = \dfrac{2\pi}{3}, t = 8\ \text{sec}$

15. $\theta = 14, t = 7\ \text{min}$ 16. $\theta = 21, t = 3\ \text{min}$

17. $\theta = \dfrac{35\pi}{4}, t = 1.5\ \text{hr}$ 18. $\theta = \dfrac{22\pi}{5}, t = 0.4\ \text{hr}$

In Exercises 19–24, find the distance traveled by a point *P* traveling on a circle of radius *r* by finding θ and then using the arc length formula, $s = r\theta$. Each value of ω is in radians/sec.

19. $r = 3\ \text{in.}, \omega = 5, t = 5\ \text{sec}$

20. $r = 4\ \text{in.}, \omega = 2, t = 8\ \text{sec}$

21. $r = 2.4\ \text{m}, \omega = \dfrac{\pi}{4}, t = 12\ \text{min}$

22. $r = 3.1\ \text{m}, \omega = \dfrac{3\pi}{2}, t = 4\ \text{min}$

23. $r = 16\ \text{ft}, \omega = \dfrac{3\pi}{4}, t = 1.2\ \text{hr}$

24. $r = 9\ \text{ft}, \omega = \dfrac{2\pi}{3}, t = 0.6\ \text{hr}$

In Exercises 25–36, θ = central angle of a circle, *r* = radius of the circle, *s* = length of the intercepted arc, *v* = linear speed, ω = angular speed, and *t* = time. In each case, find the missing quantity. Round your answer to three decimal places.

25. $r = 25\ \text{inches}, s = 7\ \text{inches}, \theta = ?$

26. $r = 5\ \text{feet}, s = 6\ \text{feet}, \theta = ?$

27. $r = 10.5\ \text{centimeters}, s = 22\ \text{centimeters}, \theta = ?$

28. $r = 60\ \text{meters}, s = 120\ \text{meters}, \theta = ?$

29. $r = 3\ \text{meters}, \theta = 25°, s = ?$

30. $r = 0.7\ \text{meter}, \theta = 357°, s = ?$

31. $r = 6.5\ \text{meters}, \theta = 12\ \text{radians}, s = ?$

32. $r = 6\ \text{meters}, \theta = \dfrac{\pi}{6}\ \text{radians}, s = ?$

33. $r = 6\ \text{meters}, \omega = 10\ \text{rad/min}, v = ?$

34. $r = 3.2\ \text{feet}, \omega = 5\ \text{rad/sec}, v = ?$

35. $v = 20\ \text{feet/sec}, r = 10\ \text{feet}, \omega = ?$

36. $v = 10\ \text{meters/min}, r = 6\ \text{meters}, \omega = ?$

B EXERCISES Applying the Concepts

37. **Bicycle wheel speed.** A bicycle's wheels are 24 inches in diameter. Assuming that the bike is traveling at a rate of 25 miles per hour, find the angular speed of the wheels. Round your answer to two decimal places.

38. **Bicycle wheel speed.** A bicycle's wheels are 30 inches in diameter. Assuming that the angular speed of the wheels is 11 radians per second, find the speed of the bicycle in inches per second.

39. **Hard disk speed.** Hard disks are circular disks that store data in computers. Suppose a circular hard disk is 3.75 inches in diameter. If the disk rotates 7200 revolutions per minute, what is the linear speed of a point on the edge of the disk (in inches per minute)?

40. **Ferris wheel motion.** A Ferris wheel in Vienna, Austria, has a diameter of approximately 61 meters. Assume that it takes 90 seconds for the Ferris wheel to make one complete revolution.
    a. Find the angular speed of the Ferris wheel. Round your answer to two decimal places.
    b. Find the linear speed of the Ferris wheel in meters per second. Round your answer to two decimal places.

41. **Microwave platter rotation.** The rotating platter in a microwave oven has a diameter of 12.5 inches. Assuming that a point on the rim of the platter has a linear speed of 4 inches per minute, find its angular speed.

42. Propeller speed. A 16-inch propeller blade has an angular speed of 16π radians per second. Find its linear speed.

43. Merry-go-round speed. A horse on the outside row of a merry-go-round is 20 feet from the center, and its linear speed is 314 feet per minute. Find its angular speed.

44. Potter wheel motion. A point on the rim of a pottery wheel with a 28-inch diameter has a linear speed of 21 inches per second. Find its angular speed.

45. Find
   a. the angular speed of every point on the minute hand of a clock.
   b. the linear speed of a point on the tip of a 6-inch minute hand.

46. Lawn roller motion. The cylindrical drum of a lawn roller has a 2-foot diameter and moves across the grass at 80 inches per second. Find the angular speed of the roller.

2 ft

47. Car wheel speed. Stacy is driving 60 mph in a car whose wheels have a 30-inch diameter. Find the angular speed of the wheels.

48. Windshield wiper motion. A 21-inch windshield wiper arm has a blade that begins 4 inches from the bottom of the arm. The wiper arm rotates through $120°$ in two seconds. Find the linear speed of
   a. a point at the tip of the blade.
   b. a point halfway up the blade (not the arm).

49. Pulley interaction. Two pulleys are connected by a belt so that when one pulley rotates, the linear speeds of the belt and both pulleys are the same. (See the figure.) The radius of the smaller pulley is 2 inches, and the radius of the larger pulley is 5 inches. A point on the belt travels at a rate of 600 inches per minute.
   a. Find the angular speed of the larger pulley.
   b. Find the angular speed of the smaller pulley.

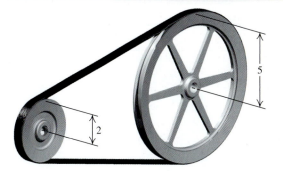

50. Rotation on Earth. Earth rotates on an axis that goes through both the north and south poles. It makes one complete revolution in 24 hours. Assuming that the distance from the axis to any location on the equator is 3960 miles, find the linear speed (in miles per hour) of a location on the equator.

51. Rotation around the sun. The earth has a nearly circular orbit around the sun. If the earth is 93,000,000 miles from the sun and completes its orbit in 365 days, find the linear velocity of the earth in miles per hour.

52. Spacecraft orbit. A NASA spacecraft has a circular orbit around Mars about 400 km above the surface of Mars. If it takes two hours to complete one orbit and the radius of Mars is 6780 km, find the linear speed of the spacecraft.

53. Satellite orbit. A geostationary satellite has a circular orbit 36,000 km above Earth's surface. It takes 24 hours for the satellite to complete its orbit, appearing to be stationary above a fixed location on Earth. Assuming that the radius of Earth is 6400 km, find the linear speed of the satellite.

54. Bicycle sprockets. The figure shows the rear wheel, pedal sprocket, and wheel sprocket system for a bicycle. The angular speed of the pedal sprocket is 65 radians per minute. Assuming that the diameter of the wheel is 28 inches and the diameter of the wheel and pedal sprockets are 3.5 inches and 7 inches, respectively, find
   a. the linear speed of a point on the chain.
   b. the angular speed of the wheel sprocket.
   c. the linear speed of the bicycle.

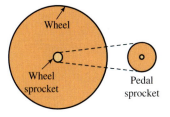

C EXERCISES Beyond the Basics

In Exercises 55 and 56, use 3960 miles for the radius of the earth.

55. Find the linear speed of any location on Earth with north latitude 30°. ($\theta = 30°$ in the figure.)

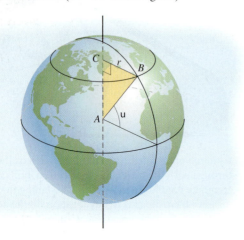

56. Find the linear speed of any location on Earth with north latitude 45°. ($\theta = 45°$ in the figure.)

57. Two pulleys are connected by a belt (see the figure) so that when one pulley rotates, the linear speeds of the belt and both pulleys are the same. Suppose the radius of the smaller pulley is r and the radius of the larger pulley is r_1. Assuming that the angular speed of the smaller pulley is ω and the angular speed of the larger pulley is ω_1, show that $\dfrac{r}{\omega_1} = \dfrac{r_1}{\omega}$.

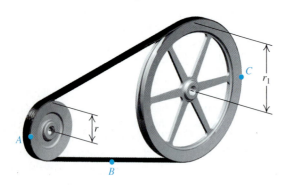

58. In Exercise 57, let $r = 6$ inches and $r_1 = 8$ inches. Assuming that the point B in the figure in Exercise 57 has a velocity of 88 feet per second, find
  a. the angular and the linear velocity of point A.
  b. the angular and the linear velocity of point C.

59. Show that if the linear speed of a point on a rotating circular disk of radius r is v, then the linear speed of the midpoint on a radius is $\dfrac{1}{2}v$.

60. A gear train is frequently used in all-terrain vehicles and other devices where a rapidly rotating device drives something that rotates more slowly. The values of the radii needed to answer each question are given in the figure. Gear 1 is rotating at 60 revolutions per second. Gear 1 turns Gear 2, which shares an axle with Gear 3, and Gear 3 turns Gear 4.
  a. Find the linear and angular speed of points on the rim of Gear 2.
  b. Find the linear and angular speed of points on the rim of Gear 3.
  c. Find the linear and angular speed of points on the rim of Gear 4.
  d. The *reduction ratio* is the ratio of the angular speed of the fastest gear to the angular speed of the slowest gear. Find the reduction ratio of this gear train.

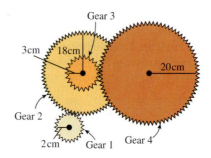

REVIEW

Definitions, Concepts, and Formulas	**Examples and Illustrations**

3.1 Radian Measure

▪ **Central angle** An angle whose vertex is at the center of a circle is called a **central angle**.

A central angle θ intercepts an arc of length 5 cm on a circle with radius 2 cm; so $\theta = \dfrac{5 \text{ cm}}{2 \text{ cm}} = 2.5$ radians.

▪ **Radian measure of a central angle** To find the radian measure of any central angle, divide the length of the intercepted arc by the radius of the circle.

If a central angle θ intercepts an arc of length s on a circle of radius r, then

$$\theta = \frac{s}{r} \text{ radians.}$$

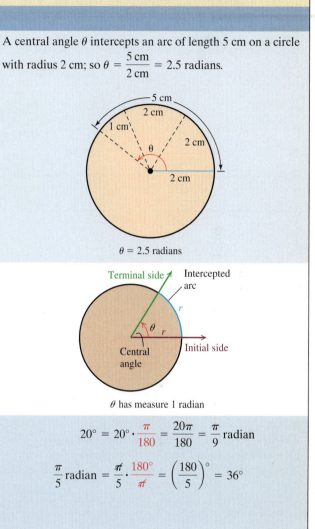

$\theta = 2.5$ radians

▪ **One radian** A central angle formed by rotating the initial ray through an arc of the circle of length equal to the radius of the circle has measure **1 radian**.

θ has measure 1 radian

▪ **Converting between degrees and radians** To convert θ degrees to radians, multiply θ by $\dfrac{\pi}{180}$. That is,

$$\theta° = \theta\left(\frac{\pi}{180}\right) \text{ radians.}$$

To convert θ radians to degrees, multiply θ by $\dfrac{180}{\pi}$. That is, θ radians $= \theta\left(\dfrac{\pi}{180}\right)$ degrees.

$$20° = 20° \cdot \frac{\pi}{180} = \frac{20\pi}{180} = \frac{\pi}{9} \text{ radian}$$

$$\frac{\pi}{5} \text{ radian} = \frac{\pi}{5} \cdot \frac{180°}{\pi} = \left(\frac{180}{5}\right)° = 36°$$

▪ **Fractional multiples of π** Angles that are fractions of a complete rotation are usually expressed in radian measure as fractional multiples of π rather than as decimals.

We write 60° as $\dfrac{\pi}{3}$ radians, which is the exact value, instead of writing the approximation $60° \approx 1.05$ radians.

■ **Degree and radian measure for some commonly used angles** Trigonometric function values can be found for angles regardless of whether the angle is given in degrees or radians. The table gives both degree and radian measures for some commonly used angles, together with the exact value of the sine and cosine of each.

The figure includes the degree and radian measures of some commonly used angles that are fractional multiples of π.

TABLE 3.1 Degree and Radian Measures for Common Angles

θ Degrees	Radians (exact)	Radians (approximate)	$\sin \theta$	$\cos \theta$
0°	0	0	0	1
30°	$\frac{\pi}{6}$	0.52	$\frac{1}{2}$	$\frac{\sqrt{3}}{2}$
45°	$\frac{\pi}{4}$	0.79	$\frac{\sqrt{2}}{2}$	$\frac{\sqrt{2}}{2}$
60°	$\frac{\pi}{3}$	1.05	$\frac{\sqrt{3}}{2}$	$\frac{1}{2}$
90°	$\frac{\pi}{2}$	1.57	1	0
180°	π	3.14	0	−1
270°	$\frac{3\pi}{2}$	4.71	−1	0
360°	2π	6.28	0	1

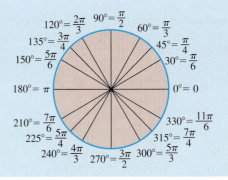

■ **Finding trigonometric function values for angles measured in radians** Compare the angle in question to the quadrantal angles to determine in which quadrant this angle lies. Use this information to find the sign of the function value. Then use the reference angle to find the numerical value.

To find $\sin \frac{5\pi}{3}$, note that $\frac{5\pi}{3} = \frac{10\pi}{6} > \frac{9\pi}{6} = \frac{3\pi}{2}$, which means that $\frac{5\pi}{3}$ is in QIV; so its sine is negative. Its reference angle is $2\pi - \frac{5\pi}{3} = \frac{6\pi}{3} - \frac{5\pi}{3} = \frac{\pi}{3}$. Then

$$\sin \frac{5\pi}{3} = -\sin \frac{\pi}{3} = -\frac{\sqrt{3}}{2}.$$

■ **Locating the terminal side of θ when θ is given in radians** Compare the given radian measure to the radian measures of the quadrantal angles to determine in which quadrant this angle lies.

For $\theta = 5.47$, we note that $4.71 < 5.47 < 6.28$, and 4.71 and 6.28 are the approximate radian measures for 270° and 360°; therefore, θ lies in QIV.

3.2 Applications of Radian Measure

ARC LENGTH FORMULA

$s = r\theta$, θ in radians

To find the length of the arc intercepted by a central angle with measure 140° in a circle of radius 36 cm, first convert 140° to radians.

$$140° = 140°\left(\frac{\pi}{180°}\right) = \frac{7\pi}{9} \text{ radians}$$

It is a formula for the length s of the arc intercepted by a central angle with radian measure θ in a circle of radius r.

Then

$$s = r\theta = 36\left(\frac{7\pi}{9}\right) = 28\pi \text{ cm.}$$

- **Area of a sector** A **sector** of a circle is a region bounded by the two sides of a central angle and the intercepted arc.

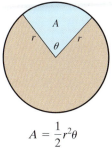

AREA OF A SECTOR

The area of a sector of a circle of radius r formed by a central angle with radian measure θ is

$$A = \frac{1}{2}r^2\theta.$$

$$A = \frac{1}{2}r^2\theta$$

To find the area of a sector of the circle of radius 8 inches formed by an angle of 60°, we convert 60° to radians.

Because $60° = \dfrac{\pi}{3}$, we have $\theta = \dfrac{\pi}{3}$ and $r = 8$. Then

$$A = \frac{1}{2}r^2\theta = \frac{1}{2}8^2\left(\frac{\pi}{3}\right) = \frac{32\pi}{3} \approx 33.51 \text{ in}^2.$$

3.3 The Unit Circle and Circular Functions

- **The unit circle** The **unit circle** is a circle of radius 1 with center $(0,0)$. Its equation is $x^2 + y^2 = 1$.

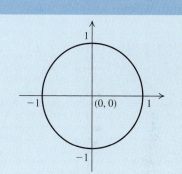

Unit circle; $x^2 + y^2 = 1$

- **Circular functions** If s is any positive real number, we measure off an arc of length s beginning on the unit circle at $(1,0)$ and ending at the point (x, y) on the unit circle. Then the point (x, y) is on the terminal ray of the central angle with radian measure θ that intercepts this arc, as shown in the figure. Because the distance from the origin to (x, y) is $r = 1$, we have

$$\cos\theta = \frac{x}{r} = \frac{x}{1} = x \quad \text{and} \quad \sin\theta = \frac{y}{r} = \frac{y}{1} = y.$$

Because $\theta = s$, we can write $\cos s = x$ and $\sin s = y$ and think of these functions as functions of the arc length, s, a real number. If s is a negative real number, we measure off an arc of length $|s|$ in a clockwise direction. Again, $\theta = s$, and we proceed as before. If $s = 0$, we let $(x, y) = (1, 0)$. All six trigonometric functions can now be defined as functions of numbers associated with arc length on a unit circle. When this is done, they are called **circular functions**.

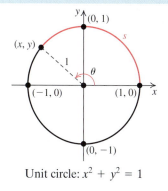

Unit circle: $x^2 + y^2 = 1$

If s is a real number and (x, y) is a point on the unit circle as described on page 125, then

$$\cos s = x \qquad\qquad \sin s = y$$

$$\tan s = \frac{y}{x} \quad (x \neq 0) \qquad \cot s = \frac{x}{y} \ (y \neq 0)$$

$$\sec s = \frac{1}{x} \quad (x \neq 0) \qquad \csc s = \frac{1}{y} \quad (y \neq 0)$$

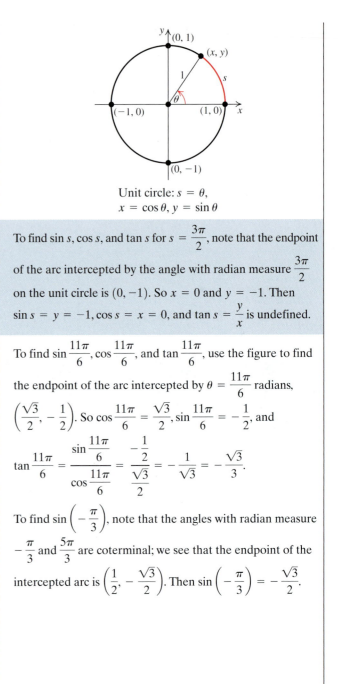

Unit circle: $s = \theta$,
$x = \cos\theta,\ y = \sin\theta$

■ **Using the definition of the circular functions** To apply the circular function definitions, you must find or be given the endpoint (x, y) of the arc intercepted by the central angle of radian measure s on the unit circle.

To find $\sin s$, $\cos s$, and $\tan s$ for $s = \dfrac{3\pi}{2}$, note that the endpoint of the arc intercepted by the angle with radian measure $\dfrac{3\pi}{2}$ on the unit circle is $(0, -1)$. So $x = 0$ and $y = -1$. Then $\sin s = y = -1$, $\cos s = x = 0$, and $\tan s = \dfrac{y}{x}$ is undefined.

■ **Degrees, radians, and ordered pairs** The figure below provides a valuable connection between degree measure, radian measure, and points on the unit circle.

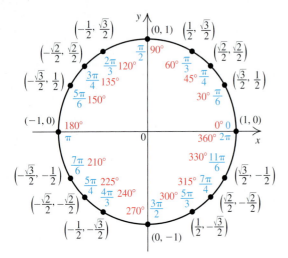

To find $\sin\dfrac{11\pi}{6}$, $\cos\dfrac{11\pi}{6}$, and $\tan\dfrac{11\pi}{6}$, use the figure to find the endpoint of the arc intercepted by $\theta = \dfrac{11\pi}{6}$ radians, $\left(\dfrac{\sqrt{3}}{2}, -\dfrac{1}{2}\right)$. So $\cos\dfrac{11\pi}{6} = \dfrac{\sqrt{3}}{2}$, $\sin\dfrac{11\pi}{6} = -\dfrac{1}{2}$, and

$$\tan\frac{11\pi}{6} = \frac{\sin\dfrac{11\pi}{6}}{\cos\dfrac{11\pi}{6}} = \frac{-\dfrac{1}{2}}{\dfrac{\sqrt{3}}{2}} = -\frac{1}{\sqrt{3}} = -\frac{\sqrt{3}}{3}.$$

To find $\sin\left(-\dfrac{\pi}{3}\right)$, note that the angles with radian measure $-\dfrac{\pi}{3}$ and $\dfrac{5\pi}{3}$ are coterminal; we see that the endpoint of the intercepted arc is $\left(\dfrac{1}{2}, -\dfrac{\sqrt{3}}{2}\right)$. Then $\sin\left(-\dfrac{\pi}{3}\right) = -\dfrac{\sqrt{3}}{2}$.

You also can use the figure to find coterminal angles that have the same functional values.

■ **Domains of the circular functions** If s is any real number, the arc intercepted by the central angle on the unit circle with radian measure s determines a point (x, y) on the unit circle. Because $\cos s = x$ and $\sin s = y$, both functions are defined at s; so the domain of these functions is the set of all real numbers. In the definitions of the other four trigonometric functions, either x or y occurs in the denominator. This restricts the domains of those functions.

The functions $\tan s = \dfrac{y}{x}$ and $\sec x = \dfrac{1}{x}$ are not defined for $x = 0$. This occurs only at the points $(0, 1)$ and $(0, -1)$, when $s = \dfrac{\pi}{2},\ -\dfrac{\pi}{2},\ \dfrac{3\pi}{2},\ -\dfrac{3\pi}{2},\ \dfrac{5\pi}{2},\ -\dfrac{5\pi}{2}$, and so on. These values can be described as "odd integer multiples of $\dfrac{\pi}{2}$," which can be written $(2n + 1)\dfrac{\pi}{2}$. So the domain of the tangent and secant

<table>
<tr><th colspan="2" align="center">DOMAINS OF THE CIRCULAR FUNCTIONS</th></tr>
<tr><td>$\sin s, \cos s$</td><td>All real numbers; $(-\infty, \infty)$</td></tr>
<tr><td>$\tan s, \sec s$</td><td>All real numbers s; $s \neq (2n + 1)\dfrac{\pi}{2}$, n any integer</td></tr>
<tr><td>$\cot s, \csc s$</td><td>All real numbers s; $s \neq n\pi$, n any integer</td></tr>
</table>

functions is all real numbers s satisfying $s \neq (2n + 1)\dfrac{\pi}{2}$, n any integer.

Similarly, because $\cot s = \dfrac{x}{y}$ and $\csc s = \dfrac{1}{y}$, these functions are not defined when $y = 0$, corresponding to the points $(1, 0)$ and $(-1, 0)$. This occurs when $s = \pi, -\pi, 2\pi, -2\pi, 3\pi, -3\pi$, and so on. To eliminate values of s that result in $y = 0$, the domain for these functions is the set of all real numbers s satisfying $s \neq n\pi$, n any integer.

- **Finding numbers having a specific circular function value** To find the number in the interval $\left[0, \dfrac{\pi}{2}\right]$ that has a specific circular function value, your calculator must be in Radian mode.

When a nonnegative number is input, the calculator keys $\boxed{\text{COS}^{-1}}$, $\boxed{\text{SIN}^{-1}}$, and $\boxed{\text{TAN}^{-1}}$ display approximate values for numbers in $\left[0, \dfrac{\pi}{2}\right]$ with the input value of cosine, sine, and tangent, respectively.

To find an approximate value for s in $\left[0, \dfrac{\pi}{2}\right]$ with $\cos s = 0.7771$, put your calculator in Radian mode, use the $\boxed{\text{COS}^{-1}}$ key to find $s = \cos^{-1}(0.7771) \approx 0.6808$.

3.4 Angular and Linear Speed

- **Angular and linear speed** Whenever an object travels along any path, the **linear speed** of the object over a given distance is the distance traveled divided by the time it took to travel that distance. When the path traveled is circular, the idea of *angular speed* can also be introduced.

To find the angular speed ω of a point on a circle that rotates through $\dfrac{3\pi}{2}$ radians in six seconds, use the formula $\omega = \dfrac{\theta}{t}$.

We have $\omega = \dfrac{\theta}{t} = \dfrac{\dfrac{3\pi}{2}}{6} = \dfrac{3\pi}{12} = \dfrac{\pi}{4}$ radians per per second.

LINEAR AND ANGULAR SPEED

Suppose an object travels around a circle of radius r. If the object travels through an angle of θ radians and an arc of length s in time t, then

1. $v = \dfrac{s}{t}$ is the (average) **linear speed** of the object.

2. $\omega = \dfrac{\theta}{t}$ is the (average) **angular speed** of the object.

- **Relationship between angular and linear speed**

RELATING ANGULAR AND LINEAR SPEED

$$v = r\omega$$

Linear Speed   Angular Speed

You can find the angular speed from this equation by dividing both sides by r to get $\omega = \dfrac{v}{r}$.

To find the linear speed of an object traveling on a circular path with radius 3 feet at an angular speed of $\omega = \dfrac{\pi}{9}$ radians per second, use the formula $v = r\omega$. Then

$$v = r\omega = 3\left(\dfrac{\pi}{9}\right) = \dfrac{\pi}{3}, \text{ or } \approx 1.05 \text{ feet per second.}$$

If an object is traveling on a circular path with radius 5 meters at a linear speed of 40 m/sec, its angular speed is

$$\omega = \dfrac{v}{r} = \dfrac{40}{5} = 8 \text{ radians per second.}$$

REVIEW EXERCISES

In Exercises 1–3, find the radian measure of the central angle θ in a circle of radius r assuming that θ intercepts an arc of length s.

1. $r = 0.5$ cm, $s = 14$ cm

2. $r = 2$ m, $s = 9$ m

3. $r = 10$ ft, $s = 0.8$ ft

In Exercises 4–6, convert each measure from degrees to radians. Express your answer as a multiple of π.

4. $120°$ 5. $210°$ 6. $-30°$

In Exercises 7–9, convert each measure from radians to degrees.

7. $\dfrac{5\pi}{4}$ 8. $\dfrac{7\pi}{2}$ 9. $-\dfrac{11\pi}{6}$

In Exercises 10 and 11, convert each measure from degrees to radians. Round your answers to two decimal places.

10. $71°$ 11. $247.51°$

In Exercises 12 and 13, convert each measure from radians to degrees. Round your answers to one decimal place.

12. 4.26 13. -7.2308

In Exercises 14–16, find the exact value of each expression.

14. $\cos \dfrac{7\pi}{6}$ 15. $\tan \dfrac{5\pi}{3}$ 16. $\sin\left(-\dfrac{5\pi}{4}\right)$

17. **Wheel slippage.** A tractor rolls backward so that its wheels turn a quarter of a revolution. If the tires have a radius of 28 inches, how many inches has the tractor moved?

18. **Angles on a clock.** What is the radian measure of the smaller central angle made by the hands of a clock at 5:00? Express your answer as a rational multiple of π.

In Exercises 19–21, find the length of the arc intercepted by a central angle θ in a circle of radius r.

19. $\theta = 5, r = 4$ cm

20. $\theta = \dfrac{\pi}{4}, r = 12$ ft

21. $\theta = 60°, r = 3.47$ m

In Exercises 22–24, find the radius of a circle where a central angle θ intercepts an arc of length s.

22. $\theta = 3.1, s = 12.4$ in.

23. $\theta = \dfrac{\pi}{3}, s = 9\pi$ ft

24. $\theta = 240°, s = 3\pi$ m

In Exercises 25–27, find the area of a sector of a circle with radius r and central angle θ.

25. $\theta = 2.9, r = 4$ ft

26. $\theta = \dfrac{3\pi}{4}, r = 8.4$ m

27. $\theta = 73°, r = 27.0$ mi

28. **Arc length.** Find the length of the arc intercepted by a central angle of $\dfrac{2\pi}{3}$ radians on a circle of radius 4.7 feet.

29. **Arc length.** Find the length of the arc intercepted by a central angle of $120°$ on a circle of radius 8.5 inches.

30. **Area of a sector.** Find the area of the sector formed by a central angle of $\dfrac{3\pi}{4}$ radians in a circle of radius 32.4 cm.

31. **Area of a sector.** Find the area of the sector formed by a central angle of $240°$ in a circle of radius 0.63 m.

32. **Distance between cities.** New Orleans, Louisiana, is due south of Dubuque, Iowa. Find the distance between New Orleans (north latitude 29°59′ N) and Dubuque (north latitude 42°31′ N). Use 3960 miles as the value of the radius of Earth.

In Exercises 33–35, use the unit circle figure and the definition of the circular functions to find the exact values for sin s, cos s, and tan s.

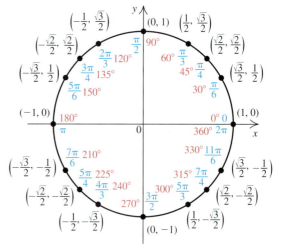

Unit Circle: degrees, radians, ordered pairs

33. $s = \dfrac{2\pi}{3}$ 34. $s = \dfrac{5\pi}{3}$

35. $s = -\dfrac{4\pi}{3}$

In Exercises 36–38, find the exact circular function value.

36. $\sin \dfrac{4\pi}{3}$ 37. $\cot \dfrac{3\pi}{4}$

38. $\cos\left(-\dfrac{13\pi}{6}\right)$

In Exercises 39–41, use a calculator to approximate each circular function value (rounded to four decimal places).

39. cos 7.14   **40.** tan 2.08

41. sin (−6.85)

In Exercises 42–44, use a calculator to find an approximate value for s in $\left[0, \dfrac{\pi}{2} \right]$ having each circular function value.

42. sin s = 0.7275

43. cos s = 0.3886

44. cot s = 2.8443

In Exercises 45 and 46, state which circular functions are undefined for the given value of s.

45. 5π

46. $-\dfrac{3\pi}{2}$

In Exercises 47 and 48, do not use a calculator. Use the unit circle figure to find an exact value of s in the specified interval with the given circular function value.

47. $\cos s = -\dfrac{1}{2}, \left[\dfrac{\pi}{2}, \pi \right]$

48. $\tan s = -\sqrt{3}, \left[\dfrac{3\pi}{2}, 2\pi \right]$

In Exercises 49–51, find the linear speed of a point traveling a circular path, where s is distance traveled in time t.

49. $s = 5$ ft, $t = 2$ sec

50. $s = 15$ m, $t = 3$ sec

51. $s = 150$ yd, $t = 8$ sec

In Exercises 52–54, find the angular speed of a point traveling through θ radians on a circle of radius r.

52. $\theta = \dfrac{\pi}{3}, t = 6$ sec

53. $\theta = 16, t = 5$ min

54. $\theta = \dfrac{16\pi}{5}, t = 8$ hr

In Exercises 55–57, find the distance traveled by a point P traveling on a circle of radius r by finding θ and then using the arc length formula, $s = r\theta$. Each value of ω is in radians/sec.

55. $r = 3$ in., $\omega = 2, t = 4$ sec

56. $r = 1.8$ m, $\omega = \dfrac{\pi}{3}, t = 10$ min

57. $r = 12$ ft, $\omega = \dfrac{5\pi}{4}, t = 1.2$ hr

58. Speed of a truck. The radius of a truck's wheels is 18 inches. Assuming that the wheels are turning through 500 revolutions per minute, find the speed of the truck (in feet per minute).

59. Merry-go-round speed. A merry-go-round has a radius of 15 feet. It takes 40 seconds to complete one revolution. What is the linear speed of a reflector on the rim of the merry-go-round (in feet per minute)?

60. Degrees on a clock. The minute hand of a clock is 1.2 inches long. How far does its tip travel in 50 minutes?

61. Distance on earth. Reno, Nevada, is 416 miles due north of Los Angles, Ca. Find the difference in latitudes of these two cities.

62. Gold jewelry. A gold pendant in the shape of a circular sector has sides of length 1.5 inches with an included angle of 40°. Find the surface area of one side of the pendant.

63. Blood pressure. Maurice's blood pressure (in millimeters of mercury) while resting is given by the function $R(t) = 20 \sin (2\pi t) + 110$, where t is time in seconds. Find his blood pressure after
   a. 1 second.
   b. 1.3 seconds.

64. Ferris wheel motion. A Ferris wheel in Paris, France, has a diameter of approximately 64 meters. Assume that it takes 80 seconds for the Ferris wheel to make one complete revolution.
   a. Find the angular speed of a point on the outside edge of the Ferris wheel. Round your answer to two decimal places.
   b. Find the linear speed of the Ferris wheel in meters per second. Round your answer to two decimal places.

65. Swinging pendulum. The pendulum of a clock, 30 inches long, swings through an arc of 21 degrees from its resting position. Find the distance that a point half the distance from the tip of the pendulum travels in one swing.

66. Earth's rotation. Earth rotates about its axis (approximately) once every 24 hours. Assuming that the radius of the earth is 3960 mi, find the (approximate) linear speed of a point on the equator of the earth.

CHAPTER TEST

1. Find the radian measure of a central angle in a circle of radius 2 cm that intercepts an arc of length 9 cm.

In Exercises 2–4, convert each degree measure to radians.

2. 160°

3. −30°

4. 7° (to four decimal places)

In Exercises 5–7, convert each radian measure to degrees.

5. $\dfrac{7\pi}{10}$

6. $-\dfrac{5\pi}{6}$

7. 2.8 (to three decimal places)

In Exercises 8–13, find the exact value of each expression.

8. $\sin\dfrac{5\pi}{4}$

9. $\cos\dfrac{11\pi}{6}$

10. $\tan\dfrac{7\pi}{6}$

11. $\sec\dfrac{7\pi}{4}$

12. $\tan(-\pi)$

13. $\cos\left(-\dfrac{5\pi}{6}\right)$

14. Find the length of the arc intercepted by a central angle of 120° in a circle of radius 10 inches.

Use the figure for Exercises 15 and 16.

15. The tip of a speedometer needle 2.8 inches long travels through an arc of length 4.71 inches. Through what angle (to the nearest degree) does the speedometer needle rotate?

16. It takes ten seconds for the speedometer needle to rotate through an angle of $\dfrac{6\pi}{14}$ radians. If the needle is 2.8 inches long, what is the linear speed of a point on the tip of the needle?

17. Find the area of a sector of a circle of radius 6 inches formed by a central angle of 45°.

18. Which two circular functions are undefined for odd integer multiples of $\dfrac{\pi}{2}$?

19. Use a calculator to find an approximate value of s in $\left[0, \dfrac{\pi}{2}\right]$ for which $\sin s = 0.8205$.

20. Find an exact value for s in $\left[\dfrac{\pi}{2}, \pi\right]$ for which $\tan s = -1$.

CHAPTER

4 Graphs of the Circular Functions

BIORHYTHMS

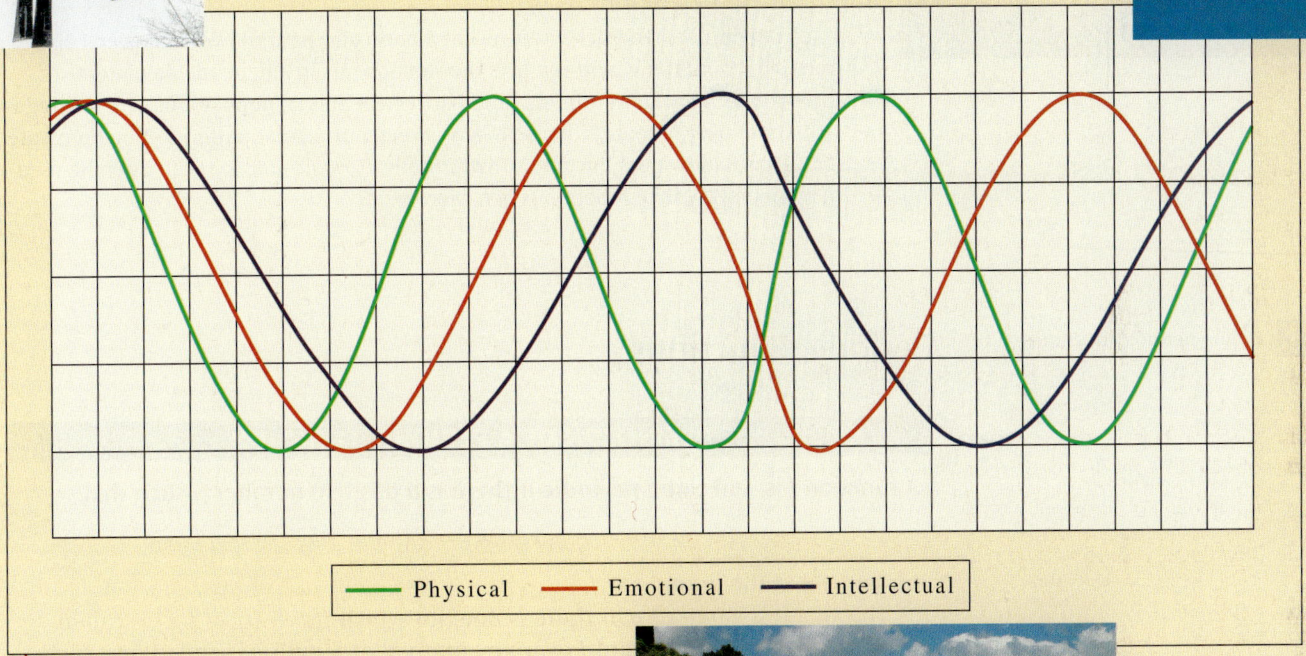
Physical
Emotional
Intellectual

TOPICS

4.1 Graphs of the Circular Functions

4.2 Amplitude and Period

4.3 Translations of the Graphs of Circular Functions

Few topics in mathematics track the pulses of life more faithfully than the trigonometric functions. Seasons of the year, biorhythms, tide patterns, and weather are just a few of the myriad natural phenomena whose behavior is reflected by these remarkable functions. In this chapter, we learn about these surprising relationships.

Graphs of the Circular Functions

Before Starting this Section, Review	Objectives
1. Equation of a circle (Appendix)	**1** Define periodic functions.
2. Transformations of functions (Appendix)	**2** Graph the sine, cosine, and tangent functions.
3. Unit circle definitions of the sine and cosine (Section 3.3)	**3** Graph the cosecant, secant, and cotangent functions.

Many phenomena and behaviors repeat a particular pattern over and over. For example, no matter where you live, the sun appears in a dependable pattern throughout the year. Naturalists find that certain animal populations vary in a regular pattern over time. Lighthouse beams sweep out regular patterns. Blood pressure for a typical individual fluctuates rhythmically. *Periodic functions* can often be used to model this type of repetitious behavior. ■

1 Define periodic functions.

Periodic Functions

DEFINITION OF A PERIODIC FUNCTION

A function f is said to be **periodic** if there is a positive number p such that

$$f(x + p) = f(x)$$

for every x in the domain of f.

The smallest value of p (if there is one) for which $f(x + p) = f(x)$ is called the **period** of f. The graph of f over any interval of length p is called one **cycle** of the graph.

Figure 4.1 shows examples of periodic functions.

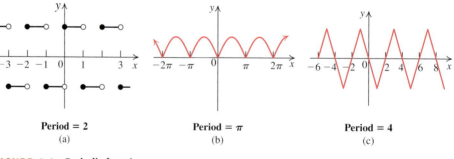

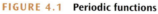

Period = 2	Period = π	Period = 4
(a)	(b)	(c)

FIGURE 4.1 Periodic functions

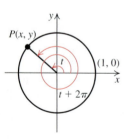

FIGURE 4.2

Let $P(x, y)$ be a point on the unit circle that corresponds to angle t, measured in radians. If we add 2π to t, we obtain the same point P on the unit circle. See Figure 4.2. Then $\sin(t + 2\pi) = \sin t = y$ and $\cos(t + 2\pi) = \cos t = x$. Therefore, $\sin t$ and $\cos t$ are periodic functions. The period for each of the sine and cosine functions is 2π. (See Exercise 61.)

> **PERIOD OF THE SINE AND COSINE FUNCTIONS**
>
> For every real number t,
>
> $$\sin (t + 2\pi) = \sin t \quad \text{and} \quad \cos (t + 2\pi) = \cos t.$$
>
> The sine and cosine functions are periodic with **period** 2π.

EXAMPLE 1   **Periodicity of the Tangent Function**

Show that $\tan t$ is periodic.

SOLUTION

In Figure 4.3, we have

$$\tan (t + \pi) = \frac{-y}{-x} = \frac{y}{x} = \tan t$$

for any angle t, measured in radians.

    Therefore, $\tan t$ is a periodic function. The period of the tangent function is π. (See Exercise 63.)   ■ ■ ■

Practice Problem 1   Show that $\cot t$ is periodic.   ■

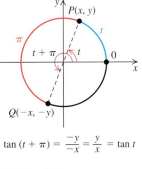

$$\tan (t + \pi) = \frac{-y}{-x} = \frac{y}{x} = \tan t$$

FIGURE 4.3

> **PERIOD OF THE TANGENT FUNCTION**
>
> For every number t in the domain of $\tan t$,
>
> $$\tan (t + \pi) = \tan t.$$
>
> The tangent function is periodic with **period** π.

2   Graph the sine, cosine, and tangent functions.

Graphs of Circular Functions

To graph the circular functions on an xy-coordinate system, we use x as the independent variable and y as the dependent variable; so we write $y = \sin x$ rather than $y = \sin t$. We can use calculus to show that the graphs of the circular functions are continuous on their domains. This means that to obtain the graph of a circular function f, we plot several ordered pairs $(x, f(x))$ and then join them by a smooth curve on the domain of f.

Graphing the Sine Function   To sketch the graph of $y = \sin x$ for $0 \le x \le 2\pi$, we use Table 4.1. This table of approximate values for $y = \sin x$ uses common values of x. That is, x is the radian measure of common angles.

TABLE 4.1

x	0	$\dfrac{\pi}{6}$	$\dfrac{\pi}{4}$	$\dfrac{\pi}{3}$	$\dfrac{\pi}{2}$	$\dfrac{2\pi}{3}$	$\dfrac{3\pi}{4}$	$\dfrac{5\pi}{6}$	π	$\dfrac{7\pi}{6}$	$\dfrac{5\pi}{6}$	$\dfrac{4\pi}{3}$	$\dfrac{3\pi}{2}$	$\dfrac{5\pi}{3}$	$\dfrac{7\pi}{4}$
$y = \sin x$	0	0.5	0.71	0.87	1	0.87	0.71	0.5	0	-0.5	-0.71	-0.87	-1	-0.87	-0.71

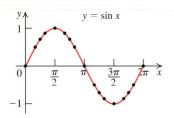

FIGURE 4.4 $y = \sin x, 0 \le x \le 2\pi$

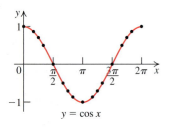

FIGURE 4.5 Graph of $y = \sin x$

Connecting the points $(x, \sin x)$ obtained from Table 4.1 with a smooth curve gives us the graph of $y = \sin x, 0 \le x \le 2\pi$. See Figure 4.4. The figure shows one cycle of the graph of $y = \sin x$.

Because the input, x, for $y = \sin x$ can be any real number, the domain of the sine function is $(-\infty, \infty)$. Since the sine function is periodic, the points

$$(x, \sin x) \text{ and } (x + 2n\pi, \sin(x + 2n\pi)) = (x + 2n\pi, \sin x)$$

on the graph have the same second coordinate for any integer n. Therefore, we may sketch the complete graph of $y = \sin x$ by extending the graph in Figure 4.4 indefinitely to the left and to the right in successive intervals of length 2π. The graph is called a **sine curve**, **sine wave**, or **sinusoid**. See Figure 4.5. A portion of this graph over any interval of length 2π is a cycle of the graph of $y = \sin x$.

Graphing the Cosine Function To sketch the graph of $y = \cos x, 0 \le x \le 2\pi$, we use Table 4.2.

TABLE 4.2

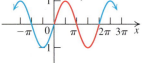

x	0	$\dfrac{\pi}{6}$	$\dfrac{\pi}{4}$	$\dfrac{\pi}{3}$	$\dfrac{\pi}{2}$	$\dfrac{2\pi}{3}$	$\dfrac{3\pi}{4}$	$\dfrac{5\pi}{6}$	π	$\dfrac{7\pi}{6}$	$\dfrac{5\pi}{6}$	$\dfrac{4\pi}{3}$	$\dfrac{3\pi}{2}$	$\dfrac{5\pi}{3}$	$\dfrac{7\pi}{4}$	$\dfrac{11\pi}{6}$	2π
$y = \cos x$	1	0.87	0.71	0.5	0	-0.5	-0.71	-0.87	-1	-0.87	-0.71	-0.5	0	0.5	0.71	0.87	1

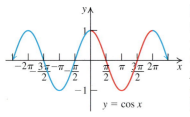

FIGURE 4.6 $y = \cos x, 0 \le x \le 2\pi$

Connecting the points $(x, \cos x)$ obtained from Table 4.2 with a smooth curve gives the graph of $y = \cos x, 0 \le x \le 2\pi$. See Figure 4.6.

As with the sine function, there is no restriction on the values of x for $y = \cos x$, so the domain of the cosine function is $(-\infty, \infty)$. The complete graph of $y = \cos x$ can be drawn by extending the graph in Figure 4.6 indefinitely to the left and right in successive intervals of length 2π. See Figure 4.7.

Using the Unit Circle Definition

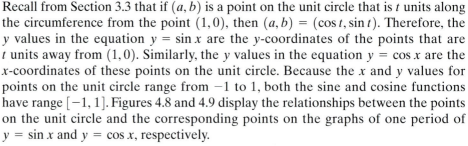

FIGURE 4.7 Graph of $y = \cos x$

Recall from Section 3.3 that if (a, b) is a point on the unit circle that is t units along the circumference from the point $(1, 0)$, then $(a, b) = (\cos t, \sin t)$. Therefore, the y values in the equation $y = \sin x$ are the y-coordinates of the points that are t units away from $(1, 0)$. Similarly, the y values in the equation $y = \cos x$ are the x-coordinates of these points on the unit circle. Because the x and y values for points on the unit circle range from -1 to 1, both the sine and cosine functions have range $[-1, 1]$. Figures 4.8 and 4.9 display the relationships between the points on the unit circle and the corresponding points on the graphs of one period of $y = \sin x$ and $y = \cos x$, respectively.

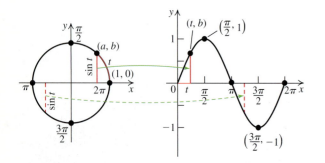

FIGURE 4.8 $y = \sin x, 0 \le x \le 2\pi$

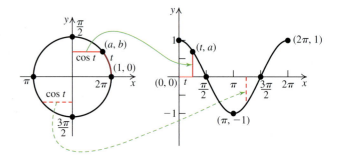

FIGURE 4.9 $y = \cos x, 0 \le x \le 2\pi$

Graphing the Tangent Function The tangent function differs from the sine and cosine functions in three significant ways.

1. The tangent function has period π.

2. Because $\tan x = \dfrac{\sin x}{\cos x}$, we have $\tan x = 0$ when $\sin x = 0$. So $\tan x = 0$ at

$x = 0, \pm\pi, \pm 2\pi, \dots$. Also, $\tan x$ is undefined when $\cos x = 0$. So $\tan x$ is

undefined at $x = \pm\dfrac{\pi}{2}, \pm\dfrac{3\pi}{2}, \pm\dfrac{5\pi}{2}, \dots$.

3. The tangent function has no minimum and maximum y-values. Another way to say this is that the range of $y = \tan x$ is $(-\infty, \infty)$.

Note that $\tan(-x) = \dfrac{\sin(-x)}{\cos(-x)} = \dfrac{-\sin x}{\cos x} = -\tan x$. Therefore, the tangent function is an odd function, so its graph is symmetric with respect to the origin.

To graph the tangent function, we use the approximate values in Table 4.3.

TABLE 4.3

x	0	$\dfrac{\pi}{6}$	$\dfrac{\pi}{4}$	$\dfrac{\pi}{3}$	$\dfrac{7\pi}{18}$	$\dfrac{4\pi}{9}$	$\dfrac{17\pi}{36}$
$y = \tan x$	0	0.6	1	1.7	2.7	5.7	11.4

As x approaches $\dfrac{\pi}{2}$, the values of $\tan x$ continue to increase; in fact, they increase indefinitely. The decimal value of $\dfrac{\pi}{2}$ is approximately 1.5707963. When $x = \dfrac{89\pi}{180} \approx 1.55$, $\tan x > 57$; when $x = 1.57$, $\tan x > 1255$; and when $x = 1.5707$, $\tan x > 10{,}000$. The graph of $y = \tan x$ approaches, but never touches, the vertical line $x = \dfrac{\pi}{2}$. See Figure 4.10. This line is called a *vertical asymptote*.

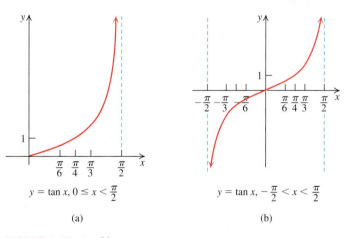

$y = \tan x,\ 0 \le x < \dfrac{\pi}{2}$

(a)

$y = \tan x,\ -\dfrac{\pi}{2} < x < \dfrac{\pi}{2}$

(b)

FIGURE 4.10 Graphing $y = \tan x$

We can extend the graph of $y = \tan x$ to the interval $\left(-\dfrac{\pi}{2}, \dfrac{\pi}{2}\right)$ by using the fact that the graph is symmetric with respect to the origin. See Figure 4.10(b).

Because the period of the tangent function is π and we have graphed $y = \tan x$ over an interval of length π, we can draw the complete graph of $y = \tan x$ by repeating the graph in Figure 4.10(b) indefinitely to the left and right over intervals of length π. Figure 4.11 shows three cycles of the graph of $y = \tan x$.

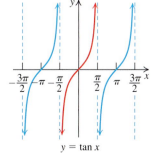

$y = \tan x$

FIGURE 4.11 Graph of $y = \tan x$

From the graphs of the sine, cosine, and tangent functions, we summarize the following useful properties.

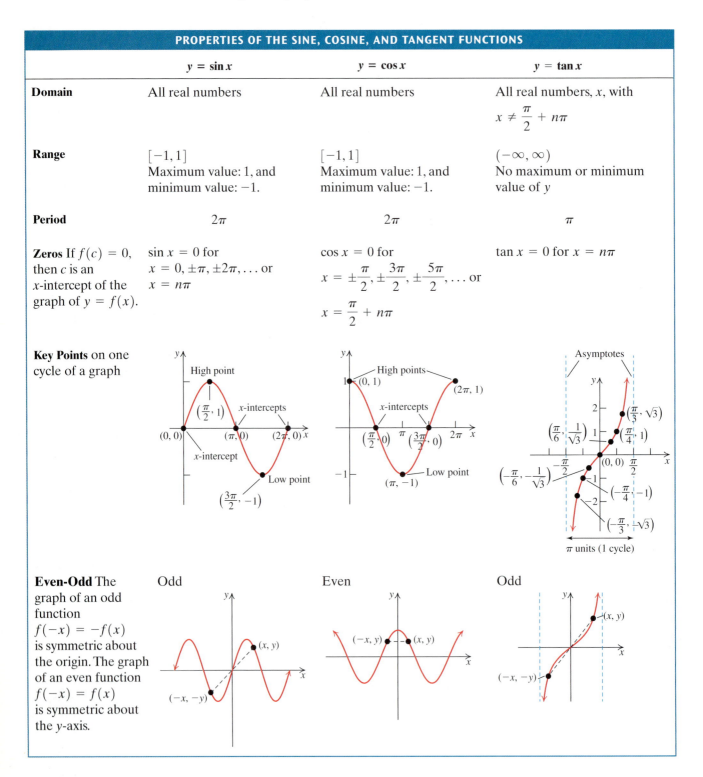

PROPERTIES OF THE SINE, COSINE, AND TANGENT FUNCTIONS		
	$y = \sin x$	$y = \cos x$	$y = \tan x$

Domain

$y = \sin x$: All real numbers

$y = \cos x$: All real numbers

$y = \tan x$: All real numbers, x, with $x \neq \dfrac{\pi}{2} + n\pi$

Range

$y = \sin x$: $[-1, 1]$ Maximum value: 1, and minimum value: -1.

$y = \cos x$: $[-1, 1]$ Maximum value: 1, and minimum value: -1.

$y = \tan x$: $(-\infty, \infty)$ No maximum or minimum value of y

Period

$y = \sin x$: 2π

$y = \cos x$: 2π

$y = \tan x$: π

Zeros If $f(c) = 0$, then c is an x-intercept of the graph of $y = f(x)$.

$y = \sin x$: $\sin x = 0$ for $x = 0, \pm\pi, \pm 2\pi, \ldots$ or $x = n\pi$

$y = \cos x$: $\cos x = 0$ for $x = \pm\dfrac{\pi}{2}, \pm\dfrac{3\pi}{2}, \pm\dfrac{5\pi}{2}, \ldots$ or $x = \dfrac{\pi}{2} + n\pi$

$y = \tan x$: $\tan x = 0$ for $x = n\pi$

Key Points on one cycle of a graph

Even-Odd The graph of an odd function $f(-x) = -f(x)$ is symmetric about the origin. The graph of an even function $f(-x) = f(x)$ is symmetric about the y-axis.

$y = \sin x$: Odd

$y = \cos x$: Even

$y = \tan x$: Odd

3 Graph the cosecant, secant, and cotangent functions.

Graphs of the Reciprocal Functions

The cosecant, secant, and cotangent functions are reciprocals of the sine, cosine, and tangent functions, respectively. We first consider some relationships between the properties of any pair of these cofunctions. We use these relationships to sketch the graph of the reciprocal function of a circular function $g(x)$.

The Graph of the Reciprocal of a Circular Function   Let $f(x)$ be the reciprocal of $g(x)$: $f(x) = \dfrac{1}{g(x)}$, where g is any circular function.

- **Periodicity** If $g(x)$ has period p, then $f(x)$ also has period p.
- **Zeros** If $g(c) = 0$, then $f(c)$ is undefined. So if c is an x-intercept of the graph of g, then the line $x = c$ is a vertical asymptote of the graph of f. Conversely, if $g(d)$ is undefined, then $f(d) = 0$.
- **Even-Odd**
  - **a.** If $g(x)$ is odd, then $f(x)$ is odd.
  - **b.** If $g(x)$ is even, then $f(x)$ is even.
- **Special Values**
  - **a.** If $g(x_1) = 1$, then $f(x_1) = 1$. Both graphs pass through the point $(x_1, 1)$.
  - **b.** If $g(x_2) = -1$, then $f(x_2) = -1$. Both graphs pass through the point $(x_2, -1)$.
- **Sign**
  - **a.** If $g(x) > 0$ on an interval (a, b), then $f(x) > 0$ on the interval (a, b). Both graphs are above the x-axis on the interval (a, b).
  - **b.** If $g(x) < 0$ on an interval (c, d), then $f(x) < 0$ on the interval (c, d). Both graphs are below the x-axis on the interval (c, d).
- **Increasing-Decreasing**
  - **a.** If $g(x)$ is increasing on an interval (a, b), then $f(x)$ is decreasing on the interval (a, b).
  - **b.** If $g(x)$ is decreasing on an interval (c, d), then $f(x)$ is increasing on the interval (c, d).
- **Magnitude**
  - **a.** If $|g(x)|$ is small, then $|f(x)|$ is large.
  - **b.** If $|g(x)|$ is large, then $|f(x)|$ is small. If c is in the domain of f and $|g(x)|$ is large as x approaches c, then $f(c) = 0$.
  - **c.** If $g(c) = 0$, then the line $x = c$ is a vertical asymptote of the graph of f.

In the exercises, you are asked to use the properties of the reciprocal functions to sketch the graphs of the cosecant, secant, and cotangent functions from the graphs of the sine, cosine, and tangent functions. Two or more cycles of these graphs along with their reciprocals are shown in the box on the next page.

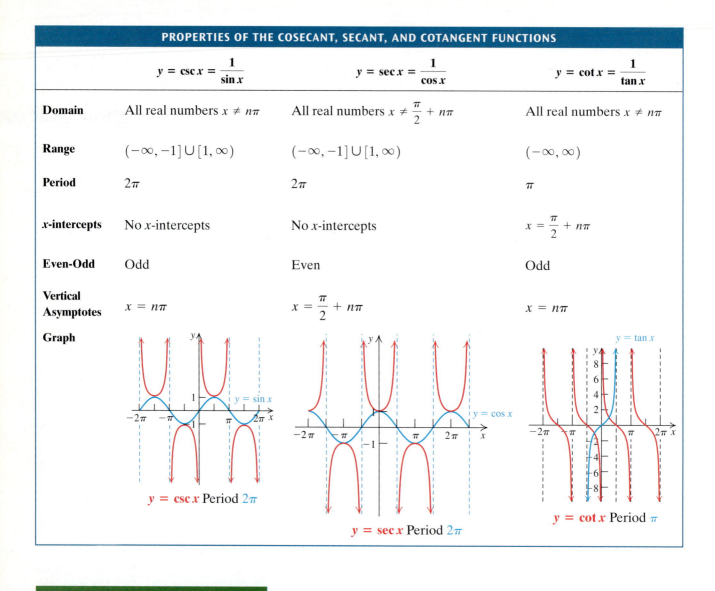

PROPERTIES OF THE COSECANT, SECANT, AND COTANGENT FUNCTIONS		
$y = \csc x = \dfrac{1}{\sin x}$	$y = \sec x = \dfrac{1}{\cos x}$	$y = \cot x = \dfrac{1}{\tan x}$
Domain All real numbers $x \neq n\pi$	All real numbers $x \neq \dfrac{\pi}{2} + n\pi$	All real numbers $x \neq n\pi$
Range $(-\infty, -1] \cup [1, \infty)$	$(-\infty, -1] \cup [1, \infty)$	$(-\infty, \infty)$
Period 2π	2π	π
x-intercepts No x-intercepts	No x-intercepts	$x = \dfrac{\pi}{2} + n\pi$
Even-Odd Odd	Even	Odd
Vertical Asymptotes $x = n\pi$	$x = \dfrac{\pi}{2} + n\pi$	$x = n\pi$
Graph $y = \csc x$ Period 2π	$y = \sec x$ Period 2π	$y = \cot x$ Period π

SECTION 4.1 ■ Exercises

A EXERCISES Basic Skills and Concepts

1. A function $f(x)$ is periodic if there is a positive number p such that $f(x + p) =$ _____ for all x in the domain of $f(x)$.

2. The domain of $\sin x$ is _____, and the domain of $\csc x$ is _____.

3. The period of $\sin x$, $\cos x$, $\csc x$, and $\sec x$ is _____, while the period of $\tan x$ and $\cot x$ is _____.

4. Among the six circular functions, the odd functions are _____ and the even functions are _____.

5. *True or False* The graph of an even function is symmetric about the origin.

6. *True or False* If c is an x-intercept of the graph of $g(x)$, then the line $x = c$ is a vertical asymptote for the graph of $f(x) = \dfrac{1}{g(x)}$.

In Exercises 7–12, write the requested information about each circular function.

	Domain	Range	Period	Odd-even	x-intercepts	y-intercepts	Asymptotes
7. $y = \sin x$							
8. $y = \cos x$							
9. $y = \tan x$							
10. $y = \cot x$							
11. $y = \sec x$							
12. $y = \csc x$							

In Exercises 13–18, describe how y values change. (Increase or decrease from each specified x-value to the next; use $\pm\infty$ as needed.)

	As x increases from 0 to $\dfrac{\pi}{2}$	As x increases from $\dfrac{\pi}{2}$ to π	As x increases from π to $\dfrac{3\pi}{2}$	As x increases from $\dfrac{3\pi}{2}$ to 2π
13. $y = \sin x$				
14. $y = \cos x$				
15. $y = \tan x$				
16. $y = \cot x$				
17. $y = \sec x$				
18. $y = \csc x$				

In Exercises 19–28, choose from the six circular functions:
$y = \sin x, y = \cos x, y = \tan x, y = \cot x, y = \sec x,$
$y = \csc x.$

19. Write all functions that are symmetric about the y-axis.

20. Write all functions that are symmetric about the origin.

21. Write all functions that are continuous on the interval $(0, 2\pi)$.

22. Write all functions that are continuous on the interval $(0, \pi)$.

23. Write all functions that are continuous on the interval $\left(0, \dfrac{\pi}{2}\right)$.

24. Write all functions that pass through the origin.

25. Write all functions that have zeros at $x = n\pi, n$ an integer.

26. Write all functions that have zeros at $x = \dfrac{\pi}{2} + n\pi, n$ an integer.

27. Write all functions that have asymptotes at $x = \dfrac{\pi}{2} + n\pi,$ n an integer.

28. Write all functions that have asymptotes at $x = n\pi, n$ an integer.

29. Show that if $g(x)$ is an odd function, then $f(x) = \dfrac{1}{g(x)}$ is also an odd function.

30. Show that if $g(x)$ is an even function, then $f(x) = \dfrac{1}{g(x)}$ is also an even function.

31. Show that $y = \sec x$ is an even function.

32. Show that $y = \csc x$ is an odd function.

33. Show that if $g(x)$ is a periodic function, then $f(x) = \dfrac{1}{g(x)}$ is also a periodic function.

34. Show that $y = \csc x$ is a periodic function.

35. Sketch one cycle of the graph of $y = \csc x$ by
   a. using the properties of reciprocal functions.
   b. making a table of values using multiples of $\dfrac{\pi}{4}$ for x.

36. Repeat Exercise 35 for $y = \sec x$.

37. Repeat Exercise 35 for $y = \cot x$.

38. Extend the graphs of $y = \tan x$ and $y = \cot x$ to the interval $[0, 2\pi]$.

In Exercises 39–56, use the appropriate extended graph to find all values of x in the interval $[-2\pi, 2\pi]$ that satisfy the given equation.

39. $\sin x = 0$ **40.** $\cos x = 0$

41. $\tan x = 0$ **42.** $\cot x = 0$

43. $\sec x = 0$ **44.** $\csc x = 0$

45. $\sin x = 1$ **46.** $\cos x = 1$

47. $\tan x = 1$ **48.** $\cot x = 1$

49. $\sec x = 1$ **50.** $\csc x = 1$

51. $\cos x = -1$ **52.** $\sin x = -1$

53. $\cot x = -1$ **54.** $\tan x = -1$

55. $\csc x = -1$ **56.** $\sec x = -1$

In Exercises 57–60, find all values of x in the interval $[-2\pi, 2\pi]$ that satisfy the given condition.

57. cot x is undefined.

58. tan x is undefined.

59. sec x is undefined.

60. csc x is undefined.

C EXERCISES Beyond the Basics

61. Show that the period of $y = \sin x$ is 2π.
[*Hint:* We know that $\sin(x + 2\pi) = \sin x$ for all real numbers x. So if 2π is not the period for $\sin x$, then $\sin(x + p) = \sin x$, where $0 < p < 2\pi$. By evaluating $\sin(x + p) = \sin x$ for $x = 0$, show that $p = \pi$. Find a value of x for which $\sin(x + \pi) \neq \sin x$ and conclude that the period of the sine function is 2π.]

62. Show that the period of $y = \cos x$ is 2π.

63. Show that the period of $y = \tan x$ is π.

64. Show that if the period of a function g is p, then the period of the reciprocal function $f(x) = \dfrac{1}{g(x)}$ is also p.
[*Hint:* Show that $f(x + p) = f(x)$. If the period of f is p_1 with $0 < p_1 < p$, show that $g(x + p_1) = g(x)$ with $p_1 < p$. This contradicts the fact that the period of g is p.]

65. Show that the period of $y = \cot x$ is π. (Use Exercises 63 and 64.)

66. Show that the period of $y = \sec x$ and $y = \csc x$ is 2π.

67. Sketch a graph of a function of period 3.

68. Sketch a graph of a function of period 2.5.

69. Find the range of each circular function if the domain of each function is restricted to the interval $\left(0, \dfrac{\pi}{4}\right)$. Use $\pm\infty$ as needed.

70. Repeat Exercise 69 with the domain restricted to $\left(-\dfrac{\pi}{4}, \dfrac{\pi}{4}\right)$.

71. Find all zeros (if any) of each circular function in the interval $(2010\pi, 2014\pi)$.

72. Find all asymptotes (if any) of each circular function in the interval $(2010\pi, 2014\pi)$.

73. Suppose f and g are functions of periods 2 and 3, respectively. Show that $y = f(x) + g(x)$ is periodic with period 6.

74. Suppose f and g are functions of periods 4 and 6, respectively. What is the period of $y = f(x) + g(x)$?

Critical Thinking

75. Suppose f is a periodic function with period p. Show that $f(x + np) = f(x)$ for any integer n.
[*Hint:* For any positive integer n, show that $f(x) = f(x + p) = f(x + 2p) \ldots = f(x + np)$ and that $f(x - p) = f(x)$.]

76. *True or False* If f is a periodic function with period p, then the points $(x, f(x))$ and $(x + np, f(x + np))$ on the graph of $y = f(x)$ have the same y-coordinate.

GROUP PROJECT

Let p and q be two positive real numbers. We define $M =$ least common multiple of p and q denoted $LCM[p, q]$ as the smallest positive number that is an integer multiple of both p and q. That is, $M = k_1 p$ and $M = k_2 q$ for some integers k_1 and k_2. For example, $LCM[4, 6] = 12$ because $12 = 3(4)$ and $12 = 2(6)$.

Verify the following:

$$LCM\left[1, \frac{2}{3}\right] = 2 \qquad LCM\left[4, \frac{2}{5}\right] = 4$$

$$LCM\left[\frac{2}{3}, \frac{5}{3}\right] = 10 \qquad LCM\left[\frac{4}{7}, \frac{6}{11}\right] = 12$$

$$LCM\left[\pi, \frac{2\pi}{3}\right] = 2\pi \qquad LCM\left[\frac{\pi}{2}, \frac{\pi}{3}\right] = \pi$$

Suppose f and g are periodic functions with periods p and q, respectively. Show that $h(x) = f(x) + g(x)$ is periodic with period $M = LCM[p, q]$.

Amplitude and Period

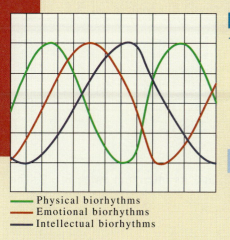

— Physical biorhythms
— Emotional biorhythms
— Intellectual biorhythms

Before Starting this Section, Review

1. Graphing circular functions (Section 4.1)

Objectives

1. Define amplitude of a periodic function.

2. Find periods of circular functions $f(Bx)$.

3. Graph circular functions $Af(Bx)$.

BIORHYTHMS

Biorhythm means "rhythm of life." The theory of biorhythms, a pseudoscience, was developed from the data of several patients in the early twentieth century by Professor Hermann Swoboda (University of Vienna) and Dr. Wilhelm Fliess, a friend of Sigmund Freud. According to the theory, every person has three fundamental biorhythm cycles. All cycles start on a person's day of birth, and each cycle has a fixed period.

1. **Physical cycle** (P) has a period of 23 days. It governs the condition of one's body.

2. **Emotional cycle** (E) has a period of 28 days. It describes one's temperament.

3. **Intellectual cycle** (I) has a period of 33 days. It influences one's thinking capacity.

The periodic functions P, E, and I can each be represented in the form $y = \sin(Bt)$; they are said to determine our biorhythm state on any day, t, since our birth. We experience a "high" or "low" in the corresponding cycle (physical, emotional, or intellectual) on the day if the curve is above or below the midline. We discuss this in Example 11. ■

---

1 Define amplitude of a periodic function.

Amplitude

In algebra, we learned (see the Appendix) that given nonzero constants A and B, we can sketch the graph of $y = Af(Bx)$ by stretching or compressing the graph of $y = f(x)$ vertically, horizontally, or both. In this section, we discuss such transformations on a circular function f.

We first look at the effect of the multiplier A in $y = Af(Bx)$. If the maximum value of $f(x)$ is M and $A > 0$, then the maximum value of $Af(x)$ is AM. The same relationship holds for the minimum value of $f(x)$. For example, the maximum value of $y = 3\sin x$ is 3 and its minimum value is -3. If the graph of $y = f(x)$ is "centered" about the x-axis, then the maximum value of $f(x)$ is the *amplitude* of $f(x)$. In general, we provide the following definition.

STUDY TIP

If a function f does not have both a maximum and a minimum value, we say that f has no amplitude or that its amplitude is undefined.

DEFINITION OF AMPLITUDE

Let f be a periodic function. Suppose M is the maximum value of f and m is the minimum value of f. The amplitude of f is defined by

$$\textbf{Amplitude} = \frac{1}{2}(M - m).$$

Because the maximum value of both functions $y = \sin x$ and $y = \cos x$ is 1 and their minimum value is -1, the amplitude for both functions is $\frac{1}{2}[1 - (-1)] = 1$.

EXAMPLE 1 **Finding Amplitude**

Find the amplitude (if any) of each function.

a. $y = 2 \sin x$ **b.** $y = -\frac{3}{2} \cos x$ **c.** $y = 2 \tan x$

SOLUTION

a. The maximum value of $y = 2 \sin x$ is 2, and its minimum value is -2. The amplitude $= \frac{1}{2}[2 - (-2)] = \frac{1}{2}(4) = 2$.

b. The maximum value of $y = -\frac{3}{2} \cos x$ is $\frac{3}{2}$, and its minimum value is $-\frac{3}{2}$. The amplitude $= \frac{1}{2}\left[\frac{3}{2} - \left(-\frac{3}{2}\right)\right] = \frac{1}{2}(3) = \frac{3}{2}$.

c. Recall that the range of $y = \tan x$ is $(-\infty, \infty)$. So the function $y = 2 \tan x$ has neither a maximum nor a minimum value. Therefore, $y = 2 \tan x$ has no amplitude. ■ ■ ■

Practice Problem 1 Find the amplitude (if any) of each function.

a. $y = 5 \cos x$ **b.** $y = -4 \sin x$ **c.** $y = 2 \csc x$ ■

The results of these examples can be generalized, and include all six circular functions.

AMPLITUDES OF CIRCULAR FUNCTIONS

The functions $y = A \sin x$ and $y = A \cos x$ have **Amplitude** $= |A|$ and **Range** $[-|A|, |A|]$. The functions $y = A \tan x$, $y = A \cot x$, $y = A \csc x$, and $y = A \sec x$ have no amplitude.

EXAMPLE 2 **Graphing $y = A \sin x$ with $A > 0$**

Graph $y = 3 \sin x$, $y = \frac{1}{3} \sin x$, and $y = \sin x$ on the same coordinate system over the interval $[-2\pi, 2\pi]$. Find the amplitude and the range of each function.

SOLUTION

We begin with the graph of $y = \sin x$. Its amplitude is 1, and its range is $[-1, 1]$. To get the graph of $y = 3 \sin x$, we multiply the y-coordinate of each point on the graph of $y = \sin x$ (including the key points) by 3. This results in stretching the graph of $y = \sin x$ vertically by a factor of 3. Because $3(0) = 0$, the x-intercepts are unchanged. However, the maximum y-value is $3(1) = 3$ and the minimum y-value is $3(-1) = -3$. See Figure 4.12. The amplitude of $y = 3 \sin x$ is $|3| = 3$ and its range is $[-3, 3]$. Similarly, we multiply each y-coordinate of the graph of $y = \sin x$ by $\frac{1}{3}$ to get the graph of $y = \frac{1}{3} \sin x$. This results in compressing the graph of $y = \sin x$ vertically by a factor of $\dfrac{1}{3}$. As before, the x-intercepts are unchanged; the maximum y value is $\dfrac{1}{3}$, and the minimum y value is $-\dfrac{1}{3}$. See Figure 4.12. The amplitude of $y = \dfrac{1}{3}\sin x$ is $\left|\dfrac{1}{3}\right| = \dfrac{1}{3}$, and its range is $\left[-\dfrac{1}{3}, \dfrac{1}{3}\right]$.

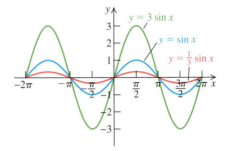

FIGURE 4.12 **Varying A in $y = A\sin x$**   ■ ■ ■

Practice Problem 2   Graph $y = 5\cos x$, $y = \dfrac{1}{5}\cos x$, and $y = \cos x$ on the same coordinate system over the interval $[-2\pi, 2\pi]$.   ■

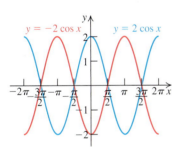

FIGURE 4.13 **Negative A in $y = A\cos x$**

EXAMPLE 3   **Graphing $y = A\cos x$**

Graph $y = -2\cos x$ over the interval $[-2\pi, 2\pi]$. Find its amplitude and range.

SOLUTION
Begin with the graph of $y = \cos x$. Multiply the y-coordinate of each point on that graph by 2; this stretches the graph vertically by a factor of 2 giving the graph of $y = 2\cos x$. Pay particular attention to the key points. Notice that the x-intercepts are unchanged. Each y value on the graph of $y = -2\cos x$ is the opposite of the corresponding y value on the graph of $y = 2\cos x$. Therefore, we reflect the graph of $y = 2\cos x$ in the x-axis to produce the graph of $y = -2\cos x$. See Figure 4.13. The largest value attained by $y = -2\cos x$ is 2, and the smallest value is -2. Therefore, the range of $y = -2\cos x$ is $[-2, 2]$ and its amplitude is $|-2| = 2$.

■ ■ ■

Practice Problem 3   Graph $y = -5\sin x$ over the interval $[-2\pi, 2\pi]$. Find the amplitude and range of the function.   ■

Generalizing from Examples 2 and 3, we have the following result.

GRAPHING $y = A\sin x$ AND $y = A\cos x$

For $A > 0$, the graph of $y = A\sin x$ or $y = A\cos x$ is obtained by stretching or compressing vertically by a factor of A the graph of $y = \sin x$ or $y = \cos x$, respectively. If $A < 0$, we sketch the graph of $y = |A|\sin x$ or $y = |A|\cos x$ and then reflect it about the x-axis.

2 Find periods of circular functions $f(Bx)$.

Period

We next investigate the effect on the graph of a periodic function $y = f(x)$ when we multiply the independent variable x by a nonzero number B.

EXAMPLE 4   **Graphing $y = \sin(Bx)$**

Graph $y = \sin 2x$ and $y = \sin x$ over the interval $[0, 2\pi]$ on the same coordinate system.

SOLUTION

We use the table of values in Table 4.4, where x values are multiples of $\dfrac{\pi}{4}$. We sketch the graphs of $y = \sin x$ and $y = \sin(2x)$ by plotting the points $(x, \sin x)$ and $(x, \sin(2x))$, respectively. See Figure 4.14.

TABLE 4.4

x	$\sin x$	$2x$	$\sin(2x)$
0	0	0	0
$\dfrac{\pi}{4}$	$\dfrac{\sqrt{2}}{2}$	$\dfrac{\pi}{2}$	1
$\dfrac{\pi}{2}$	1	π	0
$\dfrac{3\pi}{4}$	$\dfrac{\sqrt{2}}{2}$	$\dfrac{3\pi}{2}$	-1
π	0	2π	0
$\dfrac{5\pi}{4}$	$-\dfrac{\sqrt{2}}{2}$	$\dfrac{5\pi}{2}$	1
$\dfrac{3\pi}{2}$	-1	3π	0
$\dfrac{7\pi}{4}$	$-\dfrac{\sqrt{2}}{2}$	$\dfrac{7\pi}{2}$	-1
2π	0	4π	0

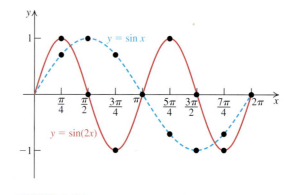

FIGURE 4.14

Notice that the graph of $y = \sin(2x)$ has period π. It completes one cycle over the interval $[0, \pi]$, and it completes two cycles over the interval $[0, 2\pi]$. So multiplying the independent variable x by 2 results in *half* the period of $y = \sin x$. Therefore, we get the graph of $y = \sin(2x)$ by compressing the graph of $y = \sin x$ horizontally to complete one cycle in $[0, \pi]$.   ■ ■ ■

Practice Problem 4   Sketch the graph of $y = \cos(2x)$ on the interval $[0, 2\pi]$.   ■

If $f(x)$ is a periodic function with period p, then $y = f(x)$ completes one cycle as x increases from 0 to p. If $B > 0$, the function $y = f(Bx)$ completes one cycle if

$$0 \le Bx \le p$$

or

$$0 \le x \le \frac{p}{B} \qquad \text{Divide by } B > 0.$$

Therefore, if the period of a function $f(x)$ is p, then for $B > 0$, the period of $f(Bx)$ is $\dfrac{p}{B}$.

PERIOD

Suppose $y = f(x)$ is a circular function with period p. Then for $B > 0$, the graph of $y = f(Bx)$ has the same shape as that of $y = f(x)$ but has period $\dfrac{p}{B}$.

EXAMPLE 5   **Graphing $y = \cos(Bx)$ with $0 < B < 1$**

Graph one cycle of $y = \cos x$ and $y = \cos\left(\dfrac{1}{3}x\right)$ on the same coordinate system.

SOLUTION
Because the period p of $\cos x$ is 2π, we graph one cycle of $y = \cos x$ on the interval $[0, 2\pi]$. The period of $\cos(Bx)$ is $\dfrac{p}{B} = \dfrac{2\pi}{B}$, so the period of $\cos\left(\dfrac{1}{3}x\right)$ is $\dfrac{2\pi}{\dfrac{1}{3}} = 6\pi$.

Therefore, one cycle of the graph of $y = \cos\left(\dfrac{1}{3}x\right)$ is sketched over the interval $[0, 6\pi]$. Divide the interval $[0, 6\pi]$ into four equal parts to get the x-coordinates of the key points: $0, \dfrac{3\pi}{2}, 3\pi, \dfrac{9\pi}{2}$, and 6π. Use Table 4.5 to sketch the graph of $y = \cos\left(\dfrac{1}{3}x\right)$. See Figure 4.15. Notice that we can get the graph of $y = \cos\left(\dfrac{1}{3}x\right)$ by stretching the graph of $y = \cos x$ horizontally by a factor of 3.

TABLE 4.5

x	$y = \cos\left(\dfrac{1}{3}x\right)$
0	1
$\dfrac{3\pi}{2}$	0
3π	-1
$\dfrac{9\pi}{2}$	0
6π	1

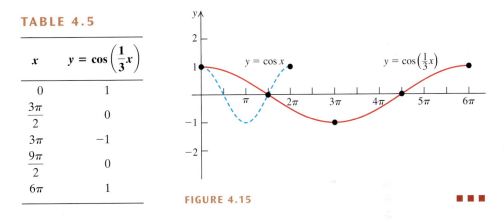

FIGURE 4.15   ■ ■ ■

Practice Problem 5   Graph one cycle of $y = \sin x$ and $y = \sin\left(\dfrac{1}{2}x\right)$ on the same coordinate system.   ■

If $B < 0$, we can use the even–odd properties of the circular functions to rewrite the function with $B > 0$. For example, $y = \sin(-2x) = -\sin(2x)$. So to sketch the graph of $y = \sin(-2x)$ on the interval $[0, 2\pi]$, we sketch the graph of $y = \sin(2x)$ and then reflect this graph about the x-axis. See Figure 4.16.

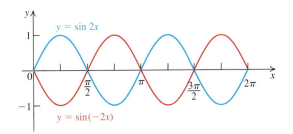

FIGURE 4.16 **Graphing $y = \sin(Bx)$ with $B < 0$**

> **GRAPHING** $y = \sin(Bx)$ **AND** $y = \cos(Bx)$
>
> For $B > 0$, the graph of $y = \sin(Bx)$ or $y = \cos(Bx)$ is obtained by stretching or compressing horizontally, by a factor of $\dfrac{1}{B}$, the graph of $y = \sin x$ or $y = \cos x$, respectively. If $B < 0$, we graph $y = \sin(|B|x)$ or $y = \cos(|B|x)$ and then use *even–odd* properties to graph $y = \sin(Bx)$ or $y = \cos(Bx)$.

3 Graph circular functions $Af(Bx)$.

Both Amplitude and Period Changes

We describe the procedure for sketching the graphs of $y = A\sin(Bx)$ and $y = A\cos(Bx)$.

When graphing these functions, it is convenient to use units for the independent variable, x, that equal one-quarter of the period of the function. This is because the x-intercepts and the maximum and minimum values occur at multiples of $\dfrac{1}{4}$ (period).

Pay particular attention to the five *key points* identified on these graphs.

FINDING THE SOLUTION: A PROCEDURE

EXAMPLE 6   **Graphing $y = A\sin(Bx)$ and $y = A\cos(Bx)$**

OBJECTIVE

Sketch the graph of $y = A\sin(Bx)$ or $y = A\cos(Bx)$.

EXAMPLE

Graph $y = 3\cos\left(\dfrac{1}{2}x\right)$.

Step 1   **Find the amplitude and the period.**

$$\text{Amplitude} = |A|$$

$$\text{Period} = \frac{2\pi}{|B|}$$

1. $y = 3\cos\left(\dfrac{1}{2}x\right)$

$$A = 3, B = \frac{1}{2}$$

$$\text{Amplitude} = 3 \qquad \text{Period} = \frac{2\pi}{\dfrac{1}{2}} = 4\pi$$

Step 2   **Find the x-coordinates for the five key points.** The x-intercepts (zeros), the maximum values, and the minimum values occur at multiples of $\dfrac{1}{4}$ (period). Start the cycle with $x_1 = 0$ and mark the x-axis in increments of $\dfrac{1}{4}$ (period).

We get $x_2 = x_1 + \dfrac{1}{4}$ (period),

$x_3 = x_2 + \dfrac{1}{4}$ (period),

$x_4 = x_3 + \dfrac{1}{4}$ (period), and

$x_5 = x_4 + \dfrac{1}{4}$ (period).

2. $\dfrac{1}{4}$ (period) $= \dfrac{1}{4}(4\pi) = \pi$

$x_1 = 0, x_2 = 0 + \pi = \pi, x_3 = \pi + \pi = 2\pi,$
$x_4 = 2\pi + \pi = 3\pi,$ and $x_5 = 3\pi + \pi = 4\pi$

continued on the next page

Step 3 **Find the *y*-coordinates for the five key points** by evaluating the function at each *x* value from Step 2.

3.

x	$y = 3 \cos \left(\dfrac{1}{2} x \right)$	Point (x, y)
0	$y = 3 \cos \left(\dfrac{1}{2} 0 \right) = 3$	$(0, 3) \leftarrow$ Maximum point
π	$y = 3 \cos \left(\dfrac{1}{2} \pi \right) = 0$	$(\pi, 0)$
2π	$y = 3 \cos \left(\dfrac{1}{2} 2\pi \right)$ $= 3 \cos (\pi) = -3$	$(2\pi, -3) \leftarrow$ Minimum point
3π	$y = 3 \cos \left(\dfrac{1}{2} 3\pi \right)$ $= 3 \cos \dfrac{3\pi}{2} = 0$	$(3\pi, 0)$
4π	$y = 3 \cos \left(\dfrac{1}{2} 4\pi \right)$ $= 3 \cos (2\pi) = 3$	$(4\pi, 3) \leftarrow$ Maximum point

Step 4 **Connect the five key points by a smooth curve** (making a wave). This is the graph of one cycle of the given function.

4. Graph of $y = 3 \cos \left(\dfrac{1}{2} x \right)$, $0 \le x \le 4\pi$

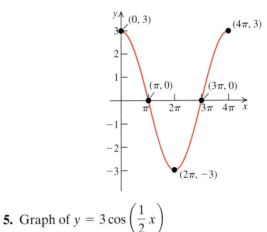

Step 5 **Sketch the graph** by repeating the graph in Step 4 to the right and to the left as needed.

5. Graph of $y = 3 \cos \left(\dfrac{1}{2} x \right)$

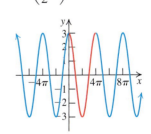

Practice Problem 6   Graph $y = 4 \sin (2x)$.

EXAMPLE 7   **Graphing $y = A \sin Bx$ with $A < 0$**

Sketch the graph of $y = -2 \sin \left(\dfrac{\pi}{3} x \right)$ over a one-period interval.

SOLUTION

Step 1   Comparing $y = -2 \sin \left(\dfrac{\pi}{3} x \right)$ with $y = A \sin (Bx)$, we have $A = -2$, and

$B = \dfrac{\pi}{3}$.

$$\text{Amplitude} = |A| = |-2| = 2$$

$$\text{Period} = \dfrac{2\pi}{|B|} = \dfrac{2\pi}{\dfrac{\pi}{3}} = 6$$

Step 2 $\dfrac{1}{4}(\text{period}) = \dfrac{1}{4}(6) = \dfrac{3}{2}$ The x-coordinates of the key points are

$$x_1 = 0, \ x_2 = x_1 + \dfrac{3}{2} = 0 + \dfrac{3}{2} = \dfrac{3}{2}$$

$$x_3 = x_2 + \dfrac{3}{2} = \dfrac{3}{2} + \dfrac{3}{2} = 3$$

$$x_4 = x_3 + \dfrac{3}{2} = 3 + \dfrac{3}{2} = \dfrac{9}{2}$$

$$x_5 = x_4 + \dfrac{3}{2} = \dfrac{9}{2} + \dfrac{3}{2} = 6.$$

Step 3   Find the five key points.

x	$y = -2 \sin \left(\dfrac{\pi}{3} x \right)$	Point (x, y)	
0	$y = -2 \sin \left(\dfrac{\pi}{3} \cdot 0 \right) = 0$	$(0, 0)$	
$\dfrac{3}{2}$	$y = -2 \sin \left(\dfrac{\pi}{3} \cdot \dfrac{3}{2} \right)$		
	$= -2 \sin \left(\dfrac{\pi}{2} \right) = -2$	$\left(\dfrac{3}{2}, -2 \right)$	← Minimum point
3	$y = -2 \sin \left(\dfrac{\pi}{3} \cdot 3 \right)$		
	$= -2 \sin (\pi) = 0$	$(3, 0)$	
$\dfrac{9}{2}$	$y = -2 \sin \left(\dfrac{\pi}{3} \cdot \dfrac{9}{2} \right)$		
	$= -2 \sin \left(\dfrac{3\pi}{2} \right) = 2$	$\left(\dfrac{9}{2}, 2 \right)$	← Maximum point
6	$y = -2 \sin \left(\dfrac{\pi}{3} \cdot 6 \right)$		
	$= -2 \sin (2\pi) = 0$	$(6, 0)$	

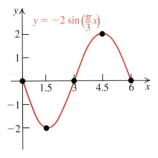

FIGURE 4.17

Step 4   Graph $y = -2\sin\left(\dfrac{\pi}{3}x\right), 0 \leq x \leq 6$ by connecting the five key points with a smooth wave. See Figure 4.17.   ■ ■ ■

Practice Problem 7   Sketch the graph of $y = -3\cos\left(\dfrac{\pi}{2}x\right)$ over a one-period interval.   ■

The procedure for graphing $y = A\tan(Bx)$ and $y = A\cot(Bx)$ is based on the essential features of the graphs of $y = \tan x$ and $y = \cot x$, respectively.

FINDING THE SOLUTION: A PROCEDURE

EXAMPLE 8	Graphing $y = A\tan(Bx)$ or $y = A\cot(Bx)$

OBJECTIVE
Graph a function of the form $y = A\tan(Bx)$ *or* $y = A\cot(Bx)$, *with* $B > 0$.

EXAMPLE
Graph $y = 3\tan(2x)$.

Step 1   **Find the period.** Because tangent and cotangent functions have period π,

$$\text{Period} = \frac{p}{B} = \frac{\pi}{B}.$$

1. $y = \underset{\uparrow}{3}\tan(\underset{\uparrow}{2}x)$

$A = 3\ B = 2$

$$\text{Period} = \frac{\pi}{B} = \frac{\pi}{2}$$

Step 2   **Locate two adjacent vertical asymptotes.**

(i) For $y = A\tan(Bx)$, solve
$$Bx = -\frac{\pi}{2} \text{ and } Bx = \frac{\pi}{2}.$$

(ii) For $y = A\cot(Bx)$, solve
$Bx = 0$ and $Bx = \pi$.

2. Solving $2x = -\dfrac{\pi}{2}$ and $2x = \dfrac{\pi}{2}$, we have the following two adjacent vertical asymptotes:

$$x = -\frac{\pi}{4} \quad \text{and} \quad x = \frac{\pi}{4}$$

Step 3   **Divide the interval** on the x-axis between the two vertical asymptotes into four equal parts, each of length
$$\frac{1}{4}(\text{period}) = \frac{1}{4}\left(\frac{\pi}{B}\right).$$

Find the x-coordinates of the division points that are in the domain of the function.

3. The interval $\left(-\dfrac{\pi}{4}, \dfrac{\pi}{4}\right)$ has length $\dfrac{\pi}{2}$, and $\dfrac{1}{4}\left(\dfrac{\pi}{2}\right) = \dfrac{\pi}{8}$. The x-coordinates of the three division points of the interval $\left(-\dfrac{\pi}{4}, \dfrac{\pi}{4}\right)$ are

$$x_1 = -\frac{\pi}{4} + \frac{\pi}{8} = -\frac{\pi}{8}$$

$$x_2 = x_1 + \frac{\pi}{8} = -\frac{\pi}{8} + \frac{\pi}{8} = 0$$

$$x_3 = x_2 + \frac{\pi}{8} = 0 + \frac{\pi}{8} = \frac{\pi}{8}.$$

continued on the next page

Step 4 **Evaluate the function** at the three x values found in Step 3. The y-values will be $\{-A, 0, A\}$.

4.

x	$y = 3\tan(2x)$	(x, y)
$-\dfrac{\pi}{8}$	$y = 3\tan 2\left(-\dfrac{\pi}{8}\right) = -3$	$\left(-\dfrac{\pi}{8}, -3\right)$
0	$y = 3\tan(0) = 0$	$(0, 0)$
$\dfrac{\pi}{8}$	$y = 3\tan 2\left(\dfrac{\pi}{8}\right) = 3$	$\left(\dfrac{\pi}{8}, 3\right)$

Step 5 **Sketch one cycle.** Sketch the vertical asymptotes (dashed lines) using the x values found in Step 2. Plot and connect the points in Step 4 with a smooth curve in the standard shape of a cycle for the given function.

5.

Step 6 **Repeat the graph** in Step 5 to the left and right over intervals of length $\dfrac{\pi}{B}$ as needed.

6.

Practice Problem 8 Graph $y = 3\cot(2x)$.

EXAMPLE 9 **Graphing $y = A \cot Bx$ with $B < 0$**

Graph $y = 3\cot\left(-\dfrac{1}{2}x\right)$ over the interval $(-2\pi, 2\pi)$.

SOLUTION

Step 1 Because the cotangent is an odd function, we have:

$$y = 3\cot\left(-\dfrac{1}{2}x\right) = -3\cot\left(\dfrac{1}{2}x\right)$$

$$\uparrow \qquad\qquad \uparrow$$

$$A = -3 \quad B = \dfrac{1}{2}$$

$$\text{Period} = \dfrac{\pi}{B} = \dfrac{\pi}{\dfrac{1}{2}} = 2\pi$$

Step 2 Solving $\dfrac{1}{2}x = 0$ and $\dfrac{1}{2}x = \pi$, we have two adjacent vertical asymptotes:

$x = 0$ and $x = 2\pi$.

Step 3 The interval $(0, 2\pi)$ has length 2π, and $\dfrac{1}{4}(2\pi) = \dfrac{\pi}{2}$. The x-coordinates of the three division points of the interval $(0, 2\pi)$ are

$$x_1 = 0 + \frac{\pi}{2} = \frac{\pi}{2}, x_2 = x_1 + \frac{\pi}{2} = \frac{\pi}{2} + \frac{\pi}{2} = \pi, \text{ and}$$

$$x_3 = x_2 + \frac{\pi}{2} = \pi + \frac{\pi}{2} = \frac{3\pi}{2}.$$

Step 4 Evaluating the function at $\dfrac{\pi}{2}, \pi$, and $\dfrac{3\pi}{2}$, we have:

x	$y = -3\cot\left(\dfrac{1}{2}x\right)$	(x, y)
$\dfrac{\pi}{2}$	$y = -3\cot\left(\dfrac{1}{2}\cdot\dfrac{\pi}{2}\right) = -3$	$\left(\dfrac{\pi}{2}, -3\right)$
π	$y = -3\cot\left(\dfrac{1}{2}\cdot\pi\right) = 0$	$(\pi, 0)$
$\dfrac{3\pi}{2}$	$y = -3\cot\left(\dfrac{1}{2}\cdot\dfrac{3\pi}{2}\right) = 3$	$\left(\dfrac{3\pi}{2}, 3\right)$

Step 5 Sketch one cycle.

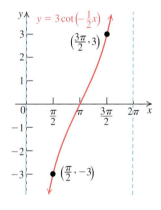

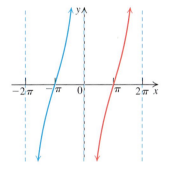

FIGURE 4.18 $y = 3\cot\left(-\dfrac{1}{2}x\right) = -3\cot\left(\dfrac{1}{2}x\right), -2\pi < x < 2\pi$

Step 6 Extend the graph to the interval $(-2\pi, 2\pi)$. See Figure 4.18. ■ ■ ■

Practice Problem 9 Graph $y = 3\tan\left(-\dfrac{1}{2}x\right)$ over the interval $(-2\pi, 2\pi)$. ■

The procedures for graphing the functions $y = A\csc(Bx)$ and $y = A\sec(Bx)$ are based on the graphs of the corresponding functions $y = A\sin(Bx)$ and $y = A\cos(Bx)$, respectively.

EXAMPLE 10 **Graphing $y = A\csc(Bx)$**

Graph $y = 3\csc(2x)$ over a two-period interval.

SOLUTION

Step 1 We first graph $y = 3\sin(2x)$.

$$A = 3 \quad B = 2$$

Amplitude $= |3| = 3$; period $= \dfrac{2\pi}{2} = \pi$. One cycle is graphed over $[0, \pi]$.

Step 2 $\dfrac{1}{4}$ (period) $= \dfrac{1}{4}(\pi) = \dfrac{\pi}{4}$

The x-coordinates of the five key points are

$$x_1 = 0, x_2 = 0 + \frac{\pi}{4} = \frac{\pi}{4}, x_3 = \frac{\pi}{4} + \frac{\pi}{4} = \frac{\pi}{2}, x_4 = \frac{\pi}{2} + \frac{\pi}{4} = \frac{3\pi}{4}, \text{ and}$$

$$x_5 = \frac{3\pi}{4} + \frac{\pi}{4} = \pi.$$

Step 3   Evaluate the function at the x values from Step 2.

x	$y = 3 \sin (2x)$	(x, y)
0	$y = 3 \sin (0) = 0$	$(0, 0)$
$\dfrac{\pi}{4}$	$y = 3 \sin \left(\dfrac{\pi}{2} \right) = 3$	$\left(\dfrac{\pi}{4}, 3 \right)$
$\dfrac{\pi}{2}$	$y = 3 \sin (\pi) = 0$	$\left(\dfrac{\pi}{2}, 0 \right)$
$\dfrac{3\pi}{4}$	$y = 3 \sin \left(\dfrac{3\pi}{2} \right) = -3$	$\left(\dfrac{3\pi}{4}, -3 \right)$
π	$y = 3 \sin (2\pi) = 0$	$(\pi, 0)$

Step 4   Sketch the sine wave for $y = 3 \sin (2x)$ through the points (x, y) found in Step 3.

Step 5   Extend the graph to the interval $[-\pi, \pi]$. See the blue graph in Figure 4.19.

Step 6   Graph $y = 3 \csc (2x)$.

Because $y = 3 \csc (2x) = 3 \left(\dfrac{1}{\sin (2x)} \right)$, the graph of $y = 3 \csc (2x)$ has vertical asymptotes at the x-intercepts of $y = 3 \sin (2x)$. In Figure 4.19, draw vertical dashed lines at $x = -\pi, x = -\dfrac{\pi}{2}, x = 0, x = \dfrac{\pi}{2},$ and $x = \pi$.

When $\sin 2x = \pm 1$, we have $3 \csc 2x = 3 \sin 2x$. This means that between two adjacent x-intercepts of $y = 3 \sin 2x$, a maximum (or a minimum) point on $y = 3 \sin 2x$ coincides with the minimum (or the maximum) point on $y = 3 \csc 2x$.

Now use the technique that generated the graph of $y = \csc x$ from that of $y = \sin x$ to graph $y = 3 \csc (2x)$. Start at the common points $\left(-\dfrac{3\pi}{4}, 3 \right)$, $\left(-\dfrac{\pi}{4}, -3 \right), \left(\dfrac{\pi}{4}, 3 \right),$ and $\left(\dfrac{3\pi}{4}, -3 \right)$; then use the reciprocal relationship $y = 3 \csc (2x) = 3 \left(\dfrac{1}{\sin (2x)} \right)$ to sketch the graph. See the red graph in Figure 4.19. ■ ■ ■

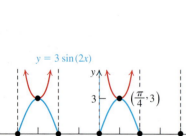
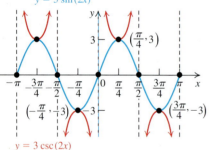

FIGURE 4.19

Practice Problem 10   Graph $y = 2 \sec (3x)$ over a two-period interval. ■

Biorhythm States

The periods for physical (P), emotional (E), and intellectual (I) states are $23, 28,$ and 33 days, respectively. So your biorhythm states on the t th day since birth are given by

$$P = \sin \left(\frac{2\pi}{23} t \right), E = \sin \left(\frac{2\pi}{28} t \right), \text{ and } I = \sin \left(\frac{2\pi}{33} t \right).$$

To calculate t on a given day, use the formula

$$t = (\text{your age})(365) + (\text{number of leap years since your birth year})$$
$$+ (\text{number of days since your last birthday}).$$

EXAMPLE 11   Finding Biorhythm States

Find the biorhythm states of Lisa on May 22, 2012, assuming that she was born on March 13, 1993.

SOLUTION

We first calculate t.

Number of years from March 13, 1993 to March 13, 2012 $= 2012 - 1993 = 19$.

Number of leap years $= 5$ (1996, 2000, 2004, 2008, 2012)

Number of days from March 13 to May 22 $= 18(\text{March}) + 30(\text{April}) + 22(\text{May}) = 70$

So, $t = (19)(365) + 5 + 70 = 7010$

$$P = \sin\left(\frac{2\pi}{23}t\right) = \sin\left(\frac{2\pi(7010)}{23}\right) \approx -0.98$$

$$E = \sin\left(\frac{2\pi}{28}t\right) = \sin\left(\frac{2\pi(7010)}{28}\right) \approx 0.78$$

$$I = \sin\left(\frac{2\pi}{33}t\right) = \sin\left(\frac{2\pi(7010)}{33}\right) \approx 0.46$$

Substitute $t = 7010$ in each equation; use a calculator in Radian mode.

Lisa's physical state is way down, her emotional state is excellent, and her intellectual state is good.   ■ ■ ■

Practice Problem 11   Find your biorhythm states today.   ■

Simple Harmonic Motion   Trigonometric functions can often describe or model motion caused by vibration, rotation, or oscillation. The motions associated with sound waves, radio waves, alternating electric current, a vibrating guitar string, or the swing of a pendulum are examples of such motion. Another example is the movement of a ball suspended by a spring. If the ball is pulled downward and then released (ignoring the effects of friction and air resistance), the ball will repeatedly move up and down past its rest, or equilibrium, position. See Figure 4.20.

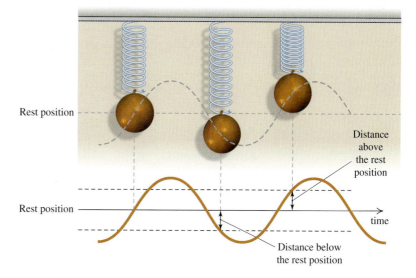

FIGURE 4.20 Simple harmonic motion

SIMPLE HARMONIC MOTION

An object whose position relative to an equilibrium position at time t that can be described by either

$$y = A \sin(\omega t) \quad \text{or} \quad y = A \cos(\omega t), \omega > 0$$

is said to be in **simple harmonic motion**.

The *amplitude*, $|A|$, is the maximum distance the object reaches from its equilibrium position. The *period* of the motion, $\dfrac{2\pi}{\omega}$, is the time it takes for the object to complete one full cycle. The **frequency** of the motion is $\dfrac{\omega}{2\pi}$ and gives the number of cycles completed per unit of time.

If the distance above and below the rest position of the ball is graphed as a function of time, a sine or a cosine curve results. The amplitude of the curve is the maximum distance above the rest position the ball travels, and one cycle is completed as the ball travels from its highest position to its lowest position and back to its highest position.

EXAMPLE 12 **Simple Harmonic Motion of a Ball Attached to a Spring**

Suppose that a ball attached to a spring is pulled down 6 inches and released and the resulting simple harmonic motion has a period of 8 seconds. Write an equation for the ball's simple harmonic motion.

SOLUTION
We must first choose between an equation of the form $y = A \sin \omega t$ or $y = A \cos \omega t$. We start tracking the motion of the ball when $t = 0$. Note that for $t = 0$,

$$y = A \sin(\omega \cdot 0) = A \cdot \sin 0 = A \cdot 0 = 0 \quad \text{and}$$
$$y = A \cos(\omega \cdot 0) = A \cdot \cos 0 = A \cdot 1 = A.$$

If we choose to start tracking the ball's motion when we release it after pulling it down 6 inches, we should choose $A = -6$ and $y = -6 \cos \omega t$. Because we pulled the ball *down* in order to start, A is negative. We now have the form of the equation of motion:

$$y = -6 \cos \omega t \qquad \text{When } t = 0, y = -6.$$

$$\text{period} = \frac{2\pi}{\omega} = 8 \qquad \text{The period is given to be 8 seconds.}$$

$$\omega = \frac{2\pi}{8} = \frac{\pi}{4} \qquad \text{Solve for } \omega.$$

Replacing ω by $\dfrac{\pi}{4}$ in $y = -6 \cos(\omega t)$ yields the equation of the ball's simple harmonic motion,

$$y = -6 \cos\left(\frac{\pi}{4} t\right) \qquad \blacksquare\blacksquare\blacksquare$$

Practice Problem 12 Rework Example 12 with the motion period of 3 seconds and the ball pulled down 4 inches. ■

SECTION 4.2 ■ Exercises

A EXERCISES Basic Skills and Concepts

1. The amplitude of $A \sin x$ or $A \cos x$ is _____ .

2. The amplitude of $A \sec x$ or $A \csc x$ is _____ .

3. The period of $\sin x$ is 2π, and the period of $\sin Bx$ is _____ .

4. The period of $\tan x$ is _____ , and the period of $\tan Bx$ is _____ .

5. *True or False* For $A > 0$, the graph of $y = A \sin x$ is obtained by stretching or compressing vertically by a factor of A the graph of $y = \sin x$.

6. *True or False* For $B > 0$, the graph of $y = \sin Bx$ is obtained by stretching or compressing horizontally by a factor of B the graph of $y = \sin x$.

In Exercises 7–18, match each function with its graph.

7. $y = \sin x$

8. $y = \cos x$

9. $y = -\cos x$

10. $y = -\sin x$

11. $y = \tan x$

12. $y = -\tan x$

13. $y = -\cot x$

14. $y = \cot x$

15. $y = \csc x$

16. $y = -\sec x$

17. $y = -\csc x$

18. $y = \sec x$

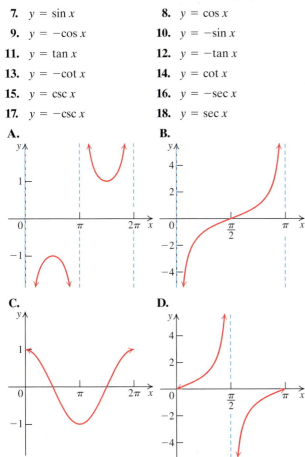

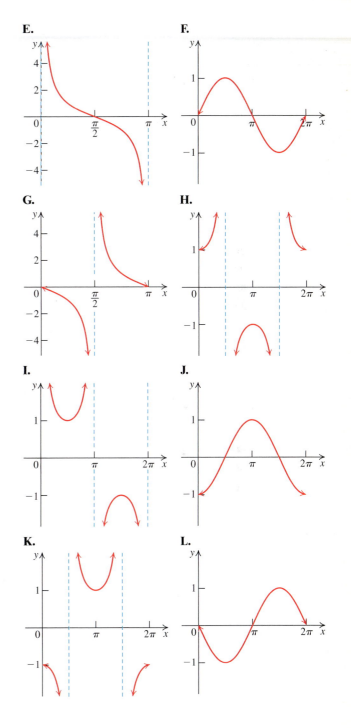

In Exercises 19–30, graph each function over the interval $[-2\pi, 2\pi]$. Find the amplitude and the range of the function.

19. $y = 6 \cos x$ **20.** $y = 4 \cos x$

21. $y = \frac{1}{2} \cos x$ **22.** $y = \frac{1}{4} \cos x$

23. $y = 2 \sin x$ **24.** $y = 6 \sin x$

25. $y = -2 \sin x$ **26.** $y = -2 \cos x$

27. $y = -4 \cos x$ **28.** $y = -5 \sin x$

29. $y = -6 \sin x$ **30.** $y = -\frac{1}{4} \cos x$

In Exercises 31–42, find the period of each function.

31. $y = 2 \sin 3x$ **32.** $y = -\cos 4x$

33. $y = -\cos(-x)$ **34.** $y = \sin(-2x)$

35. $y = 2 \tan 2x$ **36.** $y = 5 \cot 3x$

37. $y = \cot(-2x)$ **38.** $y = \tan(-3x)$

39. $y = 5 \csc 3x$ **40.** $y = -3 \sec(5x)$

41. $y = 2 \sec(-2x)$ **42.** $y = -3 \csc(-2x)$

In Exercises 43–58, graph each function.

43. $y = \sin(4x)$ **44.** $y = \cos(4x)$

45. $y = \cos\left(\frac{2}{3}x\right)$ **46.** $y = \sin\left(\frac{4}{3}x\right)$

47. $y = 2 \sin(3x)$ **48.** $y = 3 \sin(-x)$

49. $y = -3 \cos(2x)$ **50.** $y = -2 \cos(-4x)$

51. $y = 2 \sin\left(\frac{1}{2}x\right)$ **52.** $y = 4 \sin\left(\frac{1}{3}x\right)$

53. $y = -2 \cos\left(\frac{1}{4}x\right)$ **54.** $y = 5 \cos\left(\frac{1}{2}x\right)$

55. $y = 2 \cos\left(\frac{\pi x}{3}\right)$ **56.** $y = 3 \cos(\pi x)$

57. $y = 2 \sin\left(\frac{\pi x}{2}\right)$ **58.** $y = 3 \sin(-4\pi x)$

In Exercises 59–70, graph two cycles of each function.

59. $y = \tan(3x)$ **60.** $y = \cot(3x)$

61. $y = \cot\left(\frac{1}{3}x\right)$ **62.** $y = \tan\left(\frac{1}{3}x\right)$

63. $y = 2 \tan\left(\frac{1}{2}x\right)$ **64.** $y = 4 \cot\left(\frac{1}{2}x\right)$

65. $y = 3 \cot\left(\frac{1}{4}x\right)$ **66.** $y = -6 \tan\left(\frac{1}{4}x\right)$

67. $y = 4 \tan(-2x)$ **68.** $y = 5 \cot\left(-\frac{1}{2}x\right)$

69. $y = -2 \tan(-3x)$ **70.** $y = -3 \cot(-4x)$

In Exercises 71–82, graph one cycle of each function.

71. $y = \csc(2x)$ **72.** $y = \sec(2x)$

73. $y = \sec\left(\frac{1}{2}x\right)$ **74.** $y = \csc\left(\frac{1}{2}x\right)$

75. $y = 4 \csc\left(\frac{1}{3}x\right)$ **76.** $y = 2 \sec\left(\frac{1}{3}x\right)$

77. $y = 2 \sec\left(\frac{1}{4}x\right)$ **78.** $y = -2 \csc\left(\frac{1}{3}x\right)$

79. $y = 2 \sec(-2x)$ **80.** $y = 3 \csc\left(-\frac{1}{2}x\right)$

81. $y = -2 \sec\left(-\frac{1}{2}x\right)$ **82.** $y = -3 \csc(-2x)$

In Exercises 83–90, write an equation $y = A \sin(Bx)$ of the sine function with the given amplitude and period.

83. Amplitude $= \frac{1}{4}$, period $= \frac{\pi}{8}$

84. Amplitude $= 2$, period $= \frac{\pi}{6}$

85. Amplitude $= 6$, period $= 3\pi$

86. Amplitude $= \frac{1}{2}$, period $= 6\pi$

87. Amplitude $= 2.4$, period $= 6$

88. Amplitude $= 0.8$, period $= 10$

89. Amplitude $= \frac{\pi}{2}$, period $= \frac{5}{8}$

90. Amplitude $= \frac{2}{\pi}$, period $= \frac{2}{3}$

B EXERCISES   Applying the Concepts

91. Biorhythm. Find the biorhythm states of Tina on April 1, 2011, assuming that she was born on July 22, 1990.

92. Biorhythm. Find the biorhythm states of Dave on August 12, 2012, assuming that he was born on March 31, 1991.

93. Simple harmonic motion. A ball attached to a spring is pulled down 5 inches and released, and the resulting simple harmonic motion has a period of 10 seconds. Write an equation of the ball's simple harmonic motion.

94. Simple harmonic motion. The motion of a ball attached to a spring is described by the equation $x = 6 \cos(0.5 t)$, where x is the displacement in feet from the equilibrium position and t is the time elapsed in seconds. How long does it take to complete one oscillation of the ball? Where is the ball relative to the equilibrium position after three seconds?

95. Electric voltage. The voltage $V(t)$ in an electrical circuit is given by $V(t) = 4.5 \cos(160\pi t)$, where t is measured in seconds.
  a. Find the amplitude and the period for $V(t)$.
  b. Find the frequency of $V(t)$, that is, the number of cycles completed in one second.
  c. Graph $V(t)$ over the interval $\left[0, \frac{1}{40}\right]$.
  d. Use a graphing calculator to verify your graph.

96. Voltage of an electric outlet. The voltage across the terminals of a typical electric outlet is approximated by $V(t) = 156 \sin (120\pi t)$, where t is measured in seconds.

a. Find the amplitude and the period for $V(t)$.

b. Find the frequency of $V(t)$, that is, the number of cycles completed in one second.

c. Graph $V(t)$ over the interval $\left[0, \frac{1}{30}\right]$.

d. Use a graphing calculator to verify your graph.

97. Prison searchlight. A dual-beam rotating light on a movie set is positioned as a spotlight shining on a prison wall. The light is 20 feet from the wall and rotates clockwise. When the light is first turned on $(t = 0)$, it shines on point P on the wall. After t seconds, the distance (in feet) from the beam on the wall to the point P is given by the function

$$d(t) = 20 \tan \frac{\pi t}{5}.$$

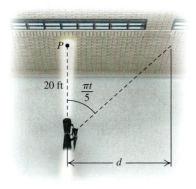

When the light beam is to the right of P, the value of d is positive, and when the beam is to the left of P, the value of d is negative.

a. Graph d over the interval $0 \le t \le 5$.

b. Because $d(t)$ is undefined for $t = 2.5$, where is the rotating light point when $t = 2.5$?

98. Prison searchlight. In the situation described in Exercise 97, find the value for b assuming that the light beam is to sweep the entire wall in ten seconds and $d(t) = 20 \tan bt$.

99. Sonic cone. When a plane travels at supersonic and hypersonic speeds, small disturbances in the atmosphere are transmitted downstream within a cone. The cone intersects the ground, and the edge of the cone's intersection with the ground can be represented as shown in the figure. The sound waves strike the edge of the cone at a right angle. The speed of the sound wave is represented by leg s of the right triangle shown in the figure. The plane is moving at speed v, which is represented by the hypotenuse of the right triangle in the figure.

The Mach number, M, is given by

$$M = M(x) = \frac{\text{Speed of the aircraft}}{\text{Speed of sound}} = \frac{v}{s} = \csc\left(\frac{x}{2}\right),$$

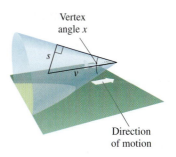

where x is the angle at the vertex of the cone. Graph the Mach number function, $M(x)$, as the angle at the vertex of the cone varies. What is the range of Mach numbers associated with the interval $\left[\frac{\pi}{4}, \pi\right)$?

100. In Exercise 99, what is the range of Mach numbers associated with the interval $\left[\frac{\pi}{8}, \frac{\pi}{4}\right]$?

C EXERCISES Beyond the Basics

101. Sketch the graph of $y = |\sin (2x)|$ on the interval $-2\pi \le x \le 2\pi$. What is its period?

102. Sketch the graph of $y = |\tan (2x)|$ on the interval $-\pi \le x \le \pi$. What is its period?

103. Sketch the graph of the function
$$y = \begin{cases} \sin x & 0 \le x \le \pi \\ 0 & \pi < x \le 2\pi \end{cases}$$
with period 2π on the interval $[0, 4\pi]$.

104. Sketch the graph of the function
$$y = \begin{cases} \cos x & -\dfrac{\pi}{2} \le x \le \dfrac{\pi}{2} \\ 0 & \dfrac{\pi}{2} < x \le \dfrac{3\pi}{2} \end{cases}$$
with period 2π on the interval $\left[-\dfrac{5\pi}{2}, \dfrac{5\pi}{2}\right]$.

In Exercises 105–108, write an equation for each graph.

105.

106.

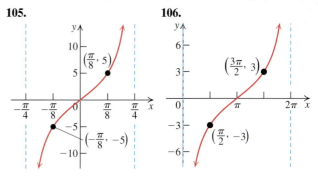

107. **108.**

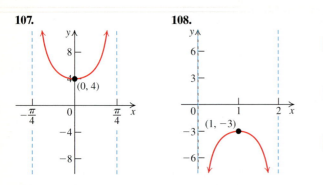

In Exercises 109–111, use the following graph of $g(x) = A \sin(Bx)$.

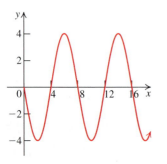

109. Find A and B.

110. Find $g(2010)$.

111. Sketch a graph of $y = A \csc(Bx)$.

112. Graph the equations $y = x$, $y = -x$, and $y = x \sin x$ over the interval $[-2\pi, 2\pi]$ on the same coordinate plane.

113. Graph the equations $y = x^2$, $y = -x^2$, and $y = x^2 \sin x$ over the interval $[-2\pi, 2\pi]$ on the same coordinate plane.

114. Graph $y = x + \sin x$ over the interval $[-2\pi, 2\pi]$.

115. Graph $y = \sin x + \cos x$ over the interval $[-2\pi, 2\pi]$.

Critical Thinking

116. For what number B does $y = \sec(Bx)$ have period $\dfrac{\pi}{3}$?

117. For what number B does $y = \tan(Bx)$ have period 5?

Translations of the Graphs of Circular Functions

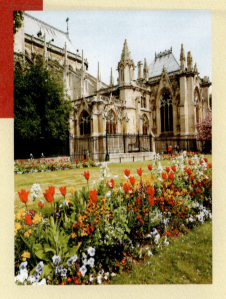

Before Starting this Section, Review

1. Amplitude and period of circular functions (Section 4.1)

2. Graphing circular functions of the form $y = Af(Bx)$ (Section 4.2)

Objectives

1. Translate graphs horizontally.

2. Translate graphs vertically.

3. Graph circular functions of the form $y = Af(Bx - C) + D$.

4. Find the equation of a sinusoidal graph.

LENGTH OF DAYS

During our winter, because the Northern Hemisphere tilts away from the sun, it receives less direct solar radiation than does the Southern Hemisphere, which tilts toward the sun. In the Northern Hemisphere, the summer solstice (the longest day of the year) occurs on or around June 21 and the winter solstice (the shortest day of the year) occurs on or about December 21. In the Southern Hemisphere, the seasons are reversed. The number of hours of daylight varies at different latitudes. The length of a day is one of the many phenomena that can be described by the trigonometric functions we study in this section. In Example 8, we model the number of daylight hours that the city of Paris enjoys throughout the year. ■

---

1 Translate graphs horizontally.

Phase Shift

We investigate the effect of replacing the expression (Bx) with $(Bx - C)$ on the graph of $y = f(Bx)$.

EXAMPLE 1 Graphing $y = \sin(x - c)$

Sketch the graphs of $y = \sin x$ and $y = \sin\left(x - \dfrac{\pi}{2}\right)$, $-\dfrac{3\pi}{2} \le x \le \dfrac{3\pi}{2}$ on the same coordinate system.

SOLUTION

The graph of $y = \sin x$ on the interval $\left[-\dfrac{3\pi}{2}, \dfrac{3\pi}{2}\right]$ is shown (in blue) in Figure 4.21 on the next page. To sketch the graph of $y = \sin\left(x - \dfrac{\pi}{2}\right)$, we use Table 4.6 to locate points on the graph. We connect these points with a sine curve to get the graph of $y = \sin\left(x - \dfrac{\pi}{2}\right)$.

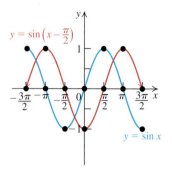

$y = \sin\left(x - \frac{\pi}{2}\right)$

$y = \sin x$

FIGURE 4.21 Phase shift

TABLE 4.6

x	$y = \sin\left(x - \dfrac{\pi}{2}\right)$	(x, y)
$-\dfrac{3\pi}{2}$	$y = \sin\left(-\dfrac{3\pi}{2} - \dfrac{\pi}{2}\right) = \sin\left(-2\pi\right) = 0$	$\left(-\dfrac{3\pi}{2}, 0\right)$
$-\pi$	$y = \sin\left(-\pi - \dfrac{\pi}{2}\right) = \sin\left(-\dfrac{3\pi}{2}\right) = 1$	$(-\pi, 1)$
$-\dfrac{\pi}{2}$	$y = \sin\left(-\dfrac{\pi}{2} - \dfrac{\pi}{2}\right) = \sin\left(-\pi\right) = 0$	$\left(-\dfrac{\pi}{2}, 0\right)$
0	$y = \sin\left(0 - \dfrac{\pi}{2}\right) = \sin\left(-\dfrac{\pi}{2}\right) = -1$	$(0, -1)$
$\dfrac{\pi}{2}$	$y = \sin\left(\dfrac{\pi}{2} - \dfrac{\pi}{2}\right) = \sin 0 = 0$	$\left(\dfrac{\pi}{2}, 0\right)$
π	$y = \sin\left(\pi - \dfrac{\pi}{2}\right) = \sin\left(\dfrac{\pi}{2}\right) = 1$	$(\pi, 1)$
$\dfrac{3\pi}{2}$	$y = \sin\left(\dfrac{3\pi}{2} - \dfrac{\pi}{2}\right) = \sin\left(\pi\right) = 0$	$\left(\dfrac{3\pi}{2}, 0\right)$

Comparing the graph of the equation $y = \sin\left(x - \dfrac{\pi}{2}\right)$ with that of $y = \sin x$, we note that the graph of $y = \sin\left(x - \dfrac{\pi}{2}\right)$ is the graph of $y = \sin x$ shifted right $\dfrac{\pi}{2}$ units. See Figure 4.21.   ■ ■ ■

Practice Problem 1   Graph $y = \cos\left(x + \dfrac{\pi}{4}\right)$, $-\dfrac{\pi}{4} \le x \le \dfrac{7\pi}{4}$.   ■

The reason the shift in Example 1 occurs is as follows:

The graph of $y = \sin x$ completes one cycle as x increases from $x = 0$ to $x = 2\pi$. So the graph of $y = \sin\left(x - \dfrac{\pi}{2}\right)$ completes one cycle when $\left(x - \dfrac{\pi}{2}\right)$ increases from 0 to 2π. In other words, $y = \sin\left(x - \dfrac{\pi}{2}\right)$ completes one cycle from

$$x - \frac{\pi}{2} = 0 \text{ to } x - \frac{\pi}{2} = 2\pi$$

or $x = \dfrac{\pi}{2}$ to $x = \dfrac{\pi}{2} + 2\pi$ Add $\dfrac{\pi}{2}$ to both sides in each equation.

This is the
x-value of the
start of a cycle.

This is the
x-value of the
end of the cycle.

Now let's compare for $B > 0$ the graph of $y = f(Bx - C)$ with that of the circular function of the form $y = f(x)$ of period p.

Because $y = f(x)$ has period p, one complete cycle of $y = f(x)$ occurs as x increases from 0 to p. So one complete cycle of $y = f(Bx - C)$ occurs as $(Bx - C)$

increases from 0 to p. In other words, we can find an interval over which $y = f(Bx - C)$ completes one cycle by solving for x in the following equations.

$$Bx - C = 0 \quad \text{and} \quad Bx - C = p$$
$$Bx = C \qquad\qquad Bx = C + p \qquad \text{Add } C \text{ to both sides of each equation.}$$
$$x = \frac{C}{B} \qquad\qquad x = \frac{C}{B} + \frac{p}{B} \qquad \text{Divide both sides of each equation by } B.$$

The numbers $\frac{C}{B}$ and $\frac{C}{B} + \frac{p}{B}$ are the x values of the start and end points of one cycle of the graph of $y = f(Bx - C)$. The number $\frac{C}{B}$ is the *phase shift* associated with the graph.

> ### PHASE SHIFT
>
> The phase shift of the graph of $y = Af(Bx - C)$ with $B > 0$ is $\frac{C}{B}$. This is the amount by which the graph of $y = Af(Bx)$ is shifted horizontally to produce the graph of $y = Af(Bx - C)$. If $\frac{C}{B} > 0$, the shift is to the right. If $\frac{C}{B} < 0$, the shift is to the left.

If $B < 0$, rewrite $Bx - C$ as $-(-Bx + C)$, then use even–odd property of the given circular functions and then graph $y = \pm Af(|B|x + C)$.

EXAMPLE 2 Finding the Phase Shift

Find the x-coordinates of a start and end point of one cycle of the graph of each function. Identify the phase shift and state whether the shift is to the right or left.

a. $y = -2\cos\left(2x - \frac{\pi}{3}\right)$ **b.** $y = \tan\left(3\pi x + \frac{\pi}{2}\right)$ **c.** $y = \csc\left(-\frac{1}{2}x + \frac{\pi}{4}\right)$

SOLUTION

a. Because $y = \cos x$ has period 2π, one cycle of $y = -2\cos\left(2x - \frac{\pi}{3}\right)$ is completed between

$$2x - \frac{\pi}{3} = 0 \quad \text{and} \quad 2x - \frac{\pi}{3} = 2\pi.$$
$$2x = \frac{\pi}{3} \qquad\qquad 2x = \frac{\pi}{3} + 2\pi \qquad \text{Add } \frac{\pi}{3} \text{ to both sides.}$$
$$x = \frac{\pi}{6} \qquad\qquad x = \frac{\pi}{6} + \pi \qquad \text{Divide both sides by 2.}$$

Start point — End point — Period

Because the phase shift $= \frac{\pi}{6} > 0$, the graph of $y = -2\cos\left(2x - \frac{\pi}{3}\right)$ is obtained by shifting the graph of $y = -2\cos(2x)$ horizontally to the right by $\frac{\pi}{6}$ unit.

b. The tangent function $y = \tan x$ has period π; so one cycle of $y = \tan\left(3\pi x + \dfrac{\pi}{2}\right)$ is completed between

$$3\pi x + \frac{\pi}{2} = 0 \quad \text{and} \quad 3\pi x + \frac{\pi}{2} = \pi.$$

$$3\pi x = -\frac{\pi}{2} \qquad\qquad 3\pi x = -\frac{\pi}{2} + \pi = \frac{\pi}{2} \qquad \text{Subtract } \frac{\pi}{2} \text{ from both sides of each equation.}$$

━━━━ Phase Shift ━━━━

$$x = -\frac{1}{6} \qquad\qquad x = \frac{1}{6} = -\frac{1}{6} + \frac{1}{3} \qquad \text{Solve for } x \text{ and rewrite.}$$

Period

$\boxed{\text{Start point}}$ $\boxed{\text{End point}}$

Because the phase shift $= -\dfrac{1}{6} < 0$, the graph of $y = \tan\left(3\pi x + \dfrac{\pi}{2}\right)$ is obtained by shifting the graph of $y = \tan(3\pi x)$ horizontally to the left by $\dfrac{1}{6}$ unit.

c. Here $B = -\dfrac{1}{2} < 0$. Because the cosecant is an odd function, we have $\csc\left[-\left(\dfrac{1}{2}x - \dfrac{\pi}{4}\right)\right] = -\csc\left(\dfrac{1}{2}x - \dfrac{\pi}{4}\right)$. The cosecant function has period 2π; so one cycle of $y = \csc\left(-\dfrac{1}{2}x + \dfrac{\pi}{4}\right)$ is completed between

$$\frac{1}{2}x - \frac{\pi}{4} = 0 \quad \text{and} \quad \frac{1}{2}x - \frac{\pi}{4} = 2\pi.$$

$$\frac{1}{2}x = \frac{\pi}{4} \qquad\qquad \frac{1}{2}x = \frac{\pi}{4} + 2\pi \qquad \text{Add } \frac{\pi}{4} \text{ to both sides.}$$

━━ Phase Shift ━━

$$x = \frac{2\pi}{4} = \frac{\pi}{2} \qquad\qquad x = \frac{\pi}{2} + 4\pi \qquad \text{Solve for } x.$$

Period

$\boxed{\text{Start point}}$ $\boxed{\text{End point}}$

Because the phase shift $= \dfrac{\pi}{2} > 0$, the graph of $y = \csc\left(-\dfrac{1}{2}x + \dfrac{\pi}{4}\right)$ is obtained by shifting the graph of $y = \csc\left(-\dfrac{1}{2}x\right) = -\csc\left(\dfrac{1}{2}x\right)$ horizontally to the right by $\dfrac{\pi}{2}$ units. ▪▪▪

Practice Problem 2   Repeat Example 2 for each function.

a. $y = \sin\left(3x + \dfrac{\pi}{4}\right)$ **b.** $y = \cot\left(-2x - \dfrac{\pi}{4}\right)$ **c.** $y = \sec\left(-\dfrac{\pi x}{2} + \dfrac{\pi}{6}\right)$ ▪

2 Translate graphs vertically.

Vertical Shifts

In the next example, we discuss the effect of adding a nonzero constant to a circular function.

EXAMPLE 3   Graphing $y = f(x) + D$

Sketch the graphs of $y = \sin x$ and $y = \sin x + 2$, $0 \le x \le 2\pi$ on the same coordinate system.

SOLUTION

The graph of $y = \sin x$ on the interval $[0, 2\pi]$ is shown (in blue) in Figure 4.22. To sketch the graph of $y = \sin x + 2$, we use Table 4.7 to locate points on this graph. We connect these points with a sine curve to get the graph of $y = \sin x + 2$.

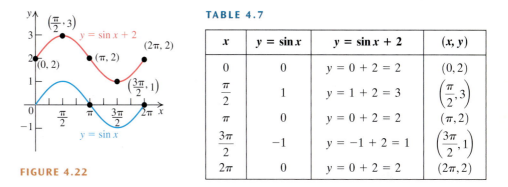

FIGURE 4.22

TABLE 4.7

x	$y = \sin x$	$y = \sin x + 2$	(x, y)
0	0	$y = 0 + 2 = 2$	$(0, 2)$
$\dfrac{\pi}{2}$	1	$y = 1 + 2 = 3$	$\left(\dfrac{\pi}{2}, 3\right)$
π	0	$y = 0 + 2 = 2$	$(\pi, 2)$
$\dfrac{3\pi}{2}$	-1	$y = -1 + 2 = 1$	$\left(\dfrac{3\pi}{2}, 1\right)$
2π	0	$y = 0 + 2 = 2$	$(2\pi, 2)$

Comparing the graph of the equation $y = \sin x + 2$ with that of $y = \sin x$, we note that the graph of $y = \sin x + 2$ is the graph of $y = \sin x$ shifted vertically two units up. See Figure 4.22.   ■ ■ ■

Practice Problem 3   Sketch the graphs of $y = \cos x$ and $y = \cos x - 2$, $0 \le x \le 2\pi$ on the same coordinate system.   ■

VERTICAL SHIFTS

The graph of $y = f(x) + D$ results by shifting the graph of $y = f(x)$ vertically D units up if $D > 0$ and $|D|$ units down if $D < 0$.

---

3 Graph circular functions of the form $y = Af(Bx - C) + D$.

Combining Transformations

Next we describe a procedure for sketching the graphs of equations of the form $y = Af(Bx - C) + D$, where f is a circular function.

FINDING THE SOLUTION: A PROCEDURE

EXAMPLE 4   Graphing $y = Af(Bx - C) + D$

OBJECTIVE
Graph $y = A \sin (Bx - C) + D$ or $y = A \cos (Bx - C) + D$.

Step 1   If necessary, use even–odd identities to write the equation in the form $y = Af(Bx - C) + D$ with $B > 0$.

EXAMPLE
Sketch the graph of $y = 2 \sin \left(\dfrac{\pi}{4} - 2x\right) + 3$.

1. $y = 2 \sin \left[-\left(2x - \dfrac{\pi}{4}\right)\right] + 3$ $\qquad \dfrac{\pi}{4} - 2x = -\left(2x - \dfrac{\pi}{4}\right)$

$y = -2 \sin \left(2x - \dfrac{\pi}{4}\right) + 3$ $\qquad$ Sine is odd, so $\sin(-\theta) = -\sin\theta$.

continued on the next page

Step 2 Write $A, B, C,$ and D.

$$\text{Amplitude} = |A|$$

$$\text{Period} = \frac{2\pi}{B}$$

2. $A = -2, B = 2, C = \dfrac{\pi}{4},$ and $D = 3.$

$$\text{Amplitude} = |-2| = 2$$

$$\text{Period} = \frac{2\pi}{B} = \frac{2\pi}{2} = \pi$$

Step 3 Find phase shift.

$$\text{Phase shift} = \frac{C}{B}$$

3. Phase shift $= \dfrac{C}{B} = \dfrac{\frac{\pi}{4}}{2} = \dfrac{\pi}{8}$

Step 4 Start the cycle with $x_1 = \dfrac{C}{B}$ and mark the x-axis in increments of $\dfrac{1}{4}$ (period).

4. $\dfrac{1}{4}(\text{period}) = \dfrac{1}{4}(\pi) = \dfrac{\pi}{4}$

$x_1 = \dfrac{\pi}{8}, x_2 = x_1 + \dfrac{\pi}{4} = \dfrac{\pi}{8} + \dfrac{\pi}{4} = \dfrac{3\pi}{8}, x_3 = x_2 + \dfrac{\pi}{4} =$

$\dfrac{3\pi}{8} + \dfrac{\pi}{4} = \dfrac{5\pi}{8}, x_4 = x_3 + \dfrac{\pi}{4} = \dfrac{5\pi}{8} + \dfrac{\pi}{4} = \dfrac{7\pi}{8},$ and

$x_5 = x_4 + \dfrac{\pi}{4} = \dfrac{7\pi}{8} + \dfrac{\pi}{4} = \dfrac{9\pi}{8}.$

Step 5 Evaluate y-values for each of the five x values from Step 4.

x	$y = -2\sin\left(2x - \dfrac{\pi}{4}\right) + 3$	(x, y)
$\dfrac{\pi}{8}$	$y = -2\sin\left(2 \cdot \dfrac{\pi}{8} - \dfrac{\pi}{4}\right) + 3 = 3$	$\left(\dfrac{\pi}{8}, 3\right)$
$\dfrac{3\pi}{8}$	$y = -2\sin\left(2 \cdot \dfrac{3\pi}{8} - \dfrac{\pi}{4}\right) + 3$ $= -2 + 3 = 1$	$\left(\dfrac{3\pi}{8}, 1\right)$ ← Minimum point
$\dfrac{5\pi}{8}$	$y = -2\sin\left(2 \cdot \dfrac{5\pi}{8} - \dfrac{\pi}{4}\right) + 3$ $= 0 + 3 = 3$	$\left(\dfrac{5\pi}{8}, 3\right)$
$\dfrac{7\pi}{8}$	$y = -2\sin\left(2 \cdot \dfrac{7\pi}{8} - \dfrac{\pi}{4}\right) + 3$ $= -2\sin\left(\dfrac{3\pi}{2}\right) + 3 = 2 + 3 = 5$	$\left(\dfrac{7\pi}{8}, 5\right)$ ← Maximum point
$\dfrac{9\pi}{8}$	$y = -2\sin\left(2 \cdot \dfrac{9\pi}{8} - \dfrac{\pi}{4}\right) + 3$ $= 0 + 3 = 3$	$\left(\dfrac{9\pi}{8}, 3\right)$

continued on the next page

Step 6   With a sine wave, connect the five key points from Step 5.

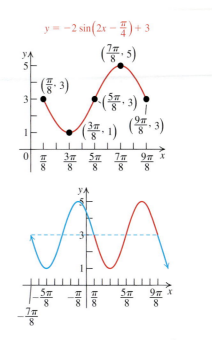

$y = -2 \sin\left(2x - \frac{\pi}{4}\right) + 3$

Step 7   Sketch the graph by repeating the graph in Step 6 to the right and left as needed.

Practice Problem 4   Sketch one cycle of the graph of $y = 3 \cos\left(2x - \frac{\pi}{2}\right) - 2$. ■

Steps, similar to those for the sine and cosine functions, are used to graph $y = A \tan(Bx - C) + D$ and $y = A \cot(Bx - C) + D$.

EXAMPLE 5   **Graphing $y = A \tan(Bx - C) + D$**

Graph one cycle of $y = 3 \tan\left(2x - \frac{\pi}{2}\right) + 1$.

SOLUTION

Step 1   Here $B = 2 > 0$.

Step 2 $A = 3, B = 2, C = \dfrac{\pi}{2}$, and $D = 1$.

Vertical stretch factor $= |A| = |3| = 3$

$$\text{Period} = \frac{\pi}{B} = \frac{\pi}{2} \qquad \text{Phase shift} = \frac{C}{B} = \frac{\dfrac{\pi}{2}}{2} = \frac{\pi}{4}$$

Step 3   Locate two adjacent asymptotes by solving the equations:

$$2x - \frac{\pi}{2} = -\frac{\pi}{2} \qquad \text{and} \qquad 2x - \frac{\pi}{2} = \frac{\pi}{2}$$

$$2x = -\frac{\pi}{2} + \frac{\pi}{2} = 0 \qquad\qquad 2x = \frac{\pi}{2} + \frac{\pi}{2} = \pi \qquad \text{Add } \frac{\pi}{2} \text{ to each side of both equations.}$$

$$x = 0 \qquad\qquad\qquad\qquad x = \frac{\pi}{2} \qquad\qquad \text{Solve for } x.$$

Step 4 Divide the interval $\left(0, \dfrac{\pi}{2}\right)$ from Step 3 on the x-axis into four equal parts, each of length $\dfrac{1}{4}$(period) $= \dfrac{1}{4}\left(\dfrac{\pi}{2}\right) = \dfrac{\pi}{8}$. The division points are $x_1 = 0$,

$x_2 = x_1 + \dfrac{\pi}{8} = 0 + \dfrac{\pi}{8} = \dfrac{\pi}{8}, x_3 = x_2 + \dfrac{\pi}{8} = \dfrac{\pi}{8} + \dfrac{\pi}{8} = \dfrac{\pi}{4}, x_4 = x_3 + \dfrac{\pi}{8} =$

$\dfrac{\pi}{4} + \dfrac{\pi}{8} = \dfrac{3\pi}{8}$, and $x_5 = x_4 + \dfrac{\pi}{8} = \dfrac{3\pi}{8} + \dfrac{\pi}{8} = \dfrac{\pi}{2}$.

Step 5 The function has vertical asymptotes at $x_1 = 0$ and at $x_5 = \dfrac{\pi}{2}$. Evaluate the function at the remaining three x-values from Step 4.

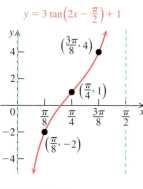

$y = 3 \tan\left(2x - \dfrac{\pi}{2}\right) + 1$

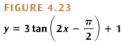

FIGURE 4.23

$y = 3 \tan\left(2x - \dfrac{\pi}{2}\right) + 1$

x	$y = 3 \tan\left(2x - \dfrac{\pi}{2}\right) + 1$	(x, y)
$\dfrac{\pi}{8}$	$y = 3 \tan\left(\dfrac{\pi}{4} - \dfrac{\pi}{2}\right) + 1 = -2$	$\left(\dfrac{\pi}{8}, -2\right)$
$\dfrac{\pi}{4}$	$y = 3 \tan\left(\dfrac{\pi}{2} - \dfrac{\pi}{2}\right) + 1 = 1$	$\left(\dfrac{\pi}{4}, 1\right)$
$\dfrac{3\pi}{8}$	$y = 3 \tan\left(\dfrac{3\pi}{4} - \dfrac{\pi}{2}\right) + 1 = 4$	$\left(\dfrac{3\pi}{8}, 4\right)$

Step 6 Sketch vertical asymptotes (dashed lines) from Step 3 at $x = 0$ and at $x = \dfrac{\pi}{2}$. Plot and connect the points from Step 5 with a smooth curve in standard shape of a cycle of the tangent function. See Figure 4.23. ■ ■ ■

Practice Problem 5 Graph one cycle of $y = 2 \cot\left(\dfrac{\pi}{4} - \dfrac{1}{2}x\right) + 3$. ■

To graph the functions of the form

$$y = A \csc(Bx - C) + D \quad \text{and} \quad y = A \sec(Bx - C) + D,$$

we note that the period, phase shift, vertical stretch factor, and vertical translation are identical to the corresponding functions $y = A \sin(Bx - C) + D$ and $y = A \cos(Bx - C) + D$, respectively.

EXAMPLE 6 Graphing $y = A \csc(Bx - C) + D$

Sketch the graph of $y = -2 \csc\left(2x - \dfrac{\pi}{2}\right) + 3$.

SOLUTION

We first sketch one cycle of the graph of the corresponding function $y = -2 \sin\left(2x - \dfrac{\pi}{2}\right) + 3$. One cycle of the graph of this equation (from Example 4) is shown in blue in Figure 4.24. Using this graph as an aid, we sketch the graph of $y = -2 \csc\left(2x - \dfrac{\pi}{2}\right) + 3$ shown in Figure 4.24. ■ ■ ■

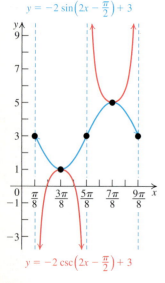

$y = -2 \sin\left(2x - \dfrac{\pi}{2}\right) + 3$

$y = -2 \csc\left(2x - \dfrac{\pi}{2}\right) + 3$

FIGURE 4.24

Practice Problem 6 Sketch one cycle of the graph of $y = 3 \sec\left(2x - \dfrac{\pi}{2}\right) - 2$. ■

4 Find the equation of a sinusoidal graph.

Determining Equations of a Sinusoidal Graph

Many real-world periodic phenomena can be modeled by sinusoidal functions. We plot the data (called *scatterplot*) and connect the points by a smooth curve. If the curve appears like a sine wave, we find an equation of the form $y = A \sin(Bx - C) + D$ that describes the curve. Once we have an equation, we can draw conclusions or make predictions about the phenomenon.

EXAMPLE 7   **Finding Equations of Sinusoidal Graphs**

Find an equation of the graph shown in Figure 4.25.

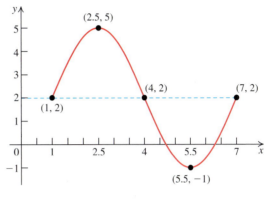

FIGURE 4.25

SOLUTION

The graph looks like a sine wave. So its equation is of the form

$$y = A \sin(Bx - C) + D.$$

We determine the constants $A, B, C,$ and D from the graph.

$$\text{Amplitude} = \frac{1}{2}(5 - (-1)) = \frac{1}{2}(6) = 3$$

The graph appears in the sine form (not reflected sine form), so $A = 3$.

By inspection, the period of the graph is 6. (Cycle starts at $x = 1$ and ends at $x = 7$.) We know that

$$\text{Period} = \frac{2\pi}{B}$$

$$6 = \frac{2\pi}{B} \qquad \text{Period} = 6$$

$$6B = 2\pi \qquad \text{Multiply by } B \text{ and simplify.}$$

$$B = \frac{2\pi}{6} = \frac{\pi}{3} \qquad \text{Solve for } B.$$

The graph starts at $(1, 2)$. So the phase shift is 1. Therefore,

$$\frac{C}{B} = 1 \qquad \text{Phase shift} = \frac{C}{B}.$$

$$C = B = \frac{\pi}{3} \qquad \text{Solve for } C \text{ and substitute for } B.$$

The average of the maximum value and the minimum value gives the vertical shift D for the sinusoidal graph.

$$D = \frac{\text{Maximum value} + \text{Minimum value}}{2}$$

$$= \frac{5 + (-1)}{2} = \frac{4}{2} = 2 \qquad \textcolor{teal}{\text{Substitute values and simplify.}}$$

Substitute the values of $A, B, C,$ and D in $y = A \sin(Bx - C) + D$, to get the equation

$$y = 3 \sin\left(\frac{\pi}{3}x - \frac{\pi}{3}\right) + 2, \qquad 1 \le x \le 7$$

The last equation represents the graph shown in Figure 4.25. We note that the graph in Figure 4.25 can also be represented by an equation of the form $y = A \cos(Bx - C) + D$ with different values of some constants. ■■■

Practice Problem 7 Show that the graph in Figure 4.25 can also be represented by the equation $y = 3 \cos\left(\frac{\pi}{3}x - \frac{5\pi}{6}\right) + 2, \ 1 \le x \le 7.$ ■

EXAMPLE 8 **Modeling the Number of Daylight Hours in Paris**

TABLE 4.8

Daylight hours in Paris

January	8.8
February	10.2
March	11.9
April	13.7
May	15.3
June	16.1
July	15.7
August	14.3
September	12.6
October	10.8
November	9.2
December	8.3

Source: http://aa.usno.navy.mil/ data/docs/Dur_One year.html

Table 4.8 gives the average number of daylight hours in Paris each month. Let y represent the number of daylight hours in Paris in month x. Find a function of the form $y = A \sin(Bx - C) + D$ that models the hours of daylight throughout the year.

SOLUTION

Plot the values given in Table 4.8, representing the months by the integers 1 through 12 (Jan. = 1,..., Dec. = 12). Then sketch a function of the form $y = A \sin(Bx - C) + D$ that models the points just graphed. See Figure 4.26.

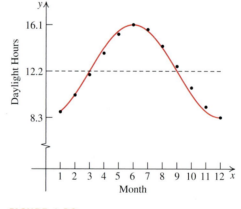

FIGURE 4.26

We want to find the values for the constants $A, B, C,$ and D that will produce the graph shown in Figure 4.26. From Table 4.8, the range of the function is $[8.3, 16.1]$, so

$$\text{Amplitude} = A = \frac{\text{highest value} - \text{lowest value}}{2} = \frac{(16.1 - 8.3)}{2} = 3.9.$$

The sine graph has been shifted vertically by $\frac{1}{2}$ (highest value + lowest value), the average of the highest and lowest values. Thus, this average value gives

$$D = \frac{1}{2}(16.1 + 8.3) = 12.2.$$

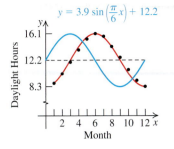

FIGURE 4.27

TABLE 4.9

Daylight Hours in Fargo	
January	9
February	10.3
March	11.9
April	13.6
May	15.1
June	15.8
July	15.4
August	14.2
September	12.5
October	10.9
November	9.4
December	8.6

Source: http://aa.usno.navy.mil/
data/docs/Dur_One year.html

The weather repeats every 12 months, so the period is 12. Because the period $= \dfrac{2\pi}{B}$, we have

$$12 = \frac{2\pi}{B} \qquad \text{\color{teal}Replace period with 12.}$$

$$B = \frac{2\pi}{12} = \frac{\pi}{6} \qquad \text{\color{teal}Solve for B.}$$

So far, we have the modeling function in the form $y = 3.9\sin\left(\dfrac{\pi}{6}x - C\right) + 12.2$.

The horizontally "unshifted" graph of $y = 3.9\sin\left(\dfrac{\pi}{6}x\right) + 12.2$ is superimposed here in Figure 4.27. This graph must be shifted to the right to fit the plotted data. To determine the phase shift, we find the value of C for which y has the highest value. This happens when $x = 6$ (in June); where $y = 16.1$. We now have

$$16.1 = 3.9\sin\left(\frac{\pi}{6}\cdot 6 - C\right) + 12.2 \qquad \text{\color{teal}Replace x with 6 and y with 16.1.}$$

$$1 = \sin(\pi - C) \qquad \text{\color{teal}Subtract 12.2 from both sides and divide by 3.9.}$$

Now $\sin(\pi - C)$ will first equal 1 when

$$\pi - C = \frac{\pi}{2} \qquad \text{\color{teal}$\sin t = 1$ when $t = \dfrac{\pi}{2}$.}$$

$$C = \frac{\pi}{2} \qquad \text{\color{teal}Solve for C.}$$

The equation describing the hours of daylight in Paris *in month x* is

$$y = 3.9\sin\left(\frac{\pi}{6}x - \frac{\pi}{2}\right) + 12.2. \qquad ■ ■ ■$$

Practice Problem 8   Rework Example 8 for the city of Fargo, North Dakota, using the values given in Table 4.9.   ■

SECTION 4.3 ■ Exercises

A EXERCISES Basic Skills and Concepts

1. In the sine curve $y = A\sin(Bx - C)$, the amplitude is
_____, the period is _____, and a cycle
starts when $Bx - C =$ _____.

2. A cycle for $y = A\cos(Bx - C)$ starts at $\dfrac{C}{B}$ and has length
_____.

3. Two adjacent vertical asymptotes of
$y = A\tan(Bx - C) + D$ may be obtained by solving
for x in the equations

$$Bx - C = -\frac{\pi}{2} \quad \text{and} \quad Bx - C = \underline{\qquad}.$$

4. The graph of $y = A\sec(Bx - C) + D$ is obtained by
first sketching as an aid the graph of the corresponding
function $y =$ _____.

5. *True or False* For $C > 0$, the graph of $y = Af(Bx - C)$
results if we shift the graph of $y = Af(Bx)$ horizontally
to the right by C units.

6. *True or False* For $D > 0$, the graph of $y = f(x) + D$
results if we shift the graph of $y = f(x)$ vertically D
units up.

In Exercises 7–24, graph each function over a one-period interval.

7. $y = \cos\left(x + \dfrac{\pi}{2}\right)$ **8.** $y = \sin\left(x + \dfrac{\pi}{4}\right)$

9. $y = \sin\left(x - \dfrac{\pi}{3}\right)$ **10.** $y = \cos\left(x - \pi\right)$

11. $y = \tan\left(x - \dfrac{\pi}{4}\right)$ **12.** $y = \tan\left(x + \dfrac{\pi}{4}\right)$

13. $y = \cot\left(x + \dfrac{\pi}{4}\right)$ **14.** $y = \cot\left(x - \dfrac{\pi}{4}\right)$

15. $y = \sec\left(x - \pi\right)$ **16.** $y = \csc\left(x - \pi\right)$

17. $y = \sin x - 1$ **18.** $y = \cos x - 1$

19. $y = -\cos x + 1$ **20.** $y = -\sin x + 2$

21. $y = -\tan x + 1$ **22.** $y = \cot x + 2$

23. $y = \sec x + 2$ **24.** $y = -\csc x + 1$

In Exercises 25–52, find amplitude (if any), period, and phase shift of the graph of each function.

25. $y = 5 \cos\left(x - \pi\right)$ **26.** $y = 3 \sin\left(x - \dfrac{\pi}{8}\right)$

27. $y = 7 \cos 9\left(x + \dfrac{\pi}{6}\right)$ **28.** $y = 11 \sin 8\left(x + \dfrac{\pi}{3}\right)$

29. $y = -6 \cos\dfrac{1}{2}(x + 2)$ **30.** $y = -8 \sin\dfrac{1}{5}(x + 9)$

31. $y = 0.9 \sin 0.25\left(x - \dfrac{\pi}{4}\right)$ **32.** $y = \sqrt{5} \cos \pi(x + 1)$

33. $y = 4 \cos\left(2x + \dfrac{\pi}{3}\right)$ **34.** $y = 5 \sin\left(3x + \dfrac{\pi}{2}\right)$

35. $y = -\dfrac{3}{2} \sin\left(2x - \pi\right)$ **36.** $y = -2 \cos\left(5x - \dfrac{\pi}{4}\right)$

37. $y = 3 \cos\left(\pi x - 1\right)$ **38.** $y = \sin\left(\dfrac{\pi x}{3} + 1\right)$

39. $y = \dfrac{1}{2} \cos\left(\dfrac{\pi x}{4} + \dfrac{\pi}{4}\right)$ **40.** $y = -\sin\left(\dfrac{\pi x}{6} + \dfrac{\pi}{6}\right)$

41. $y = 2 \sin\left(\pi x + 3\right)$ **42.** $y = -\cos\left(\pi x - \dfrac{1}{4}\right)$

43. $y = \sec 4\left(x - \dfrac{\pi}{4}\right)$ **44.** $y = \sec\dfrac{1}{2}\left(x - \dfrac{\pi}{2}\right)$

45. $y = 3 \csc\left(x + \dfrac{\pi}{2}\right)$ **46.** $y = 3 \sec 2\left(x - \dfrac{\pi}{6}\right)$

47. $y = \tan\dfrac{2}{3}\left(x - \dfrac{\pi}{2}\right)$ **48.** $y = 2 \cot 2\left(x - \dfrac{\pi}{6}\right)$

49. $y = -5 \tan 2\left(x + \dfrac{\pi}{3}\right)$ **50.** $y = -3 \cot\dfrac{1}{2}\left(x - \dfrac{\pi}{3}\right)$

51. $y = \dfrac{1}{3} \cot 2(x - \pi)$ **52.** $y = \dfrac{1}{2} \tan 4\left(x - \dfrac{\pi}{6}\right)$

In Exercises 53–68, graph each function over a one-period interval.

53. $y = 2 \cos\left(x - \dfrac{\pi}{2}\right)$ **54.** $y = 3 \sin\left(x - \dfrac{\pi}{4}\right)$

55. $y = 3 \sin\left(x + \dfrac{\pi}{6}\right)$ **56.** $y = 4 \cos\left(x + \dfrac{\pi}{6}\right)$

57. $y = -2 \sin\left(x - \dfrac{\pi}{4}\right) + 1$ **58.** $y = -3 \cos\left(x - \dfrac{\pi}{6}\right) + 2$

59. $y = -3 \cos\left(x + \dfrac{\pi}{2}\right) - 2$ **60.** $y = -4 \sin\left(x + \dfrac{\pi}{4}\right) - 3$

61. $y = 2 \cos\left(2x - \dfrac{\pi}{4}\right)$ **62.** $y = \sin\left(3x - \pi\right)$

63. $y = -4 \sin\left(2x + \pi\right) + 1$

64. $y = -3 \cos\left(2x + \dfrac{\pi}{3}\right) + 2$

65. $y = 4 \cos\left[4\left(x - \dfrac{\pi}{6}\right)\right] - 2$

66. $y = 3 \sin\left[4\left(x + \dfrac{\pi}{6}\right)\right] - 1$

67. $y = \dfrac{3}{2} \sin\left[\dfrac{1}{2}\left(x - \dfrac{\pi}{4}\right)\right]$ **68.** $y = \dfrac{5}{2} \cos\left[\pi(x - 1)\right]$

In Exercises 69–80, graph each function over a two-period interval.

69. $y = \tan\left(2x + \pi\right)$ **70.** $y = \tan\left(2x - \pi\right)$

71. $y = \cot\left(2x - \dfrac{\pi}{2}\right)$ **72.** $y = \cot\left(2x + \dfrac{\pi}{2}\right)$

73. $y = 2 \tan\left[\dfrac{1}{2}\left(x - \dfrac{\pi}{4}\right)\right]$ **74.** $y = 2 \cot\left[\dfrac{1}{2}\left(x + \dfrac{\pi}{4}\right)\right]$

75. $y = -2 \tan\left(2x + \dfrac{\pi}{4}\right)$ **76.** $y = -2 \cot\left(2x - \dfrac{\pi}{4}\right)$

77. $y = 3 \tan\left(2x - \dfrac{\pi}{4}\right) + 1$ **78.** $y = 3 \cot\left(2x + \dfrac{\pi}{4}\right) - 1$

79. $y = -2 \tan\left(2x - \dfrac{\pi}{3}\right) - 3$ **80.** $y = -2 \cot\left(2x - \dfrac{\pi}{3}\right) - 3$

In Exercises 81–88, use appropriate graphs from Exercises 53–68 to graph each function over a one-period interval.

81. $y = 2 \sec\left(x - \dfrac{\pi}{2}\right)$ **82.** $y = 3 \csc\left(x - \dfrac{\pi}{4}\right)$

83. $y = -2 \csc\left(x - \dfrac{\pi}{4}\right) + 1$

84. $y = -3 \sec\left(x - \dfrac{\pi}{6}\right) + 2$

85. $y = -4 \csc\left(2x + \pi\right) + 1$

86. $y = -3 \sec\left(2x + \dfrac{\pi}{3}\right) + 2$

87. $y = 4 \sec\left[4\left(x - \dfrac{\pi}{6}\right)\right] - 2$

88. $y = 3 \csc\left[4\left(x + \dfrac{\pi}{6}\right)\right] - 1$

In Exercises 89–96, write an equation for each graph.

89.   **90.**

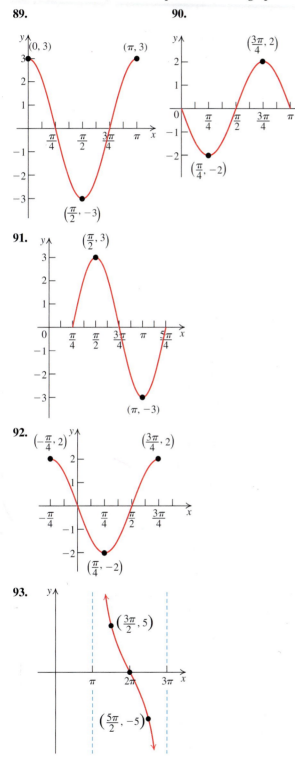

91.

92.

93.

94.

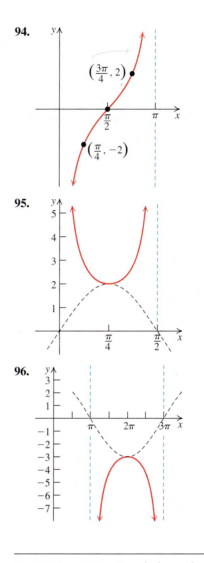

95.

96.

B EXERCISES Applying the Concepts

97. **Pulse and blood pressure.** Blood pressure is given by two numbers written as a fraction: $\dfrac{\text{systolic}}{\text{diastolic}}$. The *systolic* reading is the maximum pressure in an artery, and the *diastolic* reading is the minimum pressure in an artery. As the heart beats, the systolic measurement is taken; when the heart rests, the diastolic measurement is taken. A reading of $\dfrac{120}{80}$ is considered normal. Your pulse is the number of heartbeats per minute. Suppose Desmond's blood pressure after t minutes is given by

$$p(t) = 20 \sin(140\pi t) + 122,$$

where $p(t)$ is the pressure in millimeters of mercury.
  a. Find the period and explain how it relates to pulse.
  b. Graph the function over one period.
  c. What is Desmond's blood pressure?

98. Pulse and blood pressure. Anita's blood pressure reads $\frac{110}{75}$. Her pulse rate is 60 beats per minute. Write an equation for Anita's blood pressure, $p(t)$, as a sinusoidal function.

99. Kangaroo population. The kangaroo population in a certain region is given by the function

$$N(t) = 650 + 150 \sin 2t,$$

where the time t is measured in years.
  a. What is the largest number of kangaroos present in the region at any time?
  b. What is the smallest number of kangaroos present in the region at any time?
  c. How much time elapses between occurrences of the largest and smallest kangaroo population?

100. Lion and deer populations. The number of deer in a region is given by $D(t) = 450 \sin\left(\frac{3t}{5}\right) + 1200$ and the number of lions in that same region is given by $L(t) = 225 \sin\left(\frac{2}{5}(t - 2)\right) + 500$, where t is in years.
  a. Graph both functions on the same coordinate plane for $0 \leq t \leq 10$.
  b. What can you say about the relationship between these populations based on the graphs obtained in part (a)?
  c. Use a graphing calculator to verify your graph.

101. Daylight hours in London. The table gives the average number of daylight hours in London each month, where $x = 1$ represents January. Let y represent the number of daylight hours in London in month x. Find a function of the form $y = A \sin B(x - C) + D$ that models the hours of daylight throughout the year.

Jan	Feb	Mar	Apr	May	June
8.4	10	11.9	13.9	15.6	16.6

July	Aug	Sept	Oct	Nov	Dec
16.1	14.6	12.6	10.7	8.9	7.9

102. Daylight hours in Washington, DC. The table gives the average number of daylight hours in Washington, DC, each month, where $x = 1$ represents January. Let y represent the number of daylight hours in Washington, DC, in month x. Find a function of the form $y = A \sin B(x - C) + D$ that models the hours of daylight throughout the year.

Jan	Feb	Mar	Apr	May	June
9.8	10.8	12	13.2	14.3	14.8

July	Aug	Sept	Oct	Nov	Dec
14.6	13.6	12.4	11.2	10.1	9.5

103. Average temperature. The monthly average temperatures for Augusta, Maine, are given in the table.

Month	1	2	3	4	5	6	7	8	9	10	11	12
°F	19	22	31	43	54	63	70	67	59	48	37	24

Source: http://www.weatherbase.com/

  a. Find a function of the form $y = A \sin B(x - C) + D$ that models these temperatures.
  b. Graph the ordered pairs and the function on the same coordinate system.
  c. Compute the function values for January, April, July, and October, and compare these with the table values for these months.
  d. Use a graphing calculator to verify your graph.

104. Average temperatures. The monthly average temperatures for Nashville, Tennessee, are given in the table.

Month	1	2	3	4	5	6	7	8	9	10	11	12
°F	40	45	53	63	71	79	83	81	74	63	52	44

Source: http://www.weatherbase.com/

  a. Find a function of the form $y = A \sin B(x - C) + D$ that models these temperatures.
  b. Graph the ordered pairs and the function on the same coordinate system.
  c. Compute the function values for January, April, July, and October and compare these to the table values for these months.
  d. Use a graphing calculator to verify your graph.

C EXERCISES Beyond the Basics

105. For a sinusoidal equation $y = A \sin(Bx - C) + D$, the maximum value of y is M and its minimum value is m.

Show that $|A| = \frac{1}{2}(M - m)$ and $D = \frac{1}{2}(M + m)$.

[*Hint:* Consider two cases: $A > 0$ and $A < 0$.]

In Exercises 106–109, write a sinusoidal equation of the form $y = A \sin(Bx - C) + D$ with the given conditions.

106. Amplitude: 3; period: $\frac{\pi}{2}$; phase shift: $\frac{1}{3}$; vertical shift: 4

107. Amplitude: 4; period: π; phase shift: $-\frac{1}{2}$; vertical shift: -2

108. Maximum value at $x = 8$: 14; minimum value: 4; period: 12 months

109. Maximum value: 16; minimum value at $x = 15$: 10; period: 60 minutes

In Exercises 110–112, use the following graph of
$f(x) = A \cos(Bx) + D.$

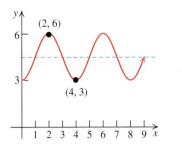

(2, 6)

(4, 3)

110. Find A, B, and D.

111. Find $f(2011)$.

112. Sketch a graph of $y = A \sec(Bx) + D$, where A, B, and D are the constants found in Exercise 109.

113. Show that the period of $f(x) = \sin(2x)\cos(2x)$ is $\dfrac{\pi}{2}$.

    a. Verify algebraically that $f\left(x + \dfrac{\pi}{2}\right) = f(x)$.

[*Hint:* Recall that $\sin(\theta + \pi) = -\sin\theta$ and $\cos(\theta + \pi) = -\cos\theta$.]

    b. Verify by using a graphing calculator.

114. Suppose $f(x)$ is neither a constant nor periodic and its domain contains the interval $[-1, 1]$. Is the function $y = f(\sin 4x)$ periodic?

115. Find the amplitude of the function $y = \sin(\sin(4x))$.

Critical Thinking

116. *True or False* If $A \neq 0$ and $B \neq 0$, then the amplitude of $A \sin(Bx - C)$ is $|A|$, period is $\dfrac{2\pi}{|B|}$, and phase shift is $\dfrac{C}{|B|}$.

117. Use a graphing calculator to sketch for $x > 0$ the graphs of $y = 2^{-x}$, $y = -2^{-x}$, and $y = 2^{-x}\sin x$. What effect does the factor 2^{-x} have on the graph of $y = \sin x$?

REVIEW

| **Definitions, Concepts, and Formulas** | **Examples and Illustrations** |

4.1 Graphs of the Circular Functions

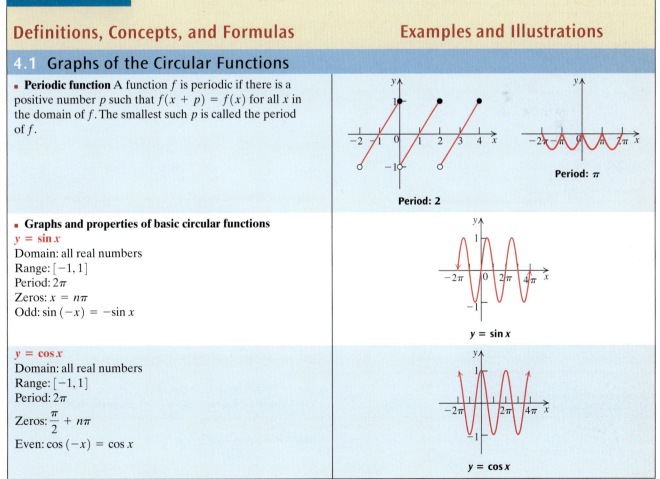

- **Periodic function** A function f is periodic if there is a positive number p such that $f(x + p) = f(x)$ for all x in the domain of f. The smallest such p is called the period of f.

Period: 2

Period: π

- **Graphs and properties of basic circular functions**
$y = \sin x$
Domain: all real numbers
Range: $[-1, 1]$
Period: 2π
Zeros: $x = n\pi$
Odd: $\sin(-x) = -\sin x$

$y = \sin x$

$y = \cos x$
Domain: all real numbers
Range: $[-1, 1]$
Period: 2π
Zeros: $\dfrac{\pi}{2} + n\pi$
Even: $\cos(-x) = \cos x$

$y = \cos x$

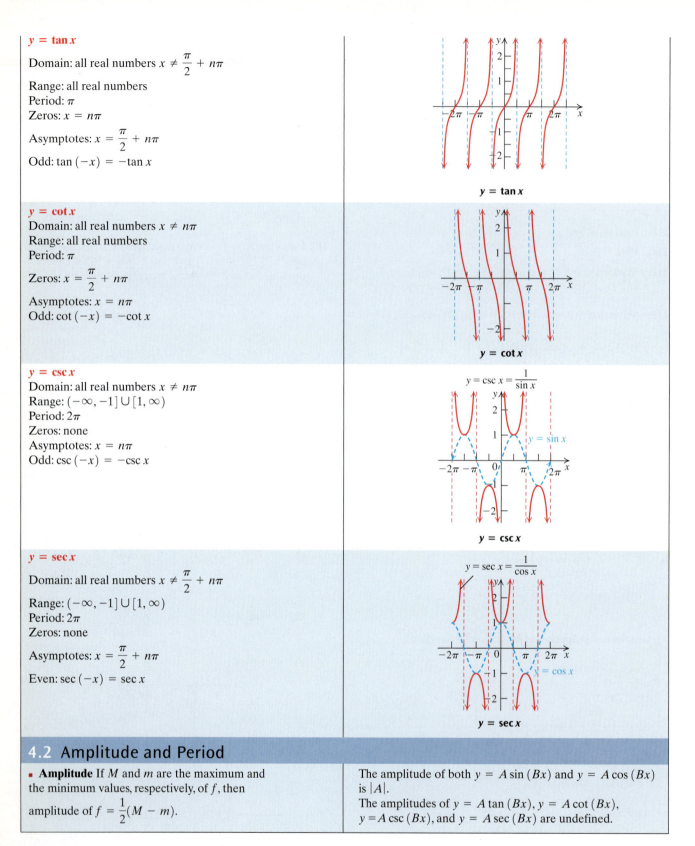

$y = \tan x$

Domain: all real numbers $x \neq \dfrac{\pi}{2} + n\pi$

Range: all real numbers

Period: π

Zeros: $x = n\pi$

Asymptotes: $x = \dfrac{\pi}{2} + n\pi$

Odd: $\tan(-x) = -\tan x$

$y = \tan x$

$y = \cot x$

Domain: all real numbers $x \neq n\pi$

Range: all real numbers

Period: π

Zeros: $x = \dfrac{\pi}{2} + n\pi$

Asymptotes: $x = n\pi$

Odd: $\cot(-x) = -\cot x$

$y = \cot x$

$y = \csc x$

Domain: all real numbers $x \neq n\pi$

Range: $(-\infty, -1] \cup [1, \infty)$

Period: 2π

Zeros: none

Asymptotes: $x = n\pi$

Odd: $\csc(-x) = -\csc x$

$y = \csc x = \dfrac{1}{\sin x}$

$y = \sin x$

$y = \csc x$

$y = \sec x$

Domain: all real numbers $x \neq \dfrac{\pi}{2} + n\pi$

Range: $(-\infty, -1] \cup [1, \infty)$

Period: 2π

Zeros: none

Asymptotes: $x = \dfrac{\pi}{2} + n\pi$

Even: $\sec(-x) = \sec x$

$y = \sec x = \dfrac{1}{\cos x}$

$y = \cos x$

$y = \sec x$

4.2 Amplitude and Period

■ **Amplitude** If M and m are the maximum and the minimum values, respectively, of f, then

$$\text{amplitude of } f = \frac{1}{2}(M - m).$$

The amplitude of both $y = A\sin(Bx)$ and $y = A\cos(Bx)$ is $|A|$.

The amplitudes of $y = A\tan(Bx)$, $y = A\cot(Bx)$, $y = A\csc(Bx)$, and $y = A\sec(Bx)$ are undefined.

■ **Graphing $y = Af(x)$** Suppose f is one of the six basic circular functions. For $A > 0$, the graph of $y = Af(x)$ is obtained by stretching or compressing vertically the graph of $y = f(x)$ by a factor of A.

If $A < 0$, we sketch the graph of $y = |A|f(x)$ and then reflect it about the x-axis.

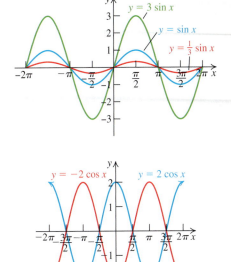

■ **Period** Suppose $y = f(x)$ is a circular function with period p. Then the period of $y = f(Bx)$ is $\dfrac{p}{|B|}$.

The period of each function $y = \sin(Bx)$, $y = \cos(Bx)$, $y = \csc(Bx)$, and $y = \sec(Bx)$ is $\dfrac{2\pi}{|B|}$.

The period of each function $y = \tan(Bx)$ and $y = \cot(Bx)$ is $\dfrac{\pi}{|B|}$.

■ **Graphing $y = f(Bx)$** For $B > 0$, the graph of $y = f(Bx)$ is obtained by stretching or compressing horizontally the graph of $y = f(x)$ by a factor of $\dfrac{1}{B}$.

If $B < 0$, we graph $y = f(|B|x)$, then use even–odd properties of f to graph $y = f(Bx)$. That is, if f is odd, we reflect the graph of $y = f(|B|x)$ about the x-axis to get the graph of $y = f(Bx)$. If f is even, the graph of $y = f(|B|x)$ is the graph of $y = f(Bx)$.

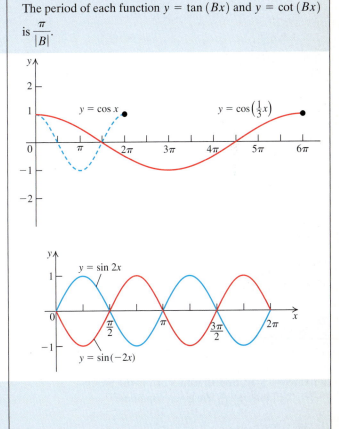

The procedure for graphing (a) $y = A\sin(Bx)$ and $y = A\cos(Bx)$ is given on page 146, (b) $y = A\tan(Bx)$ and $y = A\cot(Bx)$ is given on page 149, and (c) $y = A\csc(Bx)$ and $y = A\sec(Bx)$ is illustrated in Example 10 on page 151.

4.3 Translations of the Graphs of Circular Functions

▪ **Phase shift** Phase shift is the amount by which the graph of $y = Af(Bx)$ is shifted horizontally (left or right) to produce the graph of $y = Af(Bx - C)$.

▪ **Finding phase shift** (a) To find the period and phase shift of $y = A \sin(Bx - C)$, $y = A \cos(Bx - C)$, $y = A \csc(Bx - C)$, and $y = A \sec(Bx - C)$ solve

$$Bx - C = 0 \quad \text{and} \quad Bx - C = 2\pi.$$

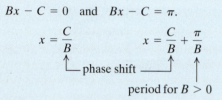

period for $B > 0$

(b) To find the period and phase shift of $y = A \tan(Bx - C)$ and $y = A \cot(Bx - C)$, solve

$$Bx - C = 0 \quad \text{and} \quad Bx - C = \pi.$$

$$x = \frac{C}{B} \qquad x = \frac{C}{B} + \frac{\pi}{B}$$

phase shift

period for $B > 0$

If $B < 0$, use even–odd properties of the circular function and then graph the resulting function.

▪ **Vertical shift** The graph of $y = f(x) + D$ results by shifting the graph of $y = f(x)$ vertically D units up if $D > 0$ and $|D|$ units down if $D < 0$.

The procedure for graphing $y = Af(Bx - C) + D$ is given on page 163.

Find the phase shift and the period for $y = 5 \sin(3x - 2)$.

Solution: We solve for x.

$$3x - 2 = 0 \quad \text{and} \quad 3x - 2 = 2\pi$$

$$x = \frac{2}{3} \qquad x = \frac{2}{3} + \frac{2\pi}{3}$$

$$\text{Phase shift} = \frac{2}{3}$$

$$\text{Period} = \frac{2\pi}{3}$$

Find the phase shift and the period for $y = -3 \cot\left(2x - \frac{\pi}{4}\right)$.

Solution: We solve for x.

$$2x - \frac{\pi}{4} = 0 \quad \text{and} \quad 2x - \frac{\pi}{4} = \pi$$

$$x = \frac{\pi}{8} \quad \text{and} \quad x = \frac{\pi}{8} + \frac{\pi}{2}$$

$$\text{Phase shift} = \frac{\pi}{8}$$

$$\text{Period} = \frac{\pi}{2}$$

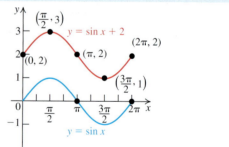

REVIEW EXERCISES

In Exercises 1–12, find all values of x in the interval $[-2\pi, 2\pi]$ that satisfy the given condition.

1. $\sin x = \dfrac{1}{2}$

2. $\cos x = \dfrac{1}{2}$

3. $\tan x = \sqrt{3}$

4. $\cot x = \sqrt{3}$

5. $\csc x = \dfrac{1}{2}$

6. $\sec x = \dfrac{1}{2}$

7. $\sec x = -\sqrt{2}$

8. $\csc x = \sqrt{2}$

9. $\tan\left(x - \dfrac{\pi}{4}\right)$ is undefined.

10. $\cot\left(x + \dfrac{\pi}{4}\right)$ is undefined.

11. $\csc\left(x + \dfrac{\pi}{8}\right)$ is undefined.

12. $\sec\left(x - \dfrac{\pi}{4}\right)$ is undefined.

In Exercises 13–24, find the range of each function.

13. $y = 2\sin 5x$

14. $y = 3\cos 2x$

15. $y = -3\sin 2x$

16. $y = -2\cos 5x$

17. $y = 3\csc x$

18. $y = 4\sec x$

19. $y = -2\sec 3x$

20. $y = -3\csc 2x$

21. $y = -3\sin(2x) + 4$

22. $y = -2\cos(3x) - 4$

23. $y = -3\sec(2x) + 1$

24. $y = 2\sec(3x) - 3$

In Exercises 25–38, find (if any) the amplitude, period, zeros, phase shift, vertical translation, and asymptotes of each function.

25. $y = -\dfrac{3}{2}\cos x$

26. $y = \dfrac{5}{2}\sin x$

27. $y = 3\sin(5x)$

28. $y = \dfrac{1}{2}\cos(5x)$

29. $y = 3\sin\left(x - \dfrac{\pi}{3}\right)$

30. $y = -2\cos(\pi x)$

31. $y = 2\tan\left(x - \dfrac{\pi}{3}\right)$

32. $y = 4\cot\left(x + \dfrac{\pi}{4}\right)$

33. $y = 2\cos\left(2x + \dfrac{\pi}{3}\right) + 1$

34. $y = -4\sin\left(3x - \dfrac{\pi}{2}\right) + 2$

35. $y = 2\tan\left(3x - \dfrac{\pi}{2}\right) + 1$

36. $y = -2\cot\left(2x + \dfrac{\pi}{4}\right) - 4$

37. $y = 3\sec\left(2x + \dfrac{\pi}{3}\right) - 2$

38. $y = 2\sec\left(3x - \dfrac{\pi}{2}\right) + 4$

In Exercises 39–50, graph each function over a two-period interval.

39. $y = -3\cos x$

40. $y = 5\cos x$

41. $y = 3\sin\left(x - \dfrac{\pi}{3}\right)$

42. $y = 4\cos\left(x + \dfrac{3\pi}{2}\right)$

43. $y = -2\cos\left(x + \dfrac{2\pi}{3}\right)$

44. $y = 3\cos(x - \pi)$

45. $y = 5\tan\left(2x - \dfrac{\pi}{2}\right)$

46. $y = -\cot\left(2x + \dfrac{\pi}{2}\right)$

47. $y = \dfrac{1}{2}\sec\left(\dfrac{x}{2}\right)$

48. $y = -3\sec\left(\dfrac{x}{2}\right)$

49. $y = 2\sin\left(3x - \dfrac{\pi}{2}\right) + 1$

50. $y = -3\cos\left(2x - \dfrac{\pi}{2}\right) + 1$

51. Biorhythm states. The physical (P), emotional (E), and intellectual (I) states of an individual who is t days old are given by $P = \sin\left(\dfrac{2\pi}{23}t\right)$, $E = \sin\left(\dfrac{2\pi}{28}t\right)$, and $I = \sin\left(\dfrac{2\pi}{33}t\right)$.

   a. Find Andy's physical state when he is 7000 days old.

   b. Find Amit's intellectual state when he is 8000 days old.

   c. Find Michelle's emotional state when she is 7600 days old.

52. Simple harmonic motion. The motion of a weight attached to a spring is described by the equation $x = 4\cos(2t)$ where x is the displacement in inches and t is the time in seconds.

   a. Find the amplitude, period, and frequency of this motion.

   b. Find the position relative to the equilibrium of the weight after three seconds.

53. Simple harmonic motion. A ball attached to a spring is pulled down 11 inches and released, and the resulting simple harmonic motion has a period of five seconds. Write an equation of the ball's motion.

54. Electric voltage. The voltage $V(t)$ in an electrical circuit is given by $V(t) = (110)\cos(120\pi t)$, where t is measured in seconds.

   a. Find the amplitude, period, and frequency for $V(t)$.

   b. Graph $V(t)$ over the interval $\left[0, \dfrac{1}{30}\right]$.

55. The table gives the average number of daylight hours in Santa Fe, New Mexico, each month. Let y represent the number of daylight hours in Santa Fe in month x, and find a function of the form $y = A\sin[B(x - C)] + D$ that models the hours of daylight throughout the year, where $x = 1$ represents January.

Jan	Feb	Mar	Apr	May	June
10.1	9.9	12.0	12.7	14.1	14.1

July	Aug	Sept	Oct	Nov	Dec
14.3	13.5	12.0	11.3	10.0	9.8

56. Ocean tides. The table gives the water levels on the shores of an island t hours after midnight on January 1, 2008.

t	Water Level in Feet
0	5
3	6 (high tide)
9.5	2 (low tide)
16	6 (high tide)

   a. Write a function of the form $y = A \cos (Bt - C) + D$ that models the water level t hours after midnight.

   b. Estimate the water level when $t = 14$.

57. Chemotherapy and WBC count. Chemotherapy is the use of chemicals to destroy cancer cells. One side effect of chemotherapy is that it damages healthy cells such as white blood cells (WBC) that fight diseases. Patients are then given other drugs to increase the WBC count.

Amilia is undergoing chemotherapy treatment administered every 21 days. Her WBC count after t days of treatment is given in the table.

t	WBC Count per Microliter ($=10^{-9}$ liter)
0	5000
10.5	2000
21	5000

   a. Find a function of the form $y = A \cos (Bt) + D$ that models the WBC count in the table.

   b. What is Amilia's WBC when $t = 7$?

CHAPTER TEST

In Problems 1–8, graph each function over a two-period interval. Identify (if applicable) the amplitude, period, phase shift, and asymptotes.

1. $y = -2 \sin x$

2. $y = 3 \cos (\pi x)$

3. $y = \tan \left(x - \dfrac{\pi}{4} \right)$

4. $y = 2 \sin \left(2x - \dfrac{\pi}{4} \right)$

5. $y = -2 - 3 \cos \left(\dfrac{\pi}{2}x - \dfrac{\pi}{4} \right)$

6. $y = -1 + \cot \left(x - \dfrac{\pi}{2} \right)$

7. $y = 2 \csc \left(\dfrac{x}{2} - 1 \right)$

8. $y = 2 - \sec \left(3x - \dfrac{\pi}{2} \right)$

In Problems, 9–12, find an equation for each graph.

9.

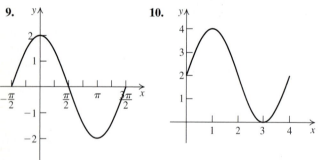

10.

11.

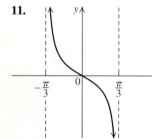

12.

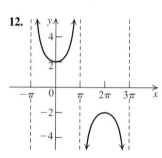

13. Assuming that $y = A \sin (Bx - C)$ has an amplitude of $\dfrac{1}{2}$, a period of 4π, and a phase shift of $\dfrac{\pi}{2}$, find A, B, and C.

14. A ball attached to a spring is pulled down 7 inches and released. The resulting simple harmonic motion has a period of four seconds. Write an equation for the ball's simple harmonic motion.

In Problems 15–20, state whether the given statement is true or false. Justify your answer.

15. The graph of $y = A \cos (Bx)$ is the same as the graph of $y = A \cos (-Bx)$.

16. The graph of $y = \sin (2x)$ can be obtained by stretching the graph of $y = \sin x$ horizontally by a factor of 2.

17. The graph of a circular function has asymptotes wherever it is undefined.

18. The functions $\sec x$ and $\tan x$ have the same domain.

19. The functions $y = 2 \cos x$ and $y = \cos (2x)$ have the same graph.

20. The functions $y = \tan x$ and $y = -\cot \left(x + \dfrac{\pi}{2} \right)$ have the same graph.

Trigonometric Identities

Everyone knows that any idea can be expressed in many ways and in many languages. The valuable information contained in the trigonometric expressions that are used in applications around the world can likewise be written many ways. In this chapter, we study various ways to rewrite familiar formulas to extend their usefulness.

Verifying Identities

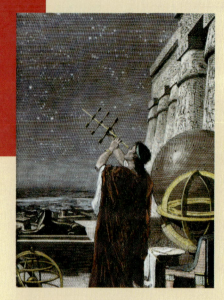

Hipparchus of Rhodes

(190–120 B.C.)

Hipparchus was born in Nicaea (now called Iznik) in Bithynia (northwest Turkey) but spent much of his life in Rhodes (Greece). Many historians consider him the founder of trigonometry. He introduced trigonometric functions in the form of a chord table—the ancestor of the sine table found in ancient Indian astronomical works. With his chord table, Hipparchus could solve the height–distance problems of plane trigonometry. In his time, there was no Greek term for trigonometry because it was not counted as a branch of mathematics. Rather, trigonometry was just an aid to solving problems in astronomy.

Before Starting this Section, Review

1. Signs of the trigonometric functions (Section 1.3)

2. Factoring and special products (Appendix)

3. Reciprocal, quotient, and Pythagorean identities (Section 1.5)

Objectives

1 Verify the even–odd identities.

2 Verify a trigonometric identity.

VISUALIZING TRIGONOMETRIC FUNCTIONS

Trigonometric functions are commonly defined as the ratios of two sides corresponding to an angle in a right triangle. The Greek mathematician Hipparchus was the first person to relate trigonometric functions to a circle. His work allows us to visualize the trigonometric functions of an acute angle θ as the length of various segments associated with a unit circle. The figure below shows several similar triangles. (See Figure 5.1.) For example, right triangles PCT and OCP are similar ($\theta = \angle CPT$); so

$$\frac{CT}{PC} = \frac{PC}{OC} \qquad \text{Sides are proportional.}$$

From Figure 5.1, we use the definitions of the trigonometric functions to get

$$PC = \sin \theta, \quad OC = \cos \theta, \quad \text{and} \quad CT = OT - OC = \sec \theta - \cos \theta.$$

Substituting those values into the equation $\dfrac{CT}{PC} = \dfrac{PC}{OC}$, we obtain

$$\frac{\sec \theta - \cos \theta}{\sin \theta} = \frac{\sin \theta}{\cos \theta}.$$

In Example 3, we verify that this equation is an identity. Recall that an *identity* is an equation that is satisfied by all numbers for which both sides are defined.

In Section 1.3, the six trigonometric functions were defined in terms of the coordinates of a point $P(x, y)$ on a unit circle. Consequently, these functions are related to each other and any expression containing these functions can be written in several equivalent ways. ■

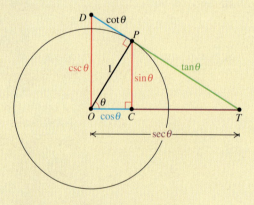

FIGURE 5.1 **The unit circle and the trigonometric functions**

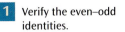 Verify the even–odd
identities.

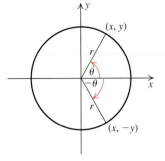

FIGURE 5.2 $\sin(-\theta) = -\sin\theta$,
$\cos(-\theta) = \cos\theta$

In Chapter 1, we proved that certain equations are identities and showed that other equations are not identities. We verified several basic identities directly from the definitions of the trigonometric functions. We verify the *even–odd identities* in a similar fashion.

If an angle θ has the point (x, y) on its terminal side, then the angle $-\theta$ has the point $(x, -y)$ on its terminal side, as suggested by Figure 5.2.

From the definition of the sine function, we have

$$\sin(-\theta) = \frac{-y}{r} = -\frac{y}{r} \quad \text{and} \quad \sin(\theta) = \frac{y}{r}$$

so

$$\sin(-\theta) = -\sin\theta.$$

Also,

$$\cos(-\theta) = \frac{x}{r} \quad \text{and} \quad \cos(\theta) = \frac{x}{r}$$

so

$$\cos(-\theta) = \cos\theta.$$

We use these results to prove that $\tan(-\theta) = -\tan\theta$.

$$\tan(-\theta) = \frac{\sin(-\theta)}{\cos(-\theta)} = \frac{-\sin\theta}{\cos\theta} = -\frac{\sin\theta}{\cos\theta} = -\tan\theta$$

The identities

$$\csc(-\theta) = -\csc\theta \qquad \sec(-\theta) = \sec\theta \qquad \cot(-\theta) = -\cot\theta$$

can be established using similar techniques.

The even–odd identities, together with the reciprocal, quotient, and Pythagorean identities are called **fundamental trigonometric identities** and are listed in the following box.

FUNDAMENTAL TRIGONOMETRIC IDENTITIES

1. **Reciprocal Identities**

$$\csc x = \frac{1}{\sin x} \qquad \sec x = \frac{1}{\cos x} \qquad \cot x = \frac{1}{\tan x}$$

$$\sin x = \frac{1}{\csc x} \qquad \cos x = \frac{1}{\sec x} \qquad \tan x = \frac{1}{\cot x}$$

2. **Quotient Identities**

$$\tan x = \frac{\sin x}{\cos x} \qquad \cot x = \frac{\cos x}{\sin x}$$

3. **Pythagorean Identities**

$$\sin^2 x + \cos^2 x = 1 \qquad 1 + \tan^2 x = \sec^2 x \qquad 1 + \cot^2 x = \csc^2 x$$

4. **Even–Odd Identities**

$$\sin(-x) = -\sin x \qquad \cos(-x) = \cos x \qquad \tan(-x) = -\tan x$$

$$\csc(-x) = -\csc x \qquad \sec(-x) = \sec x \qquad \cot(-x) = -\cot x$$

STUDY TIP

It is important to remember that the terminal side of an angle determines the quadrant in which the angle lies. It does *not* matter whether the angle is measured in radians or in degrees.

EXAMPLE 1   **Using the Even–Odd Identities**

Find the following values.

a. $\sin(-60°)$ **b.** $\tan\left(-\dfrac{\pi}{6}\right)$ **c.** $\cos\left(-\dfrac{\pi}{4}\right)$

SOLUTION

a. $\sin(-60°) = -\sin 60° = -\dfrac{\sqrt{3}}{2}$ $\sin 60° = \dfrac{\sqrt{3}}{2}$

b. $\tan\left(-\dfrac{\pi}{6}\right) = -\tan\dfrac{\pi}{6} = -\dfrac{\sqrt{3}}{3}$ $\tan\dfrac{\pi}{6} = \dfrac{\sqrt{3}}{3}$

c. $\cos\left(-\dfrac{\pi}{4}\right) = \cos\dfrac{\pi}{4} = \dfrac{\sqrt{2}}{2}$ $\cos\dfrac{\pi}{4} = \dfrac{\sqrt{2}}{2}$

■ ■ ■

Practice Problem 1   Find the following values.

a. $\cos(-30°)$ **b.** $\cot\left(-\dfrac{\pi}{3}\right)$ **c.** $\sin\left(-\dfrac{5\pi}{4}\right)$

■

2 Verify a trigonometric identity.

Process of Verifying Trigonometric Identities

Verifying a trigonometric identity differs from solving an equation. In verifying an identity, we are given an equation and want to show that the equation is satisfied by *all* values of the variable for which both sides of the equation are defined.

VERIFYING TRIGONOMETRIC IDENTITIES

To verify that an equation is an identity, transform one side of the equation into the other side by a sequence of steps, each of which produces an identity. The steps involved may be algebraic manipulations or may use known identities.

    Note that in verifying an identity, we *do not* just perform the same operation on both sides of the equation.

 In Example 2, we use a graphing calculator to graph $Y_1 = \dfrac{\csc^2 x - 1}{\cot x}$ and $Y_2 = \cot x$. Although not a definitive method of proof, the graphs appear identical; so the equation in Example 2 *appears* to be an identity.

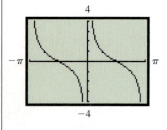

Graph of Y_1

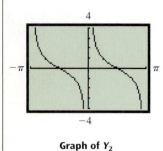

Graph of Y_2

Methods of Verifying Trigonometric Identities

Verifying trigonometric identities requires practice and experience. In the following examples, we suggest five guidelines for verifying trigonometric identities.

1. **Start with the more complicated side and transform it to the simpler side.**

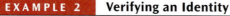

EXAMPLE 2   **Verifying an Identity**

Verify the identity:

$$\frac{\csc^2 x - 1}{\cot x} = \cot x$$

SOLUTION

We start with the left side of the equation because it appears more complicated than the right side.

$$\frac{\csc^2 x - 1}{\cot x} = \frac{\cot^2 x}{\cot x} \qquad \text{Because } \csc^2 x = 1 + \cot^2 x, \text{ we have } \csc^2 x - 1 = \cot^2 x.$$

$$= \cot x \qquad \text{Remove the common factor } \cot x.$$

We have shown that the left side of the equation is equal to the right side, which verifies the identity. ■ ■ ■

Practice Problem 2   Verify the identity:

$$\frac{1 - \sin^2 x}{\cos x} = \cos x$$

■

In Example 3, we use the TABLE feature of a graphing calculator in Radian mode to create a table of values for

$Y_1 = \dfrac{\sec\theta - \cos\theta}{\sin\theta}$ and

$Y_2 = \dfrac{\sin\theta}{\cos\theta}$ for different values of x.

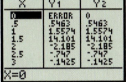

Note that Y_2 equals 0 when $x = 0$ but that Y_1 is undefined when $x = 0$. While not a definitive method of proof, the table shows that the equation in Example 3 *appears* to be an identity because the table values are identical for values of x for which both Y_1 and Y_2 are defined.

2. Stay focused on the final expression.

While working on one side of the equation, stay focused on your goal of converting it to the form on the other side. This often helps in deciding what your next step will be.

EXAMPLE 3   Verifying an Identity

Verify the identity proposed in the introduction to this section

$$\frac{\sec\theta - \cos\theta}{\sin\theta} = \frac{\sin\theta}{\cos\theta}$$

SOLUTION
We start with the more complicated left side.

$$\frac{\sec\theta - \cos\theta}{\sin\theta} = \frac{\dfrac{1}{\cos\theta} - \cos\theta}{\sin\theta} \qquad \sec\theta = \frac{1}{\cos\theta}$$

$$= \frac{\left(\dfrac{1}{\cos\theta} - \cos\theta\right)\cos\theta}{\sin\theta\cos\theta} \qquad \text{Multiply numerator and denominator by } \cos\theta.$$

$$= \frac{\dfrac{1}{\cos\theta}\cdot\cos\theta - \cos^2\theta}{\sin\theta\cos\theta} \qquad \text{Distributive property}$$

$$= \frac{1 - \cos^2\theta}{\sin\theta\cos\theta} \qquad \text{Simplify.}$$

$$= \frac{\sin^2\theta}{\sin\theta\cos\theta} \qquad \text{Variation of the Pythagorean identity } \sin^2\theta + \cos^2\theta = 1$$

$$= \frac{\sin\theta}{\cos\theta} \qquad \text{Remove the common factor } \sin\theta. \quad ■ ■ ■$$

Practice Problem 3 In Figure 5.1 on page 180, triangles OPD and TCP are similar. Thus, $\dfrac{OD}{OP} = \dfrac{PT}{CT}$ leads to

$$\frac{\csc\theta}{1} = \frac{\tan\theta}{\sec\theta - \cos\theta}.$$

Verify that this equation is an identity. ■

3. Convert to sines and cosines.

It may be helpful to rewrite all trigonometric functions in the equation in terms of sines and cosines and then simplify.

EXAMPLE 4   Verifying by Rewriting with Sines and Cosines

Verify the identity: $\cot^4 x + \cot^2 x = \cot^2 x \csc^2 x$

SOLUTION
We start with the more complicated left side.

$$\cot^4 x + \cot^2 x = \frac{\cos^4 x}{\sin^4 x} + \frac{\cos^2 x}{\sin^2 x} \qquad \cot x = \frac{\cos x}{\sin x}$$

$$= \frac{\cos^4 x}{\sin^4 x} + \frac{\cos^2 x}{\sin^2 x}\cdot\frac{\sin^2 x}{\sin^2 x} \qquad \text{The LCD is } \sin^4 x.$$

continued on the next page

$$= \frac{\cos^4 x + \cos^2 x \sin^2 x}{\sin^4 x} \qquad \text{Add fractions.}$$

$$= \frac{\cos^2 x(\cos^2 x + \sin^2 x)}{\sin^4 x} \qquad \text{Factor out } \cos^2 x.$$

$$= \frac{\cos^2 x(1)}{\sin^4 x} \qquad \cos^2 x + \sin^2 x = 1$$

$$= \frac{\cos^2 x}{\sin^2 x} \cdot \frac{1}{\sin^2 x} \qquad \begin{array}{l} \text{Factor to obtain the form on} \\ \text{the right side.} \end{array}$$

$$= \cot^2 x \csc^2 x \qquad \cot x = \frac{\cos x}{\sin x}; \quad \csc x = \frac{1}{\sin x}$$

Because the left side is identical to the right side, the given equation is an identity.
You could also verify the identity in Example 4 as follows:

$$\cot^4 x + \cot^2 x = \cot^2 x(\cot^2 x + 1) \qquad \text{Distributive property}$$
$$= \cot^2 x \csc^2 x \qquad\qquad \text{Pythagorean identity}$$

This shows that rewriting the expression using only sines and cosines is not always the quickest way to verify an identity. It is a useful approach when you are stuck, however. ■ ■ ■

Practice Problem 4 Verify the identity: $\tan^4 x + \tan^2 x = \tan^2 x \sec^2 x$ ■

4. Work on both sides.

Sometimes it is helpful to work separately on both sides of the equation. To verify the identity $P(x) = Q(x)$, for example, we transform the left side $P(x)$ into $R(x)$ by using algebraic manipulations and known identities. Then $P(x) = R(x)$ is an identity. Next, we transform the right side, $Q(x)$, into $R(x)$ so that the equation $R(x) = Q(x)$ is an identity. It then follows that $P(x) = Q(x)$ is an identity. The method is illustrated in the next example.

EXAMPLE 5 **Verifying an Identity by Transforming Both Sides Separately**

Verify the identity:

$$\frac{1}{1 - \sin x} - \frac{1}{1 + \sin x} = \frac{\tan^2 x + \sec^2 x + 1}{\csc x}$$

SOLUTION

We start with the left side of the equation.

$$\frac{1}{1 - \sin x} - \frac{1}{1 + \sin x} \qquad \text{Begin with the left-hand side.}$$

$$= \frac{1}{1 - \sin x} \cdot \frac{1 + \sin x}{1 + \sin x} - \frac{1}{1 + \sin x} \cdot \frac{1 - \sin x}{1 - \sin x} \qquad \begin{array}{l} \text{Rewrite using the LCD,} \\ (1 - \sin x)(1 + \sin x). \end{array}$$

$$= \frac{(1 + \sin x) - (1 - \sin x)}{(1 - \sin x)(1 + \sin x)} \qquad \text{Subtract fractions.}$$

$$= \frac{1 + \sin x - 1 + \sin x}{1 - \sin^2 x} \qquad \begin{array}{l} \text{Remove parentheses in} \\ \text{numerator and multiply} \\ \text{factors in denominator.} \end{array}$$

$$= \frac{2 \sin x}{\cos^2 x} \qquad \begin{array}{l} \text{Simplify numerator,} \\ 1 - \sin^2 x = \cos^2 x. \end{array}$$

We now try to convert the right side to the form $\dfrac{2\sin x}{\cos^2 x}$.

$$\dfrac{\tan^2 x + \sec^2 x + 1}{\csc x}$$

$$= \dfrac{(\tan^2 x + 1) + \sec^2 x}{\csc x} \qquad \text{Regroup terms.}$$

$$= \dfrac{\sec^2 x + \sec^2 x}{\csc x} \qquad \tan^2 x + 1 = \sec^2 x$$

$$= \dfrac{2\sec^2 x}{\csc x} \qquad \text{Simplify.}$$

$$= 2\left(\dfrac{1}{\csc x}\right)\sec^2 x \qquad \text{Rewrite.}$$

$$= 2\sin x\left(\dfrac{1}{\cos^2 x}\right) \qquad \text{Reciprocal identities}$$

$$= \dfrac{2\sin x}{\cos^2 x} \qquad \text{Multiply.}$$

From the original equation, we see that

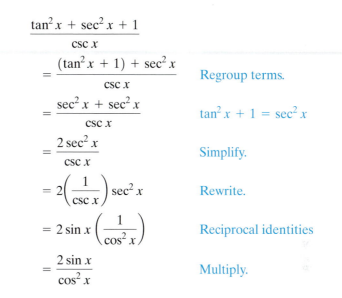

Because both sides of the original equation are equal to $\dfrac{2\sin x}{\cos^2 x}$, the identity is verified. ■ ■ ■

Practice Problem 5   Verify the identity:

$$\tan\theta + \sec\theta = \dfrac{\csc\theta + 1}{\cot\theta} \qquad ■$$

5. Use conjugates.

It may be helpful to multiply both the numerator and denominator of a fraction by the same factor. Recall that the sum $a + b$ and the difference $a - b$ are the *conjugates* of each other.

EXAMPLE 6   **Verifying an Identity by Using a Conjugate**

Verify the identity:

$$\dfrac{\cos x}{1 + \sin x} = \dfrac{1 - \sin x}{\cos x}$$

SOLUTION
We start with the left side of the equation.

$$\frac{\cos x}{1 + \sin x} = \frac{\cos x (1 - \sin x)}{(1 + \sin x)(1 - \sin x)}$$

Multiply numerator and denominator by $1 - \sin x$, the conjugate of $1 + \sin x$.

$$= \frac{\cos x (1 - \sin x)}{1 - \sin^2 x}$$

$(a + b)(a - b) = a^2 - b^2$

$$= \frac{\cos x (1 - \sin x)}{\cos^2 x}$$

$1 - \sin^2 x = \cos^2 x$

$$= \frac{1 - \sin x}{\cos x}$$

Remove the common factor $\cos x$.

This verifies the identity.　　　　　■ ■ ■

Practice Problem 6　Verify the identity: $\dfrac{\tan x}{\sec x + 1} = \dfrac{\sec x - 1}{\tan x}$　　　■

We summarize guidelines and hints to help you verify trigonometric identities.

GUIDELINES FOR VERIFYING TRIGONOMETRIC IDENTITIES

Algebra Operations

Review the procedure for combining fractions by finding the least common denominator.

Fundamental Trigonometric Identities

Review the fundamental trigonometric identities summarized on page 181. Look for an opportunity to apply the fundamental trigonometric identities when working on either side of the identity to be verified. Become thoroughly familiar with alternative forms of fundamental identities. For example, $\sin^2 x = 1 - \cos^2 x$ and $\sec^2 x - \tan^2 x = 1$ are alternative forms of the fundamental identities $\sin^2 x + \cos^2 x = 1$ and $\sec^2 x = 1 + \tan^2 x$, respectively.

1. **Start with the more complicated side.**

   It is generally helpful to start with the more complicated side of an identity and simplify until it becomes identical to the other side. (See Example 2.)

2. **Stay focused on the final expression.**

   While working on one side of the identity, stay focused on your goal of converting it to the form on the other side. (See Example 3.)

   The following techniques are *sometimes* helpful.

3. **Option: Convert to sines and cosines.**

   Rewrite each side of the identity in terms of sines and cosines. (See Example 4.)

4. **Option: Work on both sides.**

   Transform each side separately to the same equivalent expression. (See Example 5.)

5. **Option: Use conjugates.**

   In expressions containing $1 + \sin x$, $1 - \sin x$, $1 + \cos x$, $1 - \cos x$, $\sec x + \tan x$, and so on, multiply the numerator and the denominator by its conjugate and then use one of the forms of the Pythagorean identities. (See Example 6.)

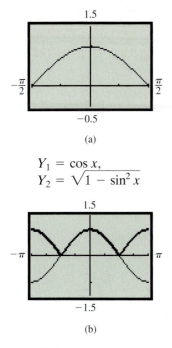

(a)

$$Y_1 = \cos x,$$
$$Y_2 = \sqrt{1 - \sin^2 x}$$

(b)

FIGURE 5.3

Identities and Graphing Calculators

To verify that an equation is a trigonometric identity, you must *prove* that both sides of the equation are equal for all values of the variable for which both sides are defined.

Consider the equation

$$\cos x = \sqrt{1 - \sin^2 x}. \qquad (1)$$

Equation (1) is satisfied by all values of x in the interval $\left[-\dfrac{\pi}{2}, \dfrac{\pi}{2}\right]$. See Figure 5.3(a).

Because the domain of both the sine and cosine functions is the interval $(-\infty, \infty)$, both sides of equation (1) are defined for all real numbers. But for any value of x in the interval $\left(\dfrac{\pi}{2}, \pi\right)$, the left side of equation (1) has a negative value (because $\cos x$ is negative in quadrant II), while the right side of equation (1) has a positive value. Therefore, equation (1) is *not* an identity. Figure 5.3(b) illustrates that a graphing calculator may help you decide that a given equation is *not* an identity. However, Figure 5.3(a) shows that a graphing calculator cannot prove that a given equation *is* an identity because you might happen to use a viewing window where the graphs coincide.

EXAMPLE 7 **Proving That an Equation Is Not an Identity**

Prove that the equation is not an identity:

$$(\sin x - \cos x)^2 = \sin^2 x - \cos^2 x$$

SOLUTION

To prove that the equation is not an identity, we find at least one value of the variable for which both sides are defined but not equal.

Let $x = 0$. We know that $\sin 0 = 0$ and $\cos 0 = 1$.

$$\text{The left side} = (\sin x - \cos x)^2 = (0 - 1)^2 = 1 \qquad \textcolor{blue}{\text{Replace } x \text{ with } 0.}$$
$$\text{The right side} = \sin^2 x - \cos^2 x = (0)^2 - (1)^2 = -1 \qquad \textcolor{blue}{\text{Replace } x \text{ with } 0.}$$

For $x = 0$, the equation's two sides are not equal; the equation is not an identity.

Practice Problem 7 Prove that the equation $\cos x = 1 - \sin x$ is not an identity. ■

SECTION 5.1 ■ Exercises

A EXERCISES Basic Skills and Concepts

1. An equation that is satisfied by all values of the variable in its domain is called a(n) _____.

2. To show that an equation is not an identity, we must find at least _____ value(s) of the variable that result(s) in both sides being defined but _____.

3. $\sin^2 x +$ _____ $= 1$; $1 +$ _____ $= \sec^2 x$; $\csc^2 x - \cot^2 x =$ _____.

4. *True or False* $\tan^2 x \cot x = \tan x$ is not an identity because $\tan^2 x \cot x$ is not defined for $x = 0$, but $\tan x$ is defined for $x = 0$.

5. *True or False* The value of $x = \dfrac{3\pi}{2}$ can be used to show that $\sin x = \sqrt{1 - \cos^2 x}$ is not an identity.

6. *True or False* Graphing calculators can sometimes be used to prove identities.

In Exercises 7–12, use the even–odd identities to evaluate each expression.

7. $\sin(-30°)$ **8.** $\tan(-225°)$ **9.** $\sin\left(-\dfrac{7\pi}{4}\right)$

10. $\cot\left(-\dfrac{11\pi}{6}\right)$ **11.** $\sec\left(-\dfrac{7\pi}{6}\right)$ **12.** $\csc\left(-\dfrac{5\pi}{3}\right)$

In Exercises 13–18, for each expression in Column I, find the expression in Column II that results in an identity when the expressions are equated.

I

II

13. $\dfrac{\cos^2 x + \sin^2 x}{\sin x \cos x}$

   a. $\cos x$

14. $\dfrac{1}{1 + \tan^2 x}$

   b. $(1 + \cos x)^2$

15. $-\cot x \sin(-x)$

   c. $\dfrac{1}{\sin x \cos x}$

16. $1 + 2 \cos x + \cos^2 x$

   d. $\sin^4 x$

17. $1 - 2 \cos^2 x + \cos^4 x$

   e. 1

18. $\sin^2 x (1 + \cot^2 x)$

   f. $\cos^2 x$

In Exercises 19–28, use the fundamental identities and simplify each expression to get a numerical value.

19. $(1 + \tan x)(1 - \tan x) + \sec^2 x$

20. $(\sec x - 1)(\sec x + 1) - \tan^2 x$

21. $(\sec x + \tan x)(\sec x - \tan x)$

22. $\dfrac{\sec^2 x - 4}{\sec x - 2} - \sec x$

23. $\csc^4 x - \cot^4 x - 2 \cot^2 x$

24. $\sin x \cos x (\tan x + \cot x)$

25. $\dfrac{\sec x \csc x (\sin x + \cos x)}{\sec x + \csc x}$

26. $\dfrac{1}{\csc x + 1} - \dfrac{1}{\csc x - 1} + 2 \tan^2 x$

27. $\dfrac{\tan^2 x - 2 \tan x - 3}{\tan x + 1} - \tan x$

28. $\dfrac{\tan^2 x + \sec x - 1}{\sec x - 1} - \sec x$

In Exercises 29–70, verify each identity.

29. $\sin x \tan x + \cos x = \sec x$

30. $\cos x \cot x + \sin x = \csc x$

31. $\dfrac{1 - 4 \cos^2 x}{1 - 2 \cos x} = 1 + 2 \cos x$

32. $\dfrac{9 - 16 \sin^2 x}{3 + 4 \sin x} = 3 - 4 \sin x$

33. $(\cos x - \sin x)(\cos x + \sin x) = 1 - 2 \sin^2 x$

34. $(\sin x - \cos x)(\sin x + \cos x) = 1 - 2 \cos^2 x$

35. $\sin^2 x \cot^2 x + \sin^2 x = 1$

36. $\tan^2 x - \sin^2 x = \sin^4 x \sec^2 x$

37. $\sin^3 x - \cos^3 x = (\sin x - \cos x)(1 + \sin x \cos x)$

38. $\sin^3 x + \cos^3 x = (\sin x + \cos x)(1 - \sin x \cos x)$

39. $\cos^4 x - \sin^4 x = 1 - 2 \sin^2 x$

40. $\cos^4 x - \sin^4 x = 2 \cos^2 x - 1$

41. $\dfrac{1}{1 - \sin x} + \dfrac{1}{1 + \sin x} = 2 \sec^2 x$

42. $\dfrac{1}{1 - \cos x} + \dfrac{1}{1 + \cos x} = 2 \csc^2 x$

43. $\dfrac{1}{\csc x - 1} - \dfrac{1}{\csc x + 1} = 2 \tan^2 x$

44. $\dfrac{1}{\sec x - 1} + \dfrac{1}{\sec x + 1} = 2 \sec x \cot^2 x$

45. $\sec^2 x + \csc^2 x = \sec^2 x \csc^2 x$

46. $\cot^2 x + \tan^2 x = \sec^2 x \csc^2 x - 2$

47. $\dfrac{1}{\sec x - \tan x} + \dfrac{1}{\sec x + \tan x} = \dfrac{2}{\cos x}$

48. $\dfrac{1}{\csc x + \cot x} + \dfrac{1}{\csc x - \cot x} = \dfrac{2}{\sin x}$

49. $(\sin x + \cos x)^2 = 1 + 2 \sin x \cos x$

50. $(\sin x - \cos x)^2 = 1 - 2 \sin x \cos x$

51. $(1 + \tan x)^2 = \sec^2 x + 2 \tan x$

52. $(1 - \cot x)^2 = \csc^2 x - 2 \cot x$

53. $\dfrac{\tan x \sin x}{\tan x + \sin x} = \dfrac{\tan x - \sin x}{\tan x \sin x}$

54. $\dfrac{\cot x \cos x}{\cot x + \cos x} = \dfrac{\cot x - \cos x}{\cot x \cos x}$

55. $(\tan x + \cot x)^2 = \sec^2 x + \csc^2 x$

56. $(1 + \cot^2 x)(1 + \tan^2 x) = \dfrac{1}{\sin^2 x \cos^2 x}$

57. $\dfrac{\sin^2 x - \cos^2 x}{\sec^2 x - \csc^2 x} = \sin^2 x \cos^2 x$

58. $\left(\tan x + \dfrac{1}{\cot x} \right)\left(\cot x + \dfrac{1}{\tan x} \right) = 4$

59. $\dfrac{\tan x}{1 + \sec x} + \dfrac{1 + \sec x}{\tan x} = 2 \csc x$

60. $\dfrac{\cot x}{1 + \csc x} + \dfrac{1 + \csc x}{\cot x} = 2 \sec x$

61. $\dfrac{\sin x + \tan x}{\cos x + 1} = \tan x$

62. $\dfrac{\sin x}{1 + \tan x} = \dfrac{\cos x}{1 + \cot x}$

63. $\dfrac{\sin x - 2 \sin^3 x}{2 \cos^3 x - \cos x} = \tan x$

64. $\dfrac{\csc x + \cot x}{\csc x - \cot x} = \dfrac{\sin^2 x}{(1 - \cos x)^2}$

65. $\dfrac{1 - \sin x}{1 - \sec x} - \dfrac{1 + \sin x}{1 + \sec x} = 2 \cot x (\cos x - \csc x)$

66. $\dfrac{\sec x + \tan x}{\csc x + \cot x} - \dfrac{\sec x - \tan x}{\csc x - \cot x} = 2(\sec x - \csc x)$

67. $(1 - \tan x)^2 + (1 - \cot x)^2 = (\sec x - \csc x)^2$

68. $\sec^6 x - \tan^6 x = 1 + 3 \tan^2 x + 3 \tan^4 x$

69. $\dfrac{\cot x + \csc x - 1}{\cot x + \csc x + 1} = \dfrac{1 - \sin x}{\cos x}$

70. $\dfrac{\tan x + \sec x - 1}{\tan x - \sec x + 1} = \dfrac{1 + \sin x}{\cos x}$

In Exercises 71–76, use a graphing calculator to determine whether the equation could be an identity by graphing each side of the equation on the same screen. Then prove or disprove the statement algebraically.

71. $\cos^2 x - \sin^2 x = 2\cos^2 x - 1$

72. $(\sin x + \cos x)^2 - 1 = 2\sin x \cos x$

73. $\sin x + \cos x = 1$

74. $\dfrac{\sin 2x}{2} = \sin x$

75. $\dfrac{\sin^2 x}{1 + \cos x} = 1 - \cos x$

76. $\sin x = \cos x \tan x$

In Exercises 77–82, use the TABLE feature of a graphing calculator in Radian mode to calculate each side of the equation for different values of x. Determine whether the equation could be an identity. Then prove or disprove the statement algebraically.

77. $\sin x \cot x = \cos x$

78. $\sec x \cot x = \csc x$

79. $\dfrac{\tan x - 1}{\tan x + 1} = \dfrac{1 - \cot x}{1 + \cot x}$

80. $\sin^2 x \sec^2 x + 1 = \sec^2 x$

81. $\tan 2x = 2\tan x$

82. $(1 - \sin x)^2 = \cos x$

B EXERCISES Applying the Concepts

83. **Length of a ladder.** A ladder x feet long makes an angle θ with the horizontal and reaches a height of 20 feet. Then $x = \dfrac{20}{\sin \theta}$. Use a reciprocal identity to rewrite this formula.

84. **Distance from a building.** From a distance of x feet to a 60-foot-high building, the angle of elevation is θ degrees. Then $x = \dfrac{60}{\tan \theta}$. Use a reciprocal identity to rewrite this formula.

C EXERCISES Beyond the Basics

In Exercises 85–94, find the exact value of each expression.

85. $(\sin u \cos v + \cos u \sin v)^2 + (\cos u \cos v - \sin u \sin v)^2$

86. $(\sin u \cos v - \cos u \sin v)^2 + (\cos u \cos v + \sin u \sin v)^2$

87. $3(\sin^4 x + \cos^4 x) - 2(\sin^6 x + \cos^6 x)$

88. $\sin^6 x + \cos^6 x + 3\cos^2 x - 3\cos^4 x$

89. $\dfrac{1 - \cos \theta}{1 + \cos \theta} + \dfrac{1 + \cos \theta}{1 - \cos \theta} - 4\cot^2 \theta$

90. $\dfrac{\cos^3 \theta + \sin^3 \theta}{\cos \theta + \sin \theta} + \dfrac{\cos^3 \theta - \sin^3 \theta}{\cos \theta - \sin \theta}$

91. $\dfrac{\sec^2 \theta + 2\tan^2 \theta}{1 + 3\tan^2 \theta}$

92. $\dfrac{\csc^2 \alpha + \sec^2 \alpha}{\csc^2 \alpha - \sec^2 \alpha} - \dfrac{1 + \tan^2 \alpha}{1 - \tan^2 \alpha}$

93. $\cos^2 x(3 - 4\cos^2 x)^2 + \sin^2 x(3 - 4\sin^2 x)^2$

94. $(\sin \theta + \csc \theta)^2 + (\cos \theta + \sec \theta)^2 - \tan^2 \theta - \cot^2 \theta$

95. If $\sin \theta = \dfrac{a^2 - b^2}{a^2 + b^2}$ and $a > b > 0$, find the values of $\cos \theta$ and $\cot \theta$.

96. Repeat Exercise 95 for $b > a > 0$.

97. If $x = r\cos u \cos v$, $y = r\cos u \sin v$, and $z = r\sin u$, verify that $x^2 + y^2 + z^2 = r^2$.

98. If $\tan x + \cot x = 2$, show that
  a. $\tan^2 x + \cot^2 x = 2$.
  b. $\tan^3 x + \cot^3 x = 2$.

99. If $\sec x + \cos x = 2$, show that
  a. $\sec^2 x + \cos^2 x = \sec^4 x + \cos^4 x = 2$.
  b. $\sec^3 x + \cos^3 x = 2$.

100. If $\sin x + \sin^2 x = 1$, show that $\cos^2 x + \cos^4 x = 1$.

Critical Thinking

101. If x and y are real numbers, explain why $\sec \theta$ cannot be equal to $\dfrac{xy}{x^2 + y^2}$.

102. Find values of t for which $\sin \theta = \dfrac{1 + t^2}{1 - t^2}$ is possible.

103. Find values of a and b for which $\cos^2 \theta = \dfrac{a^2 + b^2}{2ab}$ is possible.

104. Find values of a and b for which $\csc^2 \theta = \dfrac{2ab}{a^2 + b^2}$ is possible.

GROUP PROJECTS

1. Prove that the following inequalities are true for $0 < \theta < \dfrac{\pi}{2}$:
  a. $\sin^2 \theta + \csc^2 \theta \geq 2$
  b. $\cos^2 \theta + \sec^2 \theta \geq 2$
  c. $\sec^2 \theta + \csc^2 \theta \geq 4$

Sum and Difference Identities

Before Starting this Section, Review	Objectives
1. Distance formula (Appendix)	**1** Use the sum and difference identities for cosine.
2. Fundamental identities (Section 5.1)	**2** Use the cofunction identities.
3. Trigonometric functions of common angles (Section 1.3)	**3** Use the sum and difference identities for sine.
	4 Use the sum and difference identities for tangent.

PURE TONES IN MUSIC

A vibrating part of an instrument transmits its vibrations to the air, and they travel away as sound waves. The number of complete cycles per second traveled by a wave is called its *frequency* and is denoted by *f*. The unit of frequency, cycles per second, is also called hertz (abbreviated Hz), after Gustav Hertz, the discoverer of radio waves. The note A in the octave above middle C has a frequency of 440 Hz, or 440 cycles per second. Therefore, the time between waves is $\frac{1}{440}$ second. We define this time between waves as the period T: $T = \frac{1}{f}$. You hear the sound produced by note A when the vibration from the source travels to your ear and puts pressure on your eardrum.

A *pure tone* is a tone in which the vibration is a simple harmonic of just one frequency. The simple harmonic of a pure tone with frequency *f* can be described by the equation

$$y = a \sin (2\pi f t),$$

where |*a*| is the amplitude (indicating loudness), *t* is the time in seconds, and *y* is the pressure of a pure tone on an eardrum (in pounds per square foot). In Example 8, we consider the pressure due to two pure tones of the same frequency. ■

1 Use the sum and difference identities for cosine.

Sum and Difference Identities for Cosine

The following identities for $\cos (u + v)$ and $\cos (u - v)$ are called the sum and difference identities for cosine, respectively. The variables represent any two real numbers, or angles, in radian or degree measure.

> **SUM AND DIFFERENCE IDENTITIES FOR COSINE**
>
> $$\cos (u + v) = \cos u \cos v - \sin u \sin v$$
> $$\cos (u - v) = \cos u \cos v + \sin u \sin v$$

To prove the second identity, we assume that $0 < v < u < 2\pi$, although this identity is valid for all real numbers *u* and *v*. Figure 5.4(a) shows points *P* and *Q* on the unit circle on the terminal sides of angles *u* and *v*. Section 3.3 tells us that

$P = (\cos u, \sin u)$ and $Q = (\cos v, \sin v)$. In Figure 5.4(b), we rotated angle $(u - v)$ into standard position and labeled point B on the unit circle and the terminal side of angle $(u - v)$.

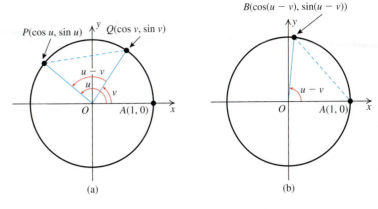

FIGURE 5.4

We know that triangle POQ in Figure 5.4(a) is congruent to triangle BOA in Figure 5.4(b) by SAS (side-angle-side congruence).

$$d(P, Q) = d(A, B)$$
$$[d(P, Q)]^2 = [d(A, B)]^2 \qquad (1) \qquad \text{Square both sides.}$$

Now use the distance formula to simplify the left side of equation (1).

$$
\begin{aligned}
[d(P, Q)]^2 &= (\cos u - \cos v)^2 + (\sin u - \sin v)^2 && \text{Distance formula} \\
&= \cos^2 u - 2\cos u \cos v + \cos^2 v && (a - b)^2 = a^2 - 2ab + b^2 \\
&\quad + \sin^2 u - 2\sin u \sin v + \sin^2 v && \\
&= (\cos^2 u + \sin^2 u) + (\cos^2 v + \sin^2 v) && \text{Combine terms.} \\
&\quad - 2(\cos u \cos v + \sin u \sin v) && \\
&= 1 + 1 - 2(\cos u \cos v + \sin u \sin v) && \text{Pythagorean identity}
\end{aligned}
$$

So

$$[d(P, Q)]^2 = 2 - 2(\cos u \cos v + \sin u \sin v) \qquad \text{Simplify.}$$

Now simplify the right side of equation (1).

$$
\begin{aligned}
[d(A, B)]^2 &= [\cos (u - v) - 1]^2 + [\sin (u - v) - 0]^2 && \text{Distance formula} \\
&= \cos^2 (u - v) - 2\cos (u - v) + 1 + \sin^2 (u - v) && \text{Expand binomial.} \\
&= [\cos^2 (u - v) + \sin^2 (u - v)] + 1 - 2\cos (u - v) && \text{Combine terms.} \\
&= 1 + 1 - 2\cos (u - v) && \text{Pythagorean identity} \\
[d(A, B)]^2 &= 2 - 2\cos (u - v) && \text{Simplify.}
\end{aligned}
$$

Now $[d(A, B)]^2 = [d(P, Q)]^2.$

$$
\begin{aligned}
2 - 2\cos (u - v) &= 2 - 2(\cos u \cos v + \sin u \sin v) && \text{Substitute on each side.} \\
-2\cos (u - v) &= -2(\cos u \cos v + \sin u \sin v) && \text{Subtract 2 from both sides.} \\
\mathbf{\cos (u - v)} &= \mathbf{\cos u \cos v + \sin u \sin v} && \text{Divide both sides by } -2.
\end{aligned}
$$

We have proved the identity for the cosine of the difference of two angles.

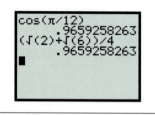
EXAMPLE 1 **Using the Difference Identity for Cosine**

Find the exact value of $\cos \dfrac{\pi}{12}$ by using $\dfrac{\pi}{12} = \dfrac{\pi}{3} - \dfrac{\pi}{4}$.

SOLUTION

We use the exact values of the trigonometric functions of $\dfrac{\pi}{3}$ and $\dfrac{\pi}{4}$ as well as the difference identity for cosine.

$$
\begin{aligned}
\cos \frac{\pi}{12} &= \cos\left(\frac{\pi}{3} - \frac{\pi}{4}\right) & & \frac{\pi}{12} = \frac{\pi}{3} - \frac{\pi}{4} \\
&= \cos \frac{\pi}{3} \cos \frac{\pi}{4} + \sin \frac{\pi}{3} \sin \frac{\pi}{4} & & \text{Identity for } \cos (u - v) \text{ with } u = \frac{\pi}{3} \\
& & & \text{and } v = \frac{\pi}{4} \\
&= \frac{1}{2} \cdot \frac{\sqrt{2}}{2} + \frac{\sqrt{3}}{2} \cdot \frac{\sqrt{2}}{2} & & \text{Use exact values. (See page 29.)} \\
&= \frac{\sqrt{2} + \sqrt{6}}{4} & & \text{Multiply and add.}
\end{aligned}
$$

Practice Problem 1 Find the exact value of $\cos 15°$ by using $15° = 45° - 30°$.

The difference identity for $\cos (u - v)$ is valid for all real numbers and angles u and v. We can use this identity and the even–odd identities to prove the identity for $\cos (u + v)$.

$$
\begin{aligned}
\cos (u + v) &= \cos [u - (-v)] & & u + v = u - (-v) \\
&= \cos u \cos (-v) + \sin u \sin (-v) & & \text{Difference identity for cosine} \\
&= \cos u \cos v + \sin u (-\sin v) & & \cos (-v) = \cos v; \\
& & & \sin (-v) = -\sin v \\
\boldsymbol{\cos (u + v)} &= \boldsymbol{\cos u \cos v - \sin u \sin v} & & \text{Simplify.}
\end{aligned}
$$

The last equation is the sum identity for cosine.

EXAMPLE 2 **Using the Sum Identity for Cosine**

Find the exact value of $\cos 75°$ by using $75° = 45° + 30°$.

SOLUTION

$$
\begin{aligned}
\cos 75° &= \cos (45° + 30°) & & 75° = 45° + 30° \\
&= \cos 45° \cos 30° - \sin 45° \sin 30° & & \text{Sum identity for cosine} \\
&= \frac{\sqrt{2}}{2} \cdot \frac{\sqrt{3}}{2} - \frac{\sqrt{2}}{2} \cdot \frac{1}{2} & & \text{Use exact values.} \\
&= \frac{\sqrt{6}}{4} - \frac{\sqrt{2}}{4} & & \text{Multiply.} \\
&= \frac{\sqrt{6} - \sqrt{2}}{4} & & \text{Simplify.}
\end{aligned}
$$

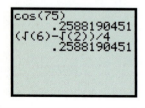
Practice Problem 2 Find the exact value of $\cos \dfrac{7\pi}{12}$ by using $\dfrac{7\pi}{12} = \dfrac{\pi}{3} + \dfrac{\pi}{4}$.

2 Use the cofunction identities.

Cofunction Identities

Two trigonometric functions f and g are called **cofunctions** if

$$f\left(\frac{\pi}{2} - x\right) = g(x) \quad \text{and} \quad g\left(\frac{\pi}{2} - x\right) = f(x).$$

We derive two cofunction identities.

$$\cos(u - v) = \cos u \cos v + \sin u \sin v \qquad \text{Difference identity for cosine.}$$

$$\cos\left(\frac{\pi}{2} - v\right) = \cos\frac{\pi}{2}\cos v + \sin\frac{\pi}{2}\sin v \qquad \text{Replace } u \text{ with } \frac{\pi}{2}.$$

$$= 0 \cdot \cos v + 1 \cdot \sin v \qquad \cos\frac{\pi}{2} = 0; \sin\frac{\pi}{2} = 1$$

$$= \sin v \qquad \text{Simplify.}$$

The result is a cofunction identity that holds for any real number v or angle in radian measure.

$$\cos\left(\frac{\pi}{2} - v\right) = \sin v$$

If we replace v with $\frac{\pi}{2} - v$ in this cofunction identity, we have

$$\cos\left(\frac{\pi}{2} - v\right) = \sin v \qquad \text{Cofunction identity}$$

$$\cos\left[\frac{\pi}{2} - \left(\frac{\pi}{2} - v\right)\right] = \sin\left(\frac{\pi}{2} - v\right) \qquad \text{Replace } v \text{ with } \frac{\pi}{2} - v.$$

$$\cos v = \sin\left(\frac{\pi}{2} - v\right) \qquad \text{Simplify.}$$

So

$$\sin\left(\frac{\pi}{2} - v\right) = \cos v$$

BASIC COFUNCTION IDENTITIES

If v is any real number or angle measured in radians, then

$$\cos\left(\frac{\pi}{2} - v\right) = \sin v$$

$$\sin\left(\frac{\pi}{2} - v\right) = \cos v.$$

If angle v is measured in degrees, replace $\frac{\pi}{2}$ with $90°$ in these identities.

EXAMPLE 3   **Using Cofunction Identities**

Prove that for any real number x,

$$\tan\left(\frac{\pi}{2} - x\right) = \cot x.$$

SOLUTION

$$\tan\left(\frac{\pi}{2} - x\right) = \frac{\sin\left(\frac{\pi}{2} - x\right)}{\cos\left(\frac{\pi}{2} - x\right)} \qquad \text{Quotient identity}$$

$$= \frac{\cos x}{\sin x} \qquad \text{Use cofunction identities.}$$

$$= \cot x \qquad \text{Quotient identity} \qquad ■ ■ ■$$

Practice Problem 3 Prove that for any real number x,

$$\sec\left(\frac{\pi}{2} - x\right) = \csc x. \qquad ■$$

3 Use the sum and difference identities for sine.

Sum and Difference Identities for Sine

To prove the difference identity for the sine function, we start with a cofunction identity.

$$\sin(u - v) = \cos\left[\frac{\pi}{2} - (u - v)\right] \qquad \text{Cofunction identity}$$

$$= \cos\left[\left(\frac{\pi}{2} - u\right) + v\right] \qquad \frac{\pi}{2} - (u - v) =$$

$$\left(\frac{\pi}{2} - u\right) + v$$

$$= \cos\left(\frac{\pi}{2} - u\right)\cos v - \sin\left(\frac{\pi}{2} - u\right)\sin v \qquad \text{Sum identity for cosine}$$

$$= \sin u \cos v - \cos u \sin v \qquad \text{Cofunction identities}$$

We have

$$\sin(u - v) = \sin u \cos v - \cos u \sin v,$$

which holds for all real numbers and angles u and v. If we replace v with $-v$, we derive the sum identity for the sine.

$$\sin(u + v) = \sin[u - (-v)] \qquad u + v = u - (-v)$$

$$= \sin u \cos(-v) - \cos u \sin(-v) \qquad \text{Difference identity for sine}$$

$$= \sin u \cos v - \cos u(-\sin v) \qquad \cos(-v) = \cos v;$$
$$\sin(-v) = -\sin v$$

$$= \sin u \cos v + \cos u \sin v \qquad \text{Simplify.}$$

So

$$\sin(u + v) = \sin u \cos v + \cos u \sin v$$

SUM AND DIFFERENCE IDENTITIES FOR SINE

$$\sin(u + v) = \sin u \cos v + \cos u \sin v$$

$$\sin(u - v) = \sin u \cos v - \cos u \sin v$$

EXAMPLE 4   **Using the Difference Identity for Sine**

Prove the identity: $\sin (\pi - x) = \sin x$

SOLUTION

$$\sin (u - v) = \sin u \cos v - \cos u \sin v \qquad \text{Difference identity for sine}$$
$$\sin (\pi - x) = \sin \pi \cos x - \cos \pi \sin x \qquad \text{Replace } u \text{ with } \pi \text{ and } v \text{ with } x.$$
$$= (0) \cos x - (-1) \sin x \qquad \sin \pi = 0; \cos \pi = -1$$
$$= \sin x \qquad \text{Simplify.} \qquad ■ ■ ■$$

Practice Problem 4   Use the sum identity for sine to prove that $\sin (\pi + x) = -\sin x$.

■

EXAMPLE 5   **Using the Sum Identity for Sine**

Find the exact value of $\sin 63° \cos 27° + \cos 63° \sin 27°$ without using a calculator.

SOLUTION

The given expression is the right side of the sum identity for sine:

$$\sin (u + v) = \sin u \cos v + \cos u \sin v$$
$$\sin 63° \cos 27° + \cos 63° \sin 27° = \sin (63° + 27°) \qquad \text{Replace } u \text{ with } 63° \text{ and } v \text{ with } 27°.$$
$$= \sin 90°$$
$$= 1 \qquad ■ ■ ■$$

Practice Problem 5   Find the exact value of $\sin 43° \cos 13° - \cos 43° \sin 13°$ without using a calculator.

■

EXAMPLE 6   **Finding the Exact Value of a Sum**

Let $\sin u = -\dfrac{3}{5}$ and $\cos v = \dfrac{12}{13}$, with $\pi < u < \dfrac{3\pi}{2}$ and $\dfrac{3\pi}{2} < v < 2\pi$. Find the exact value of $\sin (u + v)$.

SOLUTION

We are given $\sin u = -\dfrac{3}{5}$ with u in quadrant III.

$$\cos^2 u = 1 - \sin^2 u \qquad \text{Pythagorean identity}$$
$$\cos u = \pm \sqrt{1 - \sin^2 u} \qquad \text{Solve for } \cos u.$$
$$\Downarrow$$
$$\cos u = -\sqrt{1 - \sin^2 u} \qquad \cos u \text{ is negative in quadrant III.}$$
$$= -\sqrt{1 - \left(-\frac{3}{5}\right)^2} \qquad \text{Replace } \sin u \text{ with } -\frac{3}{5}.$$
$$= -\sqrt{1 - \frac{9}{25}} \qquad \left(-\frac{3}{5}\right)^2 = \frac{9}{25}$$
$$= -\sqrt{\frac{16}{25}} \qquad 1 - \frac{9}{25} = \frac{25}{25} - \frac{9}{25} = \frac{16}{25}$$
$$= -\frac{4}{5} \qquad \left(\frac{4}{5}\right)^2 = \frac{16}{25}$$

So $\cos u = -\dfrac{4}{5}$.

Similarly, given $\cos v = \dfrac{12}{13}$ with v in quadrant IV, we find the exact value of $\sin v$.

$$\sin v = \pm\sqrt{1 - \cos^2 v} \qquad \text{Solve } \sin^2 v + \cos^2 v = 1 \text{ for } \sin v.$$

$$\Downarrow$$

$$\sin v = -\sqrt{1 - \cos^2 v} \qquad \sin v \text{ is negative in quadrant IV.}$$

$$= -\sqrt{1 - \left(\frac{12}{13}\right)^2} \qquad \text{Replace } \cos v \text{ with } \frac{12}{13}.$$

$$= -\sqrt{\frac{25}{169}} \qquad 1 - \left(\frac{12}{13}\right)^2 = 1 - \frac{144}{169} = \frac{169 - 144}{169}$$

$$= -\frac{5}{13} \qquad \left(\frac{5}{13}\right)^2 = \frac{25}{169}$$

We have $\sin v = -\dfrac{5}{13}$.

$$\sin (u + v) = \sin u \cos v + \cos u \sin v \qquad \text{Sum identity for sine}$$

$$= \left(-\frac{3}{5}\right)\left(\frac{12}{13}\right) + \left(-\frac{4}{5}\right)\left(-\frac{5}{13}\right) \qquad \begin{array}{l}\text{Replace values of} \\ \sin u, \sin v, \cos u, \text{ and } \cos v.\end{array}$$

$$= -\frac{36}{65} + \frac{20}{65} \qquad \text{Multiply.}$$

$$= -\frac{16}{65} \qquad \text{Simplify.}$$

The exact value of $\sin (u + v)$ is $-\dfrac{16}{65}$. ■ ■ ■

Practice Problem 6 For the angles u and v in Example 6, find the exact value of $\cos (u + v)$. ■

EXAMPLE 7 **Verifying an Identity by Using a Sum or Difference Identity**

Verify the identity: $\dfrac{\sin (x - y)}{\cos x \cos y} = \tan x - \tan y$

SOLUTION

We start with the more complicated left side.

$$\frac{\sin (x - y)}{\cos x \cos y} = \frac{\sin x \cos y - \cos x \sin y}{\cos x \cos y} \qquad \text{Use the identity for } \sin (u - v).$$

$$= \frac{\sin x \cos y}{\cos x \cos y} - \frac{\cos x \sin y}{\cos x \cos y} \qquad \frac{a - b}{c} = \frac{a}{c} - \frac{b}{c}$$

$$= \frac{\sin x}{\cos x} - \frac{\sin y}{\cos y} \qquad \text{Remove common factors.}$$

$$= \tan x - \tan y \qquad \text{Quotient identity}$$

Because the left side is identical to the right side, the given equation is an identity. ■ ■ ■

Practice Problem 7 Verify the identity: $\dfrac{\cos (x + y)}{\sin x \sin y} = \cot x \cot y - 1$ ■

EXAMPLE 8   **Combining Two Pure Tones**

Suppose the pressure exerted by two pure tones (in pounds per square foot) after t seconds is given by

$$y_1 = 0.3 \sin (800\pi t) \quad \text{and} \quad y_2 = 0.4 \cos (800\pi t).$$

Find the amplitude, period, frequency, and phase shift for the total pressure $y = y_1 + y_2$ given that $y = A \sin (800\pi t + \theta)$, with $A > 0$.

SOLUTION

We use the facts that

$\sin (800\pi t) = 0$ when $t = 0$ and $\cos (800\pi t) = 0$ when $t = \dfrac{1}{2(800)}$.

Rewrite $\qquad\qquad\qquad y = y_1 + y_2$ as

$$A \sin (800\pi t + \theta) = 0.3 \sin (800\pi t) + 0.4 \cos (800\pi t).$$

For $t = 0$, the equation becomes

$A \sin (\theta) = 0.3 \sin 0 + 0.4 \cos 0$	$800\pi(0) + \theta = \theta, 800\pi(0) = 0$
$A \sin (\theta) = 0.3(0) + 0.4(1)$	$\sin 0 = 0$ and $\cos 0 = 1$
$A \sin \theta = 0.4$	Simplify.

For $t = \dfrac{1}{2(800)}$, the equation becomes

$A \sin \left(\dfrac{\pi}{2} + \theta\right) = 0.3 \sin \dfrac{\pi}{2} + 0.4 \cos \dfrac{\pi}{2}$	$800\pi \left(\dfrac{1}{2(800)}\right) = \dfrac{\pi}{2}$
$A \sin \left(\dfrac{\pi}{2} + \theta\right) = 0.3(1) + 0.4(0)$	$\sin \dfrac{\pi}{2} = 1, \cos \dfrac{\pi}{2} = 0$
$A \cos \theta = 0.3$	$\sin \left(\dfrac{\pi}{2} + \theta\right) = \cos \theta$

Now

$(A \cos \theta)^2 + (A \sin \theta)^2 = (0.3)^2 + (0.4)^2$	$A \cos \theta = 0.3,$ $A \sin \theta = 0.4$
$A^2 \cos^2 \theta + A^2 \sin^2 \theta = (0.3)^2 + (0.4)^2$	$(ab)^2 = a^2b^2$
$A^2(\cos^2 \theta + \sin^2 \theta) = (0.3)^2 + (0.4)^2$	Factor out A^2.
$A^2 = (0.3)^2 + (0.4)^2$	$\cos^2 \theta + \sin^2 \theta = 1$
$A = \sqrt{(0.3)^2 + (0.4)^2} = 0.5$	$A > 0$

Then

$\tan \theta = \dfrac{\sin \theta}{\cos \theta} = \dfrac{A \sin \theta}{A \cos \theta} = \dfrac{0.4}{0.3} = \dfrac{4}{3}$	$A \sin \theta = 0.4, A \cos \theta = 0.3$
$\theta = \tan^{-1}\left(\dfrac{4}{3}\right)$	One angle that will work

The total pressure is

$$y = A \sin (800\pi t + \theta)$$

$$= 0.5 \sin \left(800\pi t + \tan^{-1}\left(\dfrac{4}{3}\right)\right) \qquad \text{Replace } A \text{ and } \theta \text{ with values.}$$

Amplitude $= 0.5 \quad$ Period $= \dfrac{2\pi}{800\pi} = \dfrac{1}{400} \quad$ Frequency $= \dfrac{1}{\text{period}} = 400$

Phase shift $= -\dfrac{\theta}{800\pi} = -\dfrac{\tan^{-1}\left(\dfrac{4}{3}\right)}{800\pi} \approx -0.00037 \qquad$ Use a calculator.   ■ ■ ■

Practice Problem 8   Repeat Example 8, if

$$y_1 = 0.1 \sin (400\pi t) \quad \text{and} \quad y_2 = 0.2 \cos (400\pi t).$$ ▪

4 Use the sum and difference identities for tangent.

Sum and Difference Identities for Tangent

We use the quotient identity $\tan x = \dfrac{\sin x}{\cos x}$ and the difference identities $\sin (u - v)$ and $\cos (u - v)$ to derive the difference identity for the tangent.

$$\tan (u - v) = \frac{\sin (u - v)}{\cos (u - v)} \qquad \text{Quotient identity}$$

$$= \frac{\sin u \cos v - \cos u \sin v}{\cos u \cos v + \sin u \sin v} \qquad \text{Use identities for } \sin (u - v) \text{ and } \cos (u - v).$$

$$= \frac{\dfrac{\sin u \cos v}{\cos u \cos v} - \dfrac{\cos u \sin v}{\cos u \cos v}}{\dfrac{\cos u \cos v}{\cos u \cos v} + \dfrac{\sin u \sin v}{\cos u \cos v}} \qquad \text{Divide numerator and denominator by } \cos u \cos v.$$

$$= \frac{\dfrac{\sin u}{\cos u} - \dfrac{\sin v}{\cos v}}{1 + \dfrac{\sin u \sin v}{\cos u \cos v}} \qquad \text{Simplify.}$$

$$= \frac{\tan u - \tan v}{1 + \tan u \tan v} \qquad \text{Quotient identity}$$

We have derived the difference identity for the tangent.

DIFFERENCE IDENTITY FOR THE TANGENT

$$\tan (u - v) = \frac{\tan u - \tan v}{1 + \tan u \tan v}$$

Replacing v with $-v$ in the difference identity, we have

$$\tan (u + v) = \tan [u - (-v)] \qquad u + v = u - (-v)$$

$$= \frac{\tan u - \tan (-v)}{1 + \tan u \tan (-v)} \qquad \text{Use identity for } \tan (u - v).$$

$$= \frac{\tan u - (-\tan v)}{1 + \tan u (-\tan v)} \qquad \tan (-v) = -\tan v$$

$$= \frac{\tan u + \tan v}{1 - \tan u \tan v} \qquad \text{Simplify.}$$

We have obtained the sum identity for the tangent.

SUM IDENTITY FOR THE TANGENT

$$\tan (u + v) = \frac{\tan u + \tan v}{1 - \tan u \tan v}$$

EXAMPLE 9   **Verifying an Identity**

Verify the identity: $\tan(\pi - x) = -\tan x$

SOLUTION

Apply the difference identity for the tangent to $\tan(\pi - x)$.

$$\tan(\pi - x) = \frac{\tan \pi - \tan x}{1 + \tan \pi \tan x} \qquad \text{Replace } u \text{ with } \pi \text{ and } v \text{ with } x \text{ in the identity for } \tan(u - v).$$

$$= \frac{0 - \tan x}{1 + 0 \cdot \tan x} \qquad \tan \pi = 0$$

$$= -\tan x \qquad \text{Simplify.}$$

Thus, the given equation is an identity.   ■ ■ ■

Practice Problem 9   Verify the identity: $\tan(\pi + x) = \tan x$ ■

Summary

The important identities involving the sum, difference, and cofunctions of numbers or angles are summarized next.

SUM AND DIFFERENCE IDENTITIES

$\cos(u - v) = \cos u \cos v + \sin u \sin v$ $\quad \cos(u + v) = \cos u \cos v - \sin u \sin v$

$\sin(u - v) = \sin u \cos v - \cos u \sin v$ $\quad \sin(u + v) = \sin u \cos v + \cos u \sin v$

$$\tan(u - v) = \frac{\tan u - \tan v}{1 + \tan u \tan v} \qquad\qquad \tan(u + v) = \frac{\tan u + \tan v}{1 - \tan u \tan v}$$

COFUNCTION IDENTITIES

$$\sin\left(\frac{\pi}{2} - x\right) = \cos x \qquad \cos\left(\frac{\pi}{2} - x\right) = \sin x \qquad \tan\left(\frac{\pi}{2} - x\right) = \cot x$$

SECTION 5.2 ■ Exercises

A EXERCISES Basic Skills and Concepts

1. Fill in the correct sign: $\cos\dfrac{\pi}{12} = \cos\dfrac{\pi}{3}\cos\dfrac{\pi}{4}$

   _____ $\sin\dfrac{\pi}{3}\sin\dfrac{\pi}{4}$.

2. Fill in the correct sign: $\sin 75° = \sin 45° \cos 30°$

   _____ $\cos 45° \sin 30°$.

3. One cofunction identity states that $\tan\left(\dfrac{\pi}{2} - x\right) = $

   _____ .

4. A value of b for which $\sin 5x \cos 3x - \cos 5x \sin 3x = \sin bx$ is $b = $ _____ .

5. *True or False* $\sin\left(x - \dfrac{\pi}{2}\right) = -\cos x$.

6. *True or False* $\sin(u + v)$ is never equal to $\sin u + \sin v$.

In Exercises 7–26, find the exact value of each expression.

7. $\sin(45° + 30°)$

8. $\sin(45° - 30°)$

9. $\sin(60° - 45°)$

10. $\sin(60° + 45°)$

11. $\sin(-105°)$

12. $\cos 285°$

13. $\tan 195°$

14. $\tan(-165°)$

15. $\sin\left(\dfrac{\pi}{6} + \dfrac{\pi}{4}\right)$

16. $\cos\left(\dfrac{\pi}{3} - \dfrac{\pi}{4}\right)$

17. $\tan\left(\dfrac{\pi}{4} - \dfrac{\pi}{6}\right)$

18. $\cot\left(\dfrac{\pi}{3} - \dfrac{\pi}{4}\right)$

19. $\sec\left(\dfrac{\pi}{3} + \dfrac{\pi}{4}\right)$

20. $\csc\left(\dfrac{\pi}{4} - \dfrac{\pi}{3}\right)$

21. $\cos\dfrac{-5\pi}{12}$

22. $\sin\dfrac{7\pi}{12}$

23. $\tan\dfrac{19\pi}{12}$

24. $\sec\dfrac{\pi}{12}$

25. $\tan\dfrac{17\pi}{12}$

26. $\csc\dfrac{11\pi}{12}$

In Exercises 27–40, verify each identity.

27. $\sin\left(x + \dfrac{\pi}{2}\right) = \cos x$ **28.** $\cos\left(x + \dfrac{\pi}{2}\right) = -\sin x$

29. $\sin\left(x - \dfrac{\pi}{2}\right) = -\cos x$ **30.** $\cos\left(x - \dfrac{\pi}{2}\right) = \sin x$

31. $\tan\left(x + \dfrac{\pi}{2}\right) = -\cot x$ **32.** $\tan\left(x - \dfrac{\pi}{2}\right) = -\cot x$

33. $\csc(x + \pi) = -\csc x$ **34.** $\sec(x + \pi) = -\sec x$

35. $\cos\left(x + \dfrac{3\pi}{2}\right) = \sin x$ **36.** $\cos\left(x - \dfrac{3\pi}{2}\right) = -\sin x$

37. $\tan\left(x - \dfrac{3\pi}{2}\right) = -\cot x$

38. $\tan\left(x + \dfrac{3\pi}{2}\right) = -\cot x$

39. $\cot(3\pi - x) = -\cot x$

40. $\csc\left(\dfrac{5\pi}{2} - x\right) = \sec x$

In Exercises 41–50, find the exact value of each expression without using a calculator.

41. $\sin 56° \cos 34° + \cos 56° \sin 34°$

42. $\cos 57° \cos 33° - \sin 57° \sin 33°$

43. $\cos 331° \cos 61° + \sin 331° \sin 61°$

44. $\cos 110° \sin 70° + \sin 110° \cos 70°$

45. $\dfrac{\tan 129° - \tan 84°}{1 + \tan 129° \tan 84°}$ **46.** $\dfrac{\tan 28° + \tan 17°}{1 - \tan 28° \tan 17°}$

47. $\sin\dfrac{7\pi}{12}\cos\dfrac{3\pi}{12} - \cos\dfrac{7\pi}{12}\sin\dfrac{3\pi}{12}$

48. $\cos\dfrac{5\pi}{12}\cos\dfrac{\pi}{12} - \sin\dfrac{5\pi}{12}\sin\dfrac{\pi}{12}$

49. $\dfrac{\tan\dfrac{5\pi}{12} - \tan\dfrac{2\pi}{12}}{1 + \tan\dfrac{5\pi}{12}\tan\dfrac{2\pi}{12}}$ **50.** $\dfrac{\tan\dfrac{5\pi}{12} + \tan\dfrac{7\pi}{12}}{1 - \tan\dfrac{5\pi}{12}\tan\dfrac{7\pi}{12}}$

In Exercises 51–56, find the exact value of each expression given that $\tan u = \dfrac{3}{4}$, with u in quadrant III, and $\sin v = \dfrac{5}{13}$, with v in quadrant II.

51. $\sin(u - v)$ **52.** $\sin(u + v)$

53. $\cos(u + v)$ **54.** $\cos(u - v)$

55. $\tan(u + v)$ **56.** $\tan(u - v)$

In Exercises 57–62, find the exact value of each expression given that $\cos \alpha = -\dfrac{2}{5}$, with α in quadrant II, and $\sin \beta = -\dfrac{3}{7}$, with β in quadrant IV.

57. $\sin(\alpha - \beta)$ **58.** $\cos(\alpha - \beta)$

59. $\csc(\alpha + \beta)$ **60.** $\sec(\alpha + \beta)$

61. $\cot(\alpha - \beta)$ **62.** $\cot(\alpha + \beta)$

In Exercises 63–70, verify each identity.

63. $\dfrac{\sin(x + y)}{\cos x \cos y} = \tan x + \tan y$

64. $\dfrac{\sin(x + y)}{\sin x \sin y} = \cot x + \cot y$

65. $\dfrac{\cos(x + y)}{\cos x \cos y} = 1 - \tan x \tan y$

66. $\dfrac{\cos(x - y)}{\sin x \sin y} = \cot x \cot y + 1$

67. $\dfrac{\cos(x - y)}{\sin(x + y)} = \dfrac{1 + \cot x \cot y}{\cot x + \cot y}$

68. $\dfrac{\cos(x + y)}{\sin(x - y)} = \dfrac{1 - \cot x \cot y}{\cot x - \cot y}$

69. $\dfrac{\sin(x - y)}{\sin(x + y)} = \dfrac{\cot y - \cot x}{\cot y + \cot x}$

70. $\dfrac{\cos(x + y)}{\cos(x - y)} = \dfrac{\cot x \cot y - 1}{\cot x \cot y + 1}$

In Exercises 71 and 72, assume that $y_1 + y_2 = A \sin(x + \theta)$, with $A > 0$, and use the methods in Example 8 to find the values for A and θ. Then graph $y = A \sin(x + \theta)$.

71. $y_1 = \sin x$ and $y_2 = \cos x$

72. $y_1 = \sin x$ and $y_2 = -\cos x$

B EXERCISES Applying the Concepts

73. **Analytic geometry.** Let l be a nonvertical line in the coordinate plane. If l makes angle θ with the positive direction of the x-axis, then the slope m of the line l is given by $m = \tan \theta$. Suppose two nonvertical lines l_1 and l_2 intersect in a plane. The slope of l_1 is m_1, and the slope of l_2 is m_2. Show that the tangent of the smallest positive angle α between the lines l_1 and l_2 is given by

$$\tan \alpha = \left|\dfrac{m_2 - m_1}{1 + m_1 m_2}\right|.$$

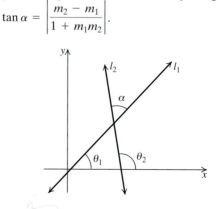

74. Combining two pure tones. The pressure exerted by two pure tones in pounds per square foot is given by the equations $y_1 = 0.4 \sin(400t)$ and $y_2 = 0.3 \cos(400t)$. Assume that $y_1 + y_2 = A \sin(t + \theta)$, with $A > 0$, and find the amplitude and the phase shift for the total pressure $y = y_1 + y_2$.

75. Combining two pure tones. Repeat Exercise 74 for $y_1 = 0.05 \sin(600t)$ and $y_2 = 0.12 \cos(600t)$.

76. Simple harmonic motion. A simple harmonic motion is described by the equation $x = 0.12 \sin 2t + 0.5 \cos 2t$, where x is the distance from the equilibrium position and t is the time in seconds. Assume that $x = A \sin(2t + \theta)$, with $A > 0$.
   a. Find the amplitude of the motion.
   b. Find the frequency and the phase shift.

77. Simple harmonic motion. Repeat Exercise 76 assuming that the motion is described by the equation
$$x = \frac{1}{2} \sin 3t + \frac{1}{3} \cos 3t \text{ and } x = A \sin(3t + \theta) \text{ with}$$
$A > 0$.

C EXERCISES Beyond the Basics

78. Difference quotient. Let $f(x) = \sin x$. Show that
$$\frac{f(x + h) - f(x)}{h} = \sin x\left(\frac{\cos h - 1}{h}\right) + \cos x\left(\frac{\sin h}{h}\right).$$

79. Difference quotient. Let $f(x) = \cos x$. Show that
$$\frac{f(x + h) - f(x)}{h} = \cos x\left(\frac{\cos h - 1}{h}\right) - \sin x\left(\frac{\sin h}{h}\right).$$

In Exercises 80–91, verify each identity.

80. $\cos u \cos(u + v) + \sin u \sin(u + v) = \cos v$

81. $\sin(x + y)\cos y - \cos(x + y)\sin y = \sin x$

82. $\sin 5x \cos 3x - \cos 5x \sin 3x = \sin 2x$

83. $\sin(2x - y)\cos y + \cos(2x - y)\sin y = \sin 2x$

84. $\sin\left(\dfrac{\pi}{2} + x - y\right) = \cos x \cos y + \sin x \sin y$

85. $\cos\left(\dfrac{\pi}{2} + x - y\right) = \cos x \sin y - \sin x \cos y$

86. $\sin(x + y)\sin(x - y) = \sin^2 x - \sin^2 y$

87. $\cos(\alpha + \beta)\cos(\alpha - \beta) = \cos^2 \alpha - \sin^2 \beta$

88. $\sin^2\left(\dfrac{\pi}{4} + \dfrac{x}{2}\right) - \sin^2\left(\dfrac{\pi}{4} - \dfrac{x}{2}\right) = \sin x$

89. $\cos^2\left(\dfrac{\pi}{4} + \dfrac{x}{2}\right) - \sin^2\left(\dfrac{\pi}{4} - \dfrac{x}{2}\right) = 0$

90. $\dfrac{\sin(\alpha - \beta)}{\sin \alpha \sin \beta} + \dfrac{\sin(\beta - \gamma)}{\sin \beta \sin \gamma} + \dfrac{\sin(\gamma - \alpha)}{\sin \gamma \sin \alpha} = 0$

91. $\dfrac{\sin(\alpha - \beta)}{\cos \alpha \cos \beta} + \dfrac{\sin(\beta - \gamma)}{\cos \beta \cos \gamma} + \dfrac{\sin(\gamma - \alpha)}{\cos \gamma \cos \alpha} = 0$

In Exercises 92–95, find the exact value of each expression.

92. $\cos^2 15° - \cos^2 30° + \cos^2 45° - \cos^2 60° + \cos^2 75°$

93. $\sin^2\left(\dfrac{\pi}{8}\right) + \sin^2\left(\dfrac{3\pi}{8}\right) + \sin^2\left(\dfrac{5\pi}{8}\right) + \sin^2\left(\dfrac{7\pi}{8}\right)$

94. $\cos 60° + \cos 80° + \cos 100°$

95. $\sin 30° - \sin 70° + \sin 110°$

96. Show that $\tan 70° - \tan 20° = 2 \tan 50°$.

97. Show that $\sin(\theta + n\pi) = (-1)^n \sin \theta$.

98. If triangle ABC is not a right triangle and $\cos A = \cos B \cos C$, show that $\tan B \tan C = 2$.

Critical Thinking

99. Find the exact value of $\tan 1° \tan 2° \tan 3° \ldots$ $\tan 88° \tan 89°$.

100. Explain why we cannot use the identity for $\tan(u - v)$ to verify that $\tan\left(\dfrac{\pi}{2} - x\right) = \cot x$.

101. In any triangle ABC, show that $\cos(B + C) = -\cos A$ and $\sin(B + C) = \sin A$.

Double-Angle and Half-Angle Identities

Before Starting this Section, Review

1. Sum identities for sine, cosine, and tangent functions (Section 5.2)

2. Pythagorean identities (Section 5.1)

3. Trigonometric functions of common angles (Section 1.3)

Objectives

1. Use double-angle identities.

2. Use power-reducing identities.

3. Use half-angle identities.

COST OF USING AN ELECTRIC BLANKET

Three basic properties of electricity—*voltage*, *current*, and *power*—together with the rate charged by your electric company, are used to find the cost of using an electric device.

Voltage (*V*) is measured in *volts*. It is the force that pushes electricity through a wire. *Current* (*I*), measured in *amperes* (amps), measures how much electricity is moving through the device per second. *Power* (*P*), measured in *watts*, gives the energy consumed per second by an electric device and is defined by the equation

$$P = VI.$$

Your electric company bills you by the kilowatt-hour. When you turn on an electric device that consumes 1000 watts for one hour, it consumes 1 kilowatt-hour. Suppose your electric company charges 8¢ per kilowatt-hour. An electric blanket might use 250 watts (depending on the setting). If you turn it on for ten hours, it will consume $250 \times 10 = 2500 = 2.5$ kilowatt-hours. This will cost you $(2.5)(8) = 20¢$.

In Example 5, we use trigonometric identities to compute the *wattage rating* of an electric blanket. ■

---

1 Use double-angle identities.

Double-Angle Identities

If an angle measures x (radians or degrees); then $x + x = 2x$ is double the measure of x. *Double-angle identities* express trigonometric functions of $2x$ in terms of functions of x. Recall the sum identities for the sine, cosine, and tangent functions.

$$\sin(u + v) = \sin u \cos v + \cos u \sin v$$

$$\cos(u + v) = \cos u \cos v - \sin u \sin v$$

$$\tan(u + v) = \frac{\tan u + \tan v}{1 - \tan u \tan v}$$

To find the double-angle identity for the sine, replace u and v with x in the sum identity for sine.

$$\sin(u + v) = \sin u \cos v + \cos u \sin v \qquad \text{Sum identity for sine}$$

$$\sin(x + x) = \sin x \cos x + \cos x \sin x \qquad \text{Replace } u \text{ and } v \text{ with } x.$$

$$\sin 2x = 2 \sin x \cos x \qquad \text{Simplify.}$$

The identity $\qquad\qquad \mathbf{\sin 2x = 2 \sin x \cos x}$

is the double-angle identity for the sine function. We derive double-angle identities for the cosine and tangent functions the same way.

$$\cos 2x = \cos^2 x - \sin^2 x \qquad \tan 2x = \frac{2\tan x}{1 - \tan^2 x}$$

To derive two other useful forms for $\cos 2x$, replace $\cos^2 x$ with $1 - \sin^2 x$ and then replace $\sin^2 x$ with $1 - \cos^2 x$ in the identity for $\cos 2x$.

$$\cos 2x = \cos^2 x - \sin^2 x \qquad\qquad \cos 2x = \cos^2 x - \sin^2 x$$
$$= (1 - \sin^2 x) - \sin^2 x \qquad\qquad = \cos^2 x - (1 - \cos^2 x)$$
$$\cos 2x = 1 - 2\sin^2 x \qquad\qquad \cos 2x = 2\cos^2 x - 1$$

DOUBLE-ANGLE IDENTITIES

$$\sin 2x = 2\sin x \cos x \qquad \cos 2x = \cos^2 x - \sin^2 x$$

$$\tan 2x = \frac{2\tan x}{1 - \tan^2 x} \qquad \cos 2x = 1 - 2\sin^2 x$$

$$\cos 2x = 2\cos^2 x - 1$$

EXAMPLE 1   Using Double-Angle Identities

If $\cos\theta = -\dfrac{3}{5}$ and θ is in quadrant II, find the exact value of each expression.

a. $\sin 2\theta$ **b.** $\cos 2\theta$ **c.** $\tan 2\theta$

SOLUTION
Before using the identity for $\sin 2\theta$, we first find $\sin\theta$.

$$\sin\theta = \sqrt{1 - \cos^2\theta} \qquad \text{In quadrant II; } \sin\theta \text{ is positive.}$$

$$= \sqrt{1 - \left(-\frac{3}{5}\right)^2} \qquad \text{Replace } \cos\theta \text{ with } -\frac{3}{5}.$$

$$= \sqrt{\frac{16}{25}} = \frac{4}{5} \qquad \text{Simplify.}$$

Then, $\tan\theta = \dfrac{\sin\theta}{\cos\theta} = -\dfrac{4}{3}$.   Replace $\sin\theta$ with $\dfrac{4}{5}$ and $\cos\theta$ with $-\dfrac{3}{5}$; simplify.

a. $\sin 2\theta = 2\sin\theta\cos\theta$ Double-angle identity for sine

$$= 2\left(\frac{4}{5}\right)\left(-\frac{3}{5}\right) \qquad \text{Replace } \sin\theta \text{ with } \frac{4}{5} \text{ and } \cos\theta \text{ with } -\frac{3}{5}.$$

$$= -\frac{24}{25} \qquad \text{Simplify.}$$

b. $\cos 2\theta = \cos^2\theta - \sin^2\theta$ Double-angle identity for cosines

$$= \left(-\frac{3}{5}\right)^2 - \left(\frac{4}{5}\right)^2 \qquad \text{Replace } \cos\theta \text{ with } -\frac{3}{5} \text{ and } \sin\theta \text{ with } \frac{4}{5}.$$

$$= \frac{9}{25} - \frac{16}{25} = -\frac{7}{25} \qquad \text{Simplify.}$$

c. $\tan 2\theta = \dfrac{2\tan\theta}{1-\tan^2\theta}$ Double-angle identity for tangent

$= \dfrac{2\left(-\dfrac{4}{3}\right)}{1-\left(-\dfrac{4}{3}\right)^2}$ Replace $\tan\theta$ with $-\dfrac{4}{3}$.

$= \dfrac{-\dfrac{8}{3}}{1-\dfrac{16}{9}} = \dfrac{24}{7}$ Simplify.

You also can find $\tan 2\theta$ by using parts **a** and **b**.

$$\tan 2\theta = \frac{\sin 2\theta}{\cos 2\theta} = \frac{-\dfrac{24}{25}}{-\dfrac{7}{25}} = \frac{24}{7}$$ ■ ■ ■

Practice Problem 1   If $\sin x = \dfrac{12}{13}$ and $\dfrac{\pi}{2} < x < \pi$, find the exact value of each expression.

a. $\sin 2x$ **b.** $\cos 2x$ **c.** $\tan 2x$ ■

EXAMPLE 2   **Using Double-Angle Identities**

Find the exact value of each expression.

a. $1 - 2\sin^2\left(\dfrac{\pi}{12}\right)$ **b.** $\dfrac{2\tan 22.5°}{1-\tan^2 22.5°}$

SOLUTION

a. The given expression is the right side of the following identity, where $\theta = \dfrac{\pi}{12}$.

$$\cos 2\theta = 1 - 2\sin^2\theta$$

$$1 - 2\sin^2\left(\frac{\pi}{12}\right) = \cos 2\left(\frac{\pi}{12}\right)$$ Replace θ with $\dfrac{\pi}{12}$; switch sides.

$$= \cos\frac{\pi}{6} = \frac{\sqrt{3}}{2}$$

b. The given expression is the right side of the following identity, where $\theta = 22.5°$.

$$\tan 2\theta = \frac{2\tan\theta}{1-\tan^2\theta}$$

$$\frac{2\tan(22.5°)}{1-\tan^2(22.5°)} = \tan 2(22.5°)$$ Replace θ with 22.5°; switch sides.

$$= \tan 45° = 1$$ ■ ■ ■

Practice Problem 2   Find the exact value of each expression.

a. $2\cos^2\left(\dfrac{\pi}{12}\right) - 1$ **b.** $\cos^2 22.5° - \sin^2 22.5°$ ■

EXAMPLE 3   **Finding a Triple-Angle Identity for Sines**

Verify the identity $\sin 3x = 3 \sin x - 4 \sin^3 x$.

SOLUTION
We begin by writing $3x$ as $2x + x$ and use the sum identity for sine and the double-angle identity to verify this identity.

$\sin 3x = \sin (2x + x)$

$= \sin 2x \cos x + \cos 2x \sin x$	Sum identity for sine
$= (2 \sin x \cos x) \cos x + (1 - 2 \sin^2 x) \sin x$	Replace $\sin 2x$ with $2 \sin x \cos x$ and $\cos 2x$ with $1 - 2 \sin^2 x$.
$= 2 \sin x \cos^2 x + \sin x - 2 \sin^3 x$	Multiply; distributive property
$= 2 \sin x(1 - \sin^2 x) + \sin x - 2 \sin^3 x$	$\cos^2 x = 1 - \sin^2 x$
$= 2 \sin x - 2 \sin^3 x + \sin x - 2 \sin^3 x$	Distributive property
$= 3 \sin x - 4 \sin^3 x$	Simplify.

We have verified the identity by showing that the left and right sides of the equation are equal.   ■ ■ ■

Practice Problem 3   Verify the identity $\cos 3x = 4 \cos^3 x - 3 \cos x$.   ■

We can use the double-angle identities to express trigonometric functions of 4θ, 6θ, and 8θ in terms of 2θ, 3θ, and 4θ, respectively. For example, the identities

$$\cos 4\theta = 2 \cos^2 2\theta - 1, \quad \sin 6\theta = 2 \sin 3\theta \cos 3\theta, \quad \text{and} \quad \tan 8\theta = \frac{2 \tan 4\theta}{1 - \tan^2 4\theta}$$

can be easily derived from the appropriate double-angle identities.

2 Use power-reducing identities.

Power-Reducing Identities

The purpose of *power-reducing identities* is to express $\sin^2 x$, $\cos^2 x$, and $\tan^2 x$ in terms of trigonometric functions with powers not greater than 1. These identities are useful in calculus.

POWER-REDUCING IDENTITIES

$$\sin^2 x = \frac{1 - \cos 2x}{2} \qquad \cos^2 x = \frac{1 + \cos 2x}{2} \qquad \tan^2 x = \frac{1 - \cos 2x}{1 + \cos 2x}$$

We can derive the first power-reducing identity by using the appropriate formula for $\cos 2x$.

$\cos 2x = 1 - 2 \sin^2 x$	Double-angle identity for $\cos 2x$ in terms of sine
$2 \sin^2 x = 1 - \cos 2x$	Add $2 \sin^2 x - \cos 2x$ to both sides and simplify.
$\sin^2 x = \dfrac{1 - \cos 2x}{2}$	Divide both sides by 2.

Similarly, we can derive the second identity.

$\cos 2x = 2 \cos^2 x - 1$	Double-angle identity for $\cos 2x$ in terms of cosine
$1 + \cos 2x = 2 \cos^2 x$	Add 1 to both sides.
$\dfrac{1 + \cos 2x}{2} = \cos^2 x$	Divide both sides by 2.

We use the quotient identity to prove the third identity.

$$\tan^2 x = \frac{\sin^2 x}{\cos^2 x} \qquad \text{Quotient identity}$$

$$= \frac{\dfrac{1 - \cos 2x}{2}}{\dfrac{1 + \cos 2x}{2}} \qquad \text{Power-reducing identities for } \sin^2 x \text{ and } \cos^2 x$$

$$= \frac{1 - \cos 2x}{1 + \cos x} \qquad \text{Multiply numerator and denominator by 2. Simplify.}$$

EXAMPLE 4   **Using Power-Reducing Identities**

Write an equivalent expression for $\cos^4 x$ that contains only first powers of cosines of multiple angles.

SOLUTION

We use power-reducing identities repeatedly.

$$\cos^4 x = (\cos^2 x)^2 \qquad a^4 = (a^2)^2$$

$$= \left(\frac{1 + \cos 2x}{2} \right)^2 \qquad \text{Power-reducing identity}$$

$$= \frac{1}{4}(1 + 2\cos 2x + \cos^2 2x) \qquad \text{Square the expression.}$$

$$= \frac{1}{4}\left(1 + 2\cos 2x + \frac{1 + \cos 4x}{2} \right) \qquad \begin{array}{l}\text{Power-reducing identity for } \cos^2 x; \\ \text{replace } x \text{ with } 2x.\end{array}$$

$$= \frac{1}{4}\left(1 + 2\cos 2x + \frac{1}{2} + \frac{1}{2}\cos 4x \right) \qquad \frac{a + b}{c} = \frac{a}{c} + \frac{b}{c}$$

$$= \frac{1}{4} + \frac{2}{4}\cos 2x + \frac{1}{8} + \frac{1}{8}\cos 4x \qquad \text{Distributive property}$$

$$= \frac{3}{8} + \frac{1}{2}\cos 2x + \frac{1}{8}\cos 4x \qquad \text{Simplify.} \qquad \blacksquare\,\blacksquare\,\blacksquare$$

Practice Problem 4   Write an equivalent expression for $\sin^4 x$ that contains only first powers of cosines of multiple angles.   ■

Alternating Current

Alternating current (AC) is the electric current that reverses direction, usually many times per second. Most electrical generators produce alternating current. The *wattage rating* of an electric device is $\dfrac{1}{\sqrt{2}} \approx 0.7071$ times the maximum wattage of the device.

EXAMPLE 5   **Finding the Wattage Rating of an Electric Blanket**

The voltage V of a household current is given by $V = 170\sin(120\pi t)$ volts, where t is in seconds. Suppose the amount of current passing through an electric blanket is $I = 0.1\sin(120\pi t)$ amps, where t is in seconds. Find the wattage rating of the blanket.

SOLUTION

We have $P = VI$ Power = Voltage × Current
                                                    Watts = Volts × Amps

$$P = [170 \sin(120\pi t)][0.1 \sin(120\pi t)]$$ Substitute the given values of
                                                    V and I.

$$= 17 \sin^2(120\pi t)$$ Multiply.

$$= 17\left[\frac{1 - \cos(240\pi t)}{2}\right]$$ Power-reducing identity

$$P = 8.5 - 8.5 \cos(240\pi t)$$ Simplify.

The maximum value of P is 17 watts when $\cos(240\pi t) = -1$; so the wattage rating

for this blanket is $\dfrac{17}{\sqrt{2}} \approx 12$ watts.   ■ ■ ■

Practice Problem 5 In Example 5, find the wattage rating of a lightbulb for which $I = 0.83 \sin(120\pi t)$ amps.   ■

3 Use half-angle identities.

Half-Angle Identities

If an angle measures θ, then $\dfrac{\theta}{2}$ is half the measure of θ. Half-angle identities express

trigonometric functions of $\dfrac{\theta}{2}$ in terms of functions of θ. To derive the half-angle

identities, we replace x with $\dfrac{\theta}{2}$ in the power-reducing identities and take the

square root of both sides. For example,

$$\cos^2 x = \frac{1 + \cos 2x}{2}$$ Power-reducing identity for cosine

$$\cos^2 \frac{\theta}{2} = \frac{1 + \cos 2\left(\frac{\theta}{2}\right)}{2}$$ Replace x with $\dfrac{\theta}{2}$.

$$\cos^2 \frac{\theta}{2} = \frac{1 + \cos \theta}{2}$$ Simplify.

$$\cos \frac{\theta}{2} = \pm\sqrt{\frac{1 + \cos \theta}{2}}$$ Square root property

We call the last equation a *half-angle identity* for cosines. The sign $+$ or $-$ depends

on the quadrant in which $\dfrac{\theta}{2}$ lies. We can derive half-angle identities for sine and

tangent in a similar manner.

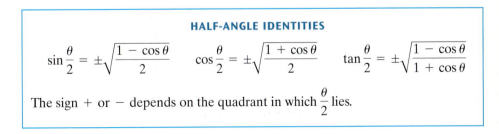

HALF-ANGLE IDENTITIES

$$\sin \frac{\theta}{2} = \pm\sqrt{\frac{1 - \cos \theta}{2}} \qquad \cos \frac{\theta}{2} = \pm\sqrt{\frac{1 + \cos \theta}{2}} \qquad \tan \frac{\theta}{2} = \pm\sqrt{\frac{1 - \cos \theta}{1 + \cos \theta}}$$

The sign $+$ or $-$ depends on the quadrant in which $\dfrac{\theta}{2}$ lies.

EXAMPLE 6   **Using Half-Angle Identities**

Use a half-angle identity to find the exact value of $\cos 157.5°$.

SOLUTION

Because $157.5° = \dfrac{315°}{2}$, we use the half-angle identity for $\cos \dfrac{\theta}{2}$ with $\theta = 315°$.

Because $\dfrac{\theta}{2} = 157.5°$ lies in quadrant II, $\cos \dfrac{\theta}{2}$ is negative.

$$\cos 157.5° = \cos \frac{315°}{2}$$

$$= -\sqrt{\frac{1 + \cos 315°}{2}} \qquad \text{Half-angle identity for cosine}$$

$$= -\sqrt{\frac{1 + \cos 45°}{2}} \qquad \begin{aligned} \cos 315° &= \cos(360° - 45°) \\ &= \cos 45° \end{aligned}$$

$$= -\sqrt{\frac{\left(1 + \dfrac{\sqrt{2}}{2}\right) \cdot 2}{2 \cdot 2}} \qquad \text{Replace } \cos 45° \text{ with } \dfrac{\sqrt{2}}{2}. \text{ Multiply}$$

numerator and denominator by 2.

$$= -\sqrt{\frac{2 + \sqrt{2}}{2 \cdot 2}} = -\frac{\sqrt{2 + \sqrt{2}}}{2} \qquad \blacksquare\,\blacksquare\,\blacksquare$$

Practice Problem 6   Find the exact value of $\sin 112.5°$.   ■

EXAMPLE 7   **Finding the Exact Value**

Given that $\sin \theta = -\dfrac{5}{13}, \pi < \theta < \dfrac{3\pi}{2}$, find the exact value of each expression.

a. $\sin \dfrac{\theta}{2}$ **b.** $\tan \dfrac{\theta}{2}$

SOLUTION

Because θ lies in quadrant III, $\cos \theta$ is negative; so

$$\cos \theta = -\sqrt{1 - \sin^2 \theta} \qquad \text{Pythagorean identity}$$

$$\cos \theta = -\sqrt{1 - \left(-\frac{5}{13}\right)^2} \qquad \text{Replace } \sin \theta \text{ with } -\frac{5}{13}.$$

$$= -\sqrt{1 - \frac{25}{169}} = -\sqrt{\frac{169 - 25}{169}} = -\frac{12}{13}$$

a. Because θ lies in quadrant III, $\dfrac{\theta}{2}$ lies in quadrant II. The half-angle identity gives

$$\sin \frac{\theta}{2} = \sqrt{\frac{1 - \cos \theta}{2}} \qquad \text{In quadrant II, } \sin \frac{\theta}{2} \text{ is positive.}$$

$$= \sqrt{\frac{1 - \left(-\dfrac{12}{13}\right)}{2}} \qquad \cos \theta = -\frac{12}{13} \text{ (from above)}$$

$$= \sqrt{\frac{\dfrac{25}{13}}{2}} = \frac{5}{\sqrt{26}} = \frac{5\sqrt{26}}{26}$$

b. From the half-angle identity, we have

$$\tan\frac{\theta}{2} = -\sqrt{\frac{1 - \cos\theta}{1 + \cos\theta}} \qquad \text{In quadrant II, } \tan\frac{\theta}{2} \text{ is negative.}$$

$$= -\sqrt{\frac{1 - \left(-\dfrac{12}{13}\right)}{1 + \left(-\dfrac{12}{13}\right)}} \qquad \cos\theta = -\frac{12}{13}$$

$$= -\sqrt{\frac{\dfrac{25}{13}}{\dfrac{1}{13}}} = -5 \qquad\qquad \blacksquare\ \blacksquare\ \blacksquare$$

Practice Problem 7   For θ in Example 7, find $\cos\dfrac{\theta}{2}$.   ■

EXAMPLE 8   **Verifying a Half-Angle Identity**

Verify the identity $\sin x \cos\dfrac{x}{2} = \sin\dfrac{x}{2}(1 + \cos x)$.

SOLUTION

The left side contains $\sin x$, and the right side contains $\sin\dfrac{x}{2}$. We replace x with $\dfrac{x}{2}$ in the double-angle identity for sine.

$$\sin 2x = 2\sin x \cos x$$

$$\sin x = 2\sin\frac{x}{2}\cos\frac{x}{2} \qquad \sin 2\left(\frac{x}{2}\right) = \sin x$$

Begin with the left side of the original equation

$$\sin x \cos\frac{x}{2} = 2\sin\frac{x}{2}\cos\frac{x}{2}\cos\frac{x}{2} \qquad\qquad \text{Replace } \sin x \text{ with } 2\sin\frac{x}{2}\cos\frac{x}{2}.$$

$$= 2\sin\frac{x}{2}\cos^2\frac{x}{2}$$

$$= 2\sin\frac{x}{2}\left(\frac{1 + \cos 2\left(\dfrac{x}{2}\right)}{2}\right) \qquad \text{Half-angle identity for cosine}$$

$$= \sin\frac{x}{2}(1 + \cos x) \qquad\qquad \cos 2\left(\frac{x}{2}\right) = \cos x$$

Because the left side is identical to the right side of the equation, the identity is verified.   ■ ■ ■

Practice Problem 8   Verify the identity $\sin\dfrac{x}{2}\sin x = \cos\dfrac{x}{2}(1 - \cos x)$.   ■

SECTION 5.3 ■ Exercises

A EXERCISES Basic Skills and Concepts

1. The double-angle identity for $\sin 2x$ is $\sin 2x = $ _____.

2. In the double-angle identity $\cos 2x = \cos^2 x - \sin^2 x$, replace $\cos^2 x$ with $1 - \sin^2 x$ to obtain a double-angle identity $\cos 2x = $ _____ in terms of $\sin^2 x$. Solve this identity for $\sin^2 x$ to obtain the power-reducing identity $\sin^2 x = $ _____.

3. The identity for $\cos 2x$ in terms of $\cos^2 x$ is $\cos 2x = $ _____. Solve this identity for $\cos^2 x$ to obtain the power-reducing identity $\cos^2 x = $ _____.

4. *True or False* $\tan 2x = \dfrac{1 - \cos 2x}{1 + \cos 2x}$.

5. *True or False* $\dfrac{1}{2}\tan 2x = \tan x$.

6. *True or False* $\cos \dfrac{\theta}{2} = -\sqrt{\dfrac{1 + \cos \theta}{2}}, \pi < \theta < 2\pi$.

In Exercises 7–12, use the given information about the angle θ to find the exact value of

a. $\sin 2\theta$.   b. $\cos 2\theta$.   c. $\tan 2\theta$.

7. $\sin \theta = \dfrac{3}{5}, \theta$ in quadrant II

8. $\cos \theta = -\dfrac{5}{13}, \theta$ in quadrant III

9. $\tan \theta = 4, \sin \theta < 0$

10. $\sec \theta = -\sqrt{3}, \sin \theta > 0$

11. $\tan \theta = -2, \dfrac{\pi}{2} < \theta < \pi$

12. $\cot \theta = -7, \dfrac{3\pi}{2} < \theta < 2\pi$

In Exercises 13–22, use a double-angle identity to find the exact value of each expression.

13. $1 - 2\sin^2 75°$

14. $\dfrac{2\tan 75°}{1 - \tan^2 75°}$

15. $2\cos^2 105° - 1$

16. $1 - 2\sin^2 165°$

17. $\dfrac{2\tan 165°}{1 - \tan^2 165°}$

18. $2\cos^2 165° - 1$

19. $1 - 2\sin^2 \dfrac{\pi}{8}$

20. $2\cos^2 \left(-\dfrac{\pi}{8}\right) - 1$

21. $\dfrac{2\tan \left(-\dfrac{5\pi}{12}\right)}{1 - \tan^2 \left(-\dfrac{5\pi}{12}\right)}$

22. $1 - 2\sin^2 \left(-\dfrac{7\pi}{12}\right)$

In Exercises 23 and 24, verify each "quadruple-angle" identity.

23. $\sin 4\theta = \cos \theta(4\sin \theta - 8\sin^3 \theta)$

24. $\cos 4\theta = 8\cos^4 \theta - 8\cos^2 \theta + 1$

In Exercises 25–32, verify each identity.

25. $\cos^4 x - \sin^4 x = \cos 2x$

26. $1 + \cos 2x + 2\sin^2 x = 2$

27. $\dfrac{1 + \sin 2x}{\cos 2x} = \dfrac{\cos x + \sin x}{\cos x - \sin x}$

28. $\dfrac{\cos 2x}{\sin 2x} + \dfrac{\sin x}{\cos x} = \csc 2x$ 29. $\dfrac{\sin 2x}{\sin x} - \dfrac{\cos 2x}{\cos x} = \sec x$

30. $\dfrac{\cos 3x}{\sin 3x} + \dfrac{\sin x}{\cos x} = \dfrac{\cos 2x}{\sin 3x \cos x}$

31. $\tan 2x + \tan x = \dfrac{\sin 3x}{\cos 2x \cos x}$

32. $\tan 2x - \tan x = \tan x \sec 2x$

In Exercises 33–42, use the power-reducing identities to rewrite each expression that does not contain trigonometric functions of power greater than 1.

33. $4\sin^2 x \cos^2 x$

34. $\sin^2 x \cos^2 x$

35. $4\sin x \cos x(1 - 2\sin^2 x)$

36. $4\sin x \cos x(2\cos^2 x - 1)$

37. $2\sin 3x \cos 3x(2\cos^2 3x - 1)$

38. $\sin 8x(1 - 2\sin^2 4x)$

39. $\sin \dfrac{x}{2}\cos \dfrac{x}{2}\left(1 - 2\sin^2 \dfrac{x}{2}\right)$

40. $\sin x\left(2\cos^2 \dfrac{x}{2} - 1\right)$

41. $8\sin^4 \dfrac{x}{2}$

42. $8\cos^4 \dfrac{x}{2}$

In Exercises 43–54, use half-angle identities to find the exact value of each expression.

43. $\sin \dfrac{\pi}{12}$

44. $\sin \dfrac{\pi}{8}$

45. $\cos \dfrac{\pi}{8}$

46. $\tan \dfrac{\pi}{8}$

47. $\sin \left(-\dfrac{3\pi}{8}\right)$

48. $\cos \left(-\dfrac{3\pi}{8}\right)$

49. $\tan \left(\dfrac{7\pi}{8}\right)$

50. $\sec \left(-\dfrac{7\pi}{8}\right)$

51. $\tan 112.5°$

52. $\cos 112.5°$

53. $\sin (-75°)$

54. $\tan (-105°)$

In Exercises 55–62, use the information about the angle θ to find the exact value of

a. $\sin \dfrac{\theta}{2}$.   b. $\cos \dfrac{\theta}{2}$.   c. $\tan \dfrac{\theta}{2}$.

55. $\sin \theta = \dfrac{4}{5}, \dfrac{\pi}{2} < \theta < \pi$

56. $\cos \theta = -\dfrac{12}{13}, \pi < \theta < \dfrac{3\pi}{2}$

57. $\tan \theta = -\dfrac{2}{3}, \dfrac{\pi}{2} < \theta < \pi$

58. $\cot \theta = \dfrac{3}{4}, \pi < \theta < \dfrac{3\pi}{2}$

59. $\sin \theta = \dfrac{1}{5}, \cos \theta < 0$ **60.** $\cos \theta = \dfrac{2}{3}, \sin \theta < 0$

61. $\sec \theta = \sqrt{5}, \sin \theta > 0$ **62.** $\csc \theta = \sqrt{7}, \tan \theta < 0$

In Exercises 63–72, verify each identity.

63. $\left(\sin \dfrac{t}{2} + \cos \dfrac{t}{2} \right)^2 = 1 + \sin t$

64. $\left(\sin \dfrac{t}{2} - \cos \dfrac{t}{2} \right)^2 = 1 - \sin t$

65. $2 \cos^2 \dfrac{x}{2} = \dfrac{\sin^2 x}{1 - \cos x}$ **66.** $2 \sin^2 \dfrac{x}{2} = \dfrac{\sin^2 x}{1 + \cos x}$

67. $\tan \dfrac{x}{2} = \dfrac{\sin x}{1 + \cos x}$ **68.** $\tan \dfrac{x}{2} = \dfrac{1 - \cos x}{\sin x}$

69. $\sin^2 \dfrac{x}{2} + \cos x = \cos^2 \dfrac{x}{2}$

70. $\cos^2 x + \cos x = 2 \cos^2 \dfrac{x}{2} - \sin^2 x$

71. $\sin x = \dfrac{2 \tan \dfrac{x}{2}}{1 + \tan^2 \dfrac{x}{2}}$

72. $\cos x = \dfrac{1 - \tan^2 \dfrac{x}{2}}{1 + \tan^2 \dfrac{x}{2}}$

B EXERCISES Applying the Concepts

In Exercises 73–79, assume that the voltage of the current is given by $V = 170 \sin (120\pi t)$, where t is in seconds. Find the wattage rating $\left(\dfrac{\text{maximum wattage}}{\sqrt{2}} \right)$ of each electric device if the current flowing through the device is I amps, and the power in watts is given by $P = VI$.

73. Light bulb. $I = 0.832 \sin (120\pi t)$.

74. Microwave oven. $I = 7.487 \sin (120\pi t)$.

75. Toaster. $I = 9.983 \sin (120\pi t)$.

76. Refrigerator. $I = 6.655 \sin (120\pi t)$.

77. Vacuum cleaner. $I = 4.991 \sin (120\pi t)$.

78. Television. $I = 2.917 \sin (120\pi t)$.

79. Throwing a football. A quarterback throws a ball with an initial velocity of v_0 feet per second at an angle θ with the horizontal. The horizontal distance x in feet

the ball is thrown is modeled by the equation

$$x = \dfrac{v_0^2}{16} \sin \theta \cos \theta.$$ For a fixed v_0, use a double–angle identity to find the angle that produces the maximum distance x.

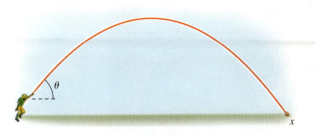

C EXERCISES Beyond the Basics

In Exercises 80–90, verify each identity.

80. $\tan 3x = \dfrac{3 \tan x - \tan^3 x}{1 - 3 \tan^2 x}$

81. $\dfrac{\sin 3x + \cos 3x}{\cos x - \sin x} = 1 + 2 \sin 2x$

82. $\dfrac{\sin x - \cos x}{\sin x + \cos x} - \dfrac{\sin x + \cos x}{\sin x - \cos x} = 2 \tan 2x$

83. $\dfrac{2}{\tan x + \cot x} = \sin x$ **84.** $\dfrac{2 \sin x}{\cos 3x} = \tan 3x - \tan x$

85. $\cot x - \tan x = 2 \cot 2x$

86. $\dfrac{1 - \tan^2 \left(\dfrac{\pi}{4} - x \right)}{1 + \tan^2 \left(\dfrac{\pi}{4} - x \right)} = \sin 2x$

87. $\dfrac{1 + \sin 2x - \cos 2x}{1 + \sin 2x + \cos 2x} = \tan x$

88. $\cos \theta \cos 2\theta \cos 4\theta = \dfrac{\sin 8\theta}{8 \sin \theta}$

89. $\sin^2 \left(\dfrac{\pi}{8} + \dfrac{x}{2} \right) - \sin^2 \left(\dfrac{\pi}{8} - \dfrac{x}{2} \right) = \dfrac{1}{\sqrt{2}} \sin x$

90. $\sqrt{2 + \sqrt{2 + 2 \cos 4x}} = 2 \cos x, 0 < x < \dfrac{\pi}{4}$

Critical Thinking

91. Use the figure to find the exact value of each expression.
   a. $\sin \theta$ **b.** $\cos \theta$
   c. $\sin 2\theta$ **d.** $\cos 2\theta$
   e. $\tan 2\theta$ **f.** $\sin \dfrac{\theta}{2}$
   g. $\cos \dfrac{\theta}{2}$ **h.** $\tan \dfrac{\theta}{2}$

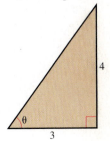

Product-to-Sum and Sum-to-Product Identities

Before Starting this Section, Review

1. Sum and difference identities for sines and cosines (Section 5.2)
2. Fundamental identities (Section 5.1)

Objectives

1 Derive product-to-sum identities.

2 Derive sum-to-product identities.

3 Verify trigonometric identities involving multiple angles.

TOUCH-TONE PHONES

Dual-tone multi-frequency (DTMF), also known as Touch-Tone, tone dialing, or push-button dialing, is a method for instructing a telephone switching network to dial a telephone number. The system was developed by Bell Labs in the late 1950s, and Touch-Tone phones were introduced to the public at the 1964 New York World's Fair. The dual-tone keypad on a Touch-Tone phone has four rows and three columns. Each row represents a *low* frequency and each column represents a *high* frequency, as shown in the figure. Pressing a button on a Touch-Tone phone produces a unique sound. The sound is produced by the combination of two tones (one of low frequency and the other of high frequency) associated with that button, as shown in the figure. In other words, the sound produced is given by $y = y_1 + y_2$, with $y_1 = \sin(2\pi l t)$ and $y_2 = \sin(2\pi h t)$, where l and h are the button's low and high frequencies, respectively (in hertz = Hz).

For example, if you press a single button such as 1, you will send a sinusoidal tone of two frequencies 697 Hz and 1209 Hz. The sound produced by pressing 1 is represented by the equation

$$y = \sin[2\pi(697)t] + \sin[2\pi(1209)t]$$

or

$$y = \sin(1394\pi t) + \sin(2418\pi t).$$

The two tones are the reason for calling such phones *dual-tone multi-frequency phones*. In Example 6, we analyze the sound produced by the sum of two sine waves. (*Source:* http://en.wikipedia.org.) ∎

---

1 Derive product-to-sum identities

Product-to-Sum Identities

The following identities enable us to rewrite products of sines or cosines as sums or differences.

> **PRODUCT-TO-SUM IDENTITIES**
>
> $$\cos x \cos y = \frac{1}{2}[\cos(x - y) + \cos(x + y)]$$
>
> $$\sin x \sin y = \frac{1}{2}[\cos(x - y) - \cos(x + y)]$$
>
> $$\sin x \cos y = \frac{1}{2}[\sin(x + y) + \sin(x - y)]$$
>
> $$\cos x \sin y = \frac{1}{2}[\sin(x + y) - \sin(x - y)]$$

These identities are fairly easy to prove. For example, to prove the first identity

$$\cos x \cos y = \frac{1}{2}[\cos(x-y) + \cos(x+y)],$$

we write the difference and sum identities for cosine and add.

$$\cos(x-y) = \cos x \cos y + \sin x \sin y$$
$$\underline{\cos(x+y) = \cos x \cos y - \sin x \sin y}$$

$\cos(x-y) + \cos(x+y) = 2\cos x \cos y + 0$	Add.
$2\cos x \cos y = \cos(x-y) + \cos(x+y)$	Switch sides.
$\mathbf{\cos x \cos y = \frac{1}{2}[\cos(x-y) + \cos(x+y)]}$	Multiply both sides by $\frac{1}{2}$.

Similarly, subtracting $\cos(x+y)$ from $\cos(x-y)$ gives the second identity.

$$\mathbf{\sin x \sin y = \frac{1}{2}[\cos(x-y) - \cos(x+y)]}$$

We can prove the third and fourth identities the same way.

EXAMPLE 1   Using a Product-to-Sum Identity

Write $\sin 5\theta \cos 3\theta$ as the sum or difference of two trigonometric functions.

SOLUTION

Use the identity $\sin x \cos y = \frac{1}{2}[\sin(x+y) + \sin(x-y)]$.

$\sin 5\theta \cos 3\theta = \frac{1}{2}[\sin(5\theta + 3\theta) + \sin(5\theta - 3\theta)]$	Replace x with 5θ and y with 3θ.
$= \frac{1}{2}[\sin 8\theta + \sin 2\theta]$	Simplify.
$= \frac{1}{2}\sin 8\theta + \frac{1}{2}\sin 2\theta$	Distributive property

■ ■ ■

Practice Problem 1   Write $\cos 3x \cos x$ as the sum or difference of two functions.   ■

EXAMPLE 2   Using a Product-to-Sum Identity

Find the exact value of $\sin 75° \sin 15°$.

SOLUTION

Use the identity $\sin x \sin y = \frac{1}{2}[\cos(x-y) - \cos(x+y)]$.

$\sin 75° \sin 15° = \frac{1}{2}[\cos(75° - 15°) - \cos(75° + 15°)]$	Replace x with $75°$ and y with $15°$.
$= \frac{1}{2}[\cos 60° - \cos 90°]$	Simplify.
$= \frac{1}{2}\left[\frac{1}{2} - 0\right] = \frac{1}{4}$	$\cos 60° = \frac{1}{2}$; $\cos 90° = 0$ ■ ■ ■

Practice Problem 2   Find the exact value of $\sin 15° \cos 75°$.   ■

2 Derive sum-to-product
identities.

Sum-to-Product Identities

The following identities enable us to do just the opposite—rewrite sums or differences of sines or cosines as products.

SUM-TO-PRODUCT IDENTITIES

$$\cos x + \cos y = 2 \cos\left(\frac{x+y}{2}\right) \cos\left(\frac{x-y}{2}\right)$$

$$\cos x - \cos y = -2 \sin\left(\frac{x+y}{2}\right) \sin\left(\frac{x-y}{2}\right)$$

$$\sin x + \sin y = 2 \sin\left(\frac{x+y}{2}\right) \cos\left(\frac{x-y}{2}\right)$$

$$\sin x - \sin y = 2 \sin\left(\frac{x-y}{2}\right) \cos\left(\frac{x+y}{2}\right)$$

We prove these identities by using the product-to-sum identities. For example, to prove the first identity, we start with the right side of the equation and use the product-to-sum identities.

$$2 \cos\left(\frac{x+y}{2}\right) \cos\left(\frac{x-y}{2}\right)$$

$$= 2 \cdot \frac{1}{2}\left[\cos\left(\frac{x+y}{2} - \frac{x-y}{2}\right) + \cos\left(\frac{x+y}{2} + \frac{x-y}{2}\right)\right] \qquad \text{Use the identity for the product of cosines.}$$

$$= \cos\left(\frac{x+y-x+y}{2}\right) + \cos\left(\frac{x+y+x-y}{2}\right) \qquad \text{Simplify.}$$

$$= \cos\left(\frac{2y}{2}\right) + \cos\left(\frac{2x}{2}\right) \qquad \text{Simplify.}$$

$$= \cos y + \cos x = \cos x + \cos y \qquad \text{Simplify and rewrite.}$$

You can verify the other three identities in the box in a similar way. (See Exercise 81.)

EXAMPLE 3   **Using Sum-to-Product Identities**

Write each expression as a product of two trigonometric functions and simplify where possible.

a. $\sin 4\theta - \sin 6\theta$ **b.** $\cos 65° + \cos 55°$

SOLUTION

a. Use the identity $\sin x - \sin y = 2 \sin\left(\frac{x-y}{2}\right) \cos\left(\frac{x+y}{2}\right)$.

$$\sin 4\theta - \sin 6\theta = 2 \sin\left(\frac{4\theta - 6\theta}{2}\right) \cos\left(\frac{4\theta + 6\theta}{2}\right) \qquad \text{Replace } x \text{ with } 4\theta \text{ and } y \text{ with } 6\theta.$$

$$= 2 \sin(-\theta) \cos(5\theta) \qquad \text{Simplify.}$$

$$= -2 \sin \theta \cos 5\theta \qquad \sin(-\theta) = -\sin\theta$$

b. Use the identity $\cos x + \cos y = 2 \cos\left(\dfrac{x+y}{2}\right) \cos\left(\dfrac{x-y}{2}\right)$.

$$\cos 65° + \cos 55° = 2 \cos\left(\dfrac{65° + 55°}{2}\right) \cos\left(\dfrac{65° - 55°}{2}\right) \qquad \text{Replace } x \text{ with } 65° \text{ and } y \text{ with } 55°.$$

$$= 2 \cos 60° \cos 5° \qquad \text{Simplify.}$$

$$= 2\left(\dfrac{1}{2}\right)\cos 5° = \cos 5° \qquad \cos 60° = \dfrac{1}{2} \quad \blacksquare \blacksquare \blacksquare$$

Practice Problem 3 Write each expression as a product of two functions and simplify where possible.

a. $\cos 2x - \cos 4x$ **b.** $\sin 43° + \sin 17°$ ■

In the next example, we show how to express a sum of a sine and a cosine as a product by first using a cofunction identity.

STUDY TIP

In Example 4, you could also write $\sin 5\theta + \cos 3\theta =$

$\sin 5\theta + \sin\left(\dfrac{\pi}{2} - 3\theta\right)$ and

then use the sum-to-product identity.

EXAMPLE 4 **Expressing a Sum of a Sine and a Cosine as a Product**

Write $\sin 5\theta + \cos 3\theta$ as a product of two trigonometric functions.

SOLUTION
Use the identity

$$\cos x + \cos y = 2 \cos\left(\dfrac{x+y}{2}\right) \cos\left(\dfrac{x-y}{2}\right)$$

$$\sin 5\theta + \cos 3\theta = \cos\left(\dfrac{\pi}{2} - 5\theta\right) + \cos 3\theta \qquad \text{Cofunction identity}$$

$$= 2 \cos\left(\dfrac{\dfrac{\pi}{2} - 5\theta + 3\theta}{2}\right) \cos\left(\dfrac{\dfrac{\pi}{2} - 5\theta - 3\theta}{2}\right) \qquad \text{Sum-to-product identity for cosines}$$

$$= 2 \cos\left(\dfrac{\pi}{4} - \theta\right) \cos\left(\dfrac{\pi}{4} - 4\theta\right) \qquad \text{Simplify.}$$

$\blacksquare \blacksquare \blacksquare$

Practice Problem 4 Write $\sin 2x + \cos x$ as a product of two trigonometric functions. ■

3 Verify trigonometric identities involving multiple angles.

Verify Trigonometric Identities

The next example illustrates the use of sum-to-product identities to verify identities.

EXAMPLE 5 **Verifying an Identity**

Verify the identity $\dfrac{\sin 5\theta + \sin 9\theta}{\cos 5\theta - \cos 9\theta} = \cot 2\theta$.

SOLUTION

$$\frac{\sin 5\theta + \sin 9\theta}{\cos 5\theta - \cos 9\theta} = \frac{2 \sin \dfrac{5\theta + 9\theta}{2} \cos \dfrac{5\theta - 9\theta}{2}}{-2 \sin \dfrac{5\theta + 9\theta}{2} \sin \dfrac{5\theta - 9\theta}{2}}$$ Use the identities for $\sin x + \sin y$ and $\cos x + \cos y$.

$$= \frac{2 \sin 7\theta \cos (-2\theta)}{-2 \sin 7\theta \sin (-2\theta)}$$ Simplify.

$$= \frac{\cos (-2\theta)}{-\sin (-2\theta)}$$ Remove the common factors.

$$= \frac{\cos 2\theta}{\sin 2\theta}$$ $\cos (-x) = \cos x$, and $\sin (-x) = -\sin x$.

$$= \cot 2\theta$$ Quotient identity ■ ■ ■

Practice Problem 5 Verify the identity $\dfrac{\cos 5x - \cos x}{\sin x - \sin 5x} = \tan 3x.$ ■

Analyzing Touch-Tone Phones

When a sound of frequency f is combined with a sound of frequency g, the resulting sound has frequency $\dfrac{f + g}{2}$. In a Touch-Tone phone, when you press a button with a low frequency l and high frequency h, the sound produced is modeled by

$$y = \sin (2\pi l t) + \sin (2\pi h t)$$ t represents time

$$y = 2 \sin \left[2\pi \left(\frac{l + h}{2} \right) t \right] \cos \left[2\pi \left(\frac{l - h}{2} \right) t \right]$$ Sum-to-product identity

$$y = 2 \cos \left[2\pi \left(\frac{h - l}{2} \right) t \right] \sin \left[2\pi \left(\frac{l + h}{2} \right) t \right]$$ Rewrite; $\cos (-\theta) = \cos \theta$

The last equation suggests that the resulting sound may be thought of as a sine wave with frequency of $\dfrac{l + h}{2}$ and variable amplitude of $2 \cos \left[2\pi \left(\dfrac{h - l}{2} \right) t \right]$.

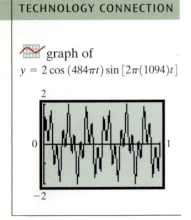

FIGURE 5.5

EXAMPLE 6 **Touch-Tone Phones**

a. Write an expression that models the tone of the sound produced by pressing the 8 button on your Touch-Tone phone. See Figure 5.5.

b. Rewrite the expression from part **a** as a product of two functions.

c. Write the frequency and the variable amplitude of the sound from part **a**.

SOLUTION

a. Pressing the 8 key produces the sound given by

$$y = \sin [2\pi (852)t] + \sin [2\pi (1336)t]$$ $l = 852; h = 1336$

b. $y = 2 \sin \left[2\pi \left(\dfrac{852 + 1336}{2} \right) t \right] \cos \left[2\pi \left(\dfrac{852 - 1336}{2} \right) t \right]$ Sum-to-product identity

$$= 2 \cos [2\pi (242)t] \sin [2\pi (1094)t]$$ $\cos (-\theta) = \cos \theta$

$$= 2 \cos (484\pi t) \sin [2\pi (1094)t]$$

c. The frequency is 1094 Hz, and the variable amplitude is $2 \cos (484\pi t)$. ■ ■ ■

Practice Problem 6 Repeat Example 6 assuming that you press the 1 button on your Touch-Tone phone. ■

TECHNOLOGY CONNECTION

graph of
$y = 2 \cos (484\pi t) \sin [2\pi (1094)t]$

A EXERCISES Basic Skills and Concepts

1. We can rewrite the product of two sines as a difference of two cosines by using the identity $\sin x \sin y =$
   _____.

2. We can rewrite the product of a sine and a cosine as the sum of two sines by using the identity $\sin x \cos y =$
   _____.

3. We can rewrite the sum of two cosines as a product of two cosines by using the identity $\cos x + \cos y =$
   _____.

4. *True or False* $\cos x - \cos y = 2 \sin\left(\dfrac{x + y}{2}\right) \sin\left(\dfrac{y - x}{2}\right)$.

5. *True or False* $\sin x + \sin y = \sin(x + y)$.

6. *True or False* $\sin(2x + 1) - \sin(2x - 1) = 2 \sin(1) \cos 2x$.

In Exercises 7–22, use the product-to-sum identities to rewrite each expression as the sum or difference of two functions. Simplify where possible.

7. $\sin x \cos x$	8. $\cos x \cos x$
9. $\sin x \sin x$	10. $\cos x \sin x$
11. $\sin 25° \cos 5°$	12. $\sin 40° \sin 20°$
13. $\cos 140° \cos 20°$	14. $\cos 70° \sin 20°$
15. $\sin \dfrac{7\pi}{12} \sin \dfrac{\pi}{12}$	16. $\sin \dfrac{3\pi}{8} \cos \dfrac{\pi}{8}$
17. $\cos \dfrac{5\pi}{8} \sin \dfrac{\pi}{8}$	18. $\cos \dfrac{5\pi}{3} \cos \dfrac{\pi}{3}$
19. $\sin 5\theta \cos \theta$	20. $\cos 3\theta \sin 2\theta$
21. $\cos 4x \cos 3x$	22. $\sin 5x \sin 2x$

In Exercises 23–30, find the exact value of each expression.

23. $\sin 37.5° \sin 7.5°$	24. $\cos 52.5° \cos 7.5°$
25. $\sin 67.5° \cos 22.5°$	26. $\cos 105° \sin 75°$
27. $\sin \dfrac{5\pi}{24} \cos \dfrac{\pi}{24}$	28. $\sin \dfrac{7\pi}{12} \sin \dfrac{\pi}{12}$
29. $\cos \dfrac{13\pi}{24} \cos \dfrac{5\pi}{24}$	30. $\cos \dfrac{7\pi}{24} \sin \dfrac{\pi}{24}$

In Exercises 31–50, use sum-to-product identities to rewrite each expression as a product. Simplify where possible.

31. $\cos 40° - \cos 20°$	32. $\sin 22° + \sin 8°$
33. $\sin 32° - \sin 16°$	34. $\cos 47° + \cos 13°$
35. $\sin \dfrac{\pi}{5} + \sin \dfrac{2\pi}{5}$	36. $\cos \dfrac{\pi}{12} + \cos \dfrac{\pi}{3}$
37. $\cos \dfrac{1}{2} + \cos \dfrac{1}{3}$	38. $\sin \dfrac{2}{3} - \sin \dfrac{1}{4}$
39. $\cos 3x + \cos 5x$	40. $\sin 5x - \sin 3x$
41. $\sin 7x + \sin(-x)$	42. $\cos 7x - \cos 3x$
43. $\sin x + \cos x$	44. $\cos x - \sin x$
45. $\sin 2x - \cos 2x$	46. $\cos 3x + \sin 3x$
47. $\sin 3x + \cos 5x$	48. $\sin 5x - \cos x$
49. $a(\sin x + \cos x)$	50. $a(\sin bx + \cos bx)$

In Exercises 51–60, verify each identity.

51. $\dfrac{\sin x + \sin 3x}{\cos x + \cos 3x} = \tan 2x$

52. $\dfrac{\sin 2x + \sin 4x}{\cos 2x + \cos 4x} = \tan 3x$

53. $\dfrac{\cos 3x - \cos 7x}{\sin 7x + \sin 3x} = \tan 2x$

54. $\dfrac{\cos 12x - \cos 4x}{\sin 4x - \sin 12x} = \tan 8x$

55. $\dfrac{\cos 2x + \cos 2y}{\cos 2x - \cos 2y} = \cot(y - x)\cot(y + x)$

56. $\dfrac{\sin 2x + \sin 2y}{\sin 2x - \sin 2y} = \dfrac{\tan(x + y)}{\tan(x - y)}$

57. $\sin x + \sin 2x + \sin 3x = \sin 2x(1 + 2\cos x)$

58. $\cos x + \cos 2x + \cos 3x = \cos 2x(1 + 2\cos x)$

59. $\sin 2x + \sin 4x + \sin 6x = 4\cos x \cos 2x \sin 3x$

60. $\cos x + \cos 3x + \cos 5x + \cos 7x = 4\cos x \cos 2x \cos 4x$

B EXERCISES Applying the Concepts

61. **Touch-Tone phone.**
    a. Write an expression that models the tone by pressing the 7 button on your Touch-Tone phone. (See Figure 5.5, page 216.)
    b. Rewrite the expression from part (a) as a product of two functions.
    c. Write the frequency and the variable amplitude of the sound from part (a).

62. **Touch-Tone phone.** Repeat Exercise 61 assuming that you press the # button on your Touch-Tone phone.

63. **Beats in music.** When two musical tones of slightly different frequencies are played, the sound you hear will fluctuate in volume according to the difference in their frequencies. These are called *beat frequencies*. (Piano tuners use the beat frequency to adjust piano wire until it is at the same frequency as the tuning fork.) Let $y_1 = 0.05 \cos(112\pi t)$ and $y_2 = 0.05 \cos(120\pi t)$ model two tones.
    a. Write $y = y_1 + y_2$ as the product of two functions.
    b. How many beats are there?

64. Beats in music. Repeat Exercise 63 for the two tones represented by $y_1 = 0.04 \sin(110\pi t)$ and $y_2 = 0.04 \sin(114\pi t)$.

C EXERCISES Beyond the Basics

In Exercises 65 and 66, sketch the graph of f. What is the amplitude and period?

65. $f(x) = \cos(2x + 1) + \cos(2x - 1)$

66. $f(x) = \sin(3x + 1) + \sin(3x - 1)$

In Exercises 67–76, verify each identity.

67. $\cos 40° + \cos 50° + \cos 70° + \cos 80°$
$\quad = \cos 10° + \cos 20°$

68. $\sin 10° + \sin 20° + \sin 40° + \sin 50° = 2 \cos 5° \cos 15°$

69. $\cos 4\theta \cos \theta - \cos 6\theta \cos 9\theta = \sin 5\theta \sin 10\theta$

70. $\cos 38° \cos 46° - \sin 14° \sin 22° = \dfrac{1}{2} \cos 24°$

71. $\sin 25° \sin 35° - \sin 25° \sin 85° - \sin 35° \sin 85° = -\dfrac{3}{4}$

72. $\cos 20° \cos 40° \cos 60° \cos 80° = \dfrac{1}{16}$

73. $\dfrac{\sin 3x \cos 5x - \sin x \cos 7x}{\sin x \sin 7x + \cos 3x \cos 5x} = \tan 2x$

74. $\dfrac{\sin 11x \sin x + \sin 7x \sin 3x}{\cos 11x \sin x + \cos 7x \sin 3x} = \tan 8x$

75. $\dfrac{\cos x + \cos 3x + \cos 5x + \cos 7x}{\sin x + \sin 3x + \sin 5x + \sin 7x} = \cot 4x$

76. $\dfrac{\sin 3x + \sin 5x + \sin 7x + \sin 9x}{\cos 3x + \cos 5x + \cos 7x + \cos 9x} = \tan 6x$

77. Verify the identity $\cos 7x = 2 \cos 6x \cos x - 2 \cos 4x \cos x + 2 \cos 2x \cos x - \cos x$.

78. a. Verify the identity
$$4 \sin \theta \sin\left(\dfrac{\pi}{3} + \theta\right) \sin\left(\dfrac{\pi}{3} - \theta\right) = \sin 3\theta.$$
[*Hint:* Recall that $\sin 3\theta = 3 \sin \theta - 4 \sin^3 \theta$.]

b. Use part (a) to show that
$$\sin 20° \sin 40° \sin 60° \sin 80° = \dfrac{3}{16}.$$

79. Verify the identity
$$\dfrac{\sin(x + 3y) + \sin(3x + y)}{\sin 2x + \sin 2y} = 2 \cos(x + y).$$

80. Verify the identity $\sin^3 x \sin 3x + \cos^3 x \cos 3x = \cos^3 2x$.

81. Verify the following sum-to-product formulas.

a. $\cos x - \cos y = -2 \sin\left(\dfrac{x + y}{2}\right) \sin\left(\dfrac{x - y}{2}\right)$

b. $\sin x + \sin y = 2 \sin\left(\dfrac{x + y}{2}\right) \cos\left(\dfrac{x - y}{2}\right)$

c. $\sin x - \sin y = 2 \sin\left(\dfrac{x - y}{2}\right) \cos\left(\dfrac{x + y}{2}\right)$

Critical Thinking

82. Supply the reason for each step in verifying the identity
$\sin \dfrac{\pi}{14} \sin \dfrac{3\pi}{14} \sin \dfrac{5\pi}{14} = \dfrac{1}{8}$.

$\sin \dfrac{\pi}{14} \sin \dfrac{3\pi}{14} \sin \dfrac{5\pi}{14} = \cos \dfrac{3\pi}{7} \cos \dfrac{2\pi}{7} \cos \dfrac{\pi}{7}$

$= \dfrac{8 \sin \dfrac{\pi}{7} \cos \dfrac{\pi}{7} \cos \dfrac{2\pi}{7} \cos \dfrac{3\pi}{7}}{8 \sin \dfrac{\pi}{7}}$

$= \dfrac{2 \sin \dfrac{4\pi}{7} \cos \dfrac{3\pi}{7}}{8 \sin \dfrac{\pi}{7}}$

$= \dfrac{\sin \pi + \sin \dfrac{\pi}{7}}{8 \sin \dfrac{\pi}{7}}$

$= \dfrac{1}{8}$

GROUP PROJECTS

Assume that $A + B + C = 180°$. Verify each identity.

1. $\sin 2A + \sin 2B + \sin 2C = 4 \sin A \sin B \sin C$

2. $\cos 2A + \cos 2B + \cos 2C = -1 - 4 \cos A \cos B \cos C$

REVIEW

Definitions, Concepts, and Formulas	Examples and Illustrations

5.1 Verifying Identities

■ **Fundamental trigonometric identities** We proved the even–odd identities to complete the **fundamental trigonometric identities** listed next.

1. Reciprocal Identities

$$\csc x = \frac{1}{\sin x} \qquad \sec x = \frac{1}{\cos x} \qquad \cot x = \frac{1}{\tan x}$$

$$\sin x = \frac{1}{\csc x} \qquad \cos x = \frac{1}{\sec x} \qquad \tan x = \frac{1}{\cot x}$$

2. Quotient Identities

$$\tan x = \frac{\sin x}{\cos x} \qquad \cot x = \frac{\cos x}{\sin x}$$

3. Pythagorean Identities

$$\sin^2 x + \cos^2 x = 1 \quad 1 + \tan^2 x = \sec^2 x \quad 1 + \cot^2 x = \csc^2 x$$

4. Even-Odd Identities

$$\sin(-x) = -\sin x \quad \cos(-x) = \cos x \quad \tan(-x) = -\tan x$$

$$\csc(-x) = -\csc x \quad \sec(-x) = \sec x \quad \cot(-x) = -\cot x$$

To find the sine and cosine of $-\frac{2\pi}{3}$, use the even-odd identities.

$$\cos\left(-\frac{2\pi}{3}\right) = \cos\frac{2\pi}{3} = -\frac{1}{2}$$

$$\sin\left(-\frac{2\pi}{3}\right) = -\sin\frac{2\pi}{3} = -\left(\frac{\sqrt{3}}{2}\right) = -\frac{\sqrt{3}}{2}$$

■ **Verifying trigonometric identities** To verify an identity, we are given an equation and want to show that the equation is satisfied by *all* values of the variable for which both sides of the equation are defined.

Algebra Operations

Review the procedure for combining fractions by finding the least common denominator.

Fundamental Trigonometric Identities

Review the fundamental trigonometric identities summarized above. Look for an opportunity to apply the fundamental trigonometric identities when working on either side of the identity to be verified. Become thoroughly familiar with alternative forms of fundamental identities. For example, $\sin^2 x = 1 - \cos^2 x$ and $\sec^2 x - \tan^2 x = 1$ are alternative forms of the fundamental identities $\sin^2 x + \cos^2 x = 1$ and $\sec^2 x = 1 + \tan^2 x$, respectively.

1. Start with the more complicated side and transform it to the simpler side.

It is generally helpful to start with the more complicated side of an identity and simplify until it becomes identical to the other side.

2. Stay focused on the final expression.

While working on one side of the identity, stay focused on your goal of converting it to the form on the other side.

To verify the identity $\cos x \tan x = \sin x$, begin with the more complicated side, the left hand side.

$$\cos x \tan x = \cos x \frac{\sin x}{\cos x}$$

$$= \frac{\cos x \sin x}{\cos x}$$

$$= \sin x$$

To verify $1 - \cot^2 x = \dfrac{\sin^4 x - \cos^4 x}{\sin^2 x}$, begin with the more complicated side and focus on the fact that there are no fourth powers in the final expression, $1 - \cot^2 x$.

$$\frac{\sin^4 x - \cos^4 x}{\sin^2 x} = \frac{(\sin^2 x - \cos^2 x)(\sin^2 x + \cos^2 x)}{\sin^2 x}$$

$$= \frac{(\sin^2 x - \cos^2 x) \cdot 1}{\sin^2 x}$$

$$= \frac{\sin^2 x}{\sin^2 x} - \frac{\cos^2 x}{\sin^2 x}$$

$$= 1 - \cot^2 x$$

The following techniques are sometimes helpful.

3. Option: Convert to sines and cosines.
Rewrite one side of the identity in terms of sines and cosines.

See Example 4 on page 183.

4. Option: Work on both sides.
Transform each side separately to the same equivalent expression.

See Example 5 on page 184.

5. Option: Use conjugates.
In expressions containing $1 + \sin x$, $1 - \sin x$, $1 + \cos x$, $1 - \cos x$, $\sec x + \tan x$, and so on, multiply the numerator and the denominator by its conjugate and then use one of the forms of the Pythagorean identities.

See Example 6 on page 185.

■ **Showing that an equation is not an identity** To prove that an equation is *not* an identity, at least one value of the variable must be found for which both sides are defined but not equal.

To show that $-\sin x \cos(-x) = \sin x \cos x$ is *not* an identity, we can use $x = \dfrac{\pi}{4}$. Then

$$-\sin x \cos(-x) = -\sin\frac{\pi}{4}\cos\left(-\frac{\pi}{4}\right)$$
$$= -\frac{\sqrt{2}}{2}\frac{\sqrt{2}}{2} = -\frac{1}{2},$$

but

$$\sin x \cos x = \sin\frac{\pi}{4}\cos\frac{\pi}{4}$$
$$= \frac{\sqrt{2}}{2}\frac{\sqrt{2}}{2} = \frac{1}{2}$$

Because $-\sin\dfrac{\pi}{4}\cos\left(-\dfrac{\pi}{4}\right) \neq \sin\dfrac{\pi}{4}\cos\left(-\dfrac{\pi}{4}\right)$, the equation $-\sin x \cos(-x) = \sin x \cos x$ is not an identity.

5.2 Sum and Difference Identities

■ **Sum and difference identities for cosine** If the variables u and v represent any real numbers or angles, we can find the values of $\cos(u \pm v)$, $\sin(u \pm v)$, and $\tan(u \pm v)$ using the values of $\cos u$ and $\cos v$, $\sin u$ and $\sin v$, and $\tan u$ and $\tan v$, respectively.

Sum and difference identities for cosine

$$\cos(u + v) = \cos u \cos v - \sin u \sin v$$
$$\cos(u - v) = \cos u \cos v + \sin u \sin v$$

To find the exact value of $\cos\dfrac{7\pi}{12}$, use the fact that

$$\frac{7\pi}{12} = \frac{\pi}{3} + \frac{\pi}{4}.$$

Then

$$\cos\left(\frac{7\pi}{12}\right) = \cos\left(\frac{\pi}{3} + \frac{\pi}{4}\right)$$
$$= \cos\frac{\pi}{3}\cos\frac{\pi}{4} - \sin\frac{\pi}{3}\sin\frac{\pi}{4}$$
$$= \frac{1}{2}\cdot\frac{\sqrt{2}}{2} - \frac{\sqrt{3}}{2}\cdot\frac{\sqrt{2}}{2}$$
$$= \frac{\sqrt{2} - \sqrt{6}}{4}$$

■ **Cofunction identities** Two trigonometric functions f and g are called cofunctions if

$$f\left(\frac{\pi}{2} - x\right) = g(x) \text{ and } g\left(\frac{\pi}{2} - x\right) = f(x).$$

The cofunction identity for cosine is derived using the difference identity for the cosine.

Basic cofunction identities

If v is any real number or angle measured in radians, then

$$\cos\left(\frac{\pi}{2} - v\right) = \sin v$$

$$\sin\left(\frac{\pi}{2} - v\right) = \cos v.$$

If angle v is measured in degrees, replace $\frac{\pi}{2}$ with $90°$ in these identities.

Other cofunction pairs are tangent and cotangent, and secant and cosecant.

We can use the cofunction identities for both positive and negative values of the variable. For example,

$$\cos\frac{\pi}{10} = \sin\left(\frac{\pi}{2} - \frac{\pi}{10}\right) = \sin\frac{2\pi}{5}$$

$$\sin 10° = \cos(90° - 10°) = \cos 80°$$

$$\tan\left(-\frac{\pi}{7}\right) = \cot\left[\frac{\pi}{2} - \left(-\frac{\pi}{7}\right)\right] = \cot\frac{9\pi}{14}$$

$$\sec(-42°) = \csc[90° - (-42°)] = \csc 132°$$

■ **Sum and difference identities for sine** The cofunction identities and the identity for $\cos(u + v)$ lead to the following:

$$\sin(u - v) = \sin u \cos v - \cos u \sin v$$

$$\sin(u + v) = \sin u \cos v + \cos u \sin v$$

We want to find the exact value of $\sin(u - v)$ when $\sin u = \frac{12}{13}$ and $\cos v = -\frac{3}{5}$ with $\frac{\pi}{2} < u < \pi$ and $\pi < v < \frac{3\pi}{2}$.

Because

$\cos^2 u = 1 - \sin^2 u$ and u is in Q II, $\cos u < 0$;

$$\cos u = -\sqrt{1 - \sin^2 u}$$

$$= -\sqrt{1 - \left(\frac{12}{13}\right)^2} = -\sqrt{\frac{25}{169}} = -\frac{5}{13}.$$

Because

$\sin^2 v = 1 - \cos^2 v$ and v is in Q III, $\sin v < 0$;

$$\sin v = -\sqrt{1 - \cos^2 v}$$

$$= -\sqrt{1 - \left(-\frac{3}{5}\right)^2} = -\sqrt{\frac{16}{25}} = -\frac{4}{5}.$$

Then

$$\sin(u - v) = \sin u \cos v - \cos u \sin v$$

$$= \left(\frac{12}{13}\right)\left(-\frac{3}{5}\right) - \left(-\frac{5}{13}\right)\left(-\frac{4}{5}\right) = -\frac{56}{65}.$$

■ **Sum and difference identities for tangent** The sum and difference identities for $\cos(u \pm v)$ and $\sin(u \pm v)$ lead to the following:

$$\tan(u - v) = \frac{\tan u - \tan v}{1 + \tan u \tan v}$$

$$\tan(u + v) = \frac{\tan u + \tan v}{1 - \tan u \tan v}$$

To find $\tan 15°$, notice that $45° - 30° = 15°$.

Then

$$\tan 15° = \tan(45° - 30°)$$

$$= \frac{\tan 45° - \tan 30°}{1 + \tan 45° \tan 30°}$$

$$= \frac{1 - \frac{1}{\sqrt{3}}}{1 + (1)\left(\frac{1}{\sqrt{3}}\right)}$$

$$= \frac{\sqrt{3} - 1}{\sqrt{3} + 1} = 2 - \sqrt{3}.$$

5.3 Double-Angle and Half-Angle Identities

■ **Double-angle identities** The sum identities for the sine, cosine, and tangent functions lead to identities called double-angle identities, for $2x$.

Double-Angle Identities

$$\sin 2x = 2 \sin x \cos x$$
$$\cos 2x = \cos^2 x - \sin^2 x$$
$$\cos 2x = 1 - 2 \sin^2 x$$
$$\cos 2x = 2 \cos^2 x - 1$$
$$\tan 2x = \frac{2 \tan x}{1 - \tan^2 x}$$

Suppose we want to find the values for $\cos 2x$, $\sin 2x$, and $\tan 2x$ given that $\sin x = \frac{1}{3}$, $\frac{\pi}{2} < x < \pi$.

Because $\frac{\pi}{2} < x < \pi$, $\cos x < 0$.

So $\cos x = -\sqrt{1 - \sin^2 x}$

$$= -\sqrt{1 - \left(\frac{1}{3}\right)^2}$$

$$= -\sqrt{\frac{8}{9}} = -\frac{2\sqrt{2}}{3}.$$

Using the double-angle identity,

$$\sin 2x = 2 \sin x \cos x$$

$$= 2\left(\frac{1}{3}\right)\left(-\frac{2\sqrt{2}}{3}\right) = -\frac{4\sqrt{2}}{9}.$$

Then

$$\cos 2x = 1 - 2 \sin^2 x$$

$$= 1 - 2\left(\frac{1}{3}\right)^2 = 1 - \frac{2}{9} = \frac{7}{9}.$$

Finally,

$$\tan 2x = \frac{\sin 2x}{\cos 2x}$$

$$= -\frac{4\sqrt{2}}{9} \div \frac{7}{9} = -\frac{4\sqrt{2}}{7}.$$

■ **Power-reducing identities** To express $\sin^2 x$, $\cos^2 x$, and $\tan^2 x$ in terms of trigonometric functions with powers less than or equal to 1, we use the power-reducing identities.

$$\sin^2 x = \frac{1 - \cos 2x}{2} \qquad \cos^2 x = \frac{1 + \cos 2x}{2}$$

$$\tan^2 x = \frac{1 - \cos 2x}{1 + \cos 2x}$$

For example,

$$\sin^2\left(\frac{\pi}{12}\right) = \frac{1 - \cos\left(2 \cdot \frac{\pi}{12}\right)}{2}$$

$$= \frac{1 - \cos \frac{\pi}{6}}{2}$$

$$= \frac{1}{2}\left(1 - \frac{\sqrt{3}}{2}\right) = \frac{2 - \sqrt{3}}{4}.$$

■ **Half-angle identities** Half-angle identities express trigonometric functions of $\frac{x}{2}$ in terms of functions of x.

Suppose we want to find $\sin \frac{x}{2}$, $\cos \frac{x}{2}$, and $\tan \frac{x}{2}$ given that $\cos x = \frac{4}{5}$ and $\frac{3\pi}{2} < x < 2\pi$.

Half-Angle Identities

$$\sin\frac{\theta}{2} = \pm\sqrt{\frac{1-\cos\theta}{2}}$$

$$\cos\frac{\theta}{2} = \pm\sqrt{\frac{1+\cos\theta}{2}}$$

$$\tan\frac{\theta}{2} = \pm\sqrt{\frac{1-\cos\theta}{1+\cos\theta}},$$

where the sign $+$ or $-$ depends on the quadrant in which $\dfrac{\theta}{2}$ lies.

Because $\dfrac{3\pi}{2} < x < 2\pi$, $\dfrac{3\pi}{4} < \dfrac{x}{2} < \pi$; so $\dfrac{x}{2}$ is in Q II.

In Q II, sine is positive and cosine is negative. The half-angle identities give:

$$\sin\frac{x}{2} = \sqrt{\frac{1-\cos x}{2}} = \sqrt{\frac{1-\frac{4}{5}}{2}}$$

$$= \sqrt{\frac{1}{10}} = \frac{\sqrt{10}}{10}$$

$$\cos\frac{x}{2} = -\sqrt{\frac{1+\cos x}{2}} = -\sqrt{\frac{1+\frac{4}{5}}{2}}$$

$$= -\sqrt{\frac{9}{10}} = -\frac{3\sqrt{10}}{10}$$

$$\tan\frac{x}{2} = \frac{\sin\dfrac{x}{2}}{\cos\dfrac{x}{2}} = \frac{\sqrt{10}}{10} \div \frac{-3\sqrt{10}}{10}$$

$$= -\frac{1}{3}$$

5.4 Product-to-Sum and Sum-to-Product Identities

■ **Product-to-sum identities** The next four identities enable us to rewrite products of sines or cosines as sums or differences.

Product-to-Sum Identities

$$\cos x \cos y = \frac{1}{2}[\cos(x-y) + \cos(x+y)]$$

$$\sin x \sin y = \frac{1}{2}[\cos(x-y) - \cos(x+y)]$$

$$\sin x \cos y = \frac{1}{2}[\sin(x+y) + \sin(x-y)]$$

$$\cos x \sin y = \frac{1}{2}[\sin(x+y) - \sin(x-y)]$$

Suppose we want to find the exact value of $\cos\dfrac{5\pi}{12}\cos\dfrac{\pi}{12}$.

Use the product-to-sum identity for $\cos x \cos y$ with $x = \dfrac{5\pi}{12}$ and $y = \dfrac{\pi}{12}$.

$$\cos\frac{5\pi}{12}\cos\frac{\pi}{12}$$

$$= \frac{1}{2}\left[\cos\left(\frac{5\pi}{12} - \frac{\pi}{12}\right) + \cos\left(\frac{5\pi}{12} + \frac{\pi}{12}\right)\right]$$

$$= \frac{1}{2}\left[\cos\frac{\pi}{3} + \cos\frac{\pi}{2}\right]$$

$$= \frac{1}{2}\left[\frac{1}{2} + 0\right] = \frac{1}{4}$$

■ **Sum-to-product identities** The next four identities enable us to rewrite sums or differences of sines or cosines as products.

Sum-to-Product Formulas

$$\cos x + \cos y = 2\cos\left(\frac{x+y}{2}\right)\cos\left(\frac{x-y}{2}\right)$$

$$\cos x - \cos y = -2\sin\left(\frac{x+y}{2}\right)\sin\left(\frac{x-y}{2}\right)$$

$$\sin x + \sin y = 2\sin\left(\frac{x+y}{2}\right)\cos\left(\frac{x-y}{2}\right)$$

$$\sin x - \sin y = 2\sin\left(\frac{x-y}{2}\right)\cos\left(\frac{x+y}{2}\right)$$

To write $\cos 12\theta + \cos 10\theta$ as a product of trigonometric functions, we use the sum-to-product identity for $\cos x + \cos y$ with $x = 12\theta$ and $y = 10\theta$.

Then $\cos 12\theta + \cos 10\theta$

$$= 2\cos\left(\frac{12\theta + 10\theta}{2}\right)\cos\left(\frac{12\theta - 10\theta}{2}\right)$$

$$= 2\cos 11\theta \cos\theta.$$

REVIEW EXERCISES

Basis Skills and Concepts

In Exercises 1–4, use the fundamental identities to find the exact value of the remaining trigonometric functions of θ.

1. $\sin \theta = -\dfrac{2}{3}$ and $\cos \theta < 0$

2. $\tan \theta = -\dfrac{1}{2}$ and $\csc \theta > 0$

3. $\sec \theta = 3$ and $\tan \theta < 0$

4. $\csc \theta = 5$ and $\cot \theta < 0$

In Exercises 5–20, verify each identity.

5. $(\sin x + \cos x)^2 + (\sin x - \cos x)^2 = 2$

6. $(1 - \tan x)^2 + (1 + \tan x)^2 = 2 \sec^2 x$

7. $\dfrac{1 - \tan^2 \theta}{1 + \tan^2 \theta} = \cos^2 \theta - \sin^2 \theta$

8. $\dfrac{\sin x + \tan x}{\csc x + \cot x} = \sin^2 x \sec x$

9. $\dfrac{\sin \theta}{1 + \cos \theta} + \dfrac{\sin \theta}{1 - \cos \theta} = 2 \csc \theta$

10. $\tan^2 x \sin^2 x = \tan^2 x - \sin^2 x$

11. $\dfrac{\sin \theta}{1 - \cot \theta} + \dfrac{\cos \theta}{1 - \tan \theta} = \cos \theta + \sin \theta$

12. $\dfrac{\tan \theta - \sin \theta}{\sin^3 \theta} = \dfrac{\sec \theta}{1 + \cos \theta}$

13. $\dfrac{\tan x}{\sec x - 1} + \dfrac{\tan x}{\sec x + 1} = 2 \csc x$

14. $\dfrac{1}{\csc x - \cot x} - \dfrac{1}{\cot x + \csc x} = 2 \cot x$

15. $\dfrac{1 + \sin \theta}{1 - \sin \theta} = (\sec \theta + \tan \theta)^2$

16. $\dfrac{1 - \cos \theta}{1 + \cos \theta} = (\csc \theta - \cot \theta)^2$

17. $\dfrac{\sec x - \tan x}{\sec x + \tan x} = (\sec x - \tan x)^2$

18. $\dfrac{\csc x + \cot x}{\csc x - \cot x} = (\csc x + \cot x)^2$

19. $\dfrac{\sin x - \cos x + 1}{\sin x + \cos x - 1} = \dfrac{\sin x + 1}{\cos x}$

    [*Hint:* Multiply the numerator and the denominator of the left side by $\sin x + (1 - \cos x)$.]

20. $\sin^2 x \cot x = \dfrac{2 \cos x}{\sin x + \csc x + \cos^2 x \csc x}$

In Exercises 21–28, find the exact value of each expression.

21. $\cos 15°$

22. $\sin 105°$

23. $\csc 75°$

24. $\tan 75°$

25. $\sin 41° \cos 49° + \cos 41° \sin 49°$

26. $\cos 50° \cos 10° - \sin 50° \sin 10°$

27. $\dfrac{\tan 69° + \tan 66°}{1 - \tan 69° \tan 66°}$

28. $2 \cos 75° \cos 15°$

In Exercises 29–32, let $\sin u = \dfrac{4}{5}$, $\cos v = \dfrac{5}{13}$ and $0 < u \le \dfrac{\pi}{2}$, $0 < v \le \dfrac{\pi}{2}$. Find the value of each expression.

29. $\sin (u - v)$

30. $\cos (u + v)$

31. $\cos (u - v)$

32. $\tan (u - v)$

In Exercises 33–50, verify each identity.

33. $\sin (x - y) \cos y + \cos (x - y) \sin y = \sin x$

34. $\cos (x - y) \cos y - \sin (x - y) \sin y = \cos x$

35. $\dfrac{\sin (u + v)}{\sin (u - v)} = \dfrac{\tan u + \tan v}{\tan u - \tan v}$

36. $\dfrac{\tan (x + y)}{\cot (x - y)} = \dfrac{\tan^2 x - \tan^2 y}{1 - \tan^2 x \tan^2 y}$

37. $\dfrac{\sin 4x}{\sin 2x} - \dfrac{\cos 4x}{\cos 2x} = \sec 2x$

38. $\dfrac{\sin 3x}{\sin x} - \dfrac{\cos 3x}{\cos x} = 2$

39. $\sin \left(x - \dfrac{\pi}{6} \right) + \cos \left(x + \dfrac{\pi}{3} \right) = 0$

40. $\cos 2x = \cos^4 x - \sin^4 x$

41. $1 + \tan \theta \tan 2\theta = \sec 2\theta$

42. $\dfrac{\sin \theta + \sin 2\theta}{1 + \cos \theta + \cos 2\theta} = \tan \theta$

43. $\dfrac{\sin \theta + \sin 2\theta}{\cos \theta + \cos 2\theta} = \tan \dfrac{3\theta}{2}$

44. $\dfrac{\sin \theta - \sin 2\theta}{\cos \theta - \cos 2\theta} = -\cot \dfrac{3\theta}{2}$

45. $\dfrac{\sin 5x - \sin 3x}{\sin 5x + \sin 3x} = \dfrac{\tan x}{\tan 4x}$

46. $\dfrac{\cos 5x - \cos 3x}{\cos 5x + \cos 3x} = -\tan x \tan 4x$

47. $\dfrac{\tan 3x + \tan x}{\tan 3x - \tan x} = 2 \cos 2x$

48. $\dfrac{\sin 4x}{2(1 + \cos 4x)} = \dfrac{\tan x}{1 - \tan^2 x}$

49. $\dfrac{\sin 3x + \sin 5x + \sin 7x + \sin 9x}{\cos 3x + \cos 5x + \cos 7x + \cos 9x} = \tan 6x$

50. $\dfrac{\cos x + \cos 3x + \cos 5x + \cos 7x}{\sin x + \sin 3x + \sin 5x + \sin 7x} = \cot 4x$

In Exercises 51 and 52, assume that $A + B + C = 180°$. Verify each identity.

51. $\sin 2A + \sin 2B - \sin 2C = 4 \cos A \cos B \sin C$

52. $\tan A + \tan B + \tan C = \tan A \tan B \tan C$

53. A jeweler wants to make a gold pendant in the shape of an isosceles triangle. Express the area of the top face

of the pendant in terms of $\dfrac{\theta}{2}$, where θ is the angle included by two sides of equal length x.

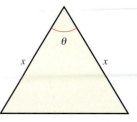

54. If the area of the pendant face in Exercise 53 is 1 square inch, find the angle included between the two sides of equal length when each measures 2 inches.

CHAPTER TEST

1. If $\sin \theta = \dfrac{3}{5}$ and $\cos \theta < 0$, find $\tan \theta$.

2. If $\tan x = \dfrac{2}{3}$ and $\csc x < 0$, find $\cos x$.

In Problems 3–10, verify each identity.

3. $\dfrac{1 - \sin^2 x}{\sin^2 x} = \cot^2 x$

4. $2 \sin x \cos x = (\sin x + \cos x + 1)(\sin x + \cos x - 1)$

5. $\sin x \sin\left(\dfrac{\pi}{2} - x\right) = \dfrac{\sin 2x}{2}$

6. $\dfrac{\sin 2x}{2(\cos x + \sin x)} = \dfrac{\sin x}{1 + \tan x}$

7. $\dfrac{\sin 2x + \sin 4x}{\cos 2x + \cos 4x} = \tan 3x$

8. $\cos(x + y)\cos(x - y) = \cos^2 x + \cos^2 y - 1$

9. $\cos(\pi - x) = -\cos x$

10. $\sin x(\csc x - \sin x) = \cos^2 x$

In Problems 11 and 12, show that the equations are not identities.

11. $\sin(2\theta) = 2 \sin \theta$

12. $\cos\left(\theta + \dfrac{\pi}{6}\right) = \cos \theta + \cos \dfrac{\pi}{6}$

In Problems 13–15, find the exact value of each expression.

13. $\sin 56° + \cos 146°$

14. $\cos 48° \cos 12° - \sin 48° \sin 12°$

15. $\sin \dfrac{5\pi}{12}$

16. If $\sin \theta = \dfrac{4}{5}$, find the exact value of $\cos 2\theta$.

17. If $\tan \theta = \dfrac{3}{4}$, find the exact value of $\sin 2\theta$.

18. Determine whether the function $y = \cos\left(\dfrac{\pi}{2} - x\right) + \tan x$ is odd, even, or neither.

19. Determine whether $\sin x + \sin y = \sin(x + y)$ is an identity.

20. The value of $\sin(2\theta)$ is positive if the terminal side of θ lies in quadrant _____ or quadrant _____.

Inverse Functions and Trigonometric Equations

Such varied phenomena as sonic booms from aircraft, musical tones, hours of daylight in a given location, current in an electric circuit, tides, and rainfall can be described using trigonometric functions. Solutions of trigonometric equations often provide answers to questions about the conditions under which specific characteristics of these phenomena occur. In this chapter, we study techniques for solving trigonometric equations.

Inverse Trigonometric Functions

Before Starting this Section, Review

1. Inverse functions (Appendix)

2. Composition of functions (Appendix)

3. Exact values of the trigonometric functions (Section 1.3)

Objectives

1 Graph and apply the inverse sine function.

2 Graph and apply the inverse cosine function.

3 Graph and apply the inverse tangent function.

4 Evaluate inverse trigonometric functions using a calculator.

5 Find exact values of composite functions involving the inverse trigonometric functions.

RETAIL THEFT

In 2005, security cameras at Filene's Basement store in Boston filmed a theft coordinated by a thief and an accomplice. The accomplice distracted the salesperson so the thief could steal a $16,000 necklace. Retail theft is a major concern for all retail outlets, from Tiffany & Co. to Walmart.

The National Retail Federation, the industry's largest trade group, and the Retail Industry Leaders Association have instituted password-protected national crime databases online. These databases allow retailers to share information about thefts and determine whether they have been targets of individual shoplifters who steal for themselves or targets of organized crime. In addition to participating in the shared databases, many large retailers have their own organized anticrime squads. One estimate puts loss to organized theft at over $30 billion annually. In Example 10, we see how methods in this section can be used in an attempt to prevent loss from theft. ■

1 Graph and apply the inverse sine function.

The Inverse Sine Function

Recall that a function f has an inverse that is also a function if no horizontal line intersects the graph of f in more than one point. Because every horizontal line $y = b$, where $-1 \leq b \leq 1$, intersects the graph of $y = \sin x$ at more than one point, the sine function fails the horizontal line test; so it is not one-to-one and consequently has no inverse.

The solid portion of the sine graph shown in Figure 6.1 is the graph of $y = \sin x$ for $-\dfrac{\pi}{2} \leq x \leq \dfrac{\pi}{2}$. If we restrict the domain of $y = \sin x$ to the interval $\left[-\dfrac{\pi}{2}, \dfrac{\pi}{2}\right]$, the resulting function

$$y = \sin x, \quad -\frac{\pi}{2} \leq x \leq \frac{\pi}{2}$$

is one-to-one. (It passes the horizontal line test.) So its inverse is also a function. Notice that the restricted function takes on all values in the range of $y = \sin x$, which is $[-1, 1]$, and that each of these y-values corresponds to exactly one x-value in the restricted domain $\left[-\dfrac{\pi}{2}, \dfrac{\pi}{2}\right]$. The inverse function for $y = \sin x, -\dfrac{\pi}{2} \leq x \leq \dfrac{\pi}{2}$, is called the **inverse sine,** or **arcsine,** function and is denoted by $\sin^{-1} x$, or by arcsin x.

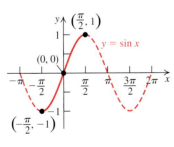

FIGURE 6.1 $y = \sin x$, $-\dfrac{\pi}{2} \leq x \leq \dfrac{\pi}{2}$

> ## INVERSE SINE FUNCTION
>
> The equation $y = \sin^{-1} x$ means that $\sin y = x$, where $-1 \le x \le 1$ and $-\dfrac{\pi}{2} \le y \le \dfrac{\pi}{2}$. Read $y = \sin^{-1} x$ as "y equals inverse sine at x."

The range of $y = \sin x$ is $[-1, 1]$, so the domain of $y = \sin^{-1} x$ is $[-1, 1]$. The domain of the restricted sine function is $\left[-\dfrac{\pi}{2}, \dfrac{\pi}{2}\right]$, so the range of $y = \sin^{-1} x$ is $\left[-\dfrac{\pi}{2}, \dfrac{\pi}{2}\right]$. We graph $y = \sin^{-1} x$ by reflecting the graph of $y = \sin x$, for $-\dfrac{\pi}{2} \le x \le \dfrac{\pi}{2}$, in the line $y = x$. See Figure 6.2.

RECALL

If two fuctions are inverses, their graphs are symmetric with respect to the line $y = x$.

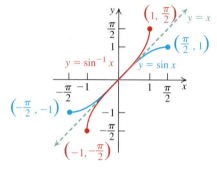

FIGURE 6.2 Graph of $y = \sin^{-1} x$

EXAMPLE 1   Finding the Exact Values for $y = \sin^{-1} x$

Find the exact values of y.

a. $y = \sin^{-1} \dfrac{\sqrt{3}}{2}$ **b.** $y = \sin^{-1}\left(-\dfrac{1}{2}\right)$ **c.** $y = \sin^{-1} 3$

SOLUTION

a. The equation $y = \sin^{-1} \dfrac{\sqrt{3}}{2}$ means that $\sin y = \dfrac{\sqrt{3}}{2}$ and $-\dfrac{\pi}{2} \le y \le \dfrac{\pi}{2}$.

Because $\sin\dfrac{\pi}{3} = \dfrac{\sqrt{3}}{2}$ and $-\dfrac{\pi}{2} \le \dfrac{\pi}{3} \le \dfrac{\pi}{2}$, we have $y = \sin^{-1} \dfrac{\sqrt{3}}{2} = \dfrac{\pi}{3}$.

STUDY TIP

You can also read $y = \sin^{-1}(x)$ as "y is the number in the interval $\left[-\dfrac{\pi}{2}, \dfrac{\pi}{2}\right]$ whose sine is x."

b. The equation $y = \sin^{-1}\left(-\dfrac{1}{2}\right)$ means that $\sin y = -\dfrac{1}{2}$ and $-\dfrac{\pi}{2} \le y \le \dfrac{\pi}{2}$.

Because $\sin\left(-\dfrac{\pi}{6}\right) = -\dfrac{1}{2}$ and $-\dfrac{\pi}{2} \le -\dfrac{\pi}{6} \le \dfrac{\pi}{2}$, we have $y = -\dfrac{\pi}{6}$.

c. Because 3 is not in the domain $[-1, 1]$ of the inverse sine function, $\sin^{-1} 3$ does not exist.   ■ ■ ■

Practice Problem 1   Find the exact values of y.

a. $y = \sin^{-1}\left(-\dfrac{\sqrt{3}}{2}\right)$ **b.** $y = \sin^{-1}(-1)$ ■

2 Graph and apply the inverse cosine function.

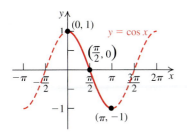

FIGURE 6.3 $y = \cos x, 0 \le x \le \pi$

The Inverse Cosine Function

When we restrict the domain of $y = \cos x$ to the interval $[0, \pi]$, the resulting function, $y = \cos x$ (with $0 \le x \le \pi$), is one-to-one. No horizontal line intersects the graph of $y = \cos x$, with $0 \le x \le \pi$, in more than one point. See Figure 6.3. Consequently, the restricted cosine function has an inverse function.

The inverse function for $y = \cos x, 0 \le x \le \pi$, is called the **inverse cosine**, or **arccosine**, function and is denoted by $\cos^{-1} x$, or by arccos x.

INVERSE COSINE FUNCTION

The equation $y = \cos^{-1} x$ means that $\cos y = x$, where $-1 \le x \le 1$ and $0 \le y \le \pi$. Read $y = \cos^{-1} x$ as "y equals inverse cosine at x."

STUDY TIP

You can also read $y = \cos^{-1} x$ as "y is the number in the interval $[0, \pi]$ whose cosine is x."

Reflecting the graph of $y = \cos x$, for $0 \le x \le \pi$, in the line, $y = x$ produces the graph of $y = \cos^{-1} x$, shown in Figure 6.4.

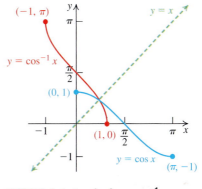

FIGURE 6.4 Graph of $y = \cos^{-1} x$

EXAMPLE 2   Finding an Exact Value for $\cos^{-1} x$

Find the exact value of y.

a. $y = \cos^{-1} \dfrac{\sqrt{2}}{2}$ **b.** $y = \cos^{-1} \left(-\dfrac{1}{2}\right)$

SOLUTION

a. The equation $y = \cos^{-1} \dfrac{\sqrt{2}}{2}$ means that $\cos y = \dfrac{\sqrt{2}}{2}$ and $0 \le y \le \pi$.

Because $\cos \dfrac{\pi}{4} = \dfrac{\sqrt{2}}{2}$ and $0 \le \dfrac{\pi}{4} \le \pi$, we have $y = \dfrac{\pi}{4}$.

b. The equation $y = \cos^{-1} \left(-\dfrac{1}{2}\right)$ means that $\cos y = -\dfrac{1}{2}$ and $0 \le y \le \pi$.

Because $\cos \dfrac{2\pi}{3} = -\dfrac{1}{2}$ and $0 \le \dfrac{2\pi}{3} \le \pi$, we have $y = \dfrac{2\pi}{3}$. ■ ■ ■

Practice Problem 2   Find the exact value of y.

a. $y = \cos^{-1} \left(-\dfrac{\sqrt{2}}{2}\right)$ **b.** $y = \cos^{-1} \dfrac{1}{2}$

3 Graph and apply the inverse tangent function.

The Inverse Tangent Function

The *inverse tangent function* results from restricting the domain of the tangent function to the interval $\left(-\dfrac{\pi}{2}, \dfrac{\pi}{2}\right)$ to obtain a one-to-one function. The inverse of this restricted tangent function is the **inverse tangent**, or **arctangent**, function.

STUDY TIP

You can also read $y = \tan^{-1} x$ as "y is the number in the interval $\left(-\dfrac{\pi}{2}, \dfrac{\pi}{2}\right)$ whose tangent is x."

INVERSE TANGENT FUNCTION

The equation $y = \tan^{-1} x$ means that $\tan y = x$, where $-\infty < x < \infty$ and $-\dfrac{\pi}{2} < y < \dfrac{\pi}{2}$. Read $y = \tan^{-1} x$ as "y equals the inverse tangent at x."

The graph of $y = \tan^{-1} x$ is obtained by reflecting the graph of $y = \tan x$, with $-\dfrac{\pi}{2} < x < \dfrac{\pi}{2}$, in the line $y = x$. Figure 6.5 shows the graph of the restricted tangent function. Figure 6.6 shows the graph of $y = \tan^{-1} x$.

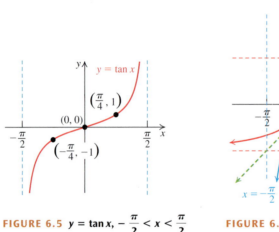

FIGURE 6.5 $y = \tan x$, $-\dfrac{\pi}{2} < x < \dfrac{\pi}{2}$

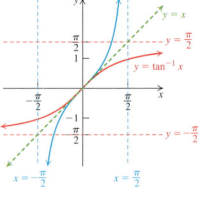

FIGURE 6.6 Graph of $y = \tan^{-1} x$

EXAMPLE 3   **Finding Exact Values for tan⁻¹ x**

Find the exact value of y.

a. $y = \tan^{-1} 0$ **b.** $y = \tan^{-1}(-\sqrt{3})$

SOLUTION

a. Because $\tan 0 = 0$ and $-\dfrac{\pi}{2} < 0 < \dfrac{\pi}{2}$, we have $y = 0$.

b. Because $\tan\left(-\dfrac{\pi}{3}\right) = -\sqrt{3}$ and $-\dfrac{\pi}{2} < -\dfrac{\pi}{3} < \dfrac{\pi}{2}$, we have $y = -\dfrac{\pi}{3}$. ■ ■ ■

Practice Problem 3   Find the exact value of $y = \tan^{-1} \dfrac{\sqrt{3}}{3}$. ■

Other Inverse Trigonometric Functions

Sometimes the ranges of the *inverse secant* and *inverse consecant* functions differ from those used in this text. Always check the definitions of the domains of these two functions when they are used outside this course.

DEFINITIONS OF OTHER TRIGONOMETRIC FUNCTIONS

Inverse cotangent $y = \cot^{-1} x$ means that $\cot y = x$, where $-\infty < x < \infty$ and $0 < y < \pi$.

Inverse cosecant $y = \csc^{-1} x$ means that $\csc y = x$, where $|x| \geq 1$ and $-\dfrac{\pi}{2} \leq y \leq \dfrac{\pi}{2}, y \neq 0$.

Inverse secant $y = \sec^{-1} x$ means that $\sec y = x$, where $|x| \geq 1$ and $0 \leq y \leq \pi, y \neq \dfrac{\pi}{2}$.

EXAMPLE 4   Finding the Exact Value for $\csc^{-1} x$

Find the exact value for $y = \csc^{-1} 2$.

SOLUTION

Because $\csc \dfrac{\pi}{6} = 2$ and $-\dfrac{\pi}{2} \leq \dfrac{\pi}{6} \leq \dfrac{\pi}{2}$, we have $y = \csc^{-1} 2 = \dfrac{\pi}{6}$.   ■ ■ ■

Practice Problem 4   Find the exact value of $y = \sec^{-1} 2$.   ■

SUMMARY
Inverse Trigonometric Functions

Inverse Function	Equivalent to	Domain	Range
$y = \sin^{-1} x$	$\sin y = x$	$[-1, 1]$	$\left[-\dfrac{\pi}{2}, \dfrac{\pi}{2} \right]$
$y = \cos^{-1} x$	$\cos y = x$	$[-1, 1]$	$[0, \pi]$
$y = \tan^{-1} x$	$\tan y = x$	$(-\infty, \infty)$	$\left(-\dfrac{\pi}{2}, \dfrac{\pi}{2} \right)$
$y = \cot^{-1} x$	$\cot y = x$	$(-\infty, \infty)$	$(0, \pi)$
$y = \csc^{-1} x$	$\csc y = x$	$(-\infty, -1] \cup [1, \infty)$	$\left[-\dfrac{\pi}{2}, 0 \right) \cup \left(0, \dfrac{\pi}{2} \right]$
$y = \sec^{-1} x$	$\sec y = x$	$(-\infty, -1] \cup [1, \infty)$	$\left[0, \dfrac{\pi}{2} \right) \cup \left(\dfrac{\pi}{2}, \pi \right]$

4 Evaluate inverse trigonometric functions using a calculator.

Using a Calculator with Inverse Functions

In Section 4.3, we defined the six trigonometric functions of *real numbers*, and in this section, we defined the corresponding six inverse trigonometric functions of real numbers. For example,

$$\sin \frac{\pi}{4} = \frac{\sqrt{2}}{2}$$

TECHNOLOGY CONNECTION

The secondary functions on your calculator, labeled $\sin^{-1}$, $\cos^{-1}$, and $\tan^{-1}$, are associated with the keys labeled $\boxed{\sin}$, $\boxed{\cos}$, and $\boxed{\tan}$, respectively. Consult your manual to learn how to access these secondary functions. The screen shows several values for the trigonometric inverse functions on a calculator set to Radian mode.

```
cos-1(3/4)
           .723
sin-1(-0.86)
          -1.035
tan-1(-6.25)
          -1.412
```

and

$$\sin^{-1}\frac{\sqrt{2}}{2} = \frac{\pi}{4}.$$

However, because we also defined the trigonometric function of *angles* in Section 4.3, it is meaningful when working with angles in degree measure to write a statement such as

$$\sin^{-1}\frac{\sqrt{2}}{2} = 45°.$$

When using a calculator to evaluate an inverse trigonometric function to find a real number (or equivalently, an angle measured in radians), make sure you set your calculator to Radian mode.

When using a calculator to find $\csc^{-1}x$ or $\sec^{-1}x$, find $\sin^{-1}\frac{1}{x}$ and $\cos^{-1}\frac{1}{x}$, respectively. For example, if $\csc^{-1}5 = \theta$, then $\csc\theta = 5$, or $\frac{1}{\sin\theta} = 5$. So $\sin\theta = \frac{1}{5}$ and $\theta = \sin^{-1}\left(\frac{1}{5}\right)$. However, to find $\cot^{-1}x$, begin by finding $\tan^{-1}\frac{1}{x}$; this gives you a value in the interval $\left(-\frac{\pi}{2}, \frac{\pi}{2}\right)$. If $x \geq 0$, this is the correct value, but **for $x < 0$, $\cot^{-1}(x) = \pi + \tan^{-1}\frac{1}{x}$** so that $\cot^{-1}(x)$ is in the interval $\left(\frac{\pi}{2}, \pi\right)$.

When using a calculator to find an unknown angle measure in degrees, make sure you set your calculator to Degree measure.

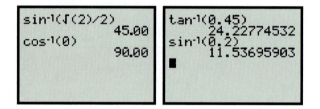

EXAMPLE 5 Using a Calculator to Find the Values of Inverse Functions

Use a calculator to find the value of y in radians rounded to four decimal places.

a. $y = \sin^{-1}0.75$ **b.** $y = \cot^{-1}2.8$ **c.** $y = \cot^{-1}(-2.3)$

SOLUTION

Set your calculator to Radian mode.

a. $y = \sin^{-1}0.75 \approx 0.8481$

b. $y = \cot^{-1}2.8 = \tan^{-1}\left(\frac{1}{2.8}\right) \approx 0.3430$

c. $y = \cot^{-1}(-2.3) = \pi + \tan^{-1}\left(-\frac{1}{2.3}\right) \approx 2.7315$ ■ ■ ■

Practice Problem 5   Use a calculator to find the value of y in radians rounded to four decimal places.

a. $y = \cos^{-1}0.22$ **b.** $y = \csc^{-1}3.5$ **c.** $y = \cot^{-1}(-4.7)$ ■

EXAMPLE 6   **Using a Calculator to Find the Values of Inverse Functions**

Use a calculator to find the value of y in degrees rounded to four decimal places.

a. $y = \tan^{-1} 0.99$ **b.** $y = \sec^{-1} 25$ **c.** $y = \cot^{-1}(-1.3)$

SOLUTION

Set your calculator to Degree mode.

a. $y = \tan^{-1} 0.99 \approx 44.7121°$

b. $y = \sec^{-1} 25 = \cos^{-1} \dfrac{1}{25} \approx 87.7076°$

c. $y = \cot^{-1}(-1.3) = 180° + \tan^{-1}\left(-\dfrac{1}{1.3}\right) \approx 142.4314°$ ■ ■ ■

Practice Problem 6   Repeat Example 6 for each expression.

a. $y = \cot^{-1} 0.75$ **b.** $y = \csc^{-1} 13$ **c.** $y = \tan^{-1}(-12)$ ■

5 Find exact values of composite functions involving the inverse trigonometric functions.

Composition of Trigonometric and Inverse Trigonometric Functions

Recall that if f is a one-to-one function with inverse f^{-1}, then $f^{-1}[f(x)] = x$ for every x in the domain of f and $f[f^{-1}(x)] = x$ for every x in the domain of f^{-1}. This leads to the following formulas for the inverse sine, cosine, and tangent functions.

Inverse Sine	Inverse Cosine	Inverse Tangent
$\sin^{-1}(\sin x) = x$,	$\cos^{-1}(\cos x) = x$,	$\tan^{-1}(\tan x) = x$,
$-\dfrac{\pi}{2} \le x \le \dfrac{\pi}{2}$	$0 \le x \le \pi$	$-\dfrac{\pi}{2} < x < \dfrac{\pi}{2}$
$\sin(\sin^{-1} x) = x$,	$\cos(\cos^{-1} x) = x$,	$\tan(\tan^{-1} x) = x$,
$-1 \le x \le 1$	$-1 \le x \le 1$	$-\infty < x < \infty$

EXAMPLE 7   **Finding the Exact Value of $\sin^{-1}(\sin x)$ and $\cos^{-1}(\cos x)$**

Find the exact value of the following.

a. $\sin^{-1}\left[\sin\left(-\dfrac{\pi}{8}\right)\right]$ **b.** $\cos^{-1}\left(\cos \dfrac{5\pi}{4}\right)$

SOLUTION

a. Because $-\dfrac{\pi}{2} \le -\dfrac{\pi}{8} \le \dfrac{\pi}{2}$, we have $\sin^{-1}\left[\sin\left(-\dfrac{\pi}{8}\right)\right] = -\dfrac{\pi}{8}$.

b. We cannot use the formula $\cos^{-1}(\cos x) = x$ for $x = \dfrac{5\pi}{4}$ because $\dfrac{5\pi}{4}$ is not in the interval $[0, \pi]$. However, $\cos \dfrac{5\pi}{4} = \cos\left(2\pi - \dfrac{5\pi}{4}\right) = \cos \dfrac{3\pi}{4}$ and $\dfrac{3\pi}{4}$ is in the interval $[0, \pi]$. Therefore,

$$\cos^{-1}\left(\cos \dfrac{5\pi}{4}\right) = \cos^{-1}\left(\cos \dfrac{3\pi}{4}\right) = \dfrac{3\pi}{4}.$$ ■ ■ ■

Practice Problem 7   Find the exact value of $\sin^{-1}\left(\sin \dfrac{3\pi}{2}\right)$.   ■

To find the exact values of expressions involving the composition of a trigonometric function and the inverse of a *different* trigonometric function, we use points on the terminal side of the corresponding angle in standard position.

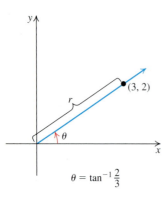

$$\theta = \tan^{-1}\frac{2}{3}$$

FIGURE 6.7

| | EXAMPLE 8 | **Finding the Exact Value of a Composite Trigonometric Expression** |

Find the exact value of the following.

a. $\cos\left(\tan^{-1}\dfrac{2}{3}\right)$ **b.** $\sin\left[\cos^{-1}\left(-\dfrac{1}{4}\right)\right]$

SOLUTION

a. Let θ represent the radian measure of the angle in the interval $\left(-\dfrac{\pi}{2}, \dfrac{\pi}{2}\right)$ with $\tan\theta = \dfrac{2}{3}$. Then because $\tan\theta$ is positive, we have

$$\theta = \tan^{-1}\frac{2}{3} \quad \text{and} \quad 0 < \theta < \frac{\pi}{2}.$$

Figure 6.7 shows θ in standard position. If (x, y) is a point on the terminal side of θ, then $\tan\theta = \dfrac{y}{x}$.

Consequently, we can choose the point with coordinates $(3, 2)$ to determine the terminal side of θ. Then $x = 3$, $y = 2$ and we have

$$\tan\theta = \frac{2}{3} \quad \text{and} \quad \cos\theta = \frac{3}{r}, \text{where}$$

$$r = \sqrt{x^2 + y^2} = \sqrt{3^2 + 2^2} = \sqrt{9 + 4} = \sqrt{13}. \text{ So}$$

$$\cos\left(\tan^{-1}\frac{2}{3}\right) = \cos\theta = \frac{3}{r} = \frac{3}{\sqrt{13}} = \frac{3\sqrt{13}}{13}.$$

b. Let θ represent the radian measure of the angle in the interval $[0, \pi]$ with $\cos\theta = -\dfrac{1}{4}$. Then because $\cos\theta$ is negative, θ is in quadrant II; so

$$\theta = \cos^{-1}\left(-\frac{1}{4}\right) \quad \text{and} \quad \frac{\pi}{2} < \theta < \pi.$$

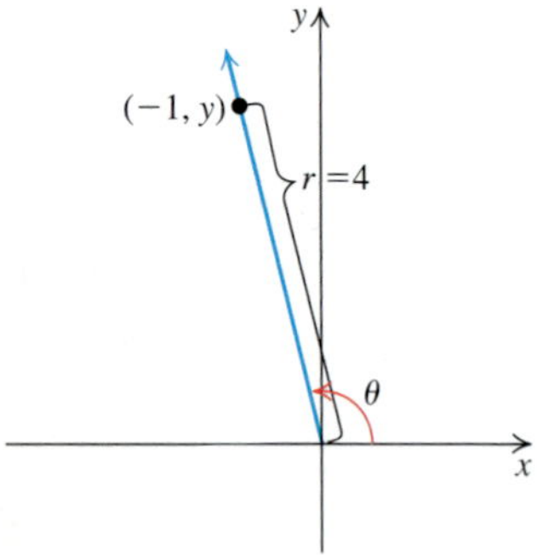

Figure 6.8 shows θ in standard position. If (x, y) is a point on the terminal side of θ and r is the distance between (x, y) and the origin, then $\sin\theta = \dfrac{y}{r}$. We choose the point with coordinates $(-1, y)$, a distance of four units from the origin, on the terminal side of θ. Then

$$\cos\theta = -\frac{1}{4} \quad \text{and} \quad \sin\theta = \frac{y}{4}, \text{where}$$

$$r = \sqrt{x^2 + y^2} = \sqrt{(-1)^2 + y^2} \text{ or } \quad r^2 = 1 + y^2$$

$$4^2 = 1 + y^2 \qquad \textcolor{blue}{\text{Replace } r \text{ with 4.}}$$

$$15 = y^2 \qquad \textcolor{blue}{\text{Simplify.}}$$

$$\sqrt{15} = y \qquad \textcolor{blue}{y \text{ is positive.}}$$

$$\theta = \cos^{-1}\left(-\frac{1}{4}\right)$$

FIGURE 6.8

Thus,

$$\sin\left[\cos^{-1}\left(-\frac{1}{4}\right)\right] = \sin\theta = \frac{y}{r} = \frac{\sqrt{15}}{4}.$$

■ ■ ■

Practice Problem 8   Find the exact value of $\cos\left[\sin^{-1}\left(-\dfrac{1}{3}\right)\right]$.

■

EXAMPLE 9 Finding the Exact Values of Composite Trigonometric Expressions

Find $\sin(\tan^{-1}(-2) + \cot^{-1}(-3))$.

SOLUTION

We let $u = \tan^{-1}(-2)$ and $v = \cot^{-1}(-3)$. Then $\tan u = -2$ and $\cot v = -3$. See Figure 6.9.

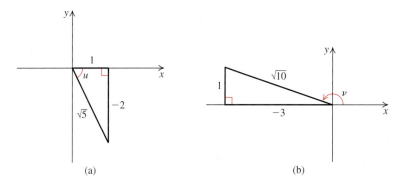

FIGURE 6.9

Note that in Figure 6.9(a), we draw $u = \tan^{-1}(-2)$ in quadrant IV because the range of the inverse tangent function is $\left(-\frac{\pi}{2}, \frac{\pi}{2}\right)$. However, in Figure 6.9(b), we draw $v = \cot^{-1}(-3)$ in quadrant II because the range of the inverse cotangent function is $(0, \pi)$. Now

$$\sin(u + v) = \sin u \cos v + \cos u \sin v \qquad \text{Sum identity for sine}$$

$$= \left(-\frac{2}{\sqrt{5}}\right)\left(-\frac{3}{\sqrt{10}}\right) + \left(\frac{1}{\sqrt{5}}\right)\left(\frac{1}{\sqrt{10}}\right) \qquad \begin{array}{l}\text{Substitute values from}\\ \text{Figure 6.9.}\end{array}$$

$$= \frac{6}{5\sqrt{2}} + \frac{1}{5\sqrt{2}} \qquad \sqrt{10} = \sqrt{2}\sqrt{5}$$

$$= \frac{7}{5\sqrt{2}} = \frac{7\sqrt{2}}{10} \qquad \text{Add and simplify.} \qquad ■■■$$

Practice Problem 9 Find $\tan\left(\cos^{-1}\left(-\frac{1}{3}\right) + \sin^{-1}\left(-\frac{4}{5}\right)\right)$. ■

EXAMPLE 10 Finding the Rotation Angle for a Security Camera

A security camera is to be installed 20 feet from the center of a jewelry counter. The counter is 30 feet long. Through what angle, to the nearest degree, should the camera rotate so that it scans the entire counter? See Figure 6.10.

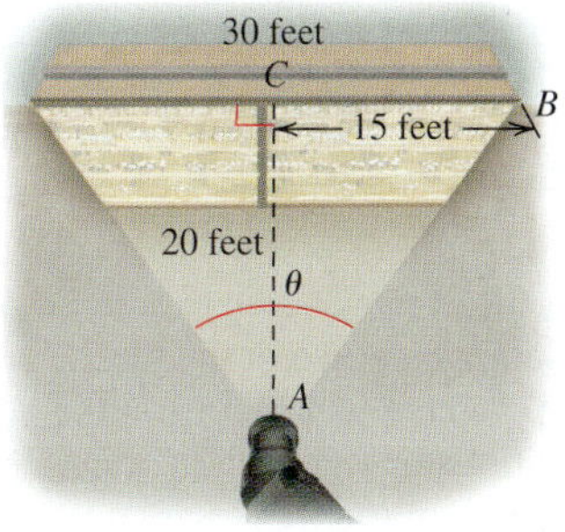

SOLUTION

The counter center C, the camera A, and a counter end B form a right triangle. The angle at vertex A is $\frac{\theta}{2}$, where θ is the angle through which the camera rotates. Note that

$$\tan\frac{\theta}{2} = \frac{15}{20} = \frac{3}{4}$$

$$\frac{\theta}{2} = \tan^{-1}\frac{3}{4} \approx 36.87° \qquad \text{Use a calculator in Degree mode.}$$

$$\theta \approx 73.74° \qquad \text{Multiply both sides by 2.}$$

The camera must rotate through 74° to scan the entire counter. ■■■

Practice Problem 10 Rework Example 10 for a counter that is 20 feet long and a camera set 12 feet from the center of the counter. ■

FIGURE 6.10

SECTION 6.1 ■ Exercises

A EXERCISES Basic Skills and Concepts

1. The domain of $f(x) = \sin^{-1} x$ is _____.

2. The range of $f(x) = \tan^{-1} x$ is _____.

3. The exact value of $y = \cos^{-1} \dfrac{1}{2}$ is _____.

4. $\sin^{-1} (\sin \pi) =$ _____.

5. *True or False* If $-1 \le x \le 0$, then $\sin^{-1} x \le 0$.

6. *True or False* If $-1 \le x \le 0$, then $\cos^{-1} x \le 0$.

7. *True or False* The domain of $f(x) = \cos^{-1} x$ is $0 \le x \le \pi$.

8. *True or False* The value of $\tan^{-1} \left(\dfrac{1}{\sqrt{3}} \right)$ is $\dfrac{\pi}{3}$.

In Exercises 9–32, find the exact value of y or state that y is undefined.

9. $y = \sin^{-1} 0$

10. $y = \cos^{-1} 0$

11. $y = \sin^{-1} \left(-\dfrac{1}{2} \right)$

12. $y = \cos^{-1} \left(-\dfrac{\sqrt{3}}{2} \right)$

13. $y = \cos^{-1} (-1)$

14. $y = \sin^{-1} \dfrac{1}{2}$

15. $y = \cos^{-1} \dfrac{\pi}{2}$

16. $y = \sin^{-1} \pi$

17. $y = \tan^{-1} \sqrt{3}$

18. $y = \tan^{-1} 1$

19. $y = \tan^{-1} (-1)$

20. $y = \tan^{-1} \left(-\dfrac{\sqrt{3}}{3} \right)$

21. $y = \cot^{-1} (-1)$

22. $y = \cot^{-1} 1$

23. $y = \sin^{-1} \left(-\dfrac{\sqrt{2}}{2} \right)$

24. $y = \cos^{-1} \left(\dfrac{\sqrt{3}}{2} \right)$

25. $y = \cot^{-1} \sqrt{3}$

26. $y = \cot^{-1} (-\sqrt{3})$

27. $y = \cos^{-1} (-2)$

28. $y = \sin^{-1} \sqrt{3}$

29. $y = \sec^{-1} (-2)$

30. $y = \sec^{-1} \sqrt{2}$

31. $y = \csc^{-1} \dfrac{2\sqrt{3}}{3}$

32. $y = \csc^{-1} (2)$

In Exercises 33–44, find the exact value of y or state that y is undefined.

33. $y = \sin \left(\sin^{-1} \dfrac{1}{8} \right)$

34. $y = \cos \left(\cos^{-1} \dfrac{1}{5} \right)$

35. $y = \cos (\cos^{-1} 0.6)$

36. $y = \sin (\sin^{-1} 0.8)$

37. $y = \tan^{-1} \left(\tan \dfrac{\pi}{7} \right)$

38. $y = \tan^{-1} \left(\tan \dfrac{\pi}{4} \right)$

39. $y = \tan (\tan^{-1} 247)$

40. $y = \tan (\tan^{-1} 7)$

41. $y = \sin^{-1} \left(\sin \dfrac{4\pi}{3} \right)$

42. $y = \cos^{-1} \left(\cos \dfrac{5\pi}{3} \right)$

43. $y = \tan^{-1} \left(\tan \dfrac{2\pi}{3} \right)$

44. $y = \tan \left(\tan^{-1} \dfrac{2\pi}{3} \right)$

In Exercises 45–54, use a calculator to find each value of y in degrees rounded to two decimal places.

45. $y = \cos^{-1} 0.6$

46. $y = \sin^{-1} 0.23$

47. $y = \sin^{-1} (-0.69)$

48. $y = \cos^{-1} (-0.57)$

49. $y = \sec^{-1} (3.5)$

50. $y = \csc^{-1} (6.8)$

51. $y = \tan^{-1} 14$

52. $y = \tan^{-1} 50$

53. $y = \tan^{-1} (-42.147)$

54. $y = \tan^{-1} (-0.3863)$

In Exercises 55–66, use a sketch to find the exact value of y.

55. $y = \cos \left(\sin^{-1} \dfrac{2}{3} \right)$

56. $y = \sin \left(\cos^{-1} \dfrac{3}{4} \right)$

57. $y = \sin \left[\cos^{-1} \left(-\dfrac{4}{5} \right) \right]$

58. $y = \cos \left(\sin^{-1} \dfrac{3}{5} \right)$

59. $y = \cos \left(\tan^{-1} \dfrac{5}{2} \right)$

60. $y = \sin \left(\tan^{-1} \dfrac{13}{5} \right)$

61. $y = \tan \left(\cos^{-1} \dfrac{4}{5} \right)$

62. $y = \tan \left[\sin^{-1} \left(-\dfrac{3}{4} \right) \right]$

63. $y = \sin (\tan^{-1} 4)$

64. $y = \cos (\tan^{-1} 3)$

65. $y = \tan (\sec^{-1} 2)$

66. $y = \tan [\csc^{-1} (-2)]$

B EXERCISES Applying the Concepts

67. **Sprinkler rotation.** A sprinkler rotates back and forth through an angle θ as shown in the figure. At a distance of 5 feet from the sprinkler, the rays that form the sides of angle θ are 6 feet apart. Find θ.

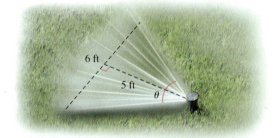

68. **Irradiating flowers.** A tray of flowers is being irradiated by a beam from a rotating lamp as shown in the figure. If the tray is 8 feet long and the lamp is 2 feet from the center of the tray, through what angle should the lamp rotate to irradiate the full length of the tray?

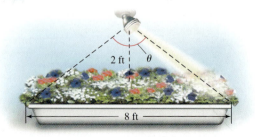

69. Motorcycle racing. A video camera is set up 110 feet at a right angle to a straight quarter-mile racetrack as shown in the figure. The starting line is to the left, and the finish line is to the right. Through what angle (to the nearest degree) must the camera rotate to film the entire race?

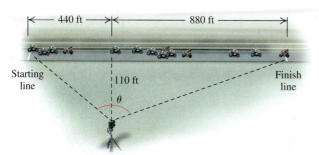

70. Camera's viewing angle. The viewing angle for the 35-millimeter camera is given (in degrees) by

$$\theta = 2\tan^{-1}\frac{18}{x},$$ where x is the focal length of the lens.

The focal length on most adjustable cameras is marked in millimeters on the lens mount.

   a. Find the viewing angle, to the nearest tenth degree, assuming that the focal length is 50 millimeters.
   b. Find the viewing angle, to the nearest tenth degree, assuming that the focal length is 200 millimeters.

C EXERCISES Beyond the Basics

In Exercises 71–73, determine whether each function is increasing or decreasing on its domain.

71. $y = \sin^{-1} x$

72. $y = \cos^{-1} x$

73. $y = \tan^{-1} x$

74. Show that

   a. $\sec^{-1} x \neq \dfrac{1}{\cos^{-1} x}$.   **b.** $\sec^{-1} x = \cos^{-1}\dfrac{1}{x}$.

75. Graph the function $y = \cot^{-1} x$.

76. Graph the function $y = \csc^{-1} x$.

77. Graph the function $y = \sec^{-1} x$.

78. For what values of x is $\cot^{-1}(\cot x) = x$ true?

79. For what values of x is $\sec^{-1}(\sec x) = x$ true?

80. For what values of x is $\csc^{-1}(\csc x) = x$ true?

In Exercises 81–86, find the exact value of each expression.

81. $\sin\left[\tan^{-1}\left(-\dfrac{3}{4}\right) + \cos^{-1}\left(\dfrac{4}{5}\right)\right]$

82. $\cos\left[\sin^{-1}\left(-\dfrac{3}{5}\right) + \cos^{-1}\left(\dfrac{3}{5}\right)\right]$

83. $\sin\left[\sin^{-1}\left(\dfrac{3}{5}\right) - \cos^{-1}\left(\dfrac{4}{5}\right)\right]$

84. $\cos\left[\sin^{-1}\left(\dfrac{3}{5}\right) + \tan^{-1}\left(-\dfrac{4}{3}\right)\right]$

85. $\tan\left[\cos^{-1}\left(\dfrac{4}{5}\right) + \tan^{-1}\left(\dfrac{2}{3}\right)\right]$

86. $\tan\left[\sin^{-1}\left(-\dfrac{3}{5}\right) + \cos^{-1}\left(\dfrac{4}{5}\right)\right]$

Critical Thinking

In Exercises 87–94, evaluate each expression in terms of x.

87. $\sin(\cos^{-1} x), |x| \leq 1$ **88.** $\tan(\sin^{-1} x), |x| < 1$

89. $\cos(\tan^{-1} x)$ **90.** $\sin(\cot^{-1} x)$

91. $\cos(\sin^{-1} x), |x| \leq 1$

92. $\tan(\cos^{-1} x), |x| \leq 1, x \neq 0$

93. $\sin(\tan^{-1} x)$ **94.** $\cos(\cot^{-1} x)$

Trigonometric Equations I

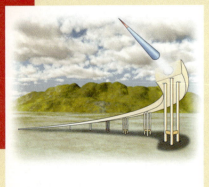

Before Starting this Section, Review

1. Reference angle (Section 1.4)
2. Periods of trigonometric functions (Section 4.1)
3. Factoring techniques (Appendix)
4. Solving linear and quadratic equations (Appendix)

Objectives

1 Solve trigonometric equations of the form $a \sin (x - c) = k$, $a \cos (x - c) = k$, and $a \tan (x - c) = k$.

2 Solve trigonometric equations by using the zero-product property.

3 Solve trigonometric equations that contain more than one trigonometric function.

4 Solve trigonometric equations by squaring both sides.

PROJECTILE MOTION

The angle that a projectile makes with a horizontal plane on which it rests at take-off and its initial velocity determine the rest of its flight. The time it takes for the projectile to hit the ground after reaching its maximum height is the same as if it had been dropped straight down from that height. The horizontal motion has no effect on the vertical motion. Suppose we ignore air resistance and measure time in seconds and distance in feet. Then the equation $h = v_0 t \sin \theta - 16t^2$ gives the height, h, of the projectile after t seconds, where θ is the initial angle the projectile makes with the ground and v_0 is the projectile's initial velocity. The horizontal distance, d, the projectile travels in t seconds is $d = t v_0 \cos \theta$. In Example 4, we use these equations to investigate the flight of a projectile.

Trigonometric Equations

Recall that a *trigonometric equation* is a conditional equation that contains a trigonometric function with a variable. An identity is an equation that is true for all values in the domain of the variable. We verified trigonometric identities in Section 5.1. Now we work with trigonometric equations that are satisfied by some but not all values of the variable. For example, $\sin x = \dfrac{1}{2}$ is satisfied by $x = \dfrac{\pi}{6}$ but not by $x = 0$.

Solving a trigonometric equation means finding its *solution set*. Some trigonometric equations do not have a solution. For example, the equation $\sin x = 2$ has no solution because $-1 \le \sin x \le 1$ for all real numbers x. However, if a trigonometric equation has a solution, it has infinitely many solutions because the trigonometric functions are periodic. Also note that we cannot find an exact solution for every equation. In such cases, we can approximate the solution by using a calculator.

In this section, we study three types of equations:

1. Equations of the form

$$a \sin (x - c) = k, \qquad a \cos (x - c) = k, \qquad a \tan (x - c) = k,$$

where a, c, and k are constants

2. Equations that can be solved by factoring using the zero-product property

3. Equations that are equivalent to a polynomial equation in one trigonometric function

1 Solve trigonometric equations of the form $a \sin(x - c) = k$, $a \cos(x - c) = k$, and $a \tan(x - c) = k$.

Trigonometric Equations of the Form $a \sin(x - c) = k$, $a \cos(x - c) = k$, and $a \tan(x - c) = k$

We begin with some simple equations.

EXAMPLE 1   Solving a Trigonometric Equation

Find all solutions of each equation. Express each answer in radians.

a. $\sin x = \dfrac{\sqrt{2}}{2}$ **b.** $\cos \theta = -\dfrac{\sqrt{3}}{2}$ **c.** $\tan x = -\sqrt{3}$

SOLUTION

a. We first find the solutions of $\sin x = \dfrac{\sqrt{2}}{2}$ in the interval $[0, 2\pi)$. We know that

$\sin \dfrac{\pi}{4} = \dfrac{\sqrt{2}}{2}$ and that $\sin x$ is positive only in quadrants I and II. See Figure 6.11.

The first and second quadrant angles with reference angle $\dfrac{\pi}{4}$ are

$$x = \frac{\pi}{4} \quad \text{and} \quad x = \pi - \frac{\pi}{4} = \frac{3\pi}{4}.$$

So $x = \dfrac{\pi}{4}$ and $x = \dfrac{3\pi}{4}$ are the only solutions in the interval $[0, 2\pi)$. Because the sine function is periodic with period 2π, adding any integer multiple of 2π to either of these values makes the sine of the resulting value still $\dfrac{\sqrt{2}}{2}$. All solutions of the equation $\sin x = \dfrac{\sqrt{2}}{2}$ are therefore given by

$$x = \frac{\pi}{4} + 2n\pi \quad \text{or} \quad x = \frac{3\pi}{4} + 2n\pi \text{ for any integer } n.$$

b. As in part **a**, we first find all solutions in the interval $[0, 2\pi)$. We know that $\cos \dfrac{\pi}{6} = \dfrac{\sqrt{3}}{2}$ and that $\cos \theta$ is negative only in quadrants II and III. See Figure 6.12. The second and third quadrant angles having reference angle $\dfrac{\pi}{6}$ are

$$\theta = \pi - \frac{\pi}{6} = \frac{5\pi}{6} \quad \text{and} \quad \theta = \pi + \frac{\pi}{6} = \frac{7\pi}{6}.$$

So $\theta = \dfrac{5\pi}{6}$ and $\theta = \dfrac{7\pi}{6}$ are the only solutions in the interval $[0, 2\pi)$.

The period of the cosine function is 2π, so all solutions are given by

$$\theta = \frac{5\pi}{6} + 2n\pi \quad \text{or} \quad \theta = \frac{7\pi}{6} + 2n\pi \text{ for any integer } n.$$

c. Because $\tan x$ is a periodic function with period π, we first find all solutions of $\tan x = -\sqrt{3}$ in the interval $[0, \pi)$. We know that $\tan \dfrac{\pi}{3} = \sqrt{3}$ and that $\tan x$ is

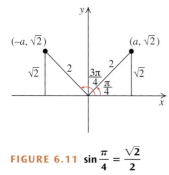

FIGURE 6.11 $\sin \dfrac{\pi}{4} = \dfrac{\sqrt{2}}{2}$

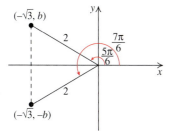

FIGURE 6.12 $\cos \dfrac{\pi}{6} = \dfrac{\sqrt{3}}{2}$

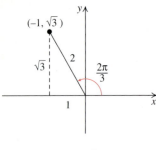

FIGURE 6.13 $\tan\dfrac{2\pi}{3} = -\sqrt{3}$

negative in quadrant II. See Figure 6.13. The second quadrant angle with reference angle $\dfrac{\pi}{3}$ is

$$x = \pi - \frac{\pi}{3} = \frac{2\pi}{3}.$$

So $x = \dfrac{2\pi}{3}$ is the only solution in the interval $[0, \pi)$. Because the period of $\tan x$ is π, all solutions of $\tan x = -\sqrt{3}$ are given by

$$x = \frac{2\pi}{3} + n\pi \text{ for any integer } n. \qquad ■■■$$

Practice Problem 1 Find all solutions of each equation. Express each answer in radians.

a. $\sin x = 1$ **b.** $\cos x = 1$ **c.** $\tan x = 1$ ■

In Example 1, we were able to find the exact solutions of trigonometric equations because the angles involved were common angles. In the next example, we find approximate solutions of trigonometric equations involving other angles.

EXAMPLE 2   **Finding Approximate Solutions**

a. Find all solutions of $\sin x = 0.3$. Round the solutions to the nearest tenth of a degree.

b. Find all solutions of $\cot x = -3.5$ in the interval $[0, 2\pi)$. Round the solutions to four decimal places.

SOLUTION

a. We use the function $\sin^{-1}$ to find the reference angle x' for any angle x with $\sin x = 0.3$.

$$\begin{aligned}
\sin x' &= |\sin x| = 0.3 && \text{Given equation} \\
x' &= \sin^{-1}(0.3) && 0° < x' < 90° \\
x' &\approx 17.5° && \text{Use a calculator in Degree mode.}
\end{aligned}$$

Because the sine function has positive values in quadrants I and II, we have

$$x \approx 17.5° \quad \text{or} \quad x \approx 180° - 17.5° = 162.5°.$$

The period of the sine function is 360°, so all solutions are given by

$$x \approx 17.5° + n \cdot 360° \quad \text{or} \quad x \approx 162.5° + n \cdot 360° \text{ for any integer } n.$$

b. Because $\cot x = -3.5 = -\dfrac{7}{2}$, we have

$$\tan x = -\frac{2}{7} \qquad \text{Reciprocal identity}$$

First, we find the reference angle x' for an angle x with $\tan x = -\dfrac{2}{7}$.

$$\begin{aligned}
\tan x' &= |\tan x| = \left| -\frac{2}{7} \right| = \frac{2}{7} \\
x' &= \tan^{-1}\left(\frac{2}{7} \right) && 0° < x' < \frac{\pi}{2} \\
x' &\approx 0.2783 && \text{Use a calculator in Radian mode.}
\end{aligned}$$

Because the cotangent function is negative in quadrants II and IV, we have

$$x \approx \pi - 0.2783 \approx 2.8633 \quad \text{and} \quad x \approx 2\pi - 0.2783 \approx 6.0049.$$

These are the only solutions in the interval $[0, 2\pi)$.   ■ ■ ■

Practice Problem 2

a. Find all solutions of $\sec x = 1.5$. Round the solutions to the nearest tenth of a degree.

b. Find all solutions of $\tan x = -2$ in the interval $[0, 2\pi)$. Round the solutions to four decimal places.   ■

In most of our examples, we find the solutions in the interval $[0, 2\pi)$ for equations involving sine, cosine, secant, and cosecant functions. To find all solutions of such equations, add $2n\pi$ to these solutions. Similarly, to find all solutions of an equation involving tangent or cotangent function, add $n\pi$ to each solution found in $[0, \pi)$. When an equation has only a finite number of solutions, we write the solutions using set notation.

> **RECALL**
>
> The period of $y = \tan x$ and $y = \cot x$ is π. The period of the other four trigonometric functions is 2π.

EXAMPLE 3   Solving a Linear Trigonometric Equation

Find all solutions in the interval $[0, 2\pi)$ of the equation

$$2 \sin \left(x - \frac{\pi}{4} \right) + 1 = 2.$$

SOLUTION

Replace $x - \dfrac{\pi}{4}$ with θ in the given equation.

$$2 \sin \theta + 1 = 2$$

$$\sin \theta = \frac{1}{2} \qquad \text{Solve for } \sin \theta.$$

The reference angle is $\dfrac{\pi}{6}$ because $\sin \dfrac{\pi}{6} = \dfrac{1}{2}$. (See page 29 or recall from memory.)

Because $\sin \theta$ is positive only in quadrants I and II, the solutions of $\sin \theta = \dfrac{1}{2}$ in $[0, 2\pi)$ are

$$\theta = \frac{\pi}{6} \quad \text{or} \quad \theta = \pi - \frac{\pi}{6} = \frac{5\pi}{6}.$$

Now $\theta = x - \dfrac{\pi}{4}$, so $\theta = \dfrac{\pi}{6}$ or $\theta = \dfrac{5\pi}{6}$ gives

$$x - \frac{\pi}{4} = \frac{\pi}{6} \qquad\qquad x - \frac{\pi}{4} = \frac{5\pi}{6} \qquad \text{Replace } \theta \text{ with } x - \frac{\pi}{4}.$$

$$x = \frac{\pi}{6} + \frac{\pi}{4} \qquad\qquad x = \frac{5\pi}{6} + \frac{\pi}{4} \qquad \text{Add } \frac{\pi}{4} \text{ to both sides.}$$

$$x = \frac{2\pi}{12} + \frac{3\pi}{12} = \frac{5\pi}{12} \qquad\qquad x = \frac{10\pi}{12} + \frac{3\pi}{12} = \frac{13\pi}{12} \qquad \text{Simplify.}$$

The solution set in the interval $[0, 2\pi)$ is $\left\{ \dfrac{5\pi}{12}, \dfrac{13\pi}{12} \right\}$.   ■ ■ ■

Practice Problem 3 Find all solutions in the interval $[0°, 360°)$ of the equation
$$2 \sec (x - 30)° + 1 = \sec (x - 30)° + 3.$$ ■

> **EXAMPLE 4**   **Finding the Angle from Which a Bullet Was Fired**

A bullet hits a target 1500 feet away 0.9 second after being fired. If the bullet's velocity is 3280 ft/sec, from what angle to the ground was the bullet fired? Give your answer to the nearest degree.

SOLUTION

We use the equation $d = tv_0 \cos \theta$ (from the section introduction) for the horizontal distance, d, that the projectile travels in t seconds, where θ is the initial angle the projectile makes with the ground and v_0 is the projectile's initial velocity. Because $d = tv_0 \cos \theta$,

$$1500 = 0.9(3280) \cos \theta \qquad \text{Replace } d \text{ with 1500, } t \text{ with 0.9, and } v_0 \text{ with 3280.}$$

$$\cos \theta = \frac{1500}{0.9(3280)} \qquad \text{Solve for } \cos \theta \text{: interchange sides.}$$

$$\theta = \cos^{-1}\left(\frac{1500}{0.9(3280)}\right) \qquad \theta \text{ is in Q 1.}$$

$$\theta \approx 59° \qquad \text{Use a calculator.} \qquad ■■■$$

Practice Problem 4 Rework Example 4 assuming that the target is 2500 feet away and the bullet takes 1 second to reach the target. ■

---

2 Solve trigonometric equations by using the zero-product property.

Trigonometric Equations and the Zero-Product Property

> **EXAMPLE 5**   **Solving an Equation by Using the Zero-Product Property**

Find all solutions of the equation $(2 \sin x - 1)(7 \tan x + 2) = 0$ in the interval $[0, 2\pi)$. Round the solutions to four decimal places.

SOLUTION

$$(2 \sin x - 1)(7 \tan x + 2) = 0 \qquad \text{Given equation}$$

$$2 \sin x - 1 = 0 \quad \text{or} \quad 7 \tan x + 2 = 0 \qquad \text{Zero-product property}$$

$$\sin x = \frac{1}{2} \qquad\qquad \tan x = -\frac{2}{7} \qquad \text{Solve for } \sin x \text{ and } \tan x.$$

$$x = \frac{\pi}{6} \quad \text{or} \quad x = \frac{5\pi}{6} \qquad x \approx \pi - 0.2783 \quad \text{or} \quad x \approx 2\pi - 0.2783$$

$$\qquad\qquad\qquad\qquad\qquad x \approx 2.8633 \quad \text{or} \quad x \approx 6.0049$$

(See Example 3.)   (See Example 2(b).)

So the solution set of the given equation is

$$\left\{\frac{\pi}{6}, \frac{5\pi}{6}, 2.8633, 6.0049\right\}. \qquad ■■■$$

Practice Problem 5 Find all solutions of the equation

$$(\sin x - 1)(\sqrt{3} \tan x + 1) = 0$$

in the interval $[0, 2\pi)$. ■

TECHNOLOGY CONNECTION

You can confirm that the equation in Example 6 has the two solutions we found in $[0, 2\pi)$ by graphing $Y_1 = 2 \sin^2 x - 5 \sin x + 2$ and inspecting the x-intercepts using TRACE.

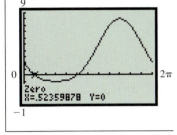

EXAMPLE 6   Solving a Quadratic Trigonometric Equation

Find all solutions of the equation $2 \sin^2 \theta - 5 \sin \theta + 2 = 0$. Express the solutions in radians.

SOLUTION

The equation is quadratic in $\sin \theta$. We use the zero-product property to solve for $\sin \theta$ and solve the resulting equation for θ.

$$2 \sin^2 \theta - 5 \sin \theta + 2 = 0 \qquad \color{blue}{2x^2 - 5x + 2 = 0 \text{ if } x = \sin \theta}$$

$$(2 \sin \theta - 1)(\sin \theta - 2) = 0 \qquad \color{blue}{(2x - 1)(x - 2) = 0; \text{ factor.}}$$

$$2 \sin \theta - 1 = 0 \quad \text{or} \quad \sin \theta - 2 = 0 \qquad \color{blue}{\text{Zero-product property}}$$

$$\sin \theta = \frac{1}{2} \qquad\qquad \sin \theta = 2 \qquad \color{blue}{\text{Solve for } \sin \theta.}$$

$$\theta = \frac{\pi}{6} \quad \text{or} \quad \theta = \frac{5\pi}{6} \qquad \color{red}{\text{No solution}} \qquad \color{blue}{-1 \le \sin \theta \le 1}$$

So $\theta = \dfrac{\pi}{6}$ and $\theta = \dfrac{5\pi}{6}$ are the only solutions in the interval $[0, 2\pi)$. Because $\sin \theta$ has period 2π, all possible solutions are

$$\theta = \frac{\pi}{6} + 2n\pi \quad \text{or} \quad \theta = \frac{5\pi}{6} + 2n\pi \text{ for any integer } n. \qquad ■ ■ ■$$

Practice Problem 6   Find all solutions of the equation $2 \cos^2 \theta - \cos \theta - 1 = 0$. Express the solutions in radians.   ■

3 Solve trigonometric equations that contain more than one trigonometric function.

Equations with More Than One Trigonometric Function

When a trigonometric equation contains more than one trigonometric function, sometimes we can use trigonometric identities to convert the equation into an equation containing only one trigonometric function.

EXAMPLE 7   Solving a Trigonometric Equation Using Identities

Find all solutions of the equation $2 \sin^2 \theta + \sqrt{3} \cos \theta + 1 = 0$ in the interval $[0, 2\pi)$.

SOLUTION

Because the equation contains both sine and cosine, we use the Pythagorean identity $\sin^2 \theta + \cos^2 \theta = 1$ to convert the equation into one containing only cosines.

$$2 \sin^2 \theta + \sqrt{3} \cos \theta + 1 = 0 \qquad \color{blue}{\text{Given equation}}$$

$$2(1 - \cos^2 \theta) + \sqrt{3} \cos \theta + 1 = 0 \qquad \color{blue}{\text{Replace } \sin^2 \theta \text{ with } 1 - \cos^2 \theta.}$$

$$2 - 2 \cos^2 \theta + \sqrt{3} \cos \theta + 1 = 0 \qquad \color{blue}{\text{Distributive property}}$$

$$3 - 2 \cos^2 \theta + \sqrt{3} \cos \theta = 0 \qquad \color{blue}{\text{Combine terms.}}$$

$$2 \cos^2 \theta - \sqrt{3} \cos \theta - 3 = 0 \qquad \color{blue}{\text{Multiply both sides by } -1.}$$

Solve the last equation for $\cos \theta$.

$$\cos \theta = \frac{-(-\sqrt{3}) \pm \sqrt{(-\sqrt{3})^2 - 4(2)(-3)}}{2(2)} \qquad \color{blue}{\text{Use } a = 2, b = -\sqrt{3}, \text{ and } c = -3 \text{ in the quadratic formula.}}$$

$$= \frac{\sqrt{3} \pm \sqrt{3 + 24}}{4} \qquad \color{blue}{\text{Simplify.}}$$

$$= \frac{\sqrt{3} \pm \sqrt{27}}{4} = \frac{\sqrt{3} \pm 3\sqrt{3}}{4} \qquad \color{blue}{\sqrt{27} = \sqrt{9 \cdot 3} = \sqrt{9}\sqrt{3} = 3\sqrt{3}}$$

So

$$\cos\theta = \frac{\sqrt{3} + 3\sqrt{3}}{4} \qquad \text{or} \qquad \cos\theta = \frac{\sqrt{3} - 3\sqrt{3}}{4}$$

$$= \frac{4\sqrt{3}}{4} = \sqrt{3} \qquad\qquad\qquad = \frac{(-2)\sqrt{3}}{4} = -\frac{\sqrt{3}}{2}$$

$$\cos\theta = \sqrt{3} > 1$$

Because $-1 \le \cos\theta \le 1$, the equation $\cos\theta = \sqrt{3}$ has no solution.

The equation $\cos\theta = -\dfrac{\sqrt{3}}{2}$ has two solutions in the interval $[0, 2\pi)$:

$$\theta = \pi - \frac{\pi}{6} = \frac{5\pi}{6} \text{ and}$$

$$\theta = \pi + \frac{\pi}{6} = \frac{7\pi}{6}$$

The solution set for the given equations in the interval $[0, 2\pi)$ is $\left\{ \dfrac{5\pi}{6}, \dfrac{7\pi}{6} \right\}$. ■ ■ ■

Practice Problem 7   Find all solutions of the equation $2\cos^2\theta + 3\sin\theta - 3 = 0$ in the interval $[0, 2\pi)$. ■

4   Solve trigonometric equations by squaring both sides.

Extraneous Solutions

Next, we solve a trigonometric equation by squaring both sides of the equation and then using an identity. Recall that squaring both sides of an equation may result in extraneous solutions. Therefore, you must check all possible solutions.

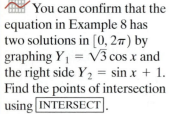
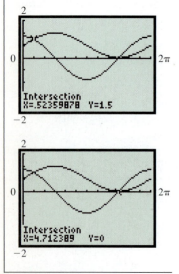
EXAMPLE 8   **Solving a Trigonometric Equation by Squaring**

Find all solutions of the equation $\sqrt{3}\cos x = \sin x + 1$ in the interval $[0, 2\pi)$.

SOLUTION

$$(\sqrt{3}\cos x)^2 = (\sin x + 1)^2 \qquad \text{Square both sides of the equation.}$$

$$3\cos^2 x = \sin^2 x + 2\sin x + 1 \qquad \text{Expand the binomial.}$$

$$3(1 - \sin^2 x) = \sin^2 x + 2\sin x + 1 \qquad \text{Pythagorean identity}$$

$$3 - 3\sin^2 x = \sin^2 x + 2\sin x + 1 \qquad \text{Distributive property}$$

$$-4\sin^2 x - 2\sin x + 2 = 0 \qquad \text{Collect like terms.}$$

$$2\sin^2 x + \sin x - 1 = 0 \qquad \text{Divide both sides by } -2.$$

$$(2\sin x - 1)(\sin x + 1) = 0 \qquad \text{Factor.}$$

$$2\sin x - 1 = 0 \quad \text{or} \quad \sin x + 1 = 0 \qquad \text{Zero-product property}$$

$$\sin x = \frac{1}{2} \qquad\qquad \sin x = -1 \qquad \text{Solve for } \sin x.$$

$$x = \frac{\pi}{6} \text{ or } x = \pi - \frac{\pi}{6} = \frac{5\pi}{6} \qquad x = \frac{3\pi}{2} \qquad \text{Solve for } x.$$

The possible solutions are $\dfrac{\pi}{6}, \dfrac{5\pi}{6}$, and $\dfrac{3\pi}{2}$.

Check:

$$x = \frac{\pi}{6} \qquad\qquad x = \frac{5\pi}{6} \qquad\qquad x = \frac{3\pi}{2}$$

$$\sqrt{3}\cos\frac{\pi}{6} \overset{?}{=} \sin\frac{\pi}{6} + 1 \quad\bigg|\quad \sqrt{3}\cos\frac{5\pi}{6} \overset{?}{=} \sin\frac{5\pi}{6} + 1 \quad\bigg|\quad \sqrt{3}\cos\frac{3\pi}{2} \overset{?}{=} \sin\frac{3\pi}{2} + 1$$

$$\sqrt{3}\left(\frac{\sqrt{3}}{2}\right) \overset{?}{=} \frac{1}{2} + 1 \quad\bigg|\quad \sqrt{3}\left(-\frac{\sqrt{3}}{2}\right) \overset{?}{=} \frac{1}{2} + 1 \quad\bigg|\quad \sqrt{3}(0) \overset{?}{=} -1 + 1$$

$$\frac{3}{2} \overset{?}{=} \frac{3}{2} \quad\bigg|\quad -\frac{3}{2} \overset{?}{=} \frac{3}{2} \quad\bigg|\quad 0 \overset{?}{=} 0$$

Yes   No   Yes

The solution set of the equation in the interval $[0, 2\pi)$ is $\left\{\dfrac{\pi}{6}, \dfrac{3\pi}{2}\right\}$.   ■ ■ ■

Practice Problem 8   Find all solutions of the equation $\sqrt{3}\cot\theta + 1 = \sqrt{3}\csc\theta$ in the interval $[0, 2\pi)$.   ■

SECTION 6.2 ■ Exercises

A EXERCISES Basic Skills and Concepts

1. The equation $\sin x = \dfrac{1}{2}$ has _____ solution(s) in $[0, 2\pi)$.

2. All solutions of $\sin x = \dfrac{1}{2}$ are given by _____ and _____ for any integer n.

3. The equation $\cos x = 1$ has _____ solution(s) in $[0, 2\pi)$.

4. All solutions of $\tan x = 1$ are given by _____, for any integer n.

5. *True or False* The equation $\sec x = \dfrac{1}{2}$ has two solutions in $[0, 2\pi)$.

6. *True or False* All solutions of $\sin x = 0$ are given by $x = n\pi$ for any integer n.

In Exercises 7–16, find all solutions of each equation. Express the solutions in radians.

7. $\cos x = 0$ **8.** $\sin x = 0$

9. $\tan x = -1$ **10.** $\cot x = -1$

11. $\cos x = \dfrac{\sqrt{2}}{2}$ **12.** $\sin x = \dfrac{\sqrt{3}}{2}$

13. $\cot x = \sqrt{3}$ **14.** $\tan x = -\dfrac{\sqrt{3}}{3}$

15. $\cos x = -\dfrac{1}{2}$ **16.** $\sin x = -\dfrac{\sqrt{3}}{2}$

In Exercises 17–26, find all solutions of each equation. Express the solutions in degrees.

17. $\tan x = \dfrac{\sqrt{3}}{3}$ **18.** $\cot x = 1$

19. $\sin x = -\dfrac{1}{2}$ **20.** $\cos x = \dfrac{1}{2}$

21. $\csc x = 1$ **22.** $\sec x = -1$

23. $\sqrt{3}\csc x - 2 = 0$ **24.** $\sqrt{3}\sec x + 2 = 0$

25. $2\sec x - 4 = 0$ **26.** $2\csc x + 4 = 0$

In Exercises 27–32, find all solutions of each equation in the interval $[0°, 360°)$. Round your answers to the nearest tenth of a degree.

27. $\sin\theta = 0.4$ **28.** $\cos\theta = 0.6$

29. $\sec\theta = 7.2$ **30.** $\csc\theta = -4.5$

31. $\tan(\theta - 30°) = -5$ **32.** $\cot(\theta + 30°) = 6$

In Exercises 33–38, find all solutions of each equation in the interval $[0, 2\pi)$. Round the solutions to four decimal places.

33. $\csc x = -3$ **34.** $3\sin x - 1 = 0$

35. $3\tan x + 4 = 0$ **36.** $2\sec x - 7 = 0$

37. $2\csc x + 5 = 0$ **38.** $\cos x = 0.1106$

In Exercises 39–46, find all solutions of each equation in the interval $[0, 2\pi)$.

39. $\sin\left(x + \dfrac{\pi}{4}\right) = \dfrac{1}{2}$ **40.** $2\cos\left(x - \dfrac{\pi}{4}\right) + 1 = 0$

41. $\sec\left(x - \dfrac{\pi}{8}\right) + 2 = 0$ **42.** $\csc\left(x + \dfrac{\pi}{8}\right) - 2 = 0$

43. $\sqrt{3}\tan\left(x - \dfrac{\pi}{6}\right) - 1 = 0$

44. $\cot\left(x + \dfrac{\pi}{6}\right) + 1 = 0$

45. $2\sin\left(x - \dfrac{\pi}{3}\right) + 1 = 0$

46. $2\cos\left(x + \dfrac{\pi}{3}\right) + \sqrt{2} = 0$

In Exercises 47–54, find all solutions of each equation in the interval $[0, 2\pi)$.

47. $(\sin x + 1)(\tan x - 1) = 0$

48. $(2\cos x + 1)(\sqrt{3}\tan x - 1) = 0$

49. $(\csc x - 2)(\cot x + 1) = 0$

50. $(\sqrt{3}\sec x - 2)(\sqrt{3}\cot x + 1) = 0$

51. $(\tan x + 1)(2\sin x - 1) = 0$

52. $(2\sin x - \sqrt{3})(2\cos x - 1) = 0$

53. $(\sqrt{2}\sec x - 2)(2\sin x + 1) = 0$

54. $(\cot x - 1)(\sqrt{2}\csc x + 2) = 0$

In Exercises 55–62, find all solutions of each equation in the interval $[0, 2\pi)$.

55. $4\sin^2 x = 1$

56. $4\cos^2 x = 1$

57. $\tan^2 x = 1$

58. $\sec^2 x = 2$

59. $3\csc^2 x = 4$

60. $3\cot^2 x = 1$

61. $2\sin^2\theta - \sin\theta - 1 = 0$ **62.** $2\cos^2\theta - 5\cos\theta + 2 = 0$

In Exercises 63–72, use trigonometric identities to solve each equation in the interval $[0, 2\pi)$.

63. $\sin x = \cos x$

64. $\sqrt{3}\sin x + \cos x = 0$

65. $3\sin^2 x = \cos^2 x$

66. $3\cos^2 x = \sin^2 x$

67. $\cos^2 x - \sin^2 x = 1$

68. $2\sin^2 x + \cos x - 1 = 0$

69. $2\cos^2 x - 3\sin x - 3 = 0$

70. $2\sin^2 x - \cos x - 1 = 0$

71. $\sqrt{3}\sec^2 x - 2\tan x - 2\sqrt{3} = 0$

72. $\csc^2 x - (\sqrt{3} + 1)\cot x + (\sqrt{3} - 1) = 0$

In Exercises 73–76, solve each trigonometric equation in the interval $[0, 2\pi)$ by first squaring both sides.

73. $\sqrt{3}\sin x = 1 + \cos x$ **74.** $\tan x + 1 = \sec x$

75. $\sqrt{3}\tan\theta + 1 = \sqrt{3}\sec\theta$ **76.** $\sqrt{3}\cot\theta + 1 = \sqrt{3}\csc\theta$

B EXERCISES Applying the Concepts

77. Angle of elevation. Find the angle of elevation of the sun if the shadow of a tree 24 feet high is $8\sqrt{3}$ feet in length.

78. Leaning Tower of Pisa. The Leaning Tower of Pisa is 179 feet high, and at noon, its shadow measures 16.5 feet. At what angle is the tower inclined from the vertical?

79. Returning spacecraft. When a spacecraft reenters the atmosphere, the angle of reentry from the horizontal must

be between 5.1° and 7.1°. Under 5.1°, the craft would "skip" back into space, and over 7.1°, the acceleration forces would be too high and the craft would crash. On reentry, a spacecraft descends 60 kilometers vertically while traveling 605 kilometers. Find the angle of reentry off the horizontal to the nearest tenth of a degree.

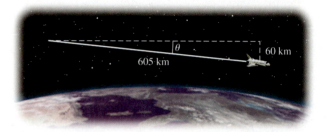

80. A flare is fired from the deck of an anchored ship at an initial velocity of 78 feet per second. After three seconds, the flare is directly over a lifeboat stalled 112 feet from the boat. At what angle to the deck was the flare fired? Give your answer to the nearest degree.

81. Find the angle that a golf ball's path makes with the ground assuming that its initial velocity is 150 feet per second and after four seconds it is 25 feet above the ground. Give your answer to the nearest degree.

82. Find the angle that a baseball's path makes with the ground assuming that its initial velocity is 140 feet per second and after two seconds it is 40 feet higher than when it was initially hit. Give your answer to the nearest degree.

C EXERCISES Beyond the Basics

In Exercises 83–88, find all solutions of each equation in the interval $[0, 2\pi)$.

83. $\sin x\cos x - \dfrac{\sqrt{3}}{2}\sin x + \dfrac{1}{2}\cos x - \dfrac{\sqrt{3}}{4} = 0$
[*Hint:* Factor by grouping.]

84. $2\sin x\tan x + 2\sin x + \tan x + 1 = 0$
[*Hint:* Factor by grouping.]

85. $5\sin^2\theta + \cos^2\theta - \sec^2\theta = 0$

86. $2\sin\theta = \cos\theta$ **87.** $2\cos x = 1 - \sin x$

88. $\cos^4 x - \cos^2 x + 1 = 0$

Critical Thinking

In Exercises 89–92, find all solutions of each equation in the interval $[0, 2\pi)$.

89. $\tan^2 x = 4$ **90.** $3\cos^2 x + \cos x = 0$

91. $\cos x - \sec x + 1 = 0$ **92.** $3\csc x + 2\cot^2 x = 5$

93. Solve the following equation: $\sin x\cos x = \dfrac{1}{2}$.

[*Hint:* Square both sides and replace $\cos^2 x$ with $1 - \sin^2 x$.]

94. Follow the hint given for Exercise 93 to show that the equation $\sin x\cos x = 1$ has no real-number solutions.

Trigonometric Equations II

Before Starting This Section, Review

1. Reference angle (Section 1.4)
2. Periods of trigonometric functions (Section 4.1)
3. Factoring techniques (Appendix)
4. Solving linear and quadratic equations (Appendix)

Objectives

1. Solve trigonometric equations involving multiple angles.
2. Solve equations using sum-to-product identities.
3. Solve equations containing inverse trigonometric functions.

BY THE WAY . . .

The expression *once in a blue moon* means "not often," but what exactly is a blue moon? The popular definition says that a second full moon in a single calendar month is called a *blue moon*. On average, a blue moon occurs once every two and one-half years.

THE PHASES OF THE MOON

The moon orbits the earth and completes one revolution in about 29.5 days (a lunar month). During this period, the angle between the sun, the earth, and the moon changes. See Figure 6.14. This causes different amounts of the illuminated moon to face the earth; consequently, the shape of the moon appears to change. The shape varies from a **new moon**—the phase of the moon when the moon is not visible from the earth (this happens when the moon is between the sun and the earth)—to a **half moon**—the phase of the moon when the moon looks like half of a circular disk—to a **full moon**—the phase of the moon when the moon looks like a full circular disk in the sky—back to a half moon and then to a new moon. The portion of the moon visible from the earth on any given day is called the **phase of the moon**. In Example 3, we express the phases of the moon by a sinusoidal equation. ■

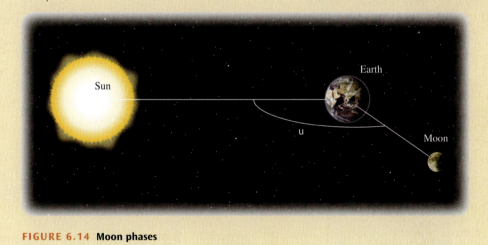

FIGURE 6.14 Moon phases

In this section, we solve equations involving trigonometric functions of multiple angles and those containing inverse trigonometric functions.

1 Solve trigonometric equations involving multiple angles.

Equations Involving Multiple Angles

If x is the measure of an angle, then for any real number k, the number kx is a **multiple angle** of x. Equations such as

$$\sin 3x = \frac{1}{2}, \qquad \cos \frac{1}{2}x = 0.7, \qquad \text{and} \qquad \sin 2x + \sin 4x = 0$$

involve multiple angles. We use the same techniques to solve the equations that we used in Section 6.2. We need to be careful when finding all solutions of such equations in the interval $[0, 2\pi)$, as you will see in Example 1.

EXAMPLE 1 **Solving a Trigonometric Equation Containing Multiple Angles**

Find all solutions of the equation $\cos 3x = \dfrac{1}{2}$ in the interval $[0, 2\pi)$.

SOLUTION

Recall that $\cos \theta = \dfrac{1}{2}$ for the acute angle $\theta = \dfrac{\pi}{3}$. Because $\cos \theta$ is positive in quadrants I and IV, we also have $\theta = 2\pi - \dfrac{\pi}{3} = \dfrac{5\pi}{3}$. The period of the cosine function is 2π; so replacing θ with $3x$, all solutions of the equation $\cos 3x = \dfrac{1}{2}$ are given by

$$3x = \frac{\pi}{3} + 2n\pi \quad \text{or} \quad 3x = \frac{5\pi}{3} + 2n\pi \qquad \text{For any integer } n$$

$$x = \frac{\pi}{9} + \frac{2n\pi}{3} \quad \text{or} \quad x = \frac{5\pi}{9} + \frac{2n\pi}{3} \qquad \text{Divide both sides by 3.}$$

To find solutions in the interval $[0, 2\pi)$, try the following:

$n = -1$	$x = \dfrac{\pi}{9} - \dfrac{2\pi}{3} = -\dfrac{5\pi}{9}$ ✗	$x = \dfrac{5\pi}{9} - \dfrac{2\pi}{3} = -\dfrac{\pi}{9}$ ✗
$n = 0$	$x = \dfrac{\pi}{9}$ ✓	$x = \dfrac{5\pi}{9}$ ✓
$n = 1$	$x = \dfrac{\pi}{9} + \dfrac{2\pi}{3} = \dfrac{7\pi}{9}$ ✓	$x = \dfrac{5\pi}{9} + \dfrac{2\pi}{3} = \dfrac{11\pi}{9}$ ✓
$n = 2$	$x = \dfrac{\pi}{9} + \dfrac{4\pi}{3} = \dfrac{13\pi}{9}$ ✓	$x = \dfrac{5\pi}{9} + \dfrac{4\pi}{3} = \dfrac{17\pi}{9}$ ✓
$n = 3$	$x = \dfrac{\pi}{9} + 2\pi = \dfrac{19\pi}{9}$ ✗	$x = \dfrac{5\pi}{9} + 2\pi = \dfrac{23\pi}{9}$ ✗

The values resulting from $n = -1$ are too small and those resulting from $n = 3$ are too large to be in the interval $[0, 2\pi)$. The solution set corresponding to $n = 0$, 1, and 2 is

$$\left\{ \frac{\pi}{9}, \frac{5\pi}{9}, \frac{7\pi}{9}, \frac{11\pi}{9}, \frac{13\pi}{9}, \frac{17\pi}{9} \right\}. \qquad ■ ■ ■$$

Practice Problem 1 Find all solutions of the equation $\sin 2x = \dfrac{1}{2}$ in the interval $[0, 2\pi)$. ■

TECHNOLOGY CONNECTION

On a graphing calculator, you can see that the graphs of $Y_1 = \cos 3x$ and $Y_2 = \dfrac{1}{2}$ intersect in six points, which correspond to the six solutions in the interval $[0, 2\pi)$.

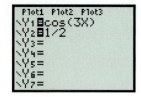

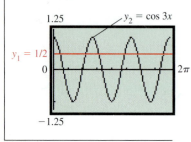

TECHNOLOGY CONNECTION

The graphs of
$$Y_1 = \sin\frac{x}{2} \text{ and } Y_2 = \frac{-\sqrt{3}}{2}$$
confirm that the equation in Example 2 has no solution.

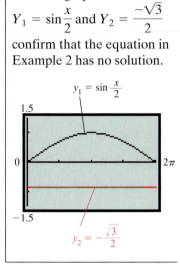

EXAMPLE 2   Solving a Trigonometric Equation Containing a Multiple Angle

Find all solutions of the equation $\sin\dfrac{x}{2} = -\dfrac{\sqrt{3}}{2}$ in the interval $[0, 2\pi)$.

SOLUTION

We know that $\sin\dfrac{\pi}{3} = \dfrac{\sqrt{3}}{2}$. Because $\sin\theta$ is negative only in quadrants III and IV, the solutions for $\sin\theta = -\dfrac{\sqrt{3}}{2}$ are

$$\theta = \pi + \frac{\pi}{3} = \frac{4\pi}{3} \quad \text{and} \quad \theta = 2\pi - \frac{\pi}{3} = \frac{5\pi}{3}.$$

Because the sine function has period 2π, all solutions of $\sin\dfrac{x}{2} = -\dfrac{\sqrt{3}}{2}$ are given by

$$\frac{x}{2} = \frac{4\pi}{3} + 2n\pi \quad \text{or} \quad \frac{x}{2} = \frac{5\pi}{3} + 2n\pi \qquad \text{For any integer } n$$

$$x = \frac{8\pi}{3} + 4n\pi \quad \text{or} \quad x = \frac{10\pi}{3} + 4n\pi \qquad \text{Multiply both sides by 2.}$$

For any integer n, the values of x in both expressions lie outside the interval $[0, 2\pi)$. For example, for $n = 0$, $x = \dfrac{8\pi}{3} > 2\pi$ and for $n = -1$, $x = \dfrac{8\pi}{3} - 4\pi = -\dfrac{2\pi}{3} < 0$. The equation $\sin\dfrac{x}{2} = -\dfrac{\sqrt{3}}{2}$, therefore, has no solution in the interval $[0, 2\pi)$; so the solution set is $\varnothing$.   ■ ■ ■

Practice Problem 2   Find all solutions of the equation $\tan\dfrac{x}{2} = \dfrac{\sqrt{3}}{3}$ in the interval $[0, 2\pi)$.   ■

EXAMPLE 3   The Phases of the Moon

The moon orbits the earth in 29.5 days. The portion F of the moon visible from the earth x days after the new moon is given by the equation

$$F = 0.5\sin\left[\frac{\pi}{14.75}\left(x - \frac{14.75}{2}\right)\right] + 0.5.$$

Find x when 75% of the moon is visible from the earth.

SOLUTION

We are asked to find x when $F = 75\% = 0.75$. We solve the equation:

$$0.75 = 0.5\sin\left[\frac{\pi}{14.75}\left(x - \frac{14.75}{2}\right)\right] + 0.5 \qquad \text{Replace } F \text{ with } 0.75.$$

$$0.25 = 0.5\sin\left[\frac{\pi}{14.75}\left(x - \frac{14.75}{2}\right)\right] \qquad \text{Subtract 0.5 from both sides.}$$

$$\frac{1}{2} = \sin\left[\frac{\pi}{14.75}\left(x - \frac{14.75}{2}\right)\right] \qquad \text{Divide both sides by 0.5.}$$

Thus, $\theta = \dfrac{\pi}{14.75}\left(x - \dfrac{14.75}{2}\right)$ is a solution of the equation $\sin\theta = \dfrac{1}{2}$.

We know that $\sin \dfrac{\pi}{6} = \dfrac{1}{2}$. Because $\sin \theta$ is positive only in quadrants I and II, we have

$$\dfrac{\pi}{14.75}\left(x - \dfrac{14.75}{2}\right) = \dfrac{\pi}{6} \qquad \text{or} \qquad \dfrac{\pi}{14.75}\left(x - \dfrac{14.75}{2}\right) = \dfrac{5\pi}{6}$$

$$x - \dfrac{14.75}{2} = \dfrac{14.75}{6} \qquad\qquad\qquad x - \dfrac{14.75}{2} = \dfrac{5(14.75)}{6} \qquad \text{Multiply both sides by } 14.75/\pi.$$

$$x = \dfrac{14.75}{2} + \dfrac{14.75}{6} \qquad\qquad\qquad x = \dfrac{14.75}{2} + \dfrac{5(14.75)}{6} \qquad \text{Solve for } x.$$

$$x \approx 10 \qquad\qquad\qquad\qquad\qquad x \approx 20 \qquad \text{Use a calculator and round to the nearest day.}$$

So 75% of the moon is visible 10 days and 20 days after the new moon. ■ ■ ■

Practice Problem 3 In Example 3, find x when 30% of the moon is visible from the earth. ■

EXAMPLE 4 **Solving a Trigonometric Equation**

Find all solutions of $\tan 2\theta = \sqrt{3}$ for $0° \le \theta < 360°$.

SOLUTION

We have $\tan x = \sqrt{3}$ for the acute angle $x = 60°$. The period of the tangent function is $\pi = 180°$; so replacing x with 2θ, all solutions of the equation $\tan 2\theta = \sqrt{3}$ are given by

$$2\theta = 60° + 180°(n) \qquad \text{For any integer } n$$
$$\theta = 30° + 90°(n) \qquad \text{Divide both sides by 2.}$$

For $n = 0, 1, 2,$ and 3, we have all values of θ between $0°$ and $360°$ that satisfy the equation $\tan 2\theta = \sqrt{3}$:

n	$\theta = 30° + 90°(n)$
0	$30° + 90°(0) = 30°$
1	$30° + 90°(1) = 120°$
2	$30° + 90°(2) = 210°$
3	$30° + 90°(3) = 300°$

The solution set is $\{30°, 120°, 210°, 300°\}$. ■ ■ ■

Practice Problem 4 Find all solutions of $\cot 3\theta = 1$ for $0° \le \theta < 360°$. ■

EXAMPLE 5 **Solving an Equation by Squaring**

Solve $\sin 2x + \cos 2x = \sqrt{2}$ over the interval $[0, 2\pi)$.

SOLUTION

$$\sin 2x + \cos 2x = \sqrt{2} \qquad \text{Original equation}$$
$$(\sin 2x + \cos 2x)^2 = (\sqrt{2})^2 \qquad \text{Square both sides.}$$
$$\sin^2 2x + \cos^2 2x + 2\sin 2x \cos 2x = 2 \qquad (a + b)^2 = a^2 + b^2 + 2ab$$
$$1 + \sin 4x = 2 \qquad \sin^2 A + \cos^2 A = 1;$$
$$\qquad\qquad\qquad\qquad\qquad 2\sin A \cos A = \sin 2A$$
$$\sin 4x = 1 \qquad \text{Solve for } \sin 4x.$$

We have $\sin \theta = 1$ for $\theta = \dfrac{\pi}{2}$. The period of the sine function is 2π; so replacing θ with $4x$, all solutions of $\sin 4x = 1$ are given by

$$4x = \frac{\pi}{2} + 2n\pi \qquad \text{For any integer } n$$

$$x = \frac{\pi}{8} + \frac{n\pi}{2} \qquad \text{Divide by 4; simplify.}$$

For $n = 0, 1, 2$, and 3, we have all possible values of x between 0 and 2π that satisfy the equation $\sin 4x = 1$:

n	$x = \dfrac{\pi}{8} + \dfrac{n\pi}{2}$
0	$\dfrac{\pi}{8} + 0 = \dfrac{\pi}{8}$
1	$\dfrac{\pi}{8} + \dfrac{\pi}{2} = \dfrac{5\pi}{8}$
2	$\dfrac{\pi}{8} + \pi = \dfrac{9\pi}{8}$
3	$\dfrac{\pi}{8} + \dfrac{3\pi}{2} = \dfrac{13\pi}{8}$

The possible solutions of the original equation are $\dfrac{\pi}{8}, \dfrac{5\pi}{8}, \dfrac{9\pi}{8}$, and $\dfrac{13\pi}{8}$. Because squaring both sides of an equation may result in extraneous solutions, we must check all possible solutions.

You can verify that the solution set of the equation is $\left\{ \dfrac{\pi}{8}, \dfrac{9\pi}{8} \right\}$.   ■ ■ ■

Practice Problem 5   Solve $\sin 3x + \cos 3x = \sqrt{\dfrac{3}{2}}$ over the interval $[0, 2\pi)$.   ■

2 Solve equations using sum-to-product identities.

Using Sum-to-Product Identities

The next example illustrates a procedure for solving a trigonometric equation of the form $\sin ax \pm \sin bx = 0$ or $\cos ax \pm \cos bx = 0$. To solve such equations, review the sum-to-product identities on page 212.

EXAMPLE 6   **Solving an Equation Using a Sum-to-Product Identity**

Solve: $\cos 2x + \cos 3x = 0$ over the interval $[0, 2\pi)$

SOLUTION

$$\cos 2x + \cos 3x = 0 \qquad \text{Original equation}$$

$$2 \cos \frac{5x}{2} \cos \frac{x}{2} = 0 \qquad \cos u + \cos v = 2 \cos \frac{u + v}{2} \cos \frac{u - v}{2}$$

So

$$\cos \frac{5x}{2} = 0 \qquad \text{or} \qquad \cos \frac{x}{2} = 0 \qquad \text{Zero-product property}$$

We know that if $\cos \theta = 0$, then for any integer n,

$$\theta = \frac{\pi}{2} + 2n\pi \quad \text{or} \quad \theta = \frac{3\pi}{2} + 2n\pi.$$

We replace θ with $\dfrac{5x}{2}$ and $\dfrac{x}{2}$ and find the values of x that lie in the interval $[0, 2\pi)$.

	$\cos\dfrac{5x}{2} = 0$		$\cos\dfrac{x}{2} = 0$	
	$\dfrac{5x}{2} = \dfrac{\pi}{2} + 2n\pi$	$\dfrac{5x}{2} = \dfrac{3\pi}{2} + 2n\pi$	$\dfrac{x}{2} = \dfrac{\pi}{2} + 2n\pi$	$\dfrac{x}{2} = \dfrac{3\pi}{2} + 2n\pi$
	$x = \dfrac{\pi}{5} + \dfrac{4n\pi}{5}$	$x = \dfrac{3\pi}{5} + \dfrac{4n\pi}{5}$	$x = \pi + 4n\pi$	$x = 3\pi + 4n\pi$
$n = 0$	$x = \dfrac{\pi}{5}$ ✓	$x = \dfrac{3\pi}{5}$ ✓	$x = \pi$ ✓	$x = 3\pi$ ✗
$n = 1$	$x = \pi$ ✓	$x = \dfrac{7\pi}{5}$ ✓	$x = 5\pi$ ✗	
$n = 2$	$x = \dfrac{9\pi}{5}$ ✓	$x = \dfrac{11\pi}{5}$ ✗		
$n = 3$	$x = \dfrac{13\pi}{5}$ ✗			

The solution set of the given equation is $\left\{\dfrac{\pi}{5}, \dfrac{3\pi}{5}, \pi, \dfrac{7\pi}{5}, \dfrac{9\pi}{5}\right\}$. ■ ■ ■

Practice Problem 6 Solve $\sin 2x + \sin 3x = 0$ over the interval $[0, 2\pi)$ ■

3 Solve equations containing inverse trigonometric functions.

Equations Containing Inverse Functions

We now consider equations containing inverse trigonometric functions.

> **EXAMPLE 7** **Solving an Equation Containing an Inverse Tangent Function**

Solve $\dfrac{\pi}{6} + 2\tan^{-1}(x - 1) = \dfrac{\pi}{2}$

SOLUTION

$$\dfrac{\pi}{6} + 2\tan^{-1}(x - 1) = \dfrac{\pi}{2} \qquad \text{Original equation}$$

$$2\tan^{-1}(x - 1) = \dfrac{\pi}{2} - \dfrac{\pi}{6} = \dfrac{\pi}{3} \qquad \text{Subtract } \dfrac{\pi}{6} \text{ and simplify.}$$

$$\tan^{-1}(x - 1) = \dfrac{\pi}{6} \qquad \text{Divide both sides by 2.}$$

$$x - 1 = \tan\dfrac{\pi}{6} \qquad \text{Definition of inverse function}$$

$$x = 1 + \tan\dfrac{\pi}{6} \qquad \text{Solve for } x.$$

$$x = 1 + \dfrac{\sqrt{3}}{3} = \dfrac{3 + \sqrt{3}}{3} \qquad \tan\dfrac{\pi}{6} = \dfrac{\sqrt{3}}{3} \qquad ■\ ■\ ■$$

Practice Problem 7 Solve $\dfrac{\pi}{4} + 3\sin^{-1}(x + 1) = \dfrac{5\pi}{4}$ ■

From the definition of the inverse sine function, the equation $\sin^{-1}\left(\dfrac{1}{2}\right) = x$ has only one solution, $x = \dfrac{\pi}{6}$. However, taking the sine of both sides gives $\sin\left(\sin^{-1}\dfrac{1}{2}\right) = \sin x$, or $\dfrac{1}{2} = \sin x$. The last equation has infinitely many solutions: $x = \dfrac{\pi}{6} + 2\pi n$ and $x = \dfrac{5\pi}{6} + 2n\pi$, n an integer. As with squaring both sides of an equation, taking the sine (or any other trigonometric function) of both sides of an equation may result in *extraneous solutions*. In such cases, you must check all solutions.

EXAMPLE 8　**Solving an Equation Containing Inverse Functions**

Solve　$\sin^{-1} x - \cos^{-1} x = \dfrac{\pi}{4}$.

SOLUTION

$$\sin^{-1} x - \cos^{-1} x = \frac{\pi}{4} \qquad \text{Original equation}$$

Let　$u = \sin^{-1} x$ and $v = \cos^{-1} x$.

Then　$\sin u = x$ and $\cos v = x$. See Figure 6.15.

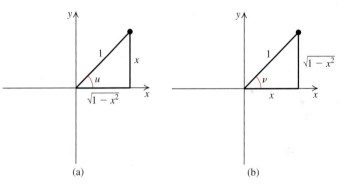

(a)　　　　　　　　　(b)

FIGURE 6.15

We have $\cos u = \sqrt{1 - x^2}$ from Figure 6.15(a) and $\sin v = \sqrt{1 - x^2}$ from Figure 6.15(b).

$$u - v = \frac{\pi}{4} \qquad \text{Original equation}$$

$$\sin(u - v) = \sin\left(\frac{\pi}{4}\right) = \frac{\sqrt{2}}{2} \qquad \text{Take sine of both sides;} \quad \sin\left(\frac{\pi}{4}\right) = \frac{\sqrt{2}}{2}$$

$$\sin u \cos v - \cos u \sin v = \frac{\sqrt{2}}{2} \qquad \text{Difference formula for sines}$$

$$x \cdot x - \left(\sqrt{1 - x^2}\right)\left(\sqrt{1 - x^2}\right) = \frac{\sqrt{2}}{2} \qquad \text{Substitute.}$$

$$x^2 - (1 - x^2) = \frac{\sqrt{2}}{2} \qquad \text{Simplify.}$$

$$2x^2 - 1 = \frac{\sqrt{2}}{2}$$

$$2x^2 = 1 + \frac{\sqrt{2}}{2} = \frac{2 + \sqrt{2}}{2} \qquad \text{Solve for } 2x^2.$$

continued on the next page

$$x^2 = \frac{2 + \sqrt{2}}{4} \qquad \text{Divide by 2.}$$

$$x = \pm\frac{\sqrt{2 + \sqrt{2}}}{2} \qquad \text{Square root property}$$

Check: Because $-\dfrac{\sqrt{2 + \sqrt{2}}}{2}$ is negative, $\sin^{-1}\left(-\dfrac{\sqrt{2 + \sqrt{2}}}{2}\right)$ is also negative. So the left side, $\sin^{-1}\left(-\dfrac{\sqrt{2 + \sqrt{2}}}{2}\right) - \cos^{-1}\left(-\dfrac{\sqrt{2 + \sqrt{2}}}{2}\right)$ is negative while the right side, $\dfrac{\pi}{4}$, is positive. We eliminate $-\dfrac{\sqrt{2 + \sqrt{2}}}{2}$ as a solution of $\sin^{-1} x - \cos^{-1} x = \dfrac{\pi}{4}$.

Use a calculator to verify that $\dfrac{\sqrt{2 + \sqrt{2}}}{2}$ is a solution.

The solution set is $\left\{\dfrac{\sqrt{2 + \sqrt{2}}}{2}\right\}$.

■ ■ ■

Practice Problem 8   Repeat Example 8 using $\cos(u - v) = \cos\dfrac{\pi}{4}$.   ■

SECTION 6.3 ■ Exercises

A EXERCISES Basic Skills and Concepts

1. If $\sin 2x_1 = \sin 2x_2$ and $0 < x_1 < x_2 < \dfrac{\pi}{2}$, then $x_2 = $ _____.

2. If $\cos 2x_1 = \cos 2x_2$ and $0 < x_1 < x_2 < \pi$, then $x_2 = $ _____.

3. If $\tan 2x_1 = \tan 2x_2$ and $0 < x_1 < x_2 < \pi$, then $x_2 = $ _____.

4. *True or False* $\sin\left(2 \sin^{-1} x\right) = 2x\sqrt{1 - x^2}$ if $-1 \le x \le 1$.

5. *True or False* $\dfrac{\sin 2x}{2} = \sin x$.

6. *True or False* $\dfrac{2 \tan \dfrac{x}{2}}{x} = \tan 1$.

In Exercises 7–26, find all solutions of each equation in the interval $[0, 2\pi)$.

7. $\cos 2x = \dfrac{1}{2}$

8. $\cos 2x = 0$

9. $\csc 2x = \dfrac{1}{2}$

10. $\sec 2x = \dfrac{\sqrt{3}}{2}$

11. $\tan 2x = \dfrac{\sqrt{3}}{3}$

12. $\cot 2x = \dfrac{\sqrt{3}}{3}$

13. $\sin 3x = \dfrac{1}{2}$

14. $\cos 3x = \dfrac{\sqrt{3}}{2}$

15. $\cos\dfrac{x}{2} = \dfrac{1}{2}$

16. $\csc\dfrac{x}{2} = 2$

17. $\tan\dfrac{x}{3} = 1$

18. $\cot\dfrac{x}{3} = \sqrt{3}$

19. $2 \sin 3x = \sqrt{2}$

20. $2 \cos 3x = \sqrt{2}$

21. $2 \cos(2x + 1) = 1$

22. $2 \sin(2x - 1) = \sqrt{3}$

23. $2 \sin(4x - 1) = 1$

24. $2 \cos(4x + 1) = \sqrt{3}$

25. $2 \cos\left(\dfrac{3x}{2} - 1\right) = \sqrt{3}$

26. $2 \sin\left(\dfrac{3x}{2} + 1\right) = 1$

In Exercises 27–38, solve each equation for θ in the interval $[0°, 360°)$. If necessary, write your answer to the nearest tenth of a degree.

27. $3 \cos 2\theta = 1$

28. $4 \sin 2\theta = 1$

29. $2 \cos 3\theta + 1 = 2$

30. $2 \sin 3\theta - 1 = -2$

31. $3 \sin 3\theta + 1 = 0$

32. $4 \cos 3\theta + 1 = 0$

33. $2 \sin\dfrac{\theta}{2} + 1 = 0$

34. $2 \cos\dfrac{\theta}{2} + \sqrt{3} = 0$

35. $2 \sec 2\theta + 3 = 7$

36. $2 \csc 2\theta + 4 = 0$

37. $3 \csc\dfrac{\theta}{2} - 1 = 5$

38. $5 \sec\dfrac{\theta}{2} - 3 = 7$

In Exercises 39–46, solve each equation by using sum-to-product identities in the interval $[0, 2\pi)$.

39. $\sin 2x + \sin x = 0$

40. $\cos 2x + \cos x = 0$

41. $\cos 3x - \cos x = 0$

42. $\sin 3x - \sin x = 0$

43. $\cos 3x + \cos 5x = 0$ **44.** $\cos 3x - \cos 5x = 0$

45. $\sin 3x - \sin 5x = 0$ **46.** $\sin 3x + \sin 5x = 0$

In Exercises 47–54, solve each equation for x.

47. $\sin^{-1} x - \cos^{-1} x = \dfrac{\pi}{6}$ **48.** $\sin^{-1} x + \cos^{-1} x = \dfrac{\pi}{6}$

49. $\sin^{-1} x + \cos^{-1} x = \dfrac{3\pi}{4}$ **50.** $\sin^{-1} x - \cos^{-1} x = \dfrac{\pi}{3}$

51. $\sin^{-1} x - \cos^{-1} x = -\dfrac{\pi}{6}$ **52.** $\sin^{-1} x + \cos^{-1} x = -\dfrac{3\pi}{4}$

53. $\sin^{-1} x - \tan^{-1} \dfrac{2}{3} = \dfrac{\pi}{4}$ **54.** $\sin^{-1} x - \cos^{-1} \dfrac{2}{3} = \dfrac{\pi}{6}$

B EXERCISES Applying the Concepts

55. Electric current. The electric current I (in amperes) produced by an alternator in time t (in seconds) is given by $I = 60 \sin(120\pi t)$. Find the smallest possible positive value of t (rounded to four decimal places) such that
  a. $I = 30$ amperes.
  b. $I = -20$ amperes.

56. Simple harmonic motion. A simple harmonic motion is described by the equation $x = 6 \sin\left(\dfrac{\pi}{2} t\right)$, where x is the displacement in feet and t is time in seconds. Find positive values of t for which the displacement is 3 feet.

57. Simple harmonic motion. Repeat Exercise 56 assuming that the simple harmonic motion is described by the equation
$x = 6 \cos\left(\dfrac{\pi}{2} t\right)$.

58. Overcoat sales. The monthly sales of overcoats at the menswear store Suit Yourself in Winterland are approximated by the equation

$$S(x) = 500 + 500 \sin\left[\frac{\pi}{4}(x - 2)\right],$$

where x is the month, with $x = 1$ for January. Find the months (after appropriate rounding) in which the number of overcoats sold is
  a. 0.
  b. 1000.
  c. 500.

59. Number of tourists. The weekly number of tourists visiting a tropical island is approximated by the equation

$$y = 20 + 10 \sin\left[\frac{\pi}{26}(x - 14)\right],$$

where y is the number of visitors (in thousands) in the xth week of the year, starting with $x = 1$ for the first

week in January. Find the week (after appropriate rounding) in which the number of tourists to the island is
  a. 30,000.
  b. 25,000.
  c. 15,000.

60. Average monthly temperature. The average monthly sea surface temperature T (in degrees Fahrenheit) on Paradise Island is approximated by the equation

$$T = 10.5 \sin\left[\frac{\pi}{6}(x - 5)\right] + 73.5,$$

where x is the month, with $x = 1$ representing January. Find the months (after appropriate rounding) when the average sea surface temperature is
  a. 78.75° F.
  b. 84° F.

61. Average monthly snowfall. The average monthly snowfall y (in inches) in Rochester, New York, in the xth month can be approximated by

$$y = 12 + 12 \sin\left[\frac{\pi}{4}(x - 2)\right], 1 \le x \le 8,$$

where October $= 1$, November $= 2, \ldots$ May $= 8$. Find the months (after appropriate rounding) when the average snowfall in Rochester is
  a. 24 inches.
  b. 18 inches.

62. Watching TV. A 3-foot-high LCD television is mounted on a wall with its base 1.5 feet above the level of the observer's eye. Let θ be the angle of vision subtended by the TV when you sit x feet from the wall.
  a. Show that $\theta = \cot^{-1}\dfrac{2x}{9} - \cot^{-1}\dfrac{2x}{3}$.
  b. Find x to the nearest foot assuming that $\tan \theta = \dfrac{1}{4}$.

C EXERCISES Beyond the Basics

In Exercises 63–80, find all solutions of each equation in the interval $[0, 2\pi)$.

63. $\sin^4 2x = 1$ **64.** $\cos^4 2x = 1$

65. $4\cos^2 \dfrac{x}{2} = 3$ **66.** $4\sin^2 \dfrac{x}{2} = 1$

67. $\tan^2 2x = 1$ **68.** $\cot^2 \dfrac{x}{2} = 1$

69. $3 \sec^2 \dfrac{x}{2} = 12$

70. $5 \csc^2 \dfrac{x}{2} - 11 = 9$

71. $(\tan 2x - 1)(\sin x + 1) = 0$

72. $(\sqrt{3} \cot 2x - 1)(2 \cos x - 1) = 0$

73. $(1 - 2 \sin 2x - 1)(\sqrt{3} + 2 \cos x) = 0$

74. $(\sqrt{3} \tan 2x + 1)(2 \cos x + 1) = 0$

75. $\sin 2x \cos 2x + \dfrac{\sqrt{3}}{2} \sin 2x + \dfrac{1}{2} \cos 2x + \dfrac{\sqrt{3}}{4} = 0$

76. $2 \sin 3x \tan 2x - 2 \sin 3x + \tan 2x - 1 = 0$

77. $\sin 2x + \sin 4x = 2 \sin 3x$

78. $\cos x + \cos 5x = 2 \cos 2x$

79. $\sin x + \sin 3x = \cos x + \cos 3x$

80. $\sin 2x + \sin 4x = \cos 2x + \cos 4x$

In Exercises 81–84, solve each equation for x in the interval $[0, 2\pi)$.

[*Hint:* write the left side of the equation in the form $A \sin (Bx - C)$.]

81. $3 \sin 2x + 4 \cos 2x = 0$

82. $3 \cos 2x - 4 \sin 2x = \dfrac{5}{2}$

83. $5 \sin 3x - 12 \cos 3x = \dfrac{13\sqrt{3}}{2}$

84. $12 \sin 3x + 5 \cos 3x = \dfrac{13}{2}$

Critical Thinking

In Exercises 85 and 86, solve each equation for x.

85. $\cos \left(2 \sin^{-1} x\right) = \dfrac{1}{2}$ **86.** $\tan \left(\tan^{-1} x + \tan^{-1} 1\right) = 5$

REVIEW

Definitions, Concepts, and Formulas	**Examples and Illustrations**

6.1 Inverse Trigonometric Functions

■ **Inverse sine function** By restricting the domain of the sine function to $\left[-\dfrac{\pi}{2}, \dfrac{\pi}{2}\right]$, we get a one-to-one function. The inverse function is called the **inverse sine** function, or **arc sine,** and is denoted by $\sin^{-1}(x)$, or arcsin x.

The equation $y = \sin^{-1} x$ means that $\sin y = x$, where $-1 \le x \le 1$ and $-\dfrac{\pi}{2} \le y \le \dfrac{\pi}{2}$. Read $y = \sin^{-1} x$ as "y equals inverse sine at x."

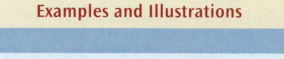

To find the value of $y = \sin^{-1}\left(-\dfrac{\sqrt{3}}{2}\right)$, we use the fact that $\sin y = -\dfrac{\sqrt{3}}{2}$ and $-\dfrac{\pi}{2} \le y \le \dfrac{\pi}{2}$. Because $\sin\left(-\dfrac{\pi}{3}\right) = -\dfrac{\sqrt{3}}{2}$ and $-\dfrac{\pi}{2} \le -\dfrac{\pi}{3} \le \dfrac{\pi}{2}$, we have $y = -\dfrac{\pi}{3}$.

■ **Inverse cosine function**
By restricting the domain of the cosine function to $[0, \pi]$, we get a one-to-one function. The inverse function is called the **inverse cosine** function, or **arccosine**, and is denoted by $\cos^{-1}(x)$, or by arccosine x.

The equation $y = \cos^{-1} x$ means that $\cos y = x$, where $-1 \le x \le 1$ and $0 \le y \le \pi$. Read $y = \cos^{-1} x$ as "y equals inverse cosine at x."

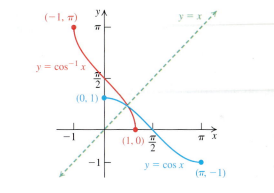

To find the value of $y = \cos^{-1} \dfrac{1}{2}$, we use the fact that

$\cos y = \dfrac{1}{2}$ and $0 \le y \le \pi$. Because $\cos \dfrac{\pi}{3} = \dfrac{1}{2}$ and

$0 \le \dfrac{\pi}{3} \le \pi$, we have $y = \dfrac{\pi}{3}$.

■ **Inverse tangent function** The *inverse tangent function* results from restricting the domain of the tangent function to the interval $\left(-\dfrac{\pi}{2}, \dfrac{\pi}{2} \right)$ to obtain a one-to-one function.

The inverse of this restricted tangent function is the **inverse tangent**, or **arctangent**, function.

The next chart summarizes all of the important facts about the inverse trigonometric functions.

To find the value of $y = \tan^{-1}(1)$, we use the fact that

$\tan y = 1$ and $-\dfrac{\pi}{2} < y < \dfrac{\pi}{2}$. Because $\tan \dfrac{\pi}{4} = 1$ and

$-\dfrac{\pi}{2} < \dfrac{\pi}{4} < \dfrac{\pi}{2}$, we have $y = \dfrac{\pi}{4}$.

i.

Inverse Trigonometric Functions

Inverse Function	Equivalent to	Domain	Range
$y = \sin^{-1} x$	$x = \sin y$	$[-1, 1]$	$\left[-\dfrac{\pi}{2}, \dfrac{\pi}{2} \right]$
$y = \cos^{-1} x$	$x = \cos y$	$[-1, 1]$	$[0, \pi]$
$y = \tan^{-1} x$	$x = \tan y$	$(-\infty, \infty)$	$\left(-\dfrac{\pi}{2}, \dfrac{\pi}{2} \right)$
$y = \cot^{-1} x$	$x = \cot y$	$(-\infty, \infty)$	$(0, \pi)$
$y = \csc^{-1} x$	$x = \csc y$	$(-\infty, -1] \cup [1, \infty)$	$\left[-\dfrac{\pi}{2}, 0 \right) \cup \left(0, \dfrac{\pi}{2} \right]$
$y = \sec^{-1} x$	$x = \sec y$	$(-\infty, -1] \cup [1, \infty)$	$\left[0, \dfrac{\pi}{2} \right) \cup \left(\dfrac{\pi}{2}, \pi \right]$

ii. Points on the terminal sides of angles in the standard position are used to find exact values of the composition of a trigonometric function and a different inverse trigonometric function.

iii. (a) $\sin^{-1}(\sin x) = x$ for $-\dfrac{\pi}{2} \le x \le \dfrac{\pi}{2}$ and

   $\sin(\sin^{-1} x) = x$ for $-1 \le x \le 1$

(b) $\cos^{-1}(\cos x) = x$ for $0 \le x \le \pi$ and

   $\cos(\cos^{-1} x) = x$ for $-1 \le x \le 1$

(c) $\tan^{-1}(\tan x) = x$ for $-\dfrac{\pi}{2} < x < \dfrac{\pi}{2}$ and

   $\tan(\tan^{-1} x) = x$ for $-\infty < x < \infty$

6.2 Trigonometric Equations I

■ **Trigonometric equations I** A trigonometric equation is an equation that contains a trigonometric function with a variable. Values of the variable that satisfy a trigonometric equation are its *solutions*. Solving a trigonometric equation means to find its *solution set*.

Algebraic techniques are used to solve equations that are in linear, quadratic, or factorable form. Sometimes trigonometric identities are used to solve trigonometric equations.

In this section, we solve three types of equations.

1. Equations of the form

$a\sin(x - c) = k$, $a\cos(x - c) = k$, and $a\tan(x - c) = k$

To solve $\sin \theta = -\dfrac{\sqrt{3}}{2}$, we first find all solutions in the interval $[0, 2\pi)$. We know that $\sin\dfrac{\pi}{3} = \dfrac{\sqrt{3}}{2}$ and that $\sin \theta$ is negative in Q III and Q IV. The third and fourth quadrant angles with reference angle $\dfrac{\pi}{3}$ are $\theta = \pi + \dfrac{\pi}{3} = \dfrac{4\pi}{3}$ and

$\theta = 2\pi - \dfrac{\pi}{3} = \dfrac{5\pi}{3}$.

2. Equations that can be solved by factoring and using the zero-product property

To solve $(\cos x + 1)(\tan x - 1) = 0$ for all solutions in the interval $[0, 2\pi)$, set each factor equal to zero; then solve the resulting equations using previous methods.

$$(\cos x + 1)(\tan x - 1) = 0$$

$$\cos x = -1 \quad \text{or} \quad \tan x = 1$$

$$x = \pi \qquad\qquad x = \dfrac{\pi}{4}$$

$$\text{or} \qquad x = \dfrac{5\pi}{4}$$

The solutions are $\dfrac{\pi}{4}, \pi, \dfrac{5\pi}{4}$.

3. Equations that are equivalent to a polynomial equation in one trigonometric function

To solve $\tan^2 x + \sec x - 1 = 0$, first use an identity relating the tangent and secant functions.

$$\tan^2 x + \sec x - 1 = 0$$
$$(\sec^2 x - 1) + \sec x - 1 = 0$$
$$\sec^2 x + \sec x - 2 = 0$$
$$(\sec x + 2)(\sec x - 1) = 0$$
$$\sec x + 2 = 0 \quad \text{or} \quad \sec x - 1 = 0$$
$$\sec x = -2 \quad \text{or} \quad \sec x = 1$$
$$x = \frac{2\pi}{3} \qquad\qquad x = 0$$
$$\text{or} \quad x = \frac{4\pi}{3}$$

The solutions are $0, \dfrac{2\pi}{3}, \dfrac{4\pi}{3}$.

6.3 Trigonometric Equations II

■ In this section, we solve trigonometric equations involving multiple angles. We use sum-to-product and other identities to solve trigonometric equations, including those containing inverse trigonometric functions.

To solve the equation $7 \tan 2\theta = 7$ for $0° \le \theta \le 360°$, we first solve for $\tan 2\theta$.

$$7 \tan 2\theta = 7$$
$$\tan 2\theta = 1$$

We know that $\tan x = 1$ for the acute angle $x = 45°$. The period of the tangent function is $\pi = 180°$; so replacing x with 2θ, all solutions of the equation $\tan 2\theta = 1$ are given by $2\theta = 45° + 180°(n)$, n any integer. Dividing by 2 gives $\theta = 22.5° + 90°(n)$. For $n = 0, 1, 2$, and 3, we get all values between $0°$ and $360°$ that satisfy the equation $7 \tan 2\theta = 7$. They are $22.5°, 112.5°, 202.5°, 292.5°$.

To solve the equation $\sin x + \cos x = 1$ over the interval $[0, 2\pi)$, begin by squaring both sides.

$$(\sin x + \cos x)^2 = 1$$
$$\sin^2 x + 2 \sin x \cos x + \cos^2 x = 1$$
$$(\sin^2 x + \cos^2 x) + 2 \sin x \cos x = 1$$
$$1 + 2 \sin x \cos x = 1$$
$$2 \sin x \cos x = 0$$
$$\sin x \cos x = 0$$
$$\sin x = 0 \quad \text{or} \quad \cos x = 0$$

So $x = 0, \pi, \dfrac{\pi}{2}$, or $\dfrac{3\pi}{2}$.

Because we squared both sides of the original equation, we must check for extraneous solutions. We find that the values $x = \pi$ and $x = \dfrac{3\pi}{2}$ are extraneous.

The solution set is $\left\{ 0, \dfrac{\pi}{2} \right\}$.

To solve $\sin^{-1} x - \cos^{-1} x = -\dfrac{\pi}{4}$, we let

$u = \sin^{-1} x$ and $v = \cos^{-1} x$.
Then $\sin u = x$ and $\cos v = x$.
Construct figures for acute angles u and v as shown next.

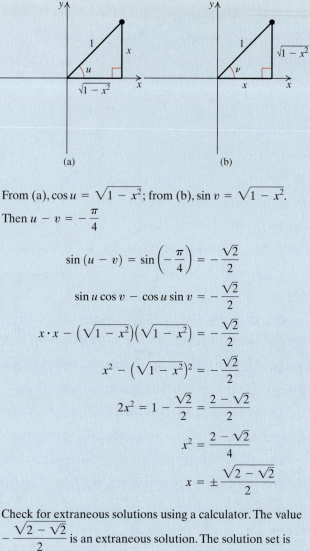

(a)   (b)

From (a), $\cos u = \sqrt{1 - x^2}$; from (b), $\sin v = \sqrt{1 - x^2}$.
Then $u - v = -\dfrac{\pi}{4}$

$$\sin (u - v) = \sin\left(-\frac{\pi}{4}\right) = -\frac{\sqrt{2}}{2}$$

$$\sin u \cos v - \cos u \sin v = -\frac{\sqrt{2}}{2}$$

$$x \cdot x - \left(\sqrt{1 - x^2}\right)\left(\sqrt{1 - x^2}\right) = -\frac{\sqrt{2}}{2}$$

$$x^2 - \left(\sqrt{1 - x^2}\right)^2 = -\frac{\sqrt{2}}{2}$$

$$2x^2 = 1 - \frac{\sqrt{2}}{2} = \frac{2 - \sqrt{2}}{2}$$

$$x^2 = \frac{2 - \sqrt{2}}{4}$$

$$x = \pm\frac{\sqrt{2 - \sqrt{2}}}{2}$$

Check for extraneous solutions using a calculator. The value
$-\dfrac{\sqrt{2 - \sqrt{2}}}{2}$ is an extraneous solution. The solution set is
$\left\{\dfrac{\sqrt{2 - \sqrt{2}}}{2}\right\}.$

REVIEW EXERCISES

Basic Skills and Concepts

In Exercises 1–16, find the exact value of y or state that y is undefined.

1. $y = \sin^{-1}\dfrac{\sqrt{2}}{2}$

2. $y = \cos^{-1} 1$

3. $y = \sin^{-1} -\pi$

4. $y = \cos^{-1}\dfrac{\pi}{2}$

5. $y = \cot^{-1}\left(\dfrac{\sqrt{3}}{3}\right)$

6. $y = \cot^{-1} 0$

7. $y = \sec^{-1} (2)$

8. $y = \sec^{-1} -\sqrt{2}$

9. $y = \cos^{-1}\left(\cos\dfrac{5\pi}{8}\right)$

10. $y = \sin^{-1}\left(\sin\dfrac{7\pi}{6}\right)$

11. $y = \tan^{-1}\left[\tan\left(-\dfrac{2\pi}{3}\right)\right]$

12. $y = \sin\left(\cos^{-1}\dfrac{1}{2}\right)$

13. $y = \cos\left(\sin^{-1}\dfrac{\sqrt{2}}{2}\right)$

14. $y = \cos\left(\tan^{-1}\dfrac{3}{4}\right)$

15. $y = \tan\left[\cos^{-1}\left(\dfrac{1}{2}\right)\right]$

16. $y = \tan\left[\sin^{-1}\left(-\dfrac{\sqrt{3}}{2}\right)\right]$

In Exercises 17–20, use a calculator to find each value of *y* in degrees rounded to two decimal places.

17. $y = \cos^{-1}(-0.43)$ 18. $y = \cos^{-1}(-0.81)$

19. $y = \sec^{-1}(2.7)$ 20. $y = \csc^{-1}(6.3)$

In Exercises 21–24, find all solutions of each equation. Express the solutions in radians.

21. $\cos x = -1$ 22. $\sin x = -\dfrac{\sqrt{2}}{2}$

23. $\tan x = 0$ 24. $\cot x = -\sqrt{3}$

In Exercises 25–30, find all solutions of each equation. Express the solutions in degrees.

25. $\tan x = \sqrt{3}$ 26. $\cot x = \sqrt{3}$

27. $\sin x = -1$ 28. $\sec x = 2$

29. $\sqrt{12}\sec x - 4 = 0$ 30. $\sqrt{12}\csc x + 4 = 0$

In Exercises 31–40, find all solutions of each equation in the interval $[0, 2\pi)$.

31. $\sin\left(x + \dfrac{\pi}{4}\right) = \dfrac{1}{2}$ 32. $2\cos\left(x - \dfrac{\pi}{4}\right) + 1 = 0$

33. $\sqrt{3}\cot\left(x - \dfrac{\pi}{6}\right) - 1 = 0$ 34. $\tan\left(x + \dfrac{\pi}{6}\right) + 1 = 0$

35. $\sin 2x = \dfrac{1}{2}$ 36. $\sec 2x = \dfrac{1}{2}$

37. $\tan 3x = -\dfrac{\sqrt{3}}{3}$ 38. $\cos 3x = -\dfrac{1}{2}$

39. $\sin\dfrac{x}{2} = \dfrac{\sqrt{3}}{2}$ 40. $\cos\dfrac{x}{2} = -\dfrac{1}{2}$

In Exercises 41–46, find all solutions of each equation in the interval $[0, 2\pi)$. Use a graphing calculator to verify your solutions.

41. $2\cos^2 x - 1 = 0$ 42. $3\tan^2 x - 1 = 0$

43. $2\cos^2 x - \cos x - 1 = 0$

44. $2\sin^2 x - 5\sin x - 3 = 0$

45. $2\sin 3x - 1 = 0$

46. $2\cos(2x - 1) - 1 = 0$

In Exercises 47–52, solve each equation for θ in the interval $(0°, 360°)$. If necessary, write the answers to the nearest tenth of a degree. Use a graphing calculator to verify your solutions.

47. $3\sin\theta - 1 = 0$

48. $4\cos\theta + 1 = 0$

49. $2\sqrt{3}\cos 2\theta - 3 = 0$

50. $(1 - 2\sin 2\theta)(\sqrt{3} + 2\cos 2\theta) = 0$

51. $(\sqrt{3}\tan\theta + 1)(2\cos\theta + 1) = 0$

52. $\sqrt{3}\cos\theta = \sin\theta + 1$

Applying the Concepts

53. A searchlight beam from a Coast Guard boat shines on a lake at an angle θ to the surface of the water. Viewed by a swimmer under water, the beam appears to make an angle α with surface of the water, as shown in the figure. Under these circumstances, $\cos\theta = \dfrac{4}{3}\cos\alpha$. Find α assuming that $\cos\theta = \dfrac{2}{3}$.

54. The rabbit population of an area is described by $N(t) = 2400 + 500\sin\pi t$, where $N(t)$ gives the number of rabbits in the area after t years. When will the rabbit population first reach 1900?

55. The voltage from an alternating current generator is given by $V(t) = 160\cos 120\pi t$, where t is measured in seconds. Find the time t when the voltage first equals 80.

56. A jeweler wants to make a gold pendant in the shape of an isosceles triangle. Express the area of the pendant in terms of $\dfrac{\theta}{2}$, where θ is the angle included by two sides of equal length x.

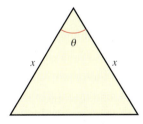

57. Assuming that the area of the pendant in Exercise 56 is 1 square inch, find the angle included between the two sides of equal length when each measures 2 inches.

CHAPTER TEST

In Exercises 1– 5, fill in the blank to form a true statement.

1. If $-1 < x < 0$, then _____ $< \cos^{-1}x <$ _____.

2. If $x > 0$, then _____ $< \tan^{-1}x <$ _____.

3. One value of x for which $\sin^{-1}(\sin x) \ne x$ is _____.

4. If $a > 0$, $\sin x = a$ has _____ solution(s) in the interval $(0, \pi)$.

5. If $a < 0$, $\tan x = a$ has _____ solution(s) in the interval $(0, \pi)$.

In Exercises 6–10, find the exact value.

6. $y = \sin^{-1}\left(-\dfrac{\sqrt{3}}{2}\right)$

7. $y = \tan^{-1}\sqrt{3}$

8. $y = \cos^{-1}\left(\cos\dfrac{4\pi}{3}\right)$

9. $y = \cos\left[\sin^{-1}\left(-\dfrac{1}{5}\right)\right]$

10. $\sin\left(\tan^{-1}\sqrt{3} + \sin^{-1}\dfrac{1}{3}\right)$

In Exercises 11–13, find all solutions of the given equation.

11. $\tan x = -1$ 12. $2\cos\theta + 1 = 0$ 13. $2\sin\dfrac{x}{2} = -1$

In Exercises 14–19, find all solutions in the interval $[0, 2\pi)$.

14. $\cos x + 1 = \sin x$

15. $(\tan x - 1)(\sqrt{3}\tan x + 1) = 0$

16. $\sin^{-1}x + \cos^{-1}x = \dfrac{\pi}{4}$

17. $\sin 2x - \cos x = 0$

18. $\tan 3x = \sqrt{3}$

19. $\cos\dfrac{x}{3} = \dfrac{\sqrt{2}}{2}$

20. A simple harmonic motion is described by the equation $x = 8\sin\left(\dfrac{\pi}{3}t\right)$, where x is the displacement in feet and t is time in seconds. Find all positive values of t for which the displacement is 4 feet.

Applications of Trigonometric Functions

Applications of trigonometry permeate virtually every field, from architecture and bionics to medicine and physics. In this chapter, we introduce vectors and polar coordinates and investigate the many applications of trigonometry to real-world problems.

The Law of Sines

Before Starting this Section, Review

1. Trigonometric functions (Section 2.1)
2. Inverse functions (Section 6.1)
3. Geometric properties of a triangle (Section 1.2)

Objectives

1 Learn vocabulary and conventions for solving triangles.

2 Derive the Law of Sines.

3 Solve AAS and ASA triangles by using the Law of Sines.

THE GREAT TRIGONOMETRIC SURVEY OF INDIA

Triangulation is the process of finding the coordinates and the distance to a point by using the Law of Sines. Triangulation was used in surveying the Indian subcontinent. The survey, which was called "one of the most stupendous works in the whole history of science," was begun by William Lambton, a British army officer, in 1802. It started in the south of India and extended north to Nepal, a distance of approximately 1600 miles. Lasting several decades and employing thousands of workers, the survey was named the Great Trigonometric Survey (GTS). In 1818, George Everest (1790–1866), a Welsh surveyor and geographer, was appointed assistant to Lambton. Everest, who succeeded Lambton in 1823 and was later promoted as surveyor general of India, completed the GTS. Mount Everest was surveyed and named after Everest by his successor Andrew Waugh. In Example 3, we use the Law of Sines to estimate the height of a mountain. ■

Mount Everest

In 1852, an unsung hero Radhanath Sickdhar managed to *calculate* the height of Peak XV, an icy peak in the Himalayas. The highest mountain in the world—later named Mount Everest—stood at 29,002 feet. Sickdhar's calculations used triangulations as well as the phenomenon called refraction—the bending of light rays by the density of Earth's atmosphere. Like George Everest, Sickdhar may have never seen Mount Everest.

1 Learn vocabulary and conventions for solving triangles.

RECALL

Two triangles are *congruent* if corresponding sides are congruent (equal in length) and corresponding angles are congruent (equal in measure). An *included side* is the side between two angles, and an *included angle* is the angle between two sides.

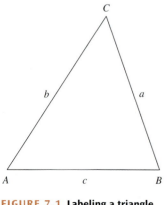

FIGURE 7.1 Labeling a triangle

Solving Oblique Triangles

The process of finding the unknown side lengths and angle measures in a triangle is called *solving a triangle*. In Section 2.2, you learned techniques of solving right triangles. We now discuss triangles that are not necessarily right triangles. A triangle with no right angle is called an **oblique triangle**. From geometry, we know that two triangles with any of the following sets of equal parts are always **congruent**. In other words, the following sets of given parts determine a unique triangle:

ASA: Two angles and the included side.

AAS: Two angles and a nonincluded side.

SAS: Two sides and the included angle.

SSS: All three sides.

Although **SSA** (two sides and a nonincluded angle) does not guarantee a unique triangle, there can be, at most, two triangles with the given parts. On the other hand, **AAA** (or **AA**) guarantees only *similar* triangles, not congruent ones, so there are infinitely many triangles with the same three angle measures.

For any triangle *ABC*, we let each letter such as *A* stand for both the vertex *A* and the measure of the angle at *A*. As usual, the angles of a triangle *ABC* are labeled *A*, *B*, and *C* and the lengths of their opposite sides are labeled, *a*, *b*, and *c*, respectively. See Figure 7.1.

To solve an oblique triangle given at least one side and two other measures, we consider four possible cases:

Case 1. Two angles and a side are known (**AAS** and **ASA** triangles).

Case 2. Two sides and an angle opposite one of the given sides are known (**SSA** triangles).

Case 3.   Two sides and their included angle are known (**SAS** triangles).

Case 4.   All three sides are known (**SSS** triangles).

We use the Law of Sines to analyze triangles in Cases 1 and 2. In Section 7.3, we use the *Law of Cosines* to solve triangles in Cases 3 and 4.

2 Derive the Law of Sines.

The Law of Sines

The Law of Sines states that in a triangle ABC with sides of length a, b, and c,

$$\frac{\sin A}{a} = \frac{\sin B}{b} = \frac{\sin C}{c}.$$

We can derive the Law of Sines by using the right triangle definition of the sine of an acute angle θ:

$$\sin \theta = \frac{\text{opposite}}{\text{hypotenuse}}$$

RECALL

An *altitude* of a triangle is a segment drawn from any vertex of the triangle perpendicular to the opposite side or to an extension of the opposite side.

We begin with an oblique triangle ABC. See Figures 7.2 and 7.3. Draw altitude CD from the vertex C to the side AB (or its extension, as in Figure 7.3). Let h be the length of segment CD.

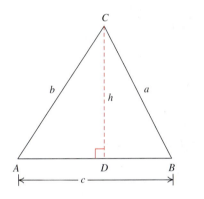

FIGURE 7.2 **Altitude *CD* with acute ∠*B***

In right triangle CDA,

$$\frac{h}{b} = \sin A \quad \text{or}$$

$$h = b \sin A.$$

In right triangle CDB,

$$\frac{h}{a} = \sin B \quad \text{or}$$

$$h = a \sin B.$$

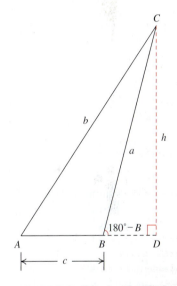

FIGURE 7.3 **Altitude *CD* with obtuse ∠*B***

In right triangle CDA,

$$\frac{h}{b} = \sin A \quad \text{or}$$

$$h = b \sin A.$$

In right triangle CDB,

$$\frac{h}{a} = \sin(180° - B) = \sin B \quad \text{or}$$

$$h = a \sin B.$$

Because in each figure $h = b \sin A$ and $h = a \sin B$, we have

$$b \sin A = a \sin B$$

$$\frac{b \sin A}{ab} = \frac{a \sin B}{ab} \qquad \text{Divide both sides by } ab.$$

$$\frac{\sin A}{a} = \frac{\sin B}{b} \qquad \text{Simplify.}$$

Similarly, by drawing altitudes from the other two vertices, we can show that

$$\frac{\sin B}{b} = \frac{\sin C}{c} \quad \text{and} \quad \frac{\sin C}{c} = \frac{\sin A}{a}.$$

We have proved the Law of Sines.

THE LAW OF SINES

In any triangle ABC with sides of length a, b, and c,

$$\frac{\sin A}{a} = \frac{\sin B}{b}, \quad \frac{\sin B}{b} = \frac{\sin C}{c}, \quad \text{and} \quad \frac{\sin C}{c} = \frac{\sin A}{a}.$$

We can rewrite these relations in compact notation.

$$\frac{\sin A}{a} = \frac{\sin B}{b} = \frac{\sin C}{c}, \quad \text{or equivalently,} \quad \frac{a}{\sin A} = \frac{b}{\sin B} = \frac{c}{\sin C}$$

---

3 | Solve AAS and ASA triangles by using the Law of Sines.

Solving AAS and ASA Triangles

We use the law of sines to solve AAS and ASA triangles of Case 1, where two angles and a side are given. Note that if two angles of a triangle are given, then you also know the third angle (because the sum of the angles of a triangle is 180°). So in Case 1, all three angles and one side of a triangle are known.

FINDING THE SOLUTION: A PROCEDURE

EXAMPLE 1   Solving the AAS and ASA Triangles

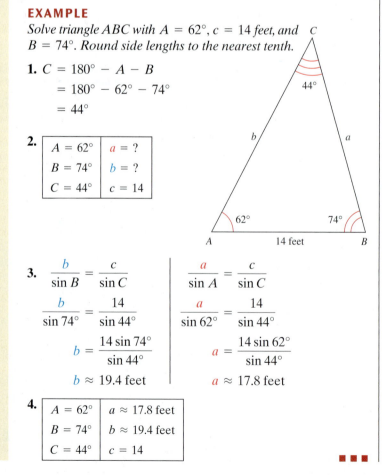

OBJECTIVE

To solve a triangle given two angles and a side.

EXAMPLE

Solve triangle ABC with $A = 62°$, $c = 14$ feet, and $B = 74°$. Round side lengths to the nearest tenth.

Step 1   Find the third angle. Find the measure of the third angle by subtracting the measures of the known angles from 180°.

1. $C = 180° - A - B$
    $= 180° - 62° - 74°$
    $= 44°$

Step 2   Make a chart. Make a chart of the six parts of the triangle, including the known and the unknown parts. Sketch the triangle.

2.

$A = 62°$	$a = ?$
$B = 74°$	$b = ?$
$C = 44°$	$c = 14$

Step 3   Apply the Law of Sines. Select two ratios from the Law of Sines in which three of the four quantities are known. Solve for the fourth quantity. Use the form of the Law of Sines in which the unknown quantity is in the numerator.

3.
$$\frac{b}{\sin B} = \frac{c}{\sin C} \qquad\qquad \frac{a}{\sin A} = \frac{c}{\sin C}$$

$$\frac{b}{\sin 74°} = \frac{14}{\sin 44°} \qquad\qquad \frac{a}{\sin 62°} = \frac{14}{\sin 44°}$$

$$b = \frac{14 \sin 74°}{\sin 44°} \qquad\qquad a = \frac{14 \sin 62°}{\sin 44°}$$

$$b \approx 19.4 \text{ feet} \qquad\qquad a \approx 17.8 \text{ feet}$$

Step 4   Show the solution. Show the solution by completing the chart.

4.

$A = 62°$	$a \approx 17.8$ feet
$B = 74°$	$b \approx 19.4$ feet
$C = 44°$	$c = 14$

■ ■ ■

Practice Problem 1 Solve triangle ABC with $C = 75°$, $B = 65°$, and $a = 12$ m. Round side lengths to the nearest tenth.   ■

EXAMPLE 2   **Using the Law of Sines to Solve an AAS Triangle**

Solve triangle ABC with $A = 46°$, $B = 100°$, and $a = 10$ meters. Round side lengths to the nearest tenth.

SOLUTION

Step 1 Find the third angle. $C = 180° - A - B$

$\quad\quad\quad\quad\quad\quad\quad\quad\quad\quad = 180 - 46° - 100°$ Replace A with $46°$ and B with $100°$.

$\quad\quad\quad\quad\quad\quad\quad\quad\quad\quad = 34°$ Simplify.

Step 2 Make a chart.

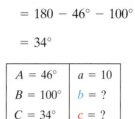

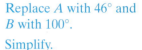

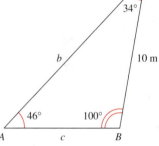

$A = 46°$	$a = 10$
$B = 100°$	$b = ?$
$C = 34°$	$c = ?$

STUDY TIP

When using your calculator to solve triangles, make sure it is in Degree mode.

Step 3 Apply the Law of Sines.

$$\frac{b}{\sin B} = \frac{a}{\sin A} \quad\quad \frac{c}{\sin C} = \frac{a}{\sin A}$$ The Law of Sines

$$b = \frac{a \sin B}{\sin A} \quad\quad\quad c = \frac{a \sin C}{\sin A}$$ Solve for the unknown length.

$$b = \frac{10 \sin 100°}{\sin 46°} \quad\quad c = \frac{10 \sin 34°}{\sin 46°}$$ Substitute known values.

$$b \approx 13.7 \text{ meters} \quad\quad c \approx 7.8 \text{ meters}$$ Use a calculator.

Step 4 Show the solution.

$A = 46°$	$a = 10$ meters
$B = 100°$	$b \approx 13.7$ meters
$C = 34°$	$c \approx 7.8$ meters

■ ■ ■

Practice Problem 2 Solve triangle ABC with $A = 70°$, $B = 65°$, and $a = 16$ inches. Round side lengths to the nearest tenth.   ■

EXAMPLE 3   **Height of a Mountain**

From a point on a level plain at the foot of a mountain, a surveyor finds the angle of elevation of the peak of the mountain to be 20°. She walks 3465 meters closer (on a direct line between the first point and the base of the mountain) and finds the angle of elevation to be 23°. Estimate the height of the mountain to the nearest meter.

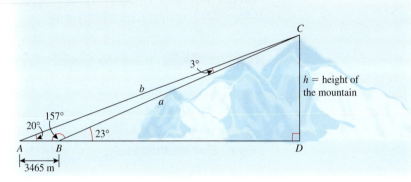

FIGURE 7.4 Height of a mountain

SOLUTION

In Figure 7.4, consider triangle ABC.

$$\angle ABC = 180° - 23° = 157° \qquad \textcolor{blue}{\angle ABC + \angle CBD = 180°}$$

In triangle ABC, we have $\angle C = \angle ACB$ and $A + B + C = 180°$. So

$$C = 180° - 20° - 157° = 3° \qquad \textcolor{blue}{\text{Substitute values and solve for } C.}$$

Apply the Law of Sines:

$$\frac{a}{\sin A} = \frac{c}{\sin C}$$

$$\frac{a}{\sin 20°} = \frac{3465}{\sin 3°} \qquad \textcolor{blue}{\text{Substitute values.}}$$

$$a = \frac{3465 \sin 20°}{\sin 3°} \approx 22{,}644 \text{ meters} \qquad \textcolor{blue}{\text{Use a calculator.}}$$

Now in triangle BCD, $\sin 23° = \dfrac{h}{a}$. So $h = a \sin 23° \approx 22{,}644 \sin 23° \approx 8848$ meters.

The mountain is approximately 8848 meters high. ■ ■ ■

Practice Problem 3 From a point on a level plain at the foot of a mountain, the angle of elevation of the peak is 40°. If you move 2500 feet farther (on a direct line extending from the first point and the base of the mountain), the angle of elevation of the peak is 35°. How high above the plain is the peak? Round your answer to the nearest foot. ■

EXAMPLE 4   **Using Bearings in Navigation**

A ship sailing due west at 20 miles per hour records the bearing of an oil rig at N 55.4° W. An hour and a half later the bearing of the same rig is N 66.8° E.

a. How far is the ship from the oil rig the second time?

b. How close did the ship pass to the oil rig?

SOLUTION

a. In an hour and a half, the ship travels $(1.5)(20) = 30$ miles due west. The oil rig (C), the starting point for the ship (A), and the position of the ship after an hour and a half (B) form the vertices of the triangle ABC shown in Figure 7.5.

Then $A = 90° - 55.4° = 34.6°$ and $B = 90° - 66.8° = 23.2°$. Therefore, $C = 180° - 34.6° - 23.2° = 122.2°$.

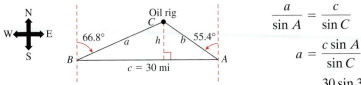

FIGURE 7.5 Navigation

$$\frac{a}{\sin A} = \frac{c}{\sin C}$$ The Law of Sines

$$a = \frac{c \sin A}{\sin C}$$ Multiply both sides by $\sin A$.

$$= \frac{30 \sin 34.6°}{\sin 122.2°} \approx 20 \text{ miles}$$ Substitute values and use a calculator.

The ship is approximately 20 miles from the oil rig when the second bearing is taken.

b. The shortest distance between the ship and the oil rig is the length of the segment h in triangle ABC.

$$\sin B = \frac{h}{a}$$ Right-triangle definition of the sine

$$h = a \sin B$$ Multiply both sides by a.

$$h \approx 20 \sin 23.2°$$ Substitute values.

$$\approx 7.9$$ Use a calculator.

The ship passes within 7.9 miles of the oil rig.   ■ ■ ■

Practice Problem 4 Rework Example 4 assuming that the second bearing is taken after two hours and is N 60.4° E and the ship is traveling due west at 25 miles per hour.   ■

SECTION 7.1 ■ Exercises

A EXERCISES Basic Skills and Concepts

1. If you know two angles of a triangle, you can determine the third angle because the sum of all three angles is _____ degrees.

2. The Law of Sines states that if a, b, and c are the sides opposite angles A, B, and C, then $\dfrac{a}{\sin A}$ = _____ = _____.

3. When solving for an angle of a triangle, we use the alternate form of the Law of Sines: $\dfrac{\sin A}{a}$ = _____ = _____.

4. If you are given any two angles and one side, exactly _____ triangle is possible.

5. *True or False* The Law of Sines allows you to solve a triangle if you know two sides and the angle between them.

6. *True or False* A triangle is uniquely determined if all three angles are given.

In Exercises 7–26, solve each triangle ABC. Round each answer to the nearest tenth.

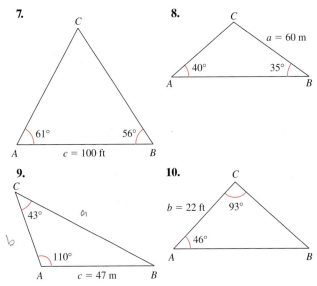

7.

8.

9.

10.

11.

A = ?	a = 100
B = 60°	b = ?
C = 45°	c = ?

12.

A = ?	a = 80
B = 45°	b = ?
C = 30°	c = ?

13.

A = 45°	a = ?
B = ?	b = 50
C = 120°	c = ?

14.

A = 130°	a = ?
B = 20°	b = ?
C = ?	c = 25

15. $A = 40°, B = 35°, a = 100$ meters

16. $A = 80°, B = 20°, a = 100$ meters

17. $A = 46°, C = 55°, a = 75$ centimeters

18. $A = 35°, C = 98°, a = 75$ centimeters

19. $A = 35°, C = 47°, c = 60$ feet

20. $A = 44°, C = 76°, c = 40$ feet

21. $B = 43°, C = 67°, b = 40$ inches

22. $B = 95°, C = 35°, b = 100$ inches

23. $B = 110°, C = 46°, c = 23.5$ feet

24. $B = 67°, C = 63°, c = 16.8$ feet

25. $A = 35.7°, B = 45.8°, c = 30$ meters

26. $A = 64.5°, B = 54.3°, c = 40$ meters

B EXERCISES Applying the Concepts

27. **Finding distance.** Angela wants to find the distance from point A to her friend Carmen's house at point C on the other side of the river. She knows that the distance from A to Betty's house at B is 540 feet. (See the figure.) The measurement of angles A and B are 57° and 46°, respectively. Calculate the distance from A to C. Round to the nearest foot.

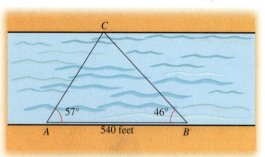

28. **Finding distance.** In Exercise 27, find the width of the river assuming that the houses are on the (very straight) banks of the river.

29. **Target.** A laser beam with an angle of elevation of 42° is reflected by a target and is received 1200 yards from the point of origin. Assume that the trajectory of the beam forms (approximately) an isosceles triangle.
  a. Find the total distance the beam travels. Round to the nearest yard.

b. What is the height of the target? Round to the nearest yard.

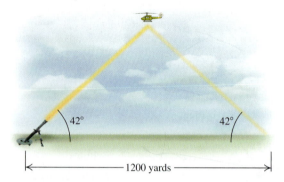

30. **Height of a flagpole.** Two surveyors stand 200 feet apart with a flagpole between them. Suppose the "transit" at each location is 5 feet high. The transit measures the angles of elevation of the top of the flagpole at the two locations to be 30° and 25°, respectively. Find the height of the flagpole. Round to the nearest foot.

31. **Radio beacon.** A ship sailing due east at the rate of 16 miles per hour records the bearing of a radio beacon at N 36.5° E. Two hours later the bearing of the same beacon is N 55.7° W. Round each answer to the nearest tenth of a mile.
  a. How far is the ship from the beacon the second time?
  b. How close to the beacon did the ship pass?

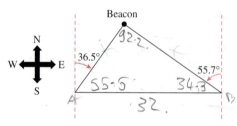

32. **Lighthouse.** A boat sailing due north at the rate of 14 miles per hour records the bearing of a lighthouse as N 8.4° E. Two hours later the bearing of the same lighthouse is N 30.9° E. Round each answer to the nearest tenth of a mile.
  a. How far is the ship from the lighthouse the second time?
  b. If the boat follows the same course and speed, how close to the lighthouse will it approach?

33. **Geostationary satellite.** A camel rider was traveling due west at night in the desert. At midnight, his angle of elevation to a satellite was 89°. After traveling west for 20 miles, his angle of elevation to the satellite was 89.05°. The satellite is at a constant height above the ground. How high is the satellite? Round your answer to the nearest mile.

34. **Height of a tower.** A flagpole 20 feet tall is placed on top of a tower. At a point on the ground, a surveyor measures the angle of elevation of the bottom of the flag pole to be 69.6° and that of the top of the flag pole to be 70.9°. What is the height of the tower to the nearest foot?

35. **Height of a building.** A vertical building stands on a street that slopes downward at an angle of 8°. At a point 120 feet from the base of the building, the angle of elevation of the top of the building is 59°. Find the height of the building to the nearest foot.

36. Height of a tree. A tree on a sloping hill casts a shadow 130 feet straight down the hill. The hill slopes downward at an angle of 12°, and the angle of elevation of the sun is 26°. Find the height of the tree to the nearest foot.

37. Distance to the airplane. The angles of elevation of an approaching enemy airplane from two antiaircraft guns are 78.25° and 53.4°. The guns are 900 feet apart, and the airplane is in a vertical plane with these guns. How far is the airplane from the nearest gun to the nearest foot?

38. Distance to the fire. Two lookout towers A and B are 5.2 miles apart with A due west of B. A column of smoke is sighted from A with a bearing of N 75.2° E and from B with a bearing of N 53.4° E. How far is the fire from B to the nearest foot?

C EXERCISES Beyond the Basics

39. Suppose CD bisects angle C of triangle ABC. Show that $\dfrac{AD}{DB} = \dfrac{AC}{CB}$. (See the figure.)

[*Hint:* Apply the Law of Sines to triangles ACD and DCB.]

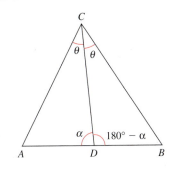

40. A flagpole 15 feet high stands on a building 75 feet high. To an observer at a height of 90 feet, the building and the flagpole intercept equal angles. Find the distance of the observer from the top of the flagpole. [*Hint:* Use Exercise 39.]

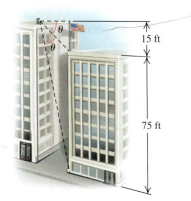

41. A side of a parallelogram is 60 inches long and makes angles of 28° and 42° with the two diagonals. What are the lengths of the diagonals? Round each answer to the nearest tenth of an inch.

42. In a triangle ABC, prove that $(b - c) \sin A + (c - a) \sin B + (a - b) \sin C = 0$.

43. In a triangle ABC, prove that $a \sin (B - C) + b \sin (C - A) + c \sin (A - B) = 0$.
[*Hint:* $\sin (B + C) \sin (B - C) = \frac{1}{2}(\cos 2C - \cos 2B)$]

44. Mollweide's formula. In a triangle ABC, prove that

$$\frac{b - c}{a} = \frac{\sin \dfrac{B - C}{2}}{\cos \dfrac{A}{2}}.$$

[*Hint:* Let $\dfrac{a}{\sin A} = \dfrac{b}{\sin B} = \dfrac{c}{\sin C} = k$. Write an expression for $\dfrac{b - c}{a}$ in terms of sines and then use sum-to-product and half-angle formulas. Note that because the formula contains all six parts of a triangle, it can be used as a check for the solutions of a triangle.]

45. Newton's formula. In a triangle ABC, prove that

$$\frac{b + c}{a} = \frac{\cos \dfrac{B - C}{2}}{\sin \dfrac{A}{2}}.$$

46. Law of Tangents. In a triangle ABC, prove that

$$\tan \frac{B - C}{2} = \frac{b - c}{b + c} \cot \frac{A}{2}.$$

47. Two sides of a triangle are $\sqrt{3} + 1$ feet and $\sqrt{3} - 1$ feet, and the measure of the angle between these sides is 60°. Use the Law of Tangents (Exercise 46) to find the measure of the difference of the remaining angles.

Critical Thinking

In Exercises 48 and 49, give the most specific description you can for a triangle satisfying the specified conditions. Explain your reasoning.

48. In a triangle ABC, $a \sin A = b \sin B$.

49. In a triangle ABC, $a \cos A = b \cos B$.

50. Use the Law of Sines to show that any isosceles triangle has two equal angles.

51. Use the Law of Sines to show that any triangle with two equal angles is isosceles.

The Law of Sines: Ambiguous Case

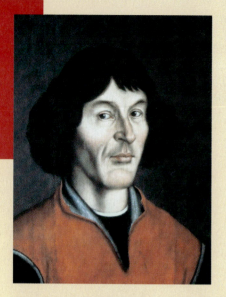

Before Starting this Section, Review	Objectives
1. The Law of Sines (Section 7.1)	**1** Discuss the ambiguous case.
2. Trigonometric functions (Section 2.1)	**2** Solve for possible SSA triangles.
	3 Solve applied problems involving SSA triangles.

PLANETARY MOTION

For a long time, people believed that Earth was the center of the universe. Polish astronomer Nicolaus Copernicus (1473–1543) changed that belief when he introduced a model of the solar system that was centered around the sun. He claimed that all of the planets (Greek for *wanderers*), including Earth, moved in orbits around the sun. Astronomers have since shown that the planets travel in elliptical (nearly circular) orbits. Table 7.1 shows the average distance of each planet to the sun in millions of miles.

Copernicus (1473-1543)

TABLE 7.1 Distance of a planet from the sun in millions of miles

Planet	Mercury	Venus	Earth	Mars	Jupiter	Saturn	Uranus	Neptune
Distance	36	67.24	93	128.42	483.77	890.71	1.79×10^3	2.8×10^3

In Exercises 43 and 44, we use the ambiguous case of the Law of Sines to find possible distances between two planets. ■

1 Discuss the ambiguous case.

The Ambiguous Case

If we know two angles and a side of triangle, we obtain a unique triangle. We solved such triangles (AAS and ASA) in Section 7.1.

However, if we know the lengths of two sides and the measure of the angle opposite one of these sides, we can have a result that is (1) not a triangle, (2) one triangle, or (3) two different triangles. For this reason, Case 2 is called the **ambiguous case**.

Suppose we want to draw triangle ABC with given measures of A, a, and b. We draw angle A with a horizontal initial side, and we place the point C on the terminal side of A so that the length of segment AC is b. We need to locate point B on the initial side of A so that the measure of the segment CB is a. See Figure 7.6.

The number of possible triangles depends upon the length h of the altitude from C to the initial side of angle A. Because $\sin A = \dfrac{h}{b}$, we have $h = b \sin A$. Various possibilities for forming triangle ACB are illustrated in Figure 7.7 (where A is an acute angle) and Figure 7.8 (where A is an obtuse angle).

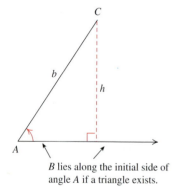

B lies along the initial side of angle A if a triangle exists.

FIGURE 7.6 Need to locate B

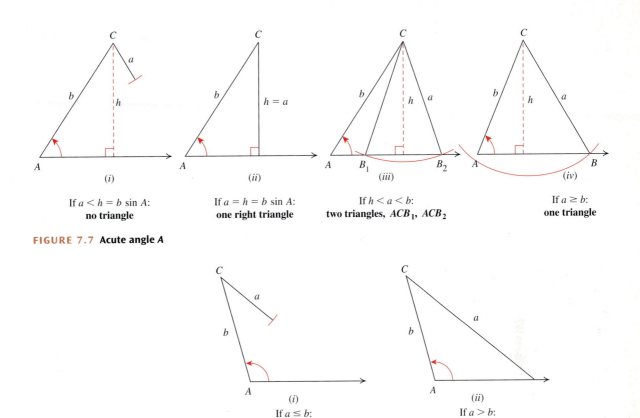

FIGURE 7.7 **Acute angle A**

We summarize these results in Table 7.2.

TABLE 7.2 If *A* is an acute angle

Case	Condition on a	Number of Triangles
1	$a < b \sin A$	None
2	$a = b \sin A$	One right triangle
3	$b \sin A < a < b$	Two
4	$a \geq b$	One

The situation is considerably simpler if the angle *A* is obtuse. The possibilities are illustrated in Figure 7.8 and summarized in Table 7.3.

TABLE 7.3 If *A* is an obtuse angle

Case	Condition on a	Number of Triangles
1	$a \leq b$	None
2	$a > b$	One

EXAMPLE 1   Finding the Number of Triangles

How many triangles can be drawn with $A = 42°$, $b = 2.4$, and $a = 2.1$?

SOLUTION

$A = 42°$ is an acute angle, and $a = 2.1 < 2.4 = b$.

We calculate

$$b \sin A = 2.4 \sin (42°)$$
$$\approx 1.6 \qquad \text{Use a calculator.}$$

We have $b \sin A < a < b$. So by Case 3 of Table 7.2, two triangles can be drawn with the given measurements. ■ ■ ■

Practice Problem 1 How many triangles can be drawn with $A = 35°, b = 6.5$, and $a = 3.5$? ■

EXAMPLE 2 Finding the Number of Triangles

How many triangles can be drawn with $A = 98°, b = 4.8$, and $a = 5.1$?

SOLUTION

$A = 98°$ is an obtuse angle, and $a = 5.1 > 4.8 = b$. So by Case 2 of Table 7.3, exactly one triangle can be drawn with the given measurements. ■ ■ ■

Practice Problem 2 How many triangles can be drawn with $A = 105°, b = 12.5$, and $a = 11.2$? ■

2 Solve for possible SSA triangles.

Solve Possible SSA Triangles

It is not necessary to memorize all of the cases involved in solving SSA triangles. Instead, we use the following procedure.

FINDING THE SOLUTION: A PROCEDURE

EXAMPLE 3 Solving the SSA Triangles

OBJECTIVE
Solve a triangle if two sides and an angle opposite one of them is given.

EXAMPLE
Solve triangle ABC with $B = 32°, b = 100$ feet, and $c = 150$ feet. Round each answer to the nearest tenth.

Step 1 Make a chart of the six parts, the known and unknown parts.

1.
$A = ?$	$a = ?$
$B = 32°$	$b = 100$
$C = ?$	$c = 150$

Three quantities are known.

Step 2 Apply the Law of Sines to the two ratios in which three of the four quantities are known. Solve for the sine of the angle opposite the other known side. Use the form of the Law of Sines in which the unknown quantity is in the numerator.

2. $\dfrac{\sin C}{c} = \dfrac{\sin B}{b}$ The Law of Sines

$\sin C = \dfrac{c \sin B}{b}$ Multiply both sides by c.

$= \dfrac{150 \sin 32°}{100}$ Substitute values.

$\sin C \approx 0.7949$ Use a calculator.

Step 3 If the sine of the angle, say θ, in Step 2 is greater than 1, there is no triangle with the given measurements. If $\sin \theta$ is between 0 and 1, go to Step 4.

3. Go to Step 4.

Step 4 Let $\sin \theta$ be x, with $0 < x \leq 1$. If $x \neq 1$, then θ has two possible values:
- $\theta_1 = \sin^{-1} x$ with $0 < \theta_1 < 90°$
- $\theta_2 = 180° - \theta_1$

4. Two possible values of C:

$$C_1 \approx \sin^{-1} (0.7949) \approx 52.6°$$
$$C_2 \approx 180° - 52.6° = 127.4°$$

Step 5 If $x \neq 1$, with (known angle) $+ \theta_1 < 180°$ and (known angle) $+ \theta_2 < 180°$, then there are two triangles. Otherwise, there is only one triangle, and if $x = 1$, it is a right triangle.

5. $B + C_1 = 32° + 52.6° = 84.6° < 180°$, and $B + C_2 = 32° + 127.4° = 159.4° < 180°$.
   We have two triangles with the given measurements.

Step 6 Find the third angle of the triangle(s).

6. $\angle BAC_1 \approx 180° - 32° - 52.6° = 95.4°$
   $\angle BAC_2 \approx 180° - 32° - 127.4° = 20.6°$

Step 7 Use the Law of Sines to find the remaining side(s).

7.
$$\frac{a_1}{\sin \angle BAC_1} = \frac{b}{\sin B} \qquad \frac{a_2}{\sin \angle BAC_2} = \frac{b}{\sin B}$$

$$a_1 = \frac{b \sin \angle BAC_1}{\sin B} \qquad a_2 = \frac{b \sin \angle BAC_2}{\sin B}$$

$$a_1 = \frac{100 \sin 95.4°}{\sin 32°} \qquad a_2 = \frac{100 \sin 20.6°}{\sin 32°}$$

$$a_1 \approx 187.9 \text{ feet} \qquad a_2 \approx 66.4 \text{ feet}$$

Step 8 Show solution(s).

8.

△BAC₁				△BAC₂		
$\angle BAC_1 \approx 95.4°$	$a_1 \approx 187.9$			$\angle BAC_2 \approx 20.6°$	$a_2 \approx 66.4$	
$B = 32°$	$b = 100$			$B = 32°$	$b = 100$	
$C_1 \approx 52.6°$	$c = 150$			$C_2 \approx 127.4°$	$c = 150$	

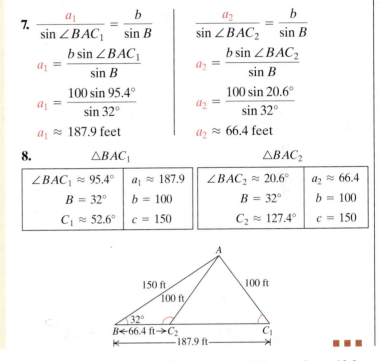

Practice Problem 3 Solve triangle ABC with $C = 35°$, $b = 15$ feet, and $c = 12$ feet. Round each answer to the nearest tenth. ■

EXAMPLE 4 **Solving an SSA Triangle (No Solution)**

Solve triangle ABC with $A = 50°$, $a = 8$ inches, and $b = 15$ inches.

SOLUTION

Step 1 **Make a chart.**

$A = 50°$	$a = 8$
$B = ?$	$b = 15$
$C = ?$	$c = ?$

Three quantities are known.

Step 2 **Apply the Law of Sines.**

$$\frac{\sin B}{b} = \frac{\sin A}{a} \qquad \text{The Law of Sines}$$

$$\sin B = \frac{b \sin A}{a} \qquad \text{Multiply both sides by } b.$$

$$\sin B = \frac{15 \sin 50°}{8} \qquad \text{Substitute values.}$$

$$\sin B \approx 1.44 \qquad \text{Use a calculator.}$$

Step 3   Because $\sin B \approx 1.44 > 1$, we conclude that no triangle has the given measures. ■■■

Practice Problem 4   Solve triangle ABC with $A = 65°, a = 16$ meters, and $b = 30$ meters. ■

EXAMPLE 5   **Solving an SSA Triangle (One Solution)**

Solve triangle ABC with $C = 40°, c = 20$ meters, and $a = 15$ meters. Round each answer to the nearest tenth.

SOLUTION

Step 1   **Make a chart.**

$A = ?$	$a = 15$	←
$B = ?$	$b = ?$	Three quantities are known.
$C = 40°$	$c = 20$	←

Step 2   **Apply the Law of Sines.**

$$\frac{\sin A}{a} = \frac{\sin C}{c} \qquad \text{The Law of Sines}$$

$$\sin A = \frac{a \sin C}{c} \qquad \text{Multiply both sides by } a.$$

$$= \frac{15 \sin 40°}{20} \qquad \text{Substitute values.}$$

$$\sin A \approx 0.4821 \qquad \text{Use a calculator.}$$

Step 3 $A = \sin^{-1}(0.4821) \approx 28.8°$. Two possible values of A are $A_1 \approx 28.8°$ and $A_2 \approx 180° - 28.8° = 151.2°$.

Step 4   Because $C + A_2 = 40° + 151.2° = 191.2° > 180°$, there is no triangle with vertex A_2. Thus, only one triangle has measure of angle $A_1 \approx 28.8°$.

Step 5   The third angle at B has measure $\approx 180° - 40° - 28.8° = 111.2°$.

Step 6   **Find the remaining side length.**

$$\frac{b}{\sin B} = \frac{c}{\sin C} \qquad \text{The Law of Sines}$$

$$b = \frac{c \sin B}{\sin C} \qquad \text{Multiply both sides by } \sin B.$$

$$= \frac{20 \sin 111.2°}{\sin 40°} \qquad \text{Substitute values.}$$

$$b \approx 29.0 \text{ m} \qquad \text{Use a calculator.}$$

Step 7   **Show the solution.** (See Figure 7.9.)

$A_1 \approx 28.8°$	$a = 15$ meters
$B \approx 111.2°$	$b \approx 29.0$ meters
$C = 40°$	$c = 20$ meters

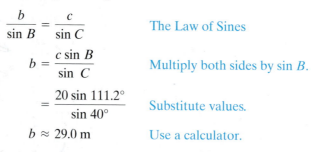

FIGURE 7.9

Practice Problem 5   Solve triangle ABC with $C = 60°, c = 50$ feet, and $a = 30$ feet. ■

SECTION 7.2 ■ Exercises

A EXERCISES Basic Skills and Concepts

1. For the given data a, A, and b, there may be no triangle formed, there may be _____ triangle, or there may be _____ triangles.

2. Given a, b, and A, there are two possible triangles if $a < b$ and $a >$ _____ .

3. If $a = b \sin A$, there is one possible triangle; it is a _____ triangle.

4. When using the Law of Sines to find an angle θ from the equation $\sin \theta = x$ with $0 < x < 1$, there are two possible values of θ: $\theta_1 = \sin^{-1}x$ with $0 < \theta_1 < 90°$ and $\theta_2 =$ _____ .

5. *True or False* The Law of Sines cannot be used if the data a, b, and A results in no triangle.

6. *True or False* Two triangles ABC and $A'B'C'$ are congruent if
   a. $\angle B = \angle B'$, **b.** $AB = A'B'$, and
   c. $AC = A'C'$.

In Exercises 7–16, determine the number of triangles that can be drawn with the given data.

7. $a = 40, b = 70, A = 30°$

8. $a = 30, b = 25\sqrt{2}, A = 60°$

9. $a = 22, b = 32, A = 42°$

10. $a = 36, b = 38, A = 62°$

11. $b = 15, c = 19, B = 58°$

12. $b = 12, c = 16, B = 32°$

13. $b = 75, c = 85, B = 135°$

14. $a = 50, b = 70, B = 120°$

15. $c = 85, a = 45, C = 150°$

16. $c = 76, a = 73, C = 135°$

In Exercises 17–20, solve each triangle ABC. Round each answer to the nearest tenth.

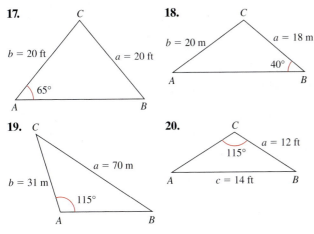

In Exercises 21–40, solve each SSA triangle. Indicate whether the given measurements result in no triangle, one triangle, or two triangles. Solve each resulting triangle. Round each answer to the nearest tenth.

21. $A = 40°, a = 23, b = 20$

22. $A = 36°, a = 30, b = 24$

23. $A = 30°, a = 25, b = 50$

24. $A = 60°, a = 20\sqrt{3}, b = 40$

25. $A = 40°, a = 10, b = 20$

26. $A = 62°, a = 30, b = 40$

27. $A = 95°, a = 18, b = 21$

28. $A = 110°, a = 37, b = 41$

29. $A = 100°, a = 40, b = 34$

30. $A = 105°, a = 70, b = 30$

31. $B = 50°, b = 22, c = 40$

32. $B = 64°, b = 45, c = 60$

33. $B = 46°, b = 35, c = 40$

34. $B = 32°, b = 50, c = 60$

35. $B = 97°, b = 27, c = 30$

36. $B = 110°, b = 19, c = 21$

37. $A = 42°, a = 55, c = 62$

38. $A = 34°, a = 6, c = 8$

39. $C = 40°, a = 3.3, c = 2.1$

40. $C = 62°, a = 50, c = 100$

B EXERCISES Applying the Concepts

41. **Hill inclination.** A vertical tree 67 feet tall grows on a sloping hill. From a point 163 feet from the base of this tree measured straight down the hill, the tree subtends an angle of 21°. Find the angle, to the nearest tenth, the sloping hill makes with the horizontal plane.

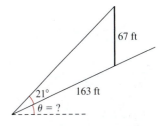

42. Hill inclination. To measure the angle that a sloping hill makes with the horizontal, a surveyor sights her transit on a small stone *S* lying 123 feet up the hill. She finds the angle of elevation to be 7.6°. The transit is 5 feet above a point *T* on the ground. Find the angle, to the nearest tenth, the sloping hill makes with the horizontal plane.

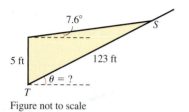

Figure not to scale

43. Distance between planets. The angle subtended at Earth by the lines joining Earth to Venus and the sun is 31°. If Venus is 67 million miles from the sun and Earth is 93 million miles from the sun, what is the distance (to the nearest million) between Earth and Venus? [*Hint:* There are two possible answers.]

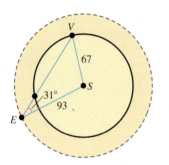

44. Distance between planets. The angle subtended at Mars by the lines joining Mars to Earth and the sun is 23°. If Mars is 128 million miles from the sun, and Earth is 93 million miles from the sun, what is the distance (to the nearest million) between Earth and Mars?

45. Navigation. A point on an island is located 24 miles southwest of a dock. A ship leaves the dock at 1 P.M. traveling west at 12 mph. At what time(s) to the nearest minute is the ship 20 miles from the point?

46. Navigation. A lighthouse is 23 miles N 55° E of a dock. A ship leaves the dock at 3 P.M. and sails due east at a speed of 15 mph. Find the time(s) to the nearest minute when the ship will be 18 miles from the lighthouse.

47. Geometry. The sides of a parallelogram are 15 m and 11 m, and the longer diagonal makes an angle of 18° with the longer side. Find the length of the longer diagonal.

48. Geometry. In the trapezoid shown, find the length *x* to the nearest tenth.

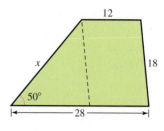

C EXERCISES Beyond the Basics

In Exercises 49–53, prove each identity for a triangle *ABC*.

49. $\dfrac{a - b}{b} = \dfrac{\sin A - \sin B}{\sin B}$ **50.** $\dfrac{a + b}{a - b} = \dfrac{\sin A + \sin B}{\sin A - \sin B}$

51. $a^2(\cos^2 B - \cos^2 C) + b^2(\cos^2 C - \cos^2 A) + c^2(\cos^2 A - \cos^2 B) = 0$

52. $a^2 \sin 2C + c^2 \sin 2A = 2ac \sin B$

53. Assuming that *ABC* is a right triangle with right angle *C*, show that

$$b = c - c \sin A \tan \frac{A}{2}.$$

54. Suppose $a \cos A = b \cos B$ in a triangle *ABC*. Show that $A = B$ or that $C = 90°$.

55. Let *ABC* be a right triangle with right angle *C*. The length of the hypotenuse is $2\sqrt{2}$ times the length of the perpendicular from *C* to the hypotenuse. Find angles *A* and *B* of the triangle. [*Hint:* Use $a^2 + b^2 = c^2$ to get $1 = 8 \sin^2 A \cos^2 A = 2 \sin^2 (2A)$.]

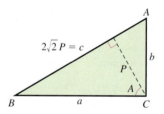

Critical Thinking

56. The length of one side of a triangle is twice the length of another side. The angles opposite these sides differ by 60°. Find the angles of the triangle.

The Law of Cosines

Before Starting this Section, Review

1. Distance formula (Appendix)
2. Inverse functions (Section 6.1)

Objectives

1 Derive the Law of Cosines.

2 Use the Law of Cosines to solve SAS triangles.

3 Use the Law of Cosines to solve SSS triangles.

GENERALIZING THE PYTHAGOREAN THEOREM

Suppose that a Boeing 747 jumbo jet is flying over Disney World in Orlando, Florida, at 552 miles per hour and is heading due south to Brazil. Twenty minutes later an F-16 fighter jet heading due east passes over Disney World at a speed of 1250 miles per hour. Using the Pythagorean Theorem, we can easily calculate the distance d between the two planes t hours after the F-16 passes over Disney World. We have the following:

$$d = \sqrt{(1250t)^2 + \left[\frac{1}{3}(552) + 552t\right]^2}$$ 20 minutes $= \frac{1}{3}$ hour

Suppose all of the other facts in the problem are unchanged except that the F-16 has a bearing of N 37°E. Now we can no longer apply the Pythagorean Theorem. In Example 2, we use the Law of Cosines, described in this section, to solve this problem. ■

1 Derive the Law of Cosines.

The Law of Cosines

The Pythagorean Theorem states that the relationship $c^2 = a^2 + b^2$ holds in a right triangle ABC, where c represents the length of the hypotenuse. This relationship is not true when the triangle is not a right triangle. The **Law of Cosines** is a generalization of the Pythagorean Theorem that is true in any triangle. This law will be used to solve triangles in which two sides and the included angle are known (SAS triangles), as well as those triangles in which all three sides are known (SSS triangles).

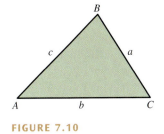

FIGURE 7.10

THE LAW OF COSINES

In triangle ABC with sides of lengths a, b, and c (as in Figure 7.10),

$$a^2 = b^2 + c^2 - 2bc \cos A,$$
$$b^2 = c^2 + a^2 - 2ca \cos B,$$
$$c^2 = a^2 + b^2 - 2ab \cos C.$$

In words, the square of any side of a triangle is equal to the sum of the squares of the length of the other two sides less twice the product of the lengths of the other sides and the cosine of their included angle.

Derivation of the Law of Cosines

To derive the Law of Cosines, place triangle ABC in a rectangular coordinate system with the vertex A at the origin and the side c along the positive x-axis. (See Figure 7.11.)

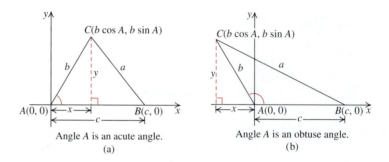

Angle A is an acute angle.

(a)

Angle A is an obtuse angle.

(b)

FIGURE 7.11 **Two cases for the Law of Cosines**

Label the coordinates of the vertices as shown in Figure 7.11. In Figures 7.11(a) and 7.11(b), the point $C(x, y)$ on the terminal side of angle A has coordinates $(b \cos A, b \sin A)$, which are found using the cosine and sine definitions.

$$\cos A = \frac{x}{b} \qquad \sin A = \frac{y}{b}$$

$$x = b \cos A \qquad y = b \sin A$$

The point B has coordinates $(c, 0)$. Applying the distance formula to the line segment joining $B(c, 0)$ and $C(b \cos A, b \sin A)$, we have

$$a = d(C, B)$$
$$a^2 = [d(C, B)]^2 \qquad \text{Square both sides.}$$
$$a^2 = (b \cos A - c)^2 + (b \sin A - 0)^2 \qquad \text{Distance formula}$$
$$a^2 = b^2 \cos^2 A - 2bc \cos A + c^2 + b^2 \sin^2 A \qquad \text{Expand binomial.}$$
$$a^2 = b^2(\sin^2 A + \cos^2 A) + c^2 - 2bc \cos A \qquad \text{Regroup terms.}$$
$$a^2 = b^2 + c^2 - 2bc \cos A \qquad \sin^2 A + \cos^2 A = 1$$

The last equation is one of the forms of the Law of Cosines. Similarly, by placing the vertex B and then the vertex C at the origin, we obtain the other two forms. Notice that the Law of Cosines becomes the Pythagorean Theorem if the included angle is $90°$ because $\cos 90° = 0$.

2 Use the Law of Cosines to solve SAS Triangles.

Solving SAS Triangles

Let's solve SAS triangles (Case 3 of Section 7.1).

FINDING THE SOLUTION: A PROCEDURE

EXAMPLE 1   **Solving the SAS Triangles**

OBJECTIVE

Solve triangles in which the measures of two sides and the included angle are known.

Step 1 Use the appropriate form of the Law of Cosines to find the side opposite the given angle.

EXAMPLE

Solve triangle ABC with $a = 15$ inches, $b = 10$ inches, and $C = 60°$. Round each answer to the nearest tenth.

1. Find side c opposite angle C.

$$c^2 = a^2 + b^2 - 2ab \cos C \qquad \text{The Law of Cosines}$$

$$c^2 = (15)^2 + (10)^2 - 2(15)(10) \cos 60° \qquad \text{Substitute values.}$$

$$c^2 = 225 + 100 - 2(15)(10)\left(\frac{1}{2}\right) \qquad \cos 60° = \frac{1}{2}$$

$$c^2 = 175 \qquad \text{Simplify.}$$

$$c = \sqrt{175} \approx 13.2 \qquad \text{Use a calculator.}$$

Step 2 Use the **Law of Sines** to find the angle opposite the shorter of the two given sides. Note that this angle is always an acute angle.

2. Find B.

$$\frac{\sin B}{b} = \frac{\sin C}{c} \qquad \text{The Law of Sines}$$

$$\sin B = \frac{b \sin C}{c} \qquad \text{Multiply both sides by } b.$$

$$\sin B = \frac{10 \sin 60°}{\sqrt{175}} \qquad \text{Substitute values.}$$

$$B = \sin^{-1}\left(\frac{10 \sin 60°}{\sqrt{175}}\right) \approx 40.9° \qquad 0° < B \le 90°$$

Step 3 Use the angle sum formula to find the third angle.

3. $A \approx 180° - 60° - 40.9° \approx 79.1° \qquad A + B + C = 180°$

Step 4 Write the solution.

4.

$A \approx 79.1°$	$a = 15$ inches
$B \approx 40.9°$	$b = 10$ inches
$C = 60°$	$c \approx 13.2$ inches

Practice Problem 1   Solve triangle ABC with $c = 25$, $a = 15$, and $B = 60°$. Round each answer to the nearest tenth.

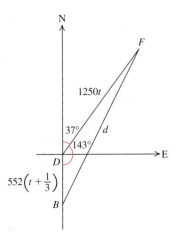

FIGURE 7.12

EXAMPLE 2   **Using the Law of Cosines**

Suppose that a Boeing 747 is flying over Disney World headed due south at 552 miles per hour. Twenty minutes later, an F-16 passes over Disney World with a bearing of N 37° E at a speed of 1250 miles per hour. Find the distance between the two planes three hours after the F-16 passes over Disney World. Round the answer to the nearest tenth.

SOLUTION

Suppose the F-16 has been traveling for t hours after passing over Disney World. Then because the Boeing 747 had a head start of 20 minutes $= \frac{1}{3}$ hour, the Boeing 747 has been traveling $\left(t + \frac{1}{3}\right)$ hours due south. The distance d between the two planes is shown in Figure 7.12. Using the Law of Cosines in triangle FDB, we have

$$d^2 = (1250t)^2 + \left[552\left(t + \frac{1}{3}\right)\right]^2 - 2(1250t) \cdot 552\left(t + \frac{1}{3}\right)\cos 143°$$

$$d^2 \approx 28{,}469{,}270.04 \qquad \text{Substitute } t = 3; \text{ use a calculator.}$$

$$d \approx 5335.7 \text{ miles} \qquad \text{Use a calculator.}$$
■ ■ ■

Practice Problem 2   Repeat Example 2 assuming that the F-16 is traveling at a speed of 1375 miles per hour due N 75°E, and the Boeing 747 is traveling with a bearing of S 12°W at 550 miles per hour. ■

3 Use the Law of Cosines to solve SSS triangles.

Solving SSS Triangles

Let's solve SSS triangles (Case 4 of Section 7.1).

FINDING THE SOLUTION: A PROCEDURE

| EXAMPLE 3 | Solving the SSS Triangles |

OBJECTIVE
Solve triangles in which the measures of the three sides are known.

EXAMPLE
Solve triangle ABC with a = 3.1 feet, b = 5.4 feet, and c = 7.2 feet. Round answers to the nearest tenths.

Step 1   Use the Law of Cosines to find the angle opposite the longest side.

1. Because c is the longest side, we find C first.

$$c^2 = a^2 + b^2 - 2ab\cos C \qquad \text{The Law of Cosines}$$
$$2ab\cos C = a^2 + b^2 - c^2 \qquad \text{Add } 2ab\cos C - c^2 \text{ to both sides.}$$
$$\cos C = \frac{a^2 + b^2 - c^2}{2ab} \qquad \text{Solve for } \cos C.$$
$$\cos C = \frac{(3.1)^2 + (5.4)^2 - (7.2)^2}{2(3.1)(5.4)} \qquad \text{Substitute values.}$$
$$\cos C \approx -0.39 \qquad \text{Use a calculator.}$$
$$C \approx \cos^{-1}(-0.39) \approx 113° \qquad 0° < C < 180°$$

Step 2   Use the Law of Sines to find either of the two remaining acute angles.

2. Find B.

$$\frac{\sin B}{b} = \frac{\sin C}{c} \qquad \text{The Law of Sines}$$
$$\sin B = \frac{b\sin C}{c} \qquad \text{Multiply both sides by } b.$$
$$B = \sin^{-1}\left(\frac{b\sin C}{c}\right) \qquad 0° < B < 90°$$
$$B = \sin^{-1}\left(\frac{5.4\sin 113°}{7.2}\right) \qquad \text{Substitute values.}$$
$$B \approx 43.7° \qquad \text{Use a calculator.}$$

Step 3   Use the angle sum formula to find the third angle.

3. $A \approx 180° - 43.7° - 113° \qquad A + B + C = 180°$
$A \approx 23.3° \qquad \text{Simplify.}$

Step 4   Write the solution.

4.

$A \approx 23.3°$	$a = 3.1$ feet
$B = 43.7°$	$b = 5.4$ feet
$C \approx 113°$	$c = 7.2$ feet

■ ■ ■

Practice Problem 3   Solve triangle ABC with $a = 4.5$, $b = 6.7$, and $c = 5.3$. Round each answer to the nearest tenth. ■

EXAMPLE 4   **Solving an SSS Triangle**

Solve triangle ABC with $a = 2$ meters, $b = 9$ meters, and $c = 5$ meters. Round each answer to the nearest tenth.

SOLUTION

We find B, the angle opposite the longest side.

$$b^2 = c^2 + a^2 - 2ca \cos B \qquad \text{The Law of Cosines}$$

$$\cos B = \frac{c^2 + a^2 - b^2}{2ca} \qquad \text{Solve for } \cos B.$$

$$\cos B = \frac{5^2 + 2^2 - 9^2}{2(5)(2)} \qquad \text{Substitute values.}$$

$$\cos B = -2.6 \qquad \text{Simplify.}$$

Because the range of the cosine function is $[-1, 1]$, there is no angle B for which $\cos B = -2.6$. This means that a triangle with the given information cannot exist. Because $2 + 5 < 9$, you also can use the Triangle Inequality from geometry to see that there is no such triangle.   ■ ■ ■

Practice Problem 4   Solve triangle ABC with $a = 2$ inches, $b = 3$ inches, and $c = 6$ inches.   ■

RECALL

The Triangle Inequality states that in any triangle, the sum of the lengths of any two sides is greater than the length of the third side.

SECTION 7.3 ■ Exercises

A EXERCISES Basic Skills and Concepts

1. One form of the Law of Cosines is
   $c^2 = a^2 + b^2 - 2ab \cos (\underline{\hspace{2cm}})$.

2. If we take the angle in the Law of Cosines to be $90°$, then we get the _____ Theorem.

3. Triangles with SAS given are solved by the Law of Cosines, as are triangles with _____ sides given.

4. When one angle is found by the Law of Cosines, the other angle can be found with the Law of _____.

5. *True or False* The Law of Cosines is used to solve triangles when two angles and a side are given.

6. *True or False* For a triangle with SSS given, we can find angle A using the formula

   $$A = \cos^{-1}\left(\frac{b^2 + c^2 - a^2}{2bc}\right).$$

In Exercises 7–10, solve each triangle. Round each answer to the nearest tenth.

7.

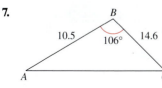

8.

9.

10.

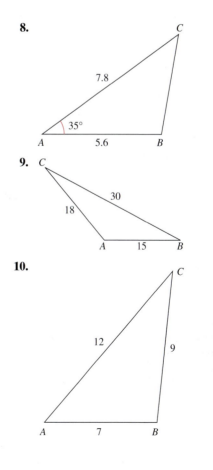

In Exercises 11–18, the sides a, b, and c of a triangle ABC are given. Find the value of the cosine of the greatest angle of the triangle. Identify the triangle as an acute, right, or obtuse triangle or as no triangle.

11. $a = 4, b = 5, c = 6$

12. $a = 5, b = 7, c = 8$

13. $a = 5, b = 12, c = 13$

14. $a = 7, b = 24, c = 25$

15. $a = 4, b = 5, c = 10$

16. $a = 6, b = 7, c = 15$

17. $a = 3, b = 6, c = 7$

18. $a = 6, b = 9, c = 12$

In Exercises 19–34, solve each triangle ABC. Round each answer to the nearest tenth. All sides are measured in feet.

19. $a = 15, b = 9, C = 120°$

20. $a = 14, b = 10, C = 75°$

21. $b = 10, c = 12, A = 62°$

22. $b = 11, c = 16, A = 110°$

23. $c = 12, a = 15, b = 11$

24. $c = 16, a = 11, b = 13$

25. $a = 9, b = 13, c = 18$

26. $a = 14, b = 6, c = 10$

27. $a = 2.5, b = 3.7, c = 5.4$

28. $a = 4.2, b = 2.9, c = 3.6$

29. $b = 3.2, c = 4.3, A = 97.7°$

30. $b = 5.4, c = 3.6, A = 79.2°$

31. $c = 4.9, a = 3.9, B = 68.3°$

32. $c = 7.8, a = 9.8, B = 95.6°$

33. $a = 2.3, b = 2.8, c = 3.7$

34. $a = 5.3, b = 2.9, c = 4.6$

B EXERCISES Applying the Concepts

In Exercises 35–45, round each answer to the nearest tenth.

35. Chord length. Find the length of the chord intercepted by a central angle of 42° in a circle of radius 8 feet.

36. Central angle. Find the measure of the central angle of a circle of radius 6 feet that intercepted a chord of length 3.5 feet.

37. Tunnel length. Engineers must bore a straight tunnel through the base of a mountain. They select a reference point C on the plain surrounding the mountain. The distance from C to portal A (the starting tunnel point) and portal B (the ending tunnel point) is 2352 yards and 1763 yards, respectively. The measure of $\angle ACB$ is 41°. How long (to the nearest yard) is the tunnel?

38. Pond length. A surveyor needs to find the length of a pond (see figure), but does so indirectly. She selects a point A on one side of the pond and measures distances to the points B and C at opposite ends of the pond to be 537 yards and

823 yards, respectively. The measure of $\angle BAC$ is 130°. (See the figure.) How long is the pond?

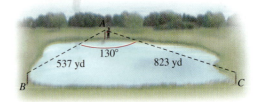

39. Roof truss. A roof truss is made in the shape of an inverted V. The lengths of the two edges are 11 feet and 23 feet. The edges meet at the peak, making a 65° angle. Find
  a. the width of the truss.
  b. the height of the peak.

40. Solar panels. A roof of a house addition is being built to accept solar energy panels as shown in the figure. Find
  a. the length of the edge AC of the truss.
  b. the measure of $\angle BAC$.

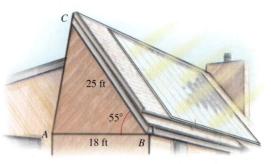

41. Hikers. Two hikers, Sonia and Tony, leave the same point at the same time. Sonia walks due east at the rate of 3 miles per hour, and Tony walks 45° northeast at the rate of 4.3 miles per hour. How far apart are the hikers after three hours?

42. Distance between ships. Two ships leave the same port— Ship A at 1:00 P.M. and ship B at 3:30 P.M. Ship A sails on a bearing of S 37° E at 18 miles per hour, and ship B sails on a bearing of N 28° E at 20 miles per hour. How far apart are the ships at 8:00 P.M.?

43. Navigation. A ship is traveling due north. At two different points A and B, the navigator of the ship sites a lighthouse at the point C, as shown in the accompanying figure.
  a. Determine the distance from B to C.
  b. How much farther due north must the ship travel to reach the point closest to the lighthouse?

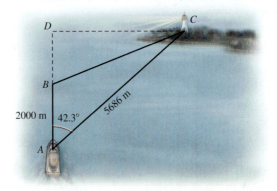

44. Tangential circles. Three circles of radii 1.2 inches, 2.2 inches, and 3.1 inches are tangent to each other externally. Find the angles of the triangle formed by joining the centers of the circles.

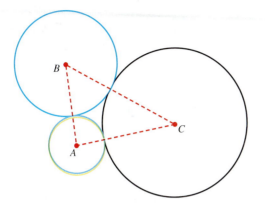

45. Height of a tree. A tree is planted at a point O on horizontal ground. Two points A and B on the ground are 100 feet apart. The angles of elevation of the top of the tree T from the points A and B are 45° and 30°, respectively. The measure of $\angle AOB$ is 60°. Find the height of the tree.

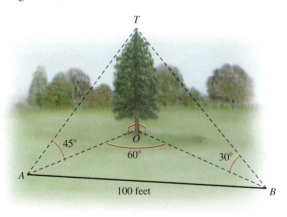

C EXERCISES Beyond the Basics

In Exercises 46–48, round each answer to the nearest tenth.

46. A parallelogram has adjacent sides 8 cm and 13 cm. Assuming that the shorter diagonal is 11 cm long, find the length of the longer diagonal.

47. A parallelogram has adjacent sides 10 cm and 15 cm long, and the angle between them is 40°. Find the length of the two diagonals.

48. The length of the two diagonals of a parallelogram are 16 cm and 22 cm. The acute angle between these diagonals is 63°. Find the length of the sides of the parallelogram. [*Hint:* The diagonals of a parallelogram bisect each other.]

In Exercises 49–58, triangle ABC has sides a, b, and c and $s = \dfrac{1}{2}(a + b + c)$. Use the Law of Cosines to prove each identity.

49. $\dfrac{\cos A}{a} + \dfrac{\cos B}{b} + \dfrac{\cos C}{c} = \dfrac{a^2 + b^2 + c^2}{2abc}$

50. $(b + c)\cos A + (c + a)\cos B + (a + b)\cos C = a + b + c$

51. $a^2 \sin(B - C) - (b^2 - c^2)\sin A = 0$

52. $\dfrac{\tan B}{\tan C} = \dfrac{a^2 + b^2 - c^2}{c^2 + a^2 - b^2}$

53. $1 - \cos A = \dfrac{(a - b + c)(a + b - c)}{2bc}$

54. $1 + \cos A = \dfrac{(b + c + a)(b + c - a)}{2bc}$

55. $\cos\dfrac{A}{2} = \sqrt{\dfrac{s(s - a)}{bc}}$

56. $\sin\dfrac{A}{2} = \sqrt{\dfrac{(s - b)(s - c)}{bc}}$

57. $4\left[ab\cos^2\dfrac{C}{2} + bc\cos^2\dfrac{A}{2} + ca\cos^2\dfrac{B}{2}\right] = (a + b + c)^2$

58. Assuming that $2a = b + c$, show that $\tan\dfrac{B}{2}\tan\dfrac{C}{2} = \dfrac{1}{3}$.

59. Use the Law of Cosines to show that for a triangle with legs of length a, b, and c (with $a \le b$), $b - a < c < b + a$.

Critical Thinking

60. Solve triangle ABC with vertices $A(-2, 1)$, $B(5, 3)$, and $C(3, 6)$.

61. Solve triangle ABC with vertices $A(-3, -5)$, $B(6, 10)$, and $C(3, -2)$.

GROUP PROJECT

You can use the Law of Cosines to solve triangle ABC in the ambiguous case of Section 6.2. For example, to solve triangle ABC with $B = 150°$, $b = 10$, and $c = 6$, use the Law of Cosines to write $b^2 = a^2 + c^2 - 2ac\cos B$.

Substitute values of b, c, and B in this equation to obtain a quadratic equation in a. Find the roots of this equation and interpret your results. Again, use the Law of Cosines to find A. Then find $C = 180° - A - B$.

Use this technique to solve each triangle ABC.

1. $B = 150°$, $b = 10$, and $c = 6$

2. $A = 30°$, $a = 6$, and $b = 10$

3. $A = 60°$, $a = 12$, and $c = 15$

Area of a Triangle

Before Starting this Section, Review

1. Area of a Triangle (Section 1.2)

Objectives

1 Find the area of SAS triangles.

2 Find the area of AAS and ASA triangles.

3 Find the area of SSS triangles.

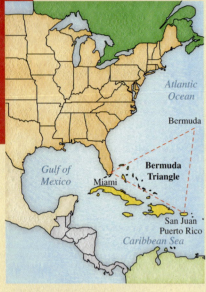

Atlantic Ocean

Bermuda

Gulf of Mexico

Miami

Bermuda Triangle

San Juan
Puerto Rico

Caribbean Sea

THE BERMUDA TRIANGLE

The Bermuda Triangle, or Devil's Triangle, is the expanse of the Atlantic Ocean between Florida, Bermuda, and Puerto Rico. This mysterious stretch of sea has an unusually high occurrence of disappearing ships and planes.

For example, on Halloween in 1991, pilot John Verdi and his copilot were flying a Grumman Cougar jet over the triangle. They radioed the nearest tower to get permission to increase their altitude. The tower agreed and watched as the jet began the ascent and then disappeared off the radar. The jet didn't fly out of range of the radar, didn't descend, and didn't radio a mayday (distress call). It just vanished, and the plane and crew were never recovered. One explanation for such disappearances is based on the theory that strange compass readings occur in crossing the Atlantic due to confusion caused by the three north poles: magnetic (toward which compasses point), grid (the real North Pole, at 90 degrees latitude), and true or celestial north (determined by Polaris, the North Star). In Exercise 31, you are asked to find the area of the Bermuda Triangle. ∎

Recall the following result from geometry.

AREA OF A TRIANGLE

The area K of a triangle is

$$K = \frac{1}{2}(\text{base})(\text{height})$$

or

$$K = \frac{1}{2}bh,$$

where b is the base and h is the height (the length of the altitude to the base).

If a base (b) and the height (h) of a triangle are given, we use the formula above to calculate the area of the triangle. In this section, we discover alternate formulas when both b and h are not known.

1 Find the area of SAS triangles.

Area of SAS Triangles

We first derive a formula for the area of a triangle in which two sides and the included angle are known.

Let ABC be a triangle with known sides b and c and included angle $A = \theta$. Let h be the altitude from B to the side b.

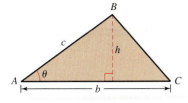

FIGURE 7.13 Acute angle A

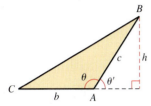

FIGURE 7.14 Obtuse angle A

If $A = \theta$ is an acute angle in a triangle (see Figure 7.13), then $\sin A = \dfrac{h}{c}$; so $h = c \sin A$. The area of this triangle is given by

$$K = \frac{1}{2}bh = \frac{1}{2}bc \sin A \qquad \text{Replace } h \text{ with } c \sin A.$$

The angle $A = \theta$ shown in Figure 7.14 is an obtuse angle. Here $\theta' = 180° - \theta$ is the reference angle for θ and $\sin \theta = \sin \theta' = \dfrac{h}{c}$.

So

$$h = c \sin \theta' = c \sin \theta = c \sin A$$

$$K = \frac{1}{2}bh = \frac{1}{2}bc \sin A \qquad \text{Replace } h \text{ with } c \sin A.$$

In both cases (A is acute or obtuse), the area K of the triangle is $\dfrac{1}{2}bc \sin A$. By dropping altitudes from A and C, we have the following result.

AREA OF AN SAS TRIANGLE

The area K of a triangle ABC with sides a, b, and c is

$$K = \frac{1}{2}bc \sin A \qquad K = \frac{1}{2}ca \sin B \qquad K = \frac{1}{2}ab \sin C.$$

In words: The area K of a triangle is one-half the product of two of its sides and the sine of the included angle.

EXAMPLE 1   **Finding the Area of a Triangle**

Find the area of the triangle ABC in Figure 7.15.

SOLUTION

We are given the angle of measure $62°$ between the sides of lengths 36 feet and 29 feet. The area K of the triangle ABC is given by

$$K = \frac{1}{2}bc \sin \theta \qquad \text{Area formula}$$

$$= \frac{1}{2}(36)(29) \sin 62° \qquad b = 36, c = 29, \theta = 62°$$

$$\approx 460.9 \text{ square feet} \qquad \text{Use a calculator.} \qquad ■\ ■\ ■$$

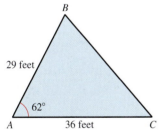

FIGURE 7.15

Practice Problem 1   Find the area of triangle ABC assuming that the lengths of the sides AC and BC are 27 feet and 38 feet, respectively, and the measure of the angle between these sides is $47°$. ■

EXAMPLE 2   **Finding a Triangular Area Determined by Cellular Telephone Towers**

Three cell towers are set up on three mountain peaks. Suppose the lines of sight from tower A to towers B and C form an angle of $120°$ and the distances between tower A and towers B and C are 3.6 miles and 4.2 miles, respectively. Find the area of the triangle having these three towers as vertices.

SOLUTION

The area of a triangle (see Figure 7.16) with angle θ included between sides of lengths b and c is

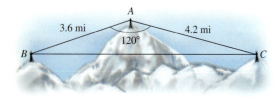

FIGURE 7.16

$$K = \frac{1}{2}bc \sin\theta$$

$$= \frac{1}{2}(4.2)(3.6)\sin 120° \qquad \text{Replace } b \text{ with } 4.2, c \text{ with } 3.6, \text{ and } \theta \text{ with } 120°.$$

$$= \frac{1}{2}(4.2)(3.6)\sin 60° \qquad \theta' = 180° - 120° = 60° \text{ and } \sin 120° = \sin 60°$$

$$= \frac{1}{2}(4.2)(3.6)\frac{\sqrt{3}}{2} \qquad \sin 60° = \frac{\sqrt{3}}{2}$$

$$\approx 6.55 \text{ square miles} \qquad \text{Use a calculator.} \qquad \blacksquare\,\blacksquare\,\blacksquare$$

Practice Problem 2   Rework Example 2, where the given distances are 5.1 and 3.8 miles and the included angle measures 150°.

 Find the area of AAS and ASA triangles.

Area of AAS and ASA Triangles

Suppose we are given two angles A and C and the side a of triangle ABC. We find the third angle B by the angle sum formula. So

$$B = 180° - A - C.$$

We find b by the Law of Sines.

$$\frac{b}{\sin B} = \frac{a}{\sin A}$$

$$b = \frac{a\sin B}{\sin A} \qquad \text{Multiply both sides by } \sin B.$$

The area, K, of triangle ABC is

$$K = \frac{1}{2}ab\sin C \qquad\qquad \text{SAS formula}$$

$$= \frac{1}{2}a\left(\frac{a\sin B}{\sin A}\right)\sin C \qquad \text{Replace } b \text{ with } \frac{a\sin B}{\sin A}.$$

$$= \frac{a^2 \sin B \sin C}{2\sin A}.$$

We obtain similar results if any two angles and the side b or the side c is given.

AREA OF AAS AND ASA TRIANGLES

The area K of a triangle ABC with sides a, b, and c is

$$K = \frac{a^2 \sin B \sin C}{2\sin A} \qquad K = \frac{b^2 \sin C \sin A}{2\sin B} \qquad K = \frac{c^2 \sin A \sin B}{2\sin C}.$$

EXAMPLE 3   **Area of an AAS Triangle**

Find the area of triangle ABC with

$$B = 36°, C = 69°, \text{ and } b = 15 \text{ ft.}$$

SOLUTION

First, we find the third angle of the triangle. We have

$$A = 180° - B - C \qquad \text{Angle sum formula}$$
$$= 180° - 36° - 69° \qquad \text{Substitute for } B \text{ and } C.$$
$$= 75°.$$

Because we are given side b, we use the area formula for an AAS triangle that contains side b. Then

$$K = \frac{b^2 \sin C \sin A}{2 \sin B} \qquad \text{Area of an AAS triangle}$$
$$= \frac{(15)^2 \sin 69° \sin 75°}{2 \sin 36°} \qquad \text{Substitute values for } b, C, A, \text{ and } B.$$
$$\approx 172.6 \, \text{ft}^2 \qquad \text{Use a calculator.} \qquad \blacksquare \blacksquare \blacksquare$$

Practice Problem 3 Find the area of triangle ABC with $A = 63°$, $B = 74°$, and $c = 18$ in.

3 ▸ Find the area of SSS triangles.

Area of SSS Triangles

The Law of Cosines can be used to derive a formula for the area of a triangle if the lengths of the three sides (SSS triangles) are known. The formula is called **Heron's formula**.

HERON'S FORMULA FOR SSS TRIANGLES

The area K of a triangle with sides of lengths a, b, and c is given by
$$K = \sqrt{s(s - a)(s - b)(s - c)},$$
where $s = \frac{1}{2}(a + b + c)$ is the **semiperimeter**.

In Exercise 40, we ask you to derive Heron's formula.

EXAMPLE 4 **Using Heron's Formula**

Find the area of triangle ABC with $a = 29$ inches, $b = 25$ inches, and $c = 40$ inches. Round the answer to the nearest tenth.

SOLUTION

We first find s:

$$s = \frac{a + b + c}{2}$$
$$= \frac{29 + 25 + 40}{2} = 47$$

$$\text{Area of the triangle} = \sqrt{s(s - a)(s - b)(s - c)} \qquad \text{Heron's formula}$$
$$= \sqrt{47(47 - 29)(47 - 25)(47 - 40)} \qquad \text{Substitute values.}$$
$$\approx 360.9 \text{ square inches} \qquad \text{Use a calculator.}$$

$$\blacksquare \blacksquare \blacksquare$$

Practice Problem 4 Find the area of triangle ABC with $a = 11$ meters, $b = 17$ meters, and $c = 20$ meters. Round the answer to the nearest tenth.

| EXAMPLE 5 | **Using Heron's Formula** |

A triangular swimming pool has side lengths 23 feet, 17 feet, and 26 feet. How many gallons of water will fill the pool to a depth of 5 feet? Round the answer to the nearest whole number.

SOLUTION

To calculate the volume of water, we first calculate the area of the triangular surface.

We have $a = 23$, $b = 17$, and $c = 26$. So $s = \frac{1}{2}(a + b + c) = 33$.

By Heron's formula, the area K of the triangular surface is

$$K = \sqrt{s(s - a)(s - b)(s - c)}$$
$$= \sqrt{33(33 - 23)(33 - 17)(33 - 26)} \qquad \text{Substitute values for } a, b, c, \text{ and } s.$$
$$\approx 192.2498 \text{ square feet.}$$

The volume of water = surface area × depth
$$\approx 192.2498 \times 5$$
$$\approx 961.25 \text{ cubic feet}$$

One cubic foot contains approximately 7.5 gallons of water. So $961.25 \times 7.5 \approx 7209$ gallons of water will fill the pool. ■ ■ ■

Practice Problem 5 Repeat Example 5 if assuming that the swimming pool has side lengths 25 feet, 30 feet, and 33 feet and the depth of the pool is 5.5 feet. ■

SECTION 7.4 ■ Exercises

A EXERCISES Basic Skills and Concepts

1. A triangle with base b and height h has area = _____ .

2. If two sides of a triangle are p and q with included angle θ, the area of the triangle is _____ .

3. If two angles of a triangle are α and β (in degrees), the third angle $\gamma =$ _____ .

4. If a, b, and c are the sides of a triangle, the number $s = \frac{1}{2}(a + b + c)$ is called the _____ .

Heron's formula for the area of a triangle is $K =$ _____ .

5. *True or False* There is no formula for finding the area of an AAA triangle.

6. *True or False* If two right triangles have the same area, then they have the same side lengths.

In Exercises 7–14, find the area of each SAS triangle *ABC*. Round your answers to the nearest tenth.

7. $A = 57°$, $b = 30$ in., $c = 52$ in.

8. $B = 110°$, $a = 20$ cm, $c = 27$ cm

9. $C = 46°$, $a = 15$ km, $b = 22$ km

10. $A = 146.7°$, $b = 16.7$ ft, $c = 18$ ft

11. $B = 38.6°$, $a = 12$ mm, $c = 16.7$ mm

12. $B = 112.5°$, $a = 151.6$ ft, $c = 221.8$ ft

13. $C = 107.3°$, $a = 271$ ft, $b = 194.3$ ft

14. $A = 131.8°$, $b = 15.7$ mm, $c = 18.2$ mm

In Exercises 15–22, find the area of each AAS or ASA triangle *ABC*. Round your answers to the nearest tenth.

15. $a = 16$ ft, $B = 57°$, $C = 49°$

16. $a = 12$ ft, $A = 73°$, $C = 64°$

17. $b = 15.3$ yd, $A = 64°$, $B = 38°$

18. $b = 10$ m, $B = 53.4°$, $C = 65.6°$

19. $c = 16.3$ cm, $B = 55°$, $C = 37.5°$

20. $c = 20.5$ ft, $A = 64°$, $B = 84.2°$

21. $a = 65.4$ ft, $A = 62°15'$, $B = 44°30'$

22. $b = 24.3$ m, $B = 56°18'$, $C = 37°36'$

In Exercises 23–30, find the area of each SSS triangle *ABC*. Round your answers to the nearest tenth.

23. $a = 2$, $b = 3$, $c = 4$

24. $a = 50$, $b = 100$, $c = 130$

25. $a = 50$, $b = 50$, $c = 75$

26. $a = 100$, $b = 100$, $c = 125$

27. $a = 7.5$, $b = 4.5$, $c = 6.0$

28. $a = 8.5$, $b = 5.1$, $c = 4.5$

29. $a = 3.7, b = 5.1, c = 4.2$

30. $a = 9.8, b = 5.7, c = 6.5$

B EXERCISES Applying the Concepts

31. **Area of the Bermuda Triangle.** The angle formed by the lines of sight from Fort Lauderdale, Florida, to Bermuda and to San Juan, Puerto Rico, is approximately 67°. The distance from Fort Lauderdale to Bermuda is 1026 miles, and the distance from Fort Lauderdale to San Juan is 1046 miles. Find the area of the Bermuda Triangle, which is formed with those cities as vertices.

32. **Landscaping.** A triangular region between the three streets shown in the figure will be landscaped for $30 a square foot. How much will the landscaping cost?

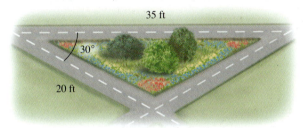

33. **Real estate.** You have inherited a commercial triangular shaped lot of side lengths 400 feet, 250 feet, and 274 feet. The neighboring property is selling for $1 million dollars per acre. How much is your lot worth? (*Hint:* 1 acre = 43,560 square feet)

34. **Real estate.** Find the area of the quadrangular lot shown in the figure. All measurements are in feet.

35. **Swimming pool.** Find the number of gallons of water in a triangular swimming pool with sides 11 feet, 16 feet, and 19 feet and a depth of 5 feet. Round your answer to the nearest whole number. [Recall: Approximately 7.5 gallons of water are in 1 cubic foot.]

36. **Swimming pool.** Find the number of gallons of water in a triangular swimming pool with adjacent sides 18.5 feet and 25.7 feet, angle between these sides 75°, and a depth of 5.5 feet. Round your answer to the nearest whole number.

37. **Parallelogram area.** A parallelogram has adjacent sides 8 cm and 13 cm. Find the area of the parallelogram assuming that the angle between the adjacent sides is 60°.

38. **Parallelogram area.** A parallelogram has adjacent sides 12 cm and 16 cm. Find the area of the parallelogram assuming that the longer diagonal is 22 cm.

C EXERCISES Beyond the Basics

39. Use Exercises 55 and 56 of Section 7.3 and the half-angle formula to show that

$$\sin A = \frac{2}{bc}\sqrt{s(s-a)(s-b)(s-c)}.$$

40. Use Exercise 39 to prove Heron's formula.

41. In triangle ABC, AD and BF are perpendicular from vertices A and B to the sides BC and CA, respectively. Assuming that $a = 18, b = 15,$ and $AD = 10$, find BF.

42. A triangle has sides of lengths 50, 72, and 78 m. Find the length of the perpendicular from the vertex opposite the side of length 72 m.

43. A regular hexagon (six-sided polygon with equal angles and equal sides) is inscribed in a circle of radius 20 cm. Find the area of the hexagon.

44. Find the area of a regular hexagon with a perimeter of 30 m.

45. The diagonals of a parallelogram divide it into four triangles. Show that the area of each triangle is one-fourth the area of the parallelogram. [*Hint:* The diagonals of a parallelogram bisect each other.]

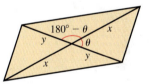

46. A triangle is called a **perfect triangle** if its sides are in whole numbers and its perimeter is numerically equal to its area. Show that the triangle with side lengths 6, 25, and 29 is a perfect triangle.

In Exercises 47–50, find the area of each polygon with indicated lengths and angles. Answers will vary, depending on rounding.

47.　　　　　　　　　　　　　**48.**

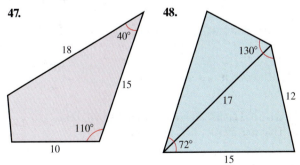

49.

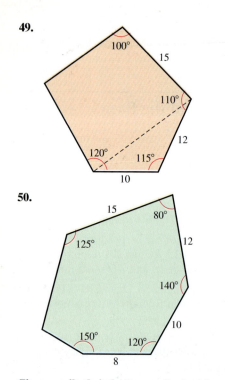

50.

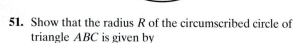

Circumscribed circle. Perpendicular bisectors of the sides of a triangle meet at a point O, and the distance from O to each of the vertices is the same number, say R. The circle with center at O and radius R is called the circumscribed circle of the triangle. (See the figure.)

51. Show that the radius R of the circumscribed circle of triangle ABC is given by

$$R = \frac{a}{2\sin A} = \frac{b}{2\sin B} = \frac{c}{2\sin C}.$$

[*Hint*: Use a theorem of geometry: $\angle BOC = 2\angle A$.]

52. Use Exercise 51 to show that

$$R = \frac{abc}{4K},$$

where K is the area of the triangle ABC. [*Hint*: Use Exercise 39.]

Inscribed circle. The bisectors of the angles of a triangle meet at a point I, and the perpendicular distance from I to each of the sides is the same number, say r. The circle with center I and radius r is called the **inscribed circle** of the triangle. (See the figure.)

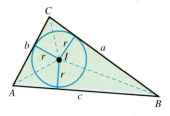

53. Show that the radius r of the inscribed circle of triangle ABC is given by

$$r = \frac{\sqrt{s(s - a)(s - b)(s - c)}}{s}.$$

[*Hint*: Show that $rs = K$.]

54. From Exercises 52 and 53, conclude that

$$rR = \frac{abc}{2(a + b + c)}.$$

55. In triangle ABC, let p_1, p_2, and p_3 be the lengths of the perpendiculars from the vertices A, B, and C to the sides a, b, and c, respectively. Show that

$$\frac{1}{p_1} + \frac{1}{p_2} + \frac{1}{p_3} = \sqrt{\frac{s}{(s - a)(s - b)(s - c)}}.$$

[*Hint*: $\frac{1}{2}ap_1 = \frac{1}{2}bp_2 = \frac{1}{2}cp_3 = K$]

56. From Exercises 53 and 55, conclude that

$$\frac{1}{p_1} + \frac{1}{p_2} + \frac{1}{p_3} = \frac{1}{r}.$$

Critical Thinking

57. Show that the area, K, of a triangle ABC is

$$K = \frac{a^2 \sin 2B + b^2 \sin 2A}{4} = \frac{b^2 \sin 2C + c^2 \sin 2B}{4}$$

$$= \frac{c^2 \sin 2A + a^2 \sin 2C}{4}.$$

58. Let r and R be the radii of the inscribed circle and the circumscribed circle, respectively, of triangle ABC. Show that $r = 4R \sin\frac{A}{2} \sin\frac{B}{2} \sin\frac{C}{2}$.

REVIEW

Definitions, Concepts, and Formulas	Examples and Illustrations

7.1 The Law of Sines

A triangle with no right angle is called an **oblique triangle**.

- **The Law of Sines** In any triangle ABC with sides a, b, and c,
$$\frac{\sin A}{a} = \frac{\sin B}{b}, \frac{\sin B}{b} = \frac{\sin C}{c}, \text{ and } \frac{\sin C}{c} = \frac{\sin A}{a}.$$

We can write those equations in compact notation:
$$\frac{\sin A}{a} = \frac{\sin B}{b} = \frac{\sin C}{c}, \text{ or equivalently,}$$
$$\frac{a}{\sin A} = \frac{b}{\sin B} = \frac{c}{\sin C}$$

In triangle ABC, find b if $a = 83.45$ in., $B = 65°$, and $C = 43°$.

Solution

1. Find A from $A + B + C = 180°$.
$$A = 180° - 65° - 43° = 72°$$

2. $\dfrac{b}{\sin B} = \dfrac{a}{\sin A}$

$$\frac{b}{\sin 65°} = \frac{83.45}{\sin 72°}$$

$$b = \frac{83.45 \sin 65°}{\sin 72°} \approx 79.52 \text{ in.}$$

7.2 The Law of Sines: Ambiguous Case

- In a triangle, if we know two sides and an angle opposite one of the sides (SSA triangles), we may have a figure that is (1) not a triangle, (2) one triangle, or (3) two triangles. Suppose in a triangle ABC we are given A, a, and b.

i. If A is an acute angle and
  a. $a < b \sin A$, then there is no triangle.
  b. $a = b \sin A$, then there is one right triangle.
  c. $b \sin A < a < b$, then there are two triangles.
  d. $a \geq b$, then there is one triangle.

ii. If A is an obtuse angle and
  a. $a \leq b$, then there is no triangle.
  b. $a > b$, then there is one triangle.

The Law of Sines can be used to solve SSA triangles.

Solve triangle ABC.

$A = 30.0°$	$a = 35.00$
$B = ?$	$b = 50.00$
$C = ?$	$c = ?$

Solution
Find angle B.

$$\frac{\sin B}{50.00} = \frac{\sin 30.0°}{35.00}$$

$$\sin B \approx 0.7143$$

There are two angles with this sine value:
$B_1 \approx 45.59°$ and $B_2 = 180° - B_1 \approx 134.41°$

$A = 30.0°$	$a = 35.00$
$B_1 = 45.59°$	$b = 50.00$
$C_1 =$	$c_1 =$

$A = 30.0°$	$a = 35.00$
$B_2 = 134.41°$	$b = 50.00$
$C_2 =$	$c_2 =$

$C_1 = 180° - A - B_1 = 104.41°$. Use the Law of Sines to find $c_1 \approx 67.8$.

$C_2 = 180° - A - B_2 = 15.59°$. Again, use the Law of Sines to find $c_2 \approx 18.81$.

There are two triangles AB_1C_1, and AB_2C_2 with the given measurements.

7.3 The Law of Cosines

■ In a triangle ABC with sides a, b, and c,

$$a^2 = b^2 + c^2 - 2bc \sin A \text{ or } \cos A = \frac{b^2 + c^2 - a^2}{2bc},$$

$$b^2 = c^2 + a^2 - 2ca \cos B \text{ or } \cos B = \frac{c^2 + a^2 - b^2}{2ca},$$

$$c^2 = a^2 + b^2 - 2ab \cos C \text{ or } \cos C = \frac{a^2 + b^2 - c^2}{2ab}.$$

The Law of Cosines is used to solve SAS and SSS triangles.

1. In triangle ABC, find a if $b = 15$ ft, $c = 10$ ft, and $A = 60°$.

Solution

$$a^2 = b^2 + c^2 - 2bc \cos A$$
$$= 15^2 + 10^2 - 2(15)(10) \cos 60°$$

So, $a = \sqrt{175}$ ft ≈ 13.2 ft.

2. In triangle ABC, find B if $a = 5$, $b = 7$, and $c = 8$.

Solution

$$\cos B = \frac{c^2 + a^2 - b^2}{2ca}$$
$$= \frac{8^2 + 5^2 - 7^2}{2(8)(5)} = \frac{1}{2}$$

So, $B = \cos^{-1}\left(\frac{1}{2}\right) = 60°$.

7.4 Area of a Triangle

■ **Area of an SAS triangle**
The area K of a triangle ABC with sides a, b, and c is

$$K = \frac{1}{2} bc \sin A = \frac{1}{2} ca \sin B = \frac{1}{2} ab \sin C.$$

Area K is one-half the product of two of its sides and the sine of the included angle.

Find the area K of triangle ABC with $a = 15.50$, $b = 17.23$, and $C = 63.7°$.

Solution

$$K = \frac{1}{2} ab \sin C$$
$$= \frac{1}{2} (15.50)(17.23) \sin 63.7°$$
$$\approx 119.71 \text{ units}^2$$

Area of AAS and ASA triangles
The area K of a triangle ABC with sides a, b, and c is

$$K = \frac{a^2 \sin B \sin C}{2 \sin A} = \frac{b^2 \sin C \sin A}{2 \sin B} = \frac{c^2 \sin A \sin B}{2 \sin C}.$$

Find the area K of triangle ABC with $b = 16.00$, $A = 62.0°$, and $C = 74.0°$.

Solution

$$B = 180° - A - C = 44.0°$$
$$K = \frac{b^2 \sin C \sin A}{2 \sin B} \approx 156.39 \text{ units}^2$$

Find the area of triangle ABC with $a = 12.0$, $b = 17.0$, and $c = 21.0$.

Solution

Area of SSS triangles

Heron's formula The area K of a triangle with sides of lengths a, b, and c is given by
$$K = \sqrt{s(s - a)(s - b)(s - c)},$$

where $s = \frac{1}{2} (a + b + c)$ is the *semiperimeter*.

$$s = \frac{1}{2} (a + b + c) = 25.0$$
$$K = \sqrt{25(25 - 12)(25 - 17)(25 - 21)}$$
$$\approx 101.98 \text{ units}^2$$

REVIEW EXERCISES

In Exercises 1–6, use the Law of Sines to find the requested measurement in each triangle ABC. Round each answer to the nearest tenth.

1. $A = 65°, B = 38°, a = 14$; find c

2. $A = 48°, B = 57°, a = 12$; find b

3. $B = 62°, b = 13, a = 8$; find A

4. $C = 74°, c = 12, b = 7$; find B

5. $A = 37.6°, B = 49.8°, a = 14.3$; find b

6. $B = 69.3°, b = 18.6, c = 7.4$; find C

In Exercises 7–14, use the Law of Sines to solve each triangle ABC. Round each answer to the nearest tenth.

7. $A = 40°, B = 35°, c = 100$

8. $B = 30°, C = 80°, a = 100$

9. $A = 45°, a = 25, b = 75$

10. $B = 36°, a = 12.5, b = 8.7$

11. $A = 48.5°, C = 57.3°, b = 47.3$

12. $A = 67°, a = 100, c = 125$

13. $A = 65.2°, a = 21.3, b = 19$

14. $C = 53°, a = 140, c = 115$

15. In triangle ABC, let $c = 20$ and $B = 60°$. Find a value of b such that C has (a) two possible values, (b) exactly one value, (c) no value.

16. Repeat Exercise 15 for $c = 20$ and $B = 150°$.

In Exercises 17–20, use the Law of Cosines to find the requested measurement in each triangle ABC. Round each answer to the nearest tenth.

17. $A = 60°, b = 12, c = 14$; find a

18. $B = 73.4°, a = 15.2, c = 11.7$; find b

19. $a = 7, b = 10, c = 14$; find B

20. $a = 9.2, b = 8.7, c = 13.8$; find A

In Exercises 21–28, use the Law of Cosines to solve each triangle ABC. Round your answers to the nearest tenth.

21. $a = 60, b = 90, c = 125$

22. $a = 15, b = 9, C = 120°$

23. $a = 40, c = 38, B = 80°$

24. $a = 10, b = 20, c = 22$

25. $a = 2.6, b = 3.7, c = 4.8$

26. $a = 15, c = 26, B = 115°$

27. $a = 12, b = 7, C = 130°$

28. $b = 75, c = 100, A = 80°$

In Exercises 29–32, find the area of each triangle ABC with the given information. Round your answers to the nearest square unit.

29. $a = 5, b = 7, c = 10$

30. $a = 2.4, b = 3.4, c = 4.4$

31. $A = 65°, b = 6$ feet, $c = 4$ feet

32. $C = 115°, b = 20$ inches, $a = 30$ inches

33. $A = 67°, B = 38°, b = 12$ m

34. $B = 46.7°, C = 29.4°, a = 7.3$ ft

35. **Geometry.** A side of a parallelogram is 60 inches long and makes angles of 32° and 46° with the two diagonals. Find the lengths of the diagonals.

36. **Height of a flagpole.** Two friends, Carmen and Latisha, stand 300 feet apart with a flagpole situated between them. Their angles of elevation of the top of the flagpole are 34° and 27°, respectively. How tall is the flagpole? How far is each girl from it?

37. **Angle of elevation of a hill.** A tower 120 feet tall is located at the top of a hill. At a point 460 feet down the hill, the angle between the surface of the hill and the line of sight to the top of the tower is 12°. Find the angle of elevation of the hill to a horizontal plane.

38. **Distance between cars.** Two cars start from a point A along two straight roads. The angle between the two roads is 72°. The speeds of the two cars are 55 miles per hour and 65 miles per hour. How far apart are the two cars after 80 minutes? Round to the nearest tenth of a mile.

39. **Length of a pond.** A surveyor wants to find the length of a pond, but can do so only indirectly. She stands at a point A on one side of the pond and locates points B and C at opposite ends of the pond. The angle BAC is 73°, $AB = 560$ yd, and $AC = 720$ yd. Find the length of the pond.

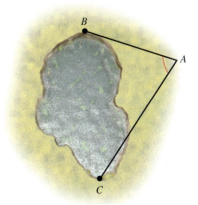

40. Geometry. A parallelogram has adjacent sides 120 and 140 feet long, and the angle between them is 48°. Find the lengths of the two diagonals of the parallelogram.

41. Tangential circles. Three circles of radii 60, 80, and 125 ft are tangent to each other externally. Find the angles of the triangle formed by joining the centers of the circles.

42. Distance between planets. The angle subtended at Earth by the lines joining Earth to Venus and the sun is 28°. If Venus is 67 million miles from the sun and Earth is 93 million miles from the sun, what is the distance (to the nearest million) between Earth and Venus?

43. In Washington, D.C., Constitution Avenue and Pennsylvania Avenue intersect at an angle of 19°. The White House is on Pennsylvania Avenue 5,600 feet from

this point of intersection. The National Academy of Sciences is on Constitution Avenue 8,600 feet from this intersection. Both buildings lie on the same side of 4th Street. How far (to the nearest foot) is the White House from the National Academy of Sciences?

44. The Lincoln Memorial in Washington, D.C., is 4,300 feet due west of the Washington Monument. The Pentagon is 7,100 feet S 15° W from the Lincoln Memorial. How far is the Pentagon from the Washington Monument?

45. Triangular plot. A triangular plot of land has sides of length 310 feet, 415 feet, and 175 feet. Find the largest angle between the sides.

46. Area. Find the area of the triangular plot of Exercise 45.

CHAPTER TEST

In Problems 1–4, find the indicated part of each triangle *ABC*. Round each answer to the nearest tenth.

1. $B = 37°, C = 63°, a = 23$ ft; find b
2. $A = 26.3°, a = 6.2, b = 3.7$; find C
3. $C = 58°, a = 4.5, b = 5.6$; find c
4. $a = 3.4, b = 5.6, c = 7.9$; find A

In Problems 5–8, solve each triangle *ABC*. Round each answer to the nearest tenth.

5.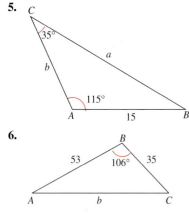

6.

7. $A = 42°, B = 37°, a = 50$ meters
8. $a = 30$ feet, $b = 20$ feet, $c = 25$ feet
9. Indicate whether the given measurements result in no triangle, one triangle, or two triangles. Solve each resulting triangle.

   $A = 43°, a = 185$ feet, $b = 248$ feet

10. Starting from point *A*, a surveyor walks 580 feet in the direction N 70.0° E. From that point, she walks 725 feet in the direction N 35.0° W. To the nearest foot, how far is she from her starting point?

In Problems 11–14, find the area of each triangle *ABC*. Round each answer to the nearest tenth square unit.

11. $a = 8, b = 12, C = 120°$
12. $C = 50°, a = 50, b = 60$
13. $A = 47°, B = 62°, c = 16$
14. $a = 2, b = 3, c = 4$

15. A side of a parallelogram is 30 cm long and makes angles of 27° and 43° with the two diagonals. Find the lengths of the two diagonals.

16. A flagpole 60 feet tall is at the top of a hill. At a point 180 feet down the hill, the angle between the surface of the hill and the line of sight to the top of the pole is 13°. Find the inclination of the hill to a horizontal plane.

17. A parallelogram has adjacent sides 70 and 90 feet long, and the angle between them is 37°. Find the lengths of the two diagonals.

18. Three circles of radii 80, 100, and 150 feet are tangent to each other externally. Find the area of the triangle formed by joining the centers of the circles.

Vectors

Moving objects have not only speed, but also direction. In fact, so many of the quantities we meet in our everyday experiences cannot be described by a number alone. Quantities that have both size (magnitude) and direction are called vector quantities. In this chapter, we describe vector quantities algebraically and geometrically and use them to solve real-world problems.

Geometric Vectors

THE MEANING OF FORCE

A **force** is a push or pull resulting from an object's *interaction* with another object. When the interacting objects are physically in contact with each other, the resulting force is called a *contact force*. Examples of contact forces include friction, tension, air resistance, and applied forces. A noncontact force is called an *action-at-a-distance* force. Examples of such forces include gravitational, electrical, and magnetic forces. The standard units of measurement for the magnitude of a force are pounds (lb) in the English system and newtons (N) in the metric system. The conversion factor between the systems is

$$1 \text{ pound of force} = 4.45 \text{ newtons.}$$

In Example 5, we discuss the *resultant* of two or more forces acting on an object. ■

---

1 Represent vectors geometrically.

Vectors

Many physical quantities such as length, area, volume, mass, and temperature are completely described by their magnitudes in appropriate units. Such quantities are called **scalar quantities**. Other physical quantities such as velocity, acceleration, and force are completely described only if *both* a magnitude (size) and a direction are specified. For example, the movement of wind is usually described by its speed (magnitude) and its direction (say, 15 miles per hour southwest). The wind speed and wind direction together form a **vector quantity** called the *wind velocity*.

Geometric Vectors

We can represent a **vector** geometrically by a directed line segment with an arrowhead. The arrow specifies the direction of the vector, and its length describes the magnitude. The tail of the arrow is the vector's **initial point**, and the tip of the arrow is its **terminal point**. We denote vectors by lowercase boldfaced type such as **a**, **b**, **i**, **j**, **u**, **v**, and **w**. When discussing vectors, we refer to real numbers as **scalars**. Scalars will be denoted by lowercase italic type such as *a*, *b*, *x*, *y*, and *z*.

As shown in Figure 8.1, if the initial point of a vector **v** is P and the terminal point is Q, we write

$$\mathbf{v} = \overrightarrow{PQ}.$$

The **magnitude** (or **norm**) of a vector $\mathbf{v} = \overrightarrow{PQ}$, denoted by $\|\mathbf{v}\|$ or $\|\overrightarrow{PQ}\|$, is the length of the vector **v** and is a scalar quantity.

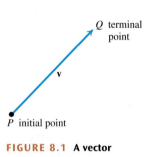

FIGURE 8.1 **A vector**

STUDY TIP

The *magnitude* of a vector is similar to the *absolute value* of a real number. Like absolute value, the magnitude of a vector cannot be negative.

Equivalent Vectors

Two vectors having the same length and same direction are called **equivalent vectors**. Because a vector is determined by its length and direction only, equivalent vectors are regarded as **equal** even though they may be located in different positions. If **v** and **w** are equivalent, we write **v** = **w**. See Figure 8.2.

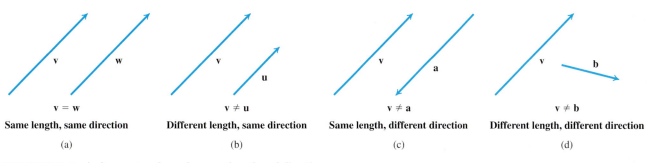

(a)	(b)	(c)	(d)
v = w	**v ≠ u**	**v ≠ a**	**v ≠ b**
Same length, same direction	Different length, same direction	Same length, different direction	Different length, different direction

FIGURE 8.2 Equivalent vectors have the same length and direction.

The vector of length zero is called the **zero vector** and is denoted by **0**. The zero vector has zero magnitude and arbitrary direction. If vectors **v** and **a**, as shown in Figure 8.2(c), have the same length and opposite direction, then **a** is the **opposite vector** of **v** and we write **a** = −**v**.

2 Add vectors geometrically.

Adding Vectors

Let's add two vectors **v** and **w**.

VECTOR ADDITIONS

Let **v** and **w** be any two vectors. Position the terminal point of **v** so that it coincides with the initial point of **w**. The *sum* **v** + **w** is the *resultant* vector whose initial point coincides with the initial point of **v**, and its terminal point coincides with the terminal point of **w**. This is called the **triangle law of vector addition**. See Figure 8.3.

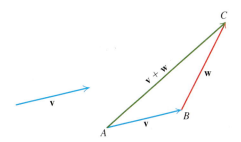

FIGURE 8.3 Triangle law for adding v and w

In Figure 8.3, if $\mathbf{v} = \overrightarrow{AB}$ and $\mathbf{w} = \overrightarrow{BC}$, then by vector addition, we have

$$\overrightarrow{AB} + \overrightarrow{BC} = \overrightarrow{AC}.$$

Note that in general, the sum of the magnitudes of $\overrightarrow{AB}$ and $\overrightarrow{BC}$ is not equal to the magnitude of $\overrightarrow{AC}$. It is only the *vector sum* $\overrightarrow{AB} + \overrightarrow{BC}$ that is equal to the vector $\overrightarrow{AC}$.

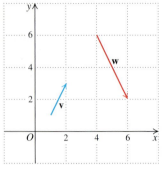

FIGURE 8.4

EXAMPLE 1   **Adding Two Vectors**

Let **v** and **w** be two vectors of Figure 8.4.

a. Draw the vector **v** + **w**.   **b.** Find $\|\mathbf{v} + \mathbf{w}\|$.

SOLUTION

a. We slide the vector **v** (without changing its length and direction) so that the terminal point of **v** coincides with the initial point of **w**. This can be accomplished by moving the vector **v** up three units and right two units. See Figure 8.5(a). We show the vector **v** + **w** in Figure 8.5(b). The initial point of **v** + **w** has coordinates $(3, 4)$, and its terminal point has coordinates $(6, 2)$.

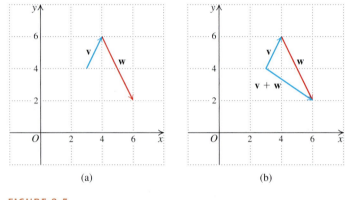

(a)   (b)

FIGURE 8.5

b. We can use the distance formula to find $\|\mathbf{v} + \mathbf{w}\|$.

$$\|\mathbf{v} + \mathbf{w}\| = \sqrt{(6 - 3)^2 + (2 - 4)^2} \qquad {\color{blue} d = \sqrt{(x_2 - x_1)^2 + (y_2 - y_1)^2}}$$
$$= \sqrt{3^2 + (-2)^2} = \sqrt{9 + 4} = \sqrt{13} \qquad {\color{blue}\text{Simplify.}} \qquad ■■■$$

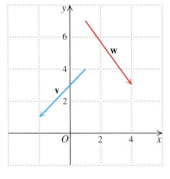

FIGURE 8.6

Practice Problem 1   Repeat Example 1 for the vectors of Figure 8.6.   ■

The definition of the sum of two vectors can be stated a different way. Given two vectors **v** and **w**, we place them so that the initial points of both vectors coincide. Next, we construct the parallelogram in which the given vectors are adjacent sides. Then as indicated in Figure 8.7, the sum **v** + **w** is the diagonal of the parallelogram directed from the common initial point to the opposite vertex. We call this the **parallelogram law of vector addition**. Figure 8.7 also illustrates that vector addition is commutative.

VECTOR ADDITION IS COMMUTATIVE

For any two vectors **v** and **w**

$$\mathbf{v} + \mathbf{w} = \mathbf{w} + \mathbf{v}.$$

In Figure 8.7, note that the vectors **v** and **w** and their sum **v** + **w** all have the same initial point O.

In summary, we have two geometric methods to use when adding two vectors **v** and **w**.

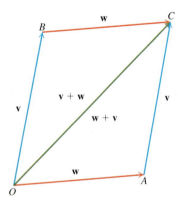

FIGURE 8.7 $\overrightarrow{OA} + \overrightarrow{OB} = \overrightarrow{OC}$

VECTOR ADDITION OF v AND w	
Triangle Method	Position **v** and **w** so that the terminal point of **v** coincides with the initial point of **w**. The vector whose initial point coincides with the initial point of **v** and whose terminal point coincides with the terminal point of **w** is **v** + **w**. See Figure 8.3.
Parallelogram Method	Position **v** and **w** so that the initial points of both vectors coincide. Construct the parallelogram in which **v** and **w** are adjacent sides. The diagonal of the parallelogram directed from the common initial point to the opposite vertex is **v** + **w**. See Figure 8.7.

Vector subtraction is defined just like the subtraction of real numbers. For any two vectors **v** and **w**, **v** − **w** = **v** + (−**w**), where −**w** is the opposite of **w**. See Figure 8.8.

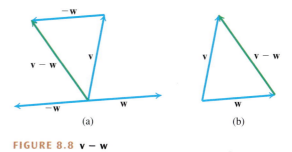

(a)   (b)

FIGURE 8.8 **v** − **w**

Figure 8.8(b) shows that you can construct the difference vector **v** − **w** without first drawing −**w**: Place the vectors **v** and **w** so that their initial points coincide. Then the vector from the terminal point of **w** to the terminal point of **v** is the vector **v** − **w**.

A second basic arithmetic operation for vectors is multiplying vectors by real numbers.

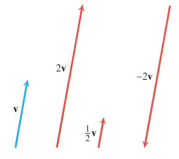

FIGURE 8.9 **Scalar multiples of v**

SCALAR MULTIPLES OF VECTORS

Let **v** be a vector and c a scalar (a real number). The vector c**v** is called the **scalar multiple** of **v**. See Figure 8.9.

If $c > 0$, c**v** has the same direction as **v** and magnitude $c\|\mathbf{v}\|$.

If $c < 0$, c**v** has the opposite direction of **v** and magnitude $|c|\|\mathbf{v}\|$.

If $c = 0$, c**v** = 0**v** = **0**.

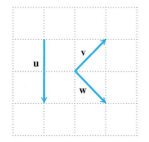

FIGURE 8.10

EXAMPLE 2   **Geometric Vectors**

Use the vectors **u**, **v**, and **w** in Figure 8.10 to graph each vector.

a. **u** − 2**w**   **b.** 2**v** − **u** + **w**

SOLUTION

The graphs are shown in Figure 8.11.

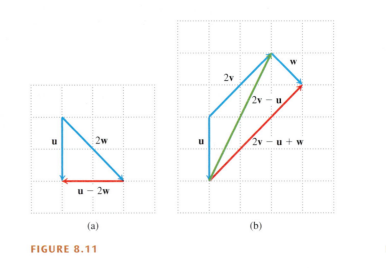

(a)   (b)

FIGURE 8.11   ▪ ▪ ▪

Practice Problem 2   Use the vectors **u**, **v**, and **w** of Figure 8.10 to graph each vector.

a. $2\mathbf{w} + \mathbf{v}$ **b.** $2\mathbf{w} + \mathbf{v} - \mathbf{u}$ ▪

EXAMPLE 3   **Writing a Vector in Terms of Other Vectors**

Let $\mathbf{v} = \overrightarrow{PQ}, \mathbf{w} = \overrightarrow{PR}$. Express $\overrightarrow{PS}$, where S is the midpoint of the segment QR in terms of **v** and **w**. See Figure 8.12.

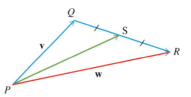

FIGURE 8.12

SOLUTION

In triangle PQR, we have $\overrightarrow{QR} = \mathbf{w} - \mathbf{v}$ Vector subtraction

So $\overrightarrow{QS} = \dfrac{1}{2}\overrightarrow{QR}$ S is midpoint of QR.

$$= \dfrac{1}{2}(\mathbf{w} - \mathbf{v})\qquad \overrightarrow{QR} = \mathbf{w} - \mathbf{v}$$

In triangle PQS, we have

$$\overrightarrow{PS} = \overrightarrow{PQ} + \overrightarrow{QS}\qquad \text{Vector addition}$$

$$= \mathbf{v} + \dfrac{1}{2}(\mathbf{w} - \mathbf{v})\qquad \text{Substitute.}$$

$$= \dfrac{1}{2}\mathbf{v} + \dfrac{1}{2}\mathbf{w}\qquad \text{Simplify.}\qquad ▪ ▪ ▪$$

Practice Problem 3   Repeat Example 3 assuming that S is $\dfrac{2}{3}$ of the way from Q to R.   ▪

3 Define and use the angle between two vectors.

Angle Between Two Vectors

In many physical applications of vectors, we require the measure of the angle between two vectors. First, we define this concept.

ANGLE BETWEEN TWO VECTORS

Let **v** and **w** be two nonzero vectors. Let $\overrightarrow{PQ}$ and $\overrightarrow{PR}$ represent **v** and **w**, respectively, with the same initial point P. The angle θ ($0° \leq \theta \leq 180°$) formed by the directed line segments $\overrightarrow{PQ}$ and $\overrightarrow{PR}$ is defined as the angle between **v** and **w**. See Figure 8.13.

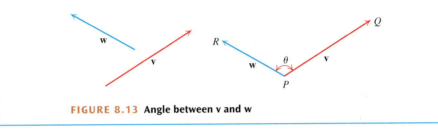

FIGURE 8.13 Angle between v and w

EXAMPLE 4   **Finding the Magnitude and Direction of the Sum of Two Vectors**

Let **v** and **w** be two vectors of magnitudes 12 and 7, respectively. The angle between **v** and **w** is 65°. Find each of the following, rounding the answers to the nearest tenth.

a. $\|\mathbf{v} + 2\mathbf{w}\|$

b. The angle θ between the vectors $\mathbf{v} + 2\mathbf{w}$ and **w**

SOLUTION

We draw the vectors **v**, **w**, 2**w**, and $\mathbf{v} + 2\mathbf{w}$. See Figure 8.14.

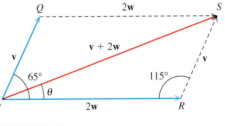

FIGURE 8.14

Note that the vector $\mathbf{v} + 2\mathbf{w}$ in Figure 8.14 is the third side of the triangle PRS. In the parallelogram $PQSR$, because the measure of $\angle QPR$ is 65°, the measure of the adjacent $\angle PRS$ is $180° - 65° = 115°$.

a. $\|\overrightarrow{PS}\|^2 = \|\overrightarrow{PR}\|^2 + \|\overrightarrow{RS}\|^2 - 2\|\overrightarrow{PR}\|\|\overrightarrow{RS}\| \cos 115°$ Apply the Law of Cosines to triangle PRS.

$\|\mathbf{v} + 2\mathbf{w}\|^2 = \|2\mathbf{w}\|^2 + \|\mathbf{v}\|^2 - 2\|2\mathbf{w}\|\|\mathbf{v}\| \cos 115°$

$= (|2|\|\mathbf{w}\|)^2 + \|\mathbf{v}\|^2 - 2|2|\|\mathbf{w}\|\|\mathbf{v}\| \cos 115°$ $\|2\mathbf{w}\| = |2|\|\mathbf{w}\|$

$\|\mathbf{v} + 2\mathbf{w}\|^2 = 481.9997$ Substitute $\|\mathbf{v}\| = 12$, $\|\mathbf{w}\| = 7$; use a calculator.

$\|\mathbf{v} + 2\mathbf{w}\| \approx 21.95$ Take the positive square root.

RECALL

From geometry, we know the following facts about parallelograms.

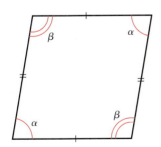

1. Opposite sides are parallel and equal.
2. Opposite angles are equal.
3. The sum of any two adjacent angles is 180°.
4. The diagonals bisect each other and are not necessarily equal.

b. To find angle θ in Figure 8.14, we apply the Law of Sines in triangle *PRS*.

$$\frac{\sin \theta}{\|\mathbf{v}\|} = \frac{\sin 115°}{\|\mathbf{v} + 2\mathbf{w}\|} \qquad \text{The Law of Sines}$$

$$\sin \theta = \frac{\|\mathbf{v}\| \sin 115°}{\|\mathbf{v} + 2\mathbf{w}\|} \qquad \text{Multiply both sides by } \|\mathbf{v}\|.$$

$$\theta = \sin^{-1}\left(\frac{\|\mathbf{v}\| \sin 115°}{\|\mathbf{v} + 2\mathbf{w}\|}\right) \qquad 0° \leq \theta \leq 90°$$

$$\theta \approx 29.7° \qquad \text{Use a calculator.} \qquad \blacksquare\,\blacksquare\,\blacksquare$$

Practice Problem 4 Repeat Example 4 assuming that $\|\mathbf{v}\| = 20$ and $\|\mathbf{w}\| = 7$. ■

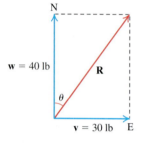

FIGURE 8.15

> **EXAMPLE 5** **Finding Resultant of Two Forces**

Find the resultant **R** of two forces, one a 40-pound force acting northward and the other a 30-pound force acting eastward.

SOLUTION

The resultant **R** is shown in Figure 8.15. The magnitude of **R** is

$$\|\mathbf{R}\| = \sqrt{40^2 + 30^2} = 50 \text{ lb.}$$

The angle θ that **R** makes with **w** is given by $\tan \theta = \dfrac{30}{40} = \dfrac{3}{4}$;

so $\theta = \tan^{-1}\left(\dfrac{3}{4}\right) \approx 36.87°$.

The resultant **R** is a 50-pound force acting in the approximate direction N 36.87° E.

$\blacksquare\,\blacksquare\,\blacksquare$

Practice Problem 5 Find the resultant of two forces, one a 60-pound force acting eastward and the other a 90-pound force acting southward. ■

4 Use vectors in navigation.

Navigation

Suppose an airplane headed due east travels with an *airspeed* (speed in still air) of 400 mph. If the wind is blowing due north at 50 mph, the plane will be blown off its course. To determine its *ground velocity* **r** (actual speed and direction relative to the ground), we argue as follows: In one hour, the airplane would travel 400 miles due east if there were no wind. But during this hour, the entire mass of the air in which the plane is moving has moved 50 miles to the north, carrying the plane with it. We expect that the plane would be at a point 400 miles east and 50 miles north of its starting point. In general, if **v** represents the air velocity of an airplane and **w** represents the wind velocity, then the ground velocity **r** of the airplane is the vector sum: **r** = **v** + **w**. The same type of argument applies to boats traveling in water.

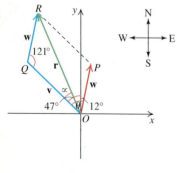

FIGURE 8.16

> **EXAMPLE 6** **Ground Velocity of a Plane**

An airplane is flying with an airspeed of 400 mph heading in the direction N 47° W. The velocity of wind is 46 mph in the direction N 12° E. Find the ground velocity of the airplane.

SOLUTION

Set up a coordinate system with north along the positive *y*-axis. See Figure 8.16. Let

$\mathbf{v} = $ Air velocity of the plane,

$\mathbf{w} = $ Wind velocity,

$\mathbf{r} = $ Ground velocity of the plane.

Figure 8.16 shows that the angle θ between **v** and **w** is $47° + 12° = 59°$.

$$\angle OQR = 180° - \theta = 180° - 59° = 121°$$ Parallelogram property

$$\|\mathbf{r}\|^2 = \|\mathbf{v}\|^2 + \|\mathbf{w}\|^2 - 2\|\mathbf{v}\|\|\mathbf{w}\| \cos 121°$$ Apply the Law of Cosines in triangle OQR.

$$\|\mathbf{r}\| = \sqrt{(400)^2 + (46)^2 - 2(400)(46)\cos(121°)}$$ Substitute values.

$$\approx 425.5$$ Use a calculator.

To find the bearing of **r**, we find the angle α between **r** and **v**. We have

$$\frac{\sin \alpha}{\|\mathbf{w}\|} = \frac{\sin 121°}{\|\mathbf{r}\|}$$ Apply the Law of Sines in triangle OQR.

$$\sin \alpha = \frac{\|\mathbf{w}\| \sin 121°}{\|\mathbf{r}\|}$$ Multiply both sides by $\|\mathbf{w}\|$.

$$\alpha = \sin^{-1}\left(\frac{46 \sin 121°}{425.5}\right) \approx 5.3°$$ Substitute values; use a calculator.

The angle between **r** and the positive y-axis is $47° - 5.3° = 41.7°$. Therefore, the ground velocity of the airplane is approximately 425.5 mph with bearing of about N 41.7° W. ■ ■ ■

Practice Problem 6   An airplane headed due east travels with an airspeed of 225 mph. The wind velocity is 40 mph in the direction N 25° E. Find the ground velocity of the airplane.   ■

SECTION 8.1 ■ Exercises

A EXERCISES Basic Skills and Concepts

1. A quantity that has both magnitude and direction is called a(n) _____ .

2. Two directed segments represent the same vector if they have the same _____ and the same _____ .

3. The vector sum **v** + **w** is represented by the diagonal of the _____ with adjacent sides **v** and **w**.

4. The angle θ between two vectors is the angle between two directed segments $\overrightarrow{PQ}$ and $\overrightarrow{PR}$ that _____ the vectors, and _____ $\leq \theta \leq$ _____ .

5. *True or False* The vector $-3\mathbf{v}$ is the vector with magnitude $-3\|\mathbf{v}\|$ and direction opposite **v**.

6. *True or False* The zero vector is the only vector with no direction specified.

In Exercises 7–12, label the vectors $\pm \mathbf{w}$ and $\pm(\mathbf{v} + \mathbf{w})$.

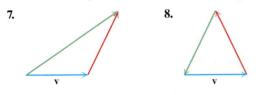

7.

8.

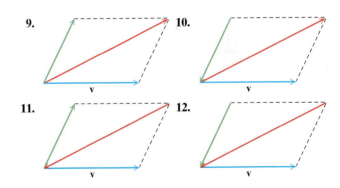

9.   10.

11.   12.

In Exercises 13–20, use the vectors u, v, and w in the accompanying figure to graph each vector.

13. **u** + **v**

14. 3**v**

15. 2**u** − **w**

16. **w** − 2**v**

17. **u** + **v** + **w**

18. 2**u** − **w** + **v**

19. **w** − 2**v** + **u**

20. 2**v** + 3**w** − **u**

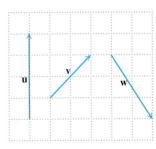

In Exercises 21–24, v = $\overrightarrow{PQ}$ and w = $\overrightarrow{PR}$. Express each vector in terms of v and w.

21. $\overrightarrow{RS}$, where S is the midpoint of the segment QR

22. $\overrightarrow{RS}$, where S is $\frac{2}{3}$ of the way from R to Q

23. $\overrightarrow{PS}$, where S is $\frac{1}{3}$ of the way from Q to R

24. $\overrightarrow{PS}$, where S is $\frac{8}{9}$ of the way from Q to R

For Exercises 25–36, refer to the vectors v_1–v_6 represented by the sides of a regular hexagon in the figure. Describe each nonzero vector in terms of a directed segment in the hexagon.
[Note that the triangles AOB, BOC, . . . in the hexagon are equilateral.]

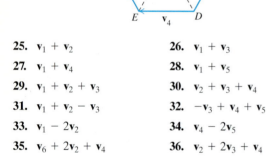

25. $v_1 + v_2$ 26. $v_1 + v_3$

27. $v_1 + v_4$ 28. $v_1 + v_5$

29. $v_1 + v_2 + v_3$ 30. $v_2 + v_3 + v_4$

31. $v_1 + v_2 - v_3$ 32. $-v_3 + v_4 + v_5$

33. $v_1 - 2v_2$ 34. $v_4 - 2v_5$

35. $v_6 + 2v_2 + v_4$ 36. $v_2 + 2v_3 + v_4$

In Exercises 37–44, the magnitudes $\|v\|$, $\|w\|$, and the angle θ between the vectors v and w are given. Round each answer of the requested magnitude to the nearest tenth.

37. $\|v\| = 3$, $\|w\| = 5$, $\theta = 60°$; find $\|v + w\|$

38. $\|v\| = 4$, $\|w\| = 6$, $\theta = 30°$; find $\|v + w\|$

39. $\|v\| = 3$, $\|w\| = 4$, $\theta = 40°$; find $\|v + 2w\|$

40. $\|v\| = 5$, $\|w\| = 8$, $\theta = 75°$; find $\|2v + w\|$

41. $\|v\| = 12$, $\|w\| = 7$, $\theta = 110°$; find $\|v - 2w\|$

42. $\|v\| = 4$, $\|w\| = 9$, $\theta = 130°$; find $\|-2v + w\|$

43. $\|v\| = 5$, $\|w\| = 7$, $\theta = 118°$; find $\|2v + 3w\|$

44. $\|v\| = 3$, $\|w\| = 5$, $\theta = 85°$; find $\|3v - 2w\|$

In Exercises 45–52, use estimates from Exercises 37–44 to round each answer to the nearest tenth degree.

45. For v, w, and θ of Exercise 37, find
    a. the angle between v + w and v.
    b. the angle between v + w and w.

46. For v, w, and θ of Exercise 38, find
    a. the angle between v + w and v.
    b. the angle between v + w and w.

47. For v, w, and θ of Exercise 39, find
    a. the angle between v + 2w and v.
    b. the angle between v + 2w and w.

48. For v, w, and θ of Exercise 40, find
    a. the angle between 2v + w and v.
    b. the angle between 2v + w and w.

49. For v, w, and θ of Exercise 41, find
    a. the angle between v − 2w and v.
    b. the angle between v − 2w and w.

50. For v, w, and θ of Exercise 42, find
    a. the angle between −2v + w and v.
    b. the angle between −2v + w and w.

51. For v, w, and θ of Exercise 43, find
    a. the angle between 2v + 3w and v.
    b. the angle between 2v + 3w and w.

52. For v, w, and θ of Exercise 44, find
    a. the angle between 3v − 2w and v.
    b. the angle between 3v − 2w and w.

B EXERCISES Applying the Concepts

In Exercises 53–62, find each answer to the nearest tenth.

53. **Resultant force.** Find the resultant **R** of two forces, one of 35 lb acting due south and the other of 46 lb acting due west.

54. **Resultant forces.** Find **R** assuming that the second force in Exercise 53 is doubled.

55. **Resultant force.** Two forces of 300 N (newtons) and 400 N act at the origin and make angles of 15° and 35°, respectively, with the positive x-axis. Find the resultant force.

56. **Resultant force.** Repeat Exercise 55 assuming that the forces have the same magnitude but that the angle each force makes with the x-axis is doubled.

57. **Angle between forces.** Two forces $F_1 = 30$ lb and $F_2 = 40$ lb act at a point with a resultant force **R** $= 33$ lb. Find the angle between the forces F_1 and F_2.

58. **Angle between forces.** Repeat Exercise 57 assuming that $F_1 = 50$ N, $F_2 = 65$ N, and **R** $= 40$ N.

59. **Ground speed.** A 40 mph wind is blowing toward the north. At what speed should a plane head due east to be on course N 75° E? Find the ground speed of the plane.

60. **Ground speed.** The pilot in Exercise 59 flies with an airspeed of 350 mph. In what direction should the pilot head the plane if she wants to travel due east? Find the ground speed of the plane.

61. **River current.** A power boat is crossing a river at 22 mph with a bearing of N 78° E. The current in the water with a bearing of N 23° E is flowing at 8 mph. Find the actual speed and direction of the boat.

62. Tugboats. Two tugboats are pulling a barge out of a harbor. Tugboat A pulls the barge with a force of 6000 lb bearing N 65° E. Find the magnitude of the force from tugboat B with bearing S 75° E that is required to pull the barge eastward.

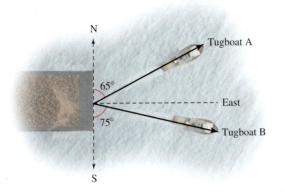

C EXERCISES Beyond the Basics

63. Associative law. For any three vectors **u**, **v**, and **w**, prove that $(\mathbf{u} + \mathbf{v}) + \mathbf{w} = \mathbf{u} + (\mathbf{v} + \mathbf{w})$.
[*Hint:* Let $\overrightarrow{OP}$, $\overrightarrow{PQ}$, and $\overrightarrow{QR}$ represent the vectors **u**, **v**, and **w**, respectively. Show that $(\overrightarrow{OP} + \overrightarrow{PQ}) + \overrightarrow{QR} = \overrightarrow{OR}$ and that $\overrightarrow{OP} + (\overrightarrow{PQ} + \overrightarrow{QR}) = \overrightarrow{OR}$.]

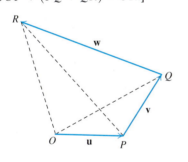

64. Let $P, Q, R, S,$ and T be five points in the plane. Show that
  a. $\overrightarrow{PQ} + \overrightarrow{QR} + \overrightarrow{RS} = \overrightarrow{PS}$.
  b. $\overrightarrow{PQ} + \overrightarrow{QR} + \overrightarrow{RS} + \overrightarrow{ST} = \overrightarrow{PT}$.

65. Use Exercise 64 a to show that in a triangle ABC, $\overrightarrow{AB} + \overrightarrow{BC} + \overrightarrow{CA} = \mathbf{0}$.

66. In a quadrilateral $ABCD$, show that $\overrightarrow{BC} + \overrightarrow{CD} + \overrightarrow{DA} + \overrightarrow{BA} = 2\overrightarrow{BA}$.

67. In a triangle ABC, let D be the midpoint of AB. Show that $\overrightarrow{CA} + \overrightarrow{CB} = 2\overrightarrow{CD}$.

68. In a quadrilateral $ABCD$, let P and Q be the midpoints of sides AB and CD, respectively. Show that $\overrightarrow{AD} + \overrightarrow{BC} = 2\overrightarrow{PQ}$.

69. In a regular pentagon $ABCDE$, show that $\overrightarrow{AB} + \overrightarrow{AE} + \overrightarrow{BC} + \overrightarrow{DC} + \overrightarrow{ED} = 2\overrightarrow{AC}$.

70. In a regular hexagon $ABCDEF$, show that $\overrightarrow{AB} + \overrightarrow{AC} + \overrightarrow{AD} + \overrightarrow{AE} + \overrightarrow{AF} = 3\overrightarrow{AD}$.

Critical Thinking

71. The following figure gives three vectors: **a**, **b**, and **c**. Which of the following is a true statement?
  a. $\mathbf{a} - \mathbf{c} + \mathbf{b} = \mathbf{0}$ **b.** $\mathbf{a} - \mathbf{b} + \mathbf{c} = \mathbf{0}$
  c. $\mathbf{a} + \mathbf{b} + \mathbf{c} = \mathbf{0}$ **d.** $\mathbf{a} - \mathbf{c} - \mathbf{b} = \mathbf{0}$

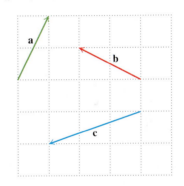

Algebraic Vectors

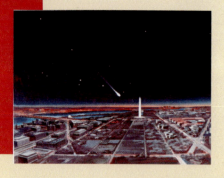

Before Starting this Section, Review	**Objectives**
1. Distance formula (Appendix)	**1** Represent vectors algebraically.
2. Slope of a line (Appendix)	**2** Find a unit vector in the direction of a vector **v**.
3. Definitions of trigonometric functions (Section 1.3)	**3** Write a vector in **i, j** form.
4. Reference angle (Section 1.4)	**4** Write a vector in terms of its magnitude and direction.
	5 Use vectors in applications.

EQUILIBRANT

If the velocity of an object is changing, we say that the object is *accelerating*. **Acceleration** is the rate of change of velocity, and **force** = mass × acceleration. So a force acting on an object will cause the object to accelerate. If a number of forces act simultaneously on an object, the *net force* on the object is the resultant (the vector sum) of all of the forces. An object is said to be in a state of **equilibrium** if the net force on the object is zero. An **equilibrant** is a single force that acts to keep a system of forces in equilibrium. Therefore, it is equal in magnitude and opposite in direction to the resultant force of the system. In Example 9, we find the equilibrant for a number of forces acting on an object. ■

1 Represent vectors algebraically.

Algebraic Vectors

We now consider vectors in the Cartesian coordinate plane. Because the location of the initial point of a vector is not relevant, we typically draw vectors with their initial point at the origin. Such a vector is called a **position vector**. Note that the terminal point of a position vector will completely determine the vector, so specifying the terminal point will specify the vector. For the position vector **v** (see Figure 8.17) with initial point at the origin O and terminal point at $P(v_1, v_2)$, we denote the vector by

$$\mathbf{v} = \overrightarrow{OP} = \langle v_1, v_2 \rangle.$$

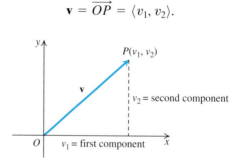

FIGURE 8.17 A position vector

We call v_1 and v_2 the **components** of the vector **v**; v_1 is the **first** (or **horizontal**) **component**, and v_2 is the **second** (or **vertical**) **component**. Note the difference between the notations for the *point* (v_1, v_2) and the *position vector* $\langle v_1, v_2 \rangle$. The magnitude of the position vector $\mathbf{v} = \langle v_1, v_2 \rangle$ follows directly from the Pythagorean Theorem. We have $\|\mathbf{v}\| = \sqrt{v_1^2 + v_2^2}$.

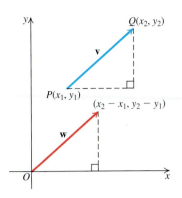

FIGURE 8.18 Two equivalent vectors

If equivalent vectors **v** and **w** are located so that their initial points are at the origin, then their terminal points must coincide (because the equivalent vectors have the same length and same direction). Thus, for the vectors

$$\mathbf{v} = \langle v_1, v_2 \rangle \quad \text{and} \quad \mathbf{w} = \langle w_1, w_2 \rangle,$$
$$\mathbf{v} = \mathbf{w} \quad \text{if and only if} \quad v_1 = w_1 \quad \text{and} \quad v_2 = w_2.$$

We can use congruent triangles to show that any vector **v** with initial point $P = (x_1, y_1)$ and terminal point $Q = (x_2, y_2)$ is equivalent to the position vector $\mathbf{w} = \langle x_2 - x_1, y_2 - y_1 \rangle$. Any vector in the Cartesian plane can therefore be represented by a position vector. See Figure 8.18.

REPRESENTING A VECTOR AS A POSITION VECTOR

The vector $\overrightarrow{PQ}$ with initial point $P = (x_1, y_1)$ and terminal point $Q = (x_2, y_2)$ is equal to the position vector

$$\mathbf{w} = \langle x_2 - x_1, y_2 - y_1 \rangle.$$

STUDY TIP

Notice that the point (v_1, v_2) has neither magnitude nor direction, whereas the nonzero position vector $\langle v_1, v_2 \rangle$ has both.

EXAMPLE 1   Representing a Vector in the Cartesian Plane

Let **v** be the vector with initial point $P = (4, -2)$ and terminal point $Q = (-1, 3)$. Write **v** as a position vector.

SOLUTION

Because **v** has initial point $P = (4, -2)$, $x_1 = 4$ and $y_1 = -2$.
Because **v** has terminal point $Q = (-1, 3)$, $x_2 = -1$ and $y_2 = 3$.

So

$$\begin{aligned}
\mathbf{w} &= \langle x_2 - x_1, y_2 - y_1 \rangle & \text{Position vector representation of } \overrightarrow{PQ} \\
&= \langle -1 - 4, 3 - (-2) \rangle & \text{Substitute values.} \\
&= \langle -5, 5 \rangle & \text{Simplify.} \quad \blacksquare\blacksquare\blacksquare
\end{aligned}$$

Practice Problem 1   Let **w** be the vector with initial point $P = (-2, 7)$ and terminal point $Q = (1, -3)$. Write **w** as a position vector. ∎

The zero vector is $\mathbf{0} = \langle 0, 0 \rangle$, and the opposite of the vector $\mathbf{v} = \langle v_1, v_2 \rangle$ is $-\mathbf{v} = \langle -v_1, -v_2 \rangle$. The following properties describe the arithmetic operations on vectors, using components.

ARITHMETIC OPERATIONS ON VECTORS

If $\mathbf{v} = \langle v_1, v_2 \rangle$ and $\mathbf{w} = \langle w_1, w_2 \rangle$ are vectors and c is any scalar, then

$$\begin{aligned}
\mathbf{v} + \mathbf{w} &= \langle v_1 + w_1, v_2 + w_2 \rangle & \text{Vector addition} \\
\mathbf{v} - \mathbf{w} &= \langle v_1 - w_1, v_2 - w_2 \rangle & \text{Vector subtraction} \\
c\mathbf{v} &= \langle cv_1, cv_2 \rangle & \text{Scalar multiplication}
\end{aligned}$$

EXAMPLE 2   Operations on Vectors

Let $\mathbf{v} = \langle 2, 3 \rangle$ and $\mathbf{w} = \langle -4, 1 \rangle$. Find each expression.

a. v + w   b. 2v

SOLUTION

a. $\mathbf{v} + \mathbf{w} = \langle 2, 3 \rangle + \langle -4, 1 \rangle = \langle 2 - 4, 3 + 1 \rangle = \langle -2, 4 \rangle$. See Figure 8.19(a).

b. $2\mathbf{v} = 2 \langle 2, 3 \rangle = \langle 2 \cdot 2, 2 \cdot 3 \rangle = \langle 4, 6 \rangle$. See Figure 8.19(b).

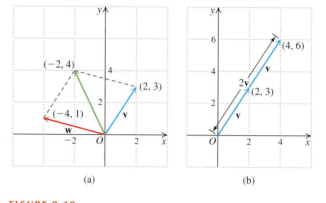

(a)   (b)

FIGURE 8.19

■ ■ ■

Practice Problem 2 Let $\mathbf{v} = \langle -1, 2 \rangle$ and $\mathbf{w} = \langle 2, -3 \rangle$. Find each expression.

a. $\mathbf{v} + \mathbf{w}$ **b.** $3\mathbf{w}$

■

EXAMPLE 3   **Finding the Magnitude of a Vector**

For the vectors $\mathbf{v}$ and $\mathbf{w}$ of Example 2, find $\|2\mathbf{v} - \mathbf{w}\|$.

SOLUTION

We have

$$2\mathbf{v} - \mathbf{w} = 2 \langle 2, 3 \rangle - \langle -4, 1 \rangle \qquad \text{\color{blue}{$\mathbf{v} = \langle 2, 3 \rangle$; $\mathbf{w} = \langle -4, 1 \rangle$}}$$
$$= \langle 4, 6 \rangle - \langle -4, 1 \rangle \qquad \text{\color{blue}{Scalar multiplication}}$$
$$= \langle 4 - (-4), 6 - 1 \rangle \qquad \text{\color{blue}{Vector subtraction}}$$
$$= \langle 8, 5 \rangle \qquad \text{\color{blue}{Simplify.}}$$

So

$$\|2\mathbf{v} - \mathbf{w}\| = \|\langle 8, 5 \rangle\|$$
$$= \sqrt{8^2 + 5^2} \qquad \text{\color{blue}{$\mathbf{v} = \langle v_1, v_2 \rangle$; $\|\mathbf{v}\| = \sqrt{v_1^2 + v_2^2}$}}$$
$$= \sqrt{64 + 25} = \sqrt{89} \approx 9.43 \qquad \text{\color{blue}{Use a calculator.}}$$

■ ■ ■

Practice Problem 3 For the vectors $\mathbf{v}$ and $\mathbf{w}$ of Practice Problem 2, find $\|3\mathbf{w} - 2\mathbf{v}\|$.

■

2 Find a unit vector in the direction of a vector $\mathbf{v}$.

Unit Vectors

Recall that if $c > 0$ and $\mathbf{v}$ is any vector, then the vector $c\mathbf{v}$ has the same direction as $\mathbf{v}$ and its length is given by

$$\|c\mathbf{v}\| = c\|\mathbf{v}\|.$$

Thus, if $\mathbf{v}$ is a nonzero vector, then letting $c = \dfrac{1}{\|\mathbf{v}\|}$, we have $\left\|\dfrac{1}{\|\mathbf{v}\|}\mathbf{v}\right\| = \dfrac{1}{\|\mathbf{v}\|}\|\mathbf{v}\| = 1.$

Consequently, $\dfrac{1}{\|\mathbf{v}\|}\mathbf{v}$ is a vector of length 1 in the same direction as $\mathbf{v}$. A vector of length 1 is called a **unit vector**.

EXAMPLE 4   **Using a Unit Vector**

a. Find a unit vector **u** in the direction of $\mathbf{v} = \langle 3, -4 \rangle$.

b. Find a vector of length 3 in the direction opposite $\mathbf{v} = \langle 3, -4 \rangle$.

SOLUTION

a. Find magnitude of $\mathbf{v} = \langle 3, -4 \rangle$.

$$\|\mathbf{v}\| = \sqrt{(3)^2 + (-4)^2} \qquad \text{Formula for magnitude}$$
$$\|\mathbf{v}\| = \sqrt{25} = 5 \qquad \text{Simplify.}$$

Now let

$$\mathbf{u} = \frac{1}{\|\mathbf{v}\|}\mathbf{v} \qquad \text{Multiply } \mathbf{v} \text{ by the scalar } \frac{1}{\|\mathbf{v}\|}.$$

$$\mathbf{u} = \frac{1}{5}\langle 3, -4 \rangle \qquad \text{Substitute values.}$$

$$\mathbf{u} = \left\langle \frac{3}{5}, -\frac{4}{5} \right\rangle \qquad \text{Scalar multiplication}$$

Check that $\|\mathbf{u}\| = 1$.

$$\|\mathbf{u}\| = \sqrt{\left(\frac{3}{5}\right)^2 + \left(-\frac{4}{5}\right)^2} = \sqrt{\frac{9}{25} + \frac{16}{25}} = \sqrt{\frac{25}{25}} = 1.$$

Hence, $\mathbf{u} = \left\langle \frac{3}{5}, -\frac{4}{5} \right\rangle$ is a unit vector in the same direction as **v**. (Note that **u** is a scalar multiple of **v**.)

b. A vector **w** of length 3 in the direction of **v** is

$$\mathbf{w} = 3\mathbf{u} = 3\left\langle \frac{3}{5}, -\frac{4}{5} \right\rangle = \left\langle \frac{9}{5}, -\frac{12}{5} \right\rangle.$$

A vector of length 3 in the direction opposite **v** is

$$-\mathbf{w} = -\left\langle \frac{9}{5}, -\frac{12}{5} \right\rangle = \left\langle -\frac{9}{5}, \frac{12}{5} \right\rangle. \qquad ■■■$$

Practice Problem 4

a. Find a unit vector in the direction of $\mathbf{v} = \langle -12, 5 \rangle$.

b. Find a vector of length 2 in the direction of $\mathbf{v} = \langle -12, 5 \rangle$.   ■

3 Write a vector in **i**, **j** form.

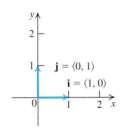

FIGURE 8.20 Standard unit vectors

Vectors in **i**, **j** Form

In a Cartesian coordinate plane, two important unit vectors lie along the positive coordinate axes.

$$\mathbf{i} = \langle 1, 0 \rangle \quad \text{and} \quad \mathbf{j} = \langle 0, 1 \rangle$$

The unit vectors **i** and **j** are called **standard unit vectors**. See Figure 8.20.
Every vector $\mathbf{v} = \langle v_1, v_2 \rangle$ can be expressed in terms of **i** and **j** as follows:

$$\mathbf{v} = \langle v_1, v_2 \rangle = \langle v_1, 0 \rangle + \langle 0, v_2 \rangle \qquad \text{Vector addition}$$
$$= v_1\langle 1, 0 \rangle + v_2\langle 0, 1 \rangle \qquad \text{Scalar multiplication}$$
$$= v_1\mathbf{i} + v_2\mathbf{j} \qquad \text{Replace } \langle 1, 0 \rangle \text{ with } \mathbf{i} \text{ and } \langle 0, 1 \rangle \text{ with } \mathbf{j}.$$

The scalars v_1 and v_2 are called the *horizontal* and *vertical components of* **v**, respectively. A vector **v** from $(0, 0)$ to (v_1, v_2) can therefore be represented in the form

$$\mathbf{v} = v_1\mathbf{i} + v_2\mathbf{j}$$

with $$\|\mathbf{v}\| = \sqrt{v_1^2 + v_2^2}.$$

EXAMPLE 5 **Vectors Involving i and j**

Find each expression for $\mathbf{u} = 4\mathbf{i} + 7\mathbf{j}$ and $\mathbf{v} = 2\mathbf{i} + 5\mathbf{j}$.

a. $\mathbf{u} - 3\mathbf{v}$ **b.** $\|\mathbf{u} - 3\mathbf{v}\|$

SOLUTION

a. $\mathbf{u} - 3\mathbf{v} = (4\mathbf{i} + 7\mathbf{j}) - 3(2\mathbf{i} + 5\mathbf{j})$

$\qquad\qquad = 4\mathbf{i} + 7\mathbf{j} - 6\mathbf{i} - 15\mathbf{j}$ Scalar multiplication

$\qquad\qquad = (4 - 6)\mathbf{i} + (7 - 15)\mathbf{j}$ Group terms.

$\qquad\qquad = -2\mathbf{i} - 8\mathbf{j}$ Simplify.

b. $\|\mathbf{u} - 3\mathbf{v}\| = \|-2\mathbf{i} - 8\mathbf{j}\|$

$\qquad\qquad\quad = \sqrt{(-2)^2 + (-8)^2}$ $\|v_1\mathbf{i} + v_2\mathbf{j}\| = \sqrt{v_1^2 + v_2^2}$

$\qquad\qquad\quad = \sqrt{68} = 2\sqrt{17}$ Simplify.   ■ ■ ■

Practice Problem 5 Find each expression for $\mathbf{u} = -3\mathbf{i} + 2\mathbf{j}$ and $\mathbf{v} = \mathbf{i} + 4\mathbf{j}$.

a. $3\mathbf{u} + 2\mathbf{v}$ **b.** $\|3\mathbf{u} + 2\mathbf{v}\|$ ■

4 Write a vector in terms of its magnitude and direction.

Vector in Terms of Magnitude and Direction

Let $\mathbf{v} = \langle v_1, v_2 \rangle$ be a position vector and suppose θ is the smallest positive angle that **v** makes with the positive x-axis. The angle θ is called the **direction angle** of **v**. See Figure 8.21.

The length (or magnitude) of the vector $\overrightarrow{OP}$ is $\|\mathbf{v}\|$; so

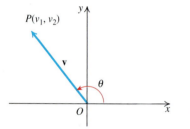

FIGURE 8.21 $\mathbf{v} = \|\mathbf{v}\|(\cos\theta\mathbf{i} + \sin\theta\mathbf{j})$

$$\frac{v_1}{\|\mathbf{v}\|} = \cos\theta \quad \text{and} \quad \frac{v_2}{\|\mathbf{v}\|} = \sin\theta \qquad \text{Definitions of cosine and sine}$$

$$v_1 = \|\mathbf{v}\|\cos\theta \qquad v_2 = \|\mathbf{v}\|\sin\theta \qquad \text{Multiply both sides by } \|\mathbf{v}\|.$$

Hence,

$$\mathbf{v} = v_1\mathbf{i} + v_2\mathbf{j} \qquad\qquad \text{Write } \mathbf{v} \text{ in terms of } \mathbf{i} \text{ and } \mathbf{j}.$$

$$\mathbf{v} = \|\mathbf{v}\|\cos\theta\mathbf{i} + \|\mathbf{v}\|\sin\theta\mathbf{j} \qquad \text{Replace values of } v_1 \text{ and } v_2.$$

$$\mathbf{v} = \|\mathbf{v}\|(\cos\theta\mathbf{i} + \sin\theta\mathbf{j}) \qquad \text{Factor out } \|\mathbf{v}\|.$$

$$= \|\mathbf{v}\|\langle\cos\theta, \sin\theta\rangle \qquad \text{Component form}$$

VECTOR IN TERMS OF MAGNITUDE AND DIRECTION

The formulas

$$\mathbf{v} = \|\mathbf{v}\|(\cos\theta\mathbf{i} + \sin\theta\mathbf{j}) \text{ and}$$

$$\mathbf{v} = \|\mathbf{v}\|\langle\cos\theta, \sin\theta\rangle$$

express a vector **v** in terms of its magnitude $\|\mathbf{v}\|$ and its direction angle θ.

Note that any angle coterminal with the direction angle θ of a vector $\mathbf{v}$ can be used in place of θ in the formula $\mathbf{v} = \|\mathbf{v}\|(\cos\theta\mathbf{i} + \sin\theta\mathbf{j})$, or $\mathbf{v} = \|\mathbf{v}\|\langle\cos\theta, \sin\theta\rangle$ in the box. The process of finding the components of a vector is called **resolving** the **vector** into components.

EXAMPLE 6   Resolving a Vector with Given Length and Direction Angle

Write in $\mathbf{i}, \mathbf{j}$ form the vector of magnitude 3 that makes an angle of $\dfrac{\pi}{3}$ with the positive x-axis.

SOLUTION
If $\mathbf{v}$ is the required vector, then

$$\mathbf{v} = \|\mathbf{v}\|(\cos\theta\mathbf{i} + \sin\theta\mathbf{j}) \qquad \text{Write } \mathbf{v} \text{ in terms of its magnitude and direction.}$$

$$\mathbf{v} = 3\left(\cos\frac{\pi}{3}\mathbf{i} + \sin\frac{\pi}{3}\mathbf{j}\right) \qquad \text{Substitute } \|\mathbf{v}\| = 3 \text{ and } \theta = \frac{\pi}{3}.$$

$$\mathbf{v} = 3\left(\frac{1}{2}\mathbf{i} + \frac{\sqrt{3}}{2}\mathbf{j}\right) \qquad \cos\frac{\pi}{3} = \frac{1}{2}; \sin\frac{\pi}{3} = \frac{\sqrt{3}}{2}$$

$$\mathbf{v} = \frac{3}{2}\mathbf{i} + \frac{3\sqrt{3}}{2}\mathbf{j} \qquad \text{Distributive property.} \qquad ■ ■ ■$$

Practice Problem 6   Write in component form the vector of magnitude 2 that makes an angle of $\dfrac{11\pi}{6}$ with the positive x-axis. ■

We can find the direction angle θ of a position vector $\mathbf{v} = \langle v_1, v_2 \rangle$ by using the equation $\tan\theta = \dfrac{v_2}{v_1}$ and the quadrant in which the point (v_1, v_2) lies.

EXAMPLE 7   Finding the Direction Angle of a Vector

Find the direction angle of the vector $\mathbf{v} = -4\mathbf{i} + 3\mathbf{j}$.

SOLUTION

$$\mathbf{v} = -4\mathbf{i} + 3\mathbf{j}$$
$$= \langle -4, 3 \rangle \qquad \text{Write } \mathbf{v} \text{ as a position vector.}$$
$$\tan\theta = \frac{3}{-4} = -\frac{3}{4}$$

The reference angle θ' is given by

$$\theta' = \left|\tan^{-1}\left(-\frac{3}{4}\right)\right| \approx |-36.87°| = 36.87°.$$

Because the point $(-4, 3)$ lies in quadrant II, we have

$$\theta = 180° - \theta' \approx 180° - 36.87° = 143.13°.$$

See Figure 8.22.   ■ ■ ■

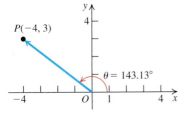

FIGURE 8.22 The direction angle of $\mathbf{v} = -4\mathbf{i} + 3\mathbf{j}$

Practice Problem 7   Find the direction angle of $\mathbf{v} = 2\mathbf{i} - 3\mathbf{j}$. ■

5 Use vectors in applications.

Applications of Vectors

EXAMPLE 8 Using Vectors in Air Navigation

An F-15 fighter jet is flying over Mount Rushmore at an airspeed (speed in still air) of 800 miles per hour on a bearing of N 30° E. The velocity of wind is 40 miles per hour in the direction of S 45° E. Find the actual speed and direction (relative to the ground) of the plane. Round each answer to the nearest tenth.

SOLUTION
Set up a coordinate system with north along the positive y-axis. See Figure 8.23.

Let **v** be the air velocity of the plane,

w be the wind velocity, and

r be the resultant ground velocity of the plane.

Writing each vector in terms of its magnitude and the direction angle θ that the vector makes with the positive x-axis, we have

$$\mathbf{v} = 800\,(\cos 60°\mathbf{i} \ + \sin 60°\mathbf{j}) \qquad 90° - 30° = 60°$$
$$\mathbf{w} = 40[\cos 315°\mathbf{i} + \sin 315°\mathbf{j}] \qquad 270° + 45° = 315°$$
$$= 40[\cos 45°\mathbf{i} - \sin 45°\mathbf{j}] \qquad \cos 315° = \cos 45°; \sin 315° = -\sin 45°$$

The resultant **r** is given by

$$\mathbf{r} = \mathbf{v} + \mathbf{w}$$
$$\mathbf{r} = 800(\cos 60°\mathbf{i} \ + \sin 60°\mathbf{j}) + 40(\cos 45°\mathbf{i} - \sin 45°\mathbf{j}) \qquad \text{Substitute values of } \mathbf{v} \text{ and } \mathbf{w}.$$

$$\mathbf{r} = (800 \cos 60° + 40 \cos 45°)\mathbf{i} + (800 \sin 60° - 40 \sin 45°)\mathbf{j} \qquad \text{Add vectors.}$$
$$\|\mathbf{r}\| = \sqrt{(800 \cos 60° + 40 \cos 45°)^2 + (800 \sin 60° - 40 \sin 45°)^2} \qquad \|v_1\mathbf{i} + v_2\mathbf{j}\| = \sqrt{v_1^2 + v_2^2}$$

$$\|\mathbf{r}\| \approx 790.6 \qquad \text{Use a calculator.}$$

The ground speed of the F-15 is approximately 790.6 miles per hour. To find the actual direction (bearing) of the plane, we first find the direction angle θ of **r**.

$$\theta = \tan^{-1}\left(\frac{800 \sin 60° \ - \ 40 \sin 45°}{800 \cos 60° \ + \ 40 \cos 45°}\right)$$
$$\approx 57.2° \qquad \text{Use a calculator.}$$

The angle between **v** and the y-axis (direction north) is

$$90° - 57.2° = 32.8°.$$

The bearing of the F-15 is approximately N 32.8° E. ■ ■ ■

Practice Problem 8 Repeat Example 8 assuming that the bearing of the plane is N 60° W and the direction of the wind is S 30° W. ■

EXAMPLE 9 Obtaining an Equilibrium

What single force (equilibrant) must be added to the system of forces shown in Figure 8.24 to obtain a system that is in equilibrium?

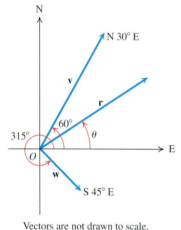

Vectors are not drawn to scale.

FIGURE 8.23

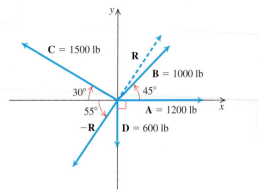

FIGURE 8.24 A system in equilibrium

SOLUTION

We first find the resultant **R** of the given system. The simplest procedure is to find the horizontal component (x-component) and the vertical component (y-component) of each force.

The horizontal component R_1 of **R** is given by

$$R_1 = A_1 \qquad + B_1 \qquad + C_1 \qquad + D_1$$
$$= 1200 \cos 0° + 1000 \cos 45° + 1500 \cos 150° + 600 \cos (270°)$$
$$\approx 608.07.$$

Similarly, the vertical component R_2 of **R** is given by

$$R_2 = A_2 \qquad + B_2 \qquad + C_2 \qquad + D_2$$
$$= 1200 \sin 0° + 1000 \sin 45° + 1500 \sin 150° + 600 \sin (270°)$$
$$\approx 857.11$$
$$\mathbf{R} = R_1\mathbf{i} \qquad + R_2\mathbf{j}$$
$$= 608.07\mathbf{i} + 857.11\mathbf{j}$$
$$\|\mathbf{R}\| = \sqrt{(608.07)^2 + (857.11)^2} \approx 1051 \text{ lb}$$
$$\theta = \tan^{-1}\left(\frac{857.11}{608.07}\right)$$
$$\approx 54.6°.$$

The force that must be added to obtain equilibrium is the negative of **R**. This is a force of approximately 1051 lb, and $-\mathbf{R}$ makes an angle of $180° + 54.6° = 234.6°$ with the positive x-axis. See Figure 8.24. ■ ■ ■

Practice Problem 9   Find the equilibrant of the following system of forces acting simultaneously at a point: $\mathbf{u} = 200$ lb in the direction N 40° E, $\mathbf{v} = 300$ lb in the direction N 70° W, and $\mathbf{w} = 400$ lb in the direction S 20° E. ■

RECALL

For a vector **v** with direction angle θ, the horizontal component $v_1 = \|\mathbf{v}\| \cos \theta$ and vertical component $v_2 = \|\mathbf{v}\| \sin \theta$.

SECTION 8.2 ■ Exercises

A EXERCISES Basic Skills and Concepts

1. If the initial point of a vector is the origin in the Cartesian plane, the vector is called a(n) _____ .

2. For a vector $\mathbf{v} = \langle v_1, v_2 \rangle$, v_1 is the horizontal _____ and v_2 is the _____ component.

3. If $P = (x_1, y_1)$ and $Q = (x_2, y_2)$, then $\overrightarrow{PQ} = \langle \text{_____} , \text{_____} \rangle$.

4. Let $\mathbf{v} = \langle v_1, v_2 \rangle$. Then $\|\mathbf{v}\| = $ _____ and a unit vector **u** in the direction of **v** is given by $\mathbf{u} = ($ _____ $)\mathbf{v}$.

5. *True or False* If $\mathbf{v} = \langle v_1, v_2 \rangle$ and θ is the direction angle for $\mathbf{v}$, then $v_1 = \|\mathbf{v}\| \sin\theta$ and $v_2 = \|\mathbf{v}\| \cos\theta$.

6. *True or False* If $\mathbf{v} = \langle v_1, v_2 \rangle = v_1\mathbf{i} + v_2\mathbf{j}$, then the reference angle θ' for the direction angle θ of $\mathbf{v}$ is given by $\theta' = \left| \tan^{-1} \dfrac{v_2}{v_1} \right|$.

In Exercises 7–14, write each vector of the adjoining figure as a position vector.

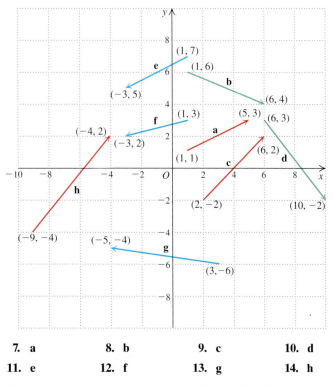

7. a	8. b	9. c	10. d
11. e	12. f	13. g	14. h

In Exercises 15–22, the vector v has initial point P and terminal point Q. Write v as a position vector.

15. $P(3, 6), Q(2, 9)$
16. $P(6, -4), Q(1, 1)$
17. $P(-5, -2), Q(-3, -4)$
18. $P(0, 0), Q(-3, -6)$
19. $P(-1, 4), Q(2, -3)$
20. $P(3.5, 2.7), Q(-1.5, 1.3)$
21. $P\left(\dfrac{1}{2}, \dfrac{3}{4}\right), Q\left(-\dfrac{1}{2}, -\dfrac{7}{4}\right)$
22. $P\left(-\dfrac{2}{3}, \dfrac{4}{9}\right), Q\left(\dfrac{1}{3}, -\dfrac{2}{3}\right)$

In Exercises 23–26, determine whether the vectors $\overrightarrow{AB}$ and $\overrightarrow{CD}$ are equivalent. [*Hint:* Write $\overrightarrow{AB}$ and $\overrightarrow{CD}$ as position vectors.]

23. $A(1, 0), B(3, 4), C(-1, 2), D(1, 6)$
24. $A(-1, 2), B(3, -2), C(2, 5), D(6, 1)$
25. $A(2, -1), B(3, 5), C(-1, 3), D(-2, -3)$
26. $A(5, 7), B(6, 3), C(-2, 1), D(-3, 5)$

In Exercises 27–34, let $\mathbf{v} = \langle -1, 2 \rangle$ and $\mathbf{w} = \langle 3, -2 \rangle$. Find each expression.

27. $\|\mathbf{v}\|$
28. $\|\mathbf{w}\|$
29. $\mathbf{v} - \mathbf{w}$
30. $\mathbf{v} + \mathbf{w}$
31. $2\mathbf{v} - 3\mathbf{w}$
32. $2\mathbf{w} - 3\mathbf{v}$
33. $\|2\mathbf{v} - 3\mathbf{w}\|$
34. $\|2\mathbf{w} - 3\mathbf{v}\|$

In Exercises 35–40, find a unit vector u in the direction of the given vector.

35. $\langle 1, -1 \rangle$
36. $\langle 1, 3 \rangle$
37. $\langle -4, 3 \rangle$
38. $\langle 5, -12 \rangle$
39. $\langle \sqrt{2}, \sqrt{2} \rangle$
40. $\langle \sqrt{5}, -2 \rangle$

In Exercises 41–46, find each expression for $\mathbf{u} = 2\mathbf{i} - 5\mathbf{j}$ and $\mathbf{v} = -3\mathbf{i} - 2\mathbf{j}$.

41. $\mathbf{u} + \mathbf{v}$
42. $\mathbf{u} - \mathbf{v}$
43. $2\mathbf{u} - 3\mathbf{v}$
44. $2\mathbf{v} + 3\mathbf{u}$
45. $\|2\mathbf{u} - 3\mathbf{v}\|$
46. $\|2\mathbf{v} + 3\mathbf{u}\|$

In Exercises 47–54, write the vector v in the form $v_1\mathbf{i} + v_2\mathbf{j}$ given $\|\mathbf{v}\|$ and the angle θ that v makes with the positive x-axis.

47. $\|\mathbf{v}\| = 2, \theta = 30°$
48. $\|\mathbf{v}\| = 5, \theta = 45°$
49. $\|\mathbf{v}\| = 4, \theta = 120°$
50. $\|\mathbf{v}\| = 3, \theta = 150°$
51. $\|\mathbf{v}\| = 3, \theta = \dfrac{5\pi}{3}$
52. $\|\mathbf{v}\| = 4, \theta = \dfrac{11\pi}{6}$
53. $\|\mathbf{v}\| = 7, \theta = -\dfrac{\pi}{3}$
54. $\|\mathbf{v}\| = 8, \theta = \dfrac{3\pi}{4}$

In Exercises 55–62, find the magnitude and the direction angle of vector v.

55. $\mathbf{v} = 10(\cos 60°\mathbf{i} + \sin 60°\mathbf{j})$
56. $\mathbf{v} = -4(\cos 30°\mathbf{i} + \sin 30°\mathbf{j})$
57. $\mathbf{v} = -3(\cos 30°\mathbf{i} - \sin 30°\mathbf{j})$
58. $\mathbf{v} = 2(\cos 300°\mathbf{i} - \sin 300°\mathbf{j})$
59. $\mathbf{v} = 5\mathbf{i} + 12\mathbf{j}$
60. $\mathbf{v} = 12\mathbf{i} - 5\mathbf{j}$
61. $\mathbf{v} = -4\mathbf{i} - 3\mathbf{j}$
62. $\mathbf{v} = -5\mathbf{i} + 12\mathbf{j}$

B EXERCISES Applying the Concepts

In Exercises 63–74 write each answer to the nearest tenth of a unit.

63. **Wind and vectors.** A wind is blowing 25 miles per hour in the direction N 67° E. Express the wind velocity $\mathbf{v}$ in the form $a\mathbf{i} + b\mathbf{j}$.

64. **Wind and vectors.** The velocity $\mathbf{v}$ of a wind is given by $\mathbf{v} = 5\mathbf{i} - 12\mathbf{j}$, where the vectors $\mathbf{i}$ and $\mathbf{j}$ represent 1-mile-per-hour winds blowing east and north, respectively. Find the speed (magnitude of $\mathbf{v}$) and the direction of the wind.

65. **Finding components.** A force of 80 lb acts in the direction N 65° W. Find its east and north components.

66. Repeat Exercise 65 assuming that a force of 60 lb acts in the direction S 32° W.

67. **Equilibrant.** Find the equilibrant for the two forces $\mathbf{F}_1$ and $\mathbf{F}_2$, where $\mathbf{F}_1$ is a force of 25 lb acting due south and $\mathbf{F}_2$ is a force of 32 lb acting due west.

68. Repeat Exercise 67 assuming that $\mathbf{F}_1$ is doubled.

69. **Equilibrant.** Two forces of 300 lb and 400 lb act at the origin and make angles of 30° and 60°, respectively, with the positive x-axis. Find the equilibrant.

70. Repeat Exercise 69 assuming that the forces have the same magnitude but that the angle each force makes with the positive *x*-axis is doubled.

71. Air navigation. A plane flies at an airspeed (speed in still air) of 500 miles per hour on a bearing of N 35° E. An east wind (wind from east to west) is blowing 30 miles per hour. Find the plane's ground speed and direction.

72. Air navigation. A plane flies at an airspeed of 550 miles per hour on a straight course from an airfield *F*. A 30-mile-per-hour wind is blowing from the west. What must be the plane's bearing so that after one hour of flying time the plane is due north of *F*?

73. River navigation. A river flowing southward has a current of 4 miles per hour. A motorboat in still water maintains a speed of 15 miles per hour. The motorboat starts at the west shore on a bearing of N 40° E. What is the actual speed and direction of the boat?

74. River crossing. A fisherwoman on the west bank of the river of Exercise 73 sees several people fishing at a spot *P* directly east of her. If she owns the boat of Exercise 73, what direction should she take to land on the spot *P*?

In Exercises 75 and 76, find a single force that must be added to the system of forces shown in the figure to obtain a system that is in equilibrium.

75.

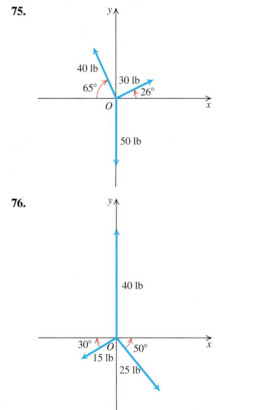

76.

C EXERCISES Beyond the Basics

In Exercises 77 and 78, calculate the magnitude of the forces F₁ and F₂ assuming that the system is in equilibrium.

77.   **78.**

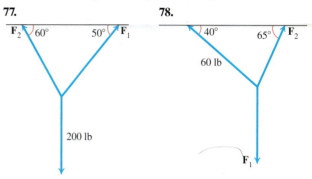

79. Find the terminal point of $\mathbf{v} = 4\mathbf{i} - 3\mathbf{j}$ assuming that the initial point is $(-2, 1)$.

80. Find the initial point of $\mathbf{v} = \langle -3, 5 \rangle$ assuming that the terminal point is $(4, 0)$.

81. Let $\mathbf{u} = \langle -1, 2 \rangle$ and $\mathbf{v} = \langle 3, 5 \rangle$. Find a vector $\mathbf{x} = \langle x_1, x_2 \rangle$ that satisfies the equation $2\mathbf{u} - \mathbf{x} = 2\mathbf{x} + 3\mathbf{v}$.

82. Let $P(3, 5)$ and $Q(7, -4)$ be two points in a coordinate plane. Use vectors to find the coordinates of the point on the line segment joining P and Q that is $\dfrac{3}{4}$ of the way from P to Q.

83. Use vectors to find the lengths of the diagonals of the parallelogram determined by $\mathbf{i} + 2\mathbf{j}$ and $\mathbf{i} - \mathbf{j}$.

84. Use vectors to find the fourth vertex of a parallelogram with three vertices at $(0, 0)$, $(2, 3)$, and $(6, 4)$. [*Hint:* There is more than one answer.]

85. Two forces $\mathbf{F}_1$ and $\mathbf{F}_2$ have a resultant of 200 lb. Assume that $\mathbf{F}_1$ acts in the direction of positive *x*-axis and $\mathbf{F}_2$ is inclined at a 50° angle above the *x*-axis. Assuming that the resultant makes an angle of 20° with the positive *x*-axis, find the magnitudes of $\mathbf{F}_1$ and $\mathbf{F}_2$.

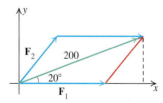

[*Hint:* Let $\|\mathbf{F}_1\| = a$ and $\|\mathbf{F}_2\| = b$; then show that
$$\begin{cases} b \sin 50° = 200 \sin 20° \\ a + b \cos 50° = 200 \cos 20°. \end{cases}$$
Solve those equations for *a* and *b*.]

Critical Thinking

Let $A = (1, 2)$, $B = (4, 3)$, and $C = (6, 1)$ be points in the plane. Find $P = (x, y)$ so that each of the following is true.

86. $\overrightarrow{AB} = \overrightarrow{CP}$ **87.** $\overrightarrow{PA} = \overrightarrow{CB}$

88. $\overrightarrow{AP} = \overrightarrow{CB}$ **89.** $\overrightarrow{PA} = \overrightarrow{BC}$

The Dot Product

Objectives

1 Define the dot product of two vectors.

2 Find the angle between two vectors.

3 Define orthogonal vectors.

4 Use the definition of work.

HOW TO MEASURE WORK

If you move an object a distance of d units by applying a force F in the direction of motion, then physicists define the work W done on the object by the force F to be

$$W = Fd$$

Work = (force)(distance).

If the force is measured in pounds and the distance is measured in feet, the unit of work is *foot-pounds*. Unfortunately, it is not always possible to exert a force in the direction you would like. For example, if you are pulling a child's wagon, you exert a force in a direction dictated by the position of the handle. In this section, we will give a precise definition of work done by a constant force; in Example 7, we compute the work done in one such instance. ■

---

1 Define the dot product of two vectors.

The Dot Product

We know that scalar multiplication and vector addition and subtraction produce vectors. A new operation, the *dot product* of two vectors, produces a *scalar*.

THE DOT PRODUCT

For two vectors $\mathbf{v} = \langle v_1, v_2 \rangle$ and $\mathbf{w} = \langle w_1, w_2 \rangle$, the dot product of $\mathbf{v}$ and $\mathbf{w}$, denoted $\mathbf{v} \cdot \mathbf{w}$, is defined as follows:

$$\mathbf{v} \cdot \mathbf{w} = \langle v_1, v_2 \rangle \cdot \langle w_1, w_2 \rangle = v_1 w_1 + v_2 w_2$$

EXAMPLE 1   **Finding the Dot Product**

Find the dot product $\mathbf{v} \cdot \mathbf{w}$.

a. $\mathbf{v} = \langle 2, -3 \rangle$ and $\mathbf{w} = \langle 3, 4 \rangle$ **b.** $\mathbf{v} = -3\mathbf{i} + 5\mathbf{j}$ and $\mathbf{w} = 2\mathbf{i} + 3\mathbf{j}$

SOLUTION

a. $\mathbf{v} \cdot \mathbf{w} = \langle 2, -3 \rangle \cdot \langle 3, 4 \rangle$

$\qquad\quad = (2)(3) + (-3)(4) = -6$ Definition of dot product

b. $\mathbf{v} \cdot \mathbf{w} = (-3\mathbf{i} + 5\mathbf{j}) \cdot (2\mathbf{i} + 3\mathbf{j})$

$\qquad = \langle -3, 5 \rangle \cdot \langle 2, 3 \rangle$ Rewrite as position vectors.

$\qquad = (-3)(2) + (5)(3) = 9$ Definition of dot product ▪ ▪ ▪

Practice Problem 1   Find the dot product $\mathbf{v} \cdot \mathbf{w}$.

a. $\mathbf{v} = \langle 1, 2 \rangle$ and $\mathbf{w} = \langle -2, 5 \rangle$ **b.** $\mathbf{v} = 4\mathbf{i} - 3\mathbf{j}$ and $\mathbf{w} = -3\mathbf{i} - 4\mathbf{j}$ ▪

2 Find the angle between two vectors.

The Angle Between Two Vectors

We use the Law of Cosines to find another formula for the dot product. The new formula is used to find the angle between two vectors.

Let θ be the angle between the two vectors $\mathbf{v} = \langle v_1, v_2 \rangle$ and $\mathbf{w} = \langle w_1, w_2 \rangle$. See Figure 8.25. Apply the Law of Cosines to the triangle OPQ in Figure 8.25.

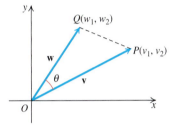

FIGURE 8.25

$[d(P, Q)]^2 = \|\mathbf{v}\|^2 + \|\mathbf{w}\|^2 - 2\|\mathbf{v}\| \|\mathbf{w}\| \cos \theta$ The Law of Cosines

$(v_1 - w_1)^2 + (v_2 - w_2)^2$

$\quad = (v_1^2 + v_2^2) + (w_1^2 + w_2^2) - 2\|\mathbf{v}\| \|\mathbf{w}\| \cos \theta$ Use the distance formula and square of the magnitudes of $\mathbf{v}$ and $\mathbf{w}$.

$v_1^2 - 2v_1 w_1 + w_1^2 + v_2^2 - 2v_2 w_2 + w_2^2$

$\quad = v_1^2 + v_2^2 + w_1^2 + w_2^2 - 2\|\mathbf{v}\| \|\mathbf{w}\| \cos \theta$ $(A - B)^2 = A^2 - 2AB + B^2$

$-2v_1 w_1 - 2v_2 w_2 = -2\|\mathbf{v}\| \|\mathbf{w}\| \cos \theta$ Subtract $v_1^2 + w_1^2 + v_2^2 + w_2^2$ from both sides.

$v_1 w_1 + v_2 w_2 = \|\mathbf{v}\| \|\mathbf{w}\| \cos \theta$ Divide both sides by -2.

$\mathbf{v} \cdot \mathbf{w} = \|\mathbf{v}\| \|\mathbf{w}\| \cos \theta$ Definition of $\mathbf{v} \cdot \mathbf{w}$

The last equation provides us with another formula for $\mathbf{v} \cdot \mathbf{w}$. Solving the last equation for $\cos \theta$ gives us a formula for finding the angle between two vectors.

THE DOT PRODUCT AND THE ANGLE BETWEEN TWO VECTORS

If θ ($0 \leq \theta \leq \pi$) is the angle between two nonzero vectors $\mathbf{v}$ and $\mathbf{w}$, then

$$\mathbf{v} \cdot \mathbf{w} = \|\mathbf{v}\| \|\mathbf{w}\| \cos \theta \quad \text{or} \quad \cos \theta = \frac{\mathbf{v} \cdot \mathbf{w}}{\|\mathbf{v}\| \|\mathbf{w}\|}.$$

EXAMPLE 2   **Finding the Dot Product**

If $\mathbf{v}$ and $\mathbf{w}$ are two vectors of magnitudes 5 and 7, respectively, and the angle between them is 75°, find $\mathbf{v} \cdot \mathbf{w}$. Round the answer to the nearest tenth.

SOLUTION

$\mathbf{v} \cdot \mathbf{w} = \|\mathbf{v}\| \|\mathbf{w}\| \cos \theta$ Formula for $\mathbf{v} \cdot \mathbf{w}$

$\mathbf{v} \cdot \mathbf{w} = (5)(7) \cos 75°$ Substitute given values.

$\mathbf{v} \cdot \mathbf{w} \approx 9.1$ Use a calculator. ▪ ▪ ▪

Practice Problem 2   Repeat Example 2 assuming that the angle between $\mathbf{v}$ and $\mathbf{w}$ is 60°.   ▪

Two vectors $\mathbf{v}$ and $\mathbf{w}$ are **parallel** if there is a nonzero scalar, c, so that $\mathbf{v} = c\mathbf{w}$. The angle θ between parallel vectors is either 0° or 180°.

EXAMPLE 3   **Deciding Whether Two Vectors Are Parallel**

Determine whether the vectors $\mathbf{v} = 2\mathbf{i} - 3\mathbf{j}$ and $\mathbf{w} = -4\mathbf{i} + 6\mathbf{j}$ are parallel.

SOLUTION

Because $\mathbf{w} = -2\mathbf{v}$, the vectors $\mathbf{v}$ and $\mathbf{w}$ are parallel. Note that

$$\cos \theta = \frac{\mathbf{v} \cdot \mathbf{w}}{\|\mathbf{v}\|\|\mathbf{w}\|} = \frac{-8 - 18}{\sqrt{13}\sqrt{52}} = \frac{-26}{\sqrt{13}(2\sqrt{13})} = \frac{-26}{26} = -1;$$

so $\theta = 180°$ is the angle between $\mathbf{v}$ and $\mathbf{w}$ and $\mathbf{v}$ and $\mathbf{w}$ are parallel.   ■ ■ ■

Practice Problem 3   Determine whether $\mathbf{v} = -\mathbf{i} - 2\mathbf{j}$ and $\mathbf{w} = 2\mathbf{i} + \mathbf{j}$ are parallel.   ■

Because the angle θ between two nonzero vectors $\mathbf{v}$ and $\mathbf{w}$ satisfies $\cos \theta = \dfrac{\mathbf{v} \cdot \mathbf{w}}{\|\mathbf{v}\|\|\mathbf{w}\|}$

and $0 \le \theta \le \pi$, we have $\theta = \cos^{-1}\left(\dfrac{\mathbf{v} \cdot \mathbf{w}}{\|\mathbf{v}\|\|\mathbf{w}\|}\right)$.

EXAMPLE 4   **Finding the Angle Between Two Vectors**

Find the angle θ between the vectors $\mathbf{v} = 2\mathbf{i} + 3\mathbf{j}$ and $\mathbf{w} = -3\mathbf{i} + 4\mathbf{j}$. Round the answer to the nearest tenth of a degree.

SOLUTION

$$\cos \theta = \frac{\mathbf{v} \cdot \mathbf{w}}{\|\mathbf{v}\| \|\mathbf{w}\|}$$ Formula for the cosine of the angle between $\mathbf{v}$ and $\mathbf{w}$

$$\cos \theta = \frac{(2\mathbf{i} + 3\mathbf{j}) \cdot (-3\mathbf{i} + 4\mathbf{j})}{\|2\mathbf{i} + 3\mathbf{j}\|\|-3\mathbf{i} + 4\mathbf{j}\|}$$ Substitute expressions for $\mathbf{v}$ and $\mathbf{w}$.

$$\cos \theta = \frac{(2)(-3) + (3)(4)}{\sqrt{2^2 + 3^2}\sqrt{(-3)^2 + 4^2}}$$ Use formulas for the dot product and the magnitude.

$$\cos \theta = \frac{6}{5\sqrt{13}}$$ Simplify.

$$\theta = \cos^{-1}\left(\frac{6}{5\sqrt{13}}\right)$$ $0° \le \theta \le 180°$

$$\theta \approx 70.6°$$ Use a calculator.   ■ ■ ■

Practice Problem 4   Find the angle between the vectors $\mathbf{v} = 2\mathbf{i} - 3\mathbf{j}$ and $\mathbf{w} = 3\mathbf{i} + 5\mathbf{j}$. Round your answer to the nearest tenth of a degree.   ■

We can verify the following properties of the dot product by writing the vectors as position vectors and using the definitions of vector addition, scalar multiplication, and the dot products.

PROPERTIES OF THE DOT PRODUCT

If $\mathbf{u}$, $\mathbf{v}$, and $\mathbf{w}$ are vectors and c is a scalar, then

1. $\mathbf{u} \cdot \mathbf{v} = \mathbf{v} \cdot \mathbf{u}$.
2. $\mathbf{u} \cdot (\mathbf{v} + \mathbf{w}) = \mathbf{u} \cdot \mathbf{v} + \mathbf{u} \cdot \mathbf{w}$.
3. $\mathbf{0} \cdot \mathbf{v} = 0$.
4. $\mathbf{v} \cdot \mathbf{v} = \|\mathbf{v}\|^2$.
5. $(c\mathbf{u}) \cdot \mathbf{v} = c(\mathbf{u} \cdot \mathbf{v}) = \mathbf{u} \cdot (c\mathbf{v})$.

EXAMPLE 5   Finding the Magnitude of the Sum of Two Vectors

Let **v** and **w** be two vectors in the plane of magnitudes 12 and 7, respectively. The angle between **v** and **w** is 65°. Find the magnitude of **v** + 2**w** to the nearest tenth.

SOLUTION

$$
\begin{aligned}
\|\mathbf{v} + 2\mathbf{w}\|^2 &= (\mathbf{v} + 2\mathbf{w}) \cdot (\mathbf{v} + 2\mathbf{w}) && \text{Property 4} \\
&= (\mathbf{v} + 2\mathbf{w}) \cdot \mathbf{v} + (\mathbf{v} + 2\mathbf{w}) \cdot (2\mathbf{w}) && \text{Property 2} \\
&= \mathbf{v} \cdot \mathbf{v} + 2(\mathbf{w} \cdot \mathbf{v}) + 2(\mathbf{v} \cdot \mathbf{w}) + 4(\mathbf{w} \cdot \mathbf{w}) && \text{Properties 1 and 5} \\
&= \|\mathbf{v}\|^2 + 4(\mathbf{v} \cdot \mathbf{w}) + 4\|\mathbf{w}\|^2 && \text{Properties 1 and 4} \\
&= \|\mathbf{v}\|^2 + 4\|\mathbf{v}\|\|\mathbf{w}\| \cos\theta + 4\|\mathbf{w}\|^2 && \mathbf{v} \cdot \mathbf{w} = \|\mathbf{v}\|\|\mathbf{w}\| \cos\theta \\
&= (12)^2 + 4(12)(7) \cos 65° + 4(7)^2 && \text{Substitute values.} \\
\|\mathbf{v} + 2\mathbf{w}\|^2 &\approx 481.9997 && \text{Use a calculator.} \\
\|\mathbf{v} + 2\mathbf{w}\| &\approx 21.95 \approx 22.0 && \text{Take positive square root.}
\end{aligned}
$$

■ ■ ■

Practice Problem 5   Repeat Example 5 assuming that $\|\mathbf{v}\| = 20$ and $\|\mathbf{w}\| = 12$ and the angle between **v** and **w** is 54°.   ■

3   Define orthogonal vectors.

Orthogonal Vectors

We know that if **v** and **w** are two nonzero vectors and $\theta (0 \le \theta \le \pi)$ is the radian measure of the angle between them, then

$$\mathbf{v} \cdot \mathbf{w} = \|\mathbf{v}\|\|\mathbf{w}\| \cos\theta \qquad \text{Form of the dot product}$$

From this equation, it follows that

$$\cos\theta = 0 \text{ if and only if } \mathbf{v} \cdot \mathbf{w} = 0.$$

Because $0 \le \theta \le \pi$, we conclude that

$$\theta = \frac{\pi}{2} \text{ if and only if } \mathbf{v} \cdot \mathbf{w} = 0.$$

DEFINITION OF ORTHOGONAL VECTORS

Two vectors **v** and **w** are **orthogonal** (perpendicular) if $\mathbf{v} \cdot \mathbf{w} = 0$.

Because $\mathbf{0} \cdot \mathbf{w} = 0$ for any vector **w**, it follows from the definition that zero vector is orthogonal to every vector **w**.

EXAMPLE 6   Deciding Whether Vectors Are Orthogonal

Determine whether $\mathbf{v} = 2\mathbf{i} - 3\mathbf{j}$ and $\mathbf{w} = 3\mathbf{i} + 2\mathbf{j}$ are orthogonal.

SOLUTION

Because $\mathbf{v} \cdot \mathbf{w} = (2\mathbf{i} - 3\mathbf{j}) \cdot (3\mathbf{i} + 2\mathbf{j}) = \langle 2, -3 \rangle \cdot \langle 3, 2 \rangle = 6 - 6 = 0$, **v** and **w** are orthogonal.

■ ■ ■

Practice Problem 6   Determine whether $\mathbf{v} = 4\mathbf{i} + 8\mathbf{j}$ and $\mathbf{w} = 2\mathbf{i} - \mathbf{j}$ are orthogonal.   ■

4 Use the definition of work.

Work

> ### DEFINITION OF WORK
>
> The work W done by a constant force **F** in moving an object from a point P to a point Q is defined by
>
> $$W = \mathbf{F} \cdot \overrightarrow{PQ} = \|\mathbf{F}\| \|\overrightarrow{PQ}\| \cos \theta,$$
>
> where θ is the angle between **F** and $\overrightarrow{PQ}$.

EXAMPLE 7 | **Computing Work**

A child pulls a wagon along level ground, with a force of 40 pounds along the wagon's handle that makes an angle of $42°$ with the horizontal. How much work has she done by pulling the wagon 150 feet?

SOLUTION

The work done is as follows.

$$
\begin{aligned}
W &= \mathbf{F} \cdot \overrightarrow{PQ} && \text{Definition of work} \\
&= \|\mathbf{F}\| \|\overrightarrow{PQ}\| \cos \theta && \mathbf{u} \cdot \mathbf{v} = \|\mathbf{u}\| \|\mathbf{v}\| \cos \theta \\
&= (40)(150) \cos 42° && \text{Substitute given values.} \\
&\approx 4458.87 \text{ foot-pounds} && \text{Use a calculator.}
\end{aligned}
$$

Practice Problem 7 In Example 7, compute the work done assuming that the handle on the wagon makes an angle of $60°$ with the horizontal. ▪

SECTION 8.3 ▪ Exercises

A EXERCISES Basic Skills and Concepts

1. The dot product of $\mathbf{v} = \langle a_1, a_2 \rangle$ and $\mathbf{w} = \langle b_1, b_2 \rangle$ is defined as $\mathbf{v} \cdot \mathbf{w} = $ _____.

2. If θ is the angle between the vectors **v** and **w**, then $\mathbf{v} \cdot \mathbf{w} = $ _____.

3. If **v** and **w** are orthogonal, then $\mathbf{v} \cdot \mathbf{w} = $ _____.

4. If **v** and **w** are nonzero vectors with $\mathbf{v} \cdot \mathbf{w} = 0$, then **v** and **w** are _____.

5. *True or False* If $\mathbf{v} \cdot \mathbf{w} < 0$, then the angle between **v** and **w** is an obtuse angle.

6. *True or False* To find a vector perpendicular to a given vector, switch components and change the sign of one of them.

In Exercises 7–14, find u · v.

7. $\mathbf{u} = \langle 1, -2 \rangle, \mathbf{v} = \langle 3, 5 \rangle$
8. $\mathbf{u} = \langle 1, 3 \rangle, \mathbf{v} = \langle -3, 1 \rangle$
9. $\mathbf{u} = \langle 2, -6 \rangle, \mathbf{v} = \langle 3, 1 \rangle$
10. $\mathbf{u} = \langle -1, -2 \rangle, \mathbf{v} = \langle -3, -4 \rangle$
11. $\mathbf{u} = \mathbf{i} - 3\mathbf{j}, \mathbf{v} = 8\mathbf{i} - 2\mathbf{j}$
12. $\mathbf{u} = 6\mathbf{i} - \mathbf{j}, \mathbf{v} = 2\mathbf{i} + 7\mathbf{j}$
13. $\mathbf{u} = 4\mathbf{i} - 2\mathbf{j}, \mathbf{v} = 3\mathbf{j}$
14. $\mathbf{u} = -2\mathbf{i}, \mathbf{v} = 5\mathbf{j}$

In Exercises 15–20, find u · v, where θ is the angle between the vectors u and v. Round your answers to the nearest tenth.

15. $\|\mathbf{u}\| = 2, \|\mathbf{v}\| = 5, \theta = \dfrac{\pi}{6}$
16. $\|\mathbf{u}\| = 3, \|\mathbf{v}\| = 4, \theta = \dfrac{\pi}{3}$
17. $\|\mathbf{u}\| = 5, \|\mathbf{v}\| = 4, \theta = 65°$
18. $\|\mathbf{u}\| = 5, \|\mathbf{v}\| = 3, \theta = 78°$
19. $\|\mathbf{u}\| = 3, \|\mathbf{v}\| = 7, \theta = 120°$
20. $\|\mathbf{u}\| = 6, \|\mathbf{v}\| = 4, \theta = 150°$

In Exercises 21–30, find the angle between the vectors v and w. Round each answer to the nearest tenth of a degree.

21. $\mathbf{v} = \langle 2, 3 \rangle, \mathbf{w} = \langle 3, 4 \rangle$
22. $\mathbf{v} = \langle -1, 1 \rangle, \mathbf{w} = \langle 5, 12 \rangle$
23. $\mathbf{v} = -2\mathbf{i} - 3\mathbf{j}, \mathbf{w} = \mathbf{i} + \mathbf{j}$
24. $\mathbf{v} = \mathbf{i} - \mathbf{j}, \mathbf{w} = 3\mathbf{i} - 4\mathbf{j}$
25. $\mathbf{v} = 2\mathbf{i} + 5\mathbf{j}, \mathbf{w} = -5\mathbf{i} + 2\mathbf{j}$
26. $\mathbf{v} = 3\mathbf{i} - 7\mathbf{j}, \mathbf{w} = 7\mathbf{i} + 3\mathbf{j}$

27. $\mathbf{v} = \mathbf{i} + \mathbf{j}, \mathbf{w} = 3\mathbf{i} + 3\mathbf{j}$

28. $\mathbf{v} = -2\mathbf{i} + 3\mathbf{j}, \mathbf{w} = -4\mathbf{i} + 6\mathbf{j}$

29. $\mathbf{v} = 2\mathbf{i} - 3\mathbf{j}, \mathbf{w} = -4\mathbf{i} + 6\mathbf{j}$

30. $\mathbf{v} = -3\mathbf{i} + 4\mathbf{j}, \mathbf{w} = 6\mathbf{i} - 8\mathbf{j}$

In Exercises 31–38, let v and w be two vectors in the plane of magnitudes 12 and 16, respectively. The angle between v and w is 50°. Find each expression. Round your answers to the nearest tenth.

31. $\|\mathbf{v} + \mathbf{w}\|$

32. $\|\mathbf{v} - \mathbf{w}\|$

33. $\|2\mathbf{v} + \mathbf{w}\|$

34. $\|2\mathbf{v} - \mathbf{w}\|$

35. Angle between $\mathbf{v} + \mathbf{w}$ and $\mathbf{w}$

36. Angle between $\mathbf{v} - \mathbf{w}$ and $\mathbf{v}$

37. Angle between $2\mathbf{v} + \mathbf{w}$ and $\mathbf{v}$

38. Angle between $2\mathbf{v} - \mathbf{w}$ and $\mathbf{w}$

In Exercises 39–44, determine whether the vectors v and w are orthogonal.

39. $\mathbf{v} = 2\mathbf{i} + 3\mathbf{j}, \mathbf{w} = -3\mathbf{i} + 2\mathbf{j}$

40. $\mathbf{v} = -4\mathbf{i} - 5\mathbf{j}, \mathbf{w} = 5\mathbf{i} - 4\mathbf{j}$

41. $\mathbf{v} = \langle 2, 7 \rangle, \mathbf{w} = \langle -7, -2 \rangle$

42. $\mathbf{v} = \langle -3, 4 \rangle, \mathbf{w} = \langle 4, -3 \rangle$

43. $\mathbf{v} = \langle 12, 6 \rangle, \mathbf{w} = \langle 2, -4 \rangle$

44. $\mathbf{v} = \langle -9, 6 \rangle, \mathbf{w} = \langle 4, 6 \rangle$

In Exercises 45–50, determine whether the vectors v and w are parallel.

45. $\mathbf{v} = 2\mathbf{i} + 3\mathbf{j}, \mathbf{w} = \dfrac{2}{3}\mathbf{i} + \mathbf{j}$

46. $\mathbf{v} = 5\mathbf{i} - 2\mathbf{j}, \mathbf{w} = -10\mathbf{i} + 4\mathbf{j}$

47. $\mathbf{v} = \langle 3, 5 \rangle, \mathbf{w} = \langle -6, 10 \rangle$

48. $\mathbf{v} = \langle -4, -2 \rangle, \mathbf{w} = \left\langle -1, \dfrac{1}{2} \right\rangle$

49. $\mathbf{v} = \langle 6, 3 \rangle, \mathbf{w} = \langle 2, 1 \rangle$

50. $\mathbf{v} = \langle 2, 5 \rangle, \mathbf{w} = \langle -4, -10 \rangle$

In Exercises 51–54, determine the scalar c so that the vectors v and w are (a) orthogonal and (b) parallel.

51. $\mathbf{v} = \langle 2, 3 \rangle, \mathbf{w} = \langle 3, c \rangle$

52. $\mathbf{v} = \langle 1, -2 \rangle, \mathbf{w} = \langle c, 4 \rangle$

53. $\mathbf{v} = \langle -4, 3 \rangle, \mathbf{w} = \langle c, -6 \rangle$

54. $\mathbf{v} = \langle -1, -3 \rangle, \mathbf{w} = \langle -2, c \rangle$

B EXERCISES Applying the Concepts

55. **Finding magnitudes.** Two forces $\mathbf{F}_1$ and $\mathbf{F}_2$ of 40 and 60 pounds, respectively, act at a point. Find the magnitude of the resultant force in each case.

a. $\mathbf{F}_1$ and $\mathbf{F}_2$ act in the same direction.

b. $\mathbf{F}_1$ and $\mathbf{F}_2$ act in opposite directions.

c. $\mathbf{F}_1$ and $\mathbf{F}_2$ act along perpendicular directions.

56. **Finding magnitudes.** The maximum and minimum magnitudes of the resultant of two forces acting at a point are 28 and 22, respectively. Find the magnitudes of the two forces.

57. **Finding resultant force.** Two forces of 6 and 8 pounds act at an angle of 30° to each other. Find the resultant force and the angle of the resultant force to each of the two forces.

58. Repeat Exercise 57 assuming that the two forces act at an angle of 60° to each other.

59. **Work.** A force $\mathbf{F} = 64\mathbf{i} - 20\mathbf{j}$ (in pounds) is applied to an object. The resulting movement of the object is represented by the vector $\mathbf{d} = 10\mathbf{i} + 4\mathbf{j}$ (in feet). Find the work done by the force.

60. **Work.** A car is pushed 150 feet on a level street by a force of 60 pounds at an angle of 18° with the horizontal. Find the work done.

61. **Inclined plane.** A car is being towed up an inclined plane making an angle of 18° with the horizontal, as shown in the figure. Find the force $\mathbf{F}$ needed to make the component of $\mathbf{F}$ parallel to the ground equal to 5250 pounds.

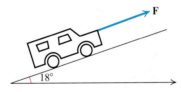

62. **Inclined plane.** In Exercise 61, find the work done by the force $\mathbf{F}$ to tow the car up 10 feet along the inclined plane.

63. **Work.** A vector $\mathbf{F}$ represents a force that has a magnitude of 10 pounds, and $\dfrac{2\pi}{3}$ is the angle for its direction. Find the work done by the force in moving an object from the origin to the point $(-6, 3)$. Distance is measured in feet.

64. **Work.** Two forces $\mathbf{F}_1 = 3\mathbf{i} - 2\mathbf{j}$ and $\mathbf{F}_2 = -4\mathbf{i} + 3\mathbf{j}$ act on an object and move it along a straight line from the point $(8, 4)$ to the point $(3, 5)$. Find the work done by the two forces acting together. The magnitudes of $\mathbf{F}_1$ and $\mathbf{F}_2$ are measured in pounds, and distance is measured in feet.

C EXERCISES Beyond the Basics

65. Orthogonality on a circle. In the figure, AB is the diameter of a circle with center O $(0, 0)$ and radius a. Show that $\overrightarrow{CA}$ and $\overrightarrow{CB}$ are perpendicular. [*Hint:* $x^2 + y^2 = a^2$.]

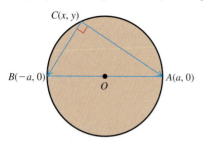

66. Cauchy-Schwarz inequality. If $\mathbf{v}$ and $\mathbf{w}$ are two vectors, then $|\mathbf{v} \cdot \mathbf{w}| \leq \|\mathbf{v}\|\|\mathbf{w}\|$. When is $|\mathbf{v} \cdot \mathbf{w}| = \|\mathbf{v}\|\|\mathbf{w}\|$? [*Hint:* $|\mathbf{v} \cdot \mathbf{w}| = \|\mathbf{v}\|\|\mathbf{w}\| \cos \theta$.]

67. Verify that for any vectors $\mathbf{u}$, $\mathbf{v}$, and $\mathbf{w}$,
$\mathbf{u} \cdot (\mathbf{v} + \mathbf{w}) = \mathbf{u} \cdot \mathbf{v} + \mathbf{u} \cdot \mathbf{w}$.

68. Prove that $(\mathbf{v} + \mathbf{w}) \cdot (\mathbf{v} + \mathbf{w}) = \|\mathbf{v}\|^2 + 2(\mathbf{v} \cdot \mathbf{w}) + \|\mathbf{w}\|^2$.

69. Triangle inequality. Use Exercises 66 and 68 to prove that $\|\mathbf{v} + \mathbf{w}\| \leq \|\mathbf{v}\| + \|\mathbf{w}\|$.

70. Show that the vectors $\mathbf{v} = \langle 2, -5 \rangle$ and $\mathbf{w} = \langle 5, 2 \rangle$ are perpendicular to each other.

71. Let $\mathbf{v} = 3\mathbf{i} + 7\mathbf{j}$. Find a vector perpendicular to $\mathbf{v}$.

72. Orthogonal unit vectors. Find a unit vector orthogonal to $\mathbf{v} = 3\mathbf{i} - 4\mathbf{j}$.

73. Orthogonal unit vectors. Let $\mathbf{u}_1$ and $\mathbf{u}_2$ be orthogonal unit vectors and $\mathbf{v} = x\mathbf{u}_1 + y\mathbf{u}_2$. Find
a. $\mathbf{v} \cdot \mathbf{u}_1$.   **b.** $\mathbf{v} \cdot \mathbf{u}_2$.

74. Right triangle. Use the dot product to show that ABC is a right triangle and identify the right angle assuming that $A = (-2, 1)$, $B = (3, 1)$, and $C = (-1, -1)$.

75. Parallelogram law. Show that for any two vectors $\mathbf{u}$ and $\mathbf{v}$,

$$\|\mathbf{u} + \mathbf{v}\|^2 + \|\mathbf{u} - \mathbf{v}\|^2 = 2\|\mathbf{u}\|^2 + 2\|\mathbf{v}\|^2.$$

[*Hint:* $\|\mathbf{a}\|^2 = \mathbf{a} \cdot \mathbf{a}$.]

76. Polarization identity. Show that for any two vectors $\mathbf{u}$ and $\mathbf{v}$,

$$\|\mathbf{u} + \mathbf{v}\|^2 - \|\mathbf{u} - \mathbf{v}\|^2 = 4(\mathbf{u} \cdot \mathbf{v}).$$

77. Show that $\mathbf{u}$ and $\mathbf{v}$ are orthogonal if and only if $\|\mathbf{u} + \mathbf{v}\| = \|\mathbf{u} - \mathbf{v}\|$.

78. Choose two points $Q(x_1, y_1)$ and $R(x_2, y_2)$ on the line $l: ax + by + c = 0$. Show that $\mathbf{n} = \langle a, b \rangle$ is perpendicular to l by showing that $\mathbf{n} \cdot \overrightarrow{QR} = 0$.

79. Perpendicular diagonals. Show that if the diagonals of a rectangle are perpendicular to each other, the rectangle is a square. [*Hint:* $(\mathbf{u} + \mathbf{v}) \cdot (\mathbf{u} - \mathbf{v}) = 0$.]

80. Equal diagonals. Show that if the diagonals of a parallelogram are equal in length, the parallelogram is a rectangle. [*Hint:* Use Exercise 75.]

Critical Thinking

81. *True or False* If $\mathbf{u} \cdot \mathbf{v} = \mathbf{u} \cdot \mathbf{w}$ and $\mathbf{u} \neq 0$, then $\mathbf{v} = \mathbf{w}$. Give reasons for your answer.

82. Prove that for any two vectors $\mathbf{v}$ and $\mathbf{w}$, $\|\mathbf{v} - \mathbf{w}\| \geq \|\mathbf{v}\| - \|\mathbf{w}\|$.

REVIEW

Definitions, Concepts, and Formulas	Examples and Illustrations

8.1 Geometric Vectors

■ **Vector** A **vector** is a quantity that has both magnitude and direction. We represent a vector by a directed line segment with an arrowhead. The length of the segment describes the magnitude of the vector, and the direction of the arrow describes its direction.

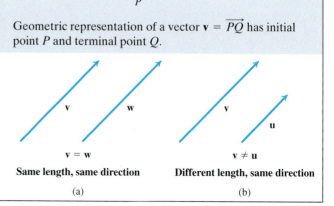

Geometric representation of a vector $\mathbf{v} = \overrightarrow{PQ}$ has initial point P and terminal point Q.

■ **Equivalent vectors** Two vectors having the same magnitude and same direction are called equivalent vectors.

$\mathbf{v} = \mathbf{w}$
Same length, same direction
(a)

$\mathbf{v} \neq \mathbf{u}$
Different length, same direction
(b)

- **Vector Addition of v and w**

1. **Triangle Method.** Position **v** and **w** so that the terminal point of **v** coincides with the initial point of **w**. The vector whose initial point coincides with the initial point of **v** and whose terminal point coincides with the terminal point of **w** is **v** + **w**.

$$\overrightarrow{AB} + \overrightarrow{BC} = \overrightarrow{AC}$$

2. **Parallelogram method.** Position **v** and **w** so that the initial points of both vectors coincide. Construct the parallelogram in which **v** and **w** are adjacent sides. The diagonal of the parallelogram directed from the common initial point to the opposite vertex is **v** + **w**.

- **Scalar multiplication** For a vector **v** and a scalar c (a real number), the vector $c\mathbf{v}$ is called the scalar multiple of **v**. The magnitude of $c\mathbf{v}$ is $|c|$ times the magnitude of **v**.

$$\|c\mathbf{v}\| = |c|\|\mathbf{v}\|$$

If $c > 0$, $c\mathbf{v}$ has the direction of **v**. If $c < 0$, $c\mathbf{v}$ has the opposite direction of **v**. The zero vector **0** has magnitude 0 but arbitrary direction.

- **Angle between two vectors** Place **v** and **w** so that $\mathbf{v} = \overrightarrow{PQ}$ and $\mathbf{w} = \overrightarrow{PR}$. The angle θ ($0° \le \theta \le 180°$) between **v** and **w** is the angle formed by the directed line segments $\overrightarrow{PQ}$ and $\overrightarrow{PR}$.

8.2 Algebraic Vectors

- **Algebraic vectors** A vector **v** with initial point at the origin and terminal point (v_1, v_2) is called a position vector and is written as $\mathbf{v} = \langle v_1, v_2 \rangle$; v_1 and v_2 are called the horizontal and vertical components of **v**, respectively. For vectors $\mathbf{v} = \langle v_1, v_2 \rangle$ and $\mathbf{w} = \langle w_1, w_2 \rangle$, $\mathbf{v} = \mathbf{w}$ if and only if $v_1 = w_1$ and $v_2 = w_2$.

A vector $\mathbf{v} = \overrightarrow{PQ}$ where $P = (x_1, y_1)$ and $Q = (x_2, y_2)$ and the position vector $\mathbf{w} = \langle x_2 - x_1, y_2 - y_1 \rangle$ are equal.

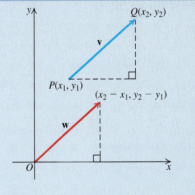

The vector $\mathbf{v} = \overrightarrow{PQ}$ where $P = (3, -1)$ and $Q = (-2, 4)$ and the position vector $\mathbf{w} = \langle -2 - 3, 4 - (-1) \rangle = \langle -5, 5 \rangle$ are equal vectors.

■ **Magnitude and direction of a vector** The magnitude (length) of a vector $\mathbf{v} = \langle v_1, v_2 \rangle$ is given by $\|\mathbf{v}\| = \sqrt{v_1^2 + v_2^2}$.

The direction angle of $\mathbf{v}$ is the angle θ that $\mathbf{v}$ makes with the positive x-axis. We can find the direction angle of a position vector $\mathbf{v} = \langle v_1, v_2 \rangle$ by using the equation $\tan \theta = \dfrac{v_2}{v_1}$, $v_1 \neq 0$ and the quadrant in which the point (v_1, v_2) lies.

For calculator use:

$$\theta = \begin{cases} \tan^{-1}\left(\dfrac{v_2}{v_1}\right) & \text{if } v_1 > 0 \\[2mm] 180° + \tan^{-1}\left(\dfrac{v_2}{v_1}\right) & \text{if } v_1 < 0 \end{cases}$$

Find the magnitude and the direction angle of each position vector.

a. $\mathbf{v} = \langle 3, -\sqrt{3} \rangle$ **b.** $\mathbf{w} = \langle -5, 12 \rangle$

Solution

a. $\|\mathbf{v}\| = \sqrt{3^2 + (-\sqrt{3})^2} = \sqrt{9 + 3} = \sqrt{12} = 2\sqrt{3}$

$\theta = \tan^{-1}\left(-\dfrac{\sqrt{3}}{3}\right) = \tan^{-1}\left(-\dfrac{1}{\sqrt{3}}\right) = -30°$ or $330°$

b. $\|\mathbf{w}\| = \sqrt{(-5)^2 + 12^2} = \sqrt{25 + 144} = \sqrt{169} = 13$

$\theta = 180° + \tan^{-1}\left(-\dfrac{12}{5}\right) \approx 112.6°$

■ **Vector operations** For vectors $\mathbf{v} = \langle v_1, v_2 \rangle$ and $\mathbf{w} = \langle w_1, w_2 \rangle$, the following operations apply:

• **Vector addition:** $\mathbf{v} + \mathbf{w} = \langle v_1 + w_1, v_2 + w_2 \rangle$

• **Scalar multiplication:** $c\mathbf{v} = \langle cv_1, cv_2 \rangle$

• **Vector subtraction:** $\mathbf{v} - \mathbf{w} = \langle v_1 - w_1, v_2 - w_2 \rangle$

$\langle 2, -5 \rangle + \langle 3, 2 \rangle = \langle 2 + 3, -5 + 2 \rangle = \langle 5, -3 \rangle$

$3\langle 2, -5 \rangle = \langle 6, -15 \rangle$

$\langle 2, -5 \rangle - \langle 3, 2 \rangle = \langle 2 - 3, -5 - 2 \rangle = \langle -1, -7 \rangle$

■ **Unit vectors** For a scalar c and vector $\mathbf{v}$, $\|c\mathbf{v}\| = |c|\|\mathbf{v}\|$.

A unit vector $\mathbf{u}$ in the direction of $\mathbf{v}$ is given by $\mathbf{u} = \dfrac{1}{\|\mathbf{v}\|}\mathbf{v}$.

Find a unit vector $\mathbf{u}$ in the direction of $\mathbf{v} = \langle -12, 5 \rangle$.

Solution
We have $\|\mathbf{v}\| = \sqrt{(-12)^2 + 5^2} = 13$.

$$\mathbf{u} = \frac{1}{13}\langle -12, 5 \rangle = \left\langle -\frac{12}{13}, \frac{5}{13} \right\rangle$$

■ **Vectors in i, j form** A vector $\mathbf{v} = \langle v_1, v_2 \rangle$ can be expressed in $\mathbf{i}, \mathbf{j}$ form as $\mathbf{v} = v_1\mathbf{i} + v_2\mathbf{j}$, where $\mathbf{i} = \langle 1, 0 \rangle$ and $\mathbf{j} = \langle 0, 1 \rangle$.

The formulas $\mathbf{v} = \|\mathbf{v}\|\langle \cos \theta, \sin \theta \rangle$ and $\mathbf{v} = \|\mathbf{v}\| \cos \theta \mathbf{i} + \|\mathbf{v}\| \sin \theta \mathbf{j}$ express a vector $\mathbf{v}$ in terms of its magnitude and direction angle θ.

$\langle 3, -7 \rangle = 3\mathbf{i} + (-7)\mathbf{j} = 3\mathbf{i} - 7\mathbf{j}$

Let $\mathbf{v} = \langle 3, -\sqrt{3} \rangle$; then $\|\mathbf{v}\| = 2\sqrt{3}$ and $\theta = 330°$.

$$\mathbf{v} = 2\sqrt{3}\langle \cos 330°, \sin 330° \rangle$$

or

$$\mathbf{v} = 2\sqrt{3} \cos 330°\mathbf{i} + 2\sqrt{3} \sin 330°\mathbf{j}$$

8.3 The Dot Product

■ **The dot product** The dot product of two vectors $\mathbf{v} = \langle v_1, v_2 \rangle$ and $\mathbf{w} = \langle w_1, w_2 \rangle$ denoted by $\mathbf{v} \cdot \mathbf{w}$ is defined by $\mathbf{v} \cdot \mathbf{w} = v_1 w_1 + v_2 w_2$.

If θ ($0° \leq \theta \leq 180°$) is the angle between two nonzero vectors $\mathbf{v}$ and $\mathbf{w}$, then $\mathbf{v} \cdot \mathbf{w} = \|\mathbf{v}\|\|\mathbf{w}\| \cos \theta$ or $\cos \theta = \dfrac{\mathbf{v} \cdot \mathbf{w}}{\|\mathbf{v}\|\|\mathbf{w}\|}$.

For $\mathbf{v} = \langle 3, -4 \rangle$ and $\mathbf{w} = \langle 5, 12 \rangle$, find the angle between $\mathbf{v}$ and $\mathbf{w}$.

Solution

$\mathbf{v} \cdot \mathbf{w} = (3)(5) + (-4)(12) = 15 - 48 = -33$

$\|\mathbf{v}\| = \sqrt{3^2 + (-4)^2} = 5$ and $\|\mathbf{w}\| = \sqrt{5^2 + 12^2} = 13$

$\cos \theta = \dfrac{-33}{(5)(13)} = -\dfrac{33}{65}$

$\theta = \cos^{-1}\left(-\dfrac{33}{65}\right) \approx 120.5°$

REVIEW EXERCISES

Basic Skills and Concepts

In Exercises 1–10, refer to the parallelogram *ABCD* with $\overrightarrow{AB}$ = v and $\overrightarrow{AD}$ = w. Write each vector in terms of v and w.

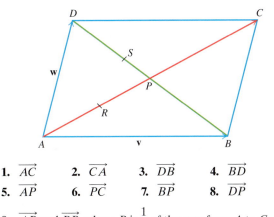

1. $\overrightarrow{AC}$	**2.** $\overrightarrow{CA}$	**3.** $\overrightarrow{DB}$	**4.** $\overrightarrow{BD}$
5. $\overrightarrow{AP}$	**6.** $\overrightarrow{PC}$	**7.** $\overrightarrow{BP}$	**8.** $\overrightarrow{DP}$

9. $\overrightarrow{AR}$ and $\overrightarrow{RP}$, where R is $\frac{1}{4}$ of the way from A to C

10. $\overrightarrow{DS}$ and $\overrightarrow{SP}$, where S is $\frac{1}{3}$ of the way from D to B

In Exercises 11 and 12, let v be the vector with initial point *P* and terminal point *Q*. Write v as a position vector in terms of i and j.

11. $P(3, 5), Q(2, 7)$ **12.** $P(-1, 3), Q(5, -4)$

In Exercises 13–16, let v = $\langle -2, 3 \rangle$ and w = $\langle 5, -6 \rangle$. Find each expression.

13. $5\mathbf{v}$ **14.** $2\mathbf{v} + \mathbf{w}$

15. $3\mathbf{v} - 2\mathbf{w}$ **16.** $\|\mathbf{v} + \mathbf{w}\|$

In Exercises 17–20, find the unit vector u in the direction of the vector v.

17. $\mathbf{v} = \mathbf{i} + \mathbf{j}$ **18.** $\mathbf{v} = 2\mathbf{i} - 7\mathbf{j}$

19. $\mathbf{v} = \langle 3, -5 \rangle$ **20.** $\mathbf{v} = \langle -5, -2 \rangle$

In Exercises 21–24, write v in terms of i and j for the given magnitude $\|\mathbf{v}\|$ and direction angle θ.

21. $\|\mathbf{v}\| = 6, \theta = 30°$ **22.** $\|\mathbf{v}\| = 20, \theta = 120°$

23. $\|\mathbf{v}\| = 12, \theta = 225°$ **24.** $\|\mathbf{v}\| = 10, \theta = -30°$

In Exercises 25–28, find the dot product v · w.

25. $\mathbf{v} = \langle 2, -3 \rangle, \mathbf{w} = \langle 3, 4 \rangle$ **26.** $\mathbf{v} = \langle -1, -2 \rangle, \mathbf{w} = \langle 4, -1 \rangle$

27. $\mathbf{v} = 2\mathbf{i} - 5\mathbf{j}, \mathbf{w} = 5\mathbf{i} + 2\mathbf{j}$ **28.** $\mathbf{v} = 2\mathbf{i} + \mathbf{j}, \mathbf{w} = 2\mathbf{i} - \mathbf{j}$

In Exercises 29–32, use the dot product to find the angle θ ($0° \leq \theta \leq 180°$) between the vectors v and w. Round your answers to the nearest tenth of a degree.

29. $\mathbf{v} = 2\mathbf{i} + 3\mathbf{j}, \mathbf{w} = -\mathbf{i} + 2\mathbf{j}$

30. $\mathbf{v} = \mathbf{i} + 4\mathbf{j}, \mathbf{w} = -4\mathbf{i} - \mathbf{j}$

31. $\mathbf{v} = \langle 1, 1 \rangle, \mathbf{w} = \langle -3, 2 \rangle$ **32.** $\mathbf{v} = \langle 1, 5 \rangle, \mathbf{w} = \langle 3, -1 \rangle$

Applying the Concepts

33. Resultant force. Two forces of 50 lb and 90 lb act at a point such that the angle between their directions is 60°. Find the magnitude of their resultant.

34. Resultant force. Two forces of 40 lb and 60 lb act at a point such that the angle between their directions is 75°. Find the magnitude of their resultant force and its angle to each of the two forces.

35. Air navigation. An airplane flying at an airspeed of 430 mph is headed due north. If an east wind of 30 mph is blowing, find the plane's ground speed and direction.

36. River navigation. A river flowing southward has a current of 8 mph. A motorboat that can travel 18 mph in still water starts on the east shore and heads in the direction S 40.3° W. What is the actual speed and direction of the boat?

37. Components. A 300 lb box slides down a plane inclined at an angle of 20°. What are the magnitudes of the forces exerted parallel to the surface and perpendicular to the surface?

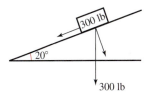

38. Equilibrant. Two forces of 200 lb and 300 lb act at the origin and make angles of 30° and 70°, respectively, with the positive *x*-axis. Find the equilibrant.

39. Work. A force of magnitude 48 lb is used to pull a wagon for 60 ft. Find the work done. The handle on the wagon makes an angle of 58° with the horizontal.

40. Work. A force $\mathbf{F} = -20\mathbf{i} + 50\mathbf{j}$ (in pounds) is applied to an object at the origin. The resulting movement of the object is represented by the vector $\mathbf{d} = 4\mathbf{i} + 6\mathbf{j}$ (units in feet). Find the work done by the force.

CHAPTER TEST

1. Liz walks 300 feet east and then walks 400 feet south. How far is she and what direction is she from the starting point?

2. A surveyor, starting from point A, walks 580 feet in the direction N 70.0° E. From that point, she walks 725 feet in the direction N 35.0° W. How far, to the nearest foot, is she from her starting point?

3. The vector $\mathbf{v}$ has initial point $P(3, 5)$ and terminal point $Q(2, -7)$. Write $\mathbf{v}$ as a position vector.

4. Assuming that $\mathbf{v} = \langle -2, 3 \rangle$ and $\mathbf{w} = \langle 1, 5 \rangle$, find $\mathbf{v} - \mathbf{w}$.

5. Assuming that $\mathbf{v} = -2\mathbf{i} + 3\mathbf{j}$ and $\mathbf{w} = \mathbf{i} + 5\mathbf{j}$, find $2\mathbf{v} - 3\mathbf{w}$.

6. Let $\|\mathbf{v}\| = 3$ and suppose $\mathbf{v}$ makes an angle of $\theta = -30°$ with the positive x-axis. Write the vector $\mathbf{v}$ in the form $v_1\mathbf{i} + v_2\mathbf{j}$.

7. Find a unit vector in the direction of $\mathbf{v} = \langle 2, -3 \rangle$.

8. Find the angle between the vectors $\mathbf{v} = \langle 4, -2 \rangle$ and $\mathbf{j}$.

9. Find the dot product $\mathbf{v} \cdot \mathbf{w}$ if $\mathbf{v} = 4\mathbf{i} + 3\mathbf{j}$ and $\mathbf{w} = -\mathbf{i} + 7\mathbf{j}$.

10. Find the angle θ ($0° \leq \theta \leq 180°$) between the vectors $\mathbf{v} = 3\mathbf{i} - 4\mathbf{j}$ and $\mathbf{w} = -2\mathbf{i} + 5\mathbf{j}$. Round your answer to the nearest tenth of a degree.

11. A 60 lb force and a 40 lb force act on an object at right angles to each other. Find the resultant and the angle it makes with the 60 lb force.

12. A plane flies at an airspeed of 460 mph with a bearing of N 30° W. A 40-mph wind is blowing in the direction N 30° E. Find the plane's direction and ground speed.

Polar Coordinates; Complex Numbers

The methods introduced in this chapter address problems of design and analysis ranging from modeling mechanical systems that imitate human characteristics to detailed analysis of the structure of coastlines around the world. You also learn about the brilliant mathematicians Archimedes, Bernoulli, De Moivre, and Mandelbrot, who were responsible for many of the ideas that provided the framework for addressing these problems.

Polar Coordinates

Before Starting this Section, Review

1. Coordinate plane (Appendix)
2. Degree and radian measure of angles (Section 3.1)
3. Trigonometric functions (Section 1.3)
4. Algebraic vectors (Section 8.2)

Objectives

1. Plot points using polar coordinates.
2. Convert points between polar and rectangular forms.
3. Convert equations between rectangular and polar forms.

BIONICS

On large construction sites and maintenance projects, it is common to see mechanical systems that lift, dig, and scoop just like biological systems having arms, legs, and hands. The technique of solving mechanical problems with our knowledge of biological systems is called **bionics**. Bionics is used to make robotic devices for the remote-control handling of radioactive materials and the machines that are sent to the moon or to Mars to scoop soil samples, bring them into the space vehicle, perform analysis on them, and radio the results back to Earth. In Example 5, we use polar coordinates to find the reach of a robotic arm. Up until now, we have used a rectangular coordinate system to identify points in the plane. In this section, we introduce another coordinate system, called a **polar coordinate system**, that allows us to describe many curves with rather simple equations. The polar coordinate system is believed to have been introduced by Jakob Bernoulli. ■

Jakob Bernoulli

The Bernoulli family includes several generations of outstanding mathematicians and scientists. After Newton and Leibniz, the Bernoulli brothers Jakob (1654–1705) and Johann (1667–1748) are considered to be the two most important founders of calculus.

---

1 Plot points using polar coordinates.

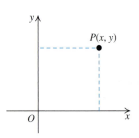

FIGURE 9.1 Rectangular coordinates

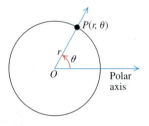

FIGURE 9.2 Polar coordinates

Polar Coordinates

In a *Cartesian*, or *rectangular*, coordinate system, a point P in the plane is described by an ordered pair of numbers (x, y), the directed distances from a pair of perpendicular axes. See Figure 9.1. In a polar coordinate system, we start with a fixed ray, called the **polar axis**, in the plane. Its endpoint O is called the **pole** or **origin**. By tradition, the polar axis is drawn horizontally pointing to the right. A point P (other than the pole) in the plane is determined by the intersection of a circle of radius r centered at $(0, 0)$ and a ray with vertex O that makes an angle θ with the polar axis. The ordered pair of numbers (r, θ) are called the **polar coordinates** of P. See Figure 9.2. The directed angle θ may be measured in degrees or radians. As usual, positive angles are measured counterclockwise from the polar axis and negative angles are measured clockwise from the polar axis.

EXAMPLE 1 **Graphing Points in Polar Coordinates**

Graph the points $(3, 60°)$, $(2, 210°)$, $(4, -30°)$, $\left(4, \dfrac{2\pi}{3}\right)$, $\left(3, -\dfrac{\pi}{3}\right)$, and $(3.5, 1.25)$ on a polar coordinate system.

SOLUTION

To locate a point with polar coordinates $(3, 60°)$, we draw an angle $\theta = 60°$ counterclockwise from the polar axis. We then measure three units along the terminal

STUDY TIP

When plotting a point in polar coordinates, measure the angle θ first. Then measure a distance of r units from the pole along the terminal ray of θ. Notice that in working with polar coordinates, you use the second coordinate first.

side of θ. See Figure 9.3. We can plot the remaining points the same way. Figure 9.4 shows these points plotted on a polar grid.

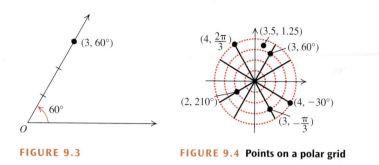

FIGURE 9.3   **FIGURE 9.4** **Points on a polar grid**   ■ ■ ■

Practice Problem 1   Graph the points $(2, 110°)$, $(3, -60°)$, $(4, 0.25)$, and $\left(3, -\dfrac{\pi}{2}\right)$ on a polar coordinate system.   ■

Sign of r

When curves are graphed in polar coordinates, it is convenient to allow r to be negative. That is why we defined r as a *directed distance*. If r is negative, then instead of the point being on the terminal side of the angle θ (ray θ), it is $|r|$ units on the extension of the terminal side, which is the ray from the pole that extends in the direction opposite the terminal side (ray $\theta + 180°$ or $\theta + \pi$). For example, the point $P = (4, 150°)$ shown in Figure 9.5 is the same point as $(-4, 330°)$ or $(-4, -30°)$.

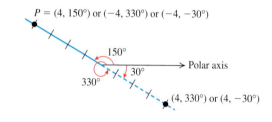

FIGURE 9.5 **Negative r**

SIGN OF r

A point $P = (r, \theta)$ in polar coordinates lies at a distance $|r|$ units from the pole.

  (i) If $r > 0$, the point P lies on the terminal side of angle θ.

  (ii) If $r < 0$, the point P lies on the terminal side of angle $\theta + 180°$ (or $\theta + \pi$). This is the ray opposite the terminal side of angle θ.

 (iii) If $r = 0$, the point P lies at the pole, regardless of the value of θ.

Multiple Representations of Points

Unlike rectangular coordinates, the polar coordinates of a point are not unique. For example, the polar coordinates $(3, 60°)$, $(3, 420°)$, and $(3, -300°)$ represent the same point. See Figure 9.6 (next page). Because adding or subtracting multiples of $360°$ to θ produces coterminal angles, there are infinitely many polar coordinate representations of a point. If a point P has polar coordinates (r, θ), then for any integer n, the point P can also be represented as

$$\underbrace{(r, \theta + n \cdot 360°)}_{\theta \text{ in degrees}} \qquad \text{or} \qquad \underbrace{(r, \ \theta + 2n\pi)}_{\theta \text{ in radians}}.$$

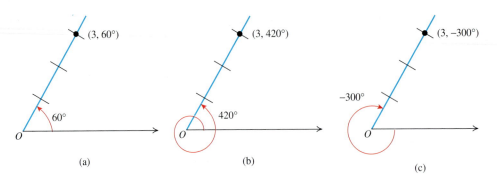

FIGURE 9.6 Multiple representations of a point

> **MULTIPLE REPRESENTATIONS OF POINTS IN POLAR COORDINATES**
>
> If a point P has polar coordinates (r, θ), then for any integer n, the point P can also be represented as
>
> $$P = (r, \theta + n \cdot 360°) \text{ or } (-r, \theta + 180° + n \cdot 360°) \qquad \text{For } \theta \text{ in degrees}$$
>
> or
>
> $$P = (r, \theta + 2n\pi) \text{ or } (-r, \theta + \pi + 2n\pi) \qquad \text{For } \theta \text{ in radians}$$

EXAMPLE 2   **Finding Different Polar Coordinates**

a. Plot the point P with polar coordinates $(3, 225°)$.
  Find another pair of polar coordinates of P with the following properties.

b. $r < 0$ and $0° < \theta < 360°$

c. $r < 0$ and $-360° < \theta < 0°$

d. $r > 0$ and $-360° < \theta < 0°$

SOLUTION

The point $P(3, 225°)$ is plotted by first drawing $\theta = 225°$ counterclockwise from the polar axis. Because $r = 3 > 0$, the point P is on the terminal side of the angle, three units from the pole. See Figure 9.7 (a).

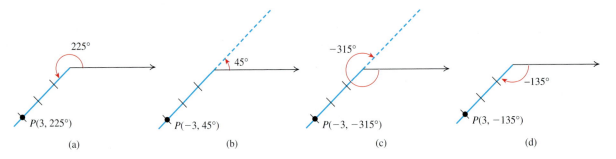

FIGURE 9.7 Plotting points

The answer to parts, **b**, **c**, and **d** are, respectively, $(-3, 45°), (-3, -315°)$, and $(3, -135°)$. See Figures 9.7 (b)–(d).   ■ ■ ■

Practice Problem 2

a. Plot the point P with polar coordinates $(2, -150°)$.
  Find another pair of polar coordinates of P with the following properties.

b. $r < 0$ and $0° < \theta < 360°$

c. $r > 0$ and $0° < \theta < 360°$

d. $r < 0$ and $-360° < \theta < 0°$

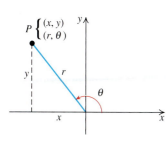

FIGURE 9.8 $P = (x, y)$ or
$P = (r, \theta)$

Converting Between Polar and Rectangular Forms

Frequently, we need to use polar and rectangular coordinates in the same problem. To do this, we let the positive x-axis of the rectangular coordinate system serve as the polar axis and the origin serve as the pole. Each point P then has polar coordinates (r, θ) and rectangular coordinates (x, y), as shown in Figure 9.8.

From Figure 9.8, we see the following relationships: $x^2 + y^2 = r^2$, $\sin \theta = \dfrac{y}{r}$, $\cos \theta = \dfrac{x}{r}$, and $\tan \theta = \dfrac{y}{x}$. These relationships hold whether $r > 0$ or $r < 0$, and they are used to convert a point's coordinates between rectangular and polar forms.

> **CONVERTING FROM POLAR TO RECTANGULAR COORDINATES**
>
> To convert the polar coordinates (r, θ) of a point to rectangular coordinates, use the equations
>
> $$x = r \cos \theta \quad \text{and} \quad y = r \sin \theta.$$

TECHNOLOGY CONNECTION

A graphing calculator can be used to check conversions from polar to rectangular coordinates. Choose the appropriate options from the ANGLE menu. The x- and y-coordinates must be calculated separately. The screen shown here is from a calculator set in Degree mode.

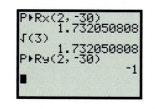

EXAMPLE 3 **Converting from Polar to Rectangular Coordinates**

Convert the polar coordinates of each point to rectangular coordinates.

a. $(2, -30°)$ **b.** $\left(-4, \dfrac{\pi}{3}\right)$

SOLUTION

a.

$x = r \cos \theta$	$y = r \sin \theta$	Conversion equations
$x = 2 \cos(-30°)$	$y = 2 \sin(-30°)$	Replace r with 2 and θ with $-30°$.
$= 2 \cos 30°$	$= -2 \sin 30°$	$\cos(-\theta) = \cos \theta$, $\sin(-\theta) = -\sin \theta$
$= 2\left(\dfrac{\sqrt{3}}{2}\right) = \sqrt{3}$	$= -2\left(\dfrac{1}{2}\right) = -1$	$\cos 30° = \dfrac{\sqrt{3}}{2}, \sin 30° = \dfrac{1}{2}$

The rectangular coordinates of $(2, -30°)$ are $(\sqrt{3}, -1)$.

b.

$x = r \cos \theta$	$y = r \sin \theta$	Conversion equations
$= -4 \cos \dfrac{\pi}{3}$	$= -4 \sin \dfrac{\pi}{3}$	Replace r with -4 and θ with $\dfrac{\pi}{3}$.
$= -4\left(\dfrac{1}{2}\right) = -2$	$= -4\left(\dfrac{\sqrt{3}}{2}\right) = -2\sqrt{3}$	$\cos \dfrac{\pi}{3} = \dfrac{1}{2}, \sin \dfrac{\pi}{3} = \dfrac{\sqrt{3}}{2}$

The rectangular coordinates of $\left(-4, \dfrac{\pi}{3}\right)$ are $(-2, -2\sqrt{3})$. ■■■

Practice Problem 3 Convert the polar coordinates of each point to rectangular coordinates.

a. $(-3, 60°)$ **b.** $\left(2, -\dfrac{\pi}{4}\right)$ ■

When converting from rectangular coordinates (x, y) of a point to polar coordinates (r, θ), remember that infinitely many representations are possible. We will find the polar coordinates (r, θ) of the point (x, y) that have $r > 0$ and $0° \le \theta < 360°$ or $(0 \le \theta < 2\pi)$.

CONVERTING FROM RECTANGULAR TO POLAR COORDINATES

To convert the rectangular coordinates (x, y) of a point to polar coordinates:

1. Find the quadrant in which the given point (x, y) lies.
2. Use $r = \sqrt{x^2 + y^2}$ to find r.
3. Find θ by using $\tan \theta = \dfrac{y}{x}$ and choose θ so that it lies in the same quadrant as the point (x, y).

A graphing calculator can also be used to check conversions from rectangular to polar coordinates. Choose the appropriate options on the ANGLE menu. The r and θ coordinates must be calculated separately. The screen shown here is from a calculator set in Radian mode.

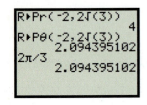

```
R▶Pr(-2,2√(3))
                    4
R▶Pθ(-2,2√(3))
          2.094395102
2π/3
          2.094395102
```

EXAMPLE 4   Converting from Rectangular to Polar Coordinates

Find polar coordinates (r, θ) of the point P with $r > 0$ and $0 \le \theta < 2\pi$ whose rectangular coordinates are $(x, y) = (-2, 2\sqrt{3})$.

SOLUTION

1. The point $P(-2, 2\sqrt{3})$ lies in quadrant II with $x = -2$ and $y = 2\sqrt{3}$.

2. $r = \sqrt{x^2 + y^2}$ Formula for computing r

   $ = \sqrt{(-2)^2 + (2\sqrt{3})^2}$ Substitute values of x and y.

   $ = \sqrt{4 + 12} = \sqrt{16} = 4$ Simplify.

3. $\tan \theta = \dfrac{y}{x}$ Definition of $\tan \theta$

   $\tan \theta = \dfrac{2\sqrt{3}}{-2} = -\sqrt{3}$ Substitute values and simplify.

Because the tangent is negative in quadrants II and IV, the solutions of $\tan \theta = -\sqrt{3}$ in the interval $[0, 2\pi)$ are $\theta = \pi - \dfrac{\pi}{3} = \dfrac{2\pi}{3}$ and $\theta = 2\pi - \dfrac{\pi}{3} = \dfrac{5\pi}{3}$. Because P lies in quadrant II, we choose $\theta = \dfrac{2\pi}{3}$. So the required polar coordinates are $\left(4, \dfrac{2\pi}{3}\right)$. ■■■

Practice Problem 4   Find the polar coordinates of the point P with $r > 0$ and $0 \le \theta < 2\pi$ whose rectangular coordinates are $(x, y) = (-1, -1)$. ■

EXAMPLE 5   Positioning a Robotic Hand

For the robotic arm of Figure 9.9, find the polar coordinates of the hand relative to the shoulder. Round all answers to the nearest tenth.

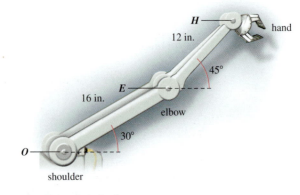

FIGURE 9.9 Robotic arm

SOLUTION

We need to find the polar coordinates (r, θ) of the hand H, with the shoulder O as the pole. Because segment $\overline{OE}$ measures 16 inches and makes an angle of 30° with the horizontal, we can write the vector $\overrightarrow{OE}$ in terms of its components:

$$\overrightarrow{OE} = \langle 16 \cos 30°, 16 \sin 30° \rangle$$

Similarly,

$$\overrightarrow{EH} = \langle 12 \cos 45°, 12 \sin 45° \rangle.$$

We know that

$$\overrightarrow{OH} = \overrightarrow{OE} + \overrightarrow{EH} \qquad \text{Resultant vector}$$
$$= \langle 16 \cos 30°, 16 \sin 30° \rangle + \langle 12 \cos 45°, 12 \sin 45° \rangle$$
$$= \langle 16 \cos 30° + 12 \cos 45°, 16 \sin 30° + 12 \sin 45° \rangle \qquad \text{Vector addition}$$

So the rectangular coordinates (x, y) of H are

$$x = 16 \cos 30° + 12 \cos 45°, \quad y = 16 \sin 30° + 12 \sin 45°.$$

We now convert the coordinates (x, y) of H to polar coordinates (r, θ).

$$r = \sqrt{x^2 + y^2} \qquad \text{Formula for } r$$
$$= \sqrt{(16 \cos 30° + 12 \cos 45°)^2 + (16 \sin 30° + 12 \sin 45°)^2} \qquad \text{Substitute values for } x \text{ and } y.$$
$$\approx 27.8 \text{ inches} \qquad \text{Use a calculator.}$$
$$\theta = \tan^{-1}\left(\frac{y}{x}\right) \qquad \text{Definition of inverse tangent}$$
$$= \tan^{-1}\left(\frac{16 \sin 30° + 12 \sin 45°}{16 \cos 30° + 12 \cos 45°}\right) \approx 36.4° \qquad \text{Substitute values and use a calculator.}$$

The polar coordinates of H relative to the pole O are $(r, \theta) = (27.8, 36.4°)$. ■ ● ■

Practice Problem 5 Repeat Example 5 with $\overline{OE} = 15$ inches and $\overline{EH} = 10$ inches.

■

3 Convert equations between rectangular and polar forms.

Converting Equations Between Rectangular and Polar Forms

An equation that has the rectangular coordinates x and y as variables is called a **rectangular** (or **Cartesian**) **equation**. Similarly, an equation where the polar coordinates r and θ are the variables is called a **polar equation**. Some examples of polar equations are

$$r = \sin \theta, \quad r = 1 + \cos \theta, \quad \text{and} \quad r = \theta.$$

To convert a rectangular equation to a polar equation, we simply replace x with $r \cos \theta$ and y with $r \sin \theta$ and then simplify where possible.

EXAMPLE 6 Converting an Equation from Rectangular to Polar Form

Convert the equation $x^2 + y^2 - 3x + 4 = 0$ to polar form.

SOLUTION

$$x^2 + y^2 - 3x + 4 = 0 \qquad \text{Given equation}$$
$$(r \cos \theta)^2 + (r \sin \theta)^2 - 3(r \cos \theta) + 4 = 0 \qquad x = r \cos \theta, y = r \sin \theta$$
$$r^2 \cos^2 \theta + r^2 \sin^2 \theta - 3r \cos \theta + 4 = 0 \qquad (ab)^2 = a^2 b^2$$

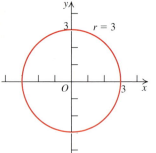

FIGURE 9.10 $x^2 + y^2 = 3^2$ or $r = 3$

$$r^2(\cos^2\theta + \sin^2\theta) - 3r\cos\theta + 4 = 0 \quad \text{Factor out } r^2 \text{ from the first two terms.}$$
$$r^2 - 3r\cos\theta + 4 = 0 \quad \sin^2\theta + \cos^2\theta = 1$$

The equation $r^2 - 3r\cos\theta + 4 = 0$ is a polar form of the given rectangular equation. ■ ■ ■

Practice Problem 6 Convert the equation $x^2 + y^2 - 2y + 3 = 0$ to polar form. ■

Converting an equation from polar to rectangular form frequently requires some ingenuity in order to use the substitutions:

$$r^2 = x^2 + y^2, \quad r\cos\theta = x, \quad r\sin\theta = y, \quad \text{and} \quad \tan\theta = \frac{y}{x}$$

FIGURE 9.11 $y = x$ or $\theta = 45°$

| EXAMPLE 7 | **Converting an Equation from Polar to Rectangular Form** |

Convert each polar equation to a rectangular equation and identify its graph.

a. $r = 3$ **b.** $\theta = 45°$ **c.** $r = \csc\theta$ **d.** $r = 2\cos\theta$

SOLUTION

a.
$$r = 3 \quad \text{Given polar equation}$$
$$r^2 = 9 \quad \text{Square both sides.}$$
$$x^2 + y^2 = 9 \quad \text{Replace } r^2 \text{ with } x^2 + y^2.$$

The graph of $r = 3$ or $x^2 + y^2 = 3^2$ is a circle with center at the pole and radius 3 units. See Figure 9.10.

b.
$$\theta = 45° \quad \text{Given polar equation}$$
$$\tan\theta = \tan 45° \quad \text{If } x = y, \text{ then } \tan x = \tan y.$$
$$\frac{y}{x} = 1 \quad \tan\theta = \frac{y}{x} \text{ and } \tan 45° = 1$$
$$y = x \quad \text{Multiply both sides by } x.$$

The graph of $\theta = 45°$ or $y = x$ is a line through the pole, making an angle of $45°$ with the polar axis. See Figure 9.11.

FIGURE 9.12 $y = 1$ or $r\sin\theta = 1$

c.
$$r = \csc\theta \quad \text{Given polar equation}$$
$$r = \frac{1}{\sin\theta} \quad \text{Reciprocal identity}$$
$$r\sin\theta = 1 \quad \text{Multiply both sides by } \sin\theta.$$
$$y = 1 \quad \text{Replace } r\sin\theta \text{ with } y.$$

The graph of $r = \csc\theta$ or $y = 1$ is a horizontal line. See Figure 9.12

d.
$$r = 2\cos\theta \quad \text{Given polar equation}$$
$$r^2 = 2r\cos\theta \quad \text{Multiply both sides by } r.$$
$$x^2 + y^2 = 2x \quad \text{Replace } r^2 \text{ with } x^2 + y^2 \text{ and } r\cos\theta \text{ with } x.$$
$$x^2 - 2x + y^2 = 0 \quad \text{Subtract } 2x \text{ from both sides and simplify.}$$
$$(x^2 - 2x + 1) + y^2 = 1 \quad \text{Add 1 to both sides to complete the square.}$$
$$(x - 1)^2 + y^2 = 1 \quad \text{Factor perfect square trinomial.}$$

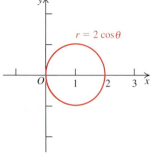

FIGURE 9.13 $(x - 1)^2 + y^2 = 1$ or $r = 2\cos\theta$

The graph of $r = 2\cos\theta$ or $(x - 1)^2 + y^2 = 1$ is a circle with center at $(1, 0)$ and radius 1 unit. See Figure 9.13. ■ ■ ■

Practice Problem 7 Convert each polar equation to a rectangular equation and identify its graph.

a. $r = 5$ **b.** $\theta = -\dfrac{\pi}{3}$ **c.** $r = \sec\theta$ **d.** $r = 2\sin\theta$ ■

SECTION 9.1 ■ Exercises

A EXERCISES Basic Skills and Concepts

1. The polar coordinates (r, θ) of a point are the directed distance r to the _____ and the directed angle θ from the polar _____.

2. The positive value of r corresponds to a distance r on the terminal side of θ, and a negative value corresponds to a distance in the _____ direction.

3. The substitutions $x =$ _____ and $y =$ _____ transform a rectangular equation into a polar equation for the same curve.

4. Polar coordinates are found from the rectangular coordinates by the formulas $r =$ _____ and $\theta =$ _____.

5. *True or False* A point has a unique pair of rectangular coordinates, but it has many pairs of polar coordinates.

6. *True or False* The points $(2, \theta)$ and $(-2, \theta)$ are on opposite sides of the line through the pole.

In Exercises 7–14, plot the point having the given polar coordinates. Then find different polar coordinates (r, θ) for the same point for which (a) $r < 0$ and $0° \le \theta < 360°$; (b) $r < 0$ and $-360° < \theta < 0°$; (c) $r > 0$ and $-360° < \theta < 0°$.

7. $(4, 45°)$ 8. $(5, 150°)$

9. $(3, 90°)$ 10. $(2, 240°)$

11. $(3, 60°)$ 12. $(4, 210°)$

13. $(6, 300°)$ 14. $(2, 270°)$

In Exercises 15–22, plot the point having the given polar coordinates. Then give two different pairs of polar coordinates of the same point, (a) one with the given value of r and (b) one with r having the opposite sign of the given value of r.

15. $\left(2, -\dfrac{\pi}{3}\right)$ 16. $\left(\sqrt{2}, -\dfrac{\pi}{4}\right)$

17. $\left(-3, \dfrac{\pi}{6}\right)$ 18. $\left(-2, \dfrac{3\pi}{4}\right)$

19. $\left(-2, -\dfrac{\pi}{6}\right)$ 20. $(-2, -\pi)$

21. $\left(4, \dfrac{7\pi}{6}\right)$ 22. $(2, 3)$

In Exercises 23–30, convert the given polar coordinates of each point to rectangular coordinates.

23. $(3, 60°)$ 24. $(-2, -30°)$

25. $(5, -60°)$ 26. $(-3, 90°)$

27. $(3, \pi)$ 28. $\left(\sqrt{2}, -\dfrac{\pi}{4}\right)$

29. $\left(-2, -\dfrac{5\pi}{6}\right)$ 30. $\left(-1, \dfrac{7\pi}{6}\right)$

In Exercises 31–38, convert the rectangular coordinates of each point to polar coordinates (r, θ) with $r > 0$ and $0 \le \theta < 2\pi$.

31. $(1, -1)$ 32. $(-\sqrt{3}, 1)$

33. $(3, 3)$ 34. $(-4, 0)$

35. $(3, -3)$ 36. $(2\sqrt{3}, 2)$

37. $(-1, \sqrt{3})$ 38. $(-2, -2\sqrt{3})$

In Exercises 39–46, convert each rectangular equation to polar form.

39. $x^2 + y^2 = 16$

40. $x + y = 1$

41. $y^2 = 4x$

42. $x^3 = 3y^2$

43. $y^2 = 6y - x^2$

44. $x^2 - y^2 = 1$

45. $xy = 1$

46. $x^2 + y^2 - 4x + 6y = 12$

In Exercises 47–54, convert each polar equation to rectangular form. Identify each curve.

47. $r = 2$ 48. $r = -3$

49. $\theta = \dfrac{3\pi}{4}$ 50. $\theta = -\dfrac{\pi}{6}$

51. $r = 4\cos\theta$ 52. $r = 4\sin\theta$

53. $r = -2\sin\theta$ 54. $r = -3\cos\theta$

In Exercises 55–62, sketch the graph of each polar equation by transforming it to rectangular coordinates.

55. $r = -2$ 56. $r\cos\theta = -1$

57. $r\sin\theta = 2$ 58. $r = \sin\theta$

59. $r = 2\sec\theta$ 60. $r + 3\cos\theta = 0$

61. $r = \dfrac{1}{\cos\theta + \sin\theta}$ 62. $r = \dfrac{6}{2\cos\theta + 3\sin\theta}$

B EXERCISES Applying the Concepts

In Exercises 63–66, determine the position of the hand relative to the shoulder by considering the robotic arm illustrated in the figure. Round all answers to the nearest tenth.

63. $\alpha = 45°, \beta = 30°$

64. $\alpha = -30°, \beta = 60°$

65. $\alpha = -70°, \beta = 0°$

66. $\alpha = 47°, \beta = 17°$

C EXERCISES Beyond the Basics

In Exercises 67 and 68, convert each rectangular equation to polar form. Assume that $x \geq 0, y \geq 0$ and that

$$\sqrt{x^2 + y^2} < \frac{\pi}{2}.$$

67. $y = x \tan \left(\sqrt{x^2 + y^2} \right)$

68. $y = x \tan \left(\ln \sqrt{x^2 + y^2} \right)$

In Exercises 69–74, convert each polar equation to rectangular form.

69. $r(1 - \sin \theta) = 3$

70. $r(1 + \cos \theta) = 2$

71. $r\left(1 + \frac{1}{2}\cos \theta \right) = 1$

72. $r\left(1 + \frac{3}{4}\sin \theta \right) = 3$

73. $r(1 - 3 \cos \theta) = 5$

74. $r(1 - 2 \sin \theta) = 4$

75. Prove that the distance between the points $P(r_1, \theta_1)$ and $Q(r_2, \theta_2)$ is given by

$$d(P, Q) = \sqrt{r_1^2 + r_2^2 - 2r_1 r_2 \cos (\theta_1 - \theta_2)}.$$

76. Prove that the equation $r = a \sin \theta + b \cos \theta$ represents a circle. Find its center and radius.

77. Prove that the area K of the triangle whose polar coordinates are $(0, 0), (r_1, \theta_1)$, and (r_2, θ_2) is given by

$$K = \frac{1}{2}r_1 r_2 \sin (\theta_2 - \theta_1). \text{ [Assume that } 0 \leq \theta_1 < \theta_2 \leq \pi$$

and $r_1 > 0, r_2 > 0.]$

78. Show that the polar equation of a circle with center (a, θ_0) and radius a is given by $r = 2a \cos (\theta - \theta_0)$.

Discuss the cases $\theta_0 = 0$ and $\theta_0 = \frac{\pi}{2}$.

Critical Thinking

79. *True or False* Explain your reasoning. Given $P = (x, y)$ in rectangular coordinates $(x \neq 0)$, one pair of polar coordinates (r, θ) of P is given by

$$r = \sqrt{x^2 + y^2}, \theta = \begin{cases} \tan^{-1}\left(\dfrac{y}{x}\right), & x > 0 \\ 180° + \tan^{-1}\left(\dfrac{y}{x}\right), & x < 0 \end{cases}.$$

Polar Equations

Before Starting this Section, Review

1. Polar coordinates (Section 9.1)
2. Cartesian equation symmetries (Appendix)
3. Graphs of sine and cosine functions (Section 4.1)

Objectives

1. Graph polar equations by plotting points.
2. Find the symmetries in a graph.
3. Graph polar equations.

ARCHIMEDES (287–212 B.C.)

Archimedes was a Greek mathematician, physicist, engineer, inventor, and astronomer. He was the first mathematician who solved physical problems by creating mathematical models. His concentration and devotion to his work was so intense that he often forgot to eat and bathe. It was this dedication to his work that cost him his life. Archimedes' genius as a military engineer kept the Roman army under General Marcellus at bay for months during the siege of Syracuse in 212 B.C. Finally, when the Romans captured the city, Marcellus gave explicit orders that Archimedes not be harmed. It is said that Archimedes was working on a mathematical diagram at that time. A Roman soldier commanded him to come and meet General Marcellus but Archimedes refused to do so until he finished his problem. The soldier was enraged by this and killed Archimedes with a sword. ■

1 Graph polar equations by plotting points.

The Graph of a Polar Equation

Many polar equations do not convert "nicely" to rectangular equations. The graph of a polar equation

$$r = f(\theta)$$

is the set of all points $P(r, \theta)$ that have at least one polar coordinate representation that satisfies the equation. To graph these equations, we make a table of several ordered pair solutions (r, θ) of the equation, plot the points, and join them with a smooth curve.

EXAMPLE 1   Sketching a Graph by Plotting Points

Sketch the graph of the polar equation $r = \theta (\theta \geq 0)$ by plotting points.

SOLUTION

We choose values of θ that are integer multiples of $\dfrac{\pi}{2}$. Because $r = \theta$, the polar coordinates of points on the curve are:

$$(0, 0), \left(\frac{\pi}{2}, \frac{\pi}{2}\right), (\pi, \pi), \left(\frac{3\pi}{2}, \frac{3\pi}{2}\right), (2\pi, 2\pi), \left(\frac{5\pi}{2}, \frac{5\pi}{2}\right), \ldots$$

Plot these points and join them with a smooth curve to obtain the graph of $r = \theta$ shown in Figure 9.14. This curve is called the **spiral of Archimedes**.

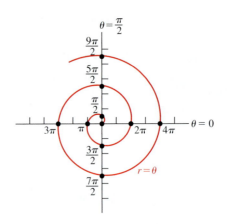

FIGURE 9.14

■ ■ ■

Practice Problem 1 Sketch the graph of the polar equation $r = 2\theta(\theta \geq 0)$ by plotting points.

■

EXAMPLE 2 **Sketching a Graph by Plotting Points**

Sketch the graph of $r = 2\cos\theta$ by plotting points.

SOLUTION

Because the period for $\cos\theta$ is $2\pi = 360°$, we make a table to find (r, θ) for $0° \leq \theta \leq 360°$. It is convenient to choose multiples of $30°$ and $45°$ for the independent variable θ.

TABLE 9.1

θ	$r = 2\cos\theta$	(r, θ)
$0°$	$r = 2\cos 0° = 2$	$(2, 0°)$
$30°$	$r = 2\cos 30° = 1.7$	$(1.7, 30°)$
$45°$	$r = 2\cos 45° = 1.4$	$(1.4, 45°)$
$60°$	$r = 2\cos 60° = 1$	$(1, 60°)$
$90°$	$r = 2\cos 90° = 0$	$(0, 90°)$
$120°$	$r = 2\cos 120° = -1$	$(-1, 120°)$
$135°$	$r = 2\cos 135° = -1.4$	$(-1.4, 135°)$
$150°$	$r = 2\cos 150° = -1.7$	$(-1.7, 150°)$
$180°$	$r = 2\cos 180° = -2$	$(-2, 180°)$
$210°$	$r = 2\cos 210° = -1.7$	$(-1.7, 210°)$
$225°$	$r = 2\cos 225° = -1.4$	$(-1.4, 225°)$
$240°$	$r = 2\cos 240° = -1$	$(-1, 240°)$
$270°$	$r = 2\cos 270° = 0$	$(0, 270°)$
$300°$	$r = 2\cos 300° = 1$	$(1, 300°)$
$315°$	$r = 2\cos 315° = 1.4$	$(1.4, 315°)$
$330°$	$r = 2\cos 330° = 1.7$	$(1.7, 330°)$
$360°$	$r = 2\cos 360° = 2$	$(2, 360°)$

We plot each point (r, θ) from Table 9.1 on a polar coordinate system and join the points with a smooth curve to obtain the graph of $r = 2\cos\theta$ shown in Figure 9.15.

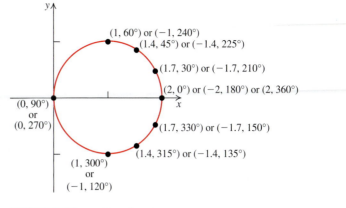

FIGURE 9.15 $r = 2 \cos \theta$ ■ ■ ■

Practice Problem 2   Sketch the graph of $r = 2 \sin \theta$ by plotting points.   ■

2 Find the symmetries in a graph.

Symmetry

As with Cartesian equations (see page 308), it is helpful to determine symmetries in the graphs of polar equations. If the graph of a polar equation has symmetry, we can sketch its graph by plotting fewer points.

TESTS FOR SYMMETRY IN POLAR COORDINATES

The graph of a polar equation has the symmetry described below if an equivalent equation results when the replacements shown are made.

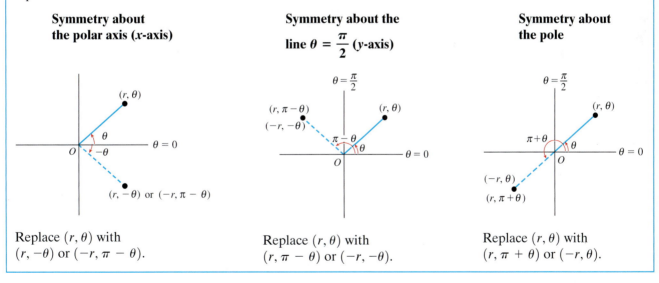

Symmetry about the polar axis (x-axis)	**Symmetry about the line $\theta = \dfrac{\pi}{2}$ (y-axis)**	**Symmetry about the pole**
Replace (r, θ) with $(r, -\theta)$ or $(-r, \pi - \theta)$.	Replace (r, θ) with $(r, \pi - \theta)$ or $(-r, -\theta)$.	Replace (r, θ) with $(r, \pi + \theta)$ or $(-r, \theta)$.

1. If a polar equation has two of these symmetries, then it must have the third symmetry.

2. Even if a polar equation fails a test for a given symmetry, its graph may show that symmetry nevertheless. (See note after Example 3.)

3. Throughout, replace π with $180°$ if θ is measured in degrees.

EXAMPLE 3 **Checking for Symmetry**

Examine the curve $r = 4 \sin 2\theta$ for symmetry.

SOLUTION

Because the sine function is an odd function, $\sin(-2\theta) = -\sin 2\theta$.

1. **Symmetry with respect to the polar axis**

   (a) Replacing (r, θ) with $(r, -\theta)$ in $r = 4 \sin 2\theta$, we have
   $$r = 4 \sin(-2\theta) = -4 \sin 2\theta.$$
   The equation $r = -4 \sin 2\theta$ is not equivalent to the original equation $r = 4 \sin 2\theta$. So this test is inconclusive.

   (b) Replacing (r, θ) with $(-r, \pi - \theta)$ in $r = 4 \sin 2\theta$, we have
   $$-r = 4 \sin[2(\pi - \theta)] = 4 \sin(2\pi - 2\theta) = 4 \sin(-2\theta) = -4 \sin 2\theta.$$
   The equation $-r = -4 \sin 2\theta$ is equivalent to the original equation, so the curve is symmetric about the polar axis.

2. **Symmetry about the line $\theta = \dfrac{\pi}{2}$**   Replacing (r, θ) with $(-r, -\theta)$ in the equation $r = 4 \sin 2\theta$, we have $-r = 4 \sin(-2\theta) = -4 \sin 2\theta$. But this is equivalent to $r = 4 \sin 2\theta$, so the curve is symmetric about the line $\theta = \dfrac{\pi}{2}$.

3. **Symmetry about the pole**   Because the curve $r = 4 \sin 2\theta$ is symmetric about the polar axis and the line $\theta = \dfrac{\pi}{2}$, it must be symmetric about the pole.   ■ ■ ■

Practice Problem 3   Examine the curve $r = 3 \cos 2\theta$ for symmetry.   ■

Note that while the curve $r = 4 \sin 2\theta$ has all three symmetries, the tests replacing (r, θ) with $(r, -\theta)$, $(-r, \pi - \theta)$, and $(-r, \theta)$ fail to reveal them. Consequently, the tests in the box (on page 341) are *sufficient* to ensure the symmetries stated but the tests are not *necessary*.

3 Graph polar equations.

Polar Equations: Graphs

We now sketch the graphs of some well-known polar equations by plotting points and using symmetry.

EXAMPLE 4 **Sketching the Graph of a Polar Equation**

Sketch the graph of the polar equation $r = 2(1 + \cos \theta)$.

SOLUTION

Because $\cos \theta$ is an even function (that is, $\cos(-\theta) = \cos \theta$), the graph of $r = 2(1 + \cos \theta)$ is symmetric about the polar axis. So, to graph this equation, it is sufficient to choose values of θ in the interval $[0, \pi]$. We construct Table 9.2 by substituting values for θ at increments of $\dfrac{\pi}{6}$ and calculating the corresponding values of r.

TABLE 9.2

θ	0	$\dfrac{\pi}{6}$	$\dfrac{\pi}{3}$	$\dfrac{\pi}{2}$	$\dfrac{2\pi}{3}$	$\dfrac{5\pi}{6}$	π
$r = 2(1 + \cos \theta)$	4	$2 + \sqrt{3} \approx 3.73$	3	2	1	$2 - \sqrt{3} \approx 0.27$	0

TECHNOLOGY CONNECTION

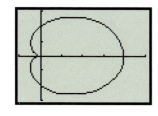 A graphing calculator can be used to graph polar equations. The calculator must be set in Polar (Pol) mode. Either Radian or Degree mode may be used, but make sure the WINDOW settings are appropriate for your choice. See your owner's manual for details on polar graphing. The screen shows the graph of $r = 2(3 + \cos\theta)$.

We plot the points (r, θ), draw a smooth curve through them, and reflect the curve in the polar axis.

The graph of the equations $r = 2(1 + \cos\theta)$ is shown in Figure 9.16. This type of curve is called a *cardioid* because it resembles a heart.

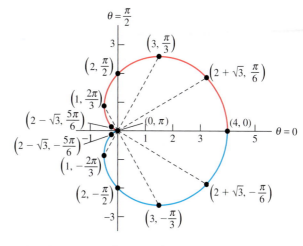

FIGURE 9.16 $r = 2(1 + \cos\theta)$ ■ ■ ■

Practice Problem 4   Sketch the graph of the polar equation $r = 2(1 + \sin\theta)$.   ■

FINDING THE SOLUTION: A PROCEDURE

EXAMPLE 5   **Graphing a Polar Equation**

OBJECTIVE	EXAMPLE
Sketch the graph of a polar equation $r = f(\theta)$, where f is a periodic function.	*Sketch the graph of $r = \cos 2\theta$.*

OBJECTIVE

Sketch the graph of a polar equation $r = f(\theta)$, where f is a periodic function.

Step 1   Test for symmetry.

Step 2   Analyze the behavior of r, and then find selected points.

EXAMPLE

Sketch the graph of $r = \cos 2\theta$.

1. Replace θ with $-\theta$.

$$\cos(-2\theta) = \cos 2\theta \qquad (1)$$

Replace θ with $\pi - \theta$.

$$\cos 2(\pi - \theta) = \cos(2\pi - 2\theta) = \cos 2\theta \qquad (2)$$

From (1) and (2), we conclude that the graph is symmetric about the polar axis and about the line $\theta = \dfrac{\pi}{2}$.

2. To get a sense of how r behaves for different values of θ, we make the following table.

As θ goes from:	r varies from:
0 to $\dfrac{\pi}{4}$	1 to 0
$\dfrac{\pi}{4}$ to $\dfrac{\pi}{2}$	0 to -1
$\dfrac{\pi}{2}$ to $\dfrac{3\pi}{4}$	-1 to 0
$\dfrac{3\pi}{4}$ to π	0 to 1

continued on the next page

Because the r values repeat from $\theta = \dfrac{\pi}{2}$ on, we find selected points for $0 \le \theta \le \dfrac{\pi}{2}$.

θ	0	$\dfrac{\pi}{6}$	$\dfrac{\pi}{4}$	$\dfrac{\pi}{3}$	$\dfrac{\pi}{2}$
$r = \cos 2\theta$	1	$\dfrac{1}{2}$	0	$-\dfrac{1}{2}$	-1

Step 3 **Sketch** the graph of $r = f(\theta)$ using the points (r, θ) found in Step 2.

3.

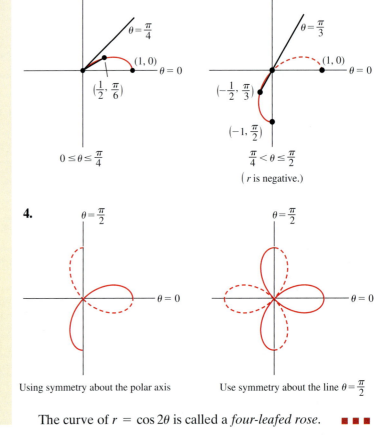

$0 \le \theta \le \dfrac{\pi}{4}$

$\dfrac{\pi}{4} < \theta \le \dfrac{\pi}{2}$
(r is negative.)

Step 4 **Use symmetries** to complete the graph.

4.

Using symmetry about the polar axis

Use symmetry about the line $\theta = \dfrac{\pi}{2}$

The curve of $r = \cos 2\theta$ is called a *four-leafed rose*. ■ ■ ■

Practice Problem 5 Sketch the graph of $r = \sin 2\theta$.

EXAMPLE 6 **Graphing a Polar Equation**

Sketch the graph of $r = 1 + 2 \sin \theta$.

SOLUTION

Step 1 **Symmetry.** Replacing (r, θ) with $(r, \pi - \theta)$, we obtain an equivalent equation. The graph is symmetric about the line $\theta = \dfrac{\pi}{2}$.

Step 2 **Analyze and make a table of values.** From Step 1, it is sufficient first to sketch the graph for $-\dfrac{\pi}{2} \le \theta \le \dfrac{\pi}{2}$. We analyze the behavior of r.

As θ goes from $-\dfrac{\pi}{2}$ to $-\dfrac{\pi}{6}$, r varies from -1 to 0.

As θ goes from $-\dfrac{\pi}{6}$ to 0, r varies from 0 to 1.

As θ goes from 0 to $\dfrac{\pi}{2}$, r varies from 1 to 3.

Table 9.3 gives the coordinates of some points on the graph for $-\dfrac{\pi}{2} \le \theta \le \dfrac{\pi}{2}$.

TABLE 9.3

θ	$-\dfrac{\pi}{2}$	$-\dfrac{\pi}{3}$	$-\dfrac{\pi}{4}$	$-\dfrac{\pi}{6}$	0	$\dfrac{\pi}{6}$	$\dfrac{\pi}{4}$	$\dfrac{\pi}{3}$	$\dfrac{\pi}{2}$
r	-1	$1 - \sqrt{3}$	$1 - \sqrt{2}$	0	1	2	$1 + \sqrt{2}$	$1 + \sqrt{3}$	3

Step 3 Sketch the graph for $-\dfrac{\pi}{2} \le \theta \le \dfrac{\pi}{2}$ using the points (r, θ) found in Step 2.

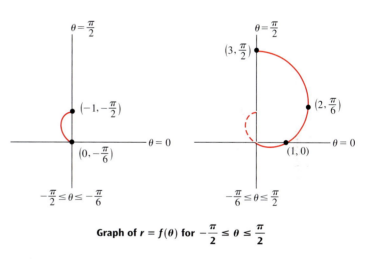

Graph of $r = f(\theta)$ for $-\dfrac{\pi}{2} \le \theta \le \dfrac{\pi}{2}$

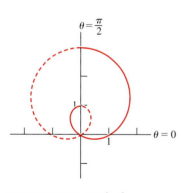

FIGURE 9.17 **Graph of** $r = 1 + 2 \sin \theta$

Step 4 Complete the graph by symmetry about the line $\theta = \dfrac{\pi}{2}$. The sketch is shown in Figure 9.17. This curve is called a *limaçon*. ■ ■ ■

Practice Problem 6 Sketch the graph of $r = 1 + 2 \cos \theta$.

The graph of an equation of the form

$$r = a \pm b \cos \theta \qquad \text{or} \qquad r = a \pm b \sin \theta$$

is a **limaçon**. If $b > a$, as in Example 6, the limaçon has a loop. If $b = a$, the limaçon is a **cardioid**, a heart-shaped curve. The curve in Example 4 is a cardioid. If $b < a$, the limaçon has a shape similar to the one shown in Example 7.

EXAMPLE 7 **Graphing a Limaçon**

Sketch a graph of $r = 3 + 2\sin\theta$.

SOLUTION

Step 1 The graph is symmetric about the line $\theta = \dfrac{\pi}{2}$ because if (r, θ) is replaced with $(r, \pi - \theta)$, an equivalent equation is obtained.

Step 2 Analyze the behavior of r. As θ goes from 0 to $\dfrac{\pi}{2}$, r increases from 3 to 5; θ as goes from $\dfrac{\pi}{2}$ to π, r decreases from 5 to 3; as θ goes from π to $\dfrac{3\pi}{2}$, r decreases from 3 to 1; and as θ goes from $\dfrac{3\pi}{2}$ to 2π, r increases from 1 to 3.

Because of symmetry about the line $\theta = \dfrac{\pi}{2}$, we find selected points for $0 \le \theta \le \dfrac{\pi}{2}$ and for $\pi \le \theta \le \dfrac{3\pi}{2}$. Table 9.4 gives polar coordinates of some points on the graph in these intervals.

TABLE 9.4

θ	0	$\dfrac{\pi}{6}$	$\dfrac{\pi}{3}$	$\dfrac{\pi}{2}$	π	$\dfrac{7\pi}{6}$	$\dfrac{4\pi}{3}$	$\dfrac{3\pi}{2}$
r	3	4	$3 + \sqrt{3}$	5	3	2	$3 - \sqrt{3}$	1

Step 3 Sketch the portion of the graph for $0 \le \theta \le \dfrac{\pi}{2}$ and for $\pi \le \theta \le \dfrac{3\pi}{2}$. See Figure 9.18.

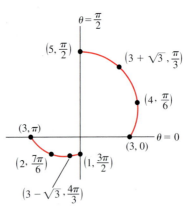

FIGURE 9.18 **Graph of $r = f(\theta)$ for $0 \le \theta \le \dfrac{\pi}{2}$ and $\pi \le \theta \le \dfrac{3\pi}{2}$**

Step 4 Complete the graph by symmetry with respect to the line $\theta = \dfrac{\pi}{2}$. See Figure 9.19.

■ ■ ■

Practice Problem 7 Sketch a graph of $r = 2 - \cos\theta$. ■

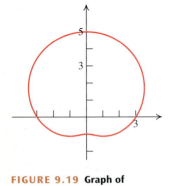

FIGURE 9.19 **Graph of**
$r = 3 + 2\sin\theta$

The following graphs have simple polar equations.

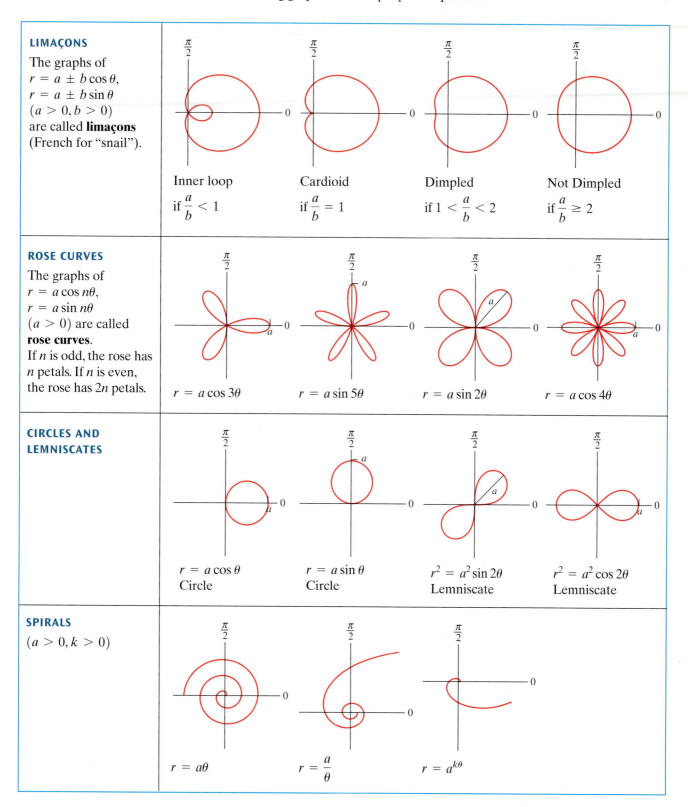

LIMAÇONS

The graphs of
$r = a \pm b \cos \theta$,
$r = a \pm b \sin \theta$
$(a > 0, b > 0)$
are called **limaçons**
(French for "snail").

Inner loop
if $\dfrac{a}{b} < 1$

Cardioid
if $\dfrac{a}{b} = 1$

Dimpled
if $1 < \dfrac{a}{b} < 2$

Not Dimpled
if $\dfrac{a}{b} \geq 2$

ROSE CURVES

The graphs of
$r = a \cos n\theta$,
$r = a \sin n\theta$
$(a > 0)$ are called
rose curves.
If n is odd, the rose has
n petals. If n is even,
the rose has $2n$ petals.

$r = a \cos 3\theta$

$r = a \sin 5\theta$

$r = a \sin 2\theta$

$r = a \cos 4\theta$

CIRCLES AND LEMNISCATES

$r = a \cos \theta$
Circle

$r = a \sin \theta$
Circle

$r^2 = a^2 \sin 2\theta$
Lemniscate

$r^2 = a^2 \cos 2\theta$
Lemniscate

SPIRALS
$(a > 0, k > 0)$

$r = a\theta$

$r = \dfrac{a}{\theta}$

$r = a^{k\theta}$

SECTION 9.2 ■ Exercises

A EXERCISES Basic Skills and Concepts

1. The points (r, θ) and $(r, -\theta)$ are symmetric about

_____ .

2. The points (r, θ) and $(-r, -\theta)$ are symmetric about

_____ .

3. The points (r, θ) and $(-r, \theta)$ are symmetric about

_____ .

4. The points $(r, -\theta)$ and $(r, \pi - \theta)$ are symmetric about

_____ .

5. *True or False* The points $(r, \pi - \theta)$ and $(-r, -\theta)$ are

symmetric about the line $\theta = \dfrac{\pi}{2}$.

6. *True or False* The points (r, θ) and $(r, \pi + \theta)$ are
symmetric about the pole.

In Exercises 7–10, graph each equation by plotting points.
Use values of θ that are multiples of 30°.

7. $r = 5 \cos \theta$ **8.** $r = 4 \sin \theta$

9. $r = -2 \sin \theta$ **10.** $r = -3 \cos \theta$

In Exercises 11–18, find the point (r, θ) for $r > 0$ and
$0° \le \theta < 360°$ that is symmetric to the given point about

a. the polar axis; b. the line $\theta = \dfrac{\pi}{2}$; c. the pole.

11. $(2, 30°)$ **12.** $(4, 120°)$

13. $(3, -45°)$ **14.** $(5, -240°)$

15. $\left(-\dfrac{1}{2}, 60°\right)$ **16.** $(-2, 210°)$

17. $\left(-\dfrac{1}{3}, -20°\right)$ **18.** $(-4, -150°)$

In Exercises 19–26, test each curve for symmetry about the
x-axis (polar axis), the y-axis $\left(\text{line } \theta = \dfrac{\pi}{2}\right)$, and the origin
(pole).

19. $r = 3 + \sin \theta$ **20.** $r = 2 + \cos \theta$

21. $r = 3 \cos 2\theta$ **22.** $r = 7 \sin 2\theta$

23. $r \cos \theta = 2$ **24.** $r \sin \theta = 4$

25. $r^2 \sin 2\theta = 4$ **26.** $r^2 \cos 2\theta = 4$

In Exercises 27–42, sketch the graph of each polar equation.
Identify the curve.

27. $r = \sin \theta$ **28.** $r = \cos \theta$

29. $r = 1 - \cos \theta$ **30.** $r = 1 + \sin \theta$

31. $r = \cos 3\theta$ **32.** $r = \sin 3\theta$

33. $r = \sin 4\theta$ **34.** $r = \cos 4\theta$

35. $r = 1 - 2 \sin \theta$ **36.** $r = 2 - 4 \sin \theta$

37. $r = 2 + 4 \cos \theta$ **38.** $r = 2 - 4 \cos \theta$

39. $r = 3 - 2 \sin \theta$ **40.** $r = 5 + 3 \sin \theta$

41. $r = 4 + 3 \cos \theta$ **42.** $r = 5 + 2 \cos \theta$

B EXERCISES Applying the Concepts

The polar equation $r = \dfrac{a(1 - e^2)}{1 + e \cos \theta}$ can be used for
calculating orbits of planets around the sun. Here a is the
average distance of a planet from the sun and is measured in
astronomical units (AU). 1 AU ≈ 93 million miles, and the
sun is located at the pole. The constant e is called the
eccentricity of the orbit with $0 < e < 1$. Note that when
$e = 0$, the equation becomes $r = a$, which is a circle.

In Exercises 43–46, for each planet with given values of a
and e, find (a) its polar equation; (b) its *perihelion* (the
smallest distance from the planet to the sun); (c) its *aphelion*
(the largest distance from the planet to the sun).

43. Mercury's Orbit: $a = 0.3871$ and $e = 0.2056$

44. Mars's Orbit: $a = 1.524$ and $e = 0.0934$

45. Jupiter's Orbit: $a = 5.203$ and $e = 0.0484$

46. Pluto's Orbit: $a = 39.44$ and $e = 0.2481$

C EXERCISES Beyond the Basics

In Exercises 47–56, use a graphing calculator to graph the
polar equation for $0 \le \theta \le 2\pi$.

47. $r = e^\theta$ (logarithmic spiral)

48. $r = e^{\theta/3}$ (logarithmic spiral)

49. $r^2 = 4 \sin 2\theta$ (lemniscate)

50. $r^2 = 9 \sin 2\theta$ (lemniscate)

51. $r^2 = 16 \cos 2\theta$ (lemniscate)

52. $r^2 = 4 \cos 2\theta$ (lemniscate)

53. $r = 2 \sin \theta \tan \theta$ (cissoid)

54. $(r - 2)^2 = 8\theta$ (parabolic spiral)

55. $r = 2 \csc \theta + 3$ (conchoid)

56. $r = 2 \sec \theta - 1$ (conchoid)

In Exercises 57–64, sketch the pair of curves and find the
points at which they intersect.

57. $r \sin \theta = 2, r = 4 \sin \theta$

58. $r \cos \theta = 2, r \sin \theta = 2\sqrt{3}$

59. $r = 2, r = 4\cos\theta$

60. $r = 2, r = 4\sin\theta$

61. $r = 2\cos\theta, r = 2\sin\theta$

62. $r = 6\cos\theta, r = 2(1 + \cos\theta)$

63. $r = 2\cos\theta + 1, r\cos\theta = 1$

64. $r = \sin 2\theta, r = \sin\theta$

65. Let Q with polar coordinates (q, α) be the foot of the perpendicular from the pole to the line l where $q > 0$. Use the accompanying figure to show that a polar equation of l is $r\cos(\theta - \alpha) = q$.

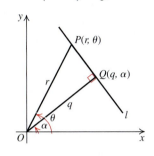

66. Use Exercise 65 to find a rectangular equation of the line with $\alpha = 30°$ and $q = 4$.

67. Use the accompanying figure to show that a polar equation of the circle with center C with polar coordinates (d, α) and radius a is $r^2 - 2rd\cos(\theta - \alpha) = a^2 - d^2$.

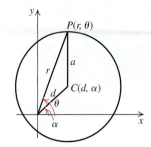

68. Use Exercise 67 to find the polar equation of a circle that passes through the origin $(d = a)$ and
   a. the center lies on the positive x-axis.
   b. the center lies on the positive y-axis.
   c. the center lies on the negative x-axis.
   d. the center lies on the negative y-axis.

Critical Thinking

69. Find the points of intersection of the two curves $r = \theta(\theta \geq 0)$ and $r = 2\theta(\theta \geq 0)$.

Complex Numbers

Before Starting this Section, Review

1. Properties of real numbers
2. Special products
3. Factoring

Objectives

1. Define complex numbers.
2. Add and subtract complex numbers.
3. Multiply complex numbers.
4. Divide complex numbers.

ALTERNATING CURRENT CIRCUITS

In the early days of the study of alternating current (AC) circuits, scientists concluded that AC circuits were somehow different from the battery-powered direct current (DC) circuits. However, both types of circuits obey the same physical and mathematical laws. The breakthrough in understanding the AC circuits came in 1893 when Charles Steinmetz explained that in AC circuits, the voltage, current, and resistance (called *impedance* in AC circuits) were not scalars, but alternate in direction, and possess frequency and phase shift that must be taken into account. He advocated the use of the polar form of complex numbers to provide a convenient method of symbolically denoting the magnitude, frequency, and phase shift simultaneously for the AC circuit quantities voltage, current, and impedance. Steinmetz eventually became known as "the wizard who generated electricity from the square root of minus one." In Example 8, we use complex numbers to compute the total impedance in an AC circuit. ■

---

1   Define complex numbers.

Complex Numbers

Because the square of a real number is nonnegative (that is, $x^2 \geq 0$ for any real number x), the equation $x^2 = -1$ has no solution in the set of real numbers. To solve such equations, we extend the real numbers to a larger set called the set of complex numbers. We first introduce a new number i whose square is -1.

DEFINITION OF i

The square root of -1 is called i.

$$i = \sqrt{-1} \text{ so that } i^2 = -1.$$

The number i is called the **imaginary unit**.

With the introduction of the number i, the equation $x^2 = -1$ has two solutions, $x = \pm\sqrt{-1} = \pm i$.

COMPLEX NUMBERS

A complex number is a number of the form

$$z = a + bi,$$

where a and b are real numbers and $i^2 = -1$.
The number a is called the **real part** of z, and we write $\operatorname{Re}(z) = a$.
The number b is called the **imaginary part** of z, and we write $b = \operatorname{Im}(z)$

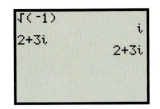 Most graphing calculators allow you to work with complex numbers by changing from "real" to $a + bi$ mode. Once the $a + bi$ mode is set, the $\sqrt{-1}$ is recognized as i. The i key is used to enter complex numbers such as $2 + 3i$.

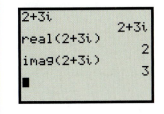 The real and imaginary parts of a complex number can then be found.

BY THE WAY . . .

In 1777, the great Swiss mathematician Leonhard Euler introduced the i symbol for $\sqrt{-1}$. However, electrical engineers often use the letter j for $\sqrt{-1}$ because in electrical engineering problems, the symbol i is traditionally reserved for the electric current.

A complex number z written in the form $a + bi$ is said to be in **standard form**. When convenient, the form $a + ib$ is used as equivalent to $a + bi$. A complex number with $a = 0$, written as just bi, is called a **pure imaginary number**. If $b = 0$, then the complex number $a + bi = a$ is a real number. So real numbers form a subset of complex numbers (with imaginary part 0). Figure 9.20 shows how various sets of numbers are contained in larger sets.

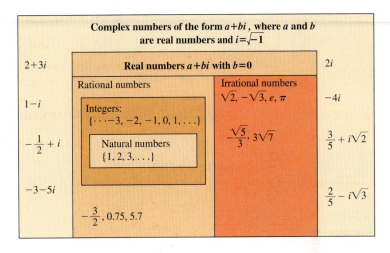

FIGURE 9.20 **Complex numbers**

We can express the square root of any negative number as a product of real number and i.

SQUARE ROOT OF A NEGATIVE NUMBER

For any positive number b,

$$\sqrt{-b} = (\sqrt{b})i = i\sqrt{b}.$$

EXAMPLE 1 **Identifying the Real and Imaginary Parts of a Complex Number**

Identify the real and imaginary parts of each complex number.

a. $2 + 5i$ **b.** $7 - \dfrac{1}{2}i$ **c.** $3i$ **d.** -9 **e.** 0 **f.** $3 + \sqrt{-25}$

SOLUTION

To identify the real and imaginary parts, we must express each number in the form $a + bi$.

a. $2 + 5i$ is already written as $a + bi$; real part 2, imaginary part 5

b. $7 - \dfrac{1}{2}i = 7 + \left(-\dfrac{1}{2}\right)i$; real part 7, imaginary part $-\dfrac{1}{2}$

c. $3i = 0 + 3i$; real part 0, imaginary part 3

d. $-9 = -9 + 0i$; real part -9, imaginary part 0

e. $0 = 0 + 0i$; real part 0, imaginary part 0

f. $3 + \sqrt{-25} = 3 + (\sqrt{25})i = 3 + 5i$; real part 3, imaginary part 5 ■ ■ ■

Practice Problem 1 Identify the real and imaginary parts of each complex number.

a. $-1 + 2i$ **b.** $-\dfrac{1}{3} - 6i$ **c.** 8 ■

EQUALITY OF COMPLEX NUMBERS

Two complex numbers $z = a + bi$ and $w = c + di$ are equal if and only if

$$a = c \text{ and } b = d.$$

That is, $z = w$ if and only if $\text{Re}(z) = \text{Re}(w)$ and $\text{Im}(z) = \text{Im}(w)$.

EXAMPLE 2 **Equality of Complex Numbers**

Find x and y if $(3x - 1) + 5i = 8 + (3 - 2y)i$.

SOLUTION

Let $z = (3x - 1) + 5i$ and $w = 8 + (3 - 2y)i$.

$\text{Re}(z) = \text{Re}(w)$		$\text{Im}(z) = \text{Im}(w)$	
$3x - 1 = 8$		$5 = 3 - 2y$	
$3x = 8 + 1$	Isolate x.	$5 - 3 = -2y$	Isolate y.
$x = 3$	Solve for x.	$-1 = y$	Solve for y.

So $x = 3$ and $y = -1$. ■■■

Practice Problem 2 Find a and b assuming that $(1 - 2a) + 3i = 5 - (2b - 5)i$. ■

---

2 Add and subtract complex numbers.

Addition and Subtraction

We find the sum or difference of two complex numbers by treating them as binomials in which i is the variable.

ADDITION AND SUBTRACTION OF COMPLEX NUMBERS

For real numbers a, b, c, and d, let $z = a + bi$ and $w = c + di$.

Sum: $z + w = (a + bi) + (c + di) = (a + c) + (b + d)i$

To add complex numbers, add their real parts, add their imaginary parts, and express the sum in standard form.

Difference: $z - w = (a + bi) - (c + di) = (a - c) + (b - d)i$

To subtract complex numbers, subtract their real parts, subtract their imaginary parts, and express the difference in standard form.

TECHNOLOGY CONNECTION

In $a + bi$ mode, most graphing calculators perform addition and subtraction of complex numbers using the ordinary addition and subtraction keys.

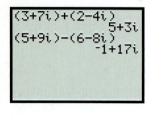

EXAMPLE 3 **Adding and Subtracting Complex Numbers**

Write the sum or difference of two complex numbers in standard form.

a. $(3 + 7i)+(2 - 4i)$ **b.** $(5 + 9i)-(6 - 8i)$ **c.** $(2 + \sqrt{-9})-(-2 + \sqrt{-4})$

SOLUTION

a. $(3 + 7i) + (2 - 4i) = (3 + 2) + [7 + (-4)]i = 5 + 3i$

b. $(5 + 9i) - (6 - 8i) = (5 - 6) + [9 - (-8)]i = -1 + 17i$

c. $(2 + \sqrt{-9}) - (-2 + \sqrt{-4}) = (2 + 3i) - (-2 + 2i)$ $\sqrt{-9} = 3i, \sqrt{-4} = 2i$
$$= 2 + 3i + 2 - 2i$$
$$= 4 + (3 - 2)i = 4 + i$$ ■ ■ ■

Practice Problem 3   Write the following complex numbers in standard form.

a. $(1 - 4i) + (3 + 2i)$ **b.** $(4 + 3i) - (5 - i)$
c. $(3 - \sqrt{-9}) - (5 - \sqrt{-64})$ ■

3 Multiply complex numbers.

Multiplying Complex Numbers

We multiply complex numbers by first using FOIL (as we do with binomials) and then replacing i^2 with -1. For example,

$$\begin{array}{cccc} \text{F} & \text{O} & \text{I} & \text{L} \end{array}$$
$$(2 + 5i)(4 + 3i) = 2 \cdot 4 + 2 \cdot 3i + 5i \cdot 4 + 5i \cdot 3i$$
$$= 8 + 6i + 20i + 15i^2$$
$$= 8 + 26i + 15(-1) \quad \text{Replace } i^2 \text{ with } -1.$$
$$= (8 - 15) + 26i$$
$$= -7 + 26i$$

You should always use the FOIL method to multiply complex numbers in standard form and replace i^2 by -1, but for completeness, we state the product rule formally.

MULTIPLYING COMPLEX NUMBERS

For all real numbers a, b, c, and d,

$$(a + bi)(c + di) = (ac - bd) + (ad + bc)i.$$

EXAMPLE 4   **Multiplying Complex Numbers**

Write the following products in standard form.

a. $(3 - 5i)(2 + 7i)$ **b.** $-2i(5 - 9i)$

SOLUTION

$$\begin{array}{cccc} \text{F} & \text{O} & \text{I} & \text{L} \end{array}$$
a. $(3 - 5i)(2 + 7i) = 6 + 21i - 10i - 35i^2$
$$= 6 + 11i + 35 \quad \text{Because } i^2 = -1, -35i^2 = 35.$$
$$= 41 + 11i \quad \text{Combine terms.}$$
b. $-2i(5 - 9i) = -10i + 18i^2 \quad \text{Distributive property}$
$$= -10i - 18 \quad \text{Because } i^2 = -1, 18i^2 = -18.$$
$$= -18 - 10i \quad ■ ■ ■$$

Practice Problem 4   Write the following products in standard form.

a. $(2 - 6i)(1 + 4i)$ **b.** $-3i(7 - 5i)$ ■

◆ **WARNING**

Recall from algebra that if a and b are positive real numbers, then

$$\sqrt{a}\sqrt{b} = \sqrt{ab}.$$

However, this property is not true for all complex numbers. For example,

$$\sqrt{-9}\sqrt{-9} = (3i)(3i) = 9i^2 = 9(-1) = -9,$$

but

$$\sqrt{(-9)(-9)} = \sqrt{81} = 9.$$

Thus,

$$\sqrt{-9}\sqrt{-9} \neq \sqrt{(-9)(-9)}.$$

When performing multiplication (or division) involving square roots of negative numbers, say $\sqrt{-b}$ with $b > 0$, always write $\sqrt{-b} = i\sqrt{b}$ before performing the operation.

EXAMPLE 5 **Multiplication Involving Square Roots of Negative Numbers**

Perform the indicated operations and write the result in standard form.

a. $\sqrt{-2}\sqrt{-8}$　　**b.** $\sqrt{-3}(2 + \sqrt{-3})$

c. $(-2 + \sqrt{-3})^2$　　**d.** $(3 + \sqrt{-2})(1 + \sqrt{-32})$

SOLUTION

a. $\sqrt{-2}\sqrt{-8} = i\sqrt{2} \cdot i\sqrt{8} = i^2\sqrt{2 \cdot 8} = i^2\sqrt{16} = (-1)(4) = -4$

b. $\sqrt{-3}(2 + \sqrt{-3}) = i\sqrt{3}(2 + i\sqrt{3})$ 　　　$\sqrt{-3} = i\sqrt{3}$

$\qquad\qquad\qquad\quad = 2i\sqrt{3} + i^2\sqrt{9}$ 　　Distributive property

$\qquad\qquad\qquad\quad = 2i\sqrt{3} + (-1)(3)$ 　　$i^2 = -1, \sqrt{9} = 3$

$\qquad\qquad\qquad\quad = -3 + 2i\sqrt{3}$ 　　　Standard form

c. $(-2 + \sqrt{-3})^2 = (-2 + i\sqrt{3})^2$ 　　　　　　$\sqrt{-3} = i\sqrt{3}$

$\qquad\qquad\qquad = (-2)^2 + 2(-2)(i\sqrt{3}) + (i\sqrt{3})^2$ 　　$(a + b)^2 = a^2 + 2ab + b^2$

$\qquad\qquad\qquad = 4 - 4i\sqrt{3} + 3i^2$ 　　$(i\sqrt{3})^2 = (i\sqrt{3})(i\sqrt{3}) = 3i^2$

$\qquad\qquad\qquad = 4 - 4i\sqrt{3} + 3(-1)$ 　　$i^2 = -1$

$\qquad\qquad\qquad = 1 - 4i\sqrt{3}$ 　　Simplify.

d. $(3 + \sqrt{-2})(1 + \sqrt{-32})$ 　　$\sqrt{-2} = i\sqrt{2},$

$\qquad = (3 + i\sqrt{2})(1 + i\sqrt{32})$ 　　$\sqrt{-32} = i\sqrt{32}$

$\qquad = 3 + 3i\sqrt{32} + i\sqrt{2} + (i\sqrt{2})(i\sqrt{32})$ 　　FOIL

$\qquad = 3 + 3i(4\sqrt{2}) + i\sqrt{2} + i^2\sqrt{64}$ 　　$\sqrt{32} = \sqrt{16 \cdot 2} = 4\sqrt{2}$

$\qquad = 3 + 12i\sqrt{2} + i\sqrt{2} + (-1)(8)$ 　　$i^2 = -1$

$\qquad = (-5) + 13i\sqrt{2}$ 　　Add. ■ ■ ■

Practice Problem 5 Perform the indicated operations and write the result in standard form.

a. $(-3 + \sqrt{-4})^2$　　**b.** $(5 + \sqrt{-2})(4 + \sqrt{-8})$ 　　■

4 Divide complex numbers.

TECHNOLOGY CONNECTION

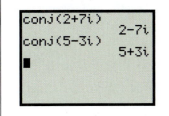 In $a + bi$ mode, most graphing calculators can compute the complex conjugate of a complex number.

Complex Conjugates and Division

To perform the division of complex numbers, it is helpful to introduce the *conjugate* of a complex number.

CONJUGATE OF A COMPLEX NUMBER

If $z = a + bi$, then the conjugate (or complex conjugate) of z is denoted by $\bar{z}$ and defined by $\overline{z} = \overline{a + bi} = a - bi$.

Note that the conjugate $\bar{z}$ of a complex number has the same real part as z does, but the sign of the imaginary part is changed. For example, $\overline{2 + 7i} = 2 - 7i$ and $\overline{5 - 3i} = \overline{5 + (-3)i} = 5 - (-3)i = 5 + 3i$.

EXAMPLE 6   **Multiplying a Complex Number by Its Conjugate**

Find the product $z\bar{z}$ for each complex number z.

a. $z = 2 + 5i$ **b.** $z = 1 - 3i$

SOLUTION

a. If $z = 2 + 5i$, then $\bar{z} = 2 - 5i$.

$$\begin{aligned} z\bar{z} = (2 + 5i)(2 - 5i) &= 2^2 - (5i)^2 && \text{Difference of squares} \\ &= 4 - 25i^2 && (5i)^2 = 5^2 i^2 = 25\, i^2 \\ &= 4 - (-25) && \text{Because } i^2 = -1, 25\, i^2 = -25. \\ &= 29 && \text{Simplify.} \end{aligned}$$

b. If $z = 1 - 3i$, then $\bar{z} = 1 + 3i$.

$$\begin{aligned} z\bar{z} = (1 - 3i)(1 + 3i) &= 1^2 - (3i)^2 && \text{Difference of squares} \\ &= 1 - 9i^2 && (3i)^2 = 3^2 i^2 \\ &= 1 - (-9) && \text{Because } i^2 = -1, 9\, i^2 = -9. \\ &= 10 && \text{Simplify.} \end{aligned}$$ ■ ■ ■

Practice Problem 6   Find the product $z\bar{z}$ for each complex number z.

a. $1 + 6i$ **b.** $-2i$ ■

The results in Example 6 correctly suggest the following theorem.

COMPLEX CONJUGATE PRODUCT THEOREM

If $z = a + bi$, then

$$z\bar{z} = a^2 + b^2.$$

To write the reciprocal of a nonzero complex number or the quotient of two complex numbers in the form $a + bi$, multiply the numerator and denominator with the conjugate of the denominator. By the Complex Conjugate Product Theorem, the resulting denominator is a real number.

In $a + bi$ mode, most graphing calculators perform division of complex numbers with the ordinary division key. The Frac option displays results using rational numbers.

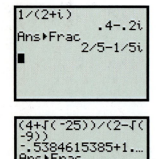

The reciprocal of a complex number can also be found using the reciprocal key.

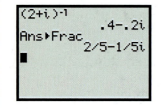

DIVIDING COMPLEX NUMBERS

To write the quotient of two complex numbers w and z in standard form, first write

$$\frac{w}{z} = \frac{w\overline{z}}{z\overline{z}}.$$

EXAMPLE 7   Dividing Complex Numbers

Write the following quotients in standard form.

a. $\dfrac{1}{2 + i}$ **b.** $\dfrac{4 + \sqrt{-25}}{2 - \sqrt{-9}}$

SOLUTION

a. The denominator is $2 + i$, so its conjugate is $2 - i$.

$$\frac{1}{2 + i} = \frac{1(2 - i)}{(2 + i)(2 - i)} \qquad \text{Multiply numerator and denominator with } 2 - i.$$

$$= \frac{2 - i}{2^2 + 1^2} \qquad (2 + i)(2 - i) = 2^2 + 1^2$$

$$= \frac{2}{5} - \frac{1}{5}i \qquad \text{Simplify.}$$

b. We write $\sqrt{-25} = 5i$ and $\sqrt{-9} = 3i$ so that $\dfrac{4 + \sqrt{-25}}{2 - \sqrt{-9}} = \dfrac{4 + 5i}{2 - 3i}.$

$$\frac{4 + 5i}{2 - 3i} = \frac{(4 + 5i)(2 + 3i)}{(2 - 3i)(2 + 3i)} \qquad \text{Multiply numerator and denominator with } 2 + 3i.$$

$$= \frac{8 + 12i + 10i + 15i^2}{2^2 + 3^2} \qquad \text{Use FOIL in the numerator:} \quad (2 - 3i)(2 + 3i) = 2^2 + 3^2.$$

$$= \frac{-7 + 22i}{13} \qquad 15i^2 = -15, 8 - 15 = -7$$

$$= -\frac{7}{13} + \frac{22}{13}i \qquad \blacksquare\blacksquare\blacksquare$$

Practice Problem 7   Write the following quotients in standard form.

a. $\dfrac{2}{1 - i}$ **b.** $\dfrac{-3i}{4 + \sqrt{-25}}$

EXAMPLE 8   Using Complex Numbers in AC Circuits

In a parallel circuit, the total impendence Z_t is given by

$$Z_t = \frac{Z_1 Z_2}{Z_1 + Z_2}.$$

Find Z_t if $Z_1 = 2 + 3i$ ohms and $Z_2 = 3 - 4i$ ohms.

SOLUTION

We first calculate $Z_1 + Z_2$ and $Z_1 Z_2$.

$$Z_1 + Z_2 = (2 + 3i) + (3 - 4i) = 5 - i$$

$$Z_1 Z_2 = (2 + 3i)(3 - 4i)$$

$$= 6 - 8i + 9i - 12i^2 \qquad \text{FOIL}$$

$$= 18 + i \qquad \text{Set } i^2 = -1 \text{ and simplify.}$$

$$Z_t = \frac{Z_1 Z_2}{Z_1 + Z_2} = \frac{18 + i}{5 - i}$$

$$= \frac{(18 + i)(5 + i)}{(5 - i)(5 + i)} \qquad \text{Multiply numerator and denominator by the conjugate of the denominator.}$$

$$= \frac{90 + 18i + 5i + i^2}{5^2 + 1^2} \qquad \begin{array}{l}\text{Use FOIL in the numerator;} \\ (5 - i)(5 + i) = 5^2 + 1^2\end{array}$$

$$= \frac{89 + 23i}{26} \qquad \text{Set } i^2 = -1 \text{ and simplify.}$$

$$= \frac{89}{26} + \frac{23}{26}i \qquad \text{Standard form}$$

Practice Problem 8   Repeat Example 8 assuming that $Z_1 = 1 + 2i$ and $Z_2 = 2 - 3i$.

SECTION 9.3 ■ Exercises

A EXERCISES Basic Skills and Concepts

1. We define $i = $ _____ so that $i^2 = $ _____.

2. A complex number in the form $a + bi$ is said to be in _____.

3. For $b > 0$, $\sqrt{-b} = $ _____.

4. The conjugate of $a + bi$ is _____, and the conjugate of $a - bi$ is _____.

5. *True or False* The product of a complex number and its conjugate is a real number.

6. *True or False* Division by a nonzero complex number z is done by multiplying the numerator and denominator by $\bar{z}$.

In Exercises 7–10, use the definition of equality of complex numbers to find the real numbers x and y so that the equation is true.

7. $2 + xi = y + 3i$
8. $x - 2i = 7 + yi$
9. $x - \sqrt{-16} = 2 + yi$
10. $3 + yi = x - \sqrt{-25}$

In Exercises 11–34, perform each operation and write the result in the standard form.

11. $(5 + 2i) + (3 + i)$
12. $(6 + i) + (1 + 2i)$
13. $(4 - 3i) - (5 + 3i)$
14. $(3 - 5i) - (3 + 2i)$
15. $(-2 - 3i) + (-3 - 2i)$
16. $(-5 - 3i) + (2 - i)$
17. $3(5 + 2i)$
18. $4(3 + 5i)$
19. $-4(2 - 3i)$
20. $-7(3 - 4i)$
21. $3i(5 + i)$
22. $2i(4 + 3i)$
23. $4i(2 - 5i)$
24. $-3i(5 - 2i)$

25. $(3 + i)(2 + 3i)$
26. $(4 + 3i)(2 + 5i)$
27. $(2 - 3i)(2 + 3i)$
28. $(4 - 3i)(4 + 3i)$
29. $(3 + 4i)(4 - 3i)$
30. $(-2 + 3i)(-3 + 10i)$
31. $(\sqrt{3} - 12i)^2$
32. $(-\sqrt{5} - 13i)^2$
33. $(2 - \sqrt{-16})(3 + 5i)$
34. $(5 - 2i)(3 + \sqrt{-25})$

In Exercises 35–40, write the conjugate $\bar{z}$ of each complex number z. Then find $z\bar{z}$.

35. $z = 2 - 3i$
36. $z = 4 + 5i$
37. $z = \frac{1}{2} - 2i$
38. $z = \frac{2}{3} + \frac{1}{2}i$
39. $z = \sqrt{2} - 3i$
40. $z = \sqrt{5} + \sqrt{3}i$

In Exercises 41–54, write each quotient in the standard form.

41. $\dfrac{5}{-i}$
42. $\dfrac{2}{-3i}$
43. $\dfrac{-1}{1 + i}$
44. $\dfrac{1}{2 - i}$
45. $\dfrac{5i}{2 + i}$
46. $\dfrac{3i}{2 - i}$
47. $\dfrac{2 + 3i}{1 + i}$
48. $\dfrac{3 + 5i}{4 + i}$
49. $\dfrac{2 - 5i}{4 - 7i}$
50. $\dfrac{3 + 5i}{1 - 3i}$
51. $\dfrac{2 + \sqrt{-4}}{1 + i}$
52. $\dfrac{5 - \sqrt{-9}}{3 + 2i}$
53. $\dfrac{-2 + \sqrt{-25}}{2 - 3i}$
54. $\dfrac{-5 - \sqrt{-4}}{5 - \sqrt{-9}}$

B EXERCISES Applying the Concepts

55. **Series circuits.** If the impedance of a resistor in a circuit is $Z_1 = 4 + 3i$ ohms and the impedance of a second resistor is $Z_2 = 5 - 2i$ ohms, find the total impedance of the two resistors when placed in series (sum of the two impedances).

Series circuit

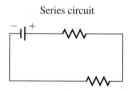

56. **Parallel circuits.** If the two resistors in Exercise 55 are connected in parallel, the total impedance is given by

$$\frac{Z_1 Z_2}{Z_1 + Z_2}.$$

Find the total impedance assuming that the resistors in Exercise 55 are connected in parallel.

Parallel circuit

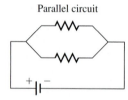

As with impedance, the current I and voltage V in a circuit can be represented by complex numbers. The three quantities (voltage, V; impedance, Z; and current, I) are related by the equation $Z = \dfrac{V}{I}$. Thus, if two of these values are given, the value of the third can be found using the equation.

In Exercises 57–62, find the value that is not specified.

57. **Finding Impedance:** $I = 7 + 5i$ $V = 35 + 70i$

58. **Finding Impedance:** $I = 7 + 4i$ $V = 45 + 88i$

59. **Finding Voltage:** $Z = 5 - 7i$ $I = 2 + 5i$

60. **Finding Voltage:** $Z = 7 - 8i$ $I = \dfrac{1}{3} + \dfrac{1}{6}i$

61. **Finding Current:** $V = 12 + 10i$ $Z = 12 + 16i$

62. **Finding Current:** $V = 29 + 18i$ $Z = 25 + 6i$

C EXERCISES Beyond the Basics

In Exercises 63–72, find each power of i and simplify the expression.

63. i^{17}

64. i^{125}

65. i^{-7}

66. i^{-24}

67. $i^{10} + 7$

68. $9 + i^3$

69. $3i^5 - 2i^3$

70. $5i^6 - 3i^4$

71. $2i^3(1 + i^4)$

72. $5i^5(i^3 - i)$

73. Prove that the reciprocal of $a + bi$, where a and b are not both zero, is $\dfrac{a}{a^2 + b^2} - \dfrac{b}{a^2 + b^2}i$.

In Exercises 74–77, let $z = a + bi$ and $w = c + di$. Prove each statement.

74. $\text{Re}(z) = \dfrac{z + \bar{z}}{2}$

75. $\text{Im}(z) = \dfrac{z - \bar{z}}{2i}$

76. $\text{Re}\left(\dfrac{z}{z + w}\right) + \text{Re}\left(\dfrac{w}{z + w}\right) = 1$

77. The product $z\bar{z} = 0$ if and only if $z = 0$.

In Exercises 78–81, use the definition of equality of complex numbers to solve for x and y.

78. $\dfrac{x}{i} + y = 3 + i$

79. $x - \dfrac{y}{i} = 4i + 1$

80. $\dfrac{x + yi}{i} = 5 - 7i$

81. $\dfrac{5x + yi}{2 - i} = 2 + i$

82. Show that $\dfrac{1 - 2i}{5 - 5i} = \dfrac{2 - 3i}{9 - 7i}$.

83. Write in standard form:

$$\frac{1 + i}{1 - i} \div \frac{2 + i}{1 + 2i}$$

84. Solve for z:

$$(1 + 3i)z + (2 + 4i) = 7 - 3i$$

85. Let $z = 2 - 3i$ and $w = 1 + 2i$.
  a. Show that $\overline{(zw)} = (\bar{z})(\bar{w})$.

  b. Show that $\overline{\left(\dfrac{z}{w}\right)} = \dfrac{\bar{z}}{\bar{w}}$.

Critical Thinking

86. State whether the following are true or false. Explain your reason.
  a. Every real number is a complex number.
  b. Every complex number is a real number.
  c. Every complex number is a pure imaginary number.
  d. A real number is a complex number whose imaginary part is 0.
  e. The product of a complex number and its conjugate is a real number.
  f. The equality $z = \bar{z}$ holds if and only if z is a real number.

GROUP PROJECT

87. Show that the set of complex numbers does not have the ordering properties of the set of real numbers. [*Hint:* Assume that ordering properties hold. Then by the law of trichotomy, $i = 0$ or $i < 0$ or $i > 0$. Show that each leads to a contradiction.]

Polar (Trigonometric) Form of Complex Numbers

Before Starting this Section, Review

1. Addition of complex numbers (Section 9.3)
2. Conversion between polar and rectangular coordinates (Section 9.1)

Objectives

1 Represent complex numbers geometrically.

2 Define absolute value of a complex number.

3 Write a complex number in polar form.

4 Find the products and quotients of complex numbers in polar form.

Mandelbrot Set Benoit Mandelbrot 1924–

Mandelbrot was born in Poland into a family with a strong academic tradition. His family moved to France in 1936, where his uncle Szolem Mandelbrot was professor of Mathematics at the Collège de France. During World War II, with the constant threat of poverty and the need to survive, Mandelbrot was unable to attend very much college. He was largely self-taught. Mandelbrot began his studies at Ecole Polytechnique in 1944. After graduation, he went to the United States where he visited the California Institute of Technology (Caltech) and Princeton University. He found work at IBM, where he used computers to create his famous Mandelbrot set. He is responsible for most of the creation of fractal geometry and chaos theory, two concepts that may have changed the way mathematics is viewed today.

FRACTALS AND MANDELBROT SETS

In 1967, mathematician Benoit Mandelbrot posed the following question: How long is the coastline of Great Britain? Mandelbrot pointed out that repeated measurements of a shoreline on a map produce a variety of different lengths. The length of the coastline will depend on detail and scale. Mandelbrot introduced the concept of fractals, which are connected to the shoreline measurement phenomenon, in his groundbreaking book *The Fractal Geometry of Nature*. Fractals are geometric patterns that display *self-similarity* at various scales; that is, the pattern looks the same on every scale. Magnifying a fractal reveals small-scale details similar to the large-scale characteristics. Coastlines and riverbanks show fractal patterns, mountains show fractal patterns, and root structures that prevent erosion show fractal patterns. It also turns out that weather patterns are related to fractal patterns. The Mandelbrot set (a famous fractal pattern) is a mathematical set, a collection of complex numbers. The computations used to determine which complex numbers are in a Mandelbrot set require that you know how to multiply and add complex numbers. We give an example of a typical computation for discovering the complex numbers in a Mandelbrot set in Example 9. The Mandelbrot set can be graphically depicted and is both stunning and elegant. ■

1 Represent complex numbers geometrically

Geometric Representation of Complex Numbers

Because each complex number $a + bi$ determines a unique ordered pair (a, b) of real numbers, we can represent the set of complex numbers geometrically by points in a rectangular coordinate system. Specifically, we represent the complex number $a + bi$ by the point (a, b) in a rectangular coordinate system. We call the plane in this system the **complex plane**. The x-axis is also called the **real axis** because the real

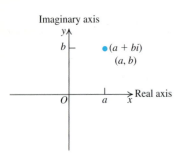

FIGURE 9.21

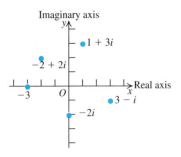

FIGURE 9.22

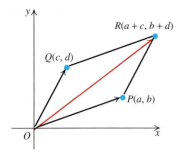

FIGURE 9.23 Geometric sum of two complex numbers

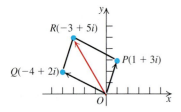

FIGURE 9.24

 Define absolute value of a complex number.

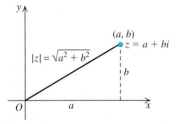

FIGURE 9.25
$|a + bi| = \sqrt{a^2 + b^2}$

part of a complex number is plotted along the x-axis. Similarly, the y-axis is also called the **imaginary axis**.

See Figure 9.21. This geometric representation of a complex number is the reason the standard for $z = a + bi$ is also called the **rectangular form** of a complex number.

EXAMPLE 1 **Plotting Complex Numbers**

Plot each complex number in the complex plane.

$$1 + 3i, \quad -2 + 2i, \quad -3, \quad -2i, \quad 3 - i$$

SOLUTION

In Figure 9.22, the points representing the complex numbers $1 + 3i$, $-2 + 2i$, -3, $-2i$, and $3 - i$ are shown. ■ ■ ■

Practice Problem 1 Plot each complex number in the complex plane.

$$2 + 3i, \quad -3 + 2i, \quad 4, \quad -2 - 3i, \quad 3 - 2i \quad ■$$

The geometric representation of complex numbers allows us to think of a complex number $z = a + bi$ as a position vector with initial point $(0, 0)$ and terminal point (a, b). Recall that the sum of two complex numbers $z = a + bi$ and $w = c + di$ (see page 352) is

$$z + w = (a + bi) + (c + di) = (a + c) + (b + d)i.$$

Geometrically, the sum $z + w$ is represented by the resultant (diagonal of the parallelogram) of the two position vectors corresponding to the complex numbers z and w. See Figure 9.23.

EXAMPLE 2 **Adding Complex Numbers Geometrically**

Add the complex numbers $1 + 3i$ and $-4 + 2i$ geometrically.

SOLUTION

In Figure 9.24, we first locate the points P and Q representing the complex numbers $1 + 3i$ and $-4 + 2i$, respectively. We draw the line segments $\overline{OP}$ and $\overline{OQ}$. We then draw the line segments through P and Q parallel to the line segments $\overline{OQ}$ and $\overline{OP}$, respectively. The point of intersection R represents the complex number $-3 + 5i$, where

$$-3 + 5i = (1 + 3i) + (-4 + 2i). \quad ■ ■ ■$$

Practice Problem 2 Add the complex numbers $2 + 3i$ and $1 - 2i$ geometrically. ■

The Absolute Value of a Complex Number

Let (a, b) represent the complex number $z = a + bi$ in a rectangular coordinate system. Then the distance from the origin O to the point (a, b) is $\sqrt{a^2 + b^2}$. See Figure 9.25. The number $\sqrt{a^2 + b^2}$ is called the *absolute value* (or **magnitude** or **modulus**) of the complex number $z = a + bi$ and is denoted by $|z|$.

ABSOLUTE VALUE OF A COMPLEX NUMBER

The **absolute value** of a complex number $z = a + bi$ is defined by

$$|z| = |a + bi| = \sqrt{a^2 + b^2}$$

EXAMPLE 3   **Finding the Absolute Value of a Complex Number**

Find the absolute value of each complex number.

a. $4 + 3i$ **b.** $2 - 3i$ **c.** $-4 + i$ **d.** $-2 - 2i$ **e.** $-3i$

SOLUTION
In each case, we use the formula $|a + bi| = \sqrt{a^2 + b^2}$ and simplify.

a. $|4 + 3i| = \sqrt{4^2 + 3^3} = \sqrt{16 + 9} = \sqrt{25} = 5$
b. $|2 - 3i| = \sqrt{2^2 + (-3)^2} = \sqrt{4 + 9} = \sqrt{13}$
c. $|-4 + i| = |-4 + 1 \cdot i| = \sqrt{(-4)^2 + (1)^2} = \sqrt{16 + 1} = \sqrt{17}$
d. $|-2 - 2i| = \sqrt{(-2)^2 + (-2)^2} = \sqrt{4 + 4} = \sqrt{4 \cdot 2} = 2\sqrt{2}$
e. $|-3i| = |0 - 3i| = \sqrt{0^2 + (-3)^2} = \sqrt{0 + 9} = 3$ ■ ■ ■

Practice Problem 3   Find the absolute value of each complex number.

a. $-5 + 12i$ **b.** -7 **c.** i **d.** $a - bi$ ▨

3 Write a complex number in polar form.

Polar Form of a Complex Number

A complex number z written as $z = a + bi$ is said to be in **rectangular form**. The point (a, b) has polar coordinates (r, θ), where $r = \sqrt{a^2 + b^2}$, $a = r\cos\theta$, and $b = r\sin\theta$. See Figure 9.26. The complex number $z = a + bi$ can therefore be written in the form

$$z = r\cos\theta + (r\sin\theta)i = r(\cos\theta + i\sin\theta).$$

We call $r(\cos\theta + i\sin\theta)$ the **polar form** or the **trigonometric form** of z.

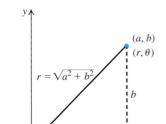

$\cos\theta = \dfrac{a}{r}$ $\sin\theta = \dfrac{b}{r}$

FIGURE 9.26

POLAR FORM OF A COMPLEX NUMBER

The complex number $z = a + bi$ can be written in **polar form**

$$z = r(\cos\theta + i\sin\theta),$$

where $a = r\cos\theta$, $b = r\sin\theta$, $r = \sqrt{a^2 + b^2}$, and $\tan\theta = \dfrac{b}{a}$.

When a nonzero complex number is written in polar form, the positive number r is the **modulus** or **absolute value** of z; the angle θ is called the **argument** of z (written $\theta = \arg z$).

Note that the angle θ in the polar representation of z is not unique because for any integer n,

$$r(\cos\theta + i\sin\theta) = r[\cos(\theta + n \cdot 360°) + i\sin(\theta + n \cdot 360°)].$$

Two complex numbers in polar form are therefore equal if and only if their *moduli* (plural of *modulus*) are equal and their arguments differ by a multiple of 360° (or a multiple of 2π).

FINDING THE SOLUTION: A PROCEDURE

EXAMPLE 4   **Writing a Complex Number in Polar Form**

OBJECTIVE
Write a complex number $z = a + bi$ in polar form.

EXAMPLE
Write $z = \sqrt{3} - i$ in polar form. Express the argument θ in degrees, $0° \leq \theta < 360°$.

Step 1   **Find r.** Identify a and b. Use the formula $r = \sqrt{a^2 + b^2}$.

1. $z = \sqrt{3} - i$, $a = \sqrt{3}$, $b = -1$
$r = \sqrt{(\sqrt{3})^2 + (-1)^2} = \sqrt{3 + 1} = 2$

continued on the next page

Step 2 Find θ. Use $\tan\theta = \dfrac{b}{a}$ to find the possible values of θ. Choose θ in the quadrant in which (a, b) lies. In general, when a calculator is used, a value of θ is given by:

$$\theta = \begin{cases} \tan^{-1}\dfrac{b}{a} & \text{if } a > 0 \\[2mm] 180° + \tan^{-1}\dfrac{b}{a} & \text{if } a < 0 \end{cases}.$$

2. $\tan\theta = \dfrac{b}{a} = \dfrac{-1}{\sqrt{3}} = -\dfrac{1}{\sqrt{3}}$. We know that $\tan 30° = \dfrac{1}{\sqrt{3}}$ and the tangent is negative in quadrants II and IV; so either $\theta = 180° - 30° = 150°$ or $\theta = 360° - 30° = 330°$. Because $(a, b) = (\sqrt{3}, -1)$ lies in quadrant IV, we have $\theta = 330°$. See the figure.

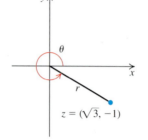

$z = (\sqrt{3}, -1)$

Step 3 Write in polar form. From Steps 1 and 2, write the polar form $z = r(\cos\theta + i\sin\theta)$.

3. $z = 2(\cos 330° + i\sin 330°)$ $r = 2, \theta = 330°$

■ ■ ■

Practice Problem 4   Write $z = -1 - i$ in polar form, letting $0 \le \theta < 2\pi$.   ■

EXAMPLE 5   **Converting from Rectangular Form to Polar Form**

Write each complex number in polar form with $0 \le \theta < 2\pi$.

a. $z = -3$ **b.** $w = -2i$

SOLUTION

a. Step 1   We have $z = -3 = -3 + 0i$. So $a = -3$ and $b = 0$ and
$$r = \sqrt{a^2 + b^2} = \sqrt{(-3)^2 + 0^2} = \sqrt{9 + 0} = \sqrt{9} = 3.$$

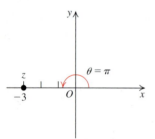

FIGURE 9.27

Step 2 $\tan\theta = \dfrac{b}{a} = \dfrac{0}{-3} = 0$. Because $\tan\theta = 0$ for $\theta = 0$ and $\theta = 180° = \pi$, we see from the graph of z in Figure 9.27 that $\theta = \pi$.

Step 3   From Steps 1 and 2, the polar form for $z = -3$ is
$$-3 = 3(\cos\pi + i\sin\pi).$$

b. Step 1   We have $w = -2i = 0 + (-2)i$. So $a = 0$ and $b = -2$ and
$$r = \sqrt{a^2 + b^2} = \sqrt{0^2 + (-2)^2} = \sqrt{0 + 4} = \sqrt{4} = 2.$$

Step 2   We cannot find θ by using $\tan\theta = \dfrac{b}{a}$ because $a = 0$. However, from the graph of $w = -2i$ in Figure 9.28, we note that $\theta = 270° = \dfrac{3\pi}{2}$.

Step 3   From Steps 1 and 2, the polar form for $w = -2i$ is
$$-2i = 2\left(\cos\frac{3\pi}{2} + i\sin\frac{3\pi}{2}\right).$$

■ ■ ■

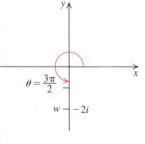

FIGURE 9.28

Practice Problem 5   Write each complex number in polar form with $0° < \theta \le 360°$.

a. $z = 5$ **b.** $w = 5i$ ■

EXAMPLE 6   **Converting from Polar Form to Rectangular Form**

Write the complex number $z = 2\left(\cos\dfrac{\pi}{6} + i\sin\dfrac{\pi}{6}\right)$ in rectangular form.

SOLUTION

$$z = 2\left(\cos\dfrac{\pi}{6} + i\sin\dfrac{\pi}{6}\right) \qquad \text{Given complex number}$$

$$= 2\cos\dfrac{\pi}{6} + 2i\sin\dfrac{\pi}{6} \qquad \text{Distributive property}$$

$$= 2\left(\dfrac{\sqrt{3}}{2}\right) + 2i\left(\dfrac{1}{2}\right) \qquad \cos\dfrac{\pi}{6} = \dfrac{\sqrt{3}}{2},\ \sin\dfrac{\pi}{6} = \dfrac{1}{2}$$

$$= \sqrt{3} + i \qquad \text{Simplify.}$$

The rectangular form of $z = 2\left(\cos\dfrac{\pi}{6} + i\sin\dfrac{\pi}{6}\right)$ is $\sqrt{3} + i$.   ■ ■ ■

Practice Problem 6   Write $z = 4\left(\cos\dfrac{5\pi}{3} + i\sin\dfrac{5\pi}{3}\right)$ in rectangular form.   ■

4 Find the products and quotients of complex numbers in polar form.

Product and Quotient in Polar Form

The polar representation of complex numbers leads to an interesting interpretation of the product and quotient of two complex numbers.

PRODUCT AND QUOTIENT OF TWO COMPLEX NUMBERS IN POLAR FORM

Let $z_1 = r_1(\cos\theta_1 + i\sin\theta_1)$ and $z_2 = r_2(\cos\theta_2 + i\sin\theta_2)$ be two complex numbers in polar form. Then

$$z_1 z_2 = r_1 r_2[\cos(\theta_1 + \theta_2) + i\sin(\theta_1 + \theta_2)] \qquad \text{Product rule}$$

and

$$\dfrac{z_1}{z_2} = \dfrac{r_1}{r_2}[\cos(\theta_1 - \theta_2) + i\sin(\theta_1 - \theta_2)],\ z_2 \neq 0. \qquad \text{Quotient rule}$$

In words:
To multiply two complex numbers in polar form, multiply their moduli and add their arguments; to divide two complex numbers, divide their moduli and subtract their arguments.

We prove the Product rule and ask you to prove the Quotient rule in the exercises.

$$z_1 z_2 = [r_1(\cos\theta_1 + i\sin\theta_1)][r_2(\cos\theta_2 + i\sin\theta_2)]$$

$$= r_1 r_2(\cos\theta_1 + i\sin\theta_1)(\cos\theta_2 + i\sin\theta_2) \qquad \text{Rearrange factors.}$$

$$= r_1 r_2(\cos\theta_1\cos\theta_2 + i\cos\theta_1\sin\theta_2 + i\sin\theta_1\cos\theta_2 + i^2\sin\theta_1\sin\theta_2) \qquad \text{Use FOIL.}$$

$$= r_1 r_2[(\cos\theta_1\cos\theta_2 - \sin\theta_1\sin\theta_2) + i(\cos\theta_1\sin\theta_2 + \sin\theta_1\cos\theta_2)] \qquad \text{Use } i^2 = -1 \text{ and rearrange terms.}$$

$$= r_1 r_2[\cos(\theta_1 + \theta_2) + i\sin(\theta_1 + \theta_2)] \qquad \text{Sum formulas for cosine and sine.}$$

EXAMPLE 7 **Finding the Product and Quotient of Two Complex Numbers**

Let $z_1 = 3(\cos 65° + i \sin 65°)$ and $z_2 = 4(\cos 15° + i \sin 15°)$. Find $z_1 z_2$ and $\dfrac{z_1}{z_2}$. Leave the answers in polar form.

SOLUTION

$$z_1 z_2 = 3(\cos 65° + i \sin 65°) \cdot 4(\cos 15° + i \sin 15°) \qquad \text{Product of given numbers}$$

$$= 3 \cdot 4[\cos (65° + 15°) + i \sin (65° + 15°)] \qquad \text{Multiply moduli and add arguments.}$$

$$= 12(\cos 80° + i \sin 80°) \qquad \text{Simplify.}$$

$$\frac{z_1}{z_2} = \frac{3(\cos 65° + i \sin 65°)}{4(\cos 15° + i \sin 15°)} \qquad \text{Quotient of given numbers}$$

$$= \frac{3}{4}[\cos (65° - 15°) + i \sin (65° - 15°)] \qquad \text{Divide moduli and subtract arguments.}$$

$$= \frac{3}{4}(\cos 50° + i \sin 50°) \qquad \text{Simplify.} \qquad ■ ■ ■$$

Practice Problem 7 Let $z_1 = 5(\cos 75° + i \sin 75°)$ and $z_2 = 2(\cos 60° + i \sin 60°)$. Find $z_1 z_2$ and $\dfrac{z_1}{z_2}$. Leave your answers in polar form. ■

EXAMPLE 8 **Converting Complex Numbers to Polar Form**

Convert all complex numbers to polar form and simplify the expression. Leave the answer in polar form with $0 \leq \arg w < 2\pi$.

$$w = \frac{(1 + i)(2 - 2i)}{-1 + i\sqrt{3}}$$

SOLUTION

Let

$$z_1 = 1 + i = r_1(\cos \theta_1 + i \sin \theta_1),$$

$$z_2 = 2 - 2i = r_2(\cos \theta_2 + i \sin \theta_2), \text{ and}$$

$$z_3 = -1 + i\sqrt{3} = r_3(\cos \theta_3 + i \sin \theta_3).$$

We find $r_k = |z_k|$ and $\arg z_k = \theta_k$ for each complex number z_k for $k = 1, 2,$ and 3.

z_k	a_k, b_k	$r_k = \lvert z_k \rvert$	Quad of z_k	$\theta_k = \tan^{-1}\left(\dfrac{b_k}{a_k}\right)$
$z_1 = 1 + i$	$a_1 = 1, b_1 = 1$	$r_1 = \sqrt{1^2 + 1^2} = \sqrt{2}$	I	$\theta_1 = \tan^{-1}(1) = \left(\dfrac{\pi}{4}\right)$
$z_2 = 2 - 2i$	$a_2 = 2, b_2 = -2$	$r_2 = \sqrt{2^2 + (-2)^2} = 2\sqrt{2}$	IV	$\theta_2 = \tan^{-1}\left(\dfrac{-2}{2}\right) = \left(\dfrac{7\pi}{4}\right)$
$z_1 = -1 + i\sqrt{3}$	$a_3 = -1, b_3 = \sqrt{3}$	$r_3 = \sqrt{(-1)^2 + (\sqrt{3})^2} = 2$	II	$\theta_3 = \tan^{-1}\left(\dfrac{\sqrt{3}}{-1}\right) = \left(\dfrac{2\pi}{3}\right)$

Substituting the values of r_k and θ_k from the table, we have

$$z_1 = \sqrt{2}\left(\cos\frac{\pi}{4} + i\sin\frac{\pi}{4}\right), z_2 = 2\sqrt{2}\left(\cos\frac{7\pi}{4} + i\sin\frac{7\pi}{4}\right), \text{ and}$$

$$z_3 = 2\left(\cos\frac{2\pi}{3} + i\sin\frac{2\pi}{3}\right).$$

So by using the product and quotient rules, we have

$$w = \frac{z_1 z_2}{z_3} = \frac{\sqrt{2}(2\sqrt{2})}{2}\left[\cos\left(\frac{\pi}{4} + \frac{7\pi}{4} - \frac{2\pi}{3}\right) + i\sin\left(\frac{\pi}{4} + \frac{7\pi}{4} - \frac{2\pi}{3}\right)\right]$$

$$= 2\left(\cos\frac{4\pi}{3} + i\sin\frac{4\pi}{3}\right) \quad \text{Simplify.} \qquad ■ ■ ■$$

Practice Problem 8 Repeat Example 8 for $w = \dfrac{(1+i)^2}{\sqrt{3}-i}$. ■

EXAMPLE 9 **Computing Mandelbrot Sets**

The basic computations used (repeatedly) to decide whether a complex number z is in the Mandelbrot set is $z^2 + c$, where c is a complex number. Compute $z^2 + c$ for

$$z = 1 + \frac{1}{4}i \text{ and } c = 2 + i.$$

SOLUTION

$$z^2 + c = \left(1 + \frac{1}{4}i\right)\left(1 + \frac{1}{4}i\right) + 2 + i \qquad z^2 = z \cdot z$$

$$= 1\cdot 1 + \frac{1}{4}i + \frac{1}{4}i + \left(\frac{1}{4}i\right)\left(\frac{1}{4}i\right) + 2 + i \qquad \text{Use FOIL.}$$

$$= 1 - \frac{1}{16} + 2 + \frac{1}{4}i + \frac{1}{4}i + i \qquad \text{Rearrange terms.}$$

$$\left(\frac{1}{4}i\right)\left(\frac{1}{4}i\right) = -\frac{1}{16}.$$

$$= \frac{47}{16} + \frac{3}{2}i \qquad \text{Combine terms.} \qquad ■ ■ ■$$

Practice Problem 9 Compute $z^2 + c$ for $z = \dfrac{1}{2} + \dfrac{1}{5}i$ and $c = 1 - i$. ■

EXAMPLE 10 **Using Complex Numbers in AC Circuits**

In a parallel circuit, the total impedance Z_t is given by

$$Z_t = \frac{Z_1 Z_2}{Z_1 + Z_2}.$$

Find Z_t assuming that

$$Z_t = 9(\cos 90° + i\sin 90°) \text{ and } Z_2 = 4[\cos(-60°) + i\sin(-60°)].$$

SOLUTION

We first calculate $Z_1 Z_2$ and $Z_1 + Z_2$.

$$Z_1 Z_2 = 9(\cos 90° + i\sin 90°) \cdot 4[\cos(-60°) + i\sin(-60°)] \qquad \text{Substitute values for } Z_1 \text{ and } Z_2.$$

$$= 9\cdot 4[\cos(90° - 60°) + i\sin(90° - 60°)] \qquad \text{Multiply moduli and add arguments.}$$

$$= 36(\cos 30° + i\sin 30°) \qquad \text{Simplify.}$$

To add complex numbers in polar form, convert to rectangular form, perform addition, and convert back to polar form.

$$Z_1 = 9\cos 90° + 9i\sin 90° = 9i \qquad \cos 90° = 0, \sin 90° = 1$$

$$Z_2 = 4[\cos(-60°) + i\sin(-60°)]$$

$$= 4\cos 60° - 4i\sin 60° \qquad \cos(-\theta) = \cos\theta, \sin(-\theta) = -\sin\theta$$

$$= 4\left(\frac{1}{2}\right) - 4i\left(\frac{\sqrt{3}}{2}\right) \qquad \cos 60° = \frac{1}{2}, \sin 60° = \frac{\sqrt{3}}{2}$$

$$= 2 - (2\sqrt{3})i \qquad \text{Simplify.}$$

$$Z_1 + Z_2 = 9i + 2 - (2\sqrt{3})i$$

$$Z_1 + Z_2 = 2 + (9 - 2\sqrt{3})i \qquad \text{Regroup.}$$

To write $Z_1 + Z_2$ in polar form, find the values of r and θ.

$$r = \sqrt{a^2 + b^2}$$

$$= \sqrt{2^2 + (9 - 2\sqrt{3})^2} \qquad \text{Replace } a \text{ with 2 and } b \text{ with } 9 - 2\sqrt{3}.$$

$$\approx 5.89 \qquad \text{Use a calculator.}$$

$$\tan\theta = \frac{b}{a} = \frac{9 - 2\sqrt{3}}{2} \approx 2.768$$

$$\theta \approx \tan^{-1}(2.768) \approx 70° \qquad \text{Use a calculator.}$$

The polar form of $Z_1 + Z_2$ is approximately $5.89(\cos 70° + i\sin 70°)$. Thus,

$$Z_t = \frac{Z_1 Z_2}{Z_1 + Z_2} = \frac{36(\cos 30° + i\sin 30°)}{5.89(\cos 70° + i\sin 70°)}$$

$$= \frac{36}{5.89}[\cos(30° - 70°) + i\sin(30° - 70°)] \qquad \begin{array}{l}\text{Substitute values for} \\ Z_1 Z_2 \text{ and } Z_1 + Z_2.\end{array}$$

$$= \frac{36}{5.89}[\cos(-40°) + i\sin(-40°)] \qquad \begin{array}{l}\text{Divide moduli and} \\ \text{subtract arguments.}\end{array}$$

$$= \frac{36}{5.89}(\cos 40° - i\sin 40°) \qquad \begin{array}{l}\cos(-\theta) = \cos\theta \\ \sin(-\theta) = -\sin\theta\end{array}$$

$$\approx 6.11(\cos 40° - i\sin 40°). \qquad ■ ■ ■$$

Practice Problem 10 Repeat Example 10 with $Z_1 = 4(\cos 45° + i\sin 45°)$ and $Z_2 = 6(\cos 0° + i\sin 0°)$. ■

SECTION 9.4 ■ Exercises

A EXERCISES Basic Skills and Concepts

1. If $z = a + bi$ is a complex number, then the modulus of z is written $|z|$ where $|z|$ = _____.

2. If $z = a + bi$ is a complex number, then the argument of z is written arg z, and arg z is the angle θ between the positive real axis and the ray from the origin to _____.

3. If $|z| = r$ and arg $z = \theta$, then the polar form of z is z = _____.

4. To multiply two complex numbers in polar form, we multiply their _____ and _____ their arguments.

5. *True or False* The argument of a negative real number is $\pi + 2n\pi$, where n is an integer.

6. *True or False* The argument of a pure imaginary number (bi) is $\frac{\pi}{2} + 2n\pi$, where n is an integer.

In Exercises 7–14, plot each complex number and find its absolute value.

7. $z = 2$

8. $z = -3$

9. $z = -4i$

10. $z = 2i$

11. $z = 3 + 4i$

12. $z = -1 + 2i$

13. $z = -2 - 3i$

14. $z = 2 - 5i$

In Exercises 15–18, add the given pair of complex numbers geometrically.

15. $z_1 = 2i, z_2 = 3$

16. $z_1 = -2, z_2 = -3i$

17. $z_1 = 2 + 3i, z_2 = 1 - 2i$

18. $z_1 = 3 - 4i, z_2 = -2 + 3i$

In Exercises 19–30, write each complex number in polar form. Express the argument θ in degrees with $0° \leq \theta < 360°$.

19. $1 + i\sqrt{3}$

20. $-1 + i\sqrt{3}$

21. $-1 + i$

22. $1 - i$

23. i

24. $-i$

25. 1

26. -1

27. $3 - 3i$

28. $4\sqrt{3} + 4i$

29. $2 - 2i\sqrt{3}$

30. $2 + 3i$

In Exercises 31–42, write each complex number in rectangular form.

31. $2(\cos 60° + i \sin 60°)$

32. $4(\cos 120° + i \sin 120°)$

33. $3(\cos \pi + i \sin \pi)$

34. $5\left(\cos \dfrac{\pi}{2} + i \sin \dfrac{\pi}{2}\right)$

35. $5(\cos 240° + i \sin 240°)$

36. $2(\cos 300° + i \sin 300°)$

37. $8(\cos 0° + i \sin 0°)$

38. $2(\cos (-90°)° + i \sin (-90°))$

39. $6\left(\cos \dfrac{5\pi}{6} + i \sin \dfrac{5\pi}{6}\right)$

40. $4\left(\cos \dfrac{3\pi}{4} + i \sin \dfrac{3\pi}{4}\right)$

41. $3\left[\cos\left(-\dfrac{\pi}{3}\right) + i \sin\left(-\dfrac{\pi}{3}\right)\right]$

42. $5\left[\cos\left(-\dfrac{7\pi}{6}\right) + i \sin\left(-\dfrac{7\pi}{6}\right)\right]$

In Exercises 43–50, find $z_1 z_2$ and $\dfrac{z_1}{z_2}$. Write each answer in polar form with the argument between $0°$ and $360°$.

43. $z_1 = 4(\cos 75° + i \sin 75°), z_2 = 2(\cos 15° + i \sin 15°)$

44. $z_1 = 6(\cos 90° + i \sin 90°), z_2 = 2(\cos 45° + i \sin 45°)$

45. $z_1 = 5(\cos 240° + i \sin 240°), z_2 = 2(\cos 60° + i \sin 60°)$

46. $z_1 = 10(\cos 135° + i \sin 135°), z_2 = 4(\cos 225° + i \sin 225°)$

47. $z_1 = 3(\cos 40° + i \sin 40°), z_2 = 5(\cos 20° + i \sin 20°)$

48. $z_1 = 5(\cos 65° + i \sin 65°), z_2 = 2(\cos 25° + i \sin 25°)$

49. $z_1 = 2(\cos 310° + i \sin 310°), z_2 = 3(\cos 165° + i \sin 165°)$

50. $z_1 = 6(\cos 249° + i \sin 249°), z_2 = 10(\cos 461° + i \sin 461°)$

In Exercises 51–56, find the product $z_1 z_2$ in standard form. Convert z_1 and z_2 to polar form and find the product in polar form. Then convert the product from polar form to standard form to show that the two products are equal.

51. $z_1 = 1 + i, z_2 = 1 - i$

52. $z_1 = 1 + i\sqrt{3}, z_2 = 1 - i\sqrt{3}$

53. $z_1 = \sqrt{3} + i, z_2 = 2 - i\sqrt{3}$

54. $z_1 = \sqrt{6} + i\sqrt{2}, z_2 = \sqrt{3} - i$

55. $z_1 = 4\sqrt{3} + 4i, z_2 = 3 - 3i$

56. $z_1 = \sqrt{3} - i, z_2 = 2 + 2i$

In Exercises 57–62, find the quotient $\dfrac{z_1}{z_2}$ in standard form. Convert z_1 and z_2 to polar form and find the quotient in polar form. Then convert the quotient from polar form to standard form to show that the two quotients are equal.

57. $z_1 = 1 + i\sqrt{3}, z_2 = 1 + i$

58. $z_1 = -3 + 3i, z_2 = \sqrt{3} - i$

59. $z_1 = -\sqrt{3} - i, z_2 = 1 + i\sqrt{3}$

60. $z_1 = 2 - 2i, z_2 = -4 + \dfrac{4\sqrt{3}}{3}i$

61. $z_1 = -5 + \dfrac{5\sqrt{3}}{3}i, z_2 = 6 + 6i$

62. $z_1 = 11\sqrt{3} - 11i, z_2 = -13 - 13i$

In Exercises 63–66, convert all complex numbers in the expression for w to polar form and simplify the expression. Leave your answer in polar form with $0° \leq \arg w < 360°$.

63. $w = \dfrac{(2 - 2i)(\sqrt{3} + i)}{-3 + i\sqrt{3}}$

64. $w = \dfrac{(3 + 3i)(-1 + i)}{\sqrt{3} + i}$

65. $w = \dfrac{(\sqrt{3} - i)(2 + 2i)}{(3 - i\sqrt{3})(1 - i)}$

66. $w = \dfrac{(\sqrt{6} + i\sqrt{2})(2 - 2i\sqrt{3})}{(-\sqrt{3} + i)(2 + 2i)}$

B EXERCISES Applying the Concepts

For a complex number c, define

$$z_0 = 0$$

$$z_1 = c$$

$$z_2 = (z_1)^2 + c = c^2 + c$$

$$z_3 = (z_2)^2 + c = (c^2 + c)^2 + c$$

$$\vdots$$

$$z_{n+1} = z_n^2 + c \text{ (Square the previous answer and add } c\text{.)}$$

The complex number c does not belong to the Mandelbrot set if for any positive integer n, $|z_n| > 2$. Otherwise, c is in the Mandelbrot set. In Exercises 67–70, determine whether the given number c belongs to the Mandelbrot set. Check for $1 \leq n \leq 6$.

67. $c = \dfrac{1}{2}i$

68. $c = 1 + i$

69. $c = \dfrac{1}{2} - \dfrac{1}{2}i$

70. $c = -1$

The Mandelbrot sets are traditionally defined by giving each complex number $c = a + bi$ a color determined by the smallest integer n for which $|z_n| > 2$. The points in the Mandelbrot set are traditionally colored black. In Exercises 71–74, find the color assigned to the given complex number.

For these exercises, use the following assignments.

Smallest value of n for which $|z_n| > 2$	Color
1	Pink
2	Yellow
3	Orange
4	Blue
5	Purple

71. $c = 1 + \dfrac{\sqrt{3}}{2}i$

72. $c = \dfrac{\sqrt{3}}{2} + \dfrac{1}{2}i$

73. $c = i$

74. $c = \dfrac{1}{2}$

75. Geometry. Show that the area, K, of a triangle with vertices at the origin O, z_1, and z_2 is given by

$$K = \frac{1}{2}|z_1||z_2| \sin\left(\left| \arg \frac{z_1}{z_2} \right| \right).$$

76. AC circuits. Use Ohm's Law, $I = \dfrac{V}{Z}$, to find the current I given voltage $V = 120(\cos 60° + i \sin 60°)$ and impedance $Z = 8(\cos 30° + i \sin 30°)$.

77. AC circuits. Use the Ohm's Law from Exercise 76 to find the voltage V given $I = 6(\cos 40° + i \sin 40°)$ and $Z = 16 \cos (110° + i \sin 110°)$.

In Exercises 78 and 79, use the formula $Z_1 = \dfrac{Z_1 Z_2}{Z_1 + Z_2}$ **to find the total impedance in a parallel circuit for the given values of Z_1 and Z_2.**

78. $Z_1 = 16(\cos 180° + i \sin 180°)$ and
$Z_2 = 2(\cos 150° + i \sin 150°)$

79. $Z_1 = 12(\cos 270° + i \sin 270°)$ and
$Z_2 = 3(\cos 60° + i \sin 60°)$

C EXERCISES Beyond the Basics

80. Prove the Quotient rule. [*Hint:* The Quotient rule can be obtained by using the product rule: If $\dfrac{z_1}{z_2} = z_3$, then $z_1 = z_2 z_3$. Let $z_k = r_k(\cos \theta_k + i \sin \theta_k)$ for $k = 1, 2,$ and 3. Apply the Product rule to $z_1 = z_2 z_3$ and solve for r_3 and θ_3.]

81. Apply the Quotient rule to show that for a nonzero $z = r(\cos \theta + i \sin \theta)$, $z^{-1} = \dfrac{1}{z} = \dfrac{1}{r}[\cos (-\theta) + i \sin (-\theta)]$.

82. If $z = r(\cos \theta + i \sin \theta)$, show that $\bar{z} = r[\cos (-\theta) + i \sin (-\theta)]$.

83. Use Exercise 82 to show that $z\bar{z} = r^2$.

84. Use Exercises 82 and 83 to show that $\dfrac{1}{z} = \dfrac{1}{r}[\cos (-\theta) + i \sin (-\theta)]$. $\left[Hint: \dfrac{1}{z} = \dfrac{\bar{z}}{z\bar{z}} \right]$

In Exercises 85 and 86, let $z = r(\cos \theta + i \sin \theta)$.

85. Write a polar representation for iz. Plot z and iz on the same complex plane. Explain the geometric effect of multiplying a complex number z by i.

86. Explain the geometric effect of dividing a complex number by i.

In Exercises 87–90, write each complex number in polar form.

87. $-\cos \theta + i \sin \theta$

88. $\sin \theta - i \cos \theta$

89. $-\sin \theta - i \cos \theta$

90. $\sin \theta + i \cos \theta$

Critical Thinking

91. Find the product $(3 + 2i)(5 + i)$ using FOIL. Then deduce the identity: $\tan^{-1}\left(\dfrac{2}{3}\right) + \tan^{-1}\left(\dfrac{1}{5}\right) = \dfrac{\pi}{4}$.

[*Hint:* $\arg(z_1 z_2) = \arg z_1 + \arg z_2$.]

92. Find the product $(p + q + i)(p^2 + pq + 1 + iq)$. Then deduce the identity:

$$\tan^{-1}\left(\frac{1}{p + q}\right) + \tan^{-1}\left(\frac{q}{p^2 + pq + 1}\right) = \tan^{-1}\left(\frac{1}{p}\right).$$

Powers and Roots of Complex Numbers

Before Starting this Section, Review

1. Polar form of complex numbers (Section 9.4)

2. Multiply two complex numbers (Section 9.3)

3. Convert rectangular form to polar form (Section 9.4)

Objectives

1 State De Moivre's Theorem.

2 Use De Moivre's Theorem to find powers of a complex number.

3 Use De Moivre's Theorem to find the nth roots of a complex number.

De Moivre 1667–1754

ABRAHAM DE MOIVRE

The French mathematician De Moivre was known for his formula that links complex numbers to trigonometry. His major mathematical work was *The Doctrine of Chances*, first published in 1718. This probability text was highly prized by gamblers. Because of his religious persecution (he was Protestant), he left France for England, never to return. There he became an intimate friend of Newton. He never realized his dream of professorship at a university, but instead made his living by tutoring and solving problems arising from games of chance. De Moivre is famed for predicting the day of his own death. He noted that he was sleeping 15 minutes longer each night and calculated he would die on the day he slept for 24 hours. He was right! ■

1 State De Moivre's Theorem.

De Moivre's Theorem

In the previous section, we saw that to multiply two complex numbers in polar form, we multiply their moduli and add their arguments. This leads to a very simple formula known as De Moivre's Theorem for calculating powers of a complex number.

Let $z = r(\cos\theta + i\sin\theta)$ be a complex number in polar form. Then

$$z^2 = z \cdot z$$
$$= r(\cos\theta + i\sin\theta) \cdot r(\cos\theta + i\sin\theta) \qquad \text{Form product } z \cdot z.$$
$$= (r \cdot r)[\cos(\theta + \theta) + i\sin(\theta + \theta)] \qquad \text{Multiply moduli and add arguments.}$$
$$z^2 = r^2(\cos 2\theta + i\sin 2\theta) \qquad \text{Simplify.}$$
$$z^3 = z^2 \cdot z$$
$$= r^2(\cos 2\theta + i\sin 2\theta) \cdot r(\cos 2\theta + i\sin 2\theta) \qquad \text{Polar form of } z^2 \text{ and } z$$
$$= (r^2 \cdot r)[\cos(2\theta + \theta) + i\sin(2\theta + \theta)] \qquad \text{Multiply moduli and add arguments.}$$
$$z^3 = r^3(\cos 3\theta + i\sin 3\theta) \qquad \text{Simplify.}$$

In a similar way, by writing $z^4 = z^3 \cdot z$, you can show that

$$z^4 = r^4(\cos 4\theta + i\sin 4\theta).$$

De Moivre's Theorem (whose proof is omitted) follows this pattern.

> **DE MOIVRE'S THEOREM**
>
> Let $z = r(\cos\theta + i\sin\theta)$ be a complex number in polar form.
> Then for any integer n,
>
> $$z^n = r^n(\cos n\theta + i\sin n\theta).$$

EXAMPLE 1   **Using De Moivre's Theorem**

For $z = 2(\cos 60° + i\sin 60°)$, find z^4. Write the answer in rectangular form.

SOLUTION

For $z = 2(\cos 60° + i\sin 60°)$, $r = 2$ and $\theta = 60°$. So

$$[2(\cos 60° + i\sin 60°)]^4 = 2^4[\cos(4 \cdot 60°) + i\sin(4 \cdot 60°)] \qquad \text{De Moivre's Theorem}$$
$$= 16(\cos 240° + i\sin 240°) \qquad \text{Simplify.}$$
$$= 16\left(-\frac{1}{2} - i\frac{\sqrt{3}}{2}\right) \qquad \cos 240° = -\frac{1}{2},$$
$$\sin 240° = -\frac{\sqrt{3}}{2}$$
$$= -8 - (8\sqrt{3})i \qquad \text{Rectangular form}$$

■ ■ ■

Practice Problem 1   For $z = 2(\cos 30° + i\sin 30°)$, find z^5 in rectangular form. ■

2 Use De Moivre's Theorem to find powers of a complex number.

Powers of a Complex Number

To find the powers of a complex number in rectangular form, convert the number to polar form and then apply De Moivre's Theorem.

EXAMPLE 2   **Finding the Power of a Complex Number**

Let $z = 1 + i$. Use De Moivre's Theorem to find z^{16}.

SOLUTION

We first convert $z = 1 + i$ to polar form. We find r and θ.
$$r = \sqrt{a^2 + b^2} = \sqrt{1^2 + 1^2} = \sqrt{2}$$

and

$$\tan\theta = \frac{b}{a} = \frac{1}{1} = 1; \text{ so } \theta = \frac{\pi}{4}.$$

$$z = \sqrt{2}\left(\cos\frac{\pi}{4} + i\sin\frac{\pi}{4}\right) \qquad \text{Polar form of } z = 1 + i$$

$$z^{16} = \left[\sqrt{2}\left(\cos\frac{\pi}{4} + i\sin\frac{\pi}{4}\right)\right]^{16} \qquad \text{Raise both sides to the 16th power.}$$

$$z^{16} = (\sqrt{2})^{16}\left[\cos\left(16 \cdot \frac{\pi}{4}\right) + i\sin\left(16 \cdot \frac{\pi}{4}\right)\right] \qquad \text{De Moivre's Theorem}$$

$$= 2^8[\cos(4\pi) + i\sin(4\pi)] \qquad (\sqrt{2})^{16} = (2^{1/2})^{16} = 2^{1/2 \cdot 16} = 2^8$$

$$= 256(1 + i \cdot 0) = 256 \qquad \cos 4\pi = 1, \sin 4\pi = 0 \qquad ■ ■ ■$$

Practice Problem 2   Let $z = -1 + i$. Use De Moivre's Theorem to find z^6. ■

EXAMPLE 3 **Using De Moivre's Theorem with a Negative Power**

Let $z = 1 + i\sqrt{3}$. Use De Moivre's Theorem to find z^{-8}. Write the answer in rectangular form.

SOLUTION

Convert $z = 1 + i\sqrt{3}$ to polar form.

$$r = \sqrt{1^2 + (\sqrt{3})^2} = \sqrt{1 + 3} = \sqrt{4} = 2$$

and

$$\tan \theta = \frac{\sqrt{3}}{1} = \sqrt{3}; \text{ so } \theta = 60°.$$

$z = 2(\cos 60° + i \sin 60°)$	Polar form of $z = 1 + i\sqrt{3}$
$z^{-8} = [2(\cos 60° + i \sin 60°)]^{-8}$	Raise both sides to the power -8.
$z^{-8} = 2^{-8}[\cos(-8 \cdot 60°) + i \sin(-8 \cdot 60°)]$	De Moivre's Theorem
$= \dfrac{1}{2^8}[\cos(-480°) + i \sin(-480°)]$	Simplify.
$= \dfrac{1}{256}[\cos(-120°) + i \sin(-120°)]$	$-480° = -360° - 120°$ Coterminal angles
$= \dfrac{1}{256}[\cos(120°) - i \sin(120°)]$	$\cos(-\theta) = \cos\theta, \sin(-\theta) = \sin\theta$
$= \dfrac{1}{256}\left[-\dfrac{1}{2} - i\dfrac{\sqrt{3}}{2}\right]$	$\cos 120° = -\dfrac{1}{2}, \sin 120° = \dfrac{\sqrt{3}}{2}$
$= -\dfrac{1}{512} - \left(\dfrac{\sqrt{3}}{512}\right)i$	Rectangular form ■ ■ ■

Practice Problem 3 Let $z = -1 + i$. Use De Moivre's Theorem to find z^{-12}. Write your answer in rectangular form. ■

3 Use De Moivre's Theorem to find the nth roots of a complex number.

Roots of Complex Numbers

In Example 1, we showed that $[2(\cos 60° + i \sin 60°)]^4 = 16(\cos 240° + i \sin 240°)$. We call $[2(\cos 60° + i \sin 60°)]$ a complex fourth root of the complex number $16(\cos 240° + i \sin 240°)$. In general, we make the following definition.

DEFINITION OF nth ROOT

For a positive integer n, the complex number z is called the **nth root** of the complex number w if

$$z^n = w.$$

Every nonzero complex number w has exactly n complex nth roots. We can use De Moivre's Theorem to find all of them.

> ### DE MOIVRE'S *n*th ROOTS THEOREM
>
> The *n* nth roots of a complex number $w = r(\cos \theta + i \sin \theta)$, with $r > 0$ and θ in degrees, are given by
>
> $$z_k = r^{1/n}\left[\cos\left(\frac{\theta + 360°k}{n}\right) + i \sin\left(\frac{\theta + 360°k}{n}\right)\right] \text{ for }$$
>
> $$k = 0, 1, 2, \ldots, n - 1.$$
>
> If θ is in radians, replace 360° with 2π in z_k.

The result in the box says that there are exactly *n* nth roots of a complex number. To verify the result, we raise z_k to power *n* and use De Moivre's Theorem to show that $z_k^n = w$.

EXAMPLE 4   Finding the Roots of a Complex Number

Find the three cube roots of $1 + i$ in polar form, with the argument in degrees.

SOLUTION

In Example 2, we showed that

$$1 + i = \sqrt{2}\left(\cos\frac{\pi}{4} + i \sin\frac{\pi}{4}\right) \qquad \text{\color{blue}Polar form of } 1 + i$$

$$1 + i = \sqrt{2}(\cos 45° + i \sin 45°) \qquad \text{\color{blue}Replace } \frac{\pi}{4} \text{ with } 45°.$$

From De Moivre's Theorem for finding complex roots, with $n = 3$, we have

$$z_k = (\sqrt{2})^{1/3}\left[\cos\left(\frac{45° + 360°k}{3}\right) + i \sin\left(\frac{45° + 360°k}{3}\right)\right], k = 0, 1, 2.$$

By substituting $k = 0, 1$, and 2 in the expression for z_k and simplifying, we find the three cube roots.

$$z_0 = (2)^{1/6}\left[\cos\left(\frac{45° + 360° \cdot 0}{3}\right) + i \sin\left(\frac{45° + 360° \cdot 0}{3}\right)\right] \qquad \text{\color{blue}} k = 0$$

$$= 2^{1/6}(\cos 15° + i \sin 15°) \qquad \text{\color{blue}Simplify.}$$

$$z_1 = 2^{1/6}\left[\cos\left(\frac{45° + 360° \cdot 1}{3}\right) + i \sin\left(\frac{45° + 360° \cdot 1}{3}\right)\right] \qquad \text{\color{blue}} k = 1$$

$$= 2^{1/6}(\cos 135° + i \sin 135°) \qquad \text{\color{blue}Simplify.}$$

$$z_2 = 2^{1/6}\left[\cos\left(\frac{45° + 360° \cdot 2}{3}\right) + i \sin\left(\frac{45° + 360° \cdot 2}{3}\right)\right] \qquad \text{\color{blue}} k = 2$$

$$= 2^{1/6}(\cos 255° + i \sin 255°) \qquad \text{\color{blue}Simplify.}$$

The complex numbers z_0, z_1, and z_2 are the three cube roots of the complex number $1 + i$.   ■ ■ ■

Practice Problem 4   Find the three cube roots of $-1 + i$ in polar form with the argument in degrees.   ■

The solutions of the so-called *cyclotomic* equation $z^n = 1$ are called the **nth roots of unity**. The name refers to the close association of the equation with the construction of regular *n*-gons inscribed in a circle.

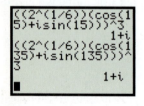

EXAMPLE 5   **Finding *n*th Roots of Unity**

Find the complex sixth roots of unity. Write the roots in polar form and represent them geometrically.

SOLUTION

The polar form for $1 = 1 + 0i$ is

$$1 = 1(\cos 0° + i \sin 0°).$$

From De Moivre's Theorem for finding complex roots with $n = 6$, we have

$$z_k = (1)^{1/6}\left[\cos\left(\frac{0° + 360° \cdot k}{6}\right) + i \sin\left(\frac{0° + 360° \cdot k}{6}\right)\right], \quad k = 0, 1, 2, 3, 4, 5.$$

$z_0 = 1(\cos 0° + i \sin 0°)$	Let $k = 0$ in z_k and simplify.
$z_1 = 1(\cos 60° + i \sin 60°)$	Let $k = 1$ in z_k and simplify.
$z_2 = 1(\cos 120° + i \sin 120°)$	Let $k = 2$ in z_k and simplify.
$z_3 = 1(\cos 180° + i \sin 180°)$	Let $k = 3$ in z_k and simplify.
$z_4 = 1(\cos 240° + i \sin 240°)$	Let $k = 4$ in z_k and simplify.
$z_k = 1(\cos 300° + i \sin 300°)$	Let $k = 5$ in z_k and simplify.

Geometrically, the six roots of unity are equally spaced at 60° intervals on a unit circle. See Figure 9.29. The six-sided polygon formed by the points z_0, z_1, z_2, z_3, z_4, and z_5 as vertices is a regular hexagon.   ■ ■ ■

Practice Problem 5   Find the complex fifth roots of unity. Write the roots in polar form and represent them geometrically.   ■

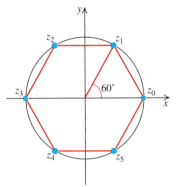

FIGURE 9.29 Sixth roots of unity

SECTION 9.5 ■ Exercises

A EXERCISES Basic Skills and Concepts

1. De Moivre's Theorem states that $[r(\cos \theta + i \sin \theta)]^n = $ _____.

2. For a positive integer n, the complex number z is called an nth root of the complex number w if _____ = _____.

3. Every nonzero complex number w has exactly _____ complex nth roots.

4. The nth roots of $r(\cos \theta + i \sin \theta)$ are given by $z_k = $ _____ for $k = 0, 1, 2, \ldots, n - 1$.

5. *True or False* If $z = r(\cos \theta + i \sin \theta)$, then

$$\frac{1}{z^n} = z^{-n} = \frac{1}{r^n}[\cos (n\theta) - i \sin (n\theta)].$$

6. *True or False* The n complex roots of 1 are

$$1, \cos\frac{2\pi}{n} + i \sin\frac{2\pi}{n}, \cos\frac{4\pi}{n} + i \sin\frac{4\pi}{n}, \ldots,$$
$$\cos\frac{2\pi(n-1)}{n} + i \sin\frac{2\pi(n-1)}{n}.$$

In Exercises 7–16, use De Moivre's Theorem to write each expression in rectangular form.

7. $[3(\cos 30° + i \sin 30°)]^3$

8. $[2(\cos 45° + i \sin 45°)]^5$

9. $\left[2\left(\cos\frac{\pi}{3} + i \sin\frac{\pi}{3}\right)\right]^{12}$

10. $\left[\sqrt{2}\left(\cos\frac{\pi}{4} + i \sin\frac{\pi}{4}\right)\right]^{20}$

11. $\left[2\left(\cos\left(\frac{3\pi}{4}\right) + i \sin\left(\frac{3\pi}{4}\right)\right)\right]^{-6}$

12. $\left(\cos\frac{\pi}{27} + i \sin\frac{\pi}{27}\right)^{-9}$

13. $\left[2\left(\cos\left(-\frac{3\pi}{4}\right) + i \sin\left(-\frac{3\pi}{4}\right)\right)\right]^6$

14. $\left[3\left(\cos\left(-\frac{5\pi}{6}\right) + i \sin\left(-\frac{5\pi}{6}\right)\right)\right]^{16}$

15. $\left[2\left(\cos\left(-\frac{\pi}{4}\right) + i \sin\left(-\frac{\pi}{4}\right)\right)\right]^{-10}$

16. $\left[\frac{1}{2}\left(\cos\left(-\frac{3\pi}{4}\right) + i \sin\left(-\frac{3\pi}{4}\right)\right)\right]^{-6}$

In Exercises 17–28, use De Moivre's Theorem to write each expression in rectangular form.

17. i^{25}

18. $(-i)^{23}$

19. $(1 - i)^{12}$

20. $(1 - i\sqrt{3})^6$

21. $(2 + 2i)^8$

22. $(\sqrt{3} - i)^6$

23. $(-3 - 3i)^3$

24. $\left(\dfrac{\sqrt{3}}{2} + \dfrac{1}{2}i\right)^{10}$

25. $(1 + i)^{-4}$

26. $(\sqrt{3} - i)^{-6}$

27. $(2 - 2i)^{-6}$

28. $\left(\dfrac{1}{2} - \dfrac{\sqrt{3}}{2}i\right)^{-8}$

In Exercises 29–46, find all complex roots. Write your answers in polar form, with $0° \le \theta < 360°$.

29. Square roots of 1

30. Square roots of -1

31. Square roots of $-i$

32. Square roots of i

33. Cube roots of 8

34. Cube roots of 27

35. Cube roots of -64

36. Cube roots of -125

37. Cube roots of $8i$

38. Cube roots of $64i$

39. Cube roots of $-27i$

40. Cube roots of $-64i$

41. Eighth roots of 1

42. Sixth roots of -1

43. Fourth roots of $-1 + i\sqrt{3}$ **44.** Square roots of $1 - i\sqrt{3}$

45. Cube roots of $4 + 4i\sqrt{3}$ **46.** Cube roots of $4 - 4i\sqrt{3}$

B EXERCISES Applying the Concepts

In Exercises 47–50, use the appropriate value of n and the binomial expansion of $(\cos \theta + i \sin \theta)^n$ and De Moivre's Theorem to verify each identity.

47. $\cos 2\theta = \cos^2 \theta - \sin^2 \theta$

48. $\sin 2\theta = 2 \sin \theta \cos \theta$

49. $\sin 3\theta = 3 \sin \theta - 4 \sin^3 \theta$

50. $\cos 3\theta = 4 \cos^3 \theta - 3 \cos \theta$

C EXERCISES Beyond the Basics

In Exercises 51–60, use De Moivre's Theorem to simplify each expression to polar form with $0° \le \theta < 360°$.

51. $(1 + i)^4(1 + i\sqrt{3})^5$

52. $(1 - i)^8(1 + i\sqrt{3})^5$

53. $\dfrac{(1 - i\sqrt{3})^{10}}{(-2 + 2i)^6}$

54. $\dfrac{\left(\dfrac{1}{2} + \dfrac{\sqrt{3}}{2}i\right)^8}{(2 - 2i)^6}$

55. $\dfrac{(3 + 3i)^3}{(\sqrt{3} + i)^4}$

56. $\dfrac{(\sqrt{3} - i)^6}{(1 + i)^4}$

57. $\left(\sin \dfrac{\pi}{6} + i \cos \dfrac{\pi}{6}\right)^{10}$

58. $\left(\sin \dfrac{2\pi}{3} + i \cos \dfrac{2\pi}{3}\right)^6$

59. $\left(-\sin \dfrac{5\pi}{3} + i \cos \dfrac{5\pi}{3}\right)^{-8}$

60. $\left(\sin \dfrac{7\pi}{6} - i \cos \dfrac{7\pi}{6}\right)^{-10}$

61. Let $z = \cos \theta + i \sin \theta$, $z \ne 0$. Prove each identity.

  a. $z + \dfrac{1}{z} = 2 \cos \theta$ **b.** $z - \dfrac{1}{z} = 2i \sin \theta$

  c. $z^n + \dfrac{1}{z^n} = 2 \cos n\theta$ **d.** $z^n - \dfrac{1}{z^n} = 2i \sin n\theta$

62. Use Exercise 61 and the binomial expansion of $\left(z + \dfrac{1}{z}\right)^4$

to show that $\cos^4 \theta = \dfrac{1}{8} \cos 4\theta + \dfrac{1}{2} \cos 2\theta + \dfrac{3}{8}$.

[*Hint:* $(a + b)^4 = a^4 + 4a^3b + 6a^2b^2 + 4ab^3 + b^4$.]

63. Use Exercise 61 and the binomial expansion of $\left(z - \dfrac{1}{z}\right)^4$

to show that $\sin^4 \theta = \dfrac{1}{8} \cos 4\theta - \dfrac{1}{2} \cos 2\theta + \dfrac{3}{8}$.

64. Use Exercise 61 and the binomial expansion of $\left(z + \dfrac{1}{z}\right)^6$

to show that $\cos^6 \theta = \dfrac{1}{32} \cos 6\theta + \dfrac{3}{16} \cos 4\theta + \dfrac{15}{32}$

$\cos 2\theta + \dfrac{5}{16}$.

65. Use De Moivre's Theorem to evaluate $(0.2 + 1.3i)^{21}$.

66. Use the Binomial Theorem to expand $(2 + 3i)^4$. Deduce

the identity: $4 \tan^{-1}\left(\dfrac{3}{2}\right) - \tan^{-1}\left(\dfrac{120}{119}\right) = \pi$.

67. Find the product $(5 + i)^4(-239 + i)$. Then deduce the

identity $4 \tan^{-1}\left(\dfrac{1}{5}\right) - \tan\left(\dfrac{1}{239}\right) = \dfrac{\pi}{4}$.

68. Prove that $(1 + \cos \theta + i \sin \theta)^n$

$= \left(2 \cos \dfrac{\theta}{2}\right)^n \left(\cos \dfrac{n\theta}{2} + i \sin \dfrac{n\theta}{2}\right)$.

69. Find the three solutions of the equation
$x^3 + x^2 + x + 1 = 0$.
[*Hint:* Multiply both sides by $(x - 1)$, solve the new equation, and reject the root $x = 1$.]

70. Find the four solutions of the equation
$x^4 + x^3 + x^2 + x + 1 = 0$.

Critical Thinking

71. Let n be a positive integer. Explain whether each of the following is true or false.

  a. $\left(\cos \dfrac{\pi}{6} + i \sin \dfrac{\pi}{6}\right)^n = \cos \dfrac{n\pi}{6} + i \sin \dfrac{n\pi}{6}$

  b. $\left(\sin \dfrac{\pi}{3} + i \cos \dfrac{\pi}{3}\right)^n = \sin \dfrac{n\pi}{3} + i \cos \dfrac{n\pi}{3}$

  c. $\left[\cos \left(-\dfrac{\pi}{3}\right) + i \sin \left(-\dfrac{\pi}{3}\right)\right]^n = \cos \dfrac{n\pi}{3} + i \sin \dfrac{n\pi}{3}$

  d. $\left(\cos \dfrac{\pi}{6} + i \sin \dfrac{\pi}{3}\right)^n = \cos \dfrac{n\pi}{6} + i \sin \dfrac{n\pi}{3}$

  e. $(\cos \theta + i \sin \theta)^n = \cos n\theta + i \sin n\theta$

  f. $(\cos \theta - i \sin \theta)^n = \cos n\theta - i \sin n\theta$

  g. $(\cos \theta + i \sin \theta)^{-n} = \cos n\theta - i \sin n\theta$

  h. $(\cos \theta - i \sin \theta)^{-n} = \cos n\theta + i \sin n\theta$

  i. $(\sin \theta + i \cos \theta)^n = \sin n\theta + i \cos n\theta$

  j. $(\sin \theta + i \cos \theta)^n$

$= \cos n\left(\dfrac{\pi}{2} - \theta\right) + i \sin n\left(\dfrac{\pi}{2} - \theta\right)$

REVIEW

Definitions, Concepts, and Formulas	**Examples and Illustrations**

9.1 Polar Coordinates

■ **Multiple representations of points** A point $P = (r, \theta)$ in polar coordinates lies at a distance $|r|$ units from the pole.

  (i) If $r > 0$, P lies on the terminal side of θ.

  (ii) If $r < 0$, P lies on the terminal side of $\theta + 180°$.

  (iii) If $r = 0$, P is the pole for any value of θ.

If $P = (r, \theta)$, then for any integer n, $P = (r, \theta + n \cdot 360°)$ or $(-r, \theta + 180° + n \cdot 360°)$.

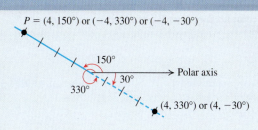

$P = (4, 150°)$ or $(-4, 330°)$ or $(-4, -30°)$

$(4, 330°)$ or $(4, -30°)$

■ **Conversion between polar and rectangular forms** If $P = (x, y)$ in rectangular coordinates and $P = (r, \theta)$ in polar coordinates, then to convert from polar to rectangular form, use $x = r \cos \theta$, $y = r \sin \theta$.
To convert from rectangular to polar form, use $r^2 = x^2 + y^2$,
$\tan \theta = \dfrac{y}{x} (x \neq 0)$.

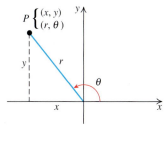

Convert the polar coordinates of $P = (3, 30°)$ to rectangular coordinates.

Solution

$$x = 3 \cos 30° = 3\left(\frac{\sqrt{3}}{2}\right) = \frac{3\sqrt{3}}{2}$$

$$y = 3 \sin 30° = 3\left(\frac{1}{2}\right) = \frac{3}{2}$$

The rectangular coordinates of P are $\left(\dfrac{3\sqrt{3}}{2}, \dfrac{3}{2}\right)$.

Convert the rectangular coordinates of $P = (-2\sqrt{3}, 2)$ to polar coordinates.

Solution

$r = \sqrt{(-2\sqrt{3})^2 + 2^2} = \sqrt{12 + 4} = \sqrt{16} = 4$

$\tan \theta = \dfrac{2}{-2\sqrt{3}} = -\dfrac{1}{\sqrt{3}}$, and θ is in quadrant II; so $\theta = 150°$.

One pair of polar coordinates is $(4, 150°)$.

9.2 Polar Equations

■ **Symmetry** The graph of a polar equation has the following symmetry if an equivalent equation results when making the replacements below.

Symmetry about the	**Replace (r, θ) with**
1. Polar axis (x-axis)	$(r, -\theta)$ or $(-r, \pi - \theta)$
2. Vertical axis $\left(\theta = \dfrac{\pi}{2} \text{ or } y\text{-axis}\right)$	$(r, \pi - \theta)$ or $(-r, -\theta)$
3. Pole (origin)	$(r, \pi + \theta)$ or $(-r, \theta)$

See page 343 for a procedure to graph a polar equation.

1. The graph of $r = 5 \cos 3\theta$ is symmetric about the polar axis.

Replacing (r, θ) with $(r, -\theta)$, we have $r = 5 \cos(-3\theta) = 5 \cos 3\theta$. $\cos(-\alpha) = \cos \alpha$

2. The graph of $r = 3 \sin 2\theta$ is symmetric about the y-axis.

Replacing (r, θ) with $(-r, -\theta)$, we have $-r = 3 \sin(-2\theta) = -3 \sin 2\theta$, which is equivalent to $r = 3 \sin 2\theta$.

3. The graph of $r = 3 \sin 2\theta$ is also symmetric about the pole because replacing (r, θ) with $(r, \pi + \theta)$ results in an equivalent equation.

9.3 Complex Numbers

■ **Definition of i** $i = \sqrt{-1}$ so that $i^2 = -1$

■ **Square root of a negative number** For $b > 0$, $\sqrt{-b} = (\sqrt{b})i = i\sqrt{b}$.

$\sqrt{-9} = 3i, \sqrt{-8} = i\sqrt{8} = 2i\sqrt{2}$

■ **Addition and subtraction of complex numbers** We find the sum or difference of two complex numbers by treating them as binomials with i as the variable.

$$(a + bi) + (c + di) = (a + c) + (b + d)i$$
$$(a + bi) - (c + di) = (a - c) + (b - d)i$$

$$(3 + 5i) + (2 - 3i) = (3 + 2) + (5 - 3)i$$
$$= 5 + 2i$$
$$(4 - 5i) - (3 + 2i) = (4 - 3) + (-5 - 2)i$$
$$= 1 - 7i$$

■ **Multiply complex numbers** We multiply complex numbers by using FOIL (as we do with binomials) and then replacing i^2 with -1.

$$(2 + 3i)(4 + i) = 8 + 2i + 12i + 3i^2 \qquad \text{FOIL}$$
$$= (8 - 3) + (2 + 12)i \qquad i^2 = -1$$
$$= 5 + 14i$$

■ **Complex conjugate** If $z = a + bi$, the complex conjugate of z is denoted by $\bar{z}$, where $\bar{z} = \overline{a + bi} = a - bi$. $z\bar{z} = a^2 + b^2$.

$$\overline{2 + 3i} = 2 - 3i, \overline{4 - 3i} = 4 + 3i,$$
$$\bar{4} = 4, \overline{2i} = -2i$$

■ **Divide complex numbers** To divide complex numbers, multiply the numerator and denominator by the conjugate of the denominator.

$$\frac{2 + 3i}{1 + i} = \frac{(2 + 3i)(1 - i)}{(1 + i)(1 - i)}$$
$$= \frac{2 - 2i + 3i - 3i^2}{1^2 - i^2}$$
$$= \frac{5 + i}{2} = \frac{5}{2} + \frac{1}{2}i \qquad i^2 = -1$$

9.4 Polar (Trigonometric) Form of Complex Numbers

■ The absolute value of a complex number

$$z = a + bi \text{ is } |z| = |a + bi| = \sqrt{a^2 + b^2}.$$

$$|2 - 3i| = \sqrt{2^2 + (-3)^2} = \sqrt{4 + 9} = \sqrt{13}$$

Write $z = 1 + i\sqrt{3}$ in polar form.

A complex number $z = a + bi$ in **rectangular form** is identified with the point (a, b). The point (a, b) has polar coordinates (r, θ), where $a = r \cos \theta$, $b = r \sin \theta$, $r = \sqrt{a^2 + b^2}$, and $\tan \theta = \dfrac{b}{a}$, $a \neq 0$. The complex number z can be written in polar form.

$$z = r(\cos \theta + i \sin \theta)$$

with $r = |z|$ and $\theta = \arg z$

Solution

$$r = |z| = \sqrt{1^2 + (\sqrt{3})^2} = \sqrt{1 + 3} = \sqrt{4} = 2$$
$$\tan \theta = \frac{\sqrt{3}}{1}, \text{ so } \theta = 60°.$$
$$1 + i\sqrt{3} = 2(\cos 60° + i \sin 60°)$$

■ **Product and quotient** Let $z_1 = r_1(\cos \theta_1 + i \sin \theta_1)$ and $z_2 = r_2(\cos \theta_2 + i \sin \theta_2)$ be two complex numbers. Then

$$z_1 z_2 = r_1 r_2 [\cos (\theta_1 + \theta_2) + i \sin (\theta_1 + \theta_2)] \text{ and}$$
$$\frac{z_1}{z_2} = \frac{r_1}{r_2} [\cos(\theta_1 - \theta_2) + i \sin(\theta_1 - \theta_2)], z_2 \neq 0.$$

If $z_1 = 6(\cos 47° + i \sin 47°)$ and $z_2 = 2(\cos 23° + i \sin 23°)$, then $z_1 z_2 = 12(\cos 70° + i \sin 70°)$ and $\dfrac{z_1}{z_2} = 3(\cos 24° + i \sin 24°)$.

9.5 Powers and Roots of Complex Numbers

■ **De Moivre's Theorem** Let $z = r(\cos \theta + i \sin \theta)$. Then for any integer n, $z^n = [r(\cos \theta + i \sin \theta)]^n$
$$= r^n(\cos n\theta + i \sin n\theta).$$

For $z = 2(\cos 45° + i \sin 45°)$,
$$z^4 = [2(\cos 45° + i \sin 45°)]^4$$
$$= 2^4(\cos 4 \cdot 45° + i \sin 4 \cdot 45°)$$
$$= 16(\cos 180° + i \sin 180°)$$
$$= 16[-1 + i(0)] = -16$$

■ **Definition of nth root** For a positive integer n, z is the nth root of w if $z^n = w$.

■ **The *n*th Root Theorem** The *n* *n*th roots of $w = r(\cos\theta + i\sin\theta)$, with $r > 0$ and θ in degrees, are given by

$$z_k = r^{1/n}\left[\cos\left(\frac{\theta + 360°k}{n}\right) + i\sin\left(\frac{\theta + 360°k}{n}\right)\right] \text{ for}$$

$$k = 0, 1, 2, \ldots, n - 1.$$

The three cube roots of $w = 8(\cos 60° + i\sin 60)$ are as follows:

$$z_0 = (8)^{1/3}\left[\cos\left(\frac{60° + 360° \cdot 0}{3}\right) + i\sin\left(\frac{60° + 360° \cdot 0}{3}\right)\right]$$
$$= 2(\cos 20° + i\sin 20°)$$

$$z_1 = (8)^{1/3}\left[\cos\left(\frac{60° + 360° \cdot 1}{3}\right) + i\sin\left(\frac{60° + 360° \cdot 1}{3}\right)\right]$$
$$= 2(\cos 140° + i\sin 140°)$$

$$z_2 = (8)^{1/3}\left[\cos\left(\frac{60° + 360° \cdot 2}{3}\right) + i\sin\left(\frac{60° + 360° \cdot 2}{3}\right)\right]$$
$$= 2(\cos 260° + i\sin 260°)$$

REVIEW EXERCISES

Basic Skills and Concepts

In Exercises 1–8, plot each point in polar coordinates and find its rectangular coordinates.

1. $(7, 30°)$
2. $(6, -60°)$
3. $(-2, 45°)$
4. $(-3, -135°)$
5. $\left(2, \dfrac{\pi}{6}\right)$
6. $\left(5, -\dfrac{\pi}{3}\right)$
7. $\left(-3, \dfrac{3\pi}{4}\right)$
8. $\left(-2, -\dfrac{2\pi}{3}\right)$

In Exercises 9–12, convert the rectangular coordinates of each point to polar coordinates (r, θ) with $r > 0$ and $0° \le \theta < 360°$.

9. $(-2, 2)$
10. $(\sqrt{3}, 1)$
11. $(2\sqrt{3}, -2)$
12. $(-2, -2\sqrt{3})$

In Exercises 13–16, convert each rectangular equation to a polar equation.

13. $3x + 2y = 12$
14. $x^2 + y^2 = 36$
15. $x^2 + y^2 = 8x$
16. $x^2 + y^2 = 6y$

In Exercises 17–22, convert each polar equation to a rectangular equation.

17. $r = -3$
18. $\theta = \dfrac{5\pi}{6}$
19. $r = 3\csc\theta$
20. $r = 2\sec\theta$
21. $r = 1 - 2\sin\theta$
22. $r = 3\cos\theta$

In Exercises 23–26, solve each quadratic equation.

23. $x^2 + 4 = 0$
24. $x^2 - 2x + 2 = 0$
25. $x(x - 4) = -13$
26. $x(x - 6) = -25$

In Exercises 27–38, perform each operation and write the result in standard form $a + bi$.

27. $(5 - 2i) + (3 + i)$
28. $(5 + i) + (2 + 3i)$
29. $(3 + 2i) - (5 + 3i)$
30. $(3 - 5i) - (2 - i)$
31. $2(3 - 4i)$
32. $3i(4 - 3i)$
33. $(4 + 3i)(4 - 3i)$
34. $(\sqrt{3} - 2i)^2$
35. $(2 - \sqrt{-16})(1 + \sqrt{-4})$
36. $\dfrac{2 - i}{1 + i}$
37. $\dfrac{-5 + \sqrt{-4}}{5 - \sqrt{-9}}$
38. $\dfrac{i^{25}}{1 + i^{-12}}$

In Exercises 39–42, write each complex number in polar form. Express the arguments in radians.

39. $-3i$
40. $-1 + i$
41. $5\sqrt{3} - 5i$
42. $-2 - 2\sqrt{3}i$

In Exercises 43–46, write each complex number in rectangular form.

43. $2(\cos 45° + i\sin 45°)$
44. $3(\cos 240° + i\sin 240°)$
45. $6\left(\cos\dfrac{3\pi}{4} + i\sin\dfrac{3\pi}{4}\right)$
46. $4\left(\cos\dfrac{7\pi}{6} + i\sin\dfrac{7\pi}{6}\right)$

In Exercises 47–50, find z_1z_2 and $\dfrac{z_1}{z_2}$. Leave your answers in polar form.

47. $z_1 = 3(\cos 25° + i\sin 25°), z_2 = 2(\cos 10° + i\sin 10°)$
48. $z_1 = 4(\cos 300° + i\sin 300°), z_2 = 2(\cos 20° + i\sin 20°)$
49. $z_1 = 2\left(\cos\dfrac{5\pi}{6} + i\sin\dfrac{5\pi}{6}\right), z_2 = 3\left(\cos\dfrac{\pi}{3} + i\sin\dfrac{\pi}{3}\right)$
50. $z_1 = 5\left(\cos\dfrac{4\pi}{3} + i\sin\dfrac{4\pi}{3}\right), z_2 = 15\left(\cos\dfrac{\pi}{3} + i\sin\dfrac{\pi}{3}\right)$

In Exercises 51–54, use De Moivre's Theorem to find the indicated power. Write your answers in polar form.

51. $[3(\cos 40° + i\sin 40°)]^3$
52. $\left[4\left(\cos\dfrac{\pi}{6} + i\sin\dfrac{\pi}{6}\right)\right]^6$
53. $(2 - 2\sqrt{3}i)^6$
54. $(2 - 2i)^7$

In Exercises 55–58, find all complex roots. Write your answers in polar form, with the arguments in degrees.

55. Cube roots of -125

56. Fourth roots of $-16i$

57. Fifth roots of $-1 + \sqrt{3}i$

58. Sixth roots of $1 - i$

Applying the Concepts

In Exercises 59–62, use the polar equation $r = \dfrac{a(1 - e^2)}{1 + e\cos\theta}$ **for planetary motion discussed on page 348 with given values of a and e to find (a) the polar equation of its orbit, (b) its perihelion, and (c) its aphelion.**

59. Venus's Orbit: $a = 0.72333$, $e = 0.0068$

60. Saturn's Orbit: $a = 9.539$, $e = 0.0543$

61. Uranus's Orbit: $a = 19.18$, $e = 0.0460$

62. Neptune's Orbit: $a = 30.06$, $e = 0.0082$

In Exercises 63–66, formulas are given for AC circuits with $I =$ current, $V =$ voltage, and $Z =$ impedance.

63. Calculate I from the formula $I = \dfrac{V}{Z}$ in rectangular form when $V = 2 + i$ and $Z = 3 - 2i$.

64. In Exercise 63, calculate I in polar form when $V = 4(\cos 60° + i\sin 60°)$ and $Z = 2(\cos 330° - i\sin 330°)$.

65. Calculate Z_t from the formula $Z_t = \dfrac{Z_1 Z_2}{Z_1 + Z_2}$ in rectangular form when $Z_1 = 2 + 3i$, and $Z_2 = 1 - 2i$.

66. Calculate Z_1 from the formula $Z_1 = \dfrac{Z_2 Z_t}{Z_2 - Z_t}$ in polar form when $Z_2 = 2 - 2i$ and $Z_t = \sqrt{3} - i$.

CHAPTER 9 TEST

1. Convert $(2, -30°)$ to rectangular coordinates.

2. Convert $(-4, 45°)$ to rectangular coordinates.

3. Convert $(-\sqrt{3}, -1)$ to polar coordinates with $r > 0$ and $0° \le \theta < 360°$.

4. Convert $(3, -\sqrt{3})$ to polar coordinates with $r < 0$ and $0° \le \theta < 360°$.

5. Convert the polar equation $r = -3$ to rectangular form. Identify the curve having this equation.

6. Convert the rectangular equation $x^2 + y^2 + 4x - 5 = 0$ to polar form.

7. Identify and graph the equation $r = 1 + \cos\theta$.

8. Express each of the following in rectangular form.
   a. i^{35} **b.** $(1 - i)^2$

9. Let $z_1 = 2 + 3i$, $z_2 = 5 + 4i$ and express each of the following in rectangular form.
   a. $z_1 + z_2$ **b.** $z_1 - z_2$
   c. $z_1 z_2$ **d.** $\dfrac{z_1}{z_2}$

10. Let $z_1 = 3 - 3i$, $z_2 = \sqrt{3} + i$ and express each of the following in polar form with argument in degrees.
   a. $z_1 z_2$ **b.** $\dfrac{z_1}{z_2}$

11. Find all solutions of the equation $4x^2 - 2x + 1 = 0$ in rectangular form.

12. Use De Moivre's Theorem to find $[\sqrt{2}(\cos 15° + i\sin 15°)]^4$. Write your answer in rectangular form.

13. Use De Moivre's Theorem to find $[\sqrt{5}(\cos 45° + i\sin 45°)]^{-6}$. Write your answer in rectangular form.

14. Find all fourth roots of $1 + i$. Express the argument in degrees.

Linear and Quadratic Equations

1 Solve linear equations in one variable.

Linear Equations

Definitions

An **equation in one variable** is a statement that two expressions, with at least one containing the variable, are equal. For example, $2x - 3 = 7$ is an equation in the variable x. The expressions $2x - 3$ and 7 are the *sides* of the equation. The **domain** of the variable in an equation is the set of all real numbers for which both sides of the equation are defined.

When the variable in an equation is replaced by a specific value from its domain, the resulting statement may be true or false. For example, in the equation $2x - 3 = 7$, if we let $x = 1$, the equation is false. However, if we replace x with 5, the equation is true. Those values (if any) of the variable that result in a true statement are called **solutions** or **roots** of the equation. Thus, 5 is a solution (or root) of the equation $2x - 3 = 7$. We also say that 5 **satisfies** the equation $2x - 3 = 7$. To **solve** an equation means to find all solutions of the equation; the set of all solutions of an equation is called its **solution set**.

An equation that is satisfied by every real number in the domain of the variable is called an **identity**. The equations

$$2(x + 3) = 2x + 6$$
$$\text{and} \quad x^2 - 9 = (x + 3)(x - 3)$$

are examples of identities. Some equations, such as $x = x + 5$, have no solution.

Solving an Equation

Equations that have the same solution set are called **equivalent equations**. For example, equations $x = 4$ and $3x = 12$ are equivalent equations with solution set $\{4\}$.

In general, to solve an equation in one variable, we replace the given equation with a sequence of equivalent equations until we obtain an equation whose solution is obvious, such as $x = 4$. The following operations yield equivalent equations.

STUDY TIP

When finding the domain of a variable, remember that

1. Division by 0 is undefined.

2. The square root (or any even root) of a negative number is not a real number.

Generating Equivalent Equations

Operations	Given Equation	Equivalent Equation
Simplify expressions on either side by eliminating parentheses, combining like terms, and so on.	$(2x - 1) - (x + 1) = 4$	$2x - 1 - x - 1 = 4$ or $x - 2 = 4$
Add (or subtract) the same expression on *both* sides of the equation.	$x - 2 = 4$	$x - 2 + 2 = 4 + 2$ or $x = 6$
Multiply (or divide) *both* sides of the equation by the same *nonzero* expression.	$2x = 8$	$\frac{1}{2} \cdot 2x = \frac{1}{2} \cdot 8$ or $x = 4$
Interchange the two sides of the equation.	$-3 = x$	$x = -3$

EXAMPLE 1   **Solving a Linear Equation**

Solve $6x - [3x - 2(x - 2)] = 11$.

SOLUTION

$6x - [3x - 2(x - 2)] = 11$	Original equation
$6x - [3x - 2x + 4] = 11$	Remove innermost parentheses by distributing $-2(x - 2) = -2x + 4$.
$6x - 3x + 2x - 4 = 11$	Remove square brackets and change the sign of each enclosed term.
$5x - 4 = 11$	Combine like terms.
$5x - 4 + 4 = 11 + 4$	Add 4 to both sides.
$5x = 15$	Simplify both sides.
$\dfrac{5x}{5} = \dfrac{15}{5}$	Divide both sides by 5.
$x = 3$	Simplify.

The apparent solution is 3.

Check: Substitute $x = 3$ into the original equation. You should obtain $11 = 11$. Thus, 3 is the only solution of the original equation; so $\{3\}$ is its solution set. ■ ■ ■

Practice Problem 1   Solve $3x - [2x - 6(x + 1)] = -1$. ■

Quadratic Equations

QUADRATIC EQUATION

A quadratic equation in the variable x is an equation equivalent to the equation

$$ax^2 + bx + c = 0,$$

where a, b, and c are real numbers and $a \neq 0$.

BY THE WAY ...

The word *quadratic* comes from the Latin *quadratus*, meaning "square."

A quadratic equation written in the form $ax^2 + bx + c = 0$ is said to be in **standard form**. Quadratic equations are also called **second-degree equations**.

2 Solve a quadratic equation by factoring.

Factoring Method

Some quadratic equations written in standard form can be solved by factoring and using the **zero-product property**.

ZERO-PRODUCT PROPERTY

Let A and B be two algebraic expressions. Then $AB = 0$ if and only if $A = 0$ or $B = 0$.

STUDY TIP

The factoring method of solving an equation works *only when one of the sides of the equation is 0*.

EXAMPLE 2   **Solving a Quadratic Equation by Factoring**

Solve by factoring: $2x^2 + 5x = 3$

SOLUTION

$$2x^2 + 5x = 3 \qquad \text{Original equation}$$
$$2x^2 + 5x - 3 = 0 \qquad \text{Write in standard form.}$$
$$(2x - 1)(x + 3) = 0 \qquad \text{Factor the left side.}$$

We now set each factor equal to 0 and solve the resulting linear equations. The vertical line separates the computations leading to the two solutions.

$2x - 1 = 0$	$x + 3 = 0$	Zero-product property
$2x = 1$	$x = -3$	Isolate the x term on one side.
$x = \dfrac{1}{2}$	$x = -3$	Solve for x.

Check: Check the two solutions in the original equation. The solution set is $\left\{ \dfrac{1}{2}, -3 \right\}$.

■ ■ ■

Practice Problem 2   Solve by factoring: $x^2 + 25x = -84$ ■

EXAMPLE 3   **Solving a Quadratic Equation by Factoring**

Solve by factoring: $x^2 + 16 = 8x$

SOLUTION
Write the equation in standard form.

$$x^2 - 8x + 16 = 0 \qquad \text{Subtract } 8x \text{ from both sides.}$$

Factor the left side of the equation.

$$(x - 4)(x - 4) = 0 \qquad \text{Perfect-square trinomial}$$

Set each factor equal to 0 and solve each resulting equation.

$x - 4 = 0$	$x - 4 = 0$
$x = 4$	$x = 4$

Check the solution, 4, in the original equation. The solution set is $\{4\}$.   ■ ■ ■

Practice Problem 3   Solve by factoring: $x^2 - 6x = -9$ ■

In Example 3, because the factor $(x - 4)$ appears twice in the solution, the number 4 is called a **double root**, or a **root of multiplicity 2**, of the given equation.

3 Solve a quadratic equation by the square root method.

Square Root Method

We can solve equations of the type $x^2 = d$ by using the square root method. Suppose we want to solve the equation $x^2 = 3$, which is equivalent to the equation $x^2 - 3 = 0$. Applying the factoring method, but *removing the restriction that coefficients and constants represent only integers*, we have

$$x^2 - 3 = 0$$
$$x^2 - (\sqrt{3})^2 = 0 \qquad \text{Because } 3 = (\sqrt{3})^2$$
$$(x + \sqrt{3})(x - \sqrt{3}) = 0 \qquad \text{Factor (using real numbers).}$$
$$x + \sqrt{3} = 0 \quad \text{or} \quad x - \sqrt{3} = 0 \qquad \text{Set each factor equal to zero.}$$
$$x = -\sqrt{3} \quad \text{or} \qquad x = \sqrt{3} \qquad \text{Solve for } x.$$

So the solutions of the equation $x^2 = 3$ are $x = -\sqrt{3}$ and $x = \sqrt{3}$, which we can write in compact form as $x = \pm\sqrt{3}$. Similarly, for any nonnegative real number d, the solutions of the quadratic equation $x^2 = d$ are $x = \pm\sqrt{d}$.

SQUARE ROOT PROPERTY

Suppose u is any algebraic expression and $d \geq 0$. If $u^2 = d$, then $u = \pm\sqrt{d}$.

EXAMPLE 4   **Solving an Equation by the Square Root Method**

Solve $(x - 3)^2 = 5$.

SOLUTION

$$(x - 3)^2 = 5 \qquad \text{Original equation}$$
$$x - 3 = \pm\sqrt{5} \qquad \text{Square root property}$$
$$x = 3 \pm \sqrt{5} \qquad \text{Add 3 to both sides.}$$

The solution set is $\{3 + \sqrt{5}, 3 - \sqrt{5}\}$.   ■ ■ ■

Practice Problem 4   Solve $(x + 2)^2 = 5$.   ■

4 Solve a quadratic equation by completing the square.

Completing the Square

We can use a method called **completing the square** to solve quadratic equations that cannot be solved by factoring and are not in the right form to use the square root method. In this method, we write a given quadratic equation in the form $(x + k)^2 = d$. Then we solve the equation $(x + k)^2 = d$ by the square root method.

Recall that

$$(x + k)^2 = x^2 + 2kx + k^2.$$

Notice that the coefficient of x on the right side is $2k$, and half of this coefficient is k. We see that the constant term, k^2, in the trinomial $x^2 + 2kx + k^2$ is the *square of one-half the coefficient of x.*

PERFECT-SQUARE TRINOMIAL

A quadratic trinomial in x with coefficient of x^2 equal to 1 is a **perfect-square trinomial** if the constant term is the square of one-half the coefficient of x.

When the constant term is *not* the square of half the coefficient of x, we subtract the constant term from both sides and add a new constant term that will result in a perfect-square trinomial.

Let's look at some examples to learn what number to add to $x^2 + bx$ to create a perfect-square trinomial.

$x^2 + bx$	b	$\dfrac{b}{2}$	Add $\left(\dfrac{b}{2}\right)^2$	Perfect Square $\left(x + \dfrac{b}{2}\right)^2$
$x^2 + 6x$	6	3	$3^2 = 9$	$x^2 + 6x + 9 = (x + 3)^2$
$x^2 - 4x$	-4	-2	$(-2)^2 = 4$	$x^2 - 4x + 4 = (x - 2)^2$
$x^2 + 3x$	3	$\dfrac{3}{2}$	$\left(\dfrac{3}{2}\right)^2 = \dfrac{9}{4}$	$x^2 + 3x + \dfrac{9}{4} = \left(x + \dfrac{3}{2}\right)^2$
$x^2 - x$	-1	$-\dfrac{1}{2}$	$\left(-\dfrac{1}{2}\right)^2 = \dfrac{1}{4}$	$x^2 - x + \dfrac{1}{4} = \left(x - \dfrac{1}{2}\right)^2$

Therefore, to make $x^2 + bx$ a perfect square, we need to add

$$\left[\frac{1}{2}(\text{coefficient of } x)\right]^2 = \left[\frac{1}{2}(b)\right]^2 = \frac{b^2}{4}$$

so that

$$x^2 + bx + \frac{b^2}{4} = \left(x + \frac{b}{2}\right)^2.$$

We say that $\dfrac{b^2}{4}$ is added to $x^2 + bx$ to *complete the square*. See Figure A.1.

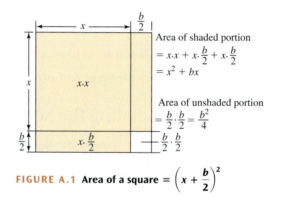

FIGURE A.1 Area of a square $= \left(x + \dfrac{b}{2}\right)^2$

METHOD OF COMPLETING THE SQUARE

Step 1 Rearrange the quadratic equation so that the terms in x^2 and x are on the left side of the equation and the constant term is on the right side.

Step 2 Make the coefficient of x^2 equal to 1 by dividing both sides of the equation by the original coefficient. (Steps 1 and 2 are interchangeable.)

Step 3 Add the square of one-half the coefficient of x to both sides of the equation.

Step 4 Write the equation in the form $(x + k)^2 = d$, using the fact that the left side is a perfect square.

Step 5 Take the square root of each side, prefixing $\pm$ to the right side.

Step 6 Solve the two equations from Step 5.

EXAMPLE 5   **Solving a Quadratic Equation by Completing the Square**

Solve by completing the square: $3x^2 - 4x - 1 = 0$

SOLUTION

$$3x^2 - 4x - 1 = 0 \qquad \text{Note that the coefficient of } x^2 \text{ is 3.}$$

$$3x^2 - 4x = 1 \qquad \text{Add 1 to both sides.}$$

$$x^2 - \frac{4}{3}x = \frac{1}{3} \qquad \text{Divide both sides by 3.}$$

$$x^2 - \frac{4}{3}x + \left(-\frac{2}{3}\right)^2 = \frac{1}{3} + \left(-\frac{2}{3}\right)^2 \qquad \text{Add } \left[\frac{1}{2}\left(-\frac{4}{3}\right)\right]^2 = \left(-\frac{2}{3}\right)^2 \text{ to both sides.}$$

$$\left(x - \frac{2}{3}\right)^2 = \frac{7}{9} \qquad x^2 - \frac{4}{3}x + \left(-\frac{2}{3}\right)^2 = \left(x - \frac{2}{3}\right)^2$$

$$x - \frac{2}{3} = \pm\sqrt{\frac{7}{9}} \qquad \text{Take the square root of both sides.}$$

$$x - \frac{2}{3} = \pm\frac{\sqrt{7}}{3} \qquad \sqrt{\frac{7}{9}} = \frac{\sqrt{7}}{\sqrt{9}} = \frac{\sqrt{7}}{3}$$

$$x = \frac{2}{3} \pm \frac{\sqrt{7}}{3} = \frac{2 \pm \sqrt{7}}{3} \qquad \text{Solve for } x.$$

The solution set is $\left\{\dfrac{2 - \sqrt{7}}{3}, \dfrac{2 + \sqrt{7}}{3}\right\}$.   ■ ■ ■

Practice Problem 5   Solve by completing the square: $4x^2 - 24x + 25 = 0$ ■

5 Solve a quadratic equation by using the quadratic formula.

Quadratic Formula

We can generalize the method of completing the square to derive a formula that gives a solution of *any* quadratic equation.

QUADRATIC FORMULA

The solutions of the quadratic equation in the standard form $ax^2 + bx + c = 0$ with $a \neq 0$ are given by the formula

$$x = \frac{-b \pm \sqrt{b^2 - 4ac}}{2a}.$$

◆ **WARNING**   To use the quadratic formula, write the given quadratic equation in standard form. Then determine the values of a (coefficient of x^2), b (coefficient of x), and c (constant term).

EXAMPLE 6 **Solving a Quadratic Equation by Using the Quadratic Formula**

Solve $3x^2 = 5x + 2$ by using the quadratic formula.

SOLUTION

We first rewrite the equation in standard form.

$$3x^2 - 5x - 2 = 0$$

Subtract $5x + 2$ from both sides.

$$3x^2 + (-5)x + (-2) = 0$$
$$\quad\uparrow\qquad\quad\uparrow\qquad\quad\uparrow$$
$$\quad a\qquad\quad b\qquad\quad c$$

Identify values of a, b, and c to be used in the quadratic formula.

$$x = \frac{-b \pm \sqrt{b^2 - 4ac}}{2a}$$

Quadratic formula

$$x = \frac{-(-5) \pm \sqrt{(-5)^2 - 4(3)(-2)}}{2(3)}$$

Substitute 3 for a, -5 for b, and -2 for c.

$$= \frac{5 \pm \sqrt{25 + 24}}{6}$$

Simplify.

$$= \frac{5 \pm \sqrt{49}}{6} = \frac{5 \pm 7}{6}$$

Simplify.

Then

$$x = \frac{5 + 7}{6} = \frac{12}{6} = 2 \text{ or } x = \frac{5 - 7}{6} = \frac{-2}{6} = -\frac{1}{3}; \text{ the solution set is } \left\{-\frac{1}{3}, 2\right\}.$$

■ ■ ■

Practice Problem 6 Solve by using the quadratic formula: $6x^2 - x - 2 = 0$ ■

SECTION A.1 ■ Exercises

A EXERCISES Basic Skills and Concepts

1. Equations that have the same solution are called _____.

2. Adding the same expression to or subtracting it from both sides of an equation results in a(n) _____.

3. Standard form for the quadratic equation $5x - 2x^2 = 8$ is _____.

4. If $ax^2 + bx + c$ does not factor readily, we can use the _____ to solve the equation $ax^2 + bx + c = 0$.

In Exercises 5–8, determine whether the given equation is an identity. If the equation is not an identity, give a value that demonstrates that fact.

5. $2x + 3 = 5x + 1$

6. $3x + 4 = 6x + 2 - (3x - 2)$

7. $\frac{1}{x} + \frac{1}{2} = \frac{2 + x}{2x}$

8. $\frac{1}{x + 3} = \frac{1}{x} + \frac{1}{3}$

In Exercises 9–34, solve each equation.

9. $3x + 5 = 14$

10. $2x - 17 = 7$

11. $-10x + 12 = 32$

12. $-2x + 5 = 6$

13. $3 - y = -4$

14. $2 - 7y = 23$

15. $7x + 7 = 2(x + 1)$

16. $3(x + 2) = 4 - x$

17. $3(2 - y) + 5y = 3y$

18. $9y - 3(y - 1) = 6 + y$

19. $4y - 3y + 7 - y = 2 - (7 - y)$

20. $3(y - 1) = 6y - 4 + 2y - 4y$

21. $2x + 3(x - 4) = 7x + 10$

22. $3(2 - 3x) - 4x = 3x - 10$

23. $3x + \frac{x}{5} - 2 = \frac{1}{10} + 2x$

24. $\frac{1}{4} + 5x - \frac{x}{7} = \frac{5x}{14} + \frac{x}{2}$

25. $4[x + 2(3 - x)] = 2x + 1$

26. $3 - [x - 3(x + 2)] = 4$

27. $3(4y - 3) = 4[y - (4y - 3)]$

28. $5 - (6y + 9) + 2y = 2(y + 1)$

29. $2x - 3(2 - x) = (x - 3) + 2x + 1$

30. $5(x - 3) - 6(x - 4) = -5$

31. $\dfrac{2x + 1}{9} - \dfrac{x + 4}{6} = 1$

32. $\dfrac{2 - 3x}{7} + \dfrac{x - 1}{3} = \dfrac{3x}{7}$

33. $\dfrac{1 - x}{4} + \dfrac{5x + 1}{2} = 3 - \dfrac{2(x + 1)}{8}$

34. $\dfrac{x + 4}{3} + 2x - \dfrac{1}{2} = \dfrac{3x + 2}{6}$

In Exercises 35–54, solve each equation by factoring.

35. $x^2 - 5x = 0$

36. $x^2 - 5x + 4 = 0$

37. $x^2 + 5x = 14$

38. $x^2 - 11x = 12$

39. $x^2 = 5x + 6$

40. $x = x^2 - 12$

41. $2x^2 + 5x - 3 = 0$

42. $2x^2 - 9x + 10 = 0$

43. $3y^2 + 5y + 2 = 0$

44. $6x^2 + 11x + 4 = 0$

45. $5x^2 + 12x + 4 = 0$

46. $3x^2 - 2x - 5 = 0$

47. $2x^2 + x = 15$

48. $6x^2 = 1 - x$

49. $12x^2 - 10x = 12$

50. $-x^2 + 10x + 1200 = 0$

51. $18x^2 - 45x = -7$

52. $18x^2 + 57x + 45 = 0$

53. $4x^2 - 10x - 750 = 0$

54. $12x^2 + 43x + 36 = 0$

In Exercises 55–60, solve each equation by the square root method.

55. $3x^2 = 48$

56. $2x^2 = 50$

57. $x^2 + 1 = 5$

58. $2x^2 - 1 = 17$

59. $(x - 1)^2 = 16$

60. $(2x - 3)^2 = 25$

In Exercises 61–70, add a constant term to the expression to make it a perfect square.

61. $x^2 + 4x$

62. $y^2 + 10y$

63. $x^2 + 6x$

64. $y^2 - 8y$

65. $x^2 - 7x$

66. $x^2 - 3x$

67. $x^2 + \dfrac{1}{3}x$

68. $x^2 - \dfrac{3}{2}x$

69. $x^2 + ax$

70. $x^2 - \dfrac{2a}{3}x$

In Exercises 71–80, solve each equation by completing the square.

71. $x^2 + 2x - 5 = 0$

72. $x^2 + 6x = -7$

73. $x^2 - 3x - 1 = 0$

74. $x^2 - x - 3 = 0$

75. $2r^2 + 3r = 9$

76. $3k^2 - 5k + 1 = 0$

77. $5x^2 - 6x = 4x^2 + 6x - 3$

78. $x^2 + 7x - 5 = x - x^2$

79. $5y^2 + 10y + 4 = 2y^2 + 3y + 1$

80. $3x^2 - 1 = 5x^2 - 3x - 5$

Graphs of Equations

1 Plot points in the Cartesian coordinate plane.

Coordinate Plane

A visually powerful device for exploring relationships between numbers is the Cartesian plane. A pair of real numbers in which the order is specified is called an **ordered pair** of real numbers. The ordered pair (a, b) has **first component** a and **second component** b. Two ordered pairs (x, y) and (a, b) are **equal**, and we write $(x, y) = (a, b)$ if and only if $x = a$ and $y = b$.

Just as the real numbers are identified with points on a line, called the **number line** or the **coordinate line**, the sets of ordered pairs of real numbers are identified with points on a plane called the **coordinate plane** or the **Cartesian plane**.

We begin with two coordinate lines, one horizontal and one vertical, that intersect at their zero points. The horizontal line (with positive numbers to the right) is usually called the **x-axis**, while the vertical line (with positive numbers up) is usually called the **y-axis**. Their point of intersection is called the **origin**. The x-axis and y-axis are called **coordinate axes**, and the plane they form is sometimes called the **xy-plane**. The axes divide the plane into four regions called **quadrants**, which are numbered as shown in Figure A.2. The points on the axes do not belong to any of the quadrants.

The notation $P(a, b)$, or $P = (a, b)$, designates the point P whose *first component* is a and whose *second component* is b. In an xy-plane, the first component, a, is called the **x-coordinate** of $P(a, b)$ and the second component, b, is called the

René Descartes

(1596–1650)

Descartes was born at La Haye, near Tours in southern France. He is often called the father of modern science. Descartes established a new, clear way of thinking about philosophy and science by accepting only those ideas that could be proved by or deduced from first principles. He took as his philosophical starting point the statement **Cogito ergo sum:** "I think; therefore, I am." Descartes made major contributions to modern mathematics, including the Cartesian coordinate system and the theory of equations.

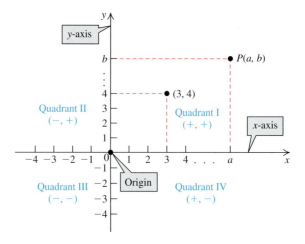

FIGURE A.2 Quadrants in a plane

y-coordinate of $P(a, b)$. The signs of the x- and y-coordinates for each quadrant are shown in Figure A.2. The point corresponding to the ordered pair (a, b) is called the **graph of the ordered pair** (a, b). However, we frequently ignore the distinction between an ordered pair and its graph.

EXAMPLE 1   **Graphing Points**

Graph the following points in the xy-plane:

$A(3, 1)$, $B(-2, 4)$, $C(-3, -4)$, $D(2, -3)$, and $E(-3, 0)$

SOLUTION

Figure A.3 shows a coordinate plane, along with the graph of the given points. These points are located by moving left, right, up, or down starting from the origin $(0, 0)$.

$A(3, 1)$	3 units right, 1 unit up	$D(2, -3)$	2 units right, 3 units down
$B(-2, 4)$	2 units left, 4 units up	$E(-3, 0)$	3 units left, 0 units up or down
$C(-3, -4)$	3 units left, 4 units down		

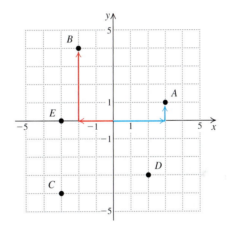

FIGURE A.3 Graphing points   ■ ■ ■

Practice Problem 1   Graph the points in the xy-plane:

$$P(-2, 2), Q(4, 0), R(5, -3), S(0, -3), \text{ and } T\left(-2, \frac{1}{2}\right)$$ ■

EXAMPLE 2   **Graphing Data on Adult Smokers in the United States**

The data in Table A.1 show the prevalence of smoking among adults aged 18 years and older in the United States over the years 1998–2004.

TABLE A.1

Year	1998	1999	2000	2001	2002	2003	2004
Percent of adult smokers	24.1	23.5	23.2	22.7	22.4	21.6	20.9

Source: Center for Disease Control and Prevention, National Health Interview Survey.

Graph the ordered pairs (year, percent of adult smokers), where the first coordinate represents a year and the second coordinate represents the percent of adult smokers in that year.

SOLUTION

We let x represent the years 1998–2004 and y represent the percent of adult smokers in each year. Because no data are given for the years 0–1997, we show a break in the x-axis. Alternately, we could declare a year—say, 1997—as 0. Similar comments apply to the y-axis. The graph of the points $(1998, 24.1)$, $(1999, 23.5)$, $(2000, 23.2)$, and so on, is shown in Figure A.4. The graph shows that the percent of adult smokers has been declining every year since 1998.

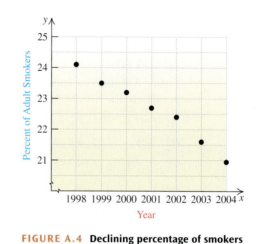

FIGURE A.4 Declining percentage of smokers

Practice Problem 2 In Example 2, suppose the percent of adult smokers shown in Table A.1 is decreased by 3 in each year. Write the corresponding ordered pairs (year, percent of adult smokers). ■

Scales on a Graphing Utility

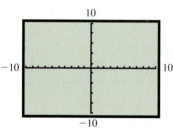

FIGURE A.5 Viewing rectangle

When drawing a graph, you can use different scales for the x- and y-axes. Similarly, the scale can be set separately for each coordinate axis on a graphing utility. Once scales are set, you get a **viewing rectangle**, where your graphs are displayed. For example, in Figure A.5, the scale for the x-axis is 1 (the distance between each tick mark), whereas the scale for the y-axis is 2. Read more about viewing rectangles in your graphing calculator manual.

2 Find the distance between two points.

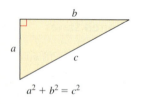

$$a^2 + b^2 = c^2$$

FIGURE A.6 Pythagorean Theorem

Distance Formula

If a Cartesian coordinate system has the same unit of measurement, such as inches or centimeters, on both axes, we can calculate the distance between any two points in that plane.

Recall that the Pythagorean Theorem states that in a **right triangle** with hypotenuse of length c and the legs of lengths a and b,

$$a^2 + b^2 = c^2, \quad \text{Pythagorean Theorem}$$

as shown in Figure A.6.

Suppose we want to compute the distance between the two points $P(x_1, y_1)$ and $Q(x_2, y_2)$. We draw a horizontal line through the point Q and a vertical line through the point P to form the right triangle PQS, as shown in Figure A.7.

The length of the horizontal side of the triangle is $|x_2 - x_1|$, and the length of the vertical side is $|y_2 - y_1|$. The distance between P and Q, denoted $d(P, Q)$, is the length of the hypotenuse.

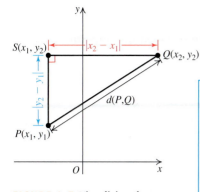

FIGURE A.7 Visualizing the distance formula

$$[d(P,Q)]^2 = |x_2 - x_1|^2 + |y_2 - y_1|^2 \quad \text{Pythagorean Theorem}$$
$$d(P,Q) = \sqrt{|x_2 - x_1|^2 + |y_2 - y_1|^2} \quad \text{Take the square root of both sides.}$$
$$d(P,Q) = \sqrt{(x_2 - x_1)^2 + (y_2 - y_1)^2} \quad |a|^2 = a^2$$

DISTANCE FORMULA IN THE COORDINATE PLANE

Let $P = (x_1, y_1)$ and $Q = (x_2, y_2)$ be any two points in the coordinate plane. Then the distance between P and Q, denoted $d(P,Q)$, is given by the **distance formula**

$$d(P,Q) = \sqrt{(x_2 - x_1)^2 + (y_2 - y_1)^2}.$$

EXAMPLE 3   **Finding the Distance Between Two Points**

Find the distance between the points $P = (-2, 5)$ and $Q = (3, -4)$.

SOLUTION

Let $(x_1, y_1) = (-2, 5)$ and $(x_2, y_2) = (3, -4)$. Then

$$x_1 = -2, y_1 = 5, x_2 = 3, \text{ and } y_2 = -4.$$
$$d(P,Q) = \sqrt{(x_2 - x_1)^2 + (y_2 - y_1)^2} \quad \text{Distance formula}$$
$$= \sqrt{3 - (-2)^2 + (-4 - 5)^2} \quad \text{Substitute the values for } x_1, x_2, y_1, y_2.$$
$$= \sqrt{5^2 + (-9)^2} = \sqrt{106} \approx 10.3 \quad \text{Use a calculator.} \quad ■■■$$

Practice Problem 3   Find the distance between the points $(-5, 2)$ and $(-4, 1)$.   ■

3 Find the midpoint of a line segment.

Midpoint Formula

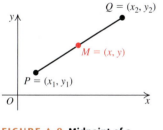

FIGURE A.8 Midpoint of a segment

MIDPOINT FORMULA

The coordinates of the midpoint $M = (x, y)$ of the line segment joining $P = (x_1, y_1)$ and $Q = (x_2, y_2)$ are given by (see Figure A.8)

$$M = (x, y) = \left(\frac{x_1 + x_2}{2}, \frac{y_1 + y_2}{2} \right).$$

The midpoint formula can be proved by showing that $d(P, M) = d(Q, M)$.

EXAMPLE 4   **Finding the Midpoint of a Line Segment**

Find the midpoint of the line segment joining the points $P(-3, 6)$ and $Q(1, 4)$.

SOLUTION

Let $(x_1, y_1) = (-3, 6)$ and $(x_2, y_2) = (1, 4)$. Then

$$x_1 = -3, y_1 = 6, x_2 = 1, \text{ and } y_2 = 4.$$
$$\text{Midpoint} = \left(\frac{x_1 + x_2}{2}, \frac{y_1 + y_2}{2} \right) = \left(\frac{-3 + 1}{2}, \frac{6 + 4}{2} \right) \quad \begin{array}{l}\text{Substitute values}\\\text{for } x_1, x_2, y_1, y_2.\end{array}$$
$$= (-1, 5) \quad \text{Simplify.}$$

The midpoint is $M = (-1, 5)$.   ■■■

Practice Problem 4   Find the midpoint of the line segment whose endpoints are $(5, -2)$ and $(6, -1)$.   ■

4 Sketch a graph by plotting points.

Graph of an Equation

We say that a *relation* exists between two quantities when one quantity changes with respect to the other quantity. The two changing (or varying) quantities are often represented by *variables*. A relation may sometimes be described by an equation or a formula. The following equations are examples of relationships between two variables.

$$y = 2x + 1 \quad x^2 + y^2 = 4 \quad y = x^2 \quad x = y^2$$

$$F = \frac{9}{5}C + 32 \quad q = -3p^2 + 30$$

An ordered pair (a, b) is said to **satisfy** an equation with variables x and y if when a is substituted for x and b is substituted for y in the equation, the resulting statement is true. For example, the ordered pair $(2, 5)$ satisfies the equation $y = 2x + 1$ because replacing x with 2 and y with 5 yields $5 = 2(2) + 1$, which is a true statement. The ordered pair $(5, -2)$ does not satisfy this equation because replacing x with 5 and y with -2 yields $-2 = 2(5) + 1$, which is false. An ordered pair that satisfies an equation is called a **solution** of the equation.

In an equation involving x and y, if the value of y can be found given the value of x, then we say that y is the **dependent variable** and x is the **independent variable**. In the equation $y = 2x + 1$, for any real number x, there is a corresponding value of y. Hence, we have infinitely many solutions of the equation $y = 2x + 1$. When these solutions are graphed or plotted as points in the coordinate plane, they constitute the *graph of the equation*. Therefore, the graph of an equation is a geometric picture of its solution set.

GRAPH OF AN EQUATION

The **graph of an equation** in two variables, such as x and y, is the graph of all ordered pairs (a, b) in the coordinate plane that satisfy the equation.

EXAMPLE 5   **Sketching a Graph by Plotting Points**

Sketch the graph of $y = x^2 - 3$.

SOLUTION

The equation has infinitely many solutions. To find a few, we choose integer values of x between -3 and 3. Then we find the corresponding values of y as shown in Table A.2.

TABLE A.2

x	$y = x^2 - 3$	(x, y)
-3	$y = (-3)^2 - 3 = 9 - 3 = 6$	$(-3, 6)$
-2	$y = (-2)^2 - 3 = 4 - 3 = 1$	$(-2, 1)$
-1	$y = (-1)^2 - 3 = 1 - 3 = -2$	$(-1, -2)$
0	$y = 0^2 - 3 = 0 - 3 = -3$	$(0, -3)$
1	$y = 1^2 - 3 = 1 - 3 = -2$	$(1, -2)$
2	$y = 2^2 - 3 = 4 - 3 = 1$	$(2, 1)$
3	$y = 3^2 - 3 = 9 - 3 = 6$	$(3, 6)$

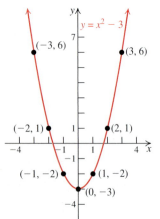

FIGURE A.9 Graph of an equation

We plot the solutions (x, y) and join them with a smooth curve to sketch the graph of $y = x^2 - 3$ shown in Figure A.9. ▪ ▪ ▪

Practice Problem 5   Sketch the graph of $y = -x^2 + 1$. ▪

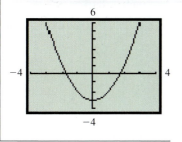

The calculator graph of $y = x^2 - 3$ reinforces the result of Example 5.

The bowl-shaped curve in Figure A.9 is called a *parabola*. You can find parabolic shapes in everyday settings such as the path of a thrown ball or the reflector behind a car's headlight.

Example 5 suggests how to sketch the graph of any equation by plotting points. We summarize the steps for this technique.

SKETCHING A GRAPH BY PLOTTING POINTS

Step 1 Make a representative table of solutions of the equation.

Step 2 Plot the solutions as ordered pairs in the Cartesian coordinate plane.

Step 3 Connect the solutions in Step 2 with a smooth curve.

Comment This technique has obvious pitfalls. For instance, many different curves pass through the four points in Figure A.10. Assume that these points are solutions of a given equation. We cannot guarantee that any curve through these points is the actual graph of the equation. However, in general, the more solutions plotted, the more accurate the graph.

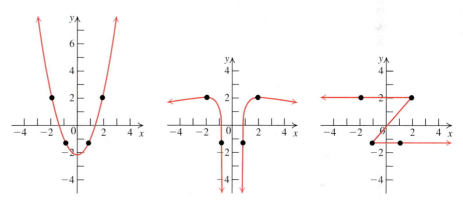

FIGURE A.10 Several graphs through four points

5 Find the intercepts of a graph.

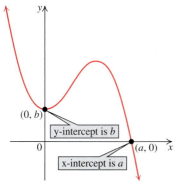

FIGURE A.11 Intercepts of a graph

Intercepts

Let's examine the points where a graph intersects (crosses or touches) the coordinate axes. Because all points on the x-axis have a y-coordinate of 0, any point where a graph intersects the x-axis has the form $(a, 0)$. See Figure A.11. The number a is called an **x-intercept** of the graph. Similarly, any point where a graph intersects the y-axis has the form $(0, b)$, and the number b is called a **y-intercept** of the graph.

FINDING THE INTERCEPTS OF THE GRAPH OF AN EQUATION

Step 1 To find the x-intercepts of the graph of an equation, set $y = 0$ in the equation and solve for x.

Step 2 To find the y-intercepts of the graph of an equation, set $x = 0$ in the equation and solve for y.

EXAMPLE 6   **Finding Intercepts**

Find the x- and y-intercepts of the graph of the equation $y = x^2 - x - 2$.

STUDY TIP

Do not try to calculate the
x-intercept by setting $x = 0$.
An x-intercept is the x-coordinate
of a point where the graph
touches or crosses the x-axis, so
the y-coordinate must be 0.

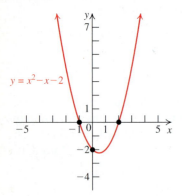

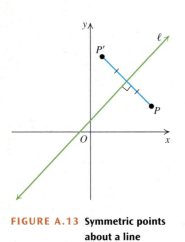

FIGURE A.12 Intercepts of a graph

6 Find the symmetries in a graph.

**FIGURE A.13 Symmetric points
about a line**

SOLUTION

Step 1   Set $y = 0$ in the equation and solve for x.

$$0 = x^2 - x - 2 \qquad \text{Set } y = 0.$$
$$0 = (x + 1)(x - 2) \qquad \text{Factor.}$$
$$x + 1 = 0 \quad \text{or} \quad x - 2 = 0 \qquad \text{Zero-product property}$$
$$x = -1 \quad \text{or} \qquad x = 2 \qquad \text{Solve each equation for } x.$$

The x-intercepts are -1 and 2.

Step 2   Set $x = 0$ in the equation and solve for y.

$$y = 0^2 - 0 - 2 \qquad \text{Set } x = 0.$$
$$y = -2 \qquad \text{Solve for } y.$$

The y-intercept is -2.

The graph of the equation $y = x^2 - x - 2$ is shown in Figure A.12.   ■ ■ ■

Practice Problem 6   Find the intercepts of the graph of $y = 2x^2 + 3x - 2$.   ■

Symmetry

The concept of **symmetry** helps us sketch graphs of equations. A graph has symmetry if one portion of the graph is a *mirror image* of another portion. As shown in
Figure A.13, if a line l is an **axis of symmetry**, or **line of symmetry**, we can construct
the mirror image of any point P not on l by first drawing the perpendicular line segment from P to l. Then we extend this segment an equal distance on the other side
to a point P' so that the line l perpendicularly bisects the line segment $\overline{PP'}$. In
Figure A.13, we say that the point P' is the *symmetric image* of the point P with
respect to the line l. Symmetry lets us use information about part of the graph to
draw the remainder of the graph.

There are three basic types of symmetries.

TESTS FOR SYMMETRIES

1. A graph is **symmetric with respect to (or about) the y-axis** if for every point
    (x, y) on the graph, the point $(-x, y)$ is also on the graph. See Figure A.14(a).

2. A graph is **symmetric with respect to (or about) the x-axis** if for every point
    (x, y) on the graph, the point $(x, -y)$ is also on the graph. See Figure A.14(b).

3. A graph is **symmetric with respect to (or about) the origin** if for every point
    (x, y) on the graph, the point $(-x, -y)$ is also on the graph. See Figure A.14(c).

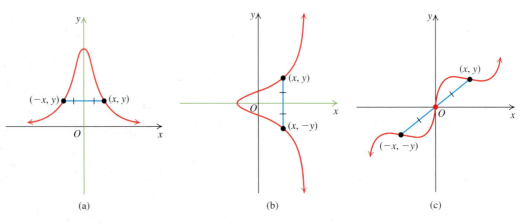

(a)   (b)   (c)

FIGURE A.14 Three types of symmetry

TECHNOLOGY CONNECTION

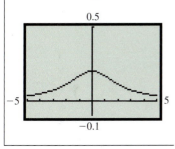

The calculator graph of $y = \dfrac{1}{x^2 + 5}$ reinforces the result of Example 7.

STUDY TIP

Note that if *only* even powers of x appear in an equation, then the graph is automatically symmetric with respect to the y-axis because for any integer n, $(-x)^{2n} = x^{2n}$. Consequently, we obtain the original equation when we replace x with $-x$.

EXAMPLE 7   Checking for Symmetry

Determine whether the graph of the equation $y = \dfrac{1}{x^2 + 5}$ is symmetric with respect to the y-axis.

SOLUTION

Replace x with $-x$ to see if $(-x, y)$ also satisfies the equation.

$$y = \frac{1}{x^2 + 5} \qquad \text{Original equation}$$

$$y = \frac{1}{(-x)^2 + 5} \qquad \text{Replace } x \text{ with } -x.$$

$$y = \frac{1}{x^2 + 5} \qquad \text{Simplify: } (-x)^2 = x^2.$$

Because replacing x with $-x$ gives us the original equation, the graph of $y = \dfrac{1}{x^2 + 5}$ is symmetric with respect to the y-axis.   ■ ■ ■

Practice Problem 7   Check the graph of $x^2 - y^2 = 1$ for symmetry with respect to the y-axis.   ■

FINDING THE SOLUTION: A PROCEDURE

EXAMPLE 8   Sketching a Graph Using Symmetry

OBJECTIVE

Use symmetry to sketch the graph of an equation.

Step 1   Test for all three symmetries.
About the x-axis: Replace y with $-y$.
About the y-axis: Replace x with $-x$.
About the origins: Replace x with $-x$ and y with $-y$.

EXAMPLE

Use symmetry to sketch the graph of $y = 4x - x^3$.

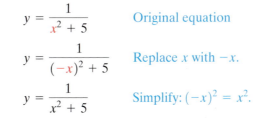

1.

x-axis	y-axis	origin
Replace y with $-y$.	Replace x with $-x$.	Replace x with $-x$ and y with $-y$.
$-y = 4x - x^3$	$y = 4(-x) - (-x)^3$	$-y = 4(-x) - (-x)^3$
$y = -4x + x^3$	$y = -4x + x^3$	$-y = -4x + x^3$
No	No	$y = 4x - x^3$
		Yes

Step 2   Make a table of values using any symmetries found in Step 1.

2.   Origin symmetry: If (x, y) is on the graph, so is $(-x, -y)$. Use only positive x values in the table.

x	0	0.5	1	1.5	2	2.5
$y = 4x - x^3$	0	1.875	3	2.625	0	-5.625

continued on the next page

Step 3 Plot the points from the table and draw a smooth curve through them.

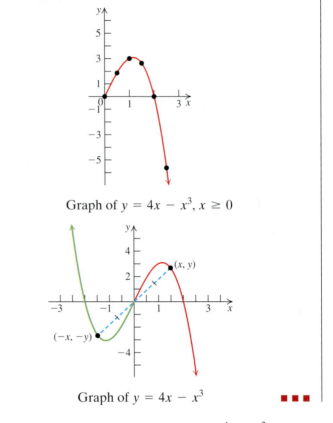

Graph of $y = 4x - x^3$, $x \geq 0$

Step 4 Extend the portion of the graph found in Step 3, using symmetry.

Graph of $y = 4x - x^3$

■■■

Practice Problem 8 Use symmetry to sketch the graph of $y = x^4 - 4x^2$. ■

7 Find the equation of a circle.

Circles

Sometimes a curve that is described geometrically can also be described by an algebraic equation. We illustrate this situation in the case of a circle.

CIRCLE

A **circle** is a set of points in a Cartesian coordinate plane that are a fixed distance r from a specified point (h, k). The fixed distance r is called the **radius** of the circle, and the specified point (h, k) is called the **center** of the circle.

A point $P(x, y)$ is on the circle if and only if its distance from the center $C(h, k)$ is r. Using the notation for the distance between the points P and C, we have

$$d(P, C) = r$$
$$\sqrt{(x - h)^2 + (y - k)^2} = r \qquad \text{Distance formula}$$
$$(x - h)^2 + (y - k)^2 = r^2 \qquad \text{Square both sides.}$$

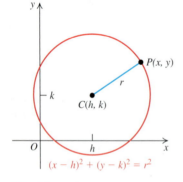

FIGURE A.15

The equation $(x - h)^2 + (y - k)^2 = r^2$ is an equation of a circle with radius r and center (h, k). A point (x, y) is on the circle of radius r and center $C(h, k)$ if and only if it satisfies this equation. Figure A.15 is the graph of a circle with center $C(h, k)$ and radius r.

TECHNOLOGY CONNECTION

To graph the equation $x^2 + y^2 = 1$ on a graphing calculator, we first solve for y.

$y^2 = 1 - x^2$ Subtract x^2 from both sides.

$y = \pm\sqrt{1 - x^2}$ Square root property

We then graph the two equations

$Y_1 = \sqrt{1 - x^2}$ and
$Y_2 = -\sqrt{1 - x^2}$

in the same window. The graph of y_1 is the upper semicircle ($y \geq 0$), and the graph of y_2 is the lower semicircle ($y \leq 0$). The calculator graph does not look quite like a circle. We use the ZSquare option to make the display look like a circle.

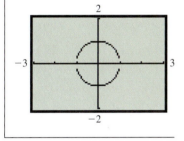

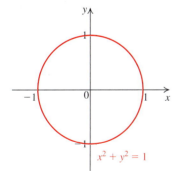

FIGURE A.16 The unit circle

STANDARD FORM OF THE EQUATION OF A CIRCLE

The equation of a circle with center (h, k) and radius r is

(1) $$(x - h)^2 + (y - k)^2 = r^2$$

and is called the **standard form** of an equation of a circle.

EXAMPLE 9   Finding the Equation of a Circle

Find the standard form of the equation of the circle with center $(-3, 4)$ and radius 7.

SOLUTION

$(x - h)^2 + (y - k)^2 = r^2$ Standard form

$[x - (-3)]^2 + (y - 4)^2 = 7^2$ Replace h with -3, k with 4, and r with 7.

$(x + 3)^2 + (y - 4)^2 = 49$ We usually eliminate double negatives. ■ ■ ■

Practice Problem 9 Find the standard form of the equation of the circle with center $(3, -6)$ and radius 10. ■

If an equation in two variables can be written in standard form, then its graph is a circle with center (h, k) and radius r.

EXAMPLE 10   Graphing a Circle

Specify the center and radius and graph each circle.

a. $x^2 + y^2 = 1$
b. $(x + 2)^2 + (y - 3)^2 = 25$

SOLUTION

a. The equation $x^2 + y^2 = 1$ can be rewritten as

$$(x - 0)^2 + (y - 0)^2 = 1^2.$$

Comparing that equation with equation (1), we conclude that the given equation is an equation of a circle with center $(0, 0)$ and radius 1. The graph is shown in Figure A.16. This circle is called the **unit circle**.

b. Rewriting the equation $(x + 2)^2 + (y - 3)^2 = 25$ as

$$[x - (-2)]^2 + (y - 3)^2 = 5^2,   x + 2 = x - (-2)$$

we see that the graph of this equation is a circle with center $(-2, 3)$ and radius 5. The graph is shown in Figure A.17 on the next page. ■ ■ ■

Practice Problem 10 Graph the equation $(x - 2)^2 + (y + 1)^2 = 36$. ■

If we expand the squared expressions in the standard equation of a circle,

(1) $$(x - h)^2 + (y - k)^2 = r^2$$

and then simplify, we obtain an equation of the form

(2) $$x^2 + y^2 + ax + by + c = 0.$$

GENERAL FORM OF THE EQUATION OF A CIRCLE

The **general form** of the equation of a circle is

$$x^2 + y^2 + ax + by + c = 0.$$

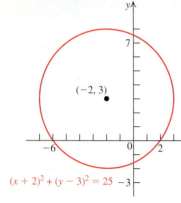

$(x + 2)^2 + (y - 3)^2 = 25$

FIGURE A.17 Circle with radius 5 and center at $(-2, 3)$

On the other hand, if we are given an equation in general form, we can convert it to standard form by completing the squares on the x- and y-terms. This gives

(3)
$$(x - h)^2 + (y - k)^2 = d.$$

If $d > 0$, the graph of equation (3) is a circle with center (h, k) and radius $\sqrt{d}$. If $d = 0$, the graph of equation (3) is the point (h, k). If $d < 0$, there is no graph.

EXAMPLE 11 **Converting the General Form to Standard Form**

Find the center and radius of the circle with equation

$$x^2 + y^2 - 6x + 8y + 10 = 0.$$

SOLUTION

Complete the squares on both the x-terms and y-terms to get standard form.

$x^2 + y^2 - 6x + 8y + 10 = 0$	Original equation
$(x^2 - 6x) + (y^2 + 8y) = -10$	Group the x-terms and y-terms.
$(x^2 - 6x + 9) + (y^2 + 8y + 16) = -10 + 9 + 16$	Complete the squares by adding 9 and 16 to both sides.
$(x - 3)^2 + (y + 4)^2 = 15$	Factor and simplify.
$(x - 3)^2 + [y - (-4)]^2 = (\sqrt{15})^2$	Rewrite in standard form.

The last equation tells us that we have $h = 3$, $k = -4$, and $r = \sqrt{15}$. Therefore, the circle has center $(3, -4)$ and radius $\sqrt{15} \approx 3.9$. ▪▪▪

Practice Problem 11 Find the center and radius of the circle with equation $x^2 + y^2 + 4x - 6y - 12 = 0$. ▪

SECTION A.2 ▪ Exercises

A EXERCISES Basic Skills and Concepts

1. A point with a negative first coordinate and a positive second coordinate lies in the _____ quadrant.

2. If $(-2, 4)$ is a point on a graph that is symmetric with respect to the y-axis, then the point _____ is also on the graph.

3. If $(0, -5)$ is a point of a graph, then -5 is a(n) _____ intercept of the graph.

4. An equation in standard form of a circle with center $(1, 0)$ and radius 2 is _____.

5. *True or False* The graph of the equation $3x^2 - 2x + y + 3 = 0$ is a circle.

6. *True or False* If a graph is symmetric about the x-axis, then it must have at least one x-intercept.

7. Plot and label each of the given points in a Cartesian coordinate plane and state the quadrant, if any,

in which each point is located. $(2, 2), (3, -1), (-1, 0),$ $(-2, -5), (0, 0), (-7, 4), (0, 3), (-4, 2)$

8. **a.** Write the coordinates of any five points on the x-axis. What do these points have in common?
   b. Graph the points $(-2, 1), (0, 1), (0.5, 1), (1, 1),$ and $(2, 1)$. Describe the set of all points of the form $(x, 1)$, where x is a real number.

9. **a.** If the x-coordinate of a point is 0, where does that point lie?
   b. Graph the points $(-1, 1), (-1, 1.5), (-1, 2),$ $(-1, 3),$ and $(-1, 4)$. Describe the set of all points of the form $(-1, y)$, where y is a real number.

10. Let $P(x, y)$ be a point in a coordinate plane. In which quadrant does P lie
    a. if x and y are both negative?
    b. if x and y are both positive?
    c. if x is positive and y is negative?
    d. if x is negative and y is positive?

In Exercises 11–16, find (a) the distance between P and Q and (b) the coordinates of the midpoint of the line segment PQ.

11. $P(2,1), Q(2,5)$

12. $P(3,5), Q(-2,5)$

13. $P(-1,-5), Q(2,-3)$

14. $P(-4,1), Q(-7,-9)$

15. $P(v-w,t), Q(v+w,t)$

16. $P(t,k), Q(k,t)$

In Exercises 17–20, determine whether the given points are collinear. Points are *collinear* if they can be labeled P, Q, and R so that $d(P,Q) + d(Q,R) = d(P,R)$.

17. $(0,0), (1,2), (-1,-2)$

18. $(3,4), (0,0), (-3,-4)$

19. $(9,6), (0,-3), (3,1)$

20. $(-2,3), (3,1), (2,-1)$

In Exercises 21–26, identify the triangle PQR as an *isosceles* (two sides of equal length), *equilateral* (three sides of equal length), or *scalene* (three sides of different lengths) triangle.

21. $P(-5,5), Q(-1,4), R(-4,1)$

22. $P(3,2), Q(6,6), R(-1,5)$

23. $P(-4,8), Q(0,7), R(-3,5)$

24. $P(6,6), Q(-1,-1), R(-5,3)$

25. $P(1,-1), Q(-1,1), R(-\sqrt{3}, -\sqrt{3})$

26. $P(-0.5,-1), Q(-1.5,1), R(\sqrt{3}-1, \sqrt{3}/2)$

In Exercises 27–30, determine whether the given points are on the graph of the equation.

	Equation	Points
27.	$y = x - 1$	$(-3,-4,), (1,0), (4,3), (2,3)$
28.	$y = \sqrt{x+1}$	$(3,2), (0,1), (8,-3), (8,3)$
29.	$y = \dfrac{1}{x}$	$\left(-3, \dfrac{1}{3}\right), (1,1), (0,0), \left(2, \dfrac{1}{2}\right)$
30.	$y^2 = x$	$(1,-1), (1,1)\ (0,0), (2,-\sqrt{2})$

In Exercises 31–42, graph each equation by plotting points. Let $x = -3, -2, -1, 0, 1, 2,$ and 3 where applicable.

31. $y = x + 1$

32. $y = x - 1$

33. $y = 2x$

34. $y = \dfrac{1}{2}x$

35. $y = |x|$

36. $y = |x + 1|$

37. $y = 4 - x^2$

38. $y = x^2 - 4$

39. $y = \sqrt{9 - x^2}$

40. $y = -\sqrt{9 - x^2}$

41. $y = x^3$

42. $y = -x^3$

43. Write the x- and y-intercepts of the graph.

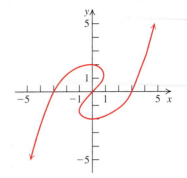

44. Write the x- and y-intercepts of the graph.

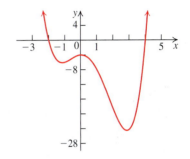

In Exercises 45–54, find the x- and y-intercepts of the graph of each equation.

45. $3x + 4y = 12$

46. $\dfrac{x}{5} + \dfrac{y}{3} = 1$

47. $2x + 3y = 5$

48. $\dfrac{x}{2} - \dfrac{y}{3} = 1$

49. $y = x^2 - 6x + 8$

50. $x = y^2 - 5y + 6$

51. $x^2 + y^2 = 4$

52. $y = \sqrt{9 - x^2}$

53. $y = \sqrt{x^2 - 1}$

54. $xy = 1$

In Exercises 55–62, test each equation for symmetry with respect to the x-axis, the y-axis, and the origin.

55. $y = x^2 + 1$

56. $x = y^2 + 1$

57. $y = x^3 + x$

58. $y = 2x^3 - x$

59. $y = 5x^4 + 2x^2$

60. $y = -3x^6 + 2x^4 + x^2$

61. $y = -3x^5 + 2x^3$

62. $y = 2x^2 - |x|$

In Exercises 63 and 64, specify the center and the radius of each circle.

63. $(x + 1)^2 + (y - 3)^2 = 16$

64. $(x + 2)^2 + (y + 3)^2 = 11$

In Exercises 65–70, find the standard form of the equation of a circle that satisfies the given conditions. Graph each equation.

65. Center $(3, 1)$; radius 3

66. Center $(-1, 2)$; radius 2

67. Center $(-3, -2)$ and touches the y-axis

68. Center $(3, -4)$ and passes through the point $(-1, 5)$

69. Diameter with endpoints $(2, -3)$ and $(8, 5)$

70. Diameter with endpoints $(7, 4)$ and $(-3, 6)$

In Exercises 71–74: a. Find the center and radius of each circle. b. Find the x- and y-intercepts of the graph of each circle.

71. $x^2 + y^2 - 2x - 2y - 4 = 0$

72. $x^2 + y^2 - 4x - 2y - 15 = 0$

73. $2x^2 + 2y^2 + 4y = 0$

74. $3x^2 + 3y^2 + 6x = 0$

B EXERCISES Applying the Concepts

In Exercises 75 and 76, use the midpoint formula to find the estimate.

75. Murders in the United States. In the United States, 22,000 murders were committed in 1995 and 18,000 in 1997. Assuming that this decline is linear, estimate the number of murders committed in 1996. (*Source:* U.S. Census Bureau.)

76. Spending on prescription drugs. Americans spent $141 billion on prescription drugs in 2001 and $252 billion in 2005. Assuming that this trend continued, estimate the amount spent on prescription drugs during 2002, 2003, and 2004. (*Source:* U.S. Census Bureau.)

77. Corporate profits. The equation $P = -0.5t^2 - 3t + 8$ describes the monthly profits (in millions of dollars) of ABCD Corp. for the year 2008, with $t = 0$ representing July 2008.

  a. How much profit did the corporation make in March 2008?

  b. How much profit did the corporation make in October 2008?

  c. Sketch the graph of the equation.

  d. Find the t-intercepts. What do they represent?

  e. Find the P-intercept. What does it represent?

78. Female students in colleges. The equation

$$P = -0.002t^2 + 0.093t + 8.18$$

models the approximate number (in millions) of female college students in the United States for the academic years 1995–2001, with $t = 0$ representing 1995.

  a. Sketch the graph of the equation.

  b. Find the positive t-intercept. What does it represent?

  c. Find the P-intercept. What does it represent?

(*Source: Statistical Abstract of the United States.*)

79. Motion. An object is thrown up from the top of a building that is 320 feet high. The equation $y = -16t^2 + 128t + 320$ gives the object's height (in feet) above the ground at any time t (in seconds) after the object is thrown.

  a. What is the height of the object after $0, 1, 2, 3, 4, 5,$ and 6 seconds?

  b. Sketch the graph of the equation $y = -16t^2 + 128t + 320$.

  c. What part of the graph represents the physical aspects of the problem?

  d. What are the intercepts of this graph, and what do they mean?

Functions

Objectives

1. Use functional notation and find function values.
2. Find the domain of a function.
3. Identify the graph of a function.

1 Use functional notation and find function values.

Functions

There are many ways of expressing a relationship between two quantities. For example, if you are paid $10 per hour, the relation between the number of hours, x, you work and the amount of money, y, you earn may be expressed by the equation $y = 10x$. Replacing x with 40 yields $y = 400$ and indicates that 40 hours of work corresponds to a $400 paycheck. A special relationship such as $y = 10x$ in which to each element x in one set there corresponds a unique element y in another set is called a *function*. We say that your pay is a function of the number of hours you work. Because the value of y depends on the given value of x, y is called the **dependent variable** and x is called the **independent variable**. Any symbol may be used for the dependent or independent variables.

DEFINITION OF FUNCTION

A **function** from a set X to a set Y is a rule that assigns to each element of X one and only one corresponding element of Y. The set X is the **domain** of the function. The set of those elements of Y that correspond (are assigned) to the elements of X is the **range** of the function.

To decide whether a correspondence is a function, we must check whether *any* domain element is paired with more than one range element. If this happens, that domain element does not have a *unique* corresponding element of Y and the correspondence is not a function. See the correspondence diagrams in Figure A.18.

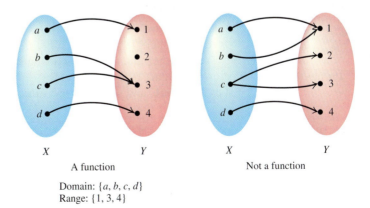

A function
Domain: $\{a, b, c, d\}$
Range: $\{1, 3, 4\}$

Not a function

FIGURE A.18 Correspondence diagrams

BY THE WAY . . .

The functional notation
$y = f(x)$ was first used by the
great Swiss mathematician
Leonhard Euler in the
*Commentarii Academia
Petropolitanae*, published
in 1735.

We usually use single letters such as f, F, g, G, h, and H as the name of a function. If we choose f as the name of a function, then for each x in the domain of f, there corresponds a unique y in its range. The number y is denoted by $f(x)$, read as "f of x" or as "f at x." We call $f(x)$ the **value of f at the number** x and say that f *assigns* the value $f(x)$ to x.

Tables and graphs can be used to describe functions. The data in Table A.3 (reproduced from Section A.2) show the prevalence of smoking among adults aged 18 years and older in the United States over the years 1998–2004.

TABLE A.3

Year	1998	1999	2000	2001	2002	2003	2004
Percent of adult smokers	24.1	23.5	23.2	22.7	22.4	21.6	20.9

Source: Centers for Disease Control, National Health Interview Survey.

The graph in Figure A.19 is a **scatter diagram** that gives a visual representation of the same information. Scatter diagrams show the relationship between two variables by displaying data as points of a graph. The variable that might be considered the independent variable is plotted on the x-axis, and the dependent variable is plotted on the y-axis. Here the percent of adult smokers depends on the year and is plotted on the y-axis.

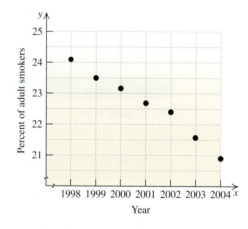

FIGURE A.19 Scatter diagram

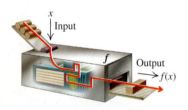

FIGURE A.20 The function f as a machine

The function described by Table A.3 and Figure A.19 has for its domain the set $\{1998, 1999, 2000, 2001, 2002, 2003, 2004\}$ and for its range the set $\{24.1, 23.5, 23.2, 22.7, 22.4, 21.6, 20.9\}$. The function assigns to each year in the domain the percent of adult smokers 18 years and older in the United States during that year.

Yet another nice way of picturing the concept of a function is as a "machine," as shown in Figure A.20. If x is in the domain of a function, then the machine accepts it as an "input" and produces the value $f(x)$ as the "output."

◆ **WARNING** In writing $y = f(x)$, do not confuse f, which is the name of the function, with $f(x)$, which is a number in the range of f that the function assigns to x. The symbol $f(x)$ does not mean "f times x."

STUDY TIP

The definition of a function is independent of the letters used to denote the function and the variables. For example,

$$s(x) = x^2, g(y) = y^2,$$
$$\text{and } h(t) = t^2$$

represent the same function.

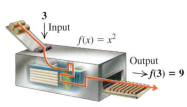

FIGURE A.21 The function f as a machine

Functions Defined by Equations When the relation defined by an equation in two variables is a function, we often can solve the equation for the dependent variable in terms of the independent variable. For example, the equation $y - x^2 = 0$ can be solved for y in terms of x.

$$y = x^2$$

Now we can replace the dependent variable, in this case, y, with functional notation $f(x)$ and express the function as

$$f(x) = x^2 \quad \text{(read "f of x equals x^2").}$$

Here $f(x)$ plays the role of y and is the value of the function f at x. For example, if $x = 3$ is an element (input value) in the domain of f, the corresponding element (output value) in the range is found by replacing x with 3 in the equation

$$f(x) = x^2$$
$$f(3) = 3^2 = 9 \qquad \text{Replace x with 3.}$$

We say that the value of the function f at 3 is 9. See Figure A.21. In other words, the number 9 in the range corresponds to the number 3 in the domain and the ordered pair $(3, 9)$ is an ordered pair of the function f.

If a function g is defined by an equation such as $y = x^2 - 6x + 8$, the notations

$$y = x^2 - 6x + 8 \quad \text{and} \quad g(x) = x^2 - 6x + 8$$

define the same function.

EXAMPLE 1   **Determining Whether an Equation Defines a Function**

Determine whether y is a function of x for each equation.

a. $6x^2 - 3y = 12$ **b.** $y^2 - x^2 = 4$

SOLUTION

Solve each equation for y in terms of x. If more than one value of y corresponds to the same value of x, then y is not a function of x.

a.
$$\begin{array}{ll} 6x^2 - 3y = 12 & \text{Original equation} \\ 6x^2 - 3y + 3y - 12 = 12 + 3y - 12 & \text{Add } 3y - 12 \text{ to both sides.} \\ 6x^2 - 12 = 3y & \text{Simplify.} \\ 2x^2 - 4 = y & \text{Divide by 3.} \end{array}$$

The last equation shows that only one value of y corresponds to each value of x. For example, if $x = 0$, then $y = 0 - 4 = -4$. So y is a function of x.

b.
$$\begin{array}{ll} y^2 - x^2 = 4 & \text{Original equation} \\ y^2 - x^2 + x^2 = 4 + x^2 & \text{Add } x^2 \text{ to both sides.} \\ y^2 = x^2 + 4 & \text{Simplify.} \\ y = \pm\sqrt{x^2 + 4} & \text{Square root property} \end{array}$$

The last equation shows that two values of y correspond to each value of x. For example, if $x = 0$, then $y = \pm\sqrt{0^2 + 4} = \pm\sqrt{4} = \pm 2$. Both $y = 2$ and $y = -2$ correspond to $x = 0$. Therefore, y is not a function of x. ■ ■ ■

Practice Problem 1 Determine whether y is a function of x for each equation.

a. $2x^2 - y^2 = 1$ **b.** $x - 2y = 5$ ■

TECHNOLOGY CONNECTION

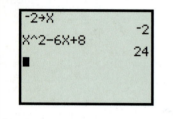 A graphing calculator allows you to store a number in a variable and then find the value of a function at that number. This screen shows the evaluation of the function $g(x) = x^2 - 6x + 8$ from Example 2(b), for $x = -2$.

```
-2→X
              -2
X^2-6X+8
              24
■
```

EXAMPLE 2   **Evaluating a Function**

Let g be the function defined by the equation

$$y = x^2 - 6x + 8.$$

Evaluate each function value.

a. $g(3)$ **b.** $g(-2)$ **c.** $g\left(\dfrac{1}{2}\right)$ **d.** $g(a + 2)$ **e.** $g(x + h)$

SOLUTION

Because the function is named g, we replace y with $g(x)$ and write

$$g(x) = x^2 - 6x + 8 \qquad \text{Replace } y \text{ with } g(x).$$

In this notation, the independent variable x is a placeholder. We can write $g(x) = x^2 - 6x + 8$ as

$$g(\ ) = (\ )^2 - 6(\ ) + 8.$$

a. $g(x) = x^2 - 6x + 8$ — The given equation
   $g(3) = 3^2 - 6(3) + 8$ — Replace x with 3 at each occurrence of x.
   $= 9 - 18 + 8 = -1$ — Simplify.

The statement $g(3) = -1$ means that the value of the function g at 3 is -1. Just as in part **a**, we can evaluate g at any value x in its domain.

$g(x) = x^2 - 6x + 8$ — Original equation

b. $g(-2) = (-2)^2 - 6(-2) + 8 = 24$ — Replace x with -2 and simplify.

c. $g\left(\dfrac{1}{2}\right) = \left(\dfrac{1}{2}\right)^2 - 6\left(\dfrac{1}{2}\right) + 8 = \dfrac{21}{4}$ — Replace x with $\dfrac{1}{2}$ and simplify.

d. $g(a + 2) = (a + 2)^2 - 6(a + 2) + 8$ — Replace x with $(a + 2)$ in $g(x)$.
   $= a^2 + 4a + 4 - 6a - 12 + 8$ — Recall: $(x + y)^2 = x^2 + 2xy + y^2$.
   $= a^2 - 2a$ — Simplify.

e. $g(x + h) = (x + h)^2 - 6(x + h) + 8$ — Replace x with $(x + h)$ in $g(x)$.
   $= x^2 + 2xh + h^2 - 6x - 6h + 8$ — Simplify.   ▪▪▪

Practice Problem 2   Let g be the function defined by the equation $y = -2x^2 + 5x$. Evaluate each function value.

a. $g(0)$ **b.** $g(-1)$ **c.** $g(x + h)$ ▪

2 Find the domain of a function.

Domain of a Function

Sometimes a function does not have a specified domain.

AGREEMENT ON DOMAIN

If the domain of a function that is defined by an equation is not specified, then we agree that the domain of the function is the largest set of real numbers that results in real numbers as outputs.

When we use our agreement to find the domain of a function, first we usually find the values of the variable that do not result in real number outputs. Then we exclude those numbers from the domain. Remember that

1. division by zero is undefined.

2. the square root (or any even root) of a negative number is not a real number.

EXAMPLE 3 **Finding the Domain of a Function**

Find the domain of each function.

a. $f(x) = \dfrac{1}{1 - x^2}$ b. $g(x) = \sqrt{x}$ c. $h(x) = \dfrac{1}{\sqrt{x - 1}}$ d. $P(t) = 2t + 1$

SOLUTION

a. The function f is not defined when the denominator $1 - x^2$ is 0. Because $1 - x^2 = 0$ if $x = 1$ or $x = -1$, the domain of f is the set $\{x | x \neq -1$ and $x \neq 1\}$, which in interval notation is written $(-\infty, -1) \cup (-1, 1) \cup (1, \infty)$.

b. Because the square root of a negative number is not a real number, negative numbers are excluded from the domain of g. The domain of $g(x) = \sqrt{x}$ is $\{x | x \geq 0\}$, or $[0, \infty)$ in interval notation.

c. The function $h(x) = \dfrac{1}{\sqrt{x - 1}}$ has *two* restrictions. The square root of a negative number is not a real number, so $\sqrt{x - 1}$ is a real number only if $x - 1 \geq 0$. However, we cannot allow $x - 1 = 0$ because $\sqrt{x - 1}$ is in the denominator. Therefore, we must have $x - 1 > 0$, or $x > 1$. The domain of h must be $\{x | x > 1\}$, or in interval notation, $(1, \infty)$.

d. When any real number is substituted for t in $y = 2t + 1$, a unique real number is determined. The domain is the set of all real numbers: $\{t | t$ is a real number$\}$, or in interval notation, $(-\infty, \infty)$.   ■ ■ ■

Practice Problem 3   Find the domain of the function

$$f(x) = \frac{1}{\sqrt{1 - x}}.$$ ■

3 Identify the graph of a function.

Graphs of Functions

The *graph of a function* f is the set of ordered pairs $(x, f(x))$ such that x is in the domain of f. That is, the graph of f is the graph of the equation $y = f(x)$. We sketch the graph of $y = f(x)$ by plotting points and joining them with a smooth curve. The graph of a function provides valuable visual information about the function.

Figure A.22 shows that not every curve in the plane is the graph of a function. In Figure A.22, a vertical line intersects the curve at two distinct points (a, b) and (a, c). This curve cannot be the graph of $y = f(x)$ for any function f because having $f(a) = b$ and $f(a) = c$ means that f assigns two different range values to the same domain element a. We express this statement in a slightly different way, as follows.

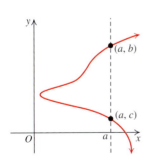

FIGURE A.22 Graph does not represent a function

VERTICAL-LINE TEST

If no vertical line intersects the graph of a curve (or scatterplot) at more than one point, then the curve (or scatterplot) is the graph of a function.

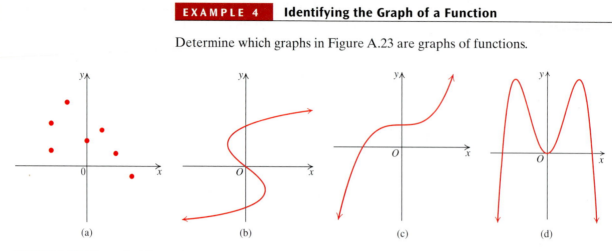

EXAMPLE 4   **Identifying the Graph of a Function**

Determine which graphs in Figure A.23 are graphs of functions.

(a)   (b)   (c)   (d)

FIGURE A.23 **The vertical-line test**

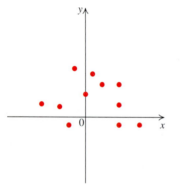

SOLUTION

The graphs in Figures A.23(a) and A.23(b) are not graphs of functions because a vertical line can be drawn through the two points farthest to the left in Figure A.23(a) and the y-axis is one of many vertical lines that contains more than one point on the graph in Figure A.23(b). The graphs in Figures A.23(c) and A.23(d) are the graphs of functions because no vertical line intersects either graph at more than one point. ■ ■ ■

Practice Problem 4   Decide whether the graph in the margin is the graph of a function. ■

EXAMPLE 5   **Examining the Graph of a Function**

Let $y = f(x) = x^2 - 2x - 3$.

a. Is the point $(1, -3)$ on the graph of f?
b. Find all values of x so that $(x, 5)$ is on the graph of f.
c. Find all y-intercepts of the graph of f.
d. Find all x-intercepts of the graph of f.

SOLUTION

a. We check whether $(1, -3)$ satisfies the equation $y = x^2 - 2x - 3$.

$$-3 \overset{?}{=} (1)^2 - 2(1) - 3 \qquad \text{Replace } x \text{ with } 1 \text{ and } y \text{ with } -3.$$
$$-3 \overset{?}{=} -4 \quad \text{No}$$

So $(1, -3)$ is *not* on the graph of f. See Figure A.24.

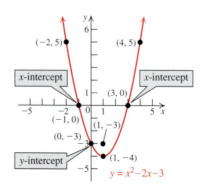

FIGURE A.24

b. Substitute 5 for y in $y = x^2 - 2x - 3$ and solve for x.

$$5 = x^2 - 2x - 3$$
$$0 = x^2 - 2x - 8 \qquad \text{Subtract 5 from both sides.}$$
$$0 = (x - 4)(x + 2) \qquad \text{Factor.}$$
$$x - 4 = 0 \quad \text{or} \quad x + 2 = 0 \qquad \text{Zero-product property}$$
$$x = 4 \quad \text{or} \quad x = -2 \qquad \text{Solve for } x.$$

The point $(x, 5)$ is on the graph of f only when $x = -2$ and $x = 4$. Both $(-2, 5)$ and $(4, 5)$ are on the graph of f. See Figure A.24.

c. Find all points (x, y) with $x = 0$ in $y = x^2 - 2x - 3$.

$$y = 0^2 - 2(0) - 3 \qquad \text{Replace } x \text{ with 0 to find the } y\text{-intercept.}$$
$$y = -3 \qquad \text{Simplify.}$$

The only y-intercept is -3. See Figure A.24.

d. Find all points (x, y) with $y = 0$ in $y = x^2 - 2x - 3$.

$$0 = x^2 - 2x - 3$$
$$0 = (x + 1)(x - 3) \qquad \text{Factor.}$$
$$x + 1 = 0 \quad \text{or} \quad x - 3 = 0 \qquad \text{Zero-product property}$$
$$x = -1 \quad \text{or} \quad x = 3 \qquad \text{Solve for } x.$$

The x-intercepts of the graph of f are -1 and 3. See Figure A.24. ■ ■ ■

Practice Problem 5 Let $y = f(x) = x^2 + 4x - 5$.

a. Is the point $(2, 7)$ on the graph of f?

b. Find all values of x so that $(x, -8)$ is on the graph of f.

c. Find the y-intercept of the graph of f.

d. Find any x-intercepts of the graph of f. ■

SUMMARY

A function is usually described in one or more of the following ways:

- A correspondence diagram
- A table of values
- An equation or a formula
- A scatter diagram or a graph

Input	Output
x	y or $f(x)$
First coordinate	Second coordinate
Independent variable	Dependent variable
Domain is the set of all inputs.	Range is the set of all outputs.

A EXERCISES Basic Skills and Concepts

1. In the functional notation $y = f(x)$, x is the _____ variable.

2. If $f(-2) = 7$, then -2 is in the _____ of the function f and 7 is in the _____ of f.

3. If the point $(9, -14)$ is on the graph of a function f, then $f(9) =$ _____.

4. If $(3, 7)$ and $(3, 0)$ are points on a graph, then the graph cannot be the graph of a(n) _____.

5. To find the x-intercepts of the graph of an equation in x and y, we solve the equation _____.

6. *True or False* If $(3, 6)$ and $(5, 22)$ are points on the graph of f, then the average rate of change of f as x changes from 3 to 5 is 14. _____

7. *True or False* If $x = -7$, then $-x$ is in the domain of $f(x) = \sqrt{x}$. _____

8. *True or False* The domain of $f(x) = \dfrac{1}{\sqrt{x + 2}}$ is all real x, $x \neq -2$. _____

In Exercises 9–14, determine the domain and range of each function. Explain why each non-function is not a function.

9.

10.

11.

12.

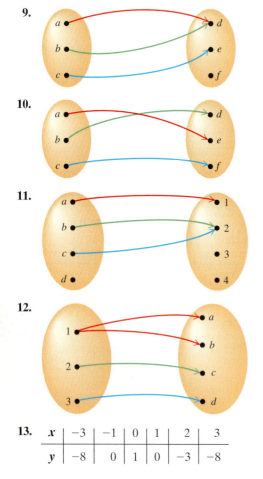

13.

x	-3	-1	0	1	2	3
y	-8	0	1	0	-3	-8

14.

x	0	3	8	0	3	8
y	-1	-2	-3	1	2	2

In Exercises 15–28, determine whether each equation defines y as a function of x.

15. $x + y = 2$

16. $x = y - 1$

17. $y = \dfrac{1}{x}$

18. $xy = -1$

19. $y = |x - 1|$

20. $x = |y|$

21. $y = \dfrac{1}{\sqrt{2x - 5}}$

22. $y = \dfrac{1}{\sqrt{x^2 - 1}}$

23. $2 - y = 3x$

24. $3x - 5y = 15$

25. $x^2 + y = 8$

26. $x = y^2$

27. $x^2 + y^3 = 5$

28. $x + y^3 = 8$

In Exercises 29–32, let $f(x) = x^2 - 3x + 1$, $g(x) = \dfrac{2}{\sqrt{x}}$, and $h(x) = \sqrt{2 - x}$.

29. Find $f(0)$, $g(0)$, $h(0)$, $f(a)$, and $f(-x)$.

30. Find $f(1)$, $g(1)$, $h(1)$, $g(a)$, and $g(x^2)$.

31. Find $f(-1)$, $g(-1)$, $h(-1)$, $h(c)$, and $h(-x)$.

32. Find $f(4)$, $g(4)$, $h(4)$, $g(2 + k)$, and $f(a + k)$.

33. Let $f(x) = \dfrac{2x}{\sqrt{4 - x^2}}$. Find each function value.

   a. $f(0)$ **b.** $f(1)$

   c. $f(2)$ **d.** $f(-2)$

   e. $f(-x)$

34. Let $g(x) = 2x + \sqrt{x^2 - 4}$. Find each function value.

   a. $g(0)$ **b.** $g(1)$

   c. $g(2)$ **d.** $g(-3)$

   e. $g(-x)$

In Exercises 35–48, find the domain of each function.

35. $f(x) = -8x + 7$

36. $f(x) = 2x^2 - 11$

37. $f(x) = \dfrac{1}{x - 9}$

38. $f(x) = \dfrac{1}{x + 9}$

39. $h(x) = \dfrac{2x}{x^2 - 1}$

40. $h(x) = \dfrac{x - 3}{x^2 - 4}$

41. $G(x) = \dfrac{\sqrt{x - 3}}{x + 2}$

42. $G(x) = \dfrac{\sqrt{x + 3}}{1 - x}$

43. $f(x) = \dfrac{3}{\sqrt{4 - x}}$

44. $f(x) = \dfrac{x}{\sqrt{2 - x}}$

45. $F(x) = \dfrac{x + 4}{x^2 + 3x + 2}$

46. $F(x) = \dfrac{1 - x}{x^2 + 5x + 6}$

47. $g(x) = \dfrac{\sqrt{x^2 + 1}}{x}$

48. $g(x) = \dfrac{1}{x^2 + 1}$

In Exercises 49–54, use the vertical-line test to determine whether the given graph represents a function.

49.

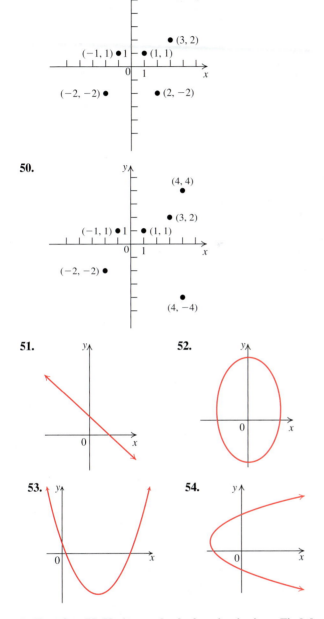

50.

51.   **52.**

53.   **54.**

In Exercises 55–58, the graph of a function is given. Find the indicated function values.

55. $f(-4), f(-1), f(3), f(5),$

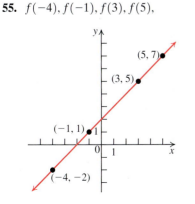

56. $g(-2), g(1), g(3), g(4)$

57. $h(-2), h(-1), h(0), h(1)$

58. $f(-1), f(0), f(1)$

59. Let $h(x) = x^2 - x + 1$. Find x such that $(x, 7)$ is on the graph of h.

60. Let $H(x) = x^2 + x + 8$. Find x such that $(x, 7)$ is on the graph of H.

61. Let $f(x) = -2(x + 1)^2 + 7$.
   a. Is $(1, 1)$ a point of the graph of f?
   b. Find all x such that $(x, 1)$ is on the graph of f.
   c. Find all y-intercepts of the graph of f.
   d. Find all x-intercepts of the graph of f.

62. Let $g(x) = -3x^2 - 12x$.
   a. Is $(-2, 10)$ a point of the graph of f?
   b. Find x such that $(x, 12)$ is on the graph of g.
   c. Find all y-intercepts of the graph of f.
   d. Find all x-intercepts of the graph of f.

Transformations of Functions

Objectives

1 Learn the meaning of transformations.
2 Use vertical or horizontal shifts to graph functions.
3 Use reflections to graph functions.
4 Use stretching or compressing to graph functions.

1 Learn the meaning of transformations.

Transformations

If a new function is formed by performing certain operations on a given function f, then the graph of the new function is called a **transformation** of the graph of f. For example, the graphs of $y = |x| + 2$ and $y = |x| - 3$ are transformations of the graph of $y = |x|$; that is, the graph of each is a special modification of the graph of $y = |x|$.

2 Use vertical or horizontal shifts to graph functions.

Vertical and Horizontal Shifts

EXAMPLE 1   **Graphing Vertical Shifts**

Let $f(x) = |x|$, $g(x) = |x| + 2$, and $h(x) = |x| - 3$. Sketch the graphs of these functions on the same coordinate plane. Describe how the graphs of g and h relate to the graph of f.

SOLUTION

Make a table of values and graph the equations $y = f(x)$, $y = g(x)$, and $y = h(x)$.

TABLE A.4

x	$y = |x|$	$y = |x| + 2$	$y = |x| - 3$
-5	5	7	2
-3	3	5	0
-1	1	3	-2
0	0	2	-3
1	1	3	-2
3	3	5	0
5	5	7	2

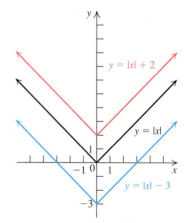

FIGURE A.25 **Vertical shifts of $y = |x|$**

Notice that in Table A.4 and Figure A.25, for each value of x, the value of $y = |x| + 2$ is 2 more than the value of $y = |x|$. So the graph of $y = |x| + 2$ is the graph of $y = |x|$ shifted two units up.

We also note that for each value of x, the value of $y = |x| - 3$ is 3 less than the value of $y = |x|$. So the graph of $y = |x| - 3$ is the graph of $y = |x|$ shifted three units down. ■ ■ ■

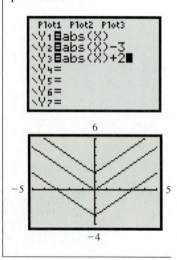

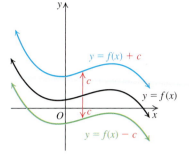

FIGURE A.26 Vertical shifts, $c > 0$

Practice Problem 1 Let

$$f(x) = x^3, g(x) = x^3 + 1, \text{ and } h(x) = x^3 - 2.$$

Sketch the graphs of all three functions on the same coordinate plane. Describe how the graphs of g and h relate to the graph of f. ■

Example 1 illustrates the concept of the vertical (up or down) shift of a graph.

VERTICAL SHIFT

Let $c > 0$. The graph of $y = f(x) + c$ is the graph of $y = f(x)$ shifted c units *up*, and the graph of $y = f(x) - c$ is the graph of $y = f(x)$ shifted c units *down*. See Figure A.26.

Next, we consider the operation that shifts a graph horizontally.

EXAMPLE 2   **Writing Functions for Horizontal Shifts**

Let $f(x) = x^2, g(x) = (x - 2)^2$, and $h(x) = (x + 3)^2$. A table of values for f, g, and h is given in Table A.5. The three functions f, g, and h are graphed on the same coordinate plane in Figure A.27. Describe how the graphs of g and h relate to the graph of f.

TABLE A.5

x	$y = x^2$	$y = (x - 2)^2$	x	$y = x^2$	$y = (x + 3)^2$
-4	**16**	36	-4	16	1
-3	**9**	25	-3	9	0
-2	**4**	16	-2	4	1
-1	**1**	9	-1	1	4
0	**0**	4	0	**0**	9
1	**1**	1	1	**1**	16
2	4	**0**	2	**4**	25
3	9	1	3	**9**	36
4	16	4	4	**16**	49
	(a)			**(b)**	

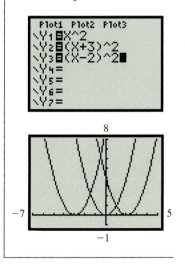
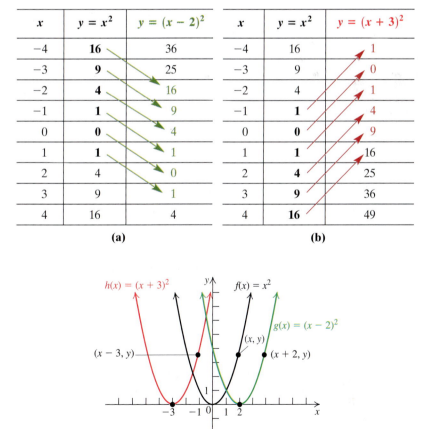

FIGURE A.27 Horizontal shifts

SOLUTION

First, notice that all three functions are squaring functions.

a. Replacing x with $x - 2$ on the right side of the defining equation for f gives the equation for g.

$$f(x) = \quad x^2 \qquad \text{Defining equation for } f$$
$$\downarrow$$
$$g(x) = (x - 2)^2 \qquad \text{Replace } x \text{ with } x - 2 \text{ to obtain the defining equation for } g.$$

The x-intercept of f is 0. We can find the x-intercept of g by solving $g(x) = (x - 2)^2 = 0$ for x. We get $x - 2 = 0$, or $x = 2$.

This means that $(2, 0)$ is a point on the graph of g, whereas $(0, 0)$ is a point on the graph of f. In general, each point (x, y) on the graph of f has a corresponding point $(x + 2, y)$ on the graph of g. So the graph of $g(x) = (x - 2)^2$ is just the graph of $f(x) = x^2$ shifted two units to the *right*. Noticing that $f(0) = 0$ and $g(2) = 0$ will help you remember which way to shift the graph. Table A.5(a) and Figure A.27 illustrate these ideas.

b. Replacing x with $x + 3$ on the right-hand side of the defining equation for f gives the equation for h.

$$f(x) = \quad x^2 \qquad \text{Defining equation for } f$$
$$\downarrow$$
$$h(x) = (x + 3)^2 \qquad \text{Replace } x \text{ with } x + 3 \text{ to obtain the defining equation for } h.$$

To find the x-intercept of h, we solve $h(x) = (x + 3)^2 = 0$. We get $x + 3 = 0$ and find that $x = -3$. This means that $(-3, 0)$ is a point on the graph of h, whereas $(0, 0)$ is a point on the graph of f. In general, each point (x, y) on the graph of f has a corresponding point $(x - 3, y)$ on the graph of h. So the graph of $h(x) = (x + 3)^2$ is just the graph of $f(x) = x^2$ shifted three units to the *left*. Noticing that $f(0) = 0$ and $h(-3) = 0$ will help you remember which way to shift the graph.

Table A.5(b) and Figure A.27 confirm these considerations. ▪ ▪ ▪

Practice Problem 2 Let

$$f(x) = x^3, g(x) = (x - 1)^3, \text{ and } h(x) = (x + 2)^3.$$

Sketch the graphs of all three functions on the same coordinate plane. Describe how the graphs of g and h relate to the graph of f. ▪

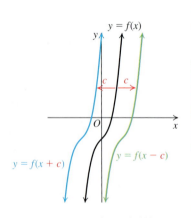

FIGURE A.28 Horizontal shifts, $c > 0$

HORIZONTAL SHIFTS

Let $c > 0$. The graph of $y = f(x - c)$ is the graph of $y = f(x)$ shifted c units to the right. The graph of $y = f(x + c)$ is the graph of $y = f(x)$ shifted c units to the left. See Figure A.28.

Replacing x with $x - c$ in the equation $y = f(x)$ results in a function whose graph is the graph of f shifted c units to the right ($c > 0$). Similarly, replacing x with $x + c$ in the equation $y = f(x)$ results in a function whose graph is the graph of f shifted c units to the left ($c > 0$).

FINDING THE SOLUTION: A PROCEDURE

EXAMPLE 3   Graphing Combined Vertical and Horizontal Shifts

OBJECTIVE	**EXAMPLE**
Sketch the graph of $g(x) = f(x - c) + b,$ *where f is a function whose graph is known.*	*Sketch the graph of* $g(x) = \sqrt{x + 2} - 3$.

Step 1 Identify and graph the known function *f*.

1. Choose $f(x) = \sqrt{x}$.

   The graph of $y = \sqrt{x}$ is shown in Step 4 below.

Step 2 Identify the constants *b* and *c*.

2. $g(x) = \sqrt{x - (-2)} + (-3)$, so $c = -2$ and $b = -3$.

Step 3 Graph $y = f(x - c)$ by shifting the graph of *f* horizontally to the

3. Because $c = -2 < 0$, the graph of $y = \sqrt{x + 2}$ is the graph of *f* shifted horizontally two units to the left. See the blue graph in Step 4 below.

   (i) right if $c > 0$.
   (ii) left if $c < 0$.

Step 4 Graph $y = f(x - c) + b$ by shifting the graph of $y = f(x - c)$ vertically

4. Graph $y = \sqrt{x + 2} - 3$ by shifting the graph of $y = \sqrt{x + 2}$ three units down.

   (i) up if $b > 0$.
   (ii) down if $b < 0$.

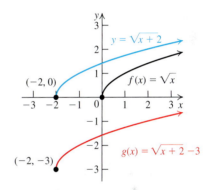

Horizontal and vertical shifts   ■ ■ ■

Practice Problem 3   Sketch the graph of

$$f(x) = \sqrt{x - 2} + 3.$$ ■

3 Use reflections to graph functions.

Reflections

Comparing the Graphs of $y = f(x)$ and $y = -f(x)$ Consider the graph of $f(x) = x^2$, shown in Figure A.29. Table A.6 gives some values for $f(x)$ and $g(x) = -f(x)$. Note that the *y*-coordinate of each point in the graph of $g(x) = -f(x)$ is the opposite of the *y*-coordinate of the corresponding point on the graph of $f(x)$. So the graph of $y = -x^2$ is the reflection of the graph of $y = x^2$ in the *x*-axis. This means that the points (x, x^2) and $(x, -x^2)$ are the same distance from but on opposite sides of the *x*-axis. See Figure A.29.

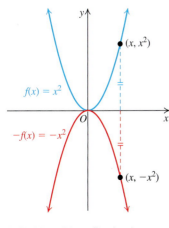

FIGURE A.29 Reflection in the *x*-axis

TABLE A.6

x	$f(x) = x^2$	$g(x) = -f(x) = -x^2$
-3	9	-9
-2	4	-4
-1	1	-1
0	0	0
1	1	-1
2	4	-4
3	9	-9

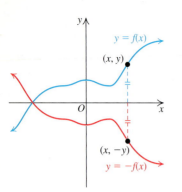

FIGURE A.30 Reflection in the *x*-axis

REFLECTION IN THE *x*-AXIS

The graph of $y = -f(x)$ is a reflection of the graph of $y = f(x)$ in the *x*-axis. If a point (x, y) is on the graph of $y = f(x)$, then the point $(x, -y)$ is on the graph of $y = -f(x)$. See Figure A.30.

Comparing the Graphs of $y = f(x)$ and $y = f(-x)$ To compare the graphs of $f(x)$ and $g(x) = f(-x)$, consider the graph of $f(x) = \sqrt{x}$. Then $f(-x) = \sqrt{-x}$. See Figure A.31. Table A.7 gives some values for $f(x)$ and $g(x) = f(-x)$. The domain of f is $[0, \infty)$, and the domain of g is $(-\infty, 0]$. Each point (x, y) on the graph of f has a corresponding point $(-x, y)$ on the graph of g. So the graph of $y = f(-x)$ is the reflection of the graph of $y = f(x)$ in the *y*-axis. This means that the points $(x, \sqrt{x})$ and $(-x, \sqrt{x})$, with $x \geq 0$, are the same distance from but on opposite sides of the *y*-axis. See Figure A.31.

TABLE A.7

x	$f(x) = \sqrt{x}$	$-x$	$g(x) = \sqrt{-x}$
-4	Undefined	4	2
-1	Undefined	1	1
0	0	0	0
1	1	-1	Undefined
4	2	-4	Undefined

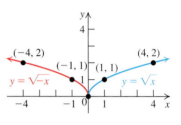

FIGURE A.31 Graphing $y = \sqrt{-x}$

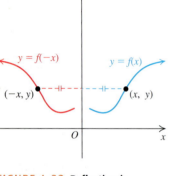

FIGURE A.32 Reflection in the *y*-axis

REFLECTION IN THE *y*-AXIS

The graph of $y = f(-x)$ is a reflection of the graph of $y = f(x)$ in the *y*-axis. If a point (x, y) is on the graph of $y = f(x)$, then the point $(-x, y)$ is on the graph of $y = f(-x)$. See Figure A.32.

EXAMPLE 4 **Combining Transformations**

Explain how the graph of $y = -|x - 2| + 3$ can be obtained from the graph of $y = |x|$.

SOLUTION

Start with the graph of $y = |x|$. Follow the point $(0, 0)$ in $y = |x|$. See Figure A.33(a).

Step 1 Shift the graph of $y = |x|$ two units to the right to obtain the graph of $y = |x - 2|$. The point $(0, 0)$ moves to $(2, 0)$. See Figure A.33(b).

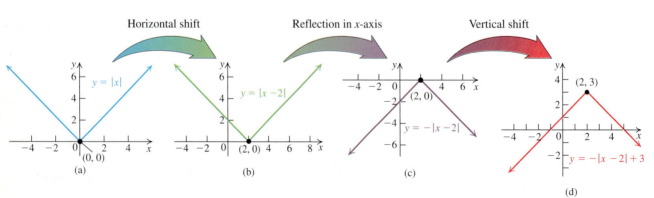

FIGURE A.33 Transformations of $y = |x|$

Step 2   Reflect the graph of $y = |x - 2|$ in the x-axis to obtain the graph of $y = -|x - 2|$. The point $(2, 0)$ remains $(2, 0)$. See Figure A.33(c).

Step 3   Finally, shift the graph of $y = -|x - 2|$ three units up to obtain the graph of $y = -|x - 2| + 3$. The point $(2, 0)$ moves to $(2, 3)$. See Figure A.33(d).

■ ■ ■

Practice Problem 4   Explain how the graph of $y = -(x - 1)^2 + 2$ can be obtained from the graph of $y = x^2$.

■

4 ▸ Use stretching or compressing to graph functions.

Stretching or Compressing

The transformations that shift or reflect a graph change only the graph's position, not its shape. Such transformations are called **rigid transformations**. We now look at transformations that distort the shape of a graph, called **nonrigid transformations**. We consider the relationship of the graphs of $y = af(x)$ and $y = f(bx)$ to the graph of $y = f(x)$.

Comparing the Graphs of $y = f(x)$ and $y = af(x)$

EXAMPLE 5   **Stretching or Compressing a Function Vertically**

Let $f(x) = |x|, g(x) = 2|x|$, and $h(x) = \dfrac{1}{2}|x|$. Sketch the graphs of f, g, and h on the same coordinate plane and describe how the graphs of g and h are related to the graph of f.

SOLUTION

The graphs of $y = |x|, y = 2|x|$, and $y = \dfrac{1}{2}|x|$ are sketched in Figure A.34. Table A.8 gives some typical function values.

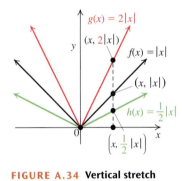

FIGURE A.34 Vertical stretch and compression

TABLE A.8

x	$f(x) = |x|$	$g(x) = 2|x|$	$h(x) = \dfrac{1}{2}|x|$
-2	2	4	1
-1	1	2	$\dfrac{1}{2}$
0	0	0	0
1	1	2	$\dfrac{1}{2}$
2	2	4	1

The graph of $y = 2|x|$ is the graph of $y = |x|$ vertically stretched (expanded) by multiplying each of its y-coordinates by 2. It is twice as high as the graph of $|x|$ at every real number x. The result is a taller V-shaped curve. See Figure A.34.

The graph $y = \dfrac{1}{2}|x|$ is the graph of $y = |x|$ vertically compressed (shrunk) by multiplying each of its y-coordinates by $\dfrac{1}{2}$. It is half as high as the graph of $|x|$ at every real number x. The result is a flatter V-shaped curve. See Figure A.34.   ■ ■ ■

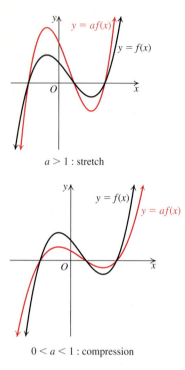

$a > 1$: stretch

$0 < a < 1$: compression

FIGURE A.35 Vertical stretch or compression

Practice Problem 5 Let $f(x) = \sqrt{x}$ and $g(x) = 2\sqrt{x}$. Sketch the graphs of f and g on the same coordinate plane and describe how the graph of g is related to the graph of f. ■

VERTICAL STRETCHING OR COMPRESSING

The graph of $y = af(x)$ is obtained from the graph of $y = f(x)$ by multiplying the y-coordinate of each point on the graph of $y = f(x)$ by a and leaving the x-coordinate unchanged. The result (see Figure A.35) is as follows:

1. A **vertical stretch** away from the x-axis if $a > 1$
2. A **vertical compression** toward the x-axis if $0 < a < 1$

If $a < 0$, graph $y = |a|f(x)$ by stretching or compressing the graph of $y = f(x)$ vertically. Then reflect the resulting graph in the x-axis.

Comparing the Graphs of $y = f(x)$ and $y = f(bx)$ Given a function $f(x)$, let's explore the effect of the constant b in graphing the function $y = f(bx)$. Consider the graphs of $y = f(x)$ and $y = f(2x)$ in Figure A.36(a). Multiplying the *independent* variable x by 2 compresses the graph $y = f(x)$ horizontally toward the y-axis. Because the value $\frac{1}{2}x$ is half the value of x, and $f\left(2\left[\frac{1}{2}x\right]\right) = f(x)$, a point on the x-axis will be only half as far from the origin when $y = f(2x)$ has the same y value as $y = f(x)$. See Figure A.36(a).

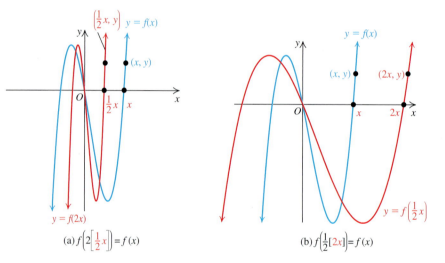

(a) $f\left(2\left[\frac{1}{2}x\right]\right) = f(x)$

(b) $f\left(\frac{1}{2}[2x]\right) = f(x)$

FIGURE A.36 Horizontal stretch or compression

Now consider the graphs of $y = f(x)$ and $y = f\left(\frac{1}{2}x\right)$ in Figure A.36(b). Multiplying the *independent* variable x by $\frac{1}{2}$ stretches the graph of $y = f(x)$ horizontally away from the y-axis. Because the value $2x$ is twice the value of x, and $f\left(\frac{1}{2}[2x]\right) = f(x)$, a point on the x-axis will be twice as far from the origin when $y = f\left(\frac{1}{2}x\right)$ has the same y value as $y = f(x)$. See Figure A.36(b).

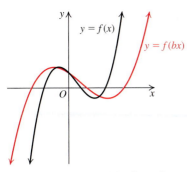

0 < b < 1 : stretch horizontally

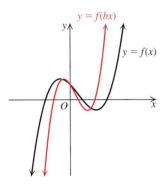

b > 1 : compress horizontally

FIGURE A.37 Horizontal stretch and compression

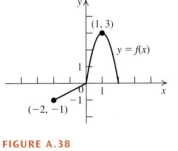

FIGURE A.38

HORIZONTAL STRETCHING OR COMPRESSING

The graph of $y = f(bx)$ is obtained from the graph of $y = f(x)$ by multiplying the x-coordinate of each point on the graph of $y = f(x)$ by $\dfrac{1}{b}$ and leaving the y-coordinate unchanged. The result (see Figure A.37) is as follows:

1. A **horizontal stretch** away from the y-axis if $0 < b < 1$
2. A **horizontal compression** toward the y-axis if $b > 1$

If $b < 0$, graph $f(|b|x)$ by stretching or compressing the graph of $y = f(x)$ horizontally. Then reflect the graph of $y = f(|b|x)$ in the y-axis.

EXAMPLE 6   **Stretching or Compressing a Function Horizontally**

Using the graph of the function $y = f(x)$ in Figure A.38, whose formula is not given, sketch the following graphs.

a. $f\left(\dfrac{1}{2}x\right)$ **b.** $f(2x)$ **c.** $f(-2x)$

SOLUTION

a. To graph $y = f\left(\dfrac{1}{2}x\right)$, we stretch the graph of $y = f(x)$ horizontally by a factor of 2. In other words, we transform each point (x, y) in Figure A.38 to the point $(2x, y)$ in Figure A.39(a).

b. To graph $y = f(2x)$, we compress the graph of $y = f(x)$ horizontally by a factor of $\dfrac{1}{2}$. Therefore, we transform each point (x, y) in Figure A.38 to $\left(\dfrac{1}{2}x, y\right)$ in Figure A.39(b).

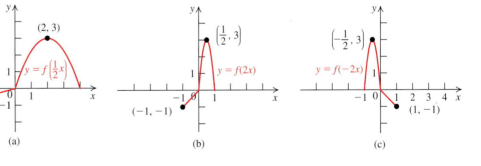

(a)   (b)   (c)

FIGURE A.39

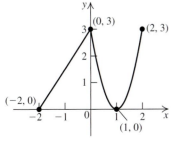

c. To graph $y = f(-2x)$, we reflect the graph of $y = f(2x)$ in Figure A.39(b) in the y-axis. So we transform each point (x, y) in Figure A.39(b) to the point $(-x, y)$ in Figure A.39(c). ■■■

Practice Problem 6   The graph of a function $y = f(x)$ is given in the margin. Sketch the graphs of the following functions.

a. $f\left(\dfrac{1}{2}x\right)$ **b.** $f(2x)$ ■

Multiple Transformations in Sequence

When graphing requires more than one transformation of a basic function, it is helpful to perform transformations in the following order:

1. Horizontal shifts   **2.** Stretch or compress   **3.** Reflections   **4.** Vertical shifts

---

EXAMPLE 7   Combining Transformations

Sketch the graph of the function $f(x) = 3 - 2(x - 1)^2$.

SOLUTION

Begin with the basic function $y = x^2$. Then apply the necessary transformations in a sequence of steps. The result of each step is shown in Figure A.40.

Step 1 $y = x^2$ Identify a related function whose graph is familiar. In this case, use $y = x^2$. See Figure A.40(a).

Step 2 $y = (x - 1)^2$ Replace x with $x - 1$; shift the graph of $y = x^2$ one unit to the right. See Figure A.40(b).

Step 3 $y = 2(x - 1)^2$ Multiply by 2; stretch the graph of $y = (x - 1)^2$ vertically by a factor of 2. See Figure A.40(c).

Step 4 $y = -2(x - 1)^2$ Multiply by -1. Reflect the graph of $y = 2(x - 1)^2$ in the x-axis. See Figure A.40(d).

Step 5 $y = 3 - 2(x - 1)^2$ Add 3. Shift the graph of $y = -2(x - 1)^2$ three units up. See Figure A.40(e).

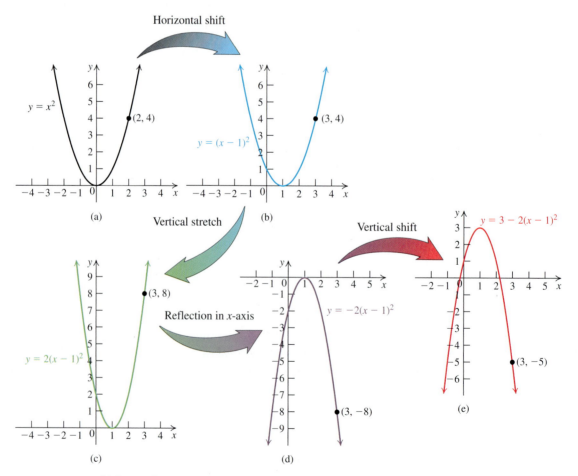

FIGURE A.40 Multiple transformations

Practice Problem 7 Sketch the graph of the function

$$f(x) = 3\sqrt{x + 1} - 2.$$

■

Summary of Transformations of $y = f(x)$

To graph	Draw the graph of f and	Make these changes to the equation $y = f(x)$	Change the graph point (x, y) to
Vertical shifts for $c > 0$:			
$y = f(x) + c$	Shift the graph of f up c units.	Add c to $f(x)$.	$(x, y + c)$
$y = f(x) - c$	Shift the graph of f down c units.	Subtract c from $f(x)$.	$(x, y - c)$
Horizontal shifts for $c > 0$:			
$y = f(x + c)$	Shift the graph of f to the left c units.	Replace x with $x + c$.	$(x - c, y)$
$y = f(x - c)$	Shift the graph of f to the right c units.	Replace x with $x - c$.	$(x + c, y)$
Reflection in the x-axis:			
$y = -f(x)$	Reflect the graph of f in the x-axis.	Multiply $f(x)$ by -1.	$(x, -y)$
Reflection in the y-axis:			
$y = f(-x)$	Reflect the graph of f in the y-axis.	Replace x with $-x$.	$(-x, y)$
Vertical stretching or compressing:			
$y = af(x)$	Multiply each y-coordinate of $y = f(x)$ by $\|a\|$. The graph of $y = f(x)$ is stretched vertically away from the x-axis if $a > 1$ and is compressed vertically toward the x-axis if $0 < a < 1$. If $a < 0$, the graph is first reflected in the x-axis and then vertically stretched or compressed.	Multiply $f(x)$ by a.	(x, ay)
Horizontal stretching or compressing:			
$y = f(bx)$	Multiply each x-coordinate of $y = f(x)$ by $\dfrac{1}{\|b\|}$. The graph of $y = f(x)$ is stretched away from the y-axis if $0 < b < 1$ and is compressed toward the y-axis if $b > 1$. If $b < 0$, sketch the graph of $y = f(\|b\|x)$; then reflect it in the y-axis.	Replace x with bx.	$\left(\dfrac{x}{b}, y\right)$

A EXERCISES Basic Skills and Concepts

1. The graph of $y = f(x) - 3$ is found by vertically shifting the graph of $y = f(x)$ three units _____.

2. The graph of $y = f(x + 5)$ is found by horizontally shifting the graph of $y = f(x)$ five units to the _____.

3. The graph of $y = f(bx)$ is a horizontal compression of the graph of $y = f(x)$ if b _____.

4. The graph of $y = f(-x)$ is found by reflecting the graph of $y = f(x)$ in the _____.

5. *True or False* The graph of $y = f(x)$ and $y = f(-x)$ cannot be the same.

6. *True or False* You get the same graph by shifting the graph of $y = x^2$ up two units, reflecting the shifted graph in the x-axis or reflecting the graph of $y = x^2$ in the x-axis, and then shifting the reflected graph up two units.

In Exercises 7–20, describe the transformations that produce the graphs of g and h from the graph of f.

7. $f(x) = \sqrt{x}$
   a. $g(x) = \sqrt{x} + 2$ b. $h(x) = \sqrt{x} - 1$

8. $f(x) = |x|$
   a. $g(x) = |x| + 1$ b. $h(x) = |x| - 2$

9. $f(x) = x^2$
   a. $g(x) = (x + 1)^2$ b. $h(x) = (x - 2)^2$

10. $f(x) = \dfrac{1}{x}$
    a. $g(x) = \dfrac{1}{x + 2}$ b. $h(x) = \dfrac{1}{x - 3}$

11. $f(x) = \sqrt{x}$
    a. $g(x) = \sqrt{x + 1} - 2$
    b. $h(x) = \sqrt{x - 1} + 3$

12. $f(x) = x^2$
    a. $g(x) = -x^2$ b. $h(x) = (-x)^2$

13. $f(x) = |x|$
    a. $g(x) = -|x|$ b. $h(x) = |-x|$

14. $f(x) = \sqrt{x}$
    a. $g(x) = 2\sqrt{x}$ b. $h(x) = \sqrt{2x}$

15. $f(x) = \dfrac{1}{x}$
    a. $g(x) = \dfrac{2}{x}$ b. $h(x) = \dfrac{1}{2x}$

16. $f(x) = x^3$
    a. $g(x) = (x - 2)^3 + 1$
    b. $h(x) = -(x + 1)^3 + 2$

17. $f(x) = \sqrt{x}$
    a. $g(x) = -\sqrt{x} + 1$ b. $h(x) = \sqrt{-x} + 1$

18. $f(x) = [\![x]\!]$
    a. $g(x) = [\![x - 1]\!] + 2$ b. $h(x) = 3[\![x]\!] - 1$

19. $f(x) = \sqrt[3]{x}$
    a. $g(x) = \sqrt[3]{x} + 1$ b. $h(x) = \sqrt[3]{x + 1}$

20. $f(x) = \sqrt[3]{x}$
    a. $g(x) = 2\sqrt[3]{1 - x} + 4$
    b. $h(x) = -\sqrt[3]{x - 1} + 3$

In Exercises 21–32, match each function with its graph (a)–(l).

21. $y = -|x| + 1$ 22. $y = -\sqrt{-x}$

23. $y = \sqrt{x^2}$ 24. $y = \dfrac{1}{2}|x|$

25. $y = \sqrt{x + 1}$ 26. $y = 2|x| - 3$

27. $y = 1 - 2\sqrt{x}$ 28. $y = -|x - 1| + 1$

29. $y = (x - 1)^2$ 30. $y = -x^2 + 3$

31. $y = -2(x - 3)^2 - 1$ 32. $y = 3 - \sqrt{1 - x}$

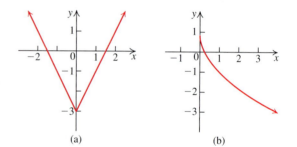

(a)   (b)

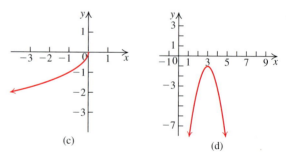

(c)   (d)

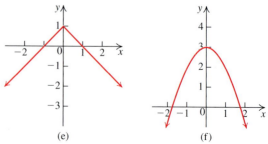

(e)   (f)

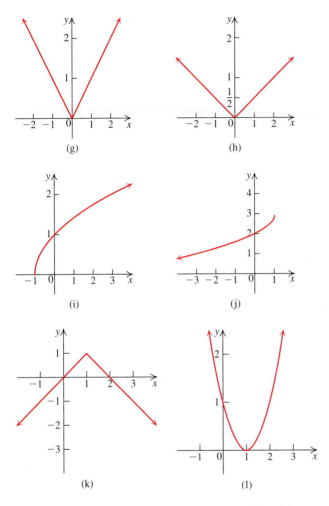

(g)

(h)

(i)

(j)

(k)

(l)

In Exercises 33–62, graph each function by starting with a function from the library of functions and then using the techniques of shifting, compressing, stretching, and/or reflecting.

33. $f(x) = x^2 - 2$

34. $f(x) = x^2 + 3$

35. $g(x) = \sqrt{x} + 1$

36. $g(x) = \sqrt{x} - 4$

37. $h(x) = |x + 1|$

38. $h(x) = |x - 2|$

39. $f(x) = (x - 3)^3$

40. $f(x) = (x + 2)^3$

41. $g(x) = (x - 2)^2 + 1$

42. $g(x) = (x + 3)^2 - 5$

43. $h(x) = -\sqrt{x}$

44. $h(x) = \sqrt{-x}$

45. $f(x) = -\dfrac{1}{x}$

46. $f(x) = -\dfrac{1}{2x}$

47. $g(x) = \dfrac{1}{2}|x|$

48. $g(x) = 4|x|$

49. $h(x) = -x^3 + 1$

50. $h(x) = -(x + 1)^3$

51. $f(x) = 2(x + 1)^2 - 1$

52. $f(x) = -(x - 1)^2$

53. $g(x) = 5 - x^2$

54. $g(x) = 2 - (x + 3)^2$

55. $h(x) = |1 - x|$

56. $h(x) = -2\sqrt{x - 1}$

57. $f(x) = -|x + 3| + 1$

58. $f(x) = 2 - \sqrt{x}$

59. $g(x) = -\sqrt{-x} + 2$

60. $g(x) = 3\sqrt{2 - x}$

61. $h(x) = 2[\![x + 1]\!]$

62. $h(x) = [\![-x]\!] + 1$

In Exercises 63–70, write an equation for a function whose graph fits the given description.

63. The graph of $f(x) = x^3$ is shifted two units up.

64. The graph of $f(x) = \sqrt{x}$ is shifted three units left.

65. The graph of $f(x) = |x|$ is reflected in the x-axis.

66. $f(x) = \sqrt{x}$ is reflected in the y-axis.

67. The graph of $f(x) = x^2$ is shifted three units right and two units up.

68. The graph of $f(x) = \sqrt{x}$ is shifted three units left, reflected in the x-axis, and shifted two units down.

69. The graph of $f(x) = x^3$ is shifted four units left, stretched vertically by a factor of 3, reflected in the y-axis, and shifted two units up.

70. The graph of $f(x) = |x|$ is shifted four units right, stretched vertically by a factor of 2, reflected in the x-axis, and shifted three units down.

In Exercises 71–78, graph the function $y = g(x)$ given the following graph of $y = f(x)$.

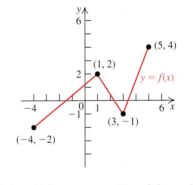

71. $g(x) = f(x) + 1$

72. $g(x) = -2f(x)$

73. $g(x) = f\left(\dfrac{1}{2}x\right)$

74. $g(x) = f(-2x)$

75. $g(x) = f(x - 1)$

76. $g(x) = f(2 - x)$

77. $g(x) = -2f(x + 1) + 3$

78. $g(x) = -f(-x + 1) - 2$

Inverse Functions

Objectives

1 Define an inverse function.

2 Find the inverse function.

3 Use inverse functions to find the range of a function.

---

1 Define an inverse function.

Inverses

DEFINITION OF A ONE-TO-ONE FUNCTION

A function is a **one-to-one function** if each y-value in its range corresponds to only one x-value in its domain.

Let f be a one-to-one function. Then the preceding definition says that for any two numbers x_1 and x_2 in the domain of f, if $x_1 \neq x_2$, then $f(x_1) \neq f(x_2)$. That is, f *is a one-to-one function if different x-values correspond to different y-values*.

Figure A.41(a) represents a one-to-one function, and Figure A.41(b) represents a function that is not one-to-one. The relation shown in Figure A.41(c) is not a function.

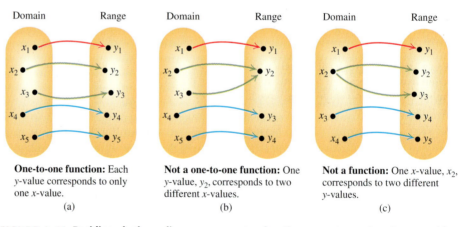

One-to-one function: Each y-value corresponds to only one x-value.

(a)

Not a one-to-one function: One y-value, y_2, corresponds to two different x-values.

(b)

Not a function: One x-value, x_2, corresponds to two different y-values.

(c)

FIGURE A.41 **Deciding whether a diagram represents a function, a one-to-one function, or neither**

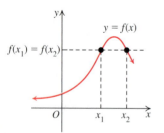

FIGURE A.42 **The function f is *not* one-to-one.**

With a one-to-one function, different x-values correspond to different y-values. Consequently, if a function f is *not* one-to-one, then there are at least two numbers x_1 and x_2 in the domain of f such that $x_1 \neq x_2$ and $f(x_1) = f(x_2)$. Geometrically, this means that the horizontal line passing through the two points $(x_1, f(x_1))$ and $(x_2, f(x_2))$ contains these *two* points on the graph of f. See Figure A.42. The geometric interpretation of a one-to-one function is called the *horizontal-line test*.

HORIZONTAL-LINE TEST

A function f is one-to-one if no horizontal line intersects the graph of f in more than one point.

EXAMPLE 1   **Using the Horizontal-Line Test**

Use the horizontal-line test to determine which of the following functions are one-to-one.

a. $f(x) = 2x + 5$ **b.** $g(x) = x^2 - 1$ **c.** $h(x) = 2\sqrt{x}$

SOLUTION

We see that no horizontal line intersects the graphs of f (Figure A.43(a)) or h (Figure A.43(c)) in more than one point; therefore, the functions f and h are one-to-one. The function g is not one-to-one because the horizontal line $y = 3$ (among others) in Figure A.43(b) intersects the graph of g at more than one point.

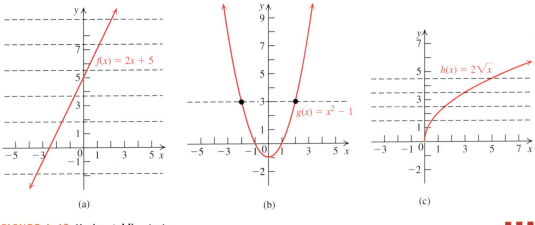

(a)   (b)   (c)

FIGURE A.43 **Horizontal-line test**   ■ ■ ■

Practice Problem 1 Use the horizontal-line test to determine whether $f(x) = (x - 1)^2$ is a one-to-one function.   ■

DEFINITION OF f^{-1} FOR A ONE-TO-ONE FUNCTION f

Let f represent a one-to-one function. Then if y is in the range of f, there is only one value of x in the domain of f such that $f(x) = y$. We define the inverse of f, called the **inverse function of f**, denoted f^{-1}, by $f^{-1}(y) = x$ if and only if $y = f(x)$.

From this definition we have the following:

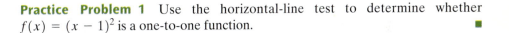

Domain of f = Range of f^{-1} and   Range of f = Domain of f^{-1}

◆ **WARNING**   The notation $f^{-1}(x)$ does not mean $\dfrac{1}{f(x)}$. The expression $\dfrac{1}{f(x)}$ represents the reciprocal of $f(x)$ and is sometimes written as $[f(x)]^{-1}$.

EXAMPLE 2   **Relating the Values of a Function and Its Inverse**

Assume that f is a one-to-one function.

a. If $f(3) = 5$, find $f^{-1}(5)$.   **b.** If $f^{-1}(-1) = 7$, find $f(7)$.

SOLUTION

By definition, $f^{-1}(y) = x$ if and only if $y = f(x)$.

a. Let $x = 3$ and $y = 5$. Now reading the definition from right to left, $5 = f(3)$ if and only if $f^{-1}(5) = 3$. Thus, $f^{-1}(5) = 3$.

b. Let $y = -1$ and $x = 7$. Now $f^{-1}(-1) = 7$ if and only if $f(7) = -1$. Thus, $f(7) = -1$.   ▪ ▪ ▪

Practice Problem 2   Assume that f is a one-to-one function.

a. If $f(-3) = 12$, find $f^{-1}(12)$.   **b.** If $f^{-1}(4) = 9$, find $f(9)$.   ▪

Consider the following input–output diagram for $f^{-1} \circ f$.

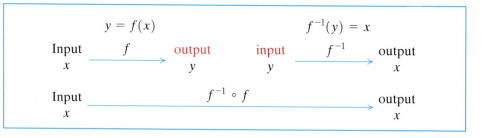

The preceding diagram suggests the following:

INVERSE FUNCTION PROPERTY

Let f denote a one-to-one function. Then

1. $f(f^{-1}(x)) = x$ for every x in the domain of f^{-1}.

2. $f^{-1}(f(x)) = x$ for every x in the domain of f.

Further, if g is any function such that (for the values of x in these equations)

$$f(g(x)) = x \quad \text{and} \quad g(f(x)) = x, \quad \text{then} \quad g = f^{-1}.$$

RECALL

The *composite* of a function f with a function g is written $f \circ g$ and defined as $(f \circ g)(x) = f(g(x))$

STUDY TIP

The reason that only a one-to-one function can have an inverse is that if $x_1 \neq x_2$ but $f(x_1) = y$ and $f(x_2) = y$, then $f^{-1}(y)$ must be x_1 as well as x_2. This is not possible because $x_1 \neq x_2$.

One interpretation of the equation $f^{-1}(f(x)) = x$ is that f^{-1} undoes anything that f does to x. For example, let

$$f(x) = x + 2 \qquad \text{\textit{f} adds 2 to any input } x.$$

To undo what f does to x, we should subtract 2 from x. That is, the inverse of f should be

$$g(x) = x - 2 \qquad \text{\textit{g} subtracts 2 from } x.$$

Let's verify that $g(x) = x - 2$ is indeed the inverse function of x.

$$f(g(x)) = f(x - 2) \qquad \text{Replace } g(x) \text{ with } x - 2.$$
$$= (x - 2) + 2 \qquad \text{Replace } x \text{ with } x - 2 \text{ in } f(x) = x + 2.$$
$$= x \qquad \text{Simplify.}$$

We leave it for you to check that $g(f(x)) = x$.

EXAMPLE 3 **Verifying Inverse Functions**

Verify that the following pairs of functions are inverses of each other.

$$f(x) = 2x + 3 \quad \text{and} \quad g(x) = \frac{x - 3}{2}$$

SOLUTION

$$f(g(x)) = f\left(\frac{x - 3}{2}\right) \qquad \text{Replace } g(x) \text{ with } \frac{x - 3}{2}.$$

$$= 2\left(\frac{x - 3}{2}\right) + 3 \qquad \text{Replace } x \text{ with } \frac{x - 3}{2} \text{ in } f(x) = 2x + 3.$$

$$= x \qquad \text{Simplify.}$$

So, $f(g(x)) = x$, for every x in the domain of g.

$$g(x) = \frac{x - 3}{2} \qquad \text{Given function } g$$

$$g(f(x)) = g(2x + 3) \qquad \text{Replace } f(x) \text{ with } 2x + 3.$$

$$= \frac{(2x + 3) - 3}{2} \qquad \text{Replace } x \text{ with } 2x + 3 \text{ in } g(x) = \frac{x - 3}{2}.$$

$$= x \qquad \text{Simplify.}$$

So, $g(f(x)) = x$ for every x in the domain of f. Because $f(g(x)) = g(f(x)) = x$, f and g are inverses of each other. ■ ■ ■

Practice Problem 3 Verify that $f(x) = 3x - 1$ and $g(x) = \frac{x + 1}{3}$ are inverses of each other. ■

In Example 3, notice how the functions f and g neutralize (undo) the effect of each other. The function f takes an input x, *multiplies* it by 2, and *adds* 3; g neutralizes (or undoes) this effect by *subtracting* 3 and *dividing* by 2. This process is illustrated in Figure A.44. Notice that g reverses the operations performed by f *and* the order in which they are done.

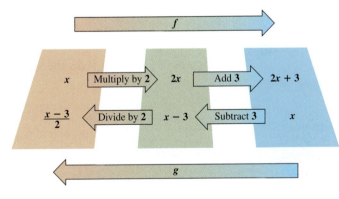

FIGURE A.44 **Function *g* undoes *f***

2 Find the inverse function.

Finding the Inverse Function

Let $y = f(x)$ be a one-to-one function; then f has an inverse function. Suppose (a, b) is a point on the graph of f. Then $b = f(a)$. This means that $a = f^{-1}(b)$; so (b, a) is a point on the graph of f^{-1}. The points (a, b) and (b, a) are symmetric with

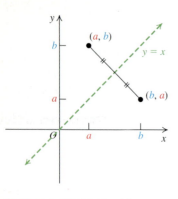

FIGURE A.45 Relationship between points (a, b) and (b, a)

respect to the line $y = x$, as shown in Figure A.45. That is, if the graph paper is folded along the line $y = x$, the points (a, b) and (b, a) will coincide. Therefore, we have the following property.

SYMMETRY PROPERTY OF THE GRAPHS OF f AND f^{-1}

The graph of a one-to-one function f and the graph of f^{-1} are symmetric with respect to the line $y = x$.

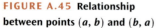 **Finding the Graph of f^{-1} from the Graph of f**

The graph of a function f is shown in Figure A.46. Sketch the graph of f^{-1}.

SOLUTION

By the horizontal-line test, f is a one-to-one function; so its inverse will also be a function.

The graph of f consists of two line segments: one joining the points $(-3, -5)$ and $(-1, 2)$ and the other joining the points $(-1, 2)$ and $(4, 3)$.

The graph of f^{-1} is the reflection of the graph of f in the line $y = x$. The reflections of the points $(-3, -5)$, $(-1, 2)$, and $(4, 3)$ in the line $y = x$ are $(-5, -3)$, $(2, -1)$, and $(3, 4)$, respectively.

STUDY TIP

It is helpful to notice that points on the x-axis, $(a, 0)$, reflect to points on the y-axis, $(0, a)$, and conversely. Also notice that points on the line $y = x$ are unaffected by reflection in the line $y = x$.

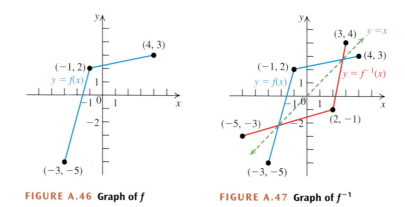

FIGURE A.46 Graph of f **FIGURE A.47** Graph of f^{-1}

The graph of f^{-1} consists of two line segments: one joining the points $(-5, -3)$ and $(2, -1)$ and the other joining the points $(2, -1)$ and $(3, 4)$. See Figure A.47. ▪ ▪ ▪

Practice Problem 4 Use the graph of a function f in Figure A.48 to sketch the graph of f^{-1}. ▪

The symmetry between the graphs of f and f^{-1} tells us that we can find an equation for the inverse function $y = f^{-1}(x)$ from the equation of a one-to-one function $y = f(x)$ by interchanging the roles of x and y in the equation $y = f(x)$. This results in the equation $x = f(y)$. Then we solve the equation $x = f(y)$ for y in terms of x to get $y = f^{-1}(x)$.

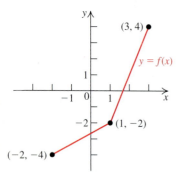

FIGURE A.48 Graphing f^{-1} from the graph of f

FINDING THE SOLUTION: A PROCEDURE

EXAMPLE 5 **Finding an Equation for f^{-1}**

OBJECTIVE	EXAMPLE
Find the inverse of a function.	*Find the inverse of $f(x) = 3x - 4$.*
Step 1 Replace $f(x)$ with y in the equation defining $f(x)$.	$y = 3x - 4$
Step 2 Interchange x and y.	$x = 3y - 4$

Step 3 Solve the equation in Step 2 for y.

$$x + 4 = 3y \qquad \text{Add 4 to both sides.}$$

$$\frac{x + 4}{3} = y \qquad \text{Divide both sides by 3.}$$

Step 4 Replace y with $f^{-1}(x)$.

$$f^{-1}(x) = \frac{x + 4}{3}$$

■ ■ ■

Practice Problem 5 Find the inverse of $f(x) = -2x + 3$.   ■

EXAMPLE 6   **Finding the Inverse Function**

Find the inverse of the one-to-one function

$$f(x) = \frac{x + 1}{x - 2}, \quad x \neq 2.$$

SOLUTION

Step 1 $\quad y = \dfrac{x + 1}{x - 2}$ Replace $f(x)$ with y.

Step 2 $\quad x = \dfrac{y + 1}{y - 2}$ Interchange x and y.

Step 3   Solve $x = \dfrac{y + 1}{y - 2}$ for y.   This is the most challenging step.

$$x(y - 2) = y + 1 \qquad \text{Multiply both sides by } y - 2.$$
$$xy - 2x = y + 1 \qquad \text{Distributive property}$$
$$xy - 2x + 2x - y = y + 1 + 2x - y \qquad \text{Add } 2x - y \text{ to both sides.}$$
$$xy - y = 2x + 1 \qquad \text{Simplify.}$$
$$y(x - 1) = 2x + 1 \qquad \text{Factor out } y.$$
$$y = \frac{2x + 1}{x - 1} \qquad \begin{array}{l}\text{Divide both sides by } x - 1 \text{ assuming} \\ \text{that } x \neq 1.\end{array}$$

Step 4 $\quad f^{-1}(x) = \dfrac{2x + 1}{x - 1}, \; x \neq 1$ Replace y with $f^{-1}(x)$.

To see if our calculations are accurate, we compute $f(f^{-1}(x))$ and $f^{-1}(f(x))$.

$$f^{-1}(f(x)) = f^{-1}\!\left(\frac{x + 1}{x - 2}\right) = \frac{2\!\left(\dfrac{x + 1}{x - 2}\right) + 1}{\dfrac{x + 1}{x - 2} - 1} = \frac{2x + 2 + x - 2}{x + 1 - x + 2} = \frac{3x}{3} = x$$

You also should check that $f(f^{-1}(x)) = x$.   ■ ■ ■

Practice Problem 6 Find the inverse of the one-to-one function $f(x) = \dfrac{x}{x + 3}$, $x \neq -3$.   ■

3 Use inverse functions to find the range of a function.

Finding the Range of a Function

It is not always easy to determine the range of a function that is defined by an equation. However, suppose a function f has inverse f^{-1}. Then the range of f is the domain of f^{-1}.

TECHNOLOGY CONNECTION

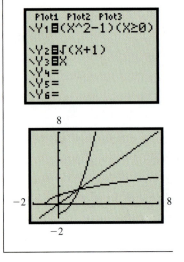

With a graphing calculator, you can also see that the graphs of $g(x) = x^2 - 1$, $x \geq 0$ and $g^{-1}(x) = \sqrt{x-1}$ are symmetric in the line $y = x$.

Enter Y_1, Y_2, and Y_3 as $g(x)$, $g^{-1}(x)$, and $f(x) = x$, respectively.

EXAMPLE 7 **Finding the Domain and Range**

Find the domain and the range of the function $f(x) = \dfrac{x+1}{x-2}$ of Example 6.

SOLUTION

The domain of $f(x) = \dfrac{x+1}{x-2}$ is the set of all real numbers x such that $x \neq 2$.

In interval notation, the domain of f is $(-\infty, 2) \cup (2, \infty)$.

From Example 6, $f^{-1}(x) = \dfrac{2x+1}{x-1}$, $x \neq 1$; therefore,

$$\text{Range of } f = \text{Domain of } f^{-1} = \{x \mid x \neq 1\}.$$

In interval notation, the range of f is $(-\infty, 1) \cup (1, \infty)$. ■ ■ ■

Practice Problem 7 Find the domain and the range of the function $f(x) = \dfrac{x}{x+3}$. ■

If a function f is not one-to-one, then it does not have an inverse function. Sometimes by changing its domain, we can produce an interesting function that does have an inverse. (This technique is frequently used in trigonometry.) We saw in Example 1(b) that $g(x) = x^2 - 1$ is not a one-to-one function; so g does not have an inverse function. However, the horizontal-line test shows that the function

$$G(x) = x^2 - 1, \quad x \geq 0$$

with domain $[0, \infty)$ is one-to-one. See Figure A.49. Therefore, G has an inverse function G^{-1}.

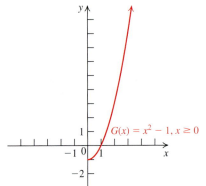

FIGURE A.49 The function G has an inverse

EXAMPLE 8 **Finding an Inverse Function**

Find the inverse of $G(x) = x^2 - 1$, $x \geq 0$.

SOLUTION

Step 1	$y = x^2 - 1, \quad x \geq 0$	Replace $G(x)$ with y.
Step 2	$x = y^2 - 1, \quad y \geq 0$	Interchange x and y.
Step 3	$x + 1 = y^2, \quad y \geq 0$	Add 1 to both sides.
	$y = \pm\sqrt{x+1}, \quad y \geq 0$	Solve for y.

Because $y \geq 0$ from Step 2, we reject $y = -\sqrt{x+1}$. So we choose

$$y = \sqrt{x+1}.$$

| Step 4 | $G^{-1}(x) = \sqrt{x+1}$ | Replace y with $G^{-1}(x)$. |

The graphs of G and G^{-1} are shown in Figure A.50. ■ ■ ■

FIGURE A.50 Graphs of G and G^{-1}

Practice Problem 8 Find the inverse of $G(x) = x^2 - 1$, $x \leq 0$. ■

SECTION A.5 ■ Exercises

A EXERCISES Basic Skills and Concepts

1. If no horizontal line intersects the graph of a function f in more than one point, then f is a(n) _____ function.

2. A function f is one-to-one when different x-values correspond to _____.

3. If $f(x) = 3x$, then $f^{-1}(x) =$ _____.

4. The graphs of a function f and its inverse f^{-1} are symmetric in the line _____.

5. *True or False* If a function f has an inverse, then the domain of the inverse function is the range of f.

6. *True or False* It is possible for a function to be its own inverse, that is, for $f = f^{-1}$.

In Exercises 7–14, the graph of a function is given. Use the horizontal-line test to determine whether the function is one-to-one.

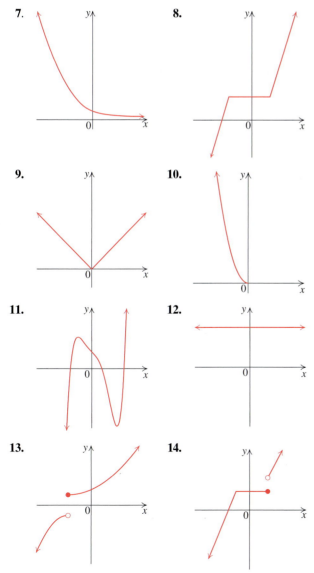

7.

8.

9.

10.

11.

12.

13.

14.

In Exercises 15–24, assume that the function f is one-to-one and that the given numbers are in the domain of f or f^{-1} as appropriate.

15. If $f(2) = 7$, find $f^{-1}(7)$.

16. If $f^{-1}(4) = -7$, find $f(-7)$.

17. If $f(-1) = 2$, find $f^{-1}(2)$.

18. If $f^{-1}(-3) = 5$, find $f(5)$.

19. If $f(a) = b$, find $f^{-1}(b)$.

20. If $f^{-1}(c) = d$, find $f(d)$.

21. Find $(f^{-1} \circ f)(337)$.

22. Find $(f \circ f^{-1})(25\pi)$.

23. Find $(f \circ f^{-1})(-1580)$.

24. Find $(f^{-1} \circ f)(9728)$.

25. For $f(x) = 2x - 3$, find each of the following.
    a. $f(3)$ b. $f^{-1}(3)$
    c. $(f \circ f^{-1})(19)$ d. $(f \circ f^{-1})(5)$

26. For $f(x) = x^3$, find each of the following.
    a. $f(2)$ b. $f^{-1}(8)$
    c. $(f \circ f^{-1})(15)$ d. $(f^{-1} \circ f)(27)$

27. For $f(x) = x^3 + 1$, find each of the following.
    a. $f(1)$ b. $f^{-1}(2)$ c. $(f \circ f^{-1})(269)$

28. For $g(x) = \sqrt[3]{2x^3 - 1}$, find each of the following.
    a. $g(1)$ b. $g^{-1}(1)$ c. $(g^{-1} \circ g)(135)$

In Exercises 29–34, show that f and g are inverses of each other by verifying that $f(g(x)) = x = g(f(x))$.

29. $f(x) = 3x + 1$; $g(x) = \dfrac{x - 1}{3}$

30. $f(x) = 2 - 3x$; $g(x) = \dfrac{2 - x}{3}$

31. $f(x) = x^3$; $g(x) = \sqrt[3]{x}$

32. $f(x) = \dfrac{1}{x}$; $g(x) = \dfrac{1}{x}$

33. $f(x) = \dfrac{x - 1}{x + 2}$; $g(x) = \dfrac{1 + 2x}{1 - x}$

34. $f(x) = \dfrac{3x + 2}{x - 1}$; $g(x) = \dfrac{x + 2}{x - 3}$

In Exercises 35–40, the graph of a function f is given. Sketch the graph of f^{-1}.

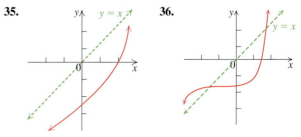

35.

36.

37.

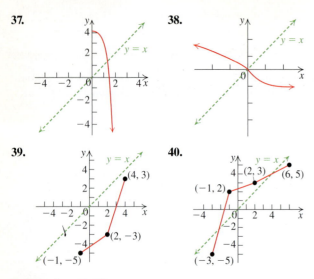

38.

39.

40.

47. $g(x) = \sqrt[3]{x + 1}$ **48.** $h(x) = \sqrt[3]{1 - x}$

49. $f(x) = \dfrac{1}{x - 1}, x \ne 1$ **50.** $g(x) = 1 - \dfrac{1}{x}, x \ne 0$

51. $f(x) = 2 + \sqrt{x + 1}$ **52.** $f(x) = -1 + \sqrt{x + 2}$

53. Find the domain and range of the function f of Exercise 33.

54. Find the domain and range of the function f of Exercise 34.

In Exercises 55–58, assume that the given function is one-to-one. Find the inverse of the function. Also find the domain and the range of the given function.

55. $f(x) = \dfrac{x + 1}{x - 2}, x \ne 2$ **56.** $g(x) = \dfrac{x + 2}{x + 1}, x \ne -1$

57. $f(x) = \dfrac{1 - 2x}{1 + x}, x \ne -1$ **58.** $h(x) = \dfrac{x - 1}{x - 3}, x \ne 3$

In Exercises 59–66, find the inverse of each function and sketch the graph of the function and its inverse on the same coordinate axes.

59. $f(x) = -x^2, x \ge 0$ **60.** $g(x) = -x^2, x \le 0$

61. $f(x) = |x|, x \ge 0$ **62.** $g(x) = |x|, x \le 0$

63. $f(x) = x^2 + 1, x \le 0$ **64.** $g(x) = x^2 + 5, x \ge 0$

65. $f(x) = -x^2 + 2, x \le 0$ **66.** $g(x) = -x^2 - 1, x \ge 0$

In Exercises 41–52,

a. determine whether the given function is a one-to-one function.

b. if the function is one-to-one, find its inverse.

c. sketch the graph of the function and its inverse on the same coordinate axes.

d. give the domain and intercepts of each one-to-one function and its inverse function.

41. $f(x) = 15 - 3x$ **42.** $g(x) = 2x + 5$

43. $f(x) = \sqrt{4 - x^2}$ **44.** $f(x) = -\sqrt{9 - x^2}$

45. $f(x) = \sqrt{x} + 3$ **46.** $f(x) = 4 - \sqrt{x}$

Answers

CHAPTER 1

Section 1.1

Practice Problems: **1.** $23°; 113°$ **2. a.** $61°28'22''$ **b.** $12°56'52''$
3. $13.16°$ **4.** $41°16'30''$ **5.**

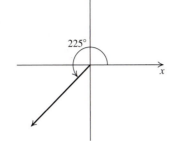

6. a. $45°; 45° + n \cdot 360°$, n any integer **b.** $150°; 150° + n \cdot 360°$,
n any integer **7.** $\theta = 225° + n \cdot 360°$ **8.** $\angle 2 = 57°; \angle 7 = 123°$

A Exercises: Basic Skills and Concepts: **1.** $360°$ **3.** initial
5. true **7. a.** $43°$ **b.** $133°$ **9. a.** No complement ($120° > 90°$)
b. $60°$ **11. a.** No complement ($210° > 90°$) **b.** No supplement
($210° > 180°$) **13.** $90° - \theta$ **15.** $180° - \theta$
17. $45°$ **19. a.** $61°17'$ **b.** $7°7'$
21. a. $60°8'$ **b.** $35°40'$ **23. a.** $29°23'$ **b.** $1°53'$
25. a. $124°30'15''$ **b.** $15°54'15''$
27. a. $20°42'58''$ **b.** $3°47'46''$
29. a. $408°31'40''$ **b.** $-32°38'34''$ **31.** $70.75°$ **33.** $23.71°$
35. $-15.72°$ **37.** $27°19'12''$ **39.** $13°20'49''$ **41.** $19°3'4''$
43. **45.**

47. **49.**

51. $40°; 40° + n \cdot 360°$, n any integer **53.** $345°; 345° + n \cdot 360°$,
n any integer **55.** $310°; 310° + n \cdot 360°$, n any integer
57. $320°; 320° + n \cdot 360°$, n any integer **59.** $45° + n \cdot 360°$, n any
integer **61.** $135° + n \cdot 360°$, n any integer **63.** $0° + n \cdot 360°$,
n any integer **65.** $180° + n \cdot 360°$, n any integer

B Exercises: Applying the Concepts: **67.** $18°$ **69.** $300°$
71. $x = 30$ **73.** $\alpha = 135°, \beta = 45°, \gamma = 135°, \theta = 45°$
75. $\alpha = 115°, \beta = 65°$ **77.** $70°$

C Exercises: Beyond the Basics: **79.** $x = 30; y = 20; z = 160$
83. $30°$

Critical Thinking: **84.** 6

Section 1.2

Practice Problems: **1.** $110°, 20°$, and $50°$ **2.** $10, 24$, and 26 ft
3. $1710\sqrt{2} \approx 2418$ ft **4.** $a = 3.5$ ft, $b = 6$ ft, and $c = 6.9$ ft
5. $x = 9; y = 4$ **6. a.** Triangles ADE and ABC are similar
because they have equal corresponding angles. **b.** $x = \dfrac{9}{2}; y = 10\dfrac{2}{3}$

A Exercises: Basic Skills and Concepts: **1.** $180°$ **3.** two; $\sqrt{3}$
5. true **7.** $58°$ **9.** $33°45'$ **11.** $68.28°$ **13.** $B = 38°; C = 82°$
15. $A = 30°; B = 60°; C = 90°$ **17.** 13 **19.** 12
21. $a = 5; b = 12$ or $a = 12; b = 5$ **23.** $a = 8; b = 15; c = 17$
25. $4\sqrt{2}$ **27.** $\dfrac{\sqrt{2}}{2}$ **29.** $3; 3$ **31.** $2\sqrt{2}; 2\sqrt{2}$ **33.** $8; 4\sqrt{3}$
35. $\dfrac{4\sqrt{3}}{3}; \dfrac{8\sqrt{3}}{3}$ **37.** $2; 2\sqrt{3}$
39. $\angle A \cong \angle Q$
$\angle B \cong \angle P$ $\dfrac{AB}{QP} = \dfrac{BC}{PR} = \dfrac{AC}{QR}$
$\angle C \cong \angle R$
41. $\angle P \cong \angle S$
$\angle R \cong \angle M$ $\dfrac{PR}{SM} = \dfrac{RQ}{MT} = \dfrac{PQ}{ST}$
$\angle Q \cong \angle T$
43. $\angle A \cong \angle A$
$\angle B \cong \angle D$ $\dfrac{AB}{AD} = \dfrac{BC}{DE} = \dfrac{AC}{AE}$
$\angle C \cong \angle E$
45. $\angle A = 180 - 64 - 43 = 73°; \angle D = 180 - 64 - 43 = 73°$
$\angle A \cong \angle D$
$\angle B \cong \angle E$
$\angle C \cong \angle F$
Corresponding angles are equal; $\dfrac{AB}{DE} = \dfrac{BC}{EF} = \dfrac{AC}{DF}$
47. $\angle A \cong \angle A'$
$\angle B \cong \angle B'$
$\angle C \cong \angle C'$
Corresponding angles are equal; $\dfrac{AB}{A'B'} = \dfrac{BC}{B'C'} = \dfrac{AC}{A'C'}$
49. $\angle A \cong \angle D$;
$\angle B \cong \angle C$;
$\angle O \cong \angle O$;
corresponding angles are equal; $x = 5$ and $y = 11.1$
51. $\angle A \cong \angle C; \angle B \cong \angle D; \angle O \cong \angle O$; corresponding angles are
equal; $x = 45$ and $y = 10\sqrt{13}$

B Exercises: Applying the Concepts: **53.** 15 ft **55.** $20\sqrt{3} \approx 34.6$ ft
57. $100\sqrt{3} \approx 173.2$ m **59.** $9\sqrt{3} \approx 15.6$ sq cm **61.** 48 ft **63.** 9 ft

C Exercises: Beyond the Basics: **77.** 45 cm
81. $180 - 2\left(180 - \dfrac{180}{n}(n - 2)\right)$ degrees

Critical Thinking: **83.** iv

Section 1.3

Practice Problems:

1. $\sin\theta = -\dfrac{12}{13}$ $\csc\theta = -\dfrac{13}{12}$

$\cos\theta = -\dfrac{5}{13}$ $\sec\theta = -\dfrac{13}{5}$

$\tan\theta = \dfrac{12}{5}$ $\cot\theta = \dfrac{5}{12}$

2. $\sin\theta = -\dfrac{5}{\sqrt{29}} = -\dfrac{5\sqrt{29}}{29}$ $\csc\theta = -\dfrac{\sqrt{29}}{5}$

$\cos\theta = \dfrac{2}{\sqrt{29}} = \dfrac{2\sqrt{29}}{29}$ $\sec\theta = \dfrac{\sqrt{29}}{2}$

$\tan\theta = -\dfrac{5}{2}$ $\cot\theta = -\dfrac{2}{5}$

3. a. $\sin 180° = 0$ $\csc 180° = $ undefined
$\cos 180° = -1$ $\sec 180° = -1$
$\tan 180° = 0$ $\cot 180° = $ undefined

b. $\sin 270° = -1$ $\csc 270° = -1$
$\cos 270° = 0$ $\sec 270° = $ undefined
$\tan 270° = $ undefined $\cot 270° = 0$

4. $\sin 1170° = \sin 90° = 1$
$\csc 1170° = \csc 90° = 1$
$\cos 1170° = \cos 90° = 0$
$\sec 1170° = \sec 90° = $ undefined
$\tan 1170° = \tan 90° = $ undefined
$\cot 1170° = \cot 90° = 0$

5. $\sin(-630°) = \sin 90° = 1$
$\csc(-630°) = \csc 90° = 1$
$\cos(-630°) = \cos 90° = 0$
$\sec(-630°) = \sec 90° = $ undefined
$\tan(-630°) = \tan 90° = $ undefined
$\cot(-630°) = \cot 90° = 0$

6. $\sin 60° = \dfrac{\sqrt{3}}{2}$ $\csc 60° = \dfrac{2}{\sqrt{3}} = \dfrac{2\sqrt{3}}{3}$

$\cos 60° = \dfrac{1}{2}$ $\sec 60° = \dfrac{2}{1} = 2$

$\tan 60° = \dfrac{\sqrt{3}}{1} = \sqrt{3}$ $\cot 60° = \dfrac{1}{\sqrt{3}} = \dfrac{\sqrt{3}}{3}$

7. $\sin 405° = \dfrac{1}{\sqrt{2}} = \dfrac{\sqrt{2}}{2}$ $\csc 405° = \dfrac{\sqrt{2}}{1} = \sqrt{2}$

$\cos 405° = \dfrac{1}{\sqrt{2}} = \dfrac{\sqrt{2}}{2}$ $\sec 405° = \dfrac{\sqrt{2}}{1} = \sqrt{2}$

$\tan 405° = \dfrac{1}{1} = 1$ $\cot 405° = \dfrac{1}{1} = 1$

8. Quadrant II   **9.** $\sin\theta = -\dfrac{4\sqrt{41}}{41}$; $\sec\theta = \dfrac{\sqrt{41}}{5}$

10. Maximum height 153 ft; range 612.5 ft

A Exercises: Basic Skills and Concepts: **1.** $\sqrt{x^2 + y^2}$

3. $\csc\theta = \dfrac{r}{y}$; $\sec\theta = \dfrac{r}{x}$; $\cot\theta = \dfrac{x}{y}$ **5.** false

7. $\sin\theta = \dfrac{4}{5}$ $\csc\theta = \dfrac{5}{4}$ **9.** $\sin\theta = \dfrac{12}{13}$ $\csc\theta = \dfrac{13}{12}$

$\cos\theta = -\dfrac{3}{5}$ $\sec\theta = -\dfrac{5}{3}$ $\cos\theta = \dfrac{5}{13}$ $\sec\theta = \dfrac{13}{5}$

$\tan\theta = -\dfrac{4}{3}$ $\cot\theta = -\dfrac{3}{4}$ $\tan\theta = \dfrac{12}{5}$ $\cot\theta = \dfrac{5}{12}$

11. $\sin\theta = \dfrac{24}{25}$ $\csc\theta = \dfrac{25}{24}$ **13.** $\sin\theta = -\dfrac{7}{25}$ $\csc\theta = -\dfrac{25}{7}$

$\cos\theta = \dfrac{7}{25}$ $\sec\theta = \dfrac{25}{7}$ $\cos\theta = -\dfrac{24}{25}$ $\sec\theta = -\dfrac{25}{24}$

$\tan\theta = \dfrac{24}{7}$ $\cot\theta = \dfrac{7}{24}$ $\tan\theta = \dfrac{7}{24}$ $\cot\theta = \dfrac{24}{7}$

15. $\sin\theta = \dfrac{1}{\sqrt{2}} = \dfrac{\sqrt{2}}{2}$ $\csc\theta = \dfrac{\sqrt{2}}{1} = \sqrt{2}$

$\cos\theta = \dfrac{1}{\sqrt{2}} = \dfrac{\sqrt{2}}{2}$ $\sec\theta = \dfrac{\sqrt{2}}{1} = \sqrt{2}$

$\tan\theta = \dfrac{1}{1} = 1$ $\cot\theta = \dfrac{1}{1} = 1$

17. $\sin\theta = \dfrac{\sqrt{2}}{2}$ $\csc\theta = \dfrac{2}{\sqrt{2}} = \sqrt{2}$

$\cos\theta = \dfrac{\sqrt{2}}{2}$ $\sec\theta = \dfrac{2}{\sqrt{2}} = \sqrt{2}$

$\tan\theta = \dfrac{\sqrt{2}}{\sqrt{2}} = 1$ $\cot\theta = \dfrac{\sqrt{2}}{\sqrt{2}} = 1$

19. $\sin\theta = -\dfrac{1}{2}$ $\csc\theta = -\dfrac{2}{1} = -2$

$\cos\theta = \dfrac{\sqrt{3}}{2}$ $\sec\theta = \dfrac{2}{\sqrt{3}} = \dfrac{2\sqrt{3}}{3}$

$\tan\theta = -\dfrac{1}{\sqrt{3}} = -\dfrac{\sqrt{3}}{3}$ $\cot\theta = -\dfrac{\sqrt{3}}{1} = -\sqrt{3}$

21. $\sin\theta = -\dfrac{2}{\sqrt{29}} = -\dfrac{2\sqrt{29}}{29}$ $\csc\theta = -\dfrac{\sqrt{29}}{2}$

$\cos\theta = \dfrac{5}{\sqrt{29}} = \dfrac{5\sqrt{29}}{29}$ $\sec\theta = \dfrac{\sqrt{29}}{5}$

$\tan\theta = -\dfrac{2}{5}$ $\cot\theta = -\dfrac{5}{2}$

23. 1   **25.** 0   **27.** Undefined   **29.** 0   **31.** Undefined

33. -1 **35.** $\dfrac{\sqrt{3}}{2} + \dfrac{1}{2}$ **37.** $\dfrac{\sqrt{3}}{2} - \dfrac{1}{2}$ **39.** $\dfrac{1}{2}$ **41.** $\dfrac{1}{2}$

43. $\dfrac{\sqrt{3}}{2} + 1$ **45.** Quadrant III   **47.** Quadrant II

49. Quadrant IV   **51.** Quadrant II   **53.** -12 **55.** 24

57. $\sin\theta = -\dfrac{12}{13}$ $\csc\theta = -\dfrac{13}{12}$ **59.** $\sin\theta = \dfrac{4}{5}$ $\csc\theta = \dfrac{5}{4}$

$\cos\theta = -\dfrac{5}{13}$ $\sec\theta = -\dfrac{13}{5}$ $\cos\theta = -\dfrac{3}{5}$ $\sec\theta = -\dfrac{5}{3}$

$\tan\theta = \dfrac{12}{5}$ $\cot\theta = \dfrac{5}{12}$ $\tan\theta = -\dfrac{4}{3}$ $\cot\theta = -\dfrac{3}{4}$

61. $\sin\theta = \dfrac{3}{5}$ $\csc\theta = \dfrac{5}{3}$

$\cos\theta = -\dfrac{4}{5}$ $\sec\theta = -\dfrac{5}{4}$

$\tan\theta = -\dfrac{3}{4}$ $\cot\theta = -\dfrac{4}{3}$

63. $\sin\theta = -\dfrac{2\sqrt{2}}{3}$ $\csc\theta = -\dfrac{3\sqrt{2}}{4}$

$\cos\theta = \dfrac{1}{3}$ $\sec\theta = 3$

$\tan\theta = -2\sqrt{2}$ $\cot\theta = -\dfrac{\sqrt{2}}{4}$

B Exercises: Applying the Concepts: **65.** $H = 7.56$ ft; $t = 1.375$ sec; $R = 52.39$ ft   **67.** $H = 22.69$ ft; $t = 2.38$ sec; $R = 52.39$ ft

69. a. $y = x\tan(45°) - \dfrac{16\sec^2(45°)}{(80)^2}x^2$ **b.** 50 ft   **71.** 3.54 sec

73. 0.98 ft   **75. a.** 50 ft   **b.** 86.6 ft

C Exercises: Beyond the Basics: **77.** $\dfrac{4}{5}$ **79.** $-\dfrac{\sqrt{3}}{2}$

81. Triangle QON **83.** Triangle SOM **85.** $\dfrac{\sqrt{2}}{2}$; $-\dfrac{\sqrt{2}}{2}$; $-\sqrt{3}$

87. $-\dfrac{\sqrt{2}}{2}$; $\dfrac{1}{2}$; $-\dfrac{\sqrt{3}}{3}$ **89. a.** $Q(-y, x)$ **91.** $A = 45°$; $B = 15°$

93. 1   **95.** The value on the left is negative, but the value on the right is positive.   **97.** The value on the left is negative, but the value on the right is positive.   **99.** False. Two sides unequal for $\theta = 90°$.

Section 1.4

Practice Problems: **1. a.** $\theta' = 5°$ **b.** $\theta' = 30°30'$ **2.** $45°$

3. $70°$ **4.** $\cos(55°) \approx 0.57358$ **5.** $-\cot(60°) = -\dfrac{\sqrt{3}}{3}$

6. $-\sin(30°) = -\dfrac{1}{2}$

7. $\sin 570° = \sin 210° = -\sin 30° = -\dfrac{1}{2}$

$\cos 570° = \cos 210° = -\cos 30° = -\dfrac{\sqrt{3}}{2}$

$\tan 570° = \tan 210° = \tan 30° = \dfrac{\sqrt{3}}{3}$

$\csc 570° = \csc 210° = -\csc 30° = -2$

$\sec 570° = \sec 210° = -\sec 30° = -\dfrac{2\sqrt{3}}{3}$

$\cot 570° = \cot 210° = \cot 30° = \sqrt{3}$

8. 101.4 m   **9.** $60° + n \cdot 360°; 240° + n \cdot 360°$

A Exercises: Basic Skills and Concepts: **1.** *x*-axis   **3.** $\theta - 180°$
5. false   **7.** $46°$ **9.** $84°$ **11.** $12°$ **13.** $70°$ **15.** $35°$

17. $80°$ **19.** $50°$ **21.** $180°$ **23.** $\dfrac{\sqrt{3}}{2}; -\sqrt{3}; \dfrac{2\sqrt{3}}{3}$

25. $\dfrac{1}{2}; -\dfrac{\sqrt{3}}{2}; -\dfrac{\sqrt{3}}{3}$ **27.** $-\dfrac{\sqrt{3}}{2}; \dfrac{\sqrt{3}}{3}; -\dfrac{2\sqrt{3}}{3}$

29. $-\dfrac{\sqrt{3}}{2}; \dfrac{\sqrt{3}}{3}; -\dfrac{2\sqrt{3}}{3}$ **31.** $-\sqrt{3}; -\dfrac{\sqrt{3}}{3}; -\dfrac{2\sqrt{3}}{3}$

33. $\dfrac{\sqrt{3}}{2}; -\dfrac{\sqrt{3}}{3}; \dfrac{2\sqrt{3}}{3}$ **35.** $\dfrac{\sqrt{3}}{2}$ **37.** 1   **39.** -2 **41.** $\dfrac{\sqrt{2}}{2}$

43. $\dfrac{\sqrt{3}}{3}$ **45.** $-\dfrac{\sqrt{3}}{2}$ **47.** $\dfrac{1}{2}$ **49.** 1   **51.** 2   **53.** $\dfrac{\sqrt{3}}{3}$

55. $60°; 300°$ **57.** $120°; 300°$ **59.** not possible   **61.** $30°; 210°$
63. $90°$ **65.** $180°$ **67.** $90°; 270°$ **69.** No value of θ
71. $225° + n \cdot 360°; 315° + n \cdot 360°, n$ any integer
73. $30° + n \cdot 360°; 210° + n \cdot 360°, n$ any integer
75. $225°$ **77.** $120°$ **79.** $120°$ **81.** $135°$ **83.** $240°$

B Exercises: Applying the Concepts: **85.** $8\sqrt{3} \approx 13.86$ ft

C Exercises: Beyond the Basics: **87.** $-135°; -315°$

89. $-(\theta + 180°)$ **91. a.** $\sin(-\theta) = -\dfrac{b}{r} = -\sin \theta$

b. $\cos(-\theta) = \dfrac{a}{r} = \cos \theta$ **c.** $\tan(-\theta) = -\dfrac{b}{a} = -\tan \theta$

93. a. $\sin(180° + \theta) = -\dfrac{b}{r} = -\sin \theta$

b. $\cos(180° + \theta) = -\dfrac{a}{r} = -\cos \theta$

c. $\tan(180° + \theta) = \dfrac{-b}{-a} = \dfrac{b}{a} = \tan \theta$ **95.** $-\dfrac{\sqrt{3}}{2}$

97. $\dfrac{\sqrt{3}}{3}$ **99.** $\alpha = 37.5°, \beta = 7.5°; \alpha = 187.5°, \beta = 37.5°;$
$\alpha = 97.5°, \beta = 307.5°; \alpha = 127.5°, \beta = 97.5°$ **101.** $135°; 315°$

Section 1.5

Practice Problems: **1. a.** $\dfrac{1}{5}$ **b.** -2 **c.** $\dfrac{11}{5}$ **2.** $-\dfrac{12}{5}$

3. $\sin \theta = -\dfrac{\sqrt{5}}{5}$

$\cos \theta = -\dfrac{2\sqrt{5}}{5}$

$\tan \theta = \dfrac{1}{2}$

$\sec \theta = -\dfrac{\sqrt{5}}{2}$

4. $\sin \theta = \dfrac{\sqrt{5}}{3}; \tan \theta = -\dfrac{\sqrt{5}}{2}$

5. $\sin \theta = \dfrac{\sqrt{2}}{2}$ $\csc \theta = \sqrt{2}$

$\cos \theta = -\dfrac{\sqrt{2}}{2}$ $\sec \theta = -\sqrt{2}$

$\tan \theta = -1$ $\cot \theta = -1$

6. $\dfrac{2}{\sin \theta}$ **7.** The equation is not an identity. Let $\theta = 30°$.

A Exercises: Basic Skills and Concepts: **1.** $\cos \theta; \sin \theta; \tan \theta$

3. $\sin^2 \theta; \cos^2 \theta$ **5.** $1; \cot^2 \theta$ **7.** $\dfrac{3}{2}$ **9.** $\dfrac{1}{5}$ **11.** $-\dfrac{7}{2}$

13. $\dfrac{5}{12}$ **15.** $\dfrac{3}{\sqrt{13}}$ **17.** $-\dfrac{3}{\sqrt{13}}$ **19.** $\dfrac{16}{\sqrt{17}}$ **21.** $-\dfrac{5}{13}$

23. $-\sqrt{10}$ **25.** $-\dfrac{\sqrt{5}}{2}$

27. $\sin \theta = -\dfrac{3}{5}$ $\csc \theta = -\dfrac{5}{3}$ **29.** $\sin \theta = \dfrac{2\sqrt{5}}{5}$ $\csc \theta = \dfrac{\sqrt{5}}{2}$

$\cos \theta = -\dfrac{4}{5}$ $\sec \theta = -\dfrac{5}{4}$ $\cos \theta = \dfrac{\sqrt{5}}{5}$ $\sec \theta = \sqrt{5}$

$\tan \theta = \dfrac{3}{4}$ $\cot \theta = \dfrac{4}{3}$ $\tan \theta = 2$ $\cot \theta = \dfrac{1}{2}$

31. $\sin \theta = -\dfrac{2}{3}$ $\csc \theta = -\dfrac{3}{2}$ **33.** $\sin \theta = \dfrac{4}{5}$ $\csc \theta = \dfrac{5}{4}$

$\cos \theta = -\dfrac{\sqrt{5}}{3}$ $\sec \theta = -\dfrac{3\sqrt{5}}{5}$ $\cos \theta = -\dfrac{3}{5}$ $\sec \theta = -\dfrac{5}{3}$

$\tan \theta = \dfrac{2\sqrt{5}}{5}$ $\cot \theta = \dfrac{\sqrt{5}}{2}$ $\tan \theta = -\dfrac{4}{3}$ $\cot \theta = -\dfrac{3}{4}$

35. $\sin \theta = \dfrac{\sqrt{3}}{3}$ $\csc \theta = \sqrt{3}$ **37.** $\sin \alpha = -\dfrac{\sqrt{5}}{5}$ $\csc \alpha = -\sqrt{5}$

$\cos \theta = \dfrac{\sqrt{6}}{3}$ $\sec \theta = \dfrac{\sqrt{6}}{2}$ $\cos \alpha = -\dfrac{2\sqrt{5}}{5}$ $\sec \alpha = -\dfrac{\sqrt{5}}{2}$

$\tan \theta = \dfrac{\sqrt{2}}{2}$ $\cot \theta = \sqrt{2}$ $\tan \alpha = \dfrac{1}{2}$ $\cot \alpha = 2$

39. $\sin \beta = \dfrac{2\sqrt{2}}{3}$ $\csc \beta = \dfrac{3\sqrt{2}}{4}$ **41.** $\sin \theta = -\dfrac{5}{13}$ $\csc \theta = -\dfrac{13}{5}$

$\cos \beta = \dfrac{1}{3}$ $\sec \beta = 3$ $\cos \theta = -\dfrac{12}{13}$ $\sec \theta = -\dfrac{13}{12}$

$\tan \beta = 2\sqrt{2}$ $\cot \beta = \dfrac{\sqrt{2}}{4}$ $\tan \theta = \dfrac{5}{12}$ $\cot \theta = \dfrac{12}{5}$

43. $\sin \theta = \dfrac{3}{4}$ $\csc \theta = \dfrac{4}{3}$

$\cos \theta = -\dfrac{\sqrt{7}}{4}$ $\sec \theta = -\dfrac{4\sqrt{7}}{7}$

$\tan \theta = -\dfrac{3\sqrt{7}}{7}$ $\cot \theta = -\dfrac{\sqrt{7}}{3}$

45. $\sin \theta = -\dfrac{2\sqrt{5}}{5}$ $\csc \theta = -\dfrac{\sqrt{5}}{2}$

$\cos \theta = -\dfrac{\sqrt{5}}{5}$ $\sec \theta = -\sqrt{5}$

$\tan \theta = 2$ $\cot \theta = \dfrac{1}{2}$

47. $\sin \theta = -\dfrac{\sqrt{21}}{5}$ $\csc \theta = -\dfrac{5\sqrt{21}}{21}$

$\cos \theta = \dfrac{2}{5}$ $\sec \theta = \dfrac{5}{2}$

$\tan \theta = -\dfrac{\sqrt{21}}{2}$ $\cot \theta = -\dfrac{2\sqrt{21}}{21}$

49. 1   **51.** 2   **53.** 1   **55.** 2   **57.** 1   **59.** 0   **61.** -3

B Exercises: Applying the Concepts: **73.** $x = 20 \csc \theta$
75. $A = nr^2 \tan \left(\dfrac{180°}{n} \right)$ **77.** $\tan \theta = \dfrac{m_1 - m_2}{1 + m_1 m_2}$

C Exercises: Beyond the Basics: **79.** 1   **81.** 1   **83.** 2
85. 1   **87.** 1   **91.** $\dfrac{1}{6}$ **93.** $\dfrac{3}{4}$

Critical Thinking: **95. a.** $\cos \theta \geq 0$ for $0 \leq \theta \leq 90°$
b. The left side is negative, and the right side is positive.

96. False. Let $\alpha = 60°$ and $\beta = 30°$.   **97.** No. From $\tan \theta = \dfrac{\sin \theta}{\cos \theta}$,
we note that if two of the functions are negative then the third has to be positive.

Review Exercises

1. 22.2°   **3.** 64.26°
5. a. Quadrant III   **b.** Quadrant III

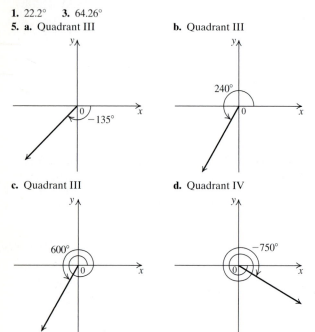

c. Quadrant III   **d.** Quadrant IV

7. a. $180° + n \cdot 360°$, n any integer   **b.** $315° + n \cdot 360°$, n any
integer   **9.** 12 cm; $6\sqrt{3}$ cm   **11.** True
13. $\sin \theta = \dfrac{4}{5}$ $\csc \theta = \dfrac{5}{4}$

$\cos \theta = -\dfrac{3}{5}$ $\sec \theta = -\dfrac{5}{3}$

$\tan \theta = -\dfrac{4}{3}$ $\cot \theta = -\dfrac{3}{4}$

15. $\sin \theta = -\dfrac{3\sqrt{13}}{13}$ $\csc \theta = -\dfrac{\sqrt{13}}{3}$

$\cos \theta = \dfrac{2\sqrt{13}}{13}$ $\sec \theta = \dfrac{\sqrt{13}}{2}$

$\tan \theta = -\dfrac{3}{2}$ $\cot \theta = -\dfrac{2}{3}$

17. $\sin \theta = 0$ $\csc \theta$ is undefined
$\cos \theta = 1$ $\sec \theta = 1$
$\tan \theta = 0$ $\cot \theta$ is undefined
19. $\sin \theta = 0$ $\csc \theta$ is undefined
$\cos \theta = -1$ $\sec \theta = -1$
$\tan \theta = 0$ $\cot \theta$ is undefined
21. Quadrant II   **23.** Quadrant III   **25.** Quadrant IV

27. $\sin \theta = \dfrac{12}{13}$ $\csc \theta = \dfrac{13}{12}$

$\cos \theta = -\dfrac{5}{13}$ $\sec \theta = -\dfrac{13}{5}$

$\tan \theta = -\dfrac{12}{5}$ $\cot \theta = -\dfrac{5}{12}$

29. $\sin \theta = \dfrac{3}{5}$ $\csc \theta = \dfrac{5}{3}$

$\cos \theta = \dfrac{4}{5}$ $\sec \theta = \dfrac{5}{4}$

$\tan \theta = \dfrac{3}{4}$ $\cot \theta = \dfrac{4}{3}$

31. 80°   **33.** 85°
35. $\sin 390° = \dfrac{1}{2}$ $\csc 390° = 2$

$\cos 390° = \dfrac{\sqrt{3}}{2}$ $\sec 390° = \dfrac{2\sqrt{3}}{3}$

$\tan 390° = \dfrac{\sqrt{3}}{3}$ $\cot 390° = \sqrt{3}$

37. $\sin (-495°) = -\dfrac{\sqrt{2}}{2}$ $\csc (-495°) = -\sqrt{2}$

$\cos (-495°) = -\dfrac{\sqrt{2}}{2}$ $\sec (-495°) = -\sqrt{2}$

$\tan (-495°) = 1$ $\cot (-495°) = 1$

39. $\sin \theta = \dfrac{5}{13}$ $\csc \theta = \dfrac{13}{5}$

$\cos \theta = \dfrac{12}{13}$ $\sec \theta = \dfrac{13}{12}$

$\tan \theta = \dfrac{5}{12}$ $\cot \theta = \dfrac{12}{5}$

41. $\sin \theta = \dfrac{1}{2}$ $\csc \theta = 2$

$\cos \theta = -\dfrac{\sqrt{3}}{2}$ $\sec \theta = -\dfrac{2\sqrt{3}}{3}$

$\tan \theta = -\dfrac{\sqrt{3}}{3}$ $\cot \theta = -\sqrt{3}$

43. $\sin \theta = -\dfrac{4\sqrt{17}}{17}$ $\csc \theta = -\dfrac{\sqrt{17}}{4}$

$\cos \theta = -\dfrac{\sqrt{17}}{17}$ $\sec \theta = -\sqrt{17}$

$\tan \theta = 4$ $\cot \theta = \dfrac{1}{4}$

45. $\sin \theta = -\dfrac{\sqrt{5}}{5}$ $\csc \theta = -\sqrt{5}$

$\cos \theta = \dfrac{2\sqrt{5}}{5}$ $\sec \theta = \dfrac{\sqrt{5}}{2}$

$\tan \theta = -\dfrac{1}{2}$ $\cot \theta = -2$

47. 0   **49.** 2

Chapter Test

1. 118°29′
2. $0° + n \cdot 360°$; $90° + n \cdot 360°$; $180° + n \cdot 360°$; $270° + n \cdot 360°$
3. 80°; 100°; 80°; 100°   **4.** 45°; 60°; 75°   **5.** 36°; 54°; 90°
6. Each side is $\dfrac{20}{\sqrt{2}} = 10\sqrt{2}$ cm.   **7.** true   **8.** 1.5 ft
9. $-\dfrac{\sqrt{5}}{5}$ **10.** $-\dfrac{\sqrt{13}}{3}$ **11.** Quadrant II   **12.** Quadrant IV
13. 55°   **14.** 80°   **15.** $-\dfrac{\sqrt{33}}{7}$ **16.** $\dfrac{13}{12}$ **19.** 0   **20.** 1

CHAPTER 2

Section 2.1

Practice Problems:

1. $\csc A = \dfrac{5}{3}, \sec A = \dfrac{5}{4}, \cot A = \dfrac{4}{3}$

   $\csc B = \dfrac{5}{4}, \sec B = \dfrac{5}{3}, \cot B = \dfrac{3}{4}$

2. **a.** $\sin 47°$ **b.** $\tan 20°$ **c.** $\csc 36°$ 3. $\theta = 25°$

4. $b = 2\sqrt{6}$

   $\sin A = \dfrac{1}{5}$ $\csc A = \dfrac{5}{1} = 5$

   $\cos A = \dfrac{2\sqrt{6}}{5}$ $\sec A = \dfrac{5}{2\sqrt{6}} = \dfrac{5\sqrt{6}}{12}$

   $\tan A = \dfrac{1}{2\sqrt{6}} = \dfrac{\sqrt{6}}{12}$ $\cot A = \dfrac{2\sqrt{6}}{1} = 2\sqrt{6}$

5. $5\sqrt{3} \approx 8.7$ feet   6. **a.** 0.9034   **b.** 0.6669

7. **a.** 56.7°   **b.** 11.2°   8. 14.5°

A Exercises: Basic Skills and Concepts:

1. $\dfrac{\text{opposite } A}{\text{hypotenuse}}; \dfrac{\text{adjacent to } A}{\text{hypotenuse}}; \dfrac{\text{opposite } A}{\text{adjacent to } A}$ 3. $\sin 63°$ 5. true

7. $\sin\theta = \dfrac{2\sqrt{5}}{25}$ $\csc\theta = \dfrac{5\sqrt{5}}{2}$

   $\cos\theta = \dfrac{11\sqrt{5}}{25}$ $\sec\theta = \dfrac{5\sqrt{5}}{11}$

   $\tan\theta = \dfrac{2}{11}$ $\cot\theta = \dfrac{11}{2}$

9. $\sin\theta = \dfrac{3}{5}$ $\csc\theta = \dfrac{5}{3}$ 11. $\sin\theta = \dfrac{9}{41}$ $\csc\theta = \dfrac{41}{9}$

   $\cos\theta = \dfrac{4}{5}$ $\sec\theta = \dfrac{5}{4}$ $\cos\theta = \dfrac{40}{41}$ $\sec\theta = \dfrac{41}{40}$

   $\tan\theta = \dfrac{3}{4}$ $\cot\theta = \dfrac{4}{3}$ $\tan\theta = \dfrac{9}{40}$ $\cot\theta = \dfrac{40}{9}$

13. $\cos 32°$ 15. $\cot 63°$ 17. $\csc 25°$ 19. $\theta = 30°$

21. $\theta = 60°$ 23. $\theta = 35°$ 25. $\theta = 15°$

27. $\sin\theta = \dfrac{3}{5}$ $\csc\theta = \dfrac{5}{3}$ 29. $\sin\theta = \dfrac{21}{29}$ $\csc\theta = \dfrac{29}{21}$

   $\cos\theta = \dfrac{4}{5}$ $\sec\theta = \dfrac{5}{4}$ $\cos\theta = \dfrac{20}{29}$ $\sec\theta = \dfrac{29}{20}$

   $\tan\theta = \dfrac{3}{4}$ $\cot\theta = \dfrac{4}{3}$ $\tan\theta = \dfrac{21}{20}$ $\cot\theta = \dfrac{20}{21}$

31. $\sin\theta = \dfrac{6}{7}$ $\csc\theta = \dfrac{7}{6}$

   $\cos\theta = \dfrac{\sqrt{13}}{7}$ $\sec\theta = \dfrac{7\sqrt{13}}{13}$

   $\tan\theta = \dfrac{6\sqrt{13}}{13}$ $\cot\theta = \dfrac{\sqrt{13}}{6}$

33. 0.5110   35. 1.1371   37. 0.6552   39. 1.1294   41. 2.8239
43. $\cos 11.8° \approx 0.9789$ 45. $\tan 31.16° \approx 0.6047$ 47. 23.6°
49. 58.1°   51. 36.7°   53. 32.6°

B Exercises: Applying the Concepts: 55. 4 feet   57. 19 feet   59. 60°

C Exercises: Beyond the Basics: 61. $\dfrac{1}{\sqrt{2}} = \dfrac{\sqrt{2}}{2}$

63. $a = 2; b = 2\sqrt{3}; c = 1; d = \sqrt{3}$
65. 4 units   67. $\sin\alpha < \sin\beta; \cos\alpha > \cos\beta$ 69. $\tan\alpha < \tan\beta$

Critical Thinking: 72. The tangent of the angle is equal to the slope of the line.

Section 2.2

Practice Problems: 1. $A = 40.8°; a \approx 11.0$ in.; $b \approx 12.8$ in.
2. $A \approx 39.0°; B \approx 51.0°; c \approx 12.3$ in.   3. 43 feet
4. 21 inches   5. 1.10 miles   6. 20,320 feet

A Exercises: Basic Skills and Concepts: 1. 514.5; 515.5   3. 63.6°
5. false   7. $B = 56°; a \approx 8.4$ in.; $b \approx 12$ in.
9. $A = 37.63°; a \approx 8.796; c \approx 14.41$
11. $A \approx 24.76°; B \approx 65.24°; c \approx 36.94$
13. $B = 66.3°; a \approx 0.937$ cm; $b \approx 2.13$ cm
15. $A = 57.4°; a \approx 54.1$ ft; $b \approx 34.6$ ft
17. $B = 27.08°; a \approx 28.8$ ft; $c \approx 32.3$ ft
19. $A = 61.53°; b \approx 2.843$ m; $c \approx 5.964$ m
21. $B = 18.63°; b \approx 14.38$ cm; $c \approx 45.02$ cm
23. $c \approx 19.9$ cm; $A \approx 51.5°; B \approx 38.5°$
25. $c \approx 19.3$ m; $A \approx 17.2°; B \approx 72.8°$
27. $B = 55°53'; a \approx 2.960$ ft; $b \approx 4.370$ ft   29. $x \approx 32; h \approx 37$
31. $h \approx 15; x \approx 11; a \approx 19$ 33. $h \approx 18; x \approx 13; a \approx 9.6$
35. $h \approx 2.8; x \approx 1.3$ 37. $B = 55°; x \approx 8.9$ 39. $r \approx 46; B = 49°$
41. $A \approx 10°; x \approx 52$

B Exercises: Applying the Concepts: 43. 258 feet   45. 43 feet
47. 37.8°   49. 25 feet   51. 94 feet

C Exercises: Beyond the Basics: 55. ≈ 20 square units   57. 40
61. **a.** $\dfrac{15}{17}$ **b.** $\dfrac{15}{8}$

Critical Thinking: 62. Find the length of the third side using the Pythagorean theorem. Find the angles using inverse trigonometric functions.   63. The triangle is similar to an infinite number of triangles having those angle measures.

Section 2.3

Practice Problems: 1. N 60° W   2. 62 miles   3. 243 feet
4. ≈ 43 ft   5. 3665 miles

A Exercises: Basic Skills and Concepts: 1. acute   3. north
5. true   7. N 10° E; N 75° E   9. S 35° W; S 65° W
11. N 45° E   13. due south   15. S 34° E

B Exercises: Applying the Concepts: 17. S 34° W
19. 136.5 miles north and 117.4 miles east   21. 51 miles
23. 7.98 miles   25. S 32.3° E   27. 106.7 feet   29. 18 feet
31. 80.7 meters   33. 15.8 feet   35. 234,884 miles
37. 32 feet   39. 2 feet   41. 16,766 square meters   43. 2.0 m
45. 2682 feet   47. 5402 meters

C Exercises: Beyond the Basics: 49. $25\sqrt{3}$ cm^2
51. $2\alpha + 2\beta = 180°$ 53. **a.** 108°   **b.** 36°; 36°
c. Draw the vertical from vertex B to the closest dashed line, splitting the length of that dashed line in half; thus, $\frac{1}{2}b$. Use this to find the cosine of the angle in the leftmost triangle at vertex A, which is $\dfrac{\frac{1}{2}b}{a}$, or $\dfrac{1}{2}\dfrac{b}{a}$.   **d.** Draw the vertical from vertex A, splitting the angle at the top of the middle triangle in half; thus, 18°. The sine of this angle is half of a over b, or $\dfrac{1}{2}\dfrac{a}{b}$.

Critical Thinking: 56. **a.** N 35° E   **b.** S 30° E   **c.** S 60° W
d. N 50° W

Review Exercises

1. $\sin \theta = \dfrac{3\sqrt{13}}{13}$ $\csc \theta = \dfrac{\sqrt{13}}{3}$

$\cos \theta = \dfrac{2\sqrt{13}}{13}$ $\sec \theta = \dfrac{\sqrt{13}}{2}$

$\tan \theta = \dfrac{3}{2}$ $\cot \theta = \dfrac{2}{3}$

3. $\sin 47°$ **5.** 90°   **7.** 25°

9. $\sin A = \dfrac{4}{8} = \dfrac{1}{2}$ $\csc A = \dfrac{8}{4} = 2$

$\cos A = \dfrac{\sqrt{3}}{2}$ $\sec A = \dfrac{2\sqrt{3}}{3}$

$\tan A = \dfrac{\sqrt{3}}{3}$ $\cot A = \sqrt{3}$

11. 0.7216   **13.** 1.0029   **15.** $\sin 14.2° \approx 0.2453$
17. 75.0°   **19.** 47.0°   **21.** $B = 54°; a \approx 11$ in.; $b \approx 15$ in.
23. $B = 68.2°; a \approx 0.713$ cm; $b \approx 1.78$ cm
25. $B = 28.58°; a \approx 27.9$ ft; $c \approx 31.8$ ft
27. $c \approx 21.7$ m; $A \approx 19.6°; B \approx 70.4°$ **29.** $h \approx 31; x \approx 25$
31. $h \approx 15; x \approx 12; y \approx 14$ **33.** $x \approx 8; B = 59°$
35. $A \approx 16°; x \approx 38$ **37.** N 45° E   **39.** S 26.6° W   **41.** 80 ft
43. 8.3 ft   **45.** 77.9 ft   **47.** 40,185 square meters
49. $\approx$8 feet 10 inches   **51.** 1013 feet   **53.** 4 feet 8 inches
55. 16.8 feet

Chapter Test

1. $\sin A = \dfrac{3}{5}; \cos A = \dfrac{4}{5}; \tan A = \dfrac{3}{4}$ **2.** $\dfrac{1}{1 + \sqrt{5}}$ **3.** 45°

4. $\sin A = \dfrac{5}{13}; \cos A = \dfrac{12}{13}; \tan A = \dfrac{5}{12}$ **5.** 4.2933

6. 21.0°   **7.** $B = 61.3°; a \approx 6.19$ in.; $b \approx 11.3$ in.
8. $c \approx 28.37$ cm; $A \approx 38.55°; B \approx 51.45°$ **9.** 17 feet
10. $x \approx 8.9; B = 58°$ **11.** 17 feet   **12.** 101.5 feet
13. 121 miles north; 70 miles west   **14.** N 38.1° W   **15.** 11.65 feet

CHAPTER 3

Section 3.1

Practice Problems: 1. $-\dfrac{\pi}{4}$ radian   **2.** 270°   **3.** $\dfrac{1}{2}$ **4.** QII

A Exercises: Basic Skills and Concepts: 1. $\dfrac{\pi}{180}$

3. $\dfrac{3}{2}$ radians   **5.** true   **7.** 4   **9.** $\dfrac{13}{5}$ **11.** 6   **13.** $\dfrac{\pi}{4}$

15. $\dfrac{5\pi}{6}$ **17.** $\dfrac{7\pi}{4}$ **19.** $-\pi$ **21.** $\dfrac{8\pi}{3}$ **23.** $-\dfrac{17\pi}{6}$ **25.** 0.33

27. 0.39   **29.** 2.19   **31.** 1.65   **33.** 90°   **35.** 480°   **37.** 300°
39. $-225°$ **41.** 450°   **43.** $-495°$ **45.** 117°   **47.** $-21°$ **49.** 401°

51. 166°   **53.** 392°   **55.** $-517°$ **57.** $\dfrac{1}{2}$ **59.** $\sqrt{3}$ **61.** $\sqrt{2}$

63. 0   **65.** $-\dfrac{\sqrt{3}}{3}$ **67.** $\dfrac{1}{2}$ **69.** 0   **71.** $2\sqrt{3}$ **73.** QI   **75.** QII

77. QIV   **79.** QIII

B Exercises: Applying the Concepts: 81. $\dfrac{2\pi}{3}$ radians

83. $\dfrac{4}{9}$ radians   **85.** 0.524 radian

C Exercises: Beyond the Basics: 87. $\dfrac{\sqrt{6} + \sqrt{2}}{4}$ **89.** 0

91. $\dfrac{\pi}{2} + \dfrac{\pi}{4}$ **93.** $\dfrac{\pi}{4} - \dfrac{\pi}{6}$ **95.** -2 **97.** $\dfrac{3\sqrt{3}}{2}$

99. new measure: $\dfrac{270°}{\pi} \approx 85.94°$; old measure: 97.18°

Critical Thinking: 100. Yes, because when changing from radians to degrees, you must multiply by a value greater than 1   **101.** No

Section 3.2

Practice Problems: 1. 7.85 meters   **2.** 3.7 feet   **3.** The radius of the wheel sprocket is one-third the radius of the pedal sprocket.
4. 790 miles   **5.** 52.36 square inches

A Exercises: Basic Skills and Concepts: 1. $r\theta$ **3.** $\dfrac{1}{2}r^2\theta$ **5.** false

7. 4π **9.** 15 m   **11.** 3π ft   **13.** 6.12π cm   **15.** $\dfrac{479}{600}\pi$ in.

17. 4 cm   **19.** 9 m   **21.** 6 ft   **23.** 4 m^2 **25.** 15.3 m^2
27. 271.44 ft^2 **29.** 33.96 cm^2 **31.** 401.43 mi^2 **33.** 9 ft
35. 4.125 radians

B Exercises: Applying the Concepts: 37. 19.9 in.   **39.** 3.1 ft

41. 0.7π radians   **43.** $\dfrac{5\pi}{6}$ radians   **45.** 84 feet   **47.** 525 miles

49. 359 miles   **51.** 8.016°   **53. a.** 0.2094155865 mile
b. 0.2094395102 mile   **c.** difference $\approx$ 0.000024; about 0.01% different   **55.** 361.28 in.^{2} **57.** 78.5 ft^2

C Exercises: Beyond the Basics: 59. 30.1 cm^2

61. a. $\dfrac{90}{\pi}$ degrees   **b.** 24 cm^2 **63.** 733 feet

Critical Thinking: 66. $3, \pi, 4, \dfrac{3\pi}{2}$ **67.** The line of latitude through 40°30'13"

Section 3.3

Practice Problems: 1. $-1; 0$; undefined   **2.** $-\dfrac{1}{2}; -\dfrac{\sqrt{3}}{2}; \dfrac{\sqrt{3}}{3}$

3. $-\dfrac{\sqrt{2}}{2}$ **4. a.** 0.1403   **b.** 1.1653   **c.** -0.8126 **5. a.** 0.2025

b. 0.2137   **6.** 49°

A Exercises: Basic Skills and Concepts: 1. origin; 1

3. $\cos s$ **5.** true   **7.** $1; 0$; undefined   **9.** $-\dfrac{\sqrt{3}}{2}; -\dfrac{1}{2}; \sqrt{3}$

11. $\dfrac{\sqrt{2}}{2}; \dfrac{\sqrt{2}}{2}; 1$ **13.** $\dfrac{1}{2}$ **15.** Undefined   **17.** $-\dfrac{\sqrt{3}}{2}$ **19.** 1

21. 0   **23.** 0   **25.** $\dfrac{2\sqrt{3}}{3}$ **27.** $\dfrac{\sqrt{3}}{2}$ **29.** 0.9887   **31.** -1.9725

33. 1.9828   **35.** -0.9978 **37.** -0.0806 **39.** -416.6671
41. Tangent, secant   **43.** Cotangent, cosecant   **45.** Cotangent, cosecant   **47.** Tangent, secant   **49.** Tangent, secant   **51.** 1.1195

53. 1.2635   **55.** 0.4162   **57.** $\dfrac{5\pi}{6}$ **59.** $\dfrac{7\pi}{4}$ **61.** $\dfrac{3\pi}{4}$

63. 0.54; 0.84   **65.** 0.28; -0.96 **67.** -0.99; -0.14

B Exercises: Applying the Concepts: 69. a. 100   **b.** 75   **71.** 1.5

C Exercises: Beyond the Basics: **73.** $\dfrac{1}{2}$ **75.** $\sqrt{2} + 5$ **77.** $-\dfrac{\sqrt{3}}{2}$

79. $-\dfrac{\sqrt{3}}{2}; -\dfrac{1}{2}$ **81.** $-0.4008; -0.9162$ **83.** $\dfrac{6001}{2}\pi; \dfrac{6003}{2}\pi; \dfrac{6005}{2}\pi;$

$\dfrac{6007}{2}\pi; \dfrac{6009}{2}\pi; \dfrac{6011}{2}\pi; \dfrac{6013}{2}\pi; \dfrac{6015}{2}\pi; \dfrac{6017}{2}\pi; \dfrac{6019}{2}\pi$ **85.** 2001

87. All real numbers $s; s \neq n\pi, n$ any integer

Critical Thinking: **89.** $\sin s = \sin t; \cos s = -\cos t$
90. $\sin s = -\sin u; \cos s = \cos u$ **91.** $\sin s = -\sin v; \cos s = -\cos v$

Section 3.4

Practice Problems: **1. a.** $\dfrac{\pi}{8}$ radian/sec **b.** four seconds

2. 36π radians per minute; ≈ 1131 feet per minute
3. a. 565 ft/min **b.** 18π radians per minute; 339 ft/min

A Exercises: Basic Skills and Concepts: **1.** average linear
3. linear speed **5.** false **7.** 3 ft/min **9.** 5 m/sec

11. 10 yd/sec **13.** $\dfrac{\pi}{10}$ radian/sec **15.** 2 radians/min

17. $\dfrac{35\pi}{6}$ radians/hr **19.** 75 in. **21.** 1357 m **23.** 162,860 ft
25. 0.28 radian **27.** 2.095 radians **29.** 1.309 m **31.** 78 m
33. 60 m/min **35.** 2 rad/sec

B Exercises: Applying the Concepts: **37.** 132,000 radians per hour
39. 84,823.00 inches per minute **41.** 0.64 radian per minute

43. 15.7 radian per minute **45. a.** $\dfrac{\pi}{30}$ radian per minute

b. $\dfrac{\pi}{5} \approx 0.628$ inch per minute **47.** 253,440 radians per hour

49. a. 120 radians per minute **b.** 300 radians per minute
51. 66,705.05 mph **53.** 11,100.29 km per hour

C Exercises: Beyond the Basics: **55.** 897.83 miles per hour

Review Exercises

1. 28 **3.** 0.08 **5.** $\dfrac{7\pi}{6}$ **7.** 225° **9.** −330° **11.** 4.32

13. −414.3° **15.** $-\sqrt{3}$ **17.** $14\pi \approx 43.98$ inches **19.** 20 cm
21. 3.63 m **23.** 27 ft **25.** 23.2 ft² **27.** 464.41 mi² **29.** 17.8 in.

31. 0.83 m² **33.** $\dfrac{\sqrt{3}}{2}; -\dfrac{1}{2}; -\sqrt{3}$ **35.** $\dfrac{\sqrt{3}}{2}; -\dfrac{1}{2}; -\sqrt{3}$ **37.** −1

39. 0.6548 **41.** −0.5369 **43.** 1.1717 **45.** cotangent, cosecant

47. $\dfrac{2\pi}{3}$ **49.** 2.5 ft/sec **51.** 18.75 yd/sec **53.** 3.2 rad/min

55. 24 in. **57.** 203,575.20 ft **59.** 141.37 ft/min **61.** 6.019°
63. a. 110 **b.** 129 **65.** 5.50 in.

Chapter Test

1. 4.5 radians **2.** $\dfrac{8\pi}{9}$ radians **3.** $-\dfrac{\pi}{6}$ radians **4.** 0.1222 radian

5. 126° **6.** −150° **7.** 160.428° **8.** $-\dfrac{\sqrt{2}}{2}$ **9.** $\dfrac{\sqrt{3}}{2}$ **10.** $\dfrac{\sqrt{3}}{3}$

11. $\sqrt{2}$ **12.** 0 **13.** $-\dfrac{\sqrt{3}}{2}$ **14.** $\dfrac{20\pi}{3} \approx 20.94$ in. **15.** 96°

16. 0.3770 in./sec **17.** $\dfrac{9\pi}{2} \approx 14.14$ in.² **18.** tangent, secant

19. 0.9623 **20.** $\dfrac{3\pi}{4}$

CHAPTER 4

Section 4.1

Practice Problems: **1.** $\cot(t + \pi) = \dfrac{-x}{-y} = \dfrac{x}{y} = \cot t$

A Exercises: Basic Skills and Concepts: **1.** $f(x)$ **3.** $2\pi; \pi$
5. false **7.** $(-\infty, \infty); [-1, 1]; 2\pi;$ odd; $x = n\pi; 0;$ none

9. $x \neq \dfrac{\pi}{2} + n\pi; (-\infty, \infty); \pi;$ odd; $x = n\pi; 0; x = \dfrac{\pi}{2} + n\pi$

11. $x \neq \dfrac{\pi}{2} + n\pi; (-\infty, -1] \cup [1, \infty); 2\pi;$ even; none; 1;

$x = \dfrac{\pi}{2} + n\pi$ **13.** increases from 0 to 1; decreases from 1 to 0;
decreases from 0 to −1; increases from −1 to 0 **15.** increases from
0 and approaches ∞; increases from values approaching −∞ to 0;
increases from 0 and approaches ∞; increases from values
approaching −∞ to 0 **17.** increases from 1 and approaches ∞;
increases from values approaching −∞ to −1; decreases from −1
and approaches −∞; decreases from values approaching ∞ to 1
19. $y = \cos x; y = \sec x$ **21.** $y = \sin x; y = \cos x$ **23.** $y = \sin x;$
$y = \cos x; y = \tan x; y = \cot x; y = \sec x; y = \csc x$ **25.** $y = \sin x;$
$y = \tan x$ **27.** $y = \tan x; y = \sec x$
35.   **37.**

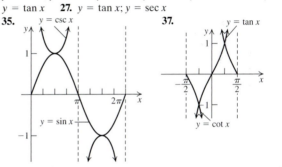

39. $0, \pm\pi, \pm 2\pi$ **41.** $0, \pm\pi, \pm 2\pi$ **43.** No x values **45.** $-\dfrac{3\pi}{2}, \dfrac{\pi}{2}$

47. $-\dfrac{7\pi}{4}, -\dfrac{3\pi}{4}, \dfrac{\pi}{4}, \dfrac{5\pi}{4}$ **49.** $0, \pm 2\pi$ **51.** $\pm\pi$ **53.** $-\dfrac{5\pi}{4}, -\dfrac{3\pi}{4}, \dfrac{3\pi}{4}, \dfrac{7\pi}{4}$

55. $-\dfrac{\pi}{2}, \dfrac{3\pi}{2}$ **57.** $0, \pm\pi, \pm 2\pi$ **59.** $\pm\dfrac{\pi}{2}, \pm\dfrac{3\pi}{2}$

C Exercises: Beyond the Basics:
67.   **69.** $\sin x: \left(0, \dfrac{\sqrt{2}}{2}\right); \cos x: \left(\dfrac{\sqrt{2}}{2}, 1\right);$

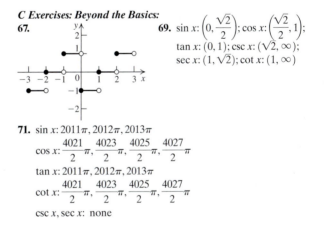

$\tan x: (0, 1); \csc x: (\sqrt{2}, \infty);$
$\sec x: (1, \sqrt{2}); \cot x: (1, \infty)$

71. $\sin x: 2011\pi, 2012\pi, 2013\pi$
$\cos x: \dfrac{4021}{2}\pi, \dfrac{4023}{2}\pi, \dfrac{4025}{2}\pi, \dfrac{4027}{2}\pi$
$\tan x: 2011\pi, 2012\pi, 2013\pi$
$\cot x: \dfrac{4021}{2}\pi, \dfrac{4023}{2}\pi, \dfrac{4025}{2}\pi, \dfrac{4027}{2}\pi$
$\csc x, \sec x:$ none

Critical Thinking: **76.** True

Section 4.2

Practice Problems: **1. a.** 5   **b.** 4   **c.** no amplitude

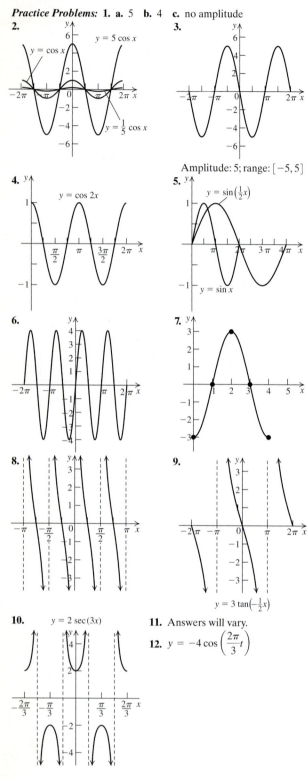

2. $y = 5 \cos x$, $y = \cos x$, $y = \frac{1}{5} \cos x$

3.   Amplitude: 5; range: $[-5, 5]$

4. $y = \cos 2x$

5. $y = \sin\left(\frac{1}{2}x\right)$, $y = \sin x$

6.

7.

8.

9. $y = 3 \tan\left(-\frac{1}{2}x\right)$

10. $y = 2 \sec(3x)$

11. Answers will vary.

12. $y = -4 \cos\left(\dfrac{2\pi}{3}t\right)$

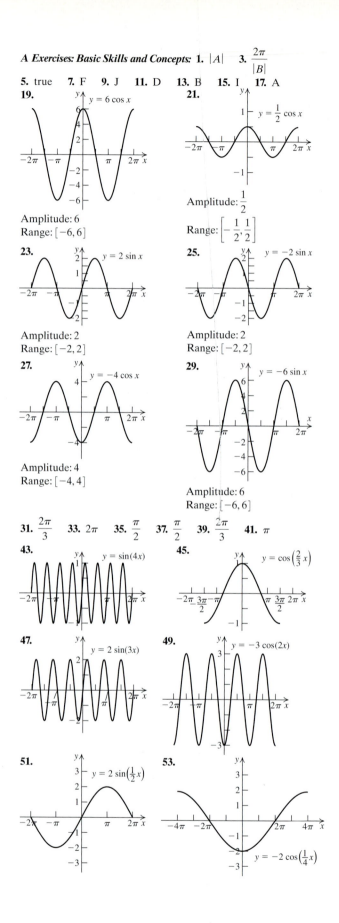

1. $|A|$ **3.** $\dfrac{2\pi}{|B|}$

5. true   **7.** F   **9.** J   **11.** D   **13.** B   **15.** I   **17.** A

19. $y = 6 \cos x$
Amplitude: 6
Range: $[-6, 6]$

21. $y = \frac{1}{2} \cos x$
Amplitude: $\dfrac{1}{2}$
Range: $\left[-\dfrac{1}{2}, \dfrac{1}{2}\right]$

23. $y = 2 \sin x$
Amplitude: 2
Range: $[-2, 2]$

25. $y = -2 \sin x$
Amplitude: 2
Range: $[-2, 2]$

27. $y = -4 \cos x$
Amplitude: 4
Range: $[-4, 4]$

29. $y = -6 \sin x$
Amplitude: 6
Range: $[-6, 6]$

31. $\dfrac{2\pi}{3}$ **33.** 2π **35.** $\dfrac{\pi}{2}$ **37.** $\dfrac{\pi}{2}$ **39.** $\dfrac{2\pi}{3}$ **41.** π

43. $y = \sin(4x)$

45. $y = \cos\left(\frac{2}{3}x\right)$

47. $y = 2 \sin(3x)$

49. $y = -3 \cos(2x)$

51. $y = 2 \sin\left(\frac{1}{2}x\right)$

53. $y = -2 \cos\left(\frac{1}{4}x\right)$

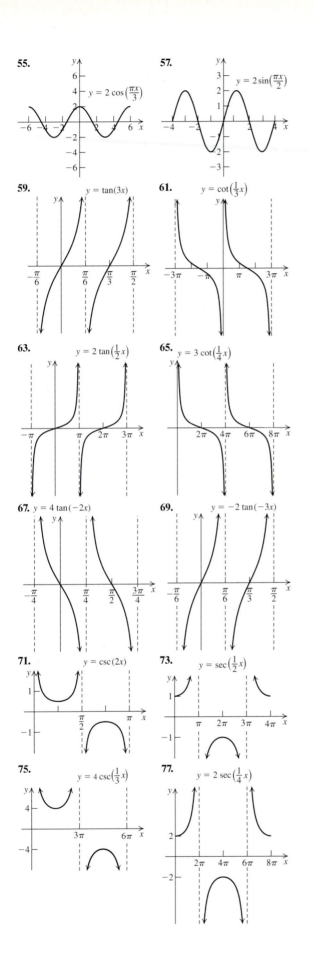

55. $y = 2\cos\left(\frac{\pi x}{3}\right)$

57. $y = 2\sin\left(\frac{\pi x}{2}\right)$

59. $y = \tan(3x)$

61. $y = \cot\left(\frac{1}{3}x\right)$

63. $y = 2\tan\left(\frac{1}{2}x\right)$

65. $y = 3\cot\left(\frac{1}{4}x\right)$

67. $y = 4\tan(-2x)$

69. $y = -2\tan(-3x)$

71. $y = \csc(2x)$

73. $y = \sec\left(\frac{1}{2}x\right)$

75. $y = 4\csc\left(\frac{1}{3}x\right)$

77. $y = 2\sec\left(\frac{1}{4}x\right)$

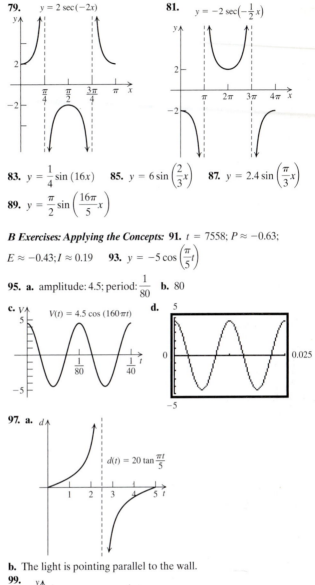

79. $y = 2\sec(-2x)$

81. $y = -2\sec\left(-\frac{1}{2}x\right)$

83. $y = \frac{1}{4}\sin(16x)$ **85.** $y = 6\sin\left(\frac{2}{3}x\right)$ **87.** $y = 2.4\sin\left(\frac{\pi}{3}x\right)$

89. $y = \frac{\pi}{2}\sin\left(\frac{16\pi}{5}x\right)$

B Exercises: Applying the Concepts: 91. $t = 7558$; $P \approx -0.63$;
$E \approx -0.43$; $I \approx 0.19$ **93.** $y = -5\cos\left(\frac{\pi}{5}t\right)$

95. a. amplitude: 4.5; period: $\frac{1}{80}$ **b.** 80

c.

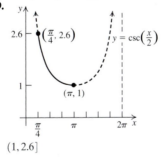

$V(t) = 4.5\cos(160\pi t)$

d.

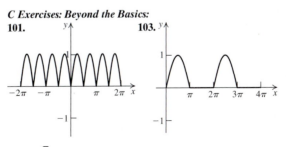

97. a.

$d(t) = 20\tan\frac{\pi t}{5}$

b. The light is pointing parallel to the wall.

99.

$\left(\frac{\pi}{4}, 2.6\right)$ $y = \csc\left(\frac{x}{2}\right)$

$(\pi, 1)$

$(1, 2.6]$

C Exercises: Beyond the Basics:

101.

103.

period: $\frac{\pi}{2}$

105. $y = 5\tan(2x)$ **107.** $y = 4\sec(2x)$ **109.** $A = -4; B = \dfrac{\pi}{4}$

111.

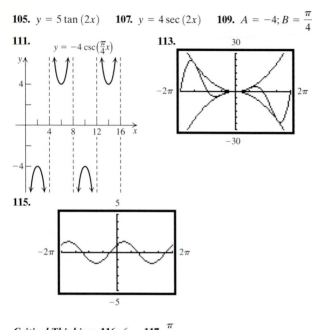

$y = -4\csc\left(\dfrac{\pi}{4}x\right)$

113.

8.

$y = 3.6\sin\left(\dfrac{\pi}{6}x - \dfrac{\pi}{2}\right) + 12.2$

A Exercises: Basic Skills and Concepts: **1.** $|A|; \dfrac{2\pi}{|B|}; 0$

3. $\dfrac{\pi}{2}$ **5.** false

7.

$y = \cos\left(x + \dfrac{\pi}{2}\right)$

9.

$y = \sin\left(x - \dfrac{\pi}{3}\right)$

115.

Critical Thinking: **116.** 6   **117.** $\dfrac{\pi}{5}$

11.

$y = \tan\left(x - \dfrac{\pi}{4}\right)$

Section 4.3

Practice Problems:

1.

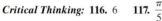

$y = \cos\left(x + \dfrac{\pi}{4}\right)$

13.

$y = \cot\left(x + \dfrac{\pi}{4}\right)$

15.

$y = \sec(x - \pi)$

2. a. start point: $-\dfrac{\pi}{12}$; end point: $\dfrac{7\pi}{12}$; phase shift: $\dfrac{\pi}{12}$ unit to the left

b. start point: $-\dfrac{\pi}{8}$; end point: $\dfrac{3\pi}{8}$; phase shift: $\dfrac{\pi}{8}$ unit to the left

c. start point: $-\dfrac{11}{3}$; end point: $\dfrac{1}{3}$; phase shift: $\dfrac{1}{3}$ unit to the right

3.

$y = \cos x$

$y = \cos x - 2$

4.

$y = 3\cos\left(2x - \dfrac{\pi}{2}\right) - 2$

17.

$y = \sin x - 1$

19.

$y = -\cos x + 1$

5.

6.

21.

$y = -\tan x + 1$

23.

$y = \sec x + 2$

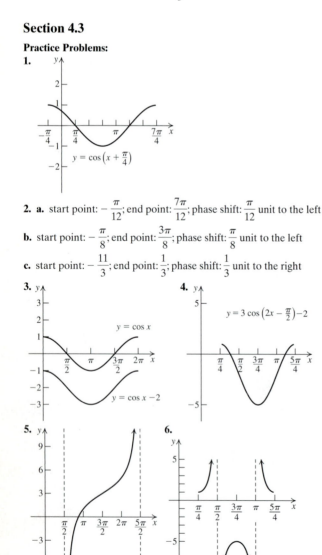

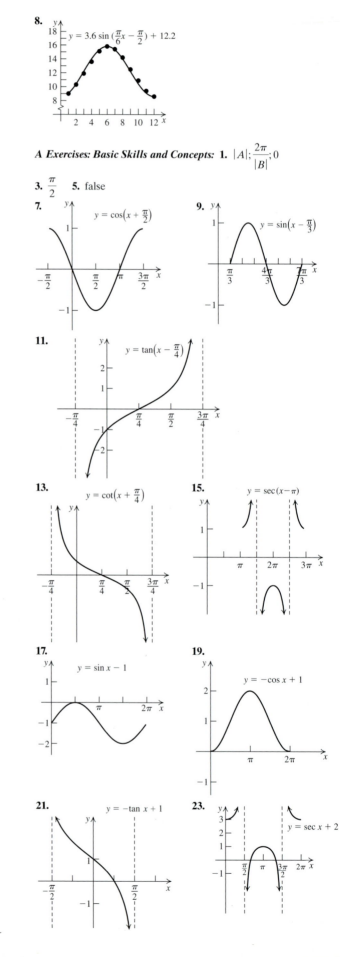

25. amplitude: 5
period: 2π
phase shift: π

27. amplitude: 7
period: $\dfrac{2\pi}{9}$
phase shift: $-\dfrac{\pi}{6}$

29. amplitude: 6
period: 4π
phase shift: -2

31. amplitude: 0.9
period: 8π
phase shift: $\dfrac{\pi}{4}$

33. amplitude: 4
period: π
phase shift: $-\dfrac{\pi}{6}$

35. amplitude: $\dfrac{3}{2}$
period: π
phase shift: $\dfrac{\pi}{2}$

37. amplitude: 3
period: 2
phase shift: $\dfrac{1}{\pi}$

39. amplitude: $\dfrac{1}{2}$
period: 8
phase shift: -1

41. amplitude: 2
period: 2
phase shift: $-\dfrac{3}{\pi}$

43. amplitude: none
period: $\dfrac{\pi}{2}$
phase shift: $\dfrac{\pi}{4}$

45. amplitude: none
period: 2π
phase shift: $-\dfrac{\pi}{2}$

47. amplitude: none
period: $\dfrac{3\pi}{2}$
phase shift: $\dfrac{\pi}{2}$

49. amplitude: none
period: $\dfrac{\pi}{2}$
phase shift: $-\dfrac{\pi}{3}$

51. amplitude: none
period: $\dfrac{\pi}{2}$
phase shift: π

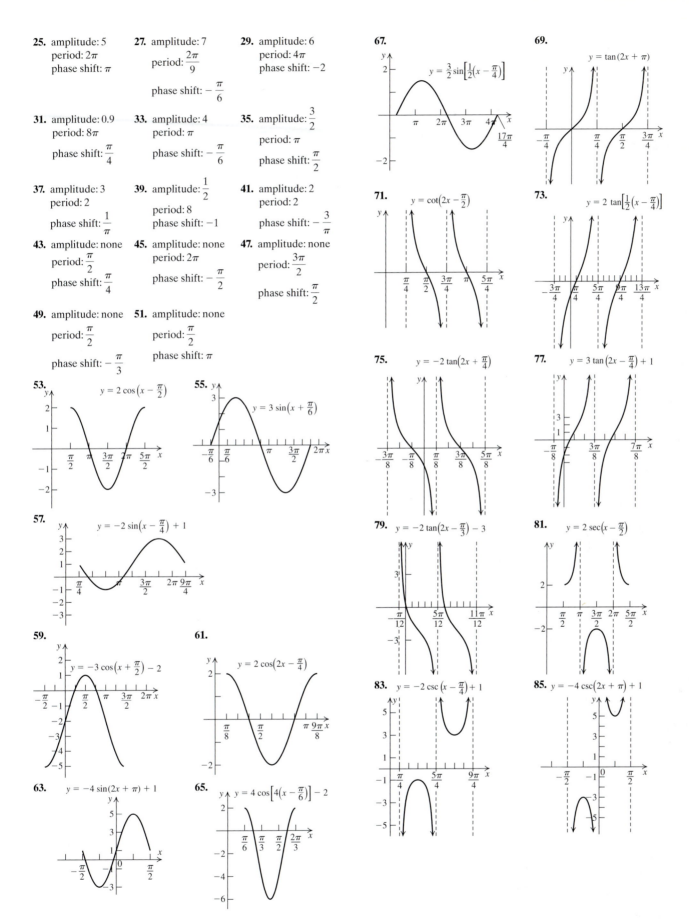

53. $y = 2\cos\left(x - \dfrac{\pi}{2}\right)$

55. $y = 3\sin\left(x + \dfrac{\pi}{6}\right)$

57. $y = -2\sin\left(x - \dfrac{\pi}{4}\right) + 1$

59. $y = -3\cos\left(x + \dfrac{\pi}{2}\right) - 2$

61. $y = 2\cos\left(2x - \dfrac{\pi}{4}\right)$

63. $y = -4\sin(2x + \pi) + 1$

65. $y = 4\cos\left[4\left(x - \dfrac{\pi}{6}\right)\right] - 2$

67. $y = \dfrac{3}{2}\sin\left[\dfrac{1}{2}\left(x - \dfrac{\pi}{4}\right)\right]$

69. $y = \tan(2x + \pi)$

71. $y = \cot\left(2x - \dfrac{\pi}{2}\right)$

73. $y = 2\tan\left[\dfrac{1}{2}\left(x - \dfrac{\pi}{4}\right)\right]$

75. $y = -2\tan\left(2x + \dfrac{\pi}{4}\right)$

77. $y = 3\tan\left(2x - \dfrac{\pi}{4}\right) + 1$

79. $y = -2\tan\left(2x - \dfrac{\pi}{3}\right) - 3$

81. $y = 2\sec\left(x - \dfrac{\pi}{2}\right)$

83. $y = -2\csc\left(x - \dfrac{\pi}{4}\right) + 1$

85. $y = -4\csc(2x + \pi) + 1$

87.

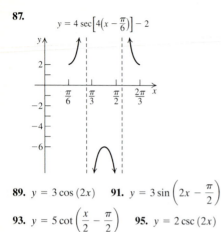

$y = 4\sec\left[4\left(x - \frac{\pi}{6}\right)\right] - 2$

89. $y = 3\cos(2x)$ **91.** $y = 3\sin\left(2x - \frac{\pi}{2}\right)$

93. $y = 5\cot\left(\frac{x}{2} - \frac{\pi}{2}\right)$ **95.** $y = 2\csc(2x)$

B Exercises: Applying the Concepts: **97. a.** period $= \dfrac{1}{70}$. The pulse is the frequency of the function; it says how many times the heart beats in one minute.

b.

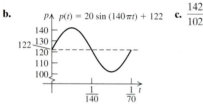

$p(t) = 20\sin(140\pi t) + 122$ **c.** $\dfrac{142}{102}$

99. a. 800 kangaroos   **b.** 500 kangaroos   **c.** $\dfrac{\pi}{2}$ years ≈ 1.57 years

101. $y = 4.35\sin\left[\frac{\pi}{6}x - \frac{\pi}{2}\right] + 12.25$

c.

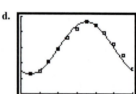

103. a. $y = 25.5\sin\left[\frac{\pi}{6}x - \frac{2\pi}{3}\right] + 44.5$

b.

$y = 25.5\sin\frac{\pi}{6}(x - 4) + 44.5$

c. January $= f(1) = 19$;
April $= f(4) = 44.5$;
July $= f(7) = 70$;
October $= f(10) = 44.5$.
The computed values are very
close to the measured values.

d.

C Exercises: Beyond the Basics: **107.** $y = 4\sin(2x + 1) - 2$

109. $y = 3\sin\left(\frac{\pi}{30}x - \pi\right) + 13$ **111.** 4.5   **115.** $\sin(1) \approx 0.841$

Critical Thinking: **116.** True

117.

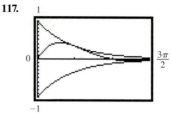

For each x, $-2^{-x} < 2^{-x}\sin x < 2^{-x}$.

Review Exercises

1. $-\dfrac{11\pi}{6}, -\dfrac{7\pi}{6}, \dfrac{\pi}{6}, \dfrac{5\pi}{6}$ **3.** $-\dfrac{5\pi}{3}, -\dfrac{2\pi}{3}, \dfrac{\pi}{3}, \dfrac{4\pi}{3}$ **5.** no x values

7. $\pm\dfrac{3\pi}{4}, \pm\dfrac{5\pi}{4}$ **9.** $-\dfrac{5\pi}{4}, -\dfrac{\pi}{4}, \dfrac{3\pi}{4}, \dfrac{7\pi}{4}$ **11.** $-\dfrac{9\pi}{8}, -\dfrac{\pi}{8}, \dfrac{7\pi}{8}, \dfrac{15\pi}{8}$

13. $[-2, 2]$ **15.** $[-3, 3]$ **17.** $(-\infty, -3] \cup [3, \infty)$
19. $(-\infty, -2] \cup [2, \infty)$ **21.** $[1, 7]$ **23.** $(-\infty, -2] \cup [4, \infty)$

25. amplitude: $\dfrac{3}{2}$

period: 2π

zeros: $\dfrac{\pi}{2} + n\pi$

phase shift: none
vertical
translation: none
asymptotes: none

27. amplitude: 3

period: $\dfrac{2\pi}{5}$

zeros: $\dfrac{n\pi}{5}$

phase shift: none
vertical
translation: none
asymptotes: none

29. amplitude: 3
period: 2π

zeros: $n\pi + \dfrac{\pi}{3}$

phase shift: $\dfrac{\pi}{3}$

vertical
translation: none
asymptotes: none

31. amplitude: none
period: π

zeros: $n\pi + \dfrac{\pi}{3}$

phase shift: $\dfrac{\pi}{3}$

vertical
translation: none
asymptotes:
$\dfrac{5\pi}{6} + n\pi$

33. amplitude: 2
period: π

zeros: $\dfrac{\pi}{2} + n\pi$ or $\dfrac{\pi}{6} + n\pi$

phase shift: $-\dfrac{\pi}{6}$

vertical
translation: up 1
asymptotes: none

35. amplitude: none

period: $\dfrac{\pi}{3}$

zeros:

$0.36904957 + \dfrac{n\pi}{3}$

phase shift: $\dfrac{\pi}{6}$

vertical translation: up 1

asymptotes: $\dfrac{n\pi}{3}$

37. amplitude: none
period: π
zeros: none

phase shift: $-\dfrac{\pi}{6}$

vertical translation: down 2

asymptotes: $\dfrac{\pi}{12} + \dfrac{n\pi}{2}$

39.

$y = -3\cos x$

41.

$y = 3\sin\left(x - \dfrac{\pi}{3}\right)$

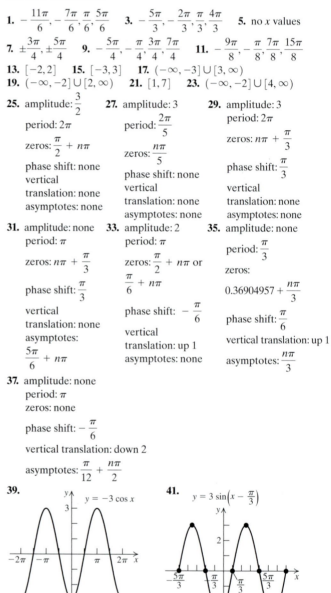

43.
$$y = -2\cos\left(x + \frac{2\pi}{3}\right)$$

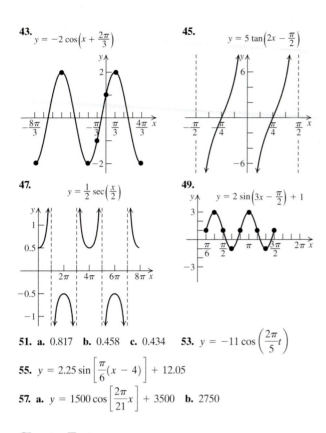

45.
$$y = 5\tan\left(2x - \frac{\pi}{2}\right)$$

47.
$$y = \frac{1}{2}\sec\left(\frac{x}{2}\right)$$

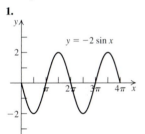

49.
$$y = 2\sin\left(3x - \frac{\pi}{2}\right) + 1$$

51. a. 0.817   **b.** 0.458   **c.** 0.434   **53.** $y = -11\cos\left(\dfrac{2\pi}{5}t\right)$

55. $y = 2.25\sin\left[\dfrac{\pi}{6}(x - 4)\right] + 12.05$

57. a. $y = 1500\cos\left[\dfrac{2\pi}{21}x\right] + 3500$ **b.** 2750

Chapter Test

1.

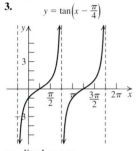

$$y = -2\sin x$$

amplitude: 2
period: 2π
phase shift: none
asymptotes: none

2.

$$y = 3\cos(\pi x)$$

amplitude: 3
period: 2
phase shift: none
asymptotes: none

3.
$$y = \tan\left(x - \frac{\pi}{4}\right)$$

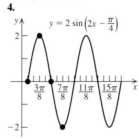

amplitude: none
period: π

phase shift: $\dfrac{\pi}{4}$

asymptotes: $\dfrac{3\pi}{4} + n\pi$

4.
$$y = 2\sin\left(2x - \frac{\pi}{4}\right)$$

amplitude: 2
period: π

phase shift: $\dfrac{\pi}{8}$

asymptotes: none

5.

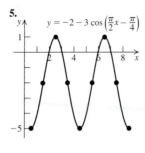

$$y = -2 - 3\cos\left(\frac{\pi}{2}x - \frac{\pi}{4}\right)$$

amplitude: 3
period: 4

phase shift: $\dfrac{1}{2}$

asymptotes: none

6.

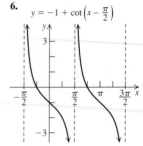

$$y = -1 + \cot\left(x - \frac{\pi}{2}\right)$$

amplitude: none
period: π

phase shift: $\dfrac{\pi}{2}$

asymptotes: $n\pi + \dfrac{\pi}{2}$

7. $y = 2\csc\left(\dfrac{x}{2} - 1\right)$

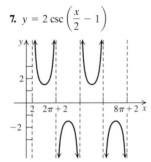

amplitude: none
period: 4π
phase shift: 2
asymptotes: $2n\pi + 2$

8. $y = 2 - \sec\left(3x - \dfrac{\pi}{2}\right)$

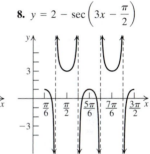

amplitude: none

period: $\dfrac{2\pi}{3}$

phase shift: $\dfrac{\pi}{6}$

asymptotes: $\dfrac{n\pi}{3}$

9. $y = 2\sin\left(x + \dfrac{\pi}{2}\right)$ **10.** $y = 2\sin\left(\dfrac{\pi}{2}x\right) + 2$

11. $y = -\tan\left(\dfrac{3}{2}x\right)$ **12.** $y = 2\csc\left(\dfrac{1}{2}x + \dfrac{\pi}{2}\right)$

13. $A = \dfrac{1}{2}; B = \dfrac{1}{2}; C = \dfrac{\pi}{4}$ **14.** $y = -7\cos\left(\dfrac{\pi}{2}t\right)$ **15.** true

16. false   **17.** true   **18.** true   **19.** false   **20.** true

CHAPTER 5

Section 5.1

Practice Problems: **1. a.** $\dfrac{\sqrt{3}}{2}$ **b.** $-\dfrac{\sqrt{3}}{3}$ **c.** $\dfrac{\sqrt{2}}{2}$ **7.** The equation
is not an identity. Let $x = \pi$.

A Exercises: Basic Skills and Concepts: **1.** identity   **3.** $\cos^2 x; \tan^2 x; 1$
5. true   **7.** $-\dfrac{1}{2}$ **9.** $\dfrac{\sqrt{2}}{2}$ **11.** $-\dfrac{2\sqrt{3}}{3}$ **13.** c   **15.** a
17. d   **21.** 1   **23.** 1   **25.** 1   **27.** -3
71.   An identity

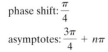

73.

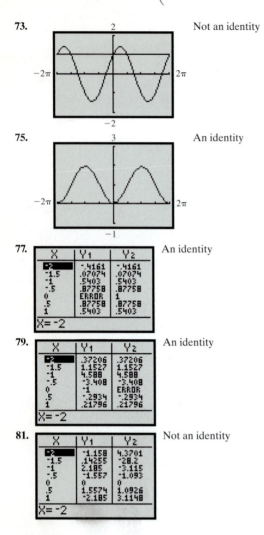

Not an identity

75.   An identity

77.   An identity

79.   An identity

81.   Not an identity

B Exercises: Applying the Concepts: 83. $20 \csc \theta$

C Exercises: Beyond the Basics: 85. 1   **87.** 1   **89.** 2   **91.** 1

93. 1   **95.** $\cos \theta = \dfrac{\pm 2ab}{a^2 + b^2}$, $\cot \theta = \dfrac{\pm 2ab}{a^2 - b^2}$.

Critical Thinking: 102. $t = 0$ **103.** $a = b$, for $a, b \neq 0$
104. $a = b$, for $a, b \neq 0$

Section 5.2

Practice Problems: 1. $\dfrac{\sqrt{6} + \sqrt{2}}{4}$ **2.** $\dfrac{\sqrt{2} - \sqrt{6}}{4}$ **5.** $\dfrac{1}{2}$

6. $-\dfrac{63}{65}$ **8.** Amplitude $= \sqrt{0.05}$, period $= \dfrac{\pi}{200}$, frequency $= \dfrac{200}{\pi}$,
phase shift ≈ -0.0028

A Exercises: Basic Skills and Concepts: 1. $+$ **3.** $\cot x$
5. true   **7.** $\dfrac{\sqrt{6} + \sqrt{2}}{4}$ **9.** $\dfrac{\sqrt{6} - \sqrt{2}}{4}$ **11.** $-\dfrac{\sqrt{6} + \sqrt{2}}{4}$

13. $2 - \sqrt{3}$ **15.** $\dfrac{\sqrt{6} + \sqrt{2}}{4}$ **17.** $2 - \sqrt{3}$ **19.** $-\sqrt{6} - \sqrt{2}$

21. $\dfrac{\sqrt{6} - \sqrt{2}}{4}$ **23.** $-2 - \sqrt{3}$ **25.** $2 + \sqrt{3}$ **41.** 1   **43.** 0

45. 1   **47.** $\dfrac{\sqrt{3}}{2}$ **49.** 1   **51.** $\dfrac{56}{65}$ **53.** $\dfrac{63}{65}$ **55.** $\dfrac{16}{63}$

57. $\dfrac{2\sqrt{210} - 6}{35}$ **59.** $\dfrac{35(\sqrt{210} - 3)}{402}$ **61.** $\dfrac{-49\sqrt{21} - 75\sqrt{10}}{402}$

71. $y = \sqrt{2} \sin\left(x + \dfrac{\pi}{4}\right)$

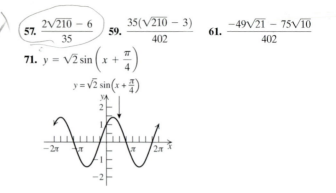

B Exercises: Applying the Concepts: 75. $A = 0.13$; $\theta \approx -0.00196$
77. a. $A = \dfrac{\sqrt{13}}{6} \approx 0.6009$ **b.** frequency $= \dfrac{3}{2\pi}$; phase shift ≈ -0.1960

C Exercises: Beyond the Basics: 93. 2   **95.** $\dfrac{1}{2}$

Critical Thinking: 99. 1

Section 5.3

Practice Problems: 1. a. $-\dfrac{120}{169}$ **b.** $-\dfrac{119}{169}$ **c.** $\dfrac{120}{119}$ **2. a.** $\dfrac{\sqrt{3}}{2}$

b. $\dfrac{\sqrt{2}}{2}$ **4.** $\dfrac{3}{8} - \dfrac{1}{2}\cos 2x + \dfrac{1}{8}\cos 4x$ **5.** $\dfrac{141.1}{\sqrt{2}} \approx 100$ watts

6. $\dfrac{\sqrt{2 + \sqrt{2}}}{2}$ **7.** $-\dfrac{\sqrt{26}}{26}$

A Exercises: Basic Skills and Concepts: 1. $2 \sin x \cos x$
3. $2\cos^2 x - 1$; $\dfrac{1 + \cos 2x}{2}$ **5.** false   **7. a.** $-\dfrac{24}{25}$ **b.** $\dfrac{7}{25}$ **c.** $-\dfrac{24}{7}$
9. a. $\dfrac{8}{17}$ **b.** $-\dfrac{15}{17}$ **c.** $-\dfrac{8}{15}$ **11. a.** $-\dfrac{4}{5}$ **b.** $-\dfrac{3}{5}$ **c.** $\dfrac{4}{3}$
13. $-\dfrac{\sqrt{3}}{2}$ **15.** $-\dfrac{\sqrt{3}}{2}$ **17.** $-\dfrac{\sqrt{3}}{3}$ **19.** $\dfrac{\sqrt{2}}{2}$ **21.** $\dfrac{\sqrt{3}}{3}$
33. $\dfrac{1 - \cos 4x}{2}$ **35.** $\sin 4x$ **37.** $\dfrac{\sin 12x}{2}$ **39.** $\dfrac{\sin 2x}{4}$
41. $\cos 2x - 4\cos x + 3$ **43.** $\dfrac{\sqrt{2 - \sqrt{3}}}{2}$ **45.** $\dfrac{\sqrt{2 + \sqrt{2}}}{2}$
47. $-\dfrac{\sqrt{2 + \sqrt{2}}}{2}$ **49.** $1 - \sqrt{2}$ **51.** $-\sqrt{2} - 1$
53. $-\dfrac{\sqrt{2 + \sqrt{3}}}{2}$ **55. a.** $\dfrac{2\sqrt{5}}{5}$ **b.** $\dfrac{\sqrt{5}}{5}$ **c.** 2
57. a. $\dfrac{1}{26}\sqrt{338 + 78\sqrt{13}}$ **b.** $\dfrac{1}{26}\sqrt{338 - 78\sqrt{13}}$ **c.** $\dfrac{11 + 3\sqrt{13}}{2}$
59. a. $\dfrac{\sqrt{30} + \sqrt{20}}{10}$ **b.** $\dfrac{\sqrt{30} - \sqrt{20}}{10}$ **c.** $5 + 2\sqrt{6}$
61. a. $\dfrac{1}{10}\sqrt{50 - 10\sqrt{5}}$ **b.** $\dfrac{1}{10}\sqrt{50 + 10\sqrt{5}}$ **c.** $\dfrac{1}{2}\sqrt{6 - 2\sqrt{5}}$

B Exercises: Applying the Concepts: 73. 100 watts   **75.** 1200 watts
77. 600 watts   **79.** $\dfrac{\pi}{4}$

Critical Thinking: 91. a. $\dfrac{4}{5}$ **b.** $\dfrac{3}{5}$ **c.** $\dfrac{24}{25}$ **d.** $-\dfrac{7}{25}$ **e.** $-\dfrac{24}{7}$
f. $\dfrac{\sqrt{5}}{5}$ **g.** $\dfrac{2\sqrt{5}}{5}$ **h.** $\dfrac{1}{2}$

Section 5.4

Practice Problems: 1. $\frac{1}{2}\cos 2x + \frac{1}{2}\cos 4x$ **2.** $\frac{2-\sqrt{3}}{4}$

3. a. $2\sin 3x \sin x$ **b.** $\cos 13°$ **4.** $2\cos\left(\frac{\pi}{4}-\frac{x}{2}\right)\cos\left(\frac{\pi}{4}-\frac{3}{2}x\right)$

6. a. $y = \sin(2\pi \cdot 697t) + \sin(2\pi \cdot 1209t)$
b. $y = 2\cos(512\pi t)\sin(2\pi(953t))$ **c.** $f = 953$ Hz; $A = 2\cos(512\pi t)$

A Exercises: Basic Skills and Concepts:

1. $\frac{1}{2}[\cos(x-y) - \cos(x+y)]$ **3.** $2\cos\left(\frac{x+y}{2}\right)\cos\left(\frac{x-y}{2}\right)$

5. false **7.** $\frac{1}{2}\sin 2x$ **9.** $\frac{1}{2}-\frac{1}{2}\cos 2x$ **11.** $\frac{1}{4}+\frac{1}{2}\sin 20°$

13. $-\frac{1}{4}+\frac{1}{2}\cos 160°$ **15.** $\frac{1}{4}$ **17.** $\frac{\sqrt{2}}{4}-\frac{1}{2}$

19. $\frac{1}{2}\sin 6\theta + \frac{1}{2}\sin 4\theta$ **21.** $\frac{1}{2}\cos x + \frac{1}{2}\cos 7x$ **23.** $\frac{\sqrt{3}}{4}-\frac{\sqrt{2}}{4}$

25. $\frac{1}{2}+\frac{\sqrt{2}}{4}$ **27.** $\frac{\sqrt{2}}{4}+\frac{1}{4}$ **29.** $\frac{1}{4}-\frac{\sqrt{2}}{4}$ **31.** $-\sin 10°$

33. $2\sin 8°\cos 24°$ **35.** $2\sin\frac{3\pi}{10}\cos\frac{\pi}{10}$ **37.** $2\cos\frac{5}{12}\cos\frac{1}{12}$

39. $2\cos 4x\cos x$ **41.** $2\sin 3x\cos 4x$ **43.** $\sqrt{2}\cos\left(x-\frac{\pi}{4}\right)$

45. $\sqrt{2}\sin\left(2x-\frac{\pi}{4}\right)$ **47.** $2\sin\left(\frac{\pi}{4}-x\right)\cos\left(4x-\frac{\pi}{4}\right)$

49. $a\sqrt{2}\cos\left(x-\frac{\pi}{4}\right)$

B Exercises: Applying the Concepts:
61. a. $y = \sin[2\pi(852)t] + \sin[2\pi(1209)t]$
b. $y = 2\cos(357\pi t)\sin[2\pi(1030.5)t]$
c. $f = 1030.5$ Hz; $A = 2\cos(357\pi t)$
63. a. $y = 0.1\cos(116\pi t)\cos(4\pi t)$ **b.** $f = 4$ beats per unit time

C Exercises: Beyond the Basics:
65. The amplitude is $2\cos 1 \approx 1.081$. The period is π.

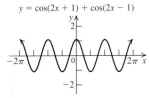
$y = \cos(2x+1) + \cos(2x-1)$

Review Exercises

1. $\cos\theta = -\frac{\sqrt{5}}{3}, \tan\theta = \frac{2\sqrt{5}}{5}, \cot\theta = \frac{\sqrt{5}}{2},$
$\sec\theta = -\frac{3\sqrt{5}}{5}, \csc\theta = -\frac{3}{2}$

3. $\sin\theta = -\frac{2\sqrt{2}}{3}, \cos\theta = \frac{1}{3}, \tan\theta = -2\sqrt{2},$
$\cot\theta = -\frac{\sqrt{2}}{4}, \csc\theta = -\frac{3\sqrt{2}}{4}$ **21.** $\frac{\sqrt{6}+\sqrt{2}}{4}$ **23.** $\sqrt{6}-\sqrt{2}$

25. 1 **27.** -1 **29.** $-\frac{16}{65}$ **31.** $\frac{63}{65}$ **53.** $x^2\sin\frac{\theta}{2}\cos\frac{\theta}{2}$

Chapter Test

1. $-\frac{3}{4}$ **2.** $-\frac{3\sqrt{13}}{13}$ **11.** Let $\theta = \frac{\pi}{2}$. **12.** Let $\theta = 0$.

13. 0 **14.** $\frac{1}{2}$ **15.** $\frac{\sqrt{6}+\sqrt{2}}{4}$ **16.** $-\frac{7}{25}$ **17.** $\frac{24}{25}$ **18.** odd

19. No, let $x = y = \frac{\pi}{2}$. **20.** I or II

CHAPTER 6

Section 6.1

Practice Problems: 1. a. $-\frac{\pi}{3}$ **b.** $-\frac{\pi}{2}$ **2. a.** $\frac{3\pi}{4}$ **b.** $\frac{\pi}{3}$ **3.** $\frac{\pi}{6}$

4. $\frac{\pi}{3}$ **5. a.** 1.3490 **b.** 0.2898 **c.** 2.9320 **6. a.** 53.1301°

b. 4.4117° **c.** $-85.2364°$ **7.** $-\frac{\pi}{2}$ **8.** $\frac{2\sqrt{2}}{3}$ **9.** $\frac{108+50\sqrt{2}}{119}$

10. 80°

A Exercises: Basic Skills and Concepts: 1. $[-1, 1]$ **3.** $\frac{\pi}{3}$

5. True **7.** False **9.** 0 **11.** $-\frac{\pi}{6}$ **13.** π **15.** Undefined

17. $\frac{\pi}{3}$ **19.** $-\frac{\pi}{4}$ **21.** $\frac{3\pi}{4}$ **23.** $-\frac{\pi}{4}$ **25.** $\frac{\pi}{6}$ **27.** Undefined

29. $\frac{2\pi}{3}$ **31.** $\frac{\pi}{3}$ **33.** $\frac{1}{8}$ **35.** 0.6 **37.** $\frac{\pi}{7}$ **39.** 247 **41.** $-\frac{\pi}{3}$

43. $-\frac{\pi}{3}$ **45.** 53.13° **47.** $-43.63°$ **49.** 73.40° **51.** 85.91°

53. $-88.64°$ **55.** $\frac{\sqrt{5}}{3}$ **57.** $\frac{3}{5}$ **59.** $\frac{2\sqrt{29}}{29}$ **61.** $\frac{3}{4}$

63. $\frac{4\sqrt{17}}{17}$ **65.** $\sqrt{3}$

B Exercises: Applying the Concepts: 67. 62° **69.** 159°

C Exercises: Beyond the Basics: 71. Increasing **73.** Increasing
75.

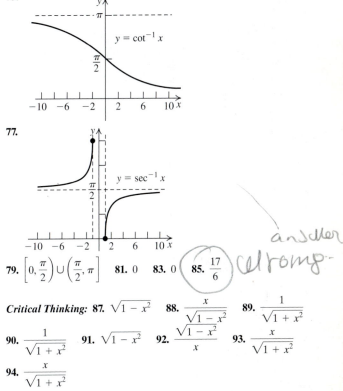
$y = \cot^{-1} x$

77.
$y = \sec^{-1} x$

79. $\left[0, \frac{\pi}{2}\right) \cup \left(\frac{\pi}{2}, \pi\right]$ **81.** 0 **83.** 0 **85.** $\frac{17}{6}$

answer wrong

Critical Thinking: 87. $\sqrt{1-x^2}$ **88.** $\frac{x}{\sqrt{1-x^2}}$ **89.** $\frac{1}{\sqrt{1+x^2}}$

90. $\frac{1}{\sqrt{1+x^2}}$ **91.** $\sqrt{1-x^2}$ **92.** $\frac{\sqrt{1-x^2}}{x}$ **93.** $\frac{x}{\sqrt{1+x^2}}$

94. $\frac{x}{\sqrt{1+x^2}}$

Section 6.2

Practice Problems: 1. a. $x = \frac{\pi}{2} + 2n\pi$ **b.** $x = 2n\pi$

c. $x = \frac{\pi}{4} + n\pi$ **2. a.** $x \approx 48.2° + n\cdot360°, x \approx 311.8° + n\cdot360°$

b. $x \approx 2.0345, x \approx 5.1761$ **3.** $x = 90°$ or $x = 330°$

4. 40°   **5.** $x = \dfrac{\pi}{2}, x = \dfrac{5\pi}{6}, x = \dfrac{11\pi}{6}$

6. $\theta = 2n\pi, \theta = \dfrac{2\pi}{3} + 2n\pi, \theta = \dfrac{4\pi}{3} + 2n\pi$

7. $\theta = \dfrac{\pi}{6}, \theta = \dfrac{\pi}{2}, \theta = \dfrac{5\pi}{6}$ **8.** $\theta = \dfrac{\pi}{3}$

A Exercises: Basic Skills and Concepts: **1.** two   **3.** one   **5.** False

7. $\dfrac{\pi}{2} + n\pi$ **9.** $\dfrac{3\pi}{4} + n\pi$ **11.** $\dfrac{\pi}{4} + 2n\pi, \dfrac{7\pi}{4} + 2n\pi$

13. $\dfrac{\pi}{6} + n\pi$ **15.** $\dfrac{2\pi}{3} + 2n\pi, \dfrac{4\pi}{3} + 2n\pi$ **17.** $30° + 180°n$

19. $210° + 360°n, 330° + 360°n$ **21.** $90° + 360°n$

23. $60° + 360°n, 120° + 360°n$ **25.** $60° + 360°n, 300° + 360°n$

27. $\{23.6°, 156.4°\}$ **29.** $\{82.0°, 278.0°\}$ **31.** $\{131.3°, 311.3°\}$

33. $\{3.4814, 5.9433\}$ **35.** $\{2.2143, 5.3559\}$ **37.** $\{3.5531, 5.8717\}$

39. $\left\{\dfrac{7\pi}{12}, \dfrac{23\pi}{12}\right\}$ **41.** $\left\{\dfrac{19\pi}{24}, \dfrac{35\pi}{24}\right\}$ **43.** $\left\{\dfrac{\pi}{3}, \dfrac{4\pi}{3}\right\}$ **45.** $\left\{\dfrac{\pi}{6}, \dfrac{3\pi}{2}\right\}$

47. $\left\{\dfrac{\pi}{4}, \dfrac{3\pi}{2}, \dfrac{5\pi}{4}\right\}$ **49.** $\left\{\dfrac{\pi}{6}, \dfrac{3\pi}{4}, \dfrac{5\pi}{6}, \dfrac{7\pi}{4}\right\}$ **51.** $\left\{\dfrac{\pi}{6}, \dfrac{3\pi}{4}, \dfrac{5\pi}{6}, \dfrac{7\pi}{4}\right\}$

53. $\left\{\dfrac{\pi}{4}, \dfrac{7\pi}{6}, \dfrac{7\pi}{4}, \dfrac{11\pi}{6}\right\}$ **55.** $\left\{\dfrac{\pi}{6}, \dfrac{5\pi}{6}, \dfrac{7\pi}{6}, \dfrac{11\pi}{6}\right\}$

57. $\left\{\dfrac{\pi}{4}, \dfrac{3\pi}{4}, \dfrac{5\pi}{4}, \dfrac{7\pi}{4}\right\}$ **59.** $\left\{\dfrac{\pi}{3}, \dfrac{2\pi}{3}, \dfrac{4\pi}{3}, \dfrac{5\pi}{3}\right\}$ **61.** $\left\{\dfrac{\pi}{2}, \dfrac{7\pi}{6}, \dfrac{11\pi}{6}\right\}$

63. $\left\{\dfrac{\pi}{4}, \dfrac{5\pi}{4}\right\}$ **65.** $\left\{\dfrac{\pi}{6}, \dfrac{5\pi}{6}, \dfrac{7\pi}{6}, \dfrac{11\pi}{6}\right\}$ **67.** $\{0, \pi\}$

69. $\left\{\dfrac{7\pi}{6}, \dfrac{3\pi}{2}, \dfrac{11\pi}{6}\right\}$ **71.** $\left\{\dfrac{\pi}{3}, \dfrac{5\pi}{6}, \dfrac{4\pi}{3}, \dfrac{11\pi}{6}\right\}$ **73.** $\left\{\dfrac{\pi}{3}, \pi\right\}$

75. $\left\{\dfrac{\pi}{6}\right\}$

B Exercises: Applying the Concepts: **77.** 60°   **79.** ≈ 5.7°   **81.** 28°

C Exercises: Beyond the Basics: **83.** $\left\{\dfrac{\pi}{6}, \dfrac{7\pi}{6}, \dfrac{11\pi}{6}\right\}$

85. $\left\{0, \dfrac{\pi}{3}, \dfrac{2\pi}{3}, \pi, \dfrac{4\pi}{3}, \dfrac{5\pi}{3}\right\}$ **87.** $\left\{\dfrac{\pi}{2}, 5.6397\right\}$

Critical Thinking: **89.** $\{1.107, 2.034, 4.249, 5.176\}$

90. $\{1.571, 1.911, 4.373, 4.712\}$ **91.** $\{0.905, 5.379\}$

92. $\{0.911, 2.231, 3.512, 5.913\}$ **93.** $\left\{\dfrac{\pi}{4}, \dfrac{5\pi}{4}\right\}$

Section 6.3

Practice Problems: **1.** $\left\{\dfrac{\pi}{12}, \dfrac{5\pi}{12}, \dfrac{13\pi}{12}, \dfrac{17\pi}{12}\right\}$ **2.** $\left\{\dfrac{\pi}{3}\right\}$

3. About 5 days and 24 days   **4.** $\{15°, 75°, 135°, 195°, 255°, 315°\}$

5. $\left\{\dfrac{\pi}{36}, \dfrac{5\pi}{36}, \dfrac{25\pi}{36}, \dfrac{29\pi}{36}, \dfrac{49\pi}{36}, \dfrac{53\pi}{36}\right\}$ **6.** $\left\{0, \dfrac{2\pi}{5}, \dfrac{4\pi}{5}, \pi, \dfrac{6\pi}{5}, \dfrac{8\pi}{5}\right\}$

7. $\left\{\dfrac{\sqrt{3} - 2}{2}\right\}$ **8.** $\left\{\dfrac{\sqrt{2} + \sqrt{2}}{2}\right\}$

A Exercises: Basic Skills and Concepts: **1.** $\dfrac{\pi}{2} - x_1$ **3.** $\dfrac{\pi}{2} + x_1$

5. False   **7.** $\left\{\dfrac{\pi}{6}, \dfrac{5\pi}{6}, \dfrac{7\pi}{6}, \dfrac{11\pi}{6}\right\}$ **9.** $\varnothing$ **11.** $\left\{\dfrac{\pi}{12}, \dfrac{7\pi}{12}, \dfrac{13\pi}{12}, \dfrac{19\pi}{12}\right\}$

13. $\left\{\dfrac{\pi}{18}, \dfrac{5\pi}{18}, \dfrac{13\pi}{18}, \dfrac{17\pi}{18}, \dfrac{25\pi}{18}, \dfrac{29\pi}{18}\right\}$ **15.** $\left\{\dfrac{2\pi}{3}\right\}$ **17.** $\left\{\dfrac{3\pi}{4}\right\}$

19. $\left\{\dfrac{\pi}{12}, \dfrac{\pi}{4}, \dfrac{3\pi}{4}, \dfrac{11\pi}{12}, \dfrac{17\pi}{12}, \dfrac{19\pi}{12}\right\}$ **21.** $\left\{\dfrac{\pi}{6} - \dfrac{1}{2}, \dfrac{5\pi}{6} - \dfrac{1}{2}, \dfrac{7\pi}{6} - \dfrac{1}{2},\right.$

$\left.\dfrac{11\pi}{6} - \dfrac{1}{2}\right\}$ **23.** $\left\{\dfrac{\pi}{24} + \dfrac{1}{4}, \dfrac{5\pi}{24} + \dfrac{1}{4}, \dfrac{13\pi}{24} + \dfrac{1}{4}, \dfrac{17\pi}{24} + \dfrac{1}{4}, \dfrac{25\pi}{24} + \dfrac{1}{4},\right.$

$\left.\dfrac{29\pi}{24} + \dfrac{1}{4}, \dfrac{37\pi}{24} + \dfrac{1}{4}, \dfrac{41\pi}{24} + \dfrac{1}{4}\right\}$ **25.** $\left\{-\dfrac{\pi}{9} + \dfrac{2}{3}, \dfrac{\pi}{9} + \dfrac{2}{3}, \dfrac{11\pi}{9} + \dfrac{2}{3},\right.$

$\left.\dfrac{13\pi}{9} + \dfrac{2}{3}\right\}$ **27.** $\{35.3°, 144.7°, 215.3°, 324.7°\}$

29. $\{20°, 100°, 140°, 220°, 260°, 340°\}$ **31.** $\{66.5°, 113.5°, 186.5°,$
$233.5°, 306.5°, 353.5°\}$ **33.** $\varnothing$ **35.** $\{30°, 150°, 210°, 330°\}$

37. $\{60°, 300°\}$ **39.** $\left\{0, \dfrac{2\pi}{3}, \pi, \dfrac{4\pi}{3}\right\}$ **41.** $\left\{0, \dfrac{\pi}{2}, \pi, \dfrac{3\pi}{2}\right\}$

43. $\left\{\dfrac{\pi}{8}, \dfrac{3\pi}{8}, \dfrac{\pi}{2}, \dfrac{5\pi}{8}, \dfrac{7\pi}{8}, \dfrac{9\pi}{8}, \dfrac{11\pi}{8}, \dfrac{3\pi}{2}, \dfrac{13\pi}{8}, \dfrac{15\pi}{8}\right\}$

45. $\left\{0, \dfrac{\pi}{8}, \dfrac{3\pi}{8}, \dfrac{5\pi}{8}, \dfrac{7\pi}{8}, \pi, \dfrac{9\pi}{8}, \dfrac{11\pi}{8}, \dfrac{13\pi}{8}, \dfrac{15\pi}{8}\right\}$

47. $\left\{\dfrac{\sqrt{3}}{2}\right\}$ **49.** $\varnothing$ **51.** $\left\{\dfrac{1}{2}\right\}$ **53.** $\left\{\dfrac{5\sqrt{26}}{26}\right\}$

B Exercises: Applying the Concepts: **55. a.** ≈ 0.0014 sec

b. ≈ 0.0092 sec   **57.** $\dfrac{2}{3} + 4n$ sec, $\dfrac{10}{3} + 4n$ sec, n an integer

59. a. 27   **b.** 18, 36   **c.** 10, 44   **61. a.** January
b. February, December

C Exercises: Beyond the Basics: **63.** $\left\{\dfrac{\pi}{4}, \dfrac{3\pi}{4}, \dfrac{5\pi}{4}, \dfrac{7\pi}{4}\right\}$

65. $\left\{\dfrac{\pi}{3}, \dfrac{5\pi}{3}\right\}$ **67.** $\left\{\dfrac{\pi}{8}, \dfrac{3\pi}{8}, \dfrac{5\pi}{8}, \dfrac{7\pi}{8}, \dfrac{9\pi}{8}, \dfrac{11\pi}{8}, \dfrac{13\pi}{8}, \dfrac{15\pi}{8}\right\}$

69. $\left\{\dfrac{2\pi}{3}, \dfrac{4\pi}{3}\right\}$ **71.** $\left\{\dfrac{\pi}{8}, \dfrac{5\pi}{8}, \dfrac{9\pi}{8}, \dfrac{3\pi}{2}, \dfrac{13\pi}{8}\right\}$

73. $\left\{0, \dfrac{\pi}{2}, \dfrac{5\pi}{6}, \pi, \dfrac{7\pi}{6}, \dfrac{3\pi}{2}\right\}$ **75.** $\left\{\dfrac{5\pi}{12}, \dfrac{7\pi}{12}, \dfrac{11\pi}{12}, \dfrac{17\pi}{12}, \dfrac{19\pi}{12}, \dfrac{23\pi}{12}\right\}$

77. $\left\{0, \dfrac{\pi}{3}, \dfrac{2\pi}{3}, \pi, \dfrac{4\pi}{3}, \dfrac{5\pi}{3}\right\}$ **79.** $\left\{\dfrac{\pi}{8}, \dfrac{\pi}{2}, \dfrac{5\pi}{8}, \dfrac{9\pi}{8}, \dfrac{3\pi}{2}, \dfrac{13\pi}{8}\right\}$

81. $\{1.107, 2.678, 4.249, 5.820\}$

83. $\{0.741, 1.090, 2.835, 3.185, 4.930, 5.279\}$

Critical Thinking: **85.** $\left\{-\dfrac{1}{2}, \dfrac{1}{2}\right\}$ **86.** $\left\{\dfrac{2}{3}\right\}$

Review Exercises

1. $\dfrac{\pi}{4}$ **3.** Undefined   **5.** $\dfrac{\pi}{3}$ **7.** $\dfrac{\pi}{3}$ **9.** $\dfrac{5\pi}{8}$ **11.** $\dfrac{\pi}{3}$ **13.** $\dfrac{\sqrt{2}}{2}$

15. $\sqrt{3}$ **17.** 115.47°   **19.** 68.26°   **21.** $\pi + 2n\pi$ **23.** $n\pi$

25. $60° + 180°n$ **27.** $270° + 360°n$ **29.** $30° + 360°n, 330° + 360°n$

31. $\left\{\dfrac{7\pi}{12}, \dfrac{23\pi}{12}\right\}$ **33.** $\left\{\dfrac{\pi}{2}, \dfrac{3\pi}{2}\right\}$ **35.** $\left\{\dfrac{\pi}{12}, \dfrac{5\pi}{12}, \dfrac{13\pi}{12}, \dfrac{17\pi}{12}\right\}$

37. $\left\{\dfrac{5\pi}{18}, \dfrac{11\pi}{18}, \dfrac{17\pi}{18}, \dfrac{23\pi}{18}, \dfrac{29\pi}{18}, \dfrac{35\pi}{18}\right\}$ **39.** $\left\{\dfrac{2\pi}{3}, \dfrac{4\pi}{3}\right\}$

41. $\left\{\dfrac{\pi}{4}, \dfrac{3\pi}{4}, \dfrac{5\pi}{4}, \dfrac{7\pi}{4}\right\}$ **43.** $\left\{0, \dfrac{2\pi}{3}, \dfrac{4\pi}{3}\right\}$

45. $\left\{\dfrac{\pi}{18}, \dfrac{5\pi}{18}, \dfrac{13\pi}{18}, \dfrac{17\pi}{18}, \dfrac{25\pi}{18}, \dfrac{29\pi}{18}\right\}$ **47.** $\{19.5°, 160.5°\}$

49. $\{15°, 165°, 195°, 345°\}$ **51.** $\{120°, 150°, 240°, 330°\}$

53. 60°   **55.** $\dfrac{1}{360}$ sec   **57.** 30°

Chapter Test

1. $\dfrac{\pi}{2}; \pi$ **2.** $0; \dfrac{\pi}{2}$ **3.** π **4.** 2 if $a < 1$, 1 if $a = 1$, 0 if $a > 1$

5. 1   **6.** $-\dfrac{\pi}{3}$ **7.** $\dfrac{\pi}{3}$ **8.** $\dfrac{2\pi}{3}$ **9.** $\dfrac{2\sqrt{6}}{5}$ **10.** $\dfrac{1 + 2\sqrt{6}}{6}$

11. $\dfrac{3\pi}{4} + n\pi$ **12.** $\dfrac{2\pi}{3} + 2n\pi, \dfrac{4\pi}{3} + 2n\pi$

13. $\dfrac{7\pi}{3} + 4n\pi, \dfrac{11\pi}{3} + 4n\pi$ **14.** $\left\{\dfrac{\pi}{2}, \pi\right\}$ **15.** $\left\{\dfrac{\pi}{4}, \dfrac{5\pi}{6}, \dfrac{5\pi}{4}, \dfrac{11\pi}{6}\right\}$

16. $\varnothing$ **17.** $\left\{\dfrac{\pi}{6}, \dfrac{\pi}{2}, \dfrac{5\pi}{6}, \dfrac{3\pi}{2}\right\}$ **18.** $\left\{\dfrac{\pi}{9}, \dfrac{4\pi}{9}, \dfrac{7\pi}{9}, \dfrac{10\pi}{9}, \dfrac{13\pi}{9}, \dfrac{16\pi}{9}\right\}$

19. $\left\{\dfrac{3\pi}{4}\right\}$ **20.** $0.5 + 6n$ sec; $2.5 + 6n$ sec

CHAPTER 7

Section 7.1

Practice Problems: **1.** $A = 40°, b \approx 16.9$ m, $c \approx 18.0$ m
2. $C = 45°, b \approx 15.4$ in., $c \approx 12.0$ in.   **3.** 10,576 ft   **4. a.** 31.5 mi
b. 15.6 mi

A Exercises: Basic Skills and Concepts: **1.** 180   **3.** $\dfrac{\sin B}{b} = \dfrac{\sin C}{c}$

5. false   **7.** $C = 63°, a \approx 98.2$ ft, $b \approx 93.0$ ft   **9.** $B = 27°,$
$a \approx 64.8$ m, $b \approx 31.3$ m   **11.** $A = 75°, b \approx 89.7, c \approx 73.2$
13. $B = 15°, a \approx 136.6, c \approx 167.3$ **15.** $C = 105°, b \approx 89.2$ m,
$c \approx 105.3$ m   **17.** $B = 79°, b \approx 102.3$ cm, $c \approx 85.4$ cm
19. $B = 98°, a \approx 47.1$ ft, $b \approx 81.2$ ft   **21.** $A = 70°, a \approx 55.1$ in,
$c \approx 54.0$ in.   **23.** $A = 24°, a \approx 13.3$ ft, $b \approx 30.7$ ft
25. $C = 98.5°, a \approx 17.7$ m, $b \approx 21.7$ m

B Exercises: Applying the Concepts: **27.** ≈ 399 ft   **29. a.** 1615 yd
b. 540 yd   **31. a.** 25.7 mi   **b.** 14.5 mi   **33.** 22,912 mi
35. 181 ft   **37.** 1719 ft

C Exercises: Beyond the Basics: **41.** 60.0 in.; 85.4 in.   **47.** 90°

Critical Thinking: **48.** An isosceles triangle with $\angle A = \angle B$
49. An isosceles right triangle

Section 7.2

Practice Problems: **1.** None   **2.** None
3. Solution 1: $A \approx 99.2°, B \approx 45.8°, a \approx 20.7$ ft
   Solution 2: $A \approx 10.8°, B \approx 134.2°, a \approx 3.9$ ft
4. No triangle exists.   **5.** $A \approx 31.3°, B \approx 88.7°, b \approx 57.7$ ft

A Exercises: Basic Skills and Concepts: **1.** one; two
3. right   **5.** true   **7.** two   **9.** two   **11.** none   **13.** none
15. one   **17.** $B = 65°, C = 50°, c \approx 16.9$ ft   **19.** $B = 23.7°, C = 41.3°,$
$c \approx 51.0$ m   **21.** $B \approx 34°, C \approx 106°, c \approx 34.4$
23. $B = 90°, C = 60°, c = 25\sqrt{3}$ **25.** No triangle exists.
27. No triangle exists.   **29.** $B \approx 56.8°, C \approx 23.2°, c \approx 16.0$
31. No triangle exists.
33. Solution 1: $C \approx 55.3°, A \approx 78.7°, a \approx 47.7$
   Solution 2: $C \approx 124.7°, A \approx 9.3°, a \approx 7.9$
35. No triangle exists.
37. Solution 1: $C \approx 49.0°, B \approx 89.0°, b \approx 82.2$
   Solution 2: $C \approx 131.0°, B \approx 7.0°, b \approx 10.0$
39. No triangle exists.

B Exercises: Applying the Concepts: **41.** 8.3°   **43.** 33 or 127 million
miles   **45.** 1:32 P.M.; 3:18 P.M.   **47.** 24.2 m

C Exercises: Beyond the Basics: **55.** $A = 22.5°; B = 67.5°$

Critical Thinking: **56.** 30°, 60°, 90°

Section 7.3

Practice Problems: **1.** $b \approx 21.8, A \approx 36.6°, C \approx 83.4°$
2. 5219.5 miles   **3.** $A \approx 42.1°, B \approx 85.9°, C \approx 52.0°$
4. No triangle exists.

A Exercises: Basic Skills and Concepts: **1.** C **3.** three
5. false   **7.** $b \approx 20.2, A \approx 44.0°, C \approx 30.0°$
9. $A \approx 130.5°, B \approx 27.1°, C \approx 22.4°$ **11.** $\cos C = 0.125$; acute
triangle   **13.** $\cos C = 0$; right triangle   **15.** $\cos C = -1.475$;
no triangle   **17.** $\cos C \approx -0.111$; obtuse triangle   **19.** $c = 21,$
$A \approx 38.2°, B \approx 21.8°$ **21.** $a \approx 11.5, B \approx 50.4°, C \approx 67.6°$
23. $A \approx 81.3°, B \approx 46.4°, C \approx 52.3°$ **25.** $A \approx 28.3°, B \approx 43.3°,$
$C \approx 108.4°$ **27.** $A \approx 23.7°, B \approx 36.4°, C \approx 119.9°$
29. $a \approx 5.7, B \approx 33.8°, C \approx 48.5°$ **31.** $b \approx 5.0 A \approx 46.3°,$
$C \approx 65.4°$ **33.** $A \approx 38.4°, B \approx 49.1°, C \approx 92.5°$

B Exercises: Applying the Concepts: **35.** 5.7 ft   **37.** 1543 yd
39. a. 20.9 ft   **b.** 11.0 ft   **41.** 9.1 mi   **43. a.** 4416.8 m
b. 2205.5 m   **45.** 66.4 ft

C Exercises: Beyond the Basics: **47.** 9.8 cm; 23.6 cm

Critical Thinking: **60.** $a = \sqrt{13}, b = 5\sqrt{2}, c = \sqrt{53}, A \approx 29.1°,$
$B \approx 72.2°, C \approx 78.7°$ **61.** $a = 3\sqrt{17}, b = 3\sqrt{5}, c = 3\sqrt{34},$
$A \approx 32.5°, B \approx 16.9°, C \approx 130.6°$

Section 7.4

Practice Problems: **1.** ≈ 375.2 sq ft   **2.** 4.845 sq mi
3. ≈ 203.4 sq in.   **4.** 93.5 sq m   **5.** 14,801 gal

A Exercises: Basic Skills and Concepts: **1.** $\dfrac{1}{2}bh$

3. $180° - \alpha - \beta$ **5.** true   **7.** 654.2 sq in.   **9.** 118.7 sq km
11. 62.5 sq mm   **13.** 25,136.6 sq ft   **15.** 84.3 sq ft
17. 167.1 sq yd   **19.** 178.6 sq cm   **21.** 1621.9 sq ft   **23.** 2.9
25. 1240.2   **27.** 13.5   **29.** 7.7

B Exercises: Applying the Concepts: **31.** 493,941 sq mi
33. $\approx \$775,668$ **35.** 3297 gal   **37.** 90.1 sq cm

C Exercises: Beyond the Basics: **41.** 12   **43.** 1039.2 sq cm
47. ≈ 112 sq units   **49.** ≈ 301 sq units

Review Exercises

1. 15.1   **3.** 32.9°   **5.** 17.9   **7.** $C = 105°, a \approx 66.5, b \approx 59.4$
9. No triangle exists.   **11.** $B = 74.2°, a \approx 36.8, c \approx 41.4$
13. $B \approx 54.1°, C \approx 60.7°, c \approx 20.5$ **15.** Answers may vary.
Sample answers: **a.** $10\sqrt{3}$, **b.** 20 **c.** 10   **17.** 13.1   **19.** 42.3°
21. $A \approx 26.6°, B \approx 42.1°, C \approx 111.3°$ **23.** $A \approx 51.7°, C \approx 48.3°,$
$b \approx 50.2$ **25.** $A \approx 32.5°, B \approx 49.8°, C \approx 97.7°$
27. $A \approx 32.0°, B \approx 18.0°, c \approx 17.3$ **29.** 16 sq ft   **31.** 11 sq ft
33. 104 sq m   **35.** 88.2 in., 65.0 in.   **37.** 25.2°   **39.** 772.2 yd
41. $A \approx 76.8°, B \approx 61.5°, C \approx 41.7°$ **43.** 3775 ft   **45.** 114.8°

Chapter Test

1. 14.1 ft   **2.** 138.4°   **3.** 5.0   **4.** 21.7°   **5.** $B = 30°, a \approx 23.7,$
$b \approx 13.1$ **6.** $A \approx 28.2°, C \approx 45.8°, b \approx 71.7$ **7.** $C = 101°,$
$b \approx 45.0$ m, $c \approx 73.4$ m   **8.** $A \approx 82.8°, B \approx 41.4°, C \approx 55.8°$
9. Two triangles: $B \approx 113.9°, C \approx 23.1°, c \approx 106.4$ ft;
$B \approx 66.1°, C \approx 70.9°, c \approx 256.3$ ft   **10.** 803 ft   **11.** 41.6 sq units
12. 1149.1 sq units   **13.** 87.4 sq units   **14.** 2.9 sq units
15. 43.5 cm, 29.0 cm   **16.** 34.6°   **17.** 54.2 ft, 151.9 ft
18. 19,899.7 sq ft

CHAPTER 8

Section 8.1

Practice Problems: **1. a.**

b. 7

2. a. 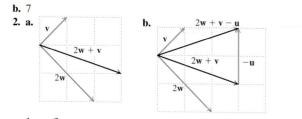   **b.**

3. $\frac{1}{3}\mathbf{v} + \frac{2}{3}\mathbf{w}$ **4. a.** 28.9   **b.** 38.8°   **5.** ≈ 108 lb force acting in the approximate direction S 33.7° E   **6.** ≈ 244.6 mph

A Exercises: Basic Skills and Concepts: **1.** vector   **3.** parallelogram
5. false

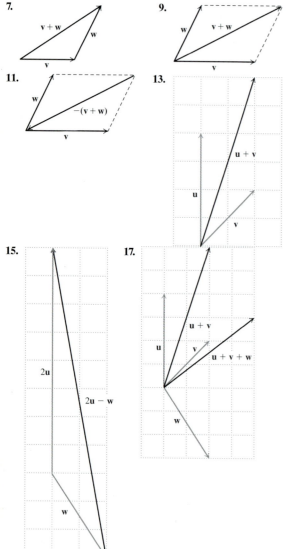

7.

9.

11.

13.

15.

17.

19.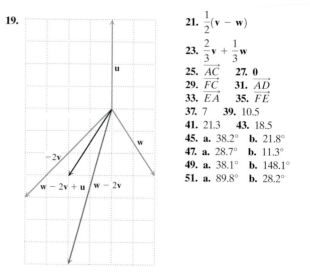

21. $\frac{1}{2}(\mathbf{v} - \mathbf{w})$

23. $\frac{2}{3}\mathbf{v} + \frac{1}{3}\mathbf{w}$

25. $\overrightarrow{AC}$ **27.** **0**
29. $\overrightarrow{FC}$ **31.** $\overrightarrow{AD}$
33. $\overrightarrow{EA}$ **35.** $\overrightarrow{FE}$
37. 7   **39.** 10.5
41. 21.3   **43.** 18.5
45. a. 38.2°   **b.** 21.8°
47. a. 28.7°   **b.** 11.3°
49. a. 38.1°   **b.** 148.1°
51. a. 89.8°   **b.** 28.2°

B Exercises: Applying the Concepts: **53.** 57.8 lb force acting in the direction S 52.7° W   **55.** 689.6 N force making an angle of 26.4° with the positive *x*-axis   **57.** 126°   **59.** 149.3 mph
61. 27.4 mph with a bearing of N 64.2° E

Critical Thinking: **71.** b

Section 8.2

Practice Problems: **1.** ⟨3, −10⟩   **2. a.** ⟨1, −1⟩   **b.** ⟨6, −9⟩
3. ≈ 15.26   **4. a.** $\left\langle -\frac{12}{13}, \frac{5}{13} \right\rangle$ **b.** $\left\langle -\frac{24}{13}, \frac{10}{13} \right\rangle$ **5. a.** −7**i** + 14**j**
b. 7√5   **6.** √3**i** − **j**   **7.** ≈ 303.69°   **8.** ≈ 801.0 mph;
≈ N 62.9° W   **9.** The magnitude of the equilibrant is approximately 121.2 lb, and the equilibrant is in the approximate direction S 7.8° E.

A Exercises: Basic Skills and Concepts: **1.** position vector
3. $x_2 - x_1, y_2 - y_1$ **5.** false   **7.** ⟨4, 2⟩   **9.** ⟨4, 4⟩
11. ⟨−4, −2⟩   **13.** ⟨−8, 2⟩   **15.** ⟨−1, 3⟩   **17.** ⟨2, −2⟩
19. ⟨3, −7⟩   **21.** $\left\langle -1, -\frac{5}{2} \right\rangle$ **23.** Equivalent   **25.** Not equivalent
27. √5   **29.** ⟨−4, 4⟩   **31.** ⟨−11, 10⟩   **33.** √221
35. $\left\langle \frac{\sqrt{2}}{2}, -\frac{\sqrt{2}}{2} \right\rangle$ **37.** $\left\langle -\frac{4}{5}, \frac{3}{5} \right\rangle$ **39.** $\left\langle \frac{\sqrt{2}}{2}, \frac{\sqrt{2}}{2} \right\rangle$ **41.** −**i** − 7**j**
43. 13**i** − 4**j**   **45.** √185   **47.** √3**i** + **j**   **49.** −2**i** + 2√3**j**
51. $\frac{3}{2}\mathbf{i} - \frac{3\sqrt{3}}{2}\mathbf{j}$ **53.** $\frac{7}{2}\mathbf{i} - \frac{7\sqrt{3}}{2}\mathbf{j}$ **55.** 10, 60°   **57.** 3, 150°
59. 13, 67.38°   **61.** 5, 216.87°

B Exercises: Applying the Concepts: **63.** 23.0**i** + 9.8**j**   **65.** −72.5; 33.8
67. A force of 40.6 lb acting in the direction N 52° E
69. The resultant is a force of 676.64 pounds making an angle of 47.19° with the positive *x*-axis.   **71.** 483.4 mph; N 32.1° E
73. 12.2 mph; N 52.2° E   **75.** A force of magnitude 10.1 pounds making an angle of 176.6° with the positive *x*-axis

C Exercises: Beyond the Basics: **77.** ‖**F₁**‖ = 106.4 lb; ‖**F₂**‖ = 136.8 lb
79. (2, −2)   **81.** $\left\langle -\frac{11}{3}, -\frac{11}{3} \right\rangle$ **83.** 3, √5
85. ‖**F₁**‖ ≈ 130.5 lb; ‖**F₂**‖ ≈ 89.3 lb

Critical Thinking: **86.** (9, 2)   **87.** (3, 0)   **88.** (−1, 4)
89. (−1, 4)

Section 8.3

Practice Problems: **1. a.** 8 **b.** 0 **2.** 17.5 **3.** Not parallel
4. 115.3° **5.** 39.2 **6.** Orthogonal **7.** 3000 foot-pounds

A Exercises: Basic Skills and Concepts: **1.** $a_1b_1 + a_2b_2$
3. 0 **5.** true **7.** -7 **9.** 0 **11.** 14 **13.** -6
15. 8.7 **17.** 8.5 **19.** -10.5 **21.** 3.2° **23.** 168.7°
25. 90° **27.** 0° **29.** 180° **31.** 25.4 **33.** 36.4 **35.** 21.2°
37. 19.7° **39.** Orthogonal **41.** Not orthogonal **43.** Orthogonal

45. Parallel **47.** Not parallel **49.** Parallel **51.** $c = -2, c = \dfrac{9}{2}$

53. $c = -\dfrac{9}{2}, c = 8$

B Exercises: Applying the Concepts: **55. a.** 100 lb **b.** 20 lb
c. 72.1 lb **57.** 13.5 lb; 12.8°; 17.2° **59.** 560 foot-pounds
61. 5520.2 pounds **63.** 56 foot-pounds

C Exercises: Beyond the Basics: **71.** $7\mathbf{i} - 3\mathbf{j}$ **73. a.** x **b.** y

Critical Thinking: **81.** False

Review Exercises

1. $\mathbf{v} + \mathbf{w}$ **3.** $\mathbf{v} - \mathbf{w}$ **5.** $\dfrac{1}{2}(\mathbf{v} + \mathbf{w})$ **7.** $\dfrac{1}{2}(\mathbf{w} - \mathbf{v})$

9. $\dfrac{1}{4}(\mathbf{v} + \mathbf{w}); \dfrac{1}{4}(\mathbf{v} + \mathbf{w})$ **11.** $-\mathbf{i} + 2\mathbf{j}$ **13.** $\langle -10, 15 \rangle$

15. $\langle -16, 21 \rangle$ **17.** $\dfrac{\sqrt{2}}{2}\mathbf{i} + \dfrac{\sqrt{2}}{2}\mathbf{j}$ **19.** $\left\langle \dfrac{3\sqrt{34}}{34}, -\dfrac{5\sqrt{34}}{34} \right\rangle$
21. $3\sqrt{3}\mathbf{i} + 3\mathbf{j}$ **23.** $-6\sqrt{2}\mathbf{i} - 6\sqrt{2}\mathbf{j}$ **25.** -6 **27.** 0 **29.** 60.3°
31. 101.3° **33.** 122.9 lb **35.** 431 mph in the direction N 4° W
37. 102.6 lb parallel to the surface; 281.9 lb perpendicular to the
surface **39.** 1526.17 foot-pounds

Chapter Test

1. 500 ft in the direction S 53.1° W **2.** 803 ft **3.** $\langle -1, -12 \rangle$
4. $\langle -3, -2 \rangle$ **5.** $-7\mathbf{i} - 9\mathbf{j}$ **6.** $\dfrac{3\sqrt{3}}{2}\mathbf{i} - \dfrac{3}{2}\mathbf{j}$ **7.** $\left\langle \dfrac{2\sqrt{13}}{13}, -\dfrac{3\sqrt{13}}{13} \right\rangle$
8. 116.6° **9.** 17 **10.** 164.9° **11.** 72.1 lb, 33.7°
12. The plane is flying N 25.9° W at 481.2 mph.

CHAPTER 9

Section 9.1

Practice Problems:
1.

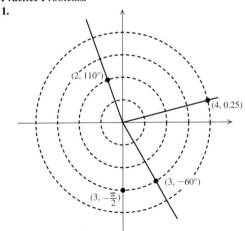

2. a.

b. $(-2, 30°)$ **c.** $(2, 210°)$

d. $(-2, -330°)$ **3. a.** $\left(-\dfrac{3}{2}, -\dfrac{3\sqrt{3}}{2} \right)$ **b.** $(\sqrt{2}, -\sqrt{2})$

4. $\left(\sqrt{2}, \dfrac{5\pi}{4} \right)$ **5.** $(24.8, 36.0°)$ **6.** $r^2 - 2r\sin\theta + 3 = 0$

7. a. $x^2 + y^2 = 25$; a circle centered at the origin with radius 5
b. $y = -x\sqrt{3}$; a line through the origin with slope $-\sqrt{3}$
c. $x = 1$; a vertical line through $x = 1$
d. $x^2 + (y - 1)^2 = 1$; a circle with center $(0, 1)$ and radius 1

A Exercises: Basic Skills and Concepts: **1.** origin; axis
3. $r\cos\theta; r\sin\theta$ **5.** true

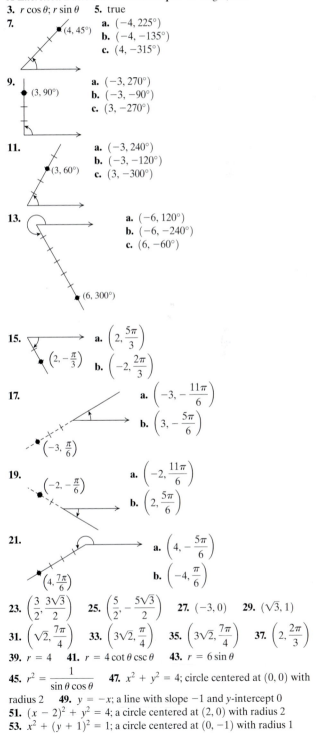

7. **a.** $(-4, 225°)$
b. $(-4, -135°)$
c. $(4, -315°)$

9. **a.** $(-3, 270°)$
b. $(-3, -90°)$
c. $(3, -270°)$

11. **a.** $(-3, 240°)$
b. $(-3, -120°)$
c. $(3, -300°)$

13. **a.** $(-6, 120°)$
b. $(-6, -240°)$
c. $(6, -60°)$

15. **a.** $\left(2, \dfrac{5\pi}{3} \right)$
b. $\left(-2, \dfrac{2\pi}{3} \right)$

17. **a.** $\left(-3, -\dfrac{11\pi}{6} \right)$
b. $\left(3, -\dfrac{5\pi}{6} \right)$

19. **a.** $\left(-2, \dfrac{11\pi}{6} \right)$
b. $\left(2, \dfrac{5\pi}{6} \right)$

21. **a.** $\left(4, -\dfrac{5\pi}{6} \right)$
b. $\left(-4, \dfrac{\pi}{6} \right)$

23. $\left(\dfrac{3}{2}, \dfrac{3\sqrt{3}}{2} \right)$ **25.** $\left(\dfrac{5}{2}, -\dfrac{5\sqrt{3}}{2} \right)$ **27.** $(-3, 0)$ **29.** $(\sqrt{3}, 1)$
31. $\left(\sqrt{2}, \dfrac{7\pi}{4} \right)$ **33.** $\left(3\sqrt{2}, \dfrac{\pi}{4} \right)$ **35.** $\left(3\sqrt{2}, \dfrac{7\pi}{4} \right)$ **37.** $\left(2, \dfrac{2\pi}{3} \right)$
39. $r = 4$ **41.** $r = 4\cot\theta\csc\theta$ **43.** $r = 6\sin\theta$

45. $r^2 = \dfrac{1}{\sin\theta\cos\theta}$ **47.** $x^2 + y^2 = 4$; circle centered at $(0, 0)$ with
radius 2 **49.** $y = -x$; a line with slope -1 and y-intercept 0
51. $(x - 2)^2 + y^2 = 4$; a circle centered at $(2, 0)$ with radius 2
53. $x^2 + (y + 1)^2 = 1$; a circle centered at $(0, -1)$ with radius 1

55.

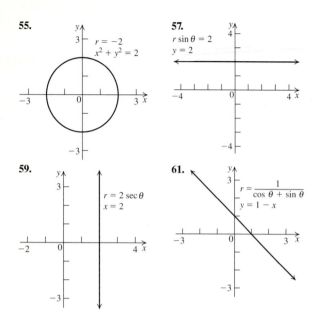

$r = -2$
$x^2 + y^2 = 2$

57.

$r \sin \theta = 2$
$y = 2$

59.

$r = 2 \sec \theta$
$x = 2$

61.

$r = \dfrac{1}{\cos \theta + \sin \theta}$
$y = 1 - x$

B Exercises: Applying the Concepts: 63. $(21.8, 39.6°)$
65. $(18.3, -45.8°)$

C Exercises: Beyond the Basics: 67. $r = \theta$ **69.** $y = \dfrac{x^2}{6} - \dfrac{3}{2}$

71. $y^2 = 1 - x - \dfrac{3x^2}{4}$ **73.** $y^2 - 8x^2 - 30x - 25 = 0$

Critical Thinking: 79. true

Section 9.2

Practice Problems:

1.

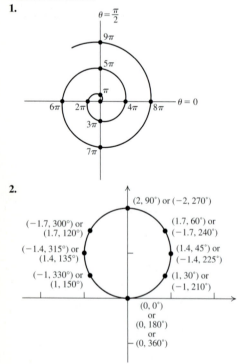

2.

(2, 90°) or (−2, 270°)
(−1.7, 300°) or (1.7, 120°)   (1.7, 60°) or (−1.7, 240°)
(−1.4, 315°) or (1.4, 135°)   (1.4, 45°) or (−1.4, 225°)
(−1, 330°) or (1, 150°)   (1, 30°) or (−1, 210°)
(0, 0°) or (0, 180°) or (0, 360°)

3. Symmetric about the polar axis, the line $\theta = \dfrac{\pi}{2}$, and the pole

4.

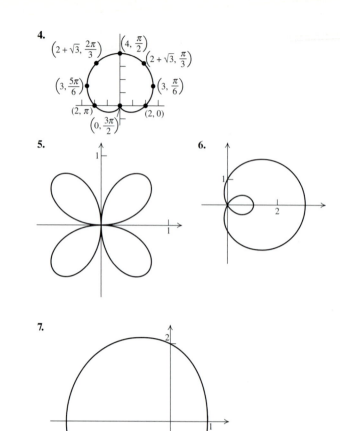

$\left(2 + \sqrt{3}, \dfrac{2\pi}{3}\right)$ $\left(4, \dfrac{\pi}{2}\right)$ $\left(2 + \sqrt{3}, \dfrac{\pi}{3}\right)$
$\left(3, \dfrac{5\pi}{6}\right)$ $\left(3, \dfrac{\pi}{6}\right)$
$(2, \pi)$ $(2, 0)$
$\left(0, \dfrac{3\pi}{2}\right)$

5.

6.

7.

A Exercises: Basic Skills and Concepts: 1. the polar axis
3. the pole   **5.** false
7.

(2.5, 60°) or (−2.5, 240°)   (4.3, 30°) or (−4.3, 210°)
(0, 90°) or (0, 270°)   (5, 0°) or (−5, 180°) or (5, 360°)
(−2.5, 120°) or (2.5, 300°)   (−4.3, 150°) or (4.3, 330°)

9.

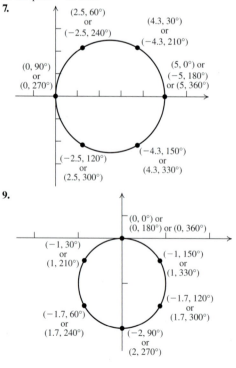

(0, 0°) or (0, 180°) or (0, 360°)
(−1, 30°) or (1, 210°)   (−1, 150°) or (1, 330°)
(−1.7, 60°) or (1.7, 240°)   (−1.7, 120°) or (1.7, 300°)
(−2, 90°) or (2, 270°)

11. a. $(2, 330°)$ **b.** $(2, 150°)$ **c.** $(2, 210°)$ **13. a.** $(3, 45°)$

b. $(3, 225°)$ **c.** $(3, 135°)$ **15. a.** $\left(\frac{1}{2}, 120°\right)$ **b.** $\left(\frac{1}{2}, 300°\right)$

c. $\left(\frac{1}{2}, 60°\right)$ **17. a.** $\left(\frac{1}{3}, 200°\right)$ **b.** $\left(\frac{1}{3}, 20°\right)$ **c.** $\left(\frac{1}{3}, 340°\right)$

19. Symmetric about the y-axis   **21.** Symmetric about the x-axis, the y-axis, and the origin   **23.** Symmetric about the x-axis
25. Symmetric about the origin
27. A circle

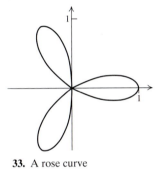

29. A cardioid

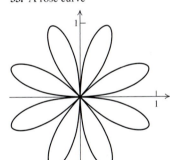

31. A rose curve

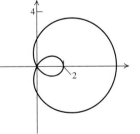

33. A rose curve

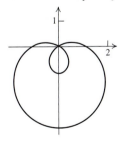

35. An inner loop limaçon

37. An inner loop limaçon

39. A dimpled limaçon

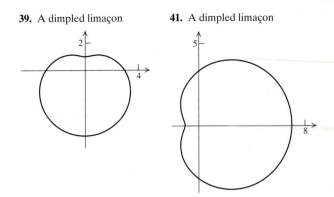

41. A dimpled limaçon

B Exercises: Applying the Concepts:

43. a. $r = \dfrac{0.370737}{1 + 0.2056 \cos \theta}$ **b.** 0.3 AU or 27.9 million miles

c. 0.5 AU or 46.5 million miles   **45. a.** $r = \dfrac{5.19081}{1 + 0.0484 \cos \theta}$

b. 5 AU or 465 million miles   **c.** 5.5 AU or 511.5 million miles

C Exercises: Beyond the Basics:

47. 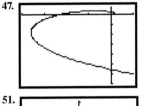   **49.**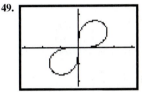

51. 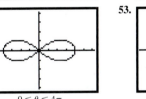   **53.**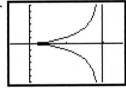

$0 \le \theta \le 4\pi$

55.

57.

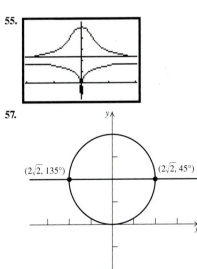

59.

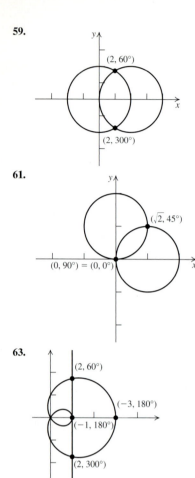

61.

63.

Critical Thinking: 69. $(0,0)$ (both curves) and $(4k\pi, 4k\pi)$, $(r = \theta)$, and $(4k\pi, 2k\pi)$ $(r = 2\theta)$, for k any positive integer

Section 9.3

Practice Problems: 1. a. real part $= -1$; imaginary part $= 2$
b. real part $= -\dfrac{1}{3}$; imaginary part $= -6$ **c.** real part $= 8$;
imaginary part $= 0$ **2.** $a = -2, b = 1$ **3. a.** $4 - 2i$ **b.** $-1 + 4i$
c. $-2 + 5i$ **4. a.** $26 + 2i$ **b.** $-15 - 21i$ **5. a.** $5 - 12i$
b. $16 + 14i\sqrt{2}$ **6. a.** 37 **b.** 4 **7. a.** $1 + i$
b. $-\dfrac{15}{41} - \dfrac{12}{41}i$ **8.** $\dfrac{23}{10} + \dfrac{11}{10}i$

A Exercises: Basic Skills and Concepts: 1. $\sqrt{-1}$; -1 **3.** $i\sqrt{b}$
5. true   **7.** $x = 3, y = 2$ **9.** $x = 2, y = -4$ **11.** $8 + 3i$
13. $-1 - 6i$ **15.** $-5 - 5i$ **17.** $15 + 6i$ **19.** $-8 + 12i$
21. $-3 + 15i$ **23.** $20 + 8i$ **25.** $3 + 11i$ **27.** 13 **29.** $24 + 7i$
31. $-141 - 24i\sqrt{3}$ **33.** $26 - 2i$ **35.** $\bar{z} = 2 + 3i, z\bar{z} = 13$
37. $\bar{z} = \dfrac{1}{2} + 2i, z\bar{z} = \dfrac{17}{4}$ **39.** $\bar{z} = \sqrt{2} + 3i, z\bar{z} = 11$ **41.** $5i$
43. $-\dfrac{1}{2} + \dfrac{1}{2}i$ **45.** $1 + 2i$ **47.** $\dfrac{5}{2} + \dfrac{1}{2}i$ **49.** $\dfrac{43}{65} - \dfrac{6}{65}i$ **51.** 2
53. $-\dfrac{19}{13} + \dfrac{4}{13}i$

B Exercises: Applying the Concepts: 55. $9 + i$
57. $Z = \dfrac{595}{74} + \dfrac{315}{74}i$ **59.** $V = 45 + 11i$ **61.** $I = \dfrac{19}{25} + \dfrac{9}{50}i$

C Exercises: Beyond the Basics: 63. i **65.** i **67.** 6 **69.** $5i$
71. $-4i$ **79.** $x = 1, y = 4$ **81.** $x = 1, y = 0$ **83.** $-\dfrac{3}{5} + \dfrac{4}{5}i$

Critical Thinking: 86. a. True   **b.** False   **c.** False   **d.** True
e. True   **f.** True

Section 9.4

Practice Problems:
1.

2. $3 + i$ **3. a.** 13 **b.** 7 **c.** 1 **d.** $\sqrt{a^2 + b^2}$
4. $z = \sqrt{2}\left(\cos\dfrac{5\pi}{4} + i\sin\dfrac{5\pi}{4}\right)$ **5. a.** $5(\cos 360° + i\sin 360°)$
b. $5(\cos 90° + i\sin 90°)$ **6.** $2 - 2\sqrt{3}i$
7. $z_1 z_2 = 10(\cos 135° + i\sin 135°)$; $\dfrac{z_1}{z_2} = \dfrac{5}{2}(\cos 15° + i\sin 15°)$
8. $\cos\dfrac{2\pi}{3} + i\sin\dfrac{2\pi}{3}$ **9.** $\dfrac{121}{100} - \dfrac{4}{5}i$ **10.** $2.6(\cos 27.2° + i\sin 27.2°)$

A Exercises: Basic Skills and Concepts: 1. $\sqrt{a^2 + b^2}$
3. $r(\cos\theta + i\sin\theta)$ **5.** true
7.–14.

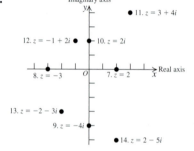

7. 2 **9.** 4 **11.** 5 **13.** $\sqrt{13}$ **15.** $3 + 2i$ **17.** $3 + i$
19. $2(\cos 60° + i\sin 60°)$ **21.** $\sqrt{2}(\cos 135° + i\sin 135°)$
23. $\cos 90° + i\sin 90°$ **25.** $\cos 0° + i\sin 0°$
27. $3\sqrt{2}(\cos 315° + i\sin 315°)$ **29.** $4(\cos 300° + i\sin 300°)$
31. $1 + \sqrt{3}i$ **33.** -3 **35.** $-\dfrac{5}{2} - \dfrac{5\sqrt{3}}{2}i$ **37.** 8
39. $-3\sqrt{3} + 3i$ **41.** $\dfrac{3}{2} - \dfrac{3\sqrt{3}}{2}i$
43. $z_1 z_2 = 8(\cos 90° + i\sin 90°)$; $\dfrac{z_1}{z_2} = 2(\cos 60° + i\sin 60°)$
45. $z_1 z_2 = 10(\cos 300° + i\sin 300°)$; $\dfrac{z_1}{z_2} = \dfrac{5}{2}(\cos 180° + i\sin 180°)$
47. $z_1 z_2 = 15(\cos 60° + i\sin 60°)$; $\dfrac{z_1}{z_2} = \dfrac{3}{5}(\cos 20° + i\sin 20°)$
49. $z_1 z_2 = 6(\cos 115° + i\sin 115°)$; $\dfrac{z_1}{z_2} = \dfrac{2}{3}(\cos 145° + i\sin 145°)$
51. $2 = 2(\cos 0° + i\sin 0°)$
53. $3\sqrt{3} - i = 2\sqrt{7}(\cos 349.1° + i\sin 349.1°)$
55. $(12 + 12\sqrt{3}) + (12 - 12\sqrt{3})i = 24\sqrt{2}(\cos 345° + i\sin 345°)$
57. $\dfrac{1 + \sqrt{3}}{2} - \dfrac{1 - \sqrt{3}}{2}i = \sqrt{2}(\cos 15° + i\sin 15°)$
59. $\dfrac{-\sqrt{3}}{2} + \dfrac{1}{2}i = \cos 150° + i\sin 150°$
61. $\dfrac{-15 + 5\sqrt{3}}{36} + \dfrac{15 + 5\sqrt{3}}{36}i = \dfrac{5\sqrt{6}}{18}(\cos 105° + i\sin 105°)$
63. $\dfrac{2\sqrt{6}}{3}(\cos 195° + i\sin 195°)$ **65.** $\dfrac{2\sqrt{3}}{3}(\cos 90° + i\sin 90°)$

B Exercises: Applying the Concepts: 67. Yes   **69.** No
71. Yellow   **73.** Black   **77.** $96(\cos 150° + i \sin 150°)$
79. $3.8(\cos 50.9° + i \sin 50.9°)$

C Exercises: Beyond the Basics: 85. $r\left[\cos\left(\theta + \dfrac{\pi}{2}\right) + i\sin\left(\theta + \dfrac{\pi}{2}\right)\right]$;
rotate z counterclockwise 90°   **87.** $\cos(\pi - \theta) + i\sin(\pi - \theta)$
89. $\cos\left(\dfrac{3\pi}{2} - \theta\right) + i\sin\left(\dfrac{3\pi}{2} - \theta\right)$

Critical Thinking: 91. $13 + 13i$
92. $p^3 + 2p^2q + p + pq^2 + (p^2 + 2pq + q^2 + 1)i$

Section 9.5

Practice Problems: 1. $-16\sqrt{3} + 16i$ **2.** $8i$ **3.** $-\dfrac{1}{64}$
4. $2^{\frac{1}{6}}(\cos 45° + i\sin 45°)$; $2^{\frac{1}{6}}(\cos 165° + i\sin 165°)$;
$2^{\frac{1}{6}}(\cos 285° + i\sin 285°)$
5. $z_0 = 1(\cos 0° + i\sin 0°)$
   $z_1 = 1(\cos 72° + i\sin 72°)$
   $z_2 = 1(\cos 144° + i\sin 144°)$
   $z_3 = 1(\cos 216° + i\sin 216°)$
   $z_4 = 1(\cos 288° + i\sin 288°)$

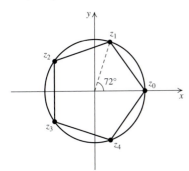

A Exercises: Basic Skills and Concepts: 1. $r^n(\cos n\theta + i\sin n\theta)$
3. n **5.** true   **7.** $27i$ **9.** $2^{12} = 4096$ **11.** $-64i$ **13.** $-64i$
15. $\dfrac{1}{2^{10}}i = \dfrac{1}{1024}i$ **17.** i **19.** -64 **21.** 4096 **23.** $54 - 54i$
25. $-\dfrac{1}{4}$ **27.** $-\dfrac{1}{512}i$ **29.** $\cos 0° + i\sin 0°, \cos 180° + i\sin 180°$
31. $\cos 135° + i\sin 135°, \cos 315° + i\sin 315°$
33. $2(\cos 0° + i\sin 0°), 2(\cos 120° + i\sin 120°),$
$2(\cos 240° + i\sin 240°)$ **35.** $4(\cos 60° + i\sin 60°),$
$4(\cos 180° + i\sin 180°), 4(\cos 300° + i\sin 300°)$
37. $2(\cos 30° + i\sin 30°), 2(\cos 150° + i\sin 150°),$
$2(\cos 270° + i\sin 270°)$ **39.** $3(\cos 90° + i\sin 90°),$
$3(\cos 210° + i\sin 210°), 3(\cos 330° + i\sin 330°)$
41. $\cos 0° + i\sin 0°, \cos 45° + i\sin 45°, \cos 90° + i\sin 90°,$
$\cos 135° + i\sin 135°, \cos 180° + i\sin 180°, \cos 225° + i\sin 225°,$
$\cos 270° + i\sin 270°, \cos 315° + i\sin 315°$
43. $2^{\frac{1}{4}}(\cos 30° + i\sin 30°), 2^{\frac{1}{4}}(\cos 120° + i\sin 120°),$
$2^{\frac{1}{4}}(\cos 210° + i\sin 210°), 2^{\frac{1}{4}}(\cos 300° + i\sin 300°)$
45. $2(\cos 20° + i\sin 20°), 2(\cos 140° + i\sin 140°),$
$2(\cos 260° + i\sin 260°)$

C Exercises: Beyond the Basics: 51. $128(\cos 120° + i\sin 120°)$
53. $2(\cos 30° + i\sin 30°)$ **55.** $\dfrac{27\sqrt{2}}{8}(\cos 15° + i\sin 15°)$
57. $\cos 240° + i\sin 240°$ **59.** $\cos 120° + i\sin 120°$
65. $-20.214 - 315.205i$ **67.** $-114{,}244 - 144{,}244i$ **69.** $\{-1, i, -i\}$

Critical Thinking: 71. a. True   **b.** False   **c.** False   **d.** False
e. True   **f.** True   **g.** True   **h.** True   **i.** False   **j.** True

Review Exercises

1. $\left(\dfrac{7\sqrt{3}}{2}, \dfrac{7}{2}\right)$

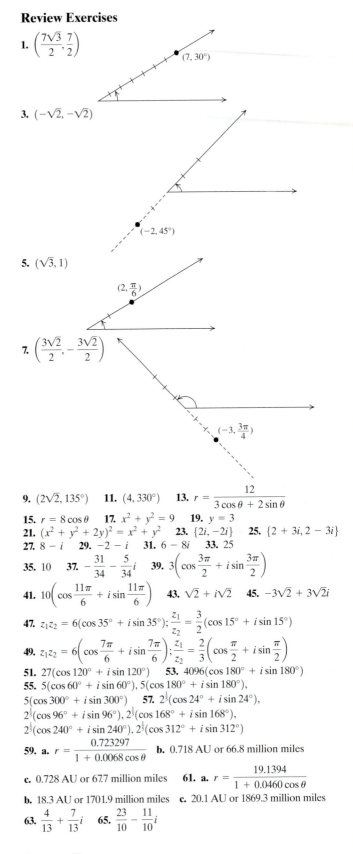

3. $(-\sqrt{2}, -\sqrt{2})$

5. $(\sqrt{3}, 1)$

7. $\left(\dfrac{3\sqrt{2}}{2}, -\dfrac{3\sqrt{2}}{2}\right)$

9. $(2\sqrt{2}, 135°)$ **11.** $(4, 330°)$ **13.** $r = \dfrac{12}{3\cos\theta + 2\sin\theta}$
15. $r = 8\cos\theta$ **17.** $x^2 + y^2 = 9$ **19.** $y = 3$
21. $(x^2 + y^2 + 2y)^2 = x^2 + y^2$ **23.** $\{2i, -2i\}$ **25.** $\{2 + 3i, 2 - 3i\}$
27. $8 - i$ **29.** $-2 - i$ **31.** $6 - 8i$ **33.** 25
35. 10 **37.** $-\dfrac{31}{34} - \dfrac{5}{34}i$ **39.** $3\left(\cos\dfrac{3\pi}{2} + i\sin\dfrac{3\pi}{2}\right)$
41. $10\left(\cos\dfrac{11\pi}{6} + i\sin\dfrac{11\pi}{6}\right)$ **43.** $\sqrt{2} + i\sqrt{2}$ **45.** $-3\sqrt{2} + 3\sqrt{2}i$
47. $z_1z_2 = 6(\cos 35° + i\sin 35°); \dfrac{z_1}{z_2} = \dfrac{3}{2}(\cos 15° + i\sin 15°)$
49. $z_1z_2 = 6\left(\cos\dfrac{7\pi}{6} + i\sin\dfrac{7\pi}{6}\right); \dfrac{z_1}{z_2} = \dfrac{2}{3}\left(\cos\dfrac{\pi}{2} + i\sin\dfrac{\pi}{2}\right)$
51. $27(\cos 120° + i\sin 120°)$ **53.** $4096(\cos 180° + i\sin 180°)$
55. $5(\cos 60° + i\sin 60°), 5(\cos 180° + i\sin 180°),$
$5(\cos 300° + i\sin 300°)$ **57.** $2^{\frac{1}{5}}(\cos 24° + i\sin 24°),$
$2^{\frac{1}{5}}(\cos 96° + i\sin 96°), 2^{\frac{1}{5}}(\cos 168° + i\sin 168°),$
$2^{\frac{1}{5}}(\cos 240° + i\sin 240°), 2^{\frac{1}{5}}(\cos 312° + i\sin 312°)$
59. a. $r = \dfrac{0.723297}{1 + 0.0068\cos\theta}$ **b.** 0.718 AU or 66.8 million miles
c. 0.728 AU or 67.7 million miles   **61. a.** $r = \dfrac{19.1394}{1 + 0.0460\cos\theta}$
b. 18.3 AU or 1701.9 million miles   **c.** 20.1 AU or 1869.3 million miles
63. $\dfrac{4}{13} + \dfrac{7}{13}i$ **65.** $\dfrac{23}{10} - \dfrac{11}{10}i$

Chapter Test

1. $(\sqrt{3}, -1)$ **2.** $(-2\sqrt{2}, -2\sqrt{2})$ **3.** $(2, 210°)$ **4.** $(-2\sqrt{3}, 150°)$
5. $x^2 + y^2 = 9$; circle with center $(0, 0)$ and radius 3

6. $r^2 + 4r \cos \theta - 5 = 0$ **7.** Cardioid

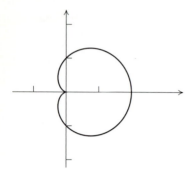

8. a. $-i$ **b.** $-2i$ **9. a.** $7 + 7i$ **b.** $-3 - i$ **c.** $-2 + 23i$

d. $\dfrac{22}{41} + \dfrac{7}{41}i$ **10. a.** $6\sqrt{2}(\cos 345° + i \sin 345°)$

b. $\dfrac{3\sqrt{2}}{2}(\cos 285° + i \sin 285°)$ **11.** $\left\{\dfrac{1}{4} + \dfrac{\sqrt{3}}{4}i, \dfrac{1}{4} - \dfrac{\sqrt{3}}{4}i\right\}$

12. $2 + 2i\sqrt{3}$ **13.** $\dfrac{1}{125}i$ **14.** $2^{\frac{1}{8}}(\cos 11.25° + i \sin 11.25°)$,
$2^{\frac{1}{8}}(\cos 101.25° + i \sin 101.25°)$, $2^{\frac{1}{8}}(\cos 191.25° + i \sin 191.25°)$,
$2^{\frac{1}{8}}(\cos 281.25° + i \sin 281.25°)$

APPENDIX

Section A.1

Practice Problems: **1.** $\{-1\}$ **2.** $\{-21, -4\}$ **3.** $\{3\}$
4. $\{-2 - \sqrt{5}, -2 + \sqrt{5}\}$ **5.** $\left\{3 - \dfrac{\sqrt{11}}{2}, 3 + \dfrac{\sqrt{11}}{2}\right\}$
6. $\left\{-\dfrac{1}{2}, \dfrac{2}{3}\right\}$

A Exercises: Basic Skills and Concepts: **1.** equivalent
3. $2x^2 - 5x + 8 = 0$ **5.** No; $x = 0$ **7.** Yes
9. $\{3\}$ **11.** $\{-2\}$ **13.** $\{7\}$ **15.** $\{-1\}$ **17.** $\{6\}$
19. $\{12\}$ **21.** $\{-11\}$ **23.** $\left\{\dfrac{7}{4}\right\}$ **25.** $\left\{\dfrac{23}{6}\right\}$ **27.** $\left\{\dfrac{7}{8}\right\}$
29. $\{2\}$ **31.** $\{28\}$ **33.** $\left\{\dfrac{4}{5}\right\}$ **35.** $\{0, 5\}$ **37.** $\{-7, 2\}$
39. $\{-1, 6\}$ **41.** $\left\{-3, \dfrac{1}{2}\right\}$ **43.** $\left\{-1, -\dfrac{2}{3}\right\}$ **45.** $\left\{-2, -\dfrac{2}{5}\right\}$
47. $\left\{-3, \dfrac{5}{2}\right\}$ **49.** $\left\{-\dfrac{2}{3}, \dfrac{3}{2}\right\}$ **51.** $\left\{\dfrac{1}{6}, \dfrac{7}{3}\right\}$ **53.** $\left\{-\dfrac{25}{2}, 15\right\}$
55. $\{-4, 4\}$ **57.** $\{-2, 2\}$ **59.** $\{-3, 5\}$ **61.** 4   **63.** 9
65. $\dfrac{49}{4}$ **67.** $\dfrac{1}{36}$ **69.** $\dfrac{a^2}{4}$ **71.** $\{-1 - \sqrt{6}, -1 + \sqrt{6}\}$
73. $\left\{\dfrac{3 - \sqrt{13}}{2}, \dfrac{3 + \sqrt{13}}{2}\right\}$ **75.** $\left\{-3, \dfrac{3}{2}\right\}$ **77.** $\{6 - \sqrt{33}, 6 + \sqrt{33}\}$
79. $\left\{\dfrac{-7 + \sqrt{13}}{6}, \dfrac{-7 - \sqrt{13}}{6}\right\}$

Section A.2

Practice Problems: **1.**

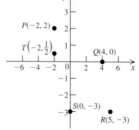

2. $(1998, 21.1), (1999, 20.5), (2000, 20.2), (2001, 19.7), (2002, 19.4),$
$(2003, 18.6), (2004, 17.9)$ **3.** $\sqrt{2} \approx 1.4$ **4.** $\left(\dfrac{11}{2}, -\dfrac{3}{2}\right)$

5. 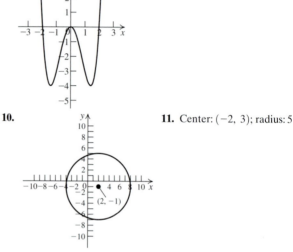   **6.** x-intercepts: $-2, \dfrac{1}{2}$
y-intercept: -2

7. Symmetric
8. 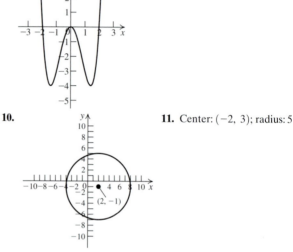   **9.** $(x - 3)^2 + (y + 6)^2 = 100$

$y = x^4 - 4x^2$

10. 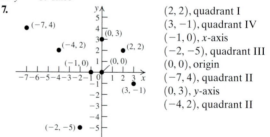   **11.** Center: $(-2, 3)$; radius: 5

A Exercises: Basic Skills and Concepts: **1.** second
3. y-   **5.** false
7.

$(2, 2)$, quadrant I
$(3, -1)$, quadrant IV
$(-1, 0)$, x-axis
$(-2, -5)$, quadrant III
$(0, 0)$, origin
$(-7, 4)$, quadrant II
$(0, 3)$, y-axis
$(-4, 2)$, quadrant II

9. a. On the y-axis   **b.** Vertical line intersecting the x-axis at -1

11. a. 4 **b.** $(2, 3)$ **13. a.** $\sqrt{13}$ **b.** $(0.5, -4)$
15. a. $2|w|$ **b.** (v, t) **17.** Yes   **19.** No   **21.** Isosceles
23. Scalene   **25.** Equilateral   **27.** On the graph: $(-3, -4)$,
$(1, 0), (4, 3)$; not on the graph: $(2, 3)$ **29.** On the graph: $(1, 1)$,
$\left(2, \dfrac{1}{2}\right)$; not on the graph: $\left(-3, \dfrac{1}{3}\right)$, $(0, 0)$

31.

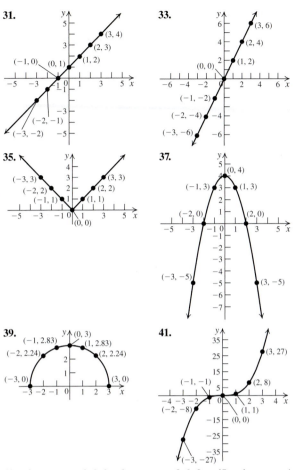

33.

35.

37.

39.

41.

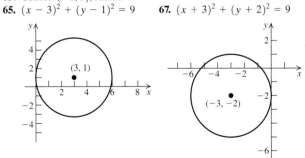

43. x-intercepts: $-3, 0, 3$; y-intercepts: $-2, 0, 2$ **45.** x-intercept: 4;

y-intercept: 3 **47.** x-intercept: $\dfrac{5}{2}$; y-intercept: $\dfrac{5}{3}$

49. x-intercepts: $2, 4$; y-intercept: 8 **51.** x-intercepts: $-2, 2$;

y-intercepts: $-2, 2$ **53.** x-intercepts: $-1, 1$; no y-intercept

55. Not symmetric with respect to the x-axis; symmetric with respect

to the y-axis; not symmetric with respect to the origin

57. Not symmetric with respect to the x-axis; not symmetric with

respect to the y-axis; symmetric with respect to the origin

59. Not symmetric with respect to the x-axis; symmetric with respect

to the y-axis; not symmetric with respect to the origin

61. Not symmetric with respect to the x-axis; not symmetric with

respect to the y-axis; symmetric with respect to the origin

63. Center: $(-1, 3)$; radius: 4

65. $(x - 3)^2 + (y - 1)^2 = 9$ **67.** $(x + 3)^2 + (y + 2)^2 = 9$

69. $(x - 5)^2 + (y - 1)^2 = 25$

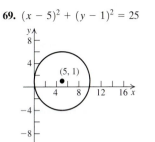

71. a. Center: $(1, 1)$; radius: $\sqrt{6}$ **b.** x-intercepts: $1 \pm \sqrt{5}$;

y-intercepts: $1 \pm \sqrt{5}$ **73. a.** Center: $(0, -1)$;

radius: 1 **b.** x-intercept: 0; y-intercepts: $-2, 0$

B Exercises: Applying the Concepts: 75. $20{,}000$

77. a. $\$12$ million   **b.** $-\$5.5$ million

c.

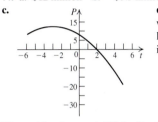

d. 2; it represents the month
when there is neither profit nor
loss.   **e.** 8; it represents the profit
in July 2008.

79. a. After 0 second: 320 ft; after 1 second: 432 ft; after

2 seconds: 512 ft; after 3 seconds: 560 ft; after 4 seconds: 576 ft;

after 5 seconds: 560 ft; after 6 seconds: 512 ft

b.

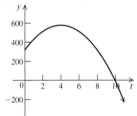

c. $0 \le t \le 10$ **d.** t-intercept:
10; it represents the time when
the object hits the ground.
y-intercept: 320; it shows the
height of the building.

Section A.3

Practice Problems: 1. a. No   **b.** Yes   **2. a.** 0 **b.** -7

c. $-2x^2 - 4hx + 5x - 2h^2 + 5h$ **3.** $(-\infty, 1)$ **4.** No

5. a. Yes   **b.** $-3, -1$ **c.** -5 **d.** $-5, 1$

A Exercises: Basic Skills and Concepts: 1. independent

3. -14 **5.** $y = 0$ **7.** true   **9.** Domain: $\{a, b, c\}$; range: $\{d, e\}$;

function   **11.** Domain: $\{a, b, c\}$; range: $\{1, 2\}$; function

13. Domain: $\{-3, -1, 0, 1, 2, 3\}$; range: $\{-8, -3, 0, 1\}$; function

15. Yes   **17.** Yes   **19.** Yes   **21.** Yes   **23.** Yes   **25.** Yes

27. Yes   **29.** $f(0) = 1, g(0)$ is not defined, $h(0) = \sqrt{2}$,

$f(a) = a^2 - 3a + 1, f(-x) = x^2 + 3x + 1$ **31.** $f(-1) = 5, g(-1)$

is not defined, $h(-1) = \sqrt{3}, h(c) = \sqrt{2 - c}, h(-x) = \sqrt{2 + x}$

33. a. 0 **b.** $\dfrac{2\sqrt{3}}{3}$ **c.** Not defined   **d.** Not defined   **e.** $\dfrac{-2x}{\sqrt{4 - x^2}}$

35. $(-\infty, \infty)$ **37.** $(-\infty, 9) \cup (9, \infty)$

39. $(-\infty, -1) \cup (-1, 1) \cup (1, \infty)$ **41.** $[3, \infty)$ **43.** $(-\infty, 4)$

45. $(-\infty, -2) \cup (-2, -1) \cup (-1, \infty)$ **47.** $(-\infty, 0) \cup (0, \infty)$

49. Yes   **51.** Yes   **53.** Yes

55. $f(-4) = -2, f(-1) = 1, f(3) = 5, f(5) = 7$

57. $h(-2) = -5, h(-1) = 4, h(0) = 3, h(1) = 4$

59. $x = -2$ or 3 **61. a.** No   **b.** $x = -1 \pm \sqrt{3}$ **c.** 5

d. $x = -1 \pm \dfrac{1}{2}\sqrt{14}$

Section A.4

Practice Problems: **1.** The graph of *g* is the graph of *f* shifted one unit up; the graph of *h* is the graph of *f* shifted two units down.

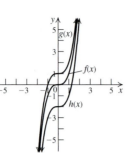

2.

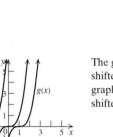

The graph of *g* is the graph of *f* shifted one unit to the right; the graph of *h* is the graph of *f* shifted two units to the left.

3.

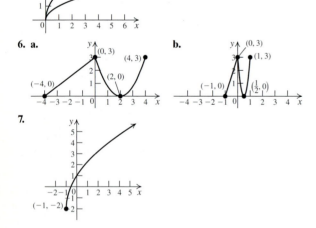

4. Shift the graph of $y = x^2$ one unit to the right, reflect the resulting graph in the *x*-axis, and shift it two units up.

5.

The graph of *g* is the graph of *f* vertically stretched by multiplying each of its *y*-coordinates by 2.

6. a.   **b.**

7.

33.

$f(x) = x^2 - 2$

35.

$g(x) = \sqrt{x} + 1$

37. $h(x) = |x + 1|$

39. $f(x) = (x - 3)^3$

41. $g(x) = (x - 2)^2 + 1$

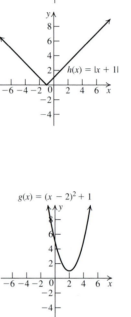

43. $h(x) = -\sqrt{x}$

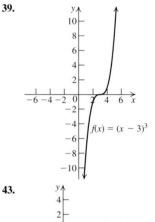

45. $f(x) = -\dfrac{1}{x}$

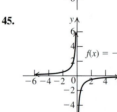

47. $g(x) = \dfrac{1}{2}|x|$

49. $h(x) = -x^3 + 1$

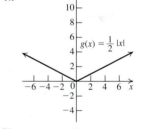

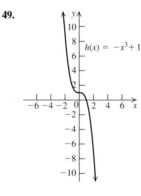

51. $f(x) = 2(x + 1)^2 - 1$

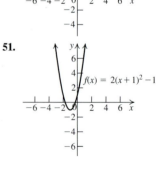

A Exercises: Basic Skills and Concepts: **1.** down   **3.** >1
5. false   **7. a.** Shift two units up   **b.** Shift one unit down
9. a. Shift one unit left   **b.** Shift two units right   **11. a.** Shift one
unit left and two units down   **b.** Shift one unit right and three units up
13. a. Reflect in *x*-axis   **b.** Reflect in *y*-axis   **15. a.** Stretch
vertically by a factor of 2   **b.** Compress horizontally by a factor of 2
17. a. Reflect in *x*-axis, shift one unit up   **b.** Reflect in *y*-axis, shift
one unit up   **19. a.** Shift one unit up   **b.** Shift one unit
left   **21.** e   **23.** g   **25.** i   **27.** b   **29.** l   **31.** d

53.
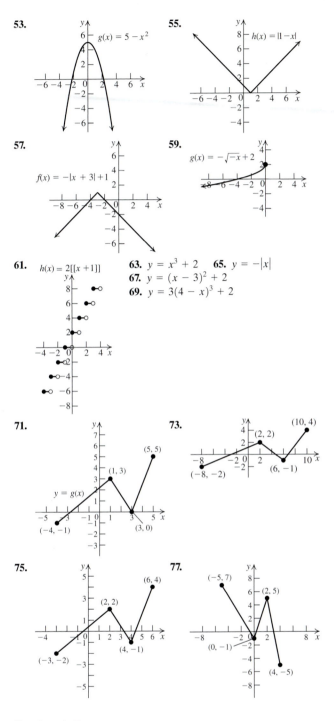
$g(x) = 5 - x^2$

55.
$h(x) = |1 - x|$

57.
$f(x) = -|x + 3| + 1$

59.
$g(x) = -\sqrt{-x} + 2$

61.
$h(x) = 2[[x + 1]]$

63. $y = x^3 + 2$ **65.** $y = -|x|$
67. $y = (x - 3)^2 + 2$
69. $y = 3(4 - x)^3 + 2$

71.
$y = g(x)$
$(1, 3)$
$(5, 5)$
$(-4, -1)$
$(3, 0)$

73.
$(10, 4)$
$(2, 2)$
$(-8, -2)$
$(6, -1)$

75.
$(6, 4)$
$(2, 2)$
$(-3, -2)$
$(4, -1)$

77.
$(-5, 7)$
$(2, 5)$
$(0, -1)$
$(4, -5)$

Section A.5

Practice Problems: 1. Not one-to-one; the horizontal line $y = 1$
intersects the graph at two different points.

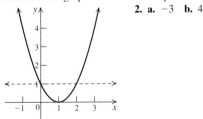

2. a. -3 **b.** 4

3. $(f \circ g)(x) = 3\left(\dfrac{x + 1}{3}\right) - 1 = (x + 1) - 1 = x$ and

$(g \circ f)(x) = \dfrac{(3x - 1) + 1}{3} = \dfrac{3x}{3} = x$; therefore, f and g are

inverses of each other.

4.
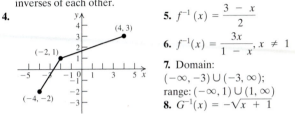
$(4, 3)$
$(-2, 1)$
$(-4, -2)$

5. $f^{-1}(x) = \dfrac{3 - x}{2}$

6. $f^{-1}(x) = \dfrac{3x}{1 - x}, x \neq 1$

7. Domain:
$(-\infty, -3) \cup (-3, \infty)$;
range: $(-\infty, 1) \cup (1, \infty)$
8. $G^{-1}(x) = -\sqrt{x + 1}$

A Exercises: Basic Skills and Concepts: 1. one-to-one

3. $\dfrac{1}{3}x$ **5.** true **7.** One-to-one **9.** Not one-to-one

11. Not one-to-one **13.** One-to-one **15.** 2 **17.** -1

19. a **21.** 337 **23.** -1580 **25. a.** 3 **b.** 3 **c.** 19 **d.** 5

27. a. 2 **b.** 1 **c.** 269

35.
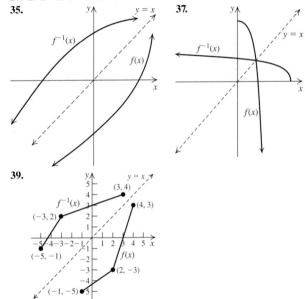
$y = x$
$f^{-1}(x)$
$f(x)$

37.
$y = x$
$f^{-1}(x)$
$f(x)$

39.
$y = x$
$(3, 4)$
$f^{-1}(x)$
$(-3, 2)$
$(4, 3)$
$(-5, -1)$
$f(x)$
$(2, -3)$
$(-1, -5)$

41. a. One-to-one **b.** $f^{-1}(x) = 5 - \dfrac{1}{3}x$

c.
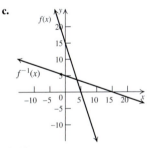
$f(x)$
$f^{-1}(x)$

d. Domain f: $(-\infty, \infty)$
x-intercept: 5
y-intercept: 15
Domain f^{-1}: $(-\infty, \infty)$
x-intercept: 15
y-intercept: 5

43. Not one-to-one
45. a. One-to-one **b.** $f^{-1}(x) = (x - 3)^2, x \geq 3$

c.
$f^{-1}(x)$
$f(x)$

d. Domain f: $[0, \infty)$
No x-intercept
y-intercept: 3
Domain f^{-1}: $[3, \infty)$
x-intercept: 3
No y-intercept

47. a. One-to-one   **b.** $g^{-1}(x) = x^3 - 1$

c.

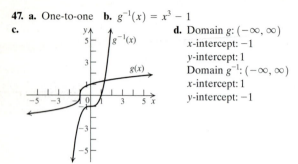

d. Domain g: $(-\infty, \infty)$
   x-intercept: -1
   y-intercept: 1
   Domain g^{-1}: $(-\infty, \infty)$
   x-intercept: 1
   y-intercept: -1

49. a. One-to-one   **b.** $f^{-1}(x) = \dfrac{x+1}{x}$, $x \neq 0$

c.

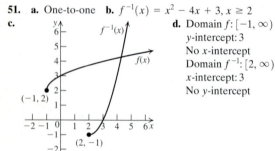

d. Domain f: $(-\infty, 1) \cup (1, \infty)$
   No x-intercept
   y-intercept: -1
   Domain f^{-1}: $(-\infty, 0) \cup (0, \infty)$
   x-intercept: -1
   No y-intercept

51. a. One-to-one   **b.** $f^{-1}(x) = x^2 - 4x + 3$, $x \geq 2$

c.

d. Domain f: $[-1, \infty)$
   y-intercept: 3
   No x-intercept
   Domain f^{-1}: $[2, \infty)$
   x-intercept: 3
   No y-intercept

53. Domain: $(-\infty, -2) \cup (-2, \infty)$; range: $(-\infty, 1) \cup (1, \infty)$

55. $f^{-1}(x) = \dfrac{2x+1}{x-1}$

Domain: $(-\infty, 2) \cup (2, \infty)$; range: $(-\infty, 1) \cup (1, \infty)$

57. $f^{-1}(x) = \dfrac{1-x}{x+2}$

Domain: $(-\infty, -1) \cup (-1, \infty)$; range: $(-\infty, -2) \cup (-2, \infty)$

59. $y = \sqrt{-x}$, $x \leq 0$ **61.** $f^{-1}(x) = x$, $x \geq 0$

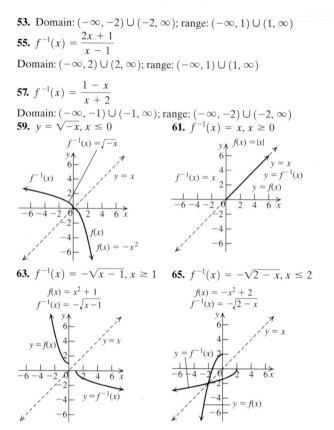

63. $f^{-1}(x) = -\sqrt{x-1}$, $x \geq 1$ **65.** $f^{-1}(x) = -\sqrt{2-x}$, $x \leq 2$

Credits

Chapter 1

p. 1, Spaceship; NASA.
p. 1, City shot; Photographer's Choice Getty RF.
p. 1, Cosmos; NASA.
p. 2, George Ferris; (public domain/Wikipedia).
p. 3, Antique transit; Photos.com.
p. 12, Euclid of Alexandria; (public domain stamp).
p. 22, Flag pole; Shutterstock.
p. 24, Golfer; Shutterstock.
p. 32, Fish with light refracting; Shutterstock.
p. 34. London Eye; Shutterstock.
p. 42, Poseidon; Shutterstock.

Chapter 2

p. 57, Triangles of light; Photos.com.
p. 57, City scene; Shutterstock.
p. 57, Plane in flight Shutterstock.
p. 58, Christmas Tree at Rockefeller Center; Photographer's Choice/Getty Royalty Free.
p. 64, Traffic light or intersection; Photos.com.
p. 66, Mount Kilimanjaro; Corbis Royalty Free.
p. 73, Alligator; Shutterstock.
p. 75, Statue of Liberty; Shutterstock.
p. 80, Ship; Photos.com.
p. 80, Hiker on top of mountain; Shutterstock.
p. 81, Empire State Building; Shutterstock.
p. 88, Acrobat on tight rope; Shutterstock.

Chapter 3

p. 91, Circles and triangles; Shutterstock.
p. 91, Ferris wheel; Shutterstock.
p. 91 and 92, Mars; NASA/John F. Kennedy Space Center.
p. 104, Motorcycle; Shutterstock.
p. 104, Rotating security camera; Photos.com.
p. 107, Blood pressure device; Shutterstock.
p. 114, Dam and water flowing under; Photos.com.
p. 116, Earth; NASA Headquarters.
p. 121, woman with potter's wheel; Photos.com.
p. 129, Blood pressure test on male; Photos.com.

Chapter 4

p. 131, Boats in a harbor; Shutterstock.
p. 131, Seasonal setting; Shutterstock.
p. 132, Mountain; Digital Vision.
p. 159, Paris during the day; Shutterstock.

Chapter 5

p. 179, Triangle and circle; Photodisc.
p. 179, Sunset landscape; Beth Anderson.
p. 179, Girl playing guitar; Corbis Royalty Free.
p. 180, Hipparchus of Rhodes; North Wind Picture Archive.
p. 190, Girl playing guitar (repeat); Corbis Royalty Free.
p. 202, Girl sleeping with electric blanket; Photodisc.
p. 212, Touch tone phone; Photodisc.

Chapter 6

p. 226, Sound waves; Shutterstock.
p. 226, Leaning Tower of Pisa; iStockphoto.
p. 226, Partial eclipse; iStockphoto.
p. 227, Blurred shoppers in mall; Gulfimages/Getty RF.
p. 247, Phases of the moon; Photo Researchers.
p. 225, Tourists in tropics; Shutterstock.

Chapter 7

p. 263, Kayaker; Photodisc.
p. 263, Mount Everest; Corbis Royalty Free.
p. 263, Factory; Digital Vision.
p. 264, Mount Everest (repeat); Corbis Royalty Free.
p. 272, Nicholas Copernicus; Photos.com.
p. 278, Lighthouse; Shutterstock.
p. 279, Fighter Jets; US Air Force.
p. 286, Bermuda Triangle; Graphic Maps and World Atlas.

Chapter 8

p. 297, Comet; NASA.
p. 297, Running leopard; Shutterstock.
p. 297, Hot air balloon; iStockphoto.
p. 298, Dog sled team; Rubberball Productions/Getty RF.
p. 308, Comet (repeat); NASA.
p. 318, Kids pulling red wagon; Digital Vision.

Chapter 9

p. 329, Robot arm; iStockphoto.
p. 329, Mandelbrot or Julia set; iStockphoto.
p. 329, Rugged coastline; iStockphoto.
p. 330, Jakob Bernouilli; public domain.
p. 339, Archimedes; public domain.
p. 350, Alternating Current circuits; Stockbyte Silver/Getty Royalty Free.
p. 359, Benoit Mandelbrot; courtesy of Benoit Mandelbrot.
p. 369, Abraham De Moivre; public domain.
p. 388, Rene Descartes (stamp); public domain.

Index of Applications

Index